ANTISEMITISM

This Companion examines the history, culture, and literature of anti-semitism from antiquity to the present. With contributions from an international team of scholars, it covers the long history of antisemit-ism starting with ancient Greece and Egypt, through the anti-Judaism of early Christianity, and the medieval era in both the Christian and Muslim worlds when Jews were defined as outsiders, especially in Christian Europe. This portrayal often led to violence, notably pogroms that often accompanied the Crusades, as well as to libels against Jews. The volume also explores antisemitism in art and literature, the roles of Luther and the Reformation, the Enlightenment, the debate over Jewish emancipation, Marxism, and the social disruptions after World War I that led to the rise of Nazism and genocide. Finally, it considers current issues, the rise of the "New Antisemitism," the dissemination of hate on social media and the internet, and questions of definition and method.

Steven T. Katz is the Alvin J. and Shirley Slater Professor of Jewish & Holocaust Studies in the Department of Religion at Boston University. Editor of the journal *Modern Judaism*, he is the author of many prize-winning books, most recently *The Holocaust and New World Slavery: A Comparison*. He serves on the academic committee of the US Holocaust Memorial Museum and from 2011 to 2017 acted as academic advisor to the thirty-six-country International Holocaust Remembrance Alliance.

(continued after the index)

THE CAMBRIDGE COMPANION TO

ANTISEMITISM

Edited by

Steven T. Katz
Boston University

CAMBRIDGE
UNIVERSITY PRESS

CAMBRIDGE
UNIVERSITY PRESS

Shaftesbury Road, Cambridge CB2 8EA, United Kingdom

One Liberty Plaza, 20th Floor, New York, NY 10006, USA

477 Williamstown Road, Port Melbourne, VIC 3207, Australia

314–321, 3rd Floor, Plot 3, Splendor Forum, Jasola District Centre, New Delhi – 110025, India

103 Penang Road, #05–06/07, Visioncrest Commercial, Singapore 238467

Cambridge University Press is part of Cambridge University Press & Assessment, a department of the University of Cambridge.

We share the University's mission to contribute to society through the pursuit of education, learning and research at the highest international levels of excellence.

www.cambridge.org
Information on this title: www.cambridge.org/9781108714525

DOI: 10.1017/9781108637725

First published 2022

A catalogue record for this publication is available from the British Library

ISBN   978-1-108-49440-3   Hardback
ISBN   978-1-108-71452-5   Paperback

Contents

Contributors

Allan Arkush is Professor of Judaic Studies and History at Binghamton University. He is the Senior Contributing Editor of the *Jewish Review of Books*.

Steven B. Bowman is Emeritus Professor of Judaic Studies, University of Cincinnati. He is author of *Jews of Byzantium 1204–1453* (1985) and *The Agony of Greek Jewry 1940–1945* (2009).

Bruno Chaouat is Professor of French and Jewish Studies at the University of Minnesota. His recent book, *Is Theory Good for the Jews?* (2016), explores the responses of French thought to the rise of antisemitism since the beginning of the millennium.

Robert Chazan is the Scheuer Professor of Hebrew and Judaic Studies Emeritus at New York University. His most recent books are: *From Anti-Judaism to Anti-Semitism* (2016) and *Refugees or Migrants: Pre-Modern Jewish Population Movement* (2018).

Bryan Cheyette is Professor of English Literature at the University of Reading. He has published four books on literary antisemitism including *Constructions of "the Jew" in English Literature and Society: Racial Representations, 1875–1945*. His most recent book is *Ghetto: A Very Short Introduction* (2020).

Jeremy Cohen is the Spiegel Family Foundation Professor of European Jewish History at Tel Aviv University. His publications focus on theological perceptions of the "other," historiography, and the history of biblical interpretation, from late antiquity until the onset of modernity.

Laura Engelstein is Henry S. McNeil Professor of Russian History Emerita at Yale University and Professor Emerita of History at Princeton University. She is the author most recently of *The Resistible Rise of Antisemitism: Exemplary Cases from Russia, Ukraine, and Poland* (2020).

Reuven Firestone is the Regenstein Professor in Medieval Judaism and Islam at Hebrew Union College in Los Angeles. His monographs include *Jihad: The Origin of Holy War in Islam* (1999) and *Holy War in Judaism: The Fall and Rise of a Controversial Idea* (2012).

Joshua Garroway is the Sol and Arlene Bronstein Professor of Judeo-Christian Studies at the Hebrew Union College–Jewish Institute of Religion in Los

Angeles, California. Among his recent publications is *The Beginning of the Gospel: Paul, Philippi, and the Origins of Christianity* (2018).

Erich S. Gruen is Gladys Rehard Wood Professor of History and Classics, Emeritus at the University of California, Berkeley. His most recent book is *Ethnicity in the Ancient World – Did it Matter?* (2020).

Andrew S. Jacobs is a Senior Fellow at the Center for the Study of World Religions at Harvard Divinity School and is editor of the *Elements in Religion in Late Antiquity* series from Cambridge University Press.

Jack Jacobs is Professor of Political Science at John Jay College and the Graduate Center, City University of New York. He is the author of *The Frankfurt School, Jewish Lives, and Antisemitism* (2015).

Debra Kaplan is Associate Professor of Jewish History and Director of the Halpern Center for the Study of Jewish Self-Perception at Bar-Ilan University. She is the author of *Beyond Expulsion: Jews, Christians and Reformation Strasbourg* (2011), and *The Patrons and Their Poor: Jewish Community and Public Charity in Early Modern Germany* (2020).

Steven T. Katz holds the Alvin J. and Shirley Slater Chair in Jewish Holocaust Studies at Boston University and edits the journal *Modern Judaism*. He served as academic advisor to the International Holocaust Remembrance Alliance from 2011 to 2017. His most recent publication is *The Holocaust and New World Slavery: A Comparison* (2019).

Deborah E. Lipstadt is the Dorot Professor of Modern Jewish History and Holocaust Studies at Emory University. Her most recent publication is *Antisemitism Here and Now* (2019).

Michael Mack (1970–2020) was Associate Professor in English Studies at Durham University. He is the author of seven books, including *German Idealism and the Jew: The Inner Antisemitism of Philosophy and German Jewish Responses* (2003). His final book is *Disappointment: Its Modern Roots from Spinoza to Contemporary Literature* (2020).

Julie Mell is Associate Professor of History at North Carolina State University and author of the two-volume work *The Myth of the Medieval Jewish Moneylender* (2017).

Pierluigi Piovanelli is Professor of Second Temple Judaism and Early Christianity at the University of Ottawa (Ontario) and Directeur d'études at the École pratique des hautes études, Sciences religieuses, Université Paris Sciences et Lettres, in Paris, France. He is the author of *Apocryphités. Études sur les textes et les traditions scripturaires du judaïsme et du christianisme anciens* (2016).

Dina Porat is the Head of the Kantor Center for the Study of Contemporary European Jewry at Tel Aviv University and also serves as chief historian of Yad Vashem. Her most recent book, *To Me Belongeth Vengeance and Recompense* (2019), deals with post-Holocaust attempts to avenge German crimes committed during the Holocaust.

Adele Reinhartz is Professor in the Department of Classics and Religious Studies at the University of Ottawa, Canada. Her most recent book is *Cast Out of the Covenant: Jews and Anti-Judaism in the Gospel of John* (2018). She was elected to the Royal Society of Canada in 2005 and served as President of the Society of Biblical Literature in 2020.

Emily M. Rose is Research Associate, Department of History, Harvard University. She is the author of *The Murder of William of Norwich: The Origins of the Blood Libel in Medieval Europe* (2015), which won the Ralph Waldo Emerson Award of the Phi Beta Kappa Society and was named a Top Ten History Book of the Year by the Sunday *Times*.

Miri Rubin is Professor of Medieval and Early Modern History at Queen Mary College, University of London. Her most recent book, *Cities of Strangers: Making Lives in Medieval Europe*, was published in 2020.

Maurice Samuels is the Betty Jane Anlyan Professor of French at Yale University, where he directs the Yale Program for the Study of Antisemitism. His most recent book is *The Betrayal of the Duchess: The Scandal That Unmade the Bourbon Monarchy and Made France Modern* (2020).

Jonathan D. Sarna is University Professor and the Joseph H. & Belle R. Braun Professor of American Jewish history at Brandeis University; he also directs the Schusterman Center for Israel Studies. His many books include *American Judaism: A History* (2019).

Debra Higgs Strickland is Professor of Medieval Art History at the University of Glasgow. She is the author of *Saracens, Demons, and Jews: Making Monsters in Medieval Art* (2003) and *The Epiphany of Hieronymus Bosch: Imagining Antichrist and Others from the Middle Ages to the Reformation* (2016).

Shulamit Volkov is Professor Emerita at Tel Aviv University and a member of the Israeli Academy of Science and the Humanities. She is the author of *Germans, Jews, and Antisemites: Trials in Emancipation* (2006) and *Walther Rathenau: Weimar's Fallen Statesman* (2012).

Esther Webman (1947–2020) was a senior researcher in the Dayan Center for Middle Eastern and African Studies and the Principal Investigator for the Program for the Study of Jews in the Middle East, both at Tel Aviv University. She coauthored the Washington Institute prize winner, *From Empathy to Denial: Arab Responses to the Holocaust* (2009).

Mark Weitzman is Chief Operating Officer of the World Jewish Restitution Organization. Previously he was Director of Government Affairs at the Simon Wiesenthal Center and past chair of the International Holocaust Remembrance Alliance's Committee on Antisemitism and Holocaust Denial. His publications include *Jews and Judaism in the Political Theology of Radical Catholic Traditionalists* (2015).

Acknowledgments

Creating a volume of new essays on a wide variety of topics and covering over 2,000 years of history required advice and assistance from many individuals. In the present case, I received important assistance from Professors David Berger (Yeshiva University) and Paula Fredriksen (Hebrew University), who were especially helpful in advising on which topics should be included in this collection. Second, I must thank all the scholars who wrote the studies that comprise this work. Distinguished scholars all, they cooperated with a smile in bringing the book to fruition. I want especially to thank Dr. Mark Weitzman, who stepped in at the last moment to supply the essential essay on the importance today of the World Wide Web as a disseminator of antisemitism in all its forms.

On a personal level, I am indebted to Professor Stephen Whitfield (Emeritus, Brandeis University), Professor Louis Dickstein (Emeritus, Wellesley College), Dr. Felice Dickstein, and Professor Sander Gilman (Emeritus, Emory University) for reading the Introduction and making helpful suggestions about its final form.

Last but not least, I owe a great deal to three very thoughtful and always helpful individuals: Ms. Lilka Elbaum, my extremely capable, very reliable, and unfailingly cooperative assistant; Ms. Beatrice Rehl, my helpful and attentive editor at Cambridge University Press, who was a pleasure to work with on this project; and my wife Rebecca, who, as always, graciously and good humoredly aided in all the steps that were involved in moving the volume from conception to publication.

To all, a most sincere "Thank You."

Steven T. Katz, Editor

Introduction

STEVEN T. KATZ

ANTI-JUDAISM IN THE PRE-CHRISTIAN WORLD

Antisemitism[1] is a late 19th-century (1870) term based on pseudo-scientific racial theory that was coined to describe in a new way opposition to, and hatred of, the Jewish People and their form of life. Though a relatively recent linguistic and ideological construction, it draws on and extends a much older tradition of anti-Jewish enmity that has its roots in the pre-Christian world of Greece, Rome, and Hellenistic Egypt and was then reinterpreted and radically reconceived in early Christianity beginning with the writings of Paul and the four Gospels that form the core of the New Testament.

Even before the rise of Christianity and its intense anti-Jewish polemic, Jews were presented in the Hellenistic world, and especially in Roman (Latin) and Egyptian literature, as being "strange," primarily due to their religious beliefs that included having only one God who could not be seen, taking off every seventh day – the Sabbath – from labor, and eating only restricted types of food that excluded pork, shellfish, and birds of prey. In addition, as historian Salo Baron has pointed out:

> The ever-noisy and quarrelsome citizenry of a Graeco-Oriental municipality resented, in particular, the peculiarities of the Jewish way of life. The segregated life of the Jewish communities injected further venom into the strained relationship. Already the Jews had a sort of ghetto. At least in Alexandria, Sardes, and Apollinopolis Magna (Edfu), perhaps also in Rome, Oxyrhynchus, Hermopolis and Halicarnassus, there existed predominantly Jewish quarters.... Life

---

[1] In this volume, the word "antisemitism" will appear in this form, following the recent trend in scholarly publications. The older spelling – anti-Semitism – is rejected because it suggests that there is such a thing as Semitism, meaning a particular Jewish racial character and distinguishable set of attributes.

within these quarters, proceeding in strange and incomprehensible ways, filled the superficial Gentile observer with awe and suspicion, or with abhorrence and contempt.[2]

That is, Jews were perceived, for many different reasons, as aliens who were destroying local social customs, pagan family life, and local religious tradition.

This led to a widespread view that Jews were misanthropic, superstitious, and arrogant, believing themselves to have a special covenantal relationship with their unseen Deity, while the gods of the pagan traditions were idols. (See Erich Gruen's essay for full details.) This negative view is present, for example, in Haman's critique of Jews in the *Book of Esther* 3:8–9:

> Haman then said to King Ahasuerus: "There is a certain people scattered and dispersed among the people in all the provinces of your kingdom; their laws are different from all other people's, and they do not keep the king's laws. Therefore, it is not fitting for the king to let them remain. If it pleases the king, let a decree be written that they be destroyed, and I will pay ten thousand talents of silver into the hands of those who do the work, to bring it into the king's treasuries." (New King James Version, Esther 3:8–9)

This paradigmatic statement, representative of pre-Christian anti-Judaism, is not only significant in itself but also important because its employment in the *Book of Esther* suggests that this theme was well known to the contemporary readers of the story (between 400 and 300 BCE is the probable date of composition). It would appear that this negative appraisal was a common idea among non-Jews, as indicated by the fact that one finds it in the writings of the Egyptian priest Manetho (early 3rd century BCE), who criticized Moses and the Jewish version of the Exodus story; in the hostile accusations made by Cicero; and in the critique of the Roman historian Lysimachus, who argued that the Jews "have no good intentions towards any man, to give not the best but the worst advice, to tear down the temples and altars of the gods." Similarly, Tacitus (c. 56–120 CE) asserts that Jews are so hostile and perverse that, "although as a race [Jews] are prone to lust, they abstain from intercourse with foreign women."[3] It was, thus,

---

[2] Salo Baron, *A Social and Religious History of the Jews*, vol. 1 (New York, 1952), 188.
[3] Ibid., 194.

not surprising that a major pogrom took place in Alexandria in 88 BCE, and another occurred in 38 CE.[4]

CHRISTIAN ANTI-JUDAISM

On reflection, it is evident that this hatred, while genuine and destructive, can reasonably be labeled "sociological" and "anthropological." That is, it operates in our world, appeals to human characteristics and actions, and explains the offenses of the "other" in terms that make no appeal to transcendental forces. This situation changed with the momentous shift introduced by the coming of Christianity and its powerful, metaphysical polemic against Judaism.

To begin to understand the profound and pervasive legacy of premodern anti-Judaism requires that one turn to early Christianity, which supplied the religious foundation of this tradition. For despite the various competing and supporting ancillary theories of the causes of this malignancy, its base, its strength, its endurance, and its dissemination in Western culture are primarily, though not solely, rooted in religious claims.

It is impossible to read the Pauline epistles, the synoptic Gospels, and later patristic sources, that is, the writings of the Church Fathers, without seeing them as affirming two salient claims: (1) Judaism is, since the coming of Christ, a spiritual cadaver, and (2) Jews and Judaism stand in dishonoring opposition, at least since the first Easter, to God's salvific plan for humankind. In these two theses lie the roots of that religious anti-Judaism that has reverberated through the last two millennia and that has laid the basis for modern antisemitism.

To appreciate what this denigration of Judaism signifies and why its civilizational legacy is so wounding, one must grasp the dynamics of early Christian anti-Jewish writings. The struggle between the nascent church and the established Jewish community was over the entitlement to the "promises" of the Torah and their meaning. Who are the "children of the promise," the "Israel" in whom "all the nations will be blessed"? Was it the "Israel of the Flesh," the biological descendants of Abraham? Or was it the new messianic community of those faithful to

---

[4] Readers need to remember that criticism of Jews in different times and places is influenced by the context, that is, the intellectual and religious civilization, of the period in question. Thus, the "Jew" criticized by Cicero and Tacitus is not exactly like the "Jew" of Paul, or Matthew, or the Quran. Nor is Luther's "Jew" the same as the "Jew" imagined in the current BDS movement or by contemporary white, right-wing nationalists.

Jesus? Self-evidently, it was the second, and accordingly, in self-justification, it was necessary to impugn the religious integrity of Judaism for were the "Israel of the Flesh" faithful, the Jewish reading of Torah valid, the Hebraic account of salvation correct, then what reason would there be for the "promises" passing to a new, gentile Israel? Only if the Torah were *not* a source of "righteousness," of "justification," and the "Old" Israel found unfaithful and guilty, could there be cause for God to seek a new covenantal partner. As Paul famously insists: "If justification were through the law [Torah], then Christ died in vain.... For all who rely on works of the law are under a curse" (*Galatians* 3:10–14 and see also 3:21).

As a consequence of the spiritual darkness in which Jews live, due to their rejection of Jesus as the promised Messiah, they are, according to Paul, "a rebellious and apostate people" (Romans 10:21). He has God say, "All day long I have held out my hands to a disobedient and contrary people" (ibid.). Stephen in *Acts of the Apostles* is still more explicit: "You stiff-necked people uncircumcised in heart and ears, you always resist the Holy Spirit. As your fathers did so do you. Which of the prophets did not your fathers persecute? And they killed those that beforehand announced the coming of the Righteous One" (Acts 7:51–53). Not only is the "Israel of the Flesh" corrupt, but it consciously chooses its corruption. Not only does it fatally follow a law that is dysfunctional, but it persists in maintaining this rebellious course even when God would open the eyes of the Jewish People and return them to Himself. Israel is not only blind but radically disobedient; not only does it not know God's true purpose, but it wills not to know it. So "the Jew" becomes the enemy of man and God, and the main root of the development that leads to medieval and modern antisemitism is set in place.

This heinous tradition of apostasy, according to the synoptic (Gospel) authors writing in the decades after Paul's death, reaches its climax in the key role that Israel is said to have played in the Crucifixion. According to Mark:

> And Pilate again said to them, "Then what shall I do with the man whom you call the King of the Jews?" And they cried out again, "Crucify him." And Pilate said to them, "Why, what evil has he done?" But they shouted all the more, "Crucify him." So, Pilate, wishing to satisfy the crowd, released for them Barabbas; and having scourged Jesus, he delivered him to be crucified. (Mark 15:12–15)

Matthew retells this same sinister tale nearly exactly but adds the pregnant, enduring phrase, so costly in Jewish lives, "[Pilate said] I am innocent of this man's blood ... and all the [Jewish] people answered, 'His blood be upon us and our children'" (27:15–26). John, writing most probably in the early 2nd century, goes even further, emphasizing that the Jews themselves crucified Jesus: "Then [Pilate] handed him over to them [the priests] to be crucified" (19:16). The full perversity, the unrestricted obstinacy of Israel as manifest in this titanic act of treason against heaven, must be properly and completely understood. When the Almighty, in his great mercy, sent the prophets to call the Jews to keep the law, they persecuted and killed them. Now, when God, in his infinite graciousness, sends his only Son to free the Jews from "the curse of the law," perverse community that they are, they kill him and continue to keep the law. Whatever Heaven wills, the Jewish people will choose the opposite. The consequence of this final, overwhelming act of disobedience, of deicide, is the rejection of the Jews by God. The "new covenant," therefore, is with the gentiles.

This censure reaches a climax in the metaphysical revaluations of the Gospel of John. Here "the Jew" is seen as a wholly negative "other." "You [Jews] are of your Father, the devil," John affirms, "and your will is to do your Father's desires" (8:43–44). However one reads this Johannine description of the tragic encounter of Christ and "the Jews," there can be no denying that in John's harsh rendition the clash has come to be seen as the temporal locus of more than historical actualities. The unconscionable role that the Jews, as the Devil's henchmen, play in the Crucifixion proves, as John has Jesus say, "[The Jews] do not belong to God" (8:47).

One, therefore, discerns in the New Testament – in this anti-Jewish theology of fulfillment, displacement, and negation, in these accusations of apostasy and deicide (deciphered more completely in the essay by Adele Reinhartz) – the origination of the abiding and tragic conflict between Judaism and Christianity.[5]

The early, post–New Testament Christian sources – primarily the product of gentile authors unconnected to Jews and Judaism by ties of biology, family, sociology, or common political needs – continued to amplify the anti-Jewish critique that they had inherited. The famous

---

[5] On the growing friction as seen from the Jewish perspective, see Steven T. Katz, "Issues in the Separation of Judaism and Christianity after 70 CE: A Reconsideration," *Journal of Biblical Literature* 103.1 (April 1984), 43–76; and Steven T. Katz, "The Rabbinic Response to Christianity," in Steven T. Katz, ed., *The Cambridge History of Judaism*, vol. 4: *The Late Roman Rabbinic Period* (Cambridge, 2006), 259–298.

Church Father, Justin Martyr (d. c. 165), chastised Israel in what became paradigmatic terms:

> For the circumcision according to the flesh, which is from Abraham, was given for a sign; that you may be separated from other nations, and from us; and that you alone may suffer that which you now justly suffer; and that your land may be desolate, and your cities burned with fire; and that strangers may eat your fruit in your presence, and not one of you may go up to Jerusalem.[6]

"Accordingly," claimed Justin, "these things have happened to you in fairness and justice, for you have slain the Just One." What transpires, what has transpired, is a new revelation through which the Jewish people are recognized as God's enemies, their outcast political status a sign of rejection: "The city where Jesus suffered was necessarily destroyed, the Jewish nation was driven from its country, and another people called by God to the blessed election."[7]

By the patristic era – as analyzed in the contributions by Joshua Garroway, Andrew Jacobs, and Steven Bowman – the encounter between Jew and Christian, between synagogue and church, was perceived as the embodiment of Satan's clash with Jesus, of Evil's rebellion against the Good, of the assault of the Sons of Darkness against the Sons of Light, of the Powers of Hell arrayed in deadly opposition to the Powers of Heaven. "If a person," John Chrysostom wrote in the 4th century, "should call the Synagogue a brothel today, or a criminals' hangout, or a resort of demons, or a citadel of the Devil, or the ruin of souls, or a cliff and a pit of complete destruction, or any other name whatever, he would speak more kindly than the place deserves."[8] "The Jews" had become and were to remain perfidious, more than human, opponents of God Himself. "The demons inhabit the very souls of the Jews."[9] They are the very "devil's teeth" who snatch away God's people and make sacrifice of them to the Devil.

What is all-important about these theological caricatures is that they continue to consign the conflict between synagogue and church to the realm of myth and metaphysics. Though the patristic writers did

---

[6] Thomas Halton, Thomas Falls, and Michael Slusser, eds., *Dialogue with Trypho* (Washington, DC, 2003), 202.
[7] Origen, *Contra Celsum*, trans. Henry Chadwick (Cambridge, 1965), 4:23.
[8] St. John Chrysostom, *Adversus Judaeos* [*Eight Homilies against the Jews*], 4:23, trans. C. M. Maxwell, PhD diss., University of Chicago, 1967. There are also standard published translations available.
[9] Ibid., 2:3.

not invent this interpretive form – the authors of the New Testament already spoke in these idioms, for example, John on the link between Jews and the Devil – they gave it extensive room for growth, heartily nurtured its most unsavory elements, and consciously assured that it would become the fixed pattern for all subsequent readings of the Jewish–Christian encounter. After the combined hermeneutical assault of the New Testament and the patristic writings, the Jew is never again to be "a man like other men." He has become a *mythic* creature. (See the essay by Pierluigi Piovanelli.)

These theological images and understandings, not surprisingly, would come to have weighty and enduring practical and legal consequences with the conversion of Constantine the Great in 312 CE and the Christianization of the Roman Empire in the first quarter of the 4th century. Jews now were legally defined as theological enemies and "outsiders" relative to all the main private and communal areas of life, as explained in Chapter 5 by Andrew Jacobs.

As the Church expanded significantly in the first three centuries after the Crucifixion of Jesus, and eventually gained real power with the conversion of Constantine, its hostility toward Jews and Judaism grew in every direction, including, most importantly, in its political influence within the Roman Empire. Now the Jewish–Christian conflict was not simply rhetorical. The Church had the power to translate its anti-Jewish views into concrete legislation that increasingly marginalized the Jew. Accordingly, Jews were pushed out of the mainstream of the social, economic, and political order.

Among the Church Fathers there is one whose understanding of Jewish–Christian relations requires separate consideration given its historical consequence in limiting anti-Jewish violence. This, of course, is Augustine (354–430 CE). Over against the extremism of John Chrysostom and other Christian writers of the 2nd to 5th centuries, Augustine's position was more constrained and his revisionist position significantly influenced the Church's official teaching on the Jews from the 5th century onward.

Augustine's analysis of the Jewish situation represents a creative conservative innovativeness. Its conservatism is reflected in its doctrinal Paulinism and in its inherited, shared anti-Judaism. His representative tract, *Contra judaeos*, his derogatory pronouncements in *Contra faustum*, and his eschatological observations on Jewish apostasy and its eventual overcoming in the *City of God* (books 18 and 20), are all, on one level, unoriginal recyclings of the unforgiving patristic idiom.

On a second level, however, amid this dogmatic continuity, Augustine contributes an important innovation as to how the Church should understand and correspondingly react to the Jewish people. He does this by emphasizing in a new and central way the meaning of the seminal doctrine of the "wandering Jew." Though he does not invent this idea, his ideological reinterpretation of it proves historically consequential for the actual practices embodied in Christian anti-Judaism. According to Augustine's ironic reading, "the Jews," above all else, are seen as a people who, in their homelessness, constitute the strange, theologically fertile, "witness of unbelief." Furthermore, he interpreted the Cain and Abel story (Genesis 4:1–16) as an allegory of the relationship that obtains between "the Jews" (Cain) and Christ (Abel) – "the Jews" (Cain) find their offering to God rejected, whereas the faith of Abel is preferred on high. But in the same way that God warned the generation of Cain and Abel that Cain was not to be harmed by man as God would supply the retribution, so, too, Christians should not do evil to the Jews.

Moreover, the rejection of "the Jews" is, in some mysterious way, a gift that makes it possible for the gentiles to become part of the covenantal community of the elect. Israel's apostasy and subsequent punishment, as well as its continued proclamation of the Torah – even though blind to its supreme meaning (Christ Jesus) – reveal important lessons for Christian society. Just as Cain's treachery verified and exalted Abel's faithfulness, so the skepticism of "the Jews," their consequent fall from favor, the destruction of their Temple, and their exile, reinforce the truth of Christianity in an overwhelmingly visible and experiential way.[10] Accordingly, "the Jews" (real Jews) are not to be harmed by Christians but, rather, are to wander the earth as proof of their rejected status.[11] In God's good time, as part of the eschaton, in conjunction with the return of Christ in glory, this exilic status will end as the ultimate sign of Christ's power and graciousness. In this accounting, Jewish survival thus becomes, paradoxically, a Christian theological imperative. Both Jewry's present exile and its final redemption play central, inescapable roles in this influential version of Christian belief. Until today, as seen among Christian fundamentalists, though no less part of the dogmatics of mainline Protestants and the Catholic and Orthodox churches, this connection of Jewish wandering, Jewish survival, and Christian eschatological hope remains alive.

---

[10] See here Augustine's *The City of God* 18.46, trans. John Healy (London, 1931).
[11] The scenario is described in Augustine's *The Reply to Faustus*, ed. and trans. Frank Talmage in his *Disputation and Dialogue* (New York, 1975).

The Theodosian Code created in 438 CE, and the Justinian Code, or *Corpus juris civilis* of 534 CE, formalized this exclusion of Jews from the main centers of civil society and set the foundations for the anti-Judaism – social, economic, political, cultural, and theological – of the medieval and modern eras. (The many crucial developments in the Christian medieval period are discussed in chapters by Robert Chazan, Emily Rose, Julie Mell, Miri Rubin, and Debra Higgs Strickland). By the 6th century CE, disabilities and exclusions vis-à-vis Jews were the norm in the Roman Empire and then in the Byzantine era (described by Steven Bowman). And this became the common existential and political circumstance of Jews in Christian society until the 18th century.[12] (See the essay by Jeremy Cohen.)

Christianity's anti-Jewish understanding, along with its state power, would continue to grow, especially with the encouragement of Martin Luther (as explained by Debra Kaplan) until the Age of Enlightenment and the late 18th-century debate over Jewish Emancipation (analyzed by Allan Arkush). But even in the post-emancipation era, as fundamental changes in the status of Jews and Judaism were inaugurated, the toxic teaching of the "Jew" as diabolical and more than an ordinary human enemy remained – and still remains – within segments of Western cultural and political traditions. So powerful was this antisemitic inheritance that it ultimately generated new social and economic doctrines that, for example, explained the older anti-Jewish restrictions by the conception of *racial* antisemitism. According to this new explanation, race not only decided one's physical features – tall or short, black or white – but also predetermined one's character and moral virtues, as well as the rise and fall of nations. Moreover, while the earlier, theological anti-Judaism allowed for conversion and hence a change in political and theological status, race was immutable and allowed no escape. This eventually became the doctrine that led to and supported antisemitic political parties and state actions, and, ultimately, Nazi Death Camps. (This crucial issue is analyzed in my "Weimar" essay and in the essays of Shulamit Volkov and Laura Engelstein.)

Consider as evidence of this "staying power" the following facts:

(1) Jews in the modern era, as was widely believed in the medieval era, are negatively associated with disease. Today, in 2021, the internet

---

[12] On these significant developments, see A. H. M. Jones, *The Decline of the Ancient World* (London, 1960), 945–947; and Marcel Simon, *Versus Israel: A Study of the Relations between Christians and Jews in the Roman Empire (AD 135–425)* (Paris, 1983; New York, 1986).

is saturated with articles linking the medieval myth that Jews caused the Black Death in 1348–1349 with the claim that Jews are the cause and prime spreaders of COVID-19. There are thousands of items on the Web spreading this lie.

(2) Jews are said to be continuing their practice of killing non-Jewish children for their blood, especially using it in the making of Passover matzoh (unleavened bread). This falsehood continued to circulate in modern, that is, post-1800, history in famous cases like those in Tiszaeszlár, Hungary (1882–1883), and Damascus, Syria (1840). It was recycled in Czarist Russia in the notorious Beilis trial in 1913, and again in Poland after the Holocaust – in Kielce on July 4, 1946, in Rzeszow on June 12, 1945, and then in Krakow shortly thereafter.[13] Today, this idea has been recycled in the libelous claim that Israeli soldiers are killing Palestinian children in order to harvest their organs.

(3) The blood libel was the theme of a fifty-two-part series on Syrian TV sponsored by the Syrian government.[14]

(4) The belief that Jews are physically misshapen, understood as a sign of their moral and spiritual degeneracy, played a part in the hotly contested, January 5, 2021, US Senate runoff in Georgia. Some political advertisements against the Jewish Democratic Party candidate, Jon Ossoff, pictured him with an elongated "Jewish" nose.[15]

(5) The continual emphasis on the connection between Jews and money that began to circulate in the medieval era, centered around usury, received a major boost in the mid-19th century from Karl Marx (whose controversial position is deciphered by Jack Jacobs). Marx wrote: "What is the object of the Jew's worship in this world: Usury. What is his worldly god? Money." This theme has reverberated in both left-wing and right-wing circles: see, for example, the caricaturing of candidate Ossoff with the theme of "buying Georgia" employed by his rival, Republican Senator David Perdue, in political advertisements. Similarly, Louis Farrakhan, in a speech in Dallas, asked his audience: "Is the Federal Reserve owned by the

---

[13] On the Blood Libel, see Magda Teter, *Blood Libel: On the Trail of an Antisemitic Myth* (Cambridge, MA, 2020), and Elissa Bemporad, *Legacy of Blood: Jews, Pogroms and Ritual Murder in the Lands of the Soviets* (Oxford, 2019).

[14] Robert Wistrich, *Muslim Anti-Semitism: A Clear and Present Danger* (New York, 2002), 31.

[15] Dave Schechter, "Perdue Campaign Removes Ad Ossoff Called 'Anti-Semitic,'" *Atlanta Jewish Times*, July 28, 2020: https://atlantajewishtimes.timesofisrael.com/2020-yir-perdue-campaign-removes-ad-ossoff-called-anti-semitic/.

government?" Audience: "No." Farrakhan: "Who owns the Federal Reserve?" Audience: "Jews."[16]

Here myth manifests itself as extreme paranoia.

In both Europe and America this same theme has been widely used to smear George Soros, whose liberal views are anathema in his native Hungary, as well as in Poland, and also in 2021 antisemitic circles in the United States. Some examples of recent Web postings:

- Soros owns company where Coronavirus broke out.
- Israel-linked Dr. Charles *Lieber* arrested for receiving payment and smuggling biomaterials to Wuhan University.
- Israel was "already working on a vaccine"
- That's some MIGHTY BIG COHENCIDENCES.

Then there is the accusation made by former Wisconsin Sheriff David A. Clark, Jr., who, without evidence, tweeted that George Soros was involved with the spread of the coronavirus: "Not ONE media outlet has asked about George Soros's involvement in this FLU panic. He is SOMEWHERE involved in this." Conservative commentator Candace Owens has accused Soros (via tweets on May 28, 2020) of "funding the chaos" in Minneapolis following the death of George Floyd by hiring protestors to demonstrate. He has also been accused of fomenting the violent riots in Washington on January 6, 2021, in order to discredit President Trump. The Network Contagion Research Institute at Rutgers University reports that on an average day there are between 2,000 and 3,000 postings attacking George Soros. In May 2020, when the George Floyd racial protests were at a height, according to the Rutgers Institute there were 500,000 hostile protests against Soros in one day. (For more on the issue of antisemitism in America, see the chapter by Jonathan Sarna.)

ISLAMIC ANTISEMITISM

The majority of the essays included in this collection discuss various anti-Jewish elements in Western Christian tradition that run from the New Testament to the Holocaust and that color, with a unique depth and intensity, almost every aspect of social, cultural, political, and

---

[16] Called to my attention by Deborah Lipstadt, "*The Protocols of the Elders of Zion* on the Contemporary American Scene," in Richard Landes and Steven T. Katz, eds., *The Paranoid Apocalypse* (London, 2018), 180.

economic life in the countries of Europe (and was then carried to colonies in the Americas, Australia, and South Africa). It is essential, however, to recognize that the phenomenon of Judeophobia also existed centrally in Islam.

Contrary to the invented image of a "golden age" that is said to have existed between Jews and Muslims before the intrusion of Zionism, the reality is that since the initial period of the emergence of Islam, which came about through the preaching of Mohammed (571–632 CE), the relationship between the two religious communities has been unequal and distorted and led, in most Muslim societies, from the medieval to the modern era, to the articulation of an anti-Jewish theology, the passage of anti-Jewish social legislation, and the practice of taxing Jews unfairly.

The encounter between Jews and Mohammed that the new Prophet thought would lead Jews to accept his revelation led, instead, to anti-Jewish violence in Mecca and Medina. The height of this action is described in Islamic tradition as resulting from the angel Gabriel's command to Mohammed: "The [Jewish] men [of the Banu Qurayza tribe] should be killed [then], the property divided, and the women and children taken as captives." In response, Mohammed, in 627, "sent for [the Jews] and struck off their heads ... There were 600 to 700 in all, though some put the figure as high as 800 to 900."[17] Because they rejected the new teaching and were repeatedly described as plotting against Mohammed, the Jews were, according to Quranic tradition, punished by Allah. In a statement that essentially repeats Acts 7:51–53, the Quran states: "humiliation and wretchedness were stamped upon them and they (the Jews) were visited with God's wrath" (Quran 2:61).

As the Muslim forces created by Muhammed began to conquer the Middle East, including Jerusalem in 636–637 CE, Islam, from its position of dominance, formulated rules as to how non-Muslims were to be treated. Jews, like the Christians and Zoroastrians, were defined as "people of the book" (*Ahl al-Kitāb*), that is, as having a true, but inferior religion. As such they were not to be forced to convert to Islam. Defined as *dhimmis* ("protected minorities"), they were permitted to continue to practice their own religious traditions but, in return for this privilege, were required to assume a status as second-class members of Islamic society and to pay a special tax known as the *jizya*.

---

[17] David Nirenberg, *Anti-Judaism: The Western Tradition* (New York, 2013), 159–160.

The overall result of this arrangement established by Islamic law, most prominently set out in the Pact of Omar formulated about 637 by Omar I, after the conquest of Jerusalem, produced a culture and tradition, including a theological teaching, that while discriminatory was far less lethal than that dominant in Christian Europe.[18] There were instances of violence and the intensification of anti-Jewish actions, but these were not common. The myth of the "diabolization" of the Jew, and the claim that Jews represented a special, negative, subclan of humanity, was not developed and widely taught. Yet the relationship of Jews and Muslims was continually affected by anti-Jewish teachings in the Quran and the extra-Quranic traditions linked to Muhammad known as *hadiths*.

The status of Jews in medieval Muslim societies continued this nonviolent tradition – relative tolerance of Jews under conditions dictated by Islamic law. Over time, the financial demands made on *dhimmis* became exceedingly important to the fiscal health of various Muslim caliphates, assuring that Jews (and others) would neither be murdered en masse, nor even sought as converts because each act of apostasy entailed a decrease in much-needed state revenue. There were local persecutions of Jews in Islamic lands in violation of Quranic teaching, including occasions of forced conversion and the public mistreatment of Jews, even including the instigation of pogroms – as took place in Egypt in 1008 under the ruler al-Hakim, in Granada in 1066 following the death of the famous courtier Joseph ha-Nagid (son of the great Samuel ha-Nagid), during the Almohad persecutions in 12th-century Spain and North Africa, and the more stringent restrictions placed on *dhimmis* in 1301 by the Mamluk state. Nevertheless, such occurrences do not force any major revision of this comparative judgment regarding Islam and Christianity. In each of these (and other) cases, the causes of the antinomian atrocities are to be located in anomalous and provincial conditions and are, even then, to be viewed as temporary aberrations that *never* entailed genocidal-like violence.[19] In sum, Muslim policy toward Jews was demeaning

---

[18] For more on this topic, consult Arthur Stanley Tritton, *The Caliphs and Their Non-Muslim Subjects: A Critical Study of the Covenant of "Umar"* (London, 1970).

[19] Norman Stillman reports that "There is no more than half a dozen [instances of organized, collective acts of forced conversion of Jews to Islam] over a period of thirteen centuries – [and] all occurred under heterodox fanatics" (*Jews of Arab Lands* [Philadelphia, 1979], 76). Also see Bernard Lewis's pioneering work, *Semites and Antisemites: An Inquiry into Conflict and Prejudice* (New York, 1987).

and abusive, calculatedly exploitative, and socially debilitating – at times even deadly – but it operated under theological (as well as socioeconomic) restraints.

The details of this history are discussed in the essay by Reuven Firestone, so I will not extend this summary description of the medieval and early modern era relative to Jewish–Muslim relations. However, when continuing the discussion of this history it is necessary to note that Islamic antisemitism entered a new phase in the late 19th and early 20th century with the coming of modernization and the improvement of Jewish life in Muslim countries, a circumstance that resulted from the assistance of European countries and the rise of political Zionism. Now, borrowing from the antisemitic discourse of Christianity, Muslim culture began to import and circulate canards such as the blood libel and saw the translation of *The Protocols of the Elders of Zion* into Arabic. Under the influence of these mythic teachings, Islamic anti-Judaism took on a new, more extreme, character.

Today these accusations are standard fare in the Muslim campaign against Israel, most notably in Iran and among the Palestinians. Israel is again said to be practicing the blood libel, and Jewish doctors are accused of intentionally infecting and killing their Palestinian patients. Then, too, Abu Mazen (Mohammed Abbas), the leader of the Palestinian National Authority, did his doctorate on *The Protocols* at the University of Moscow,[20] and the historian Dr. Attalah Abu Al-Farah, believing the lies, has asked: "Can there be, in practice, co-existence on Palestinian land between ourselves and the Jews, in light of their mentality which stems from *The Protocols of the Elders of Zion?*"[21] In addition, Israel (and the Jews) are said to control the banks, the world's stock markets, the media (especially in America), and Hollywood. A conference of Muslim scholars and clerics, held at the prestigious Al-Azhar University in Cairo, defined Jews as "the worst enemies of Islam" and "the best friends of Satan."[22]

---

[20] Egyptian TV produced a series entitled *Rider without a Horse* based on the *Protocols* in the first decade of the twenty-first century. In 1988, Hamas' Charter stated that the Jews were behind the French Revolution, the Communist Revolution, World War II, Rotary Clubs, and Freemasons (Clemens Heni, *Antisemitism, a Specific Phenomenon: Holocaust Trivialization, Islamism, Post-colonial and Cosmopolitan Anti-Zionism Antisemitism* [Berlin, 2013], 489–491).

[21] Itamar Marcus and Barbara Cook, "*The Protocols of the Elders of Zion*: An Authentic Document in Palestinian Authority Ideology," in Landes and Katz, eds., *The Paranoid Apocalypse*, 154.

[22] Avi Becker, *The Chosen: The History of an Idea, the Anatomy of an Obsession* (New York, 2008), 58–59.

Though there is much more to say on this crucial contemporary issue, I will not continue the discussion here as the topic is well covered by Esther Webman's contribution to this collection. I would, however, add that in the 21st century anti-Israelism is the most fertile and continuous source of antisemitism in the world.

DEFINING ANTISEMITISM

Each chapter in the present collection has been written by an expert and represents the best contemporary scholarship regarding all the main issues. There is only one major topic that has not been adequately covered relative to the study of antisemitism in the Western and Islamic world and that is the definition of antisemitism.

The term "antisemitism" was coined in 1870 by Wilhelm Marr, a German Jew-hater; it drew on the rising racial theory that posited that different groups were defined by their biological racial characteristics. According to this new thesis there were many different racial communities, the two most prominent in modern Europe being defined and divided as Semites and antisemites. The latter were primarily identified with Northern Western Europeans – Germans, Austrians, Dutch, Norwegians, and Swedes – and the former with Jews.[23]

Over the years, many learned efforts have been devoted to framing a coherent and broadly inclusive determination of the word – and concept of – antisemitism, but none has fully succeeded in providing a definition that is adequately comprehensive. The difficulty in supplying an explanation was already recognized by the rabbinic sages of the Roman era, who were reduced to simply saying that anti-Judaism – and what we today, recognizing needed nuances, would label antisemitism – is akin to natural events: "Esau hates Jacob." The great Jewish historian Salo Baron did only little better when he defined Judeophobia as "the dislike of the unlike." This is true but is far from being an adequate deconstruction. A more recent account provides more substantial pointers regarding its meaning:

> [antisemitism] is a persisting latent structure of hostile beliefs towards Jews as a collectivity manifested in individuals as attitudes, and in culture as myth, ideology, folklore, and imagery, and in *actions* – social or legal discrimination, political

---

[23] Though the term also correctly applies to Arabs, this is not how it was ever employed.

mobilization against Jews, and collective or state violence – which results in and/or is designed to distance, displace, or destroy Jews as Jews. (some emphases omitted)[24]

This version provides a complex mix of sociology and psychology that emphasizes that hatred of Jews is a social construction rather than a response to individual Jewish behavior. However, the question of this definition's usefulness as a practical tool is not altogether clear.

A more recent effort by Kenneth Marcus proposes the following understanding:

> Following the work of Theodor Adorno and Helen Fein, we may define anti-Semitism as a set of negative attitudes, ideologies, and practices directed at Jews as Jews, individually or collectively, based upon and sustained by a repetitive and potentially self-fulfilling latent structure of hostile erroneous beliefs and assumptions that flow from the application of double standards toward Jews as a collectivity, manifested culturally in myth, ideology, folklore, and imagery, and urging various forms of restriction, exclusion, and suppression. This definition builds on Adorno's formulation: "This ideology [of antisemitism] consists... of stereotyped negative opinions describing the Jews as threatening, immoral, and categorically different from non-Jews, and of hostile attitudes urging various forms of restriction, exclusion, and suppression as a means of solving 'the Jewish problem.'" (emphasis omitted).[25]

This proposal is better than its predecessors, having the virtues of increased clarity and more contact with concrete cultural phenomena, though it, too, is not free of conceptual ambiguity.

In further work, Anthony Julius, the English barrister and historian of antisemitism, has added necessary nuance to the issue of definition. He tells us that English antisemitism – some of the character of which can be extrapolated to modern European states more generally – has four different types: "radical antisemitism of defamation, expropriation, murder, and expulsion; a literary antisemitism, or antisemitic discourse; a modern quotidian antisemitism of insult and partial exclusion;

---

[24] This is Helen Fein's definition, cited in Alvin Rosenfeld, ed., *Deciphering the New Antisemitism* (Bloomington, IN, 2015), 21. See also Deborah Lipstadt's comments on this definition in her essay in this collection.

[25] Ibid., 23. Note that not all anti-Zionist and anti-Israel writing is antisemitic. The complexity of when it is and when it isn't poses one of the main contemporary scholarly challenges.

and the new configuration of anti-Zionism."[26] All of these types are clearly evidenced in modern culture and literature and continue to exert influence, as evidenced by the essays of Maurice Samuels, Michael Mack, and Bryan Cheyette dealing with French, German, and English literature, respectively.

A more traditional construal can be found in the 2004 "Working Definition of Anti-Semitism" produced by the Organization for Security and Cooperation in Europe (OSCE). The definition reads:

> "Antisemitism is a certain perception of Jews, which may be expressed as hatred toward Jews. Rhetorical and physical manifestations of antisemitism are directed toward Jewish or non-Jewish individuals and/or their property, toward Jewish community institutions and religious facilities."
>
> ... The Centre also made clear that manifestations of antisemitism "could also target the state of Israel, conceived as a Jewish collectivity." It continues: "Antisemitism frequently charges Jews with conspiring to harm humanity and it is often used to blame Jews for 'why things go wrong.'"[27]

Alternatively, far removed from earlier efforts, as recently as 2015, Bernard Harrison has defined the elusive subject this way:

> as I see it – antisemitism is not, at least intrinsically, an aberration of the individual mind, but an aberration of Western civilization. Killing every antisemite, were such a thing possible, would not, in other words, rid the world of antisemitism, because vast and influential tracts of Western literature and public debate, sometimes openly, more often in thoroughly opaque and whitewashed ways, stink of it. Antisemitism, in other words, understood as I understand it, is not, or not primarily, a pathological disposition or function of the individual mind, but rather a type of *social* or *cultural* pathology: a self-replicating structure of temptations and apparently explanatory delusions embodied, independently of the individual mind, in a multitude of enduring written and quasi-proverbial forms, that stands permanently ready to introduce itself, like the scrap of

---

[26] I here cite Elhanan Yakira's summary of Julius's view, "Virtuous Antisemitism," in Rosenfeld, *Deciphering the New Antisemitism*, 98 n. 4.

[27] R. Amy Elman, "The EU's Response to Contemporary Antisemitism: A Shell Game," in Rosenfeld, *Deciphering the New Antisemitism*, 413–414. The Centre referred to is the European Union Monitoring Centre, now known as the Fundamental Rights Agency (FRA) of the EU.

self-replicating genetic material that constitutes a virus, into the minds of people struggling to define their relationship to society, and of society to them, in moments of political crisis. It is so deeply embedded in the culture that the only way to damage it, and perhaps in time get rid of it, is to attack it at the cultural, [and legal, SK] rather than the individual, level.[28]

This more philosophical reflection, concentrating on communal and societal factors rather than hatred of individuals, is important to keep in mind. Then, too, there is Jerome Chanes's streamlined definition: "antisemitism is all forms of hostility manifested towards the Jews throughout history that results from no legitimate cause."[29]

The recent definition, that today is the most widely used and has been adopted by many national governments (including the United States[30]) and international agencies, is the one formulated by the International Holocaust Remembrance Alliance (IHRA) in 2016. (See the Appendix.) The particular value of this version is that not only does it provide an explanation, but it also supplies informed examples of the concrete forms in which antisemitism manifests itself in our time. These include both traditional Judeophobic themes as well as newer forms related to the State of Israel. Though it has aroused opposition[31] because of its delineation of certain forms of anti-Israel criticism as antisemitism, it is, on the whole, persuasive, and its wide adoption – by the thirty-four member nations of the IHRA and by over twenty-five other countries and international organizations such as the UN – is evidence of this. Readers can see a detailed explanation of this definition in Dina Porat's discussion of anti-Zionism as antisemitism.

All of these efforts provide insight into the phenomenon of antisemitism, personal and societal, and throw light on its social, economic, and psychological causes and effects. But, as readers can appreciate, this is a very complex matter on which still further reflection is required.

---

[28] Bernard Harrison, "The Uniqueness Debate Revisited," in Rosenfeld, *Deciphering*, 318. See also Bernard Harrison, *Blaming the Jews: Politics and Delusion* (Bloomington, 2020).

[29] Jerome Chanes, *Antisemitism: A Reference Book* (Santa Barbara, CA, 2004), 2. This definition, however, leads to the always difficult but unavoidable issue of who decides what is legitimate.

[30] Reaffirmed February 1, 2021, on behalf of the Biden administration by Kara McDonald, Deputy Assistant Secretary of State.

[31] As represented, for example, by the Jerusalem Declaration on Antisemitism published on March 25, 2021. Available at https://jerusalemdeclaration.org.

THE PRESENT IMPORTANCE OF THIS VOLUME

The contributions to this volume are arranged chronologically according to era covered. This was the most reasonable approach to adopt given that each generation draws on, and is influenced by, its predecessors. As to the work's content, there was a pressing need to include essays on our contemporary situation as rabid antisemitism has again been let loose in our 21st-century world. The belief, widely held since 1945, that the Holocaust had "cured" the world of antisemitism is now seen to have been a tragic illusion, as is made evident by Deborah Lipstadt's essay on "New Issues" and Mark Weitzman's analysis of the role of the internet and social media as main disseminators of anti-Jewish hate. Antisemitism is again a daily experience in many parts of the globe, including America (as considered also by Jonathan Sarna). Contemporary manifestations include anti-Israelism, through which anti-Israel groups propagate antisemitism under the guise of anti-Zionism; Holocaust denial; and, not least, the dissemination of hate by political elites such as the British Labour Party under its former leader, Jeremy Corbyn, and the present Hungarian and Polish governments, not to speak of Iran and many Muslim states. False anti-Jewish claims appear daily in the fabrications propagated by Iran, Jihadists, right-wing activists, white supremacists, certain groups of Christian fundamentalists, and the Nation of Islam. It appears at even United Nations–sponsored events like the UN World Conference against Racism held in Durban, South Africa, in September 2001. As Joëlle Fiss of the European Union of Jewish Students wrote, reflecting on the outpouring of the vilest forms of Jew hatred at this event, "Durban reminded [us that] hatred can surface with no prior notice."[32]

As discussed, the completely fictional conspiracy theory propagated by *The Protocols of the Elders of Zion* continues to circulate widely. Take as an example: "In January 2002 the *New Statesman*, an august journal of the British Centre-Left, published a cover story about the 'Zionist lobby' in Britain. The magazine's cover displayed a golden Star of David stabbing a pliant Union flag and carried the legend: 'A Kosher *Conspiracy*?'"[33]

This same conspiracy myth of Jewish world domination also provided the basis of the lie that "the Jews" – or perhaps more specifically

---

[32] Joëlle Fiss, *The Durban Diaries* (New York, 2008), 43.

[33] Efraim Sicher, *Multiculturalism, Globalization and Antisemitism: The British Case* (Jerusalem, 2009), 40.

Mossad, the Israeli secret service – had planned and carried out the bombing of the World Trade Center in New York City on September 11, 2001. This fantasy required no real evidence as *The Protocols* had laid the foundation for such accusations. *The Protocols* could even be found for sale in Walmart stores in 2004. In reply to criticism, Walmart put out a justification that its executives had not seen "a clear and convincing" argument that *The Protocols* was a lie. In effect, Walmart was endorsing the conspiracy theory articulated by this hoax. The same occurred regarding a UNESCO-sponsored exhibit organized in connection with the new library in Alexandria, Egypt. The theme of the exhibition was monotheism; to represent Jewish monotheism the organizers displayed two items, a Torah scroll and a copy of *The Protocols*, both described as sacred books of Judaism. Finally, I cite a posting of June 2, 2020, explaining the violence and lawlessness then unfolding in American cities as a protest against police brutality and the killing of George Floyd. The posting read: "White buses marked 'Soros Riot Dance Squad' spotted in Michigan: Its official, the riots are staged."[34]

All of these examples are fabrications. But even when one recognizes that these are lies, there is a pernicious twist, as Michael Barkun has explained:[35]

> There is a subculture of those for whom stigmatized knowledge claims are considered authoritative precisely because they have been stigmatized. To be rejected, to be denied access to university curricula, to respected newspapers, to the pulpits of major religious organizations, to scientific and medical text-books – for some, it is precisely such rejection that confers the ultimate form of validation. To those already disposed to suspect authority, what could be more persuasive than the cultural products that authority itself rejects? For them, the *Protocols* is compelling because it has been rejected, not in spite of it.

One of the most famous philosophers of the twentieth century, the Nazi sympathizer Martin Heidegger, when told that the *Protocols* were a forgery, still did not give up his false beliefs about them, replying instead: "But the dangerous international alliance of the Jews still exists."[36]

---

[34] Posted on www.intellihub.com, June 2, 2020.
[35] On this, see Michael Barkun, "Anti-Semitism from Outer Space: The Protocols in the UFO Subculture," in Landes and Katz, eds., *The Paranoid Apocalypse*, 170.
[36] Reported in Elżbieta Ettinger, *Hannah Arendt, Martin Heidegger* (New York, 1995), 48.

TOPICS THAT STILL REQUIRE CONSIDERATION

In concluding these introductory remarks, I will add only that, in spite of all the empirical and theoretical research done on the subject of antisemitism, there is much that we do not wholly understand about this phenomenon and all of the kaleidoscopic forms that it takes. These unresolved issues include three that are of primary importance. First is the provision of a really convincing explanation of the causes of contemporary Judeophobia in a world that has moved on from traditional Christian anti-Judaism. (For more on this, see the discussion of Bruno Chaouat.) Second is providing a way to accurately measure this phenomenon in any given society at any given time. In taking up this question, one enters the extremely complex area of trying to discern what people think and feel – not only what they do. Third is the problem of replying to, and fighting against, antisemitism – that is, finding ways and actions that work to counter and reduce antisemitism in general as well as within individual cultures and/or traditions. The attempt to respond to anti-Jewish assaults is already found in the classical world in such famous defenses as Philo's *Contra Flaccus*[37] and Josephus's *Contra Apion*.[38] This tradition continued in the rabbinic and medieval eras, most famously represented in Moses Ben Nahman's (Nahmanides) debate with Jewish converts to Christianity in Spain in 1263. Unfortunately, such efforts swayed neither ancient Egyptians nor Romans nor medieval Spanish friars and political elites. What steps would be effective in today's world is a subject of intense debate. So one asks: Is pointing out the falsehoods uttered by antisemites sufficient to disabuse others of the false views they express? Can hate be falsified so that it loses its potency? Is the recent push to seek relevant legislation and resolution in the courts a successful defensive response?

There is also the difficult question of how this poisonous attitude is translated into sociopolitical movements. This concern is of major importance in that the employment of antisemitism is meant to bring about meaningful change in the socioeconomic and political landscape. But how exactly does the relationship between ideas and mass movements take form, and how are concepts, especially those that are so

---

[37] With his usual broad learning, S. Baron fully describes Philo's defense of Judaism in his *Social and Religious History of the Jews*, vol. 12, 199–209.

[38] Josephus, *Contra Apion* [*Against Apion*], trans. H. St. J. Thackery (Cambridge, MA, 1926).

dark, propelled forward? Moreover, why do some ideas continue to resonate while others disappear without consequence?

Last, for now: Why do otherwise rational people believe in the absurdities that make up the inventory of antisemitic claims? What psychological processes cause individuals, even well-educated ones, to act on bizarre claims and become mass killers? What makes it possible for usually sensible men and women to believe absurdities like the following: that Jews have a particular odor that can be eliminated only through baptism; that Jews do not need to drink water and therefore can poison the public water supply (the explanation of the Black Death); that Jewish bodies are fundamentally different from non-Jewish bodies, for example, they have horns; that Jewish men menstruate; that Jewish doctors murder one out of ten of their non-Jewish patients; that while Jews give off a noxious odor, the cadavers of Christians killed by Jews for ritual purposes give off an unusually sweet smell; and that Jews kill Christian children for their blood?

There are still other substantial issues that could be added to this list, but space precludes doing so. I will, therefore, conclude by noting the obvious: antisemitism is a heinous, irrational phenomenon that has plagued, and continues to plague, Western, Muslim, Asian (in parts), and New World civilizations. It is a diseased ideology that should be of concern to all who value liberal, democratic, and just societies.

Part I

The Classical Period

1 Antisemitism in the Pagan World

ERICH S. GRUEN

Jean-Paul Sartre famously remarked that "If the Jew did not exist, the anti-Semite would invent him."[1] And he proceeds to assert that "it is not the Jewish character that provokes antisemitism, but rather the anti-Semite who creates the Jew."[2] These pungent statements convey an uncomfortable ring of truth. The image of the Jew, at least the negative image, is in part, perhaps in large part, a hostile construct, a perception by Gentiles who transformed the Jew as victim into the Jew as culprit.

One can, however, turn this conception on its head and ask whether the notion of antisemitism is not itself a construct. That, of course, is not to deny that animosity toward Jews existed or that it sometimes issued in horrific measures, actions, and consequences. But it does raise the tangled question of just what constitutes antisemitism. How do you know it when you see it?

Definitions of problematic terms are notoriously tricky and inescapably arbitrary. As is well known, the term "antisemitism" is a modern invention, first surfacing in 19th-century Germany. No equivalent of the phrase occurs in Greek or Latin. That makes the application of any definition to antiquity all the more problematic, especially so when the controversial phrase is loaded with ambiguity and rouses highly charged emotions.

Did antisemitism exist among Greeks and Romans? Or anti-Judaism? Or Judeophobia? Was there a difference among these labels? How far (and how deep) did hostility to Jews extend in the pagan and pre-Christian world? What impact did it have on Jewish experience in that period? In short, was there a "Jewish problem" in Greco-Roman antiquity?

Modern explorations of the subject have pursued diverse paths. Some have viewed the conflict in religious or ideological terms. Jewish

[1] Jean-Paul Sartre, *Anti-Semite and Jew* (New York, 1948), 13.
[2] Ibid., 143.

monotheism, it is argued, was incompatible with pagan pluralism and multiple divinities, not to mention the imperial cult and worship of the emperor to which no believing Jew could subscribe. Others view the roots of antisemitism in political terms: Jews isolated themselves from their larger communities, shunned civic responsibilities, and undermined solidarity in the cities and nations in which they dwelled. Alternatively, antipathy toward Jews could stem from ethnic prejudice, a form of racism that branded them as outsiders, unworthy and inferior by nature, a largely irrational predilection, a matter of psychology. Or was it a feature of "Judeophobia," a fear that Jewish proselytizing or infiltrating into pagan institutions constituted a menace to the established order?[3]

The Jews certainly had their share of distress and occasional calamity. A number of notorious episodes, with frightful effects, mar their history. A most memorable one occurred in the Greek city of Alexandria in Egypt in 38 CE, an event often characterized as a pogrom. Some unsavory Greek leaders, so we are told by the 1st-century Jewish philosopher Philo, pressured the Roman governor of Egypt, during the reign of the emperor Caligula, into implementing restrictions on Jewish privileges in that city. The measures encouraged attacks by native Egyptians against Jews, resulting in mob action, beatings, torture, and killings of Jews.[4] A shattering experience, and by no means the only one. The Jewish historian Josephus reports that the Jews in Babylon encountered hostility from the Babylonians, and moved to Seleucia on the Tigris, where they were caught up in an internal struggle and were victimized by both sides, with the result that 50,000 Jews were killed and others fled the city.[5] At Caesarea clashes between Jews and Syrians around 59 CE brought the intervention of a Roman prefect who turned his forces primarily against the Jews, thus victimized once again.[6]

[3] Earlier scholarship on "antisemitism" in antiquity is conveniently summarized by John Gager, *The Origins of Anti-Semitism: Attitudes toward Judaism in Pagan and Christian Antiquity* (New York, 1983), 11–34. See further Nicholas de Lange, "The Origins of Anti-Semitism: Ancient Evidence and Modern Interpretations," in Sander L. Gilman and Steven Katz, eds., *Anti-Semitism in Times of Crisis* (New York, 1991), 21–37; Peter Schäfer, *Judeophobia: Attitudes toward the Jews in the Ancient World* (Cambridge, MA, 1997), 1–6, 197–211.
[4] See the discussion and bibliography in Erich S. Gruen, *Diaspora: Jews amidst Greeks and Romans* (Cambridge, MA, 2002), 54–68, 277–282; P. van der Horst, *Philo's Flaccus. The First Pogrom* (Leiden, 2003); and J. E. Atkinson, "Ethnic Cleansing in Roman Alexandria," *Acta Classica* 49 (2006), 31–54.
[5] Jos. *Ant.* 18.371–379.
[6] Jos. *BJ*, 2.266–270; *Ant.* 20.173–178. See the valuable notes of Steve Mason, *Flavius Josephus: Translation and Commentary*, vol. 1b: *Judean War 2* (Leiden, 2008), 215–221.

A decade later Caesarea was again the site of an uprising of its citizens against the resident Jews, who suffered fatal casualties of 20,000, thus emptying the city of its entire Jewish population.[7] The events triggered still more widespread atrocities in numerous cities of greater Syria. Josephus paints lurid pictures of massacres and pillaging, piles of corpses, no sparing of the elderly, women, or even infants.[8] These episodes leave a searing image on the record.

On the face of it, such events, with their heinous horrors, would appear to be emblematic of a thoroughgoing antisemitism, however one may wish to define it. But that may be a hasty conclusion. Do these attacks reflect a consistent pattern? Are they rooted in racial bias, or in religious differences, or in political concerns, or in anxiety over Jewish increase in numbers and influence? And a related question should be posed. Were Jews a special target singled out for their peculiar characteristics or were they simply one among a large group of aliens and "others" disparaged by Greco-Roman bigotry and xenophobia?

Answers can come only with a closer look at the ancient testimony viewed in its own contexts rather than through categories framed by modern reconstructions. One notable feature needs comment right at the outset. Gentiles did not write much about Jews. They were evidently of little interest to the intellectuals. The monumental three-volume collection of texts by Greek and Latin authors on Jews and Judaism compiled a generation ago by Menachem Stern is an invaluable, indeed indispensable, resource. But it consists simply of fragments, a sentence here, a paragraph there, very rarely so much as a page or two. Not a single treatise devoted to Jews survives from pagan antiquity, and it is unclear whether anyone ever bothered to write one.[9] Furthermore, a remarkable number of the extracts that do exist are riddled with misinformation, errors, or fallacious inferences. The first Greek historian known to us who took any interest in the Jews was Hecataeus of Abdera, writing in the late 4th century BCE. He evidently did do some research on the Jews in Egypt in connection with his work on Egyptian history and institutions. But it was hardly a thorough or scrupulous investigation. Among other things, Hecataeus reported that the Jews never had kings, that they chose High Priests on the basis of virtue and wisdom, and that Moses founded both Jerusalem

---

[7] Jos. *BJ*, 2:457.

[8] Jos. *BJ*, 2:458–468, with the commentary of Mason, *Flavius Josephus*, 337–344.

[9] Menahem Stern, *Greek and Latin Authors on Jews and Judaism*, 3 vols. (Jerusalem, 1974, 1980, 1984).

and the Temple.[10] Every one of those statements is wrong. The Greek
historian did not indulge in deliberate fabrication. Nor was he motivated by either advocacy or hostility. His comments show no polemical
edge. Hecataeus simply did not trouble to conduct a searching inquiry.

That is merely a single instance. One could easily produce a litany
of lapses on the part of classical authors whose understanding of Jews
was shallow and superficial. The great geographer Strabo, for example,
maintained that Moses criticized the Greeks for producing their gods in
human form.[11] Just where Moses might have encountered any Greeks is
beyond comprehension. Strabo also thought that the Sabbath was a day
of fasting, a delusion that many Romans shared, including the emperor
Augustus. The biographer Suetonius supplies the interesting report that
Augustus once boasted that he had fasted so diligently that day that not
even a Jew on the Sabbath could have outdone him.[12] There is plainly no
animosity in any of this, just ignorance.[13] The subject of the Jews did
not drive Greek or Roman intellectuals to feats of scholarly research. It
simply was not all that important.

The idea of a fundamental religious divide that put Jews beyond the
pale has been embraced by some scholars. It generally carries the label
of "anti-Judaism" rather than "antisemitism," a reference to the notion
that it was the belief system rather than irrational prejudice or racism
that prompted the animosity. But did pagans really find Jewish theological commitments a reason for suppression and persecution? Neither
the Hellenistic kingdoms nor the Roman authorities engaged in destruction of synagogues or repression of cultic worship.[14] The fact that
multiple divinities peopled the pagan religious landscape did not mean
that non-Jews determined to stamp out monotheism. Roman tolerance,
even incorporation, of foreign gods marked their history from its very
beginning and accelerated when they adopted alien divinities like
Asklepios, Venus Erycina, Cybele, and Isis, making them part of their

---

[10] Hecataeus, *apud* Diod. Sic. 40.3.3–5.
[11] Strabo, 16.2.35. He also has Moses found the Temple in Jerusalem.
[12] Strabo, 16.2.40. On Augustus, see Suet. *Aug.* 76.2. See also Trogus, *apud* Justin,
36.2.14; Petronius, fr. 37; Martial, 4.4.7.
[13] For some of what follows, with regard to Roman perspectives, see Gruen, *Diaspora*,
27–42. Also the balanced remarks of Martin Goodman, *Rome and Jerusalem: The
Clash of Ancient Civilizations* (New York, 2007), 366–376.
[14] The Jewish temple at Elephantine in Upper Egypt was destroyed in 410 BCE. But this
was an exceptional incident, an attack by Egyptians evidently at the behest of the
priests at the neighboring shrine of the Egyptian divinity Khnum. The target was not
Judaism itself but a Jewish garrison at Elephantine that housed the temple.

own religious sensibility.[15] They would certainly not have found Yahweh offensive. Nor would the Greeks. The *Letter of Aristeas*, a Jewish composition of the 2nd century BCE, puts into the mouth of a Greek admirer the statement that "Jews revere God, the overseer and creator of all things, whom we all revere, though we call him Zeus."[16] Although the author was Jewish, the syncretistic sentiment is plainly Greek. In Hellenic eyes, the supreme deity was the same for both Jews and Greeks, only the names differed. Monotheism was not a Jewish monopoly – and certainly not a source of religious conflict. Even the great Roman historian Tacitus, who conveyed a number of opinions hostile to the Jews, had no problem with their monotheism. On the contrary: he makes a point of noting that Jews have but a single deity, and one who is apprehended solely through the mind, not through the senses, plainly an admiring statement.[17]

Nor is there any reason to believe that Greeks or Romans were offended by Jewish aniconism. Indeed, the Roman polymath Varro in the late 1st century BCE even praised the Jews' refusal to countenance images of divinity, something, he claimed, the Romans themselves practiced in their earlier (and better) days.[18] A similar observation comes from the Greek geographer Strabo, who notes that Moses rejected the Egyptian and Libyan practice of representing their deities in the form of animals of every variety, and, for good measure, he denounced Greeks too for idolatry in casting their gods in human form.[19] And Tacitus himself, in the same passage noted above, pointedly contrasts the Jews' religious position with that of the worst of the idolators, namely, the Egyptians, who revere not only images but images of animals and monstrous creatures.[20] What appears to be perhaps the harshest Tacitean remark of a religious nature about Jews is the assertion that they were hateful to the gods. But that outburst has too often been misconstrued. It comes in the context of the Hebrews' expulsion from Egypt on the orders of the Pharaoh, the biblical exodus.[21] The gods to whom the Jews were hateful, in other words, were the Egyptian gods,

---

[15] Eric Orlin, *Temples, Religion and Politics in the Roman Republic* (Leiden, 1997) and *Foreign Cults in Rome: Creating a Roman Empire* (Oxford, 2010).
[16] *Letter of Aristeas*, 16.
[17] Tacitus, *Hist.* 5.5.4.
[18] Varro, *apud* Augustine, *CD*, 4.31.
[19] Strabo, 16.2.35.
[20] Tacitus, *Hist.* 5.5.4.
[21] Ibid., 5.3.1–2.

those very bestial divinities themselves. If Jews are hated by ram-gods, dog-gods, and crocodile-gods, they come off rather well.

Jewish refusal to participate in the imperial cult might appear to be a fundamental and irreconcilable religious issue that branded Jews as enemies of pagan society. Adherence to the cult of the emperor represented a critical symbol of allegiance to the regime and a key element in the solidarity of the Roman empire. Jews, of course, however loyal they might be on other matters, could not engage in worship of the emperor. The issue was pressed on a celebrated occasion when the emperor Caligula insisted on direct homage to him as a divinity. But that potentially explosive situation cannot be taken as representative – far from it. Caligula, as is well known, was either a madman or, at best, a diabolical practical joker. The effort failed, and the crisis passed. The situation reverted to a compromise solution that had held hitherto and endured subsequently: Jews would not make sacrifice to the emperor but were perfectly happy to sacrifice to Yahweh on behalf of the emperor.[22] The issue did not provide grounds for pagan odium toward Jews. In short, the notion of "anti-Judaism," in the sense of theological differences, as a motivation for animosity toward Jews, by contrast with "antisemitism," the more virulent and irrational form of Jew-hatred, does not really fit the bill.[23]

If religion fails to account for pagan antipathy toward the Jews in their midst, does it stem from ethnic bias, a form of racism that stamped Jews as inferior beings, an ineluctable nature? A raft of remarks in Greek or Roman authors can be deployed to support that conclusion. One can readily find a plethora of passages in which Jews are stigmatized for one failing or another. Many of them express mockery or derision, amused characterization or caricature of Jewish practices and customs.

The observance of the Sabbath struck the gentiles as rather comical. They had nothing against it but found it a puzzling eccentricity that lent itself to black humor. So, for instance, Seneca, the Stoic philosopher, criticized the practice for allowing the Jews to skip work every seventh day, thus devoting one-seventh of their lives to idleness.[24] The satirical poet Persius branded the Sabbath as "the day of

---

[22] Philo, *Legat.* 280, 355–357; Josephus, *BJ*, 2.197; *CAp.* 2.77. On Jews and the imperial cult, see James S. McLaren, "Jews and the Imperial Cult: From Augustus to Domitian," *Journal for the Study of the New Testament* 27 (2005), 257–278.

[23] On this terminology, see David Nirenberg, *Anti-Judaism: The Western Tradition* (New York, 2012); and Robert Chazan, *From Anti-Judaism to Anti-Semitism* (Cambridge, 2016).

[24] Seneca, *apud* Augustine, *CD*, 6.11.

Herod," noting with scorn the dishes and drinks served, and lighting of lamps that issue in clouds of smoke, here too underscoring a worthless expenditure of time. Pliny the Elder carried the caricature a step further to a *reductio ad absurdum*, pointing to a river in Judea that stops running every Sabbath.[25]

The dietary laws also stimulated some comic disparagement. Abstention from pork, considered a delicacy by most pagans, prompted puzzlement. The satirical writer Petronius insinuated that refusal to eat pork must mean that Jews were worshippers of a pig-god.[26] The caustic satirist Juvenal added, with tongue firmly in cheek, that in Judea, by long-standing tradition, clemency is extended to pigs who can thus live to a ripe old age.[27] The emperor Augustus himself famously tapped into that same source of amusement. In speaking of king Herod of Judea who was notorious for the execution of various members of his own family, Augustus quipped that "it would be better to be Herod's pig than Herod's son."[28]

The most distinguishing feature of the Jews for gentiles was the one that was least obvious, but everyone knew about it, namely, circumcision. It was also the one that drew the most laughs. As Philo, the Jewish philosopher, acknowledged, circumcision is an object of ridicule among many persons.[29] Juvenal took mockery to another level, portraying Jews as a group so dedicated to their private creed that they would not even give directions in the street to those outside their own religion and would not guide to his destination anyone who was uncircumcised![30]

Jewish customs and conduct thus struck the Greeks and Romans as idiosyncratic, eccentric, and weird, a stimulus to satirists and a prod for jokesters. And many more instances of such material can readily be cited.[31] But where in any of this does one find racial prejudice? Nowhere is there a suggestion that these rituals and mores, outlandish as they might seem to pagans, stemmed from the genetic makeup of Jews. Nothing in the texts makes reference to Jewish physical appearance, speech, descent, ethnic traits, or qualities ascribable to hereditary lineage. The idea that racism or ethnic hatred prompted gentile reactions to Jews is simply unsustainable.

[25] Pliny, *NH*, 31.24.
[26] Petronius, fr. 37.
[27] Juvenal, 6.159
[28] Macrobius, *Sat.* 2.4.11.
[29] Philo, *Spec. Leg.* 1.1–2; cf. Josephus, *CAp.* 2.137.
[30] Juvenal, 14.100–104.
[31] See references and discussion in Gruen, *Diaspora*, 27–42.

Was there such a thing as "Judeophobia" in antiquity?[32] Are we to believe that there was considerable *fear* of Jews in the pagan world? Does some form of gentile anxiety lie at the root of hostility to Jews?

A principal argument for that conclusion rests on a few texts that suggest pagan worries about the growing number of Jews, the apostasy of many gentiles, and the negative impact of converts to Judaism on pagan society. Tacitus denounces with virulence those of his compatriots who entered the Jewish fold. He deplores their willingness to undergo circumcision, and he castigates them for despising their own gods, for neglecting their ancestral traditions, and for holding in contempt their own families.[33] Juvenal expresses comparable displeasure with gentiles who embraced Judaism. He upbraids them for observing the Sabbath, abstaining from pork, allowing themselves to be circumcised, and worshipping no gods but the clouds and some divinity of the sky. Worse still, they scorned Roman laws and devoted themselves to the codes handed down by Moses in some secret volume.[34] The philosopher Seneca goes further still. He maintains that the ways of this most criminal nation prevail so extensively that they are accepted in all lands, to the point that the vanquished now impose laws on the victors.[35]

This combination of texts has led some to infer that Judeophobia had gained a foothold in the Roman disposition toward Jews.[36] But a closer scrutiny of those passages fails to sustain that inference. Tacitus trains his vitriol primarily on gentile proselytes who, by embracing Judaism, abandoned their own gods, nation, and families. He does not, however, sound an alarm against Jews, nor does he imply that the conversion of pagans represented a menace to pagan society as a whole. Nor do the caustic verses of Juvenal support such a conclusion. The satirist grumbles about converts adopting bizarre Jewish habits, decries their reverence for the Mosaic code, and complains of their contempt for Roman laws. Most of this is satirical exaggeration and hyperbole. Nothing else in our evidence attests to Jews or proselytes violating Roman laws – or even being accused of doing so. Nor does

[32] The term was advocated independently by two distinguished scholars in the 1990s and retains force. See Zvi Yavetz, "Judeophobia" (1993); and Schäfer, *Judeophobia* (1997).

[33] Tacitus, *Hist.* 5.5.2.

[34] Juvenal, 14.96–102.

[35] Seneca, *apud* Augustine, *CD*, 6.11.

[36] See, e.g., Jerry L. Daniel, "Anti-Semitism in the Hellenistic-Roman World," *Journal of Biblical Literature* 98 (1979), 62–64; Gager, *Origins of Anti-Semitism*, 59–61; and Schafer, *Judeophobia*, 183–192.

Juvenal suggest that pagans in any significant numbers were induced by Jews to reject their roots and embrace the alien cult. No hint surfaces in this text about an epidemic of conversions that might fill the gentiles with dread.

Only Seneca's notice might raise alarm. His remark that Jewish practice is received throughout the world and that the conquered now dictate laws to the conqueror would seem, on the face of it, to suggest that Jews have the upper hand everywhere. The notion, of course, is preposterous. To be sure, Jews had spread widely in the diaspora through the Mediterranean and beyond. And both Philo and Josephus boast of embrace of the Sabbath and Yom Kippur by pagans in every corner of the world.[37] The rhetorical outbursts are doubtless exaggerations and embellishments, but not altogether fanciful. That many gentiles may have found certain Jewish conventions and customs appealing is perfectly plausible.[38] But was this perceived as a threat to paganism and thus grounds for Judeophobia? Seneca's testimony is a very slender reed. First of all, it comes secondhand through St. Augustine four centuries later. And, second, there is no trace of anything like it elsewhere in Seneca's very large corpus, which indeed lacks any other mention of Jews. Further, his (if it is his) allegation that the conquered imposed their laws on the conqueror need mean no more than that the observance of the Sabbath and other practices associated with the Jews had gained wide welcome in the Greco-Roman world. Seneca may not have approved of it. But even he does not say that pagans panicked over the increase of Jewish numbers and influence.

The very idea of Judeophobia is surely counterintuitive. That there should be widespread apprehension about a "Jewish problem" among those who dwelled in Greek cities or among the officialdom of the Roman empire is most implausible on the face of it. Certainly, the snide remarks about alien practices or the quips of acerbic satirists do not remotely suggest anxiety about Jewish infiltration. And the few texts that might at first sight allude to it dissolve on inspection. The very concept of Judeophobia in antiquity is a red herring.

Even if pagans had no reason to harbor concerns about increasing numbers or expanding influence by Jews, however, might there have been a different and more subtle political element that insinuated itself into the situation? Modern scholars have at times found ingenious explanations for what they identify as "antisemitism." So, for example,

---

[37] Philo, *Mos.* 2.20–21; Josephus, *CAp.* 2.282; cf. *BJ*, 7.34.
[38] Cf. Suetonius, *Dom.* 12.2.

some have proposed that Greek animus toward Jews was really a disguised form of anti-Romanism. Jews enjoyed certain civic privileges in Alexandria under Roman authority which caused resentment among Greeks and Egyptians in that city, leading to a violent assault on Jews in 38 CE. And Greek authorities in various cities of Asia Minor interfered with and restricted Jewish practices at the end of the 1st century BCE, causing Jews to appeal to Rome and receive backing from Roman officials. In the view of some interpreters, attacks on Jews in those various communities would be an indirect but much safer way to vent their wrath against the Romans.[39] The suggestion, however, is singularly unsatisfactory. Would a massacre of Jews in Alexandria be reckoned as an affront to Rome? A Roman governor might well be expected to repress any turmoil that occurred in his province, but the perpetrators could hardly have expected that Roman interests would have been damaged by an attack on Jews. It is worth noting that, after the assaults on the Jewish community in Alexandria in 38, a Jewish delegation to the emperor Caligula was greeted with derision.[40] So much for alleged amalgamation of Jewish and Roman interests. Roman prestige was plainly not at stake in an onslaught on Jews. A different interpretation turns this one on its head. It proposes that pagan propaganda against Jews actually aimed at currying the favor of the Romans. On that reconstruction, Greeks employed tactics to blacken Jews in the eyes of Rome, in order to prove to their Roman overlords that the Hellenized peoples of the east were more reliable than the untrustworthy Semites.[41] That hypothesis has no more plausibility than the reverse. How likely is it that the Romans would be favorably impressed by Hellenic criticism of Jews? When complaints about mistreatment or loss of privileges came to Roman officials from Jews in the Greek cities of Asia Minor, Roman judgments regularly favored the Jews.[42]

That Greeks and Romans harbored prejudices about alien peoples and reckoned themselves as superior in culture and accomplishment will come as a surprise to no one. But is there any reason to believe that

---

[39] This interpretation can be found in a variety of works, including Mary Smallwood, *The Jews under Roman Rule from Pompey to Diocletian: A Study in Political Relations* (Leiden, 1981), 233–234; Gager, *Origins of Anti-Semitism*, 44, 49–50; John M. G. Barclay, *Jews in the Mediterranean Diaspora: From Alexander to Trajan (323 BCE–17 CE)* (Edinburgh, 1996), 266–278.

[40] Philo, *Leg.* 355–373.

[41] Yavetz, "Judeophobia," 21–22.

[42] See the thorough treatment by Miriam Pucci Ben Zeev, *Jewish Rights in the Roman World* (Tübingen, 1998); cf. Gruen, *Diaspora*, 82–104.

Jews were singled out for special opprobrium or set into a category apart that might lead to something resembling antisemitism?

Jews did develop a reputation for separatism. They preferred their own company to everyone else's. That attitude and practice lent itself to comments by Greek and Latin writers who found the self-segregation opprobrious and likened it to misanthropy. Some truth surely adheres to that perception, particularly for Jews in the diaspora who felt it important to hold together for the maintenance of their traditions and identity. Did this self-isolation stimulate hostile reaction that could induce Jew-hatred?[43] Some pagans likened Jewish isolation to xenophobia. The characterization goes back as far as Hecataeus of Abdera in the late 4th century BCE, who remarked that Moses, as consequence of the Hebrews' expulsion from Egypt, introduced a somewhat unsocial and xenophobic style of life.[44] Comparable sentiments appear in a narrative provided, in slightly different forms, by two authors, the Greek historian Diodorus Siculus and the Jewish historian Josephus, ultimately deriving from a single source. Both report that advisors of the Seleucid king Antiochus VII pressed upon him a policy of eradicating the Jews on the grounds of the exclusivity of their way of life and their unwillingness to mingle with other peoples since they regard them all as their enemies.[45] But it is noteworthy that even the Greek historian refrains from endorsing this form of characterization. He has the king reject the advice of his counselors and clear the Jews unequivocally of all the charges leveled against them.[46] A different pagan author also acknowledges Jewish hesitancy to mingle freely with other peoples but ascribes this attitude to the trauma of the Exodus, which he understands as an expulsion caused by suspicion that they carried a deadly infection.[47] Tacitus delivers a harsher judgment. In his view, Jews are steadfast in their loyalty to one another, with compassion always at the ready, but toward all others they feel hatred and animosity.[48] The historian, however, bases that judgment essentially on the Jewish predilection to maintain their distance from other peoples, setting themselves apart at meals, avoiding sexual intercourse with non-Jews, and practicing

---

[43] For views along those lines, see Jan N. Sevenster, *The Roots of Pagan Anti-Semitism in the Ancient World* (Leiden, 1975), 89–108; and Louis H. Feldman, *Jew and Gentile in the Ancient World* (Princeton, NJ, 1993), 125–133.

[44] Hecataeus, *apud* Diod. Sic. 40.3.4.

[45] Diod. Sic. 34/5.1–5; Josephus, *Ant.* 13.245, 13.247.

[46] Diod. Sic. 34/5.1.5.

[47] Pompeius Trogus, *apud* Justin, 36.2.15.

[48] Tacitus, *Hist.* 5.5.1.

circumcision in order to distinguish themselves from everybody else.[49]
Yet Tacitus follows that declaration immediately with his denunciation
of fellow gentiles for their conversion to Jewish practices.[50] The idea of
Jews gaining converts while insisting on keeping their distance from
non-Jews presents a pretty paradox that Tacitus leaves without pursuing
the matter, a not untypical form of irony with which he teases his
readers.[51] And we do know from abundant testimony that Jews welcomed converts and brought into their communities numerous gentiles
who were attracted by their ways and shared their customs.[52] This
feature casts substantial doubt on the perception of Jews as misan-
thropes and xenophobes. Jews may have felt themselves most comfortable in their own company. But the notion that this proclivity
engendered any substantial hatred of Jews would be quite a stretch.

It would be equally difficult to infer that Jews stood out as a special
target for pagan wrath or cultural bias. The Greeks reckoned all non-
Greeks as "barbarians," which meant basically that they did not speak
Greek or have the benefit of Greek culture. And Romans considered all
other nations inferior in stature and destiny for they lacked the favor of
the gods. But Jews were not singled out as especially deficient. Much has
been made of Cicero's sneer in one of his speeches, branding Jews and
Syrians as born to be slaves.[53] When circumstances called for it in other
speeches, however, particularly in forensic contexts, he could spout
comparable vitriol at Gauls or Sardinians, at Phrygians, Mysians,
Lydians, and Carians, all of whom emerge at least as unworthy as
Jews.[54] Tacitus hardly reserves his fire for Jews. He blasts Britons and
Germans too, he is contemptuous of Egyptian religion, and he despises
Christianity.[55] And one surely does not have to belabor the point in the
case of satirists like Juvenal for whom easterners of every stripe are
offensive.[56] Jews had no monopoly as objects of invective.[57]

---

[49] Ibid. 5.5.2.
[50] Tacitus, *Hist.* 5.5.2.
[51] See the interpretation by Gruen, *Rethinking the Other in Antiquity* (Berlin, 2011),
179–196.
[52] See, n. 37 above.
[53] Cicero, *Prov. Cons.* 10.
[54] See, e.g., Cicero, *Font.* 33; *Scauro*, 17, 20, 37, 38, 40; *Flacco*, 65; also the discussion in
Gruen, "Cicero and the Alien," in Donald Lateiner et al., eds., *Roman Literature,
Gender, and Reception* (New York, 2013), 13–27.
[55] Tacitus, *Germ.* 4.1, 14.2–3, 22.1, 39.1, 45.4; *Agr.* 11–12; *Hist.* 1.11.1, 5.5; *Ann.* 15.44.3–5.
[56] Juvenal, 3.60–62, 15.1–8.
[57] See the assemblage of material by John P. Balsdon, *Romans and Aliens* (Chapel Hill,
NC, 1979), 214–259.

Some conclusions are warranted. A search for the roots of antisemitism in classical antiquity runs into various blind alleys. The absence of satisfactory answers itself tells a revealing story. Logical assumptions and expectations repeatedly fail to correspond to the ancient evidence. What might seem the most obvious source of conflict between Jew and non-Jew, the broad gulf between monotheism and polytheism, falls well short of a solution. Prior to the advent of Christianity (indeed well after its advent) pagans felt no need or advantage in persecuting peoples on theological grounds. There was, after all, no such religion as "paganism," a pure concoction invented as a contrast with Christianity. Pluralism prevailed. Embrace of multiple creeds could readily encompass monotheists. Synagogues sprang up in numerous cities and principalities in east and west, some even funded by non-Jews, without hindrance or resistance. Jews had a fierce revulsion of idolatry, to be sure. But some pagans shared that attitude, and the issue never arose as a motivation for suppression. Jews could even live with the imperial cult. Sacrifice to Yahweh for the welfare of the emperor sufficed as substitute for emperor worship. Religious belief was never a centerpiece for friction, let alone for oppression.

Nor did racism rear its ugly head. A myriad of acerbic remarks flowed from Greek and Roman writers about Jewish separatism and penchant for isolation, unintelligible Sabbath observance, bizarre dietary restrictions, and the unthinkable practice of circumcision. Such rituals and behavior provoked puzzlement, scorn, mockery, and even disdain. But none amounted to active hostility or set a path for persecution. More striking still, the cavils and disparagement omitted any ethnic slurs or references to innate characteristics that might associate Jews with hereditary liabilities or inescapable inferiority.

The case for "Judeophobia," that is, a dread of expanding Jewish influence on the political and social scene of the ancient Mediterranean, is even harder to make. Jews did enjoy some civic prerogatives in various Greek cities and occasionally made their voices heard and argued successfully even in Rome or before Roman officials when their own interests were involved. None of that, however, could have struck fear in the hearts of Greeks or Romans. Numerous gentiles adopted Jewish practices and became part of Jewish congregations. But there is little or no sign of any active proselytizing that might have been offensive. Anxiety over Jewish infiltration did not grip the pagan consciousness.

Both Greeks and Romans had a strong sense of their own superiority over other peoples and nations. Jews fell into the category of those who could not measure up to the quality and achievements of their superiors.

But so did Gauls, Germans, Britons, Spaniards, Phoenicians, Egyptians, and the rest of the world. Jews had no distinctive place in that panorama of inferiors and would hardly have provided reason for a singular campaign of vilification. Antisemitism in whatever meaning one might wish to allot to it has little correspondence to the attitudes and experience of the classical world.

Yet one cannot leave it at that. The grisly episodes outlined at the beginning of this chapter remain a looming presence for the thesis presented here. The shattering pogrom in Alexandria and the lethal uprisings in Seleucia and Caesarea demand attention. And others too followed, unleashing passions in city after city and multiplying Jewish fatalities in Caesarea once again, in Scythopolis, Ascalon, Ptolemais, Tyre, Damascus, and communities throughout Syria, with yet another assault in Alexandria.[58] These are chilling events, dramatic and powerful, not to be readily dismissed, even if they do not signal a form of antisemitism. And evidence for hostility can be found in other events and circumstances. Measures taken by the officialdom of various Greek cities to limit Jewish privileges included restrictions on observing the Sabbath, conducting rituals, building synagogues, and providing funds for the Temple in Jerusalem. Further, Rome itself took action against Jews, expelling them from the city on three separate occasions in this period.

The recurring instances of actions and measures directed against Jews might, at first sight, suggest a continuing motif of discrimination and oppression. Yet closer scrutiny sets these episodes too in a broader perspective and a clearer light. Context is crucial. The "pogrom" in Alexandria in 38 CE was, in many ways a unique event, a concatenation of features involving a contest over civic entitlements between Greeks and Jews, a deep resentment by Egyptians who did not possess similar entitlements, and an incompetent Roman prefect who allowed matters to get out of hand.[59] Almost all of the subsequent murderous occasions at Caesarea, Damascus, Tyre, and elsewhere took place within a short period of time, one that was gripped by a much wider upheaval, namely, the Jewish rebellion against Rome from 66 to 70 CE. Under those circumstances, cities scrambled to demonstrate their loyalty to the great western power by leveling their firepower against the much more vulnerable and exposed Jews. These actions did not constitute a coordinated campaign driven by long-standing antisemitic motivation.

---

[58] Josephus, *BJ*, 2.458–468, 2.477–478, 2.487–498, 2.559–561, 7.43–60.
[59] On the complex and intertwining issues that embroiled Alexandria at this time, see above, n. 4.

Special circumstances also engendered the rash of measures in Greek cities of Asia Minor limiting or curtailing the freedom of Jews in those cities to carry on their customary sacred duties. Almost all the measures fall within a relatively short period at the end of the Roman Republic and the beginning of the Principate, a most turbulent era engulfed in civil wars that stretched across the Mediterranean. The events fragmented loyalties as communities took sides and changed sides depending on shifts in power among Roman contenders for ascendancy. They also intensified internal friction within the communities, sometimes at the expense of the Jews. Roman adjudication depended heavily on the particular situation. But the incidents were episodic and infrequent, often readily resolved, and far from representing any systematic persecution by Greeks of Jews living in their midst.[60]

Roman orders did expel Jews from the city of Rome on three separate occasions. Was there a pattern of prejudice there? It would be very hard to discern. The expulsions were widely scattered in time, in 139 BCE, 19 CE, and 49 CE. No connecting threads tied them together. And Jews were not the sole victims. Forced deportation included astrologers in 139 BCE and worshippers of Isis in 19 CE. Nor did they stay away for very long. Evidence shows that Jews were back in Rome within a short time after each ostensible expulsion. That notable feature suggests that the incidents may have been largely matters of public relations, a display of Roman piety toward their traditional cults and rituals in times of stress for the nation as a whole.[61] In any case, three such short-term banishments over a span of two hundred years (and probably much longer) hardly represent anything like a continuing concern about Jewish presence.

In short, the actions conventionally understood as illustrative of antisemitic proclivity and biased animus toward Jews in pagan antiquity actually point in a very different direction. The evidence shows that hostile outbursts were quite rare and unrepresentative, engendered by contingent circumstances and brief in duration. For the vast proportion of the time Jewish practices and beliefs went unhindered, synagogues flourished, advocacy for Jewish causes was generally successful, many gentiles embraced Jewish observances and rituals, and Jews maintained a network of connections among themselves between Jerusalem and the far-flung diaspora. Antisemitism, whether on

---

[60] The complexity of the issue and the contingency of individual circumstances is stressed in Gruen, *Diaspora*, 84–104.

[61] For this interpretation, see the analysis in ibid., 15–19, 29–41.

religious, ideological, racial, or political grounds, was, on the whole, conspicuous by its absence.

It does not follow that one should replace a lachrymose version of Jewish history in antiquity with a joyous one. The outbursts against Jews, even though few and brief, could be horrendous in character, and must have left their scars. The deadly encounters cannot be dismissed or erased. The Jews, as is well known, held tenaciously to traits and traditions that gave them a distinctive character. And one can readily imagine that the more they became a familiar feature of pagan society, the greater the motivation to emphasize their own particular heritage and the practices that were integral to it, thus to demonstrate their special identity. Such self-expression doubtless represented a source of pride. But it carried its own risks. Through most of the era of classical antiquity, the Jewish commitment to singularity was harmless and internally affirmative. In periods of crisis, however, whether political upheaval, regional conflict, or war, local tensions become intensified and cultural differences take on greater meaning. Under such conditions, the marginal group is more easily identifiable and more vulnerable, a ready prey to scapegoating. Eccentric traits can then be reconceived as unwelcome and divisive. The Jews' very insistence on their special attributes and mores meant that, when crises came, they were conspicuous and thus constituted a convenient target for victimization. They may not have suffered from antisemitism, but they could not escape altogether the perils of a precarious marginality.

Further Reading

Chazan, R., *From Anti-Judaism to Anti-Semitism: Ancient and Medieval Christian Constructions of Jewish History* (Cambridge, 2016). Confines itself largely to early Christian and medieval attitudes toward Jews but makes a useful distinction between anti-Judaism and antisemitism.

Feldman, L. H., *Jew and Gentile in the Ancient World* (Princeton, NJ, 1993). A broad-gauged survey of Jews' relations with non-Jews from the Hellenistic period through late antiquity.

Gager, J. G., *The Origins of Anti-Semitism* (Oxford, 1985). A balanced and intelligent presentation of opinions about Jews by pagans, ancient Christians, and modern scholars.

Gruen, E. S., *Diaspora: Jews amidst Greeks and Romans* (Cambridge, MA, 2002). Treats the Jewish experience in ancient Alexandria, Asia Minor, and Rome.

Rethinking the Other in Antiquity (Princeton, NJ, 2011). Discusses Greek and Roman attitudes toward a wide variety of peoples, including Jews.

Isaac, B., *The Invention of Racism in Classical Antiquity* (Princeton, NJ, 2004). A wide-ranging study of "proto-racism" in antiquity, with an important long chapter on the Jews.

Nirenberg, D., *Anti-Judaism: The Western Tradition* (New York, 2013). Traces the concept of anti-Judaism from antiquity to the Holocaust and finds its roots in ancient Egyptian attitudes.

Schäfer, P. *Judeophobia: Attitudes toward the Jews in the Ancient World* (Cambridge, MA, 1997). Makes a strong argument for widespread hostility toward Jews, stemming from Egypt and spreading throughout.

Sevenster, J. N. *The Roots of Pagan Anti-Semitism in the Ancient World* (Leiden, 1975). An extended argument tracing antisemitism to the perception of Jews as separatists and xenophobes.

2 New Testament Origins of Christian Anti-Judaism

ADELE REINHARTZ

THE BASIC DISCUSSION

In 1974, Rosemary Ruether's book, *Faith and Fratricide*, made a controversial claim: that anti-Judaism was deeply embedded in Christian theology, fostered and sustained by the New Testament itself.[1] Ruether's book confirmed what some scholars and theologians already thought.[2] It was also heavily critiqued by both Jewish and Christian scholars as a misreading of the New Testament, a misunderstanding of early Christology (early Christian views about Christ), and an oversimplification of the history of Christianity and the causes of modern antisemitism, including its most insidious expression in the Holocaust.[3] Among New Testament scholars and Christian pastors and communities, the debate still rages over whether the New Testament itself is anti-Jewish or whether its statements about Jews and Jewishness have been distorted in an anti-Jewish direction by Christian interpreters over the past twenty centuries.

The issue of whether Christology, and the New Testament, are inherently anti-Jewish is not easily addressed. What constitutes anti-Judaism? Our answers to this question will depend on how we define the criteria for judging whether a statement, idea, or belief is or is not anti-Jewish. These criteria will inevitably reflect some prior sense of what we think the answer is or should be.

The matter is further complicated by two additional points. One is the canonical status of the New Testament for Christians. It may be easier for Jews, including Jewish New Testament scholars like myself, to condemn a theological tenet or New Testament passage as

---

[1] Rosemary R. Ruether, *Faith and Fratricide: The Theological Roots of Anti-Semitism* (New York, 1974), 7.

[2] See Gregory Baum's frank introduction to ibid., 1–22.

[3] See, for example, A. Idinopulos and Roy B. Ward, "Is Christology Inherently Anti-Semitic? A Critical Review of Rosemary Ruether's: 'Faith and Fratricide,'" *Journal of the American Academy of Religion* 45.2 (1977), 193–214.

anti-Jewish than for Christians, including scholars, who may be reluctant to describe their scriptures in this manner. The other is the long reception history of the New Testament, in which many of its verses have been taken out of their literary and historical contexts, generalized in particular ways, and used to justify certain attitudes and behaviours.[4] Paul's argument that Gentile Christ-confessors should not observe the laws of circumcision and kashrut was later generalized historically to argue that Judaism was a legalistic and moribund religious system.[5] It can then be difficult to read Paul in ways that do not support this anachronistic reading.[6]

It is not possible to approach a text completely uninfluenced by reception history and one's own theological convictions. But the attempt to consider the New Testament origins of anti-Judaism is greatly aided by a historically contextualized approach that strives to situate the Gospels, letters, and other New Testament books in their ancient historical, social, and political milieux, and to acknowledge the polemical and apologetic usages to which they were put by later readers.

My approach to the question of criteria focuses on the possible rhetorical impact that a phrase, verse, or concept would have on a (hypothetical) ancient reader or hearer. If it seems likely that a certain formulation would have led an ancient audience to form negative views or feelings about that group that it referred to as "Jews," then I consider that verse or passage to be anti-Jewish. For example, I conjecture that anyone who read or heard that the Jews have the devil as their father (John 8:44) would have been inclined to form negative views about Jews. This criterion is hardly foolproof; the term "Jews" in ancient, as in modern, times is extremely difficult to define (are Jews a "religion," an "ethnicity"?) and it is likely that then, as now, any given text would elicit different responses in different hearers or readers.[7]

---

[4] This process is not limited to anti-Judaism, which also served the purposes of antisemitism. It also concerns stances towards LGBTQIA and Black individuals and communities. For discussion, see, for example, Joseph A. Marchal, "LGBTIQ Strategies of Interpretation," in *Oxford Handbook of New Testament, Gender, and Sexuality*, edited by Benjamin H. Dunning (New York, 2019), 177–96; and Adrian Thatcher, "'Cursed Be Canaan!': The Bible, Racism, and Slavery," in *The Savage Text: The Use and Abuse of the Bible* (Oxford, 2009).

[5] For detailed discussion, see E. P. Sanders, *Paul and Palestinian Judaism: A Comparison of Patterns of Religion* (Philadelphia, 1977), 33–59.

[6] For a critique of such a move, see Margaret M. Mitchell, "Gift Histories," *Journal for the Study of the New Testament* 39.3 (2017), 221–22.

[7] On the fraught question of "who is a Jew" in the ancient world, see Adele Reinhartz et al., "Jew and Judean: A Forum on Politics and Historiography in the Translation of

Nevertheless, attention to the potential rhetorical impact of hostile statements about those whom a given text refers to as Jews can be a helpful starting point.

The contribution of the New Testament to Christian anti-Judaism is a broad and complex question, and it has generated a vast amount of scholarship especially in the post-Holocaust era.[8] In this brief essay I will focus on three most important and potent issues: supersessionism, the deicide charge, and the association of Jews with Satan. In each case, I will concentrate on a few of the New Testament passages that express these issues most directly and powerfully. I will conclude with brief comments on the theological and exegetical questions with which I began: Are the New Testament, and Christian theology, anti-Jewish?

SUPERSESSIONISM

The term "supersessionism" refers to the view that Christ-confessors or, later, Christians, have superseded or replaced Jews as God's covenantal people.[9] For Jews, the Torah is God's revelation, and it also constitutes a contract – a covenant – between God and Israel. The terms of the covenant are set out in the book of Exodus. In Exodus 19:5 God conveys this message to the Israelites via Moses: "Now therefore, if you obey my voice and keep my covenant, you shall be my treasured possession out of all the peoples." The people respond as one: "Everything that the LORD has spoken we will do" (Exod. 19:8). The authors of the New Testament, most if not all of them Jewish, considered the Torah to be divine. But they also believed in Jesus as God's new and improved revelation who fulfils the "Old Testament" prophecies and now mediates Israel's covenantal relationship with God. According to this view, since Christ's coming, the term Israel referred not to the Jewish people but only to those Jews and Gentiles who believed in Christ. Everyone – including Jews – could participate in the covenant with the God of Israel only by believing in Jesus.

Ancient Texts," *Marginalia: A Los Angeles Review of Books Channel*, 26 August 2014, http://marginalia.lareviewofbooks.org/jew-judean-forum/; Steve Mason, "Jews, Judaeans, Judaizing, Judaism: Problems of Categorization in Ancient History," *Journal for the Study of Judaism in the Persian, Hellenistic and Roman Period* 38 (2007), 457–512.

[8] For a short list, see the Further References section at the end of this essay.

[9] The term "Christian" was not used widely to refer to someone who believed Jesus until the post–New Testament period; I generally use Christ-confessor for the 1st- and early 2nd-century believers in Jesus as the Christ.

The theme of supersessionism is pervasive throughout the New Testament and is expressed in a number of different ways. I will address only two of the most obvious: the limitation of the Torah's temporal authority to the period preceding Christ, and the emphasis on Jesus as a source of revelation that improves on and surpasses the Torah.

THE ERA OF TORAH HAS ENDED

Paul's letter to the Galatians is a detailed defence of his conviction that Gentile adherents to the Jesus movement, such as the members of the Galatian church itself, are not bound by – and should not follow – the laws of circumcision or kashrut. Paul does not deny that Torah is divine revelation, but he assigns to it a preliminary role in the divine plan for human salvation. He supports this view by pointing out that God gave his covenantal promises to Abraham (Gen. 12:1–3; 15:1–17; 17:1–8) centuries before the Torah was given on Mount Sinai (Exod. 19–10), which, in turn, occurred centuries before the coming of Christ.

Genesis 17 is very clear that the covenant to Abraham was given on condition that he, the males in his household, and all males in subsequent generations undergo circumcision (Gen. 17:10–14). But throughout Galatians Paul mounts a vigorous argument that this stipulation does not apply to Gentile believers in Christ. In Galatians 3:17–18 Paul asserts that "the law [Torah], which came four hundred thirty years later [after Abraham], does not annul a covenant previously ratified by God, so as to nullify the promise. For if the inheritance comes from the law, it no longer comes from the promise; but God granted it to Abraham through the promise [in Gen. 15:5]."

Paul then asks the logical question: "Why then the law?" (3:19a). His answer: "It was added because of transgressions, until the offspring would come to whom the promise had been made; and it was ordained through angels by a mediator" (3:19b). Before Christ's coming, the law served an important purpose as a guardian or disciplinarian, to keep humankind in line until Christ came and provided the opportunity to be "justified by faith" (Gal. 3:23–24). Now that Christ has come, however, humankind is no longer subject to a disciplinarian (Gal. 3:25–26). Now faith in Christ, not obedience to Torah, provides relationship to God.

But the temporal limitation of the law's authority does not imply that the Torah has lost its divine status – on the contrary. Paul relies extensively on biblical passages to support his claims, including the very claims that limit the law's authority on matters such as circumcision. In a mere seven verses, Galatians 3:8–14, for example, Paul draws on five different verses from the Hebrew Bible as prooftexts for the "gospel" that he has been preaching to Gentiles:

> Gal. 3:8 And the scripture, foreseeing that God would justify the Gentiles by faith, declared the gospel beforehand to Abraham, saying, "All the Gentiles shall be blessed in you." (Gen. 12:3; 18:8)
>
> Gal. 3:10 For all who rely on the works of the law are under a curse; for it is written, "Cursed is everyone who does not observe and obey all the things written in the book of the law." (Deut. 27:26)
>
> Gal. 3:11 Now it is evident that no one is justified before God by the law; for "The one who is righteous will live by faith." (Gen. 15:6)
>
> Gal. 3:12 But the law does not rest on faith; on the contrary, "Whoever does the works of the law will live by them." (Lev. 18:5)
>
> Gal. 3:13 Christ redeemed us from the curse of the law by becoming a curse for us – for it is written, "Cursed is everyone who hangs on a tree." (Deut. 21:23).

Like other ancient authors, Paul took the prooftexts out of their contexts in the Pentateuch. This practice was very common in midrashic readings of the Torah.[10] What was important to Paul was that these verses provided the language that he needed to show that his message to the Gentiles was divinely ordained and approved, in order that "in Christ Jesus the blessing of Abraham might come to the Gentiles, so that we might receive the promise of the Spirit through faith" (Gal. 3:14).

JESUS AS THE NEW AND IMPROVED REVELATION

Jesus' role as a superior divine revelation is sometimes expressed as a comparison between Moses (as the one through whom the Torah was given) and Jesus. The Prologue to the Gospel of John (John 1:1–18) concludes with these words: "The law indeed was given through Moses; grace and truth came through Jesus Christ. No one has ever seen God. It is God the only Son, who is close to the Father's heart, who has made him known" (John 1:17–18). These words sum up the message of the Prologue, which describes Jesus as the pre-existent Word who parallels, or

---

[10] Martin C. Albl, *"And Scripture Cannot Be Broken": The Form and Function of the Early Christian Testimonia Collections* (Leiden, 1999); Tzvi Novick, *Piyyut and Midrash: Form, Genre, and History* (Göttingen, 2019).

perhaps is identified with, the figure of Wisdom as divine revelation. Like Wisdom, the Word was in the beginning with God (John 1:2; see Prov. 8:22–29 and the Wisdom of Ben Sira 24:9) and was an agent of creation (John 1:3; see Prov. 8:30–31). And just as Wisdom was identified with Torah (Ben Sira 24:23), so is Jesus identified as divine revelation. John 1:18 insists that only the Son – and not, it is implied, previous revelations such as the Torah given through Moses – makes God known.

The Letter to the Hebrews, attributed to but certainly not written by Paul, makes this same point more directly. Hebrews 3:2 acknowledges that Moses "was faithful in all God's house" but then continues: "Yet Jesus is worthy of more glory than Moses, just as the builder of a house has more honor than the house itself.... Now Moses was faithful in all God's house as a servant, to testify to the things that would be spoken later. Christ, however, was faithful over God's house as a son ..." (Heb. 3:3–6).

The conviction that the revelation through Christ surpasses and supersedes the Torah – and its 1st-century interpreters – comes to the fore in the section of the Sermon on the Mount known as the Antitheses (Matt. 5:21–48). Throughout this section, Jesus refers to a number of statements from the Decalogue and other biblical passages, using the formula: "You have heard it said ... But I say to you." In Matthew 5:21, for example, Jesus states, "You have heard that it was said to those of ancient times, 'You shall not murder'; and 'whoever murders shall be liable to judgment.'" He continues in Matthew 5:22: "But I say to you that if you are angry with a brother or sister, you will be liable to judgment; and if you insult a brother or sister, you will be liable to the council; and if you say, 'You fool,' you will be liable to the hell of fire." Similarly, in Matthew 5:27, Jesus states: "You have heard that it was said, 'You shall not commit adultery.'" And he continues in 5:28: "But I say to you that everyone who looks at a woman with lust has already committed adultery with her in his heart." The pattern is repeated four more times (Matt. 5:31, 33, 38, 43), with reference to the corban sacrifice, divorce, the taking of oaths, and the "golden rule."

In each section, Matthew's Jesus creates the sense of an antithesis using the term "but." In what follows, however, Jesus does not negate the Mosaic ruling but extends it from the realm of action into the realms of emotion, intent, and speech. "You shall not murder" is extended to include anger and insults; "you shall not commit adultery" is extended to include lust even if that emotion does not lead to physical adultery. The Golden Rule of loving one's neighbour is broadened to include loving one's enemy (Matt. 5:44–47).

These extensions do not negate the biblical law. Rather, they imply that Jesus has now exposed the true meaning of the law that others – perhaps Jewish interpreters – have read in a more limited fashion. If there is an antithesis, it is not between two sets of laws but two interpretations. If we read this in the context of Matthew's diatribe against the Pharisees in Matthew 23 ("woe to you, scribes and Pharisees, hypocrites!," 23:13 and throughout), then the contrast may be between what Matthew's Jesus views as a narrow interpretation of the law and Jesus' extended, compassionate interpretation. The basic message is that the true meaning of the biblical law can be understood only through the lenses that Jesus provides.

A related point is made in John 5:39–47, in which Jesus accuses his Jewish opponents of misreading their own scriptures. Jesus describes Jews as "searching the scriptures" for the key to eternal life but failing to understand that "it is they [the scriptures] that testify on my behalf" (John 5:39). He then admonishes: "Yet you refuse to come to me to have life" (5:40). A few verses later he admonishes: "Do not think that I will accuse you before the Father; your accuser is Moses, on whom you have set your hope. If you believed Moses, you would believe me, for he wrote about me" (5:45–46). In the Gospel of John, the critique is not of the Torah but of the Jews' failure, or refusal, to read the Torah christologically as a set of prophecies of the coming of Christ as the messiah.

These are but a few of the many expressions of supersessionism in the New Testament. It is not surprising that a new movement would describe itself as a new and improved version of the very same worldview that provided the framework for its own perspective on the relationship between God and humankind. I doubt that the New Testament authors imagined that within two or three centuries, the power relationship between Jews and Christians would tilt from Jews to Christians and grant Christian authorities the power to enact measures against Jews. Nor did they foresee the elaborate theology that would develop around supersessionism, a theology that included the description of Judaism as a moribund and spiritless religion that would surely die out in time. Yet it is a fact that such descriptions, and the supersessionism upon which they are based, contributed to the denigration of both Jews and Judaism well into the 20th century.[11]

---

[11] For example, Wilhelm Bousset, *What Is Religion?*, trans. F. B. Low (London, 1907), 155. For detailed discussion of the focus on legalism in German New Testament scholarship, see Anders Gerdmar, *Roots of Theological Anti-Semitism: German Biblical Interpretation and the Jews, from Herder and Semler to Kittel and Bultmann* (Leiden, 2010).

THE JEWS AND SATAN

One of the most potent aspects of Christian anti-Judaism, and modern antisemitism, is the association of Jews and Satan. The association is expressed vividly in Revelation 2:9 and 3:9. In Revelation 2:9, the seer writes: "I know the blasphemy of them that say they are Jews and are not, but are the synagogue of Satan." This statement occurs in a letter to "the angel of the church in Ephesus" (2:1). Revelation 3:9 conveys much the same sentiment, in a letter to "the angel of the church in Philadelphia" (3:7): "I will make those of the synagogue of Satan who say that they are Jews and are not, but are lying – I will make them come and bow down before your feet, and they will learn that I have loved you."

While it is clear that "synagogue of Satan" is a negative term, its exact meaning remains uncertain. Is the seer referring to a congregation of Jewish Christ-confessors? A group of Gentile Christ-Confessors who have adopted Jewish practices?[12] Ironically, while the phrase itself conveys hostility towards "the synagogue," the reference to those "who say that they are Jews and are not" indicates that the target is a group of Christ-confessors, and not Jews who do not confess Jesus as messiah.

The association of Jews and Satan likely stems not from Revelation but from the Gospel of John, where, in contrast to Revelation, it is indeed directed at non-Christ-confessing Jews. The key verse is John 8:44, in which Jesus tells a group of Jews: "You are from your father the devil, and you choose to do your father's desires. He was a murderer from the beginning and does not stand in the truth, because there is no truth in him."

Some scholars have attempted to explain away the hostility conveyed by this verse by arguing that it reflects a standard convention of ancient rhetoric, akin to schoolyard name-calling[13]. Labelling it so does not, however, empty the verse of its hostile content or emotional impact. Furthermore, the idea that Jews have the devil as their father is deeply intertwined with the Gospel's Christology, that is, its understanding of Jesus' own identity, in at least two ways.

First, it is embedded in an argument drawn from the Aristotelian theory of epigenesis. According to this theory, a child's father, that is, his semen, contributes the personal traits and attributes of a child, while

---

[12] See John W. Marshall, *Parables of War: Reading John's Jewish Apocalypse* (Waterloo, 2001).

[13] Luke T. Johnson, "The New Testament's Anti-Jewish Slander and the Conventions of Ancient Polemic," *Journal of Biblical Literature* 108.3 (1989), 419–41.

the mother contributes the medium of growth, that is, her uterus, in which the embryo grows into a baby ready to be born. Under ideal circumstances, the child will resemble the father perfectly, sharing his identity in every way from gender through to personality.

Epigenesis was the most widely accepted theory of animal and human reproduction in the ancient Mediterranean world.[14] Although the term does not appear in the Gospel, it undergirds the Gospel's claims that Jesus is God's son, and that he acts only as God acts, and on God's behalf.[15] It also explains John 8:44. John's Jesus proclaims that by murdering and lying, the Jews demonstrate that they are not the children of God, as they assert in 8:41, but the children of the devil. As Jesus states in John 8:42, "If God were your Father, you would love me, for I came from God and now I am here." But because they do not accept him (8:43), the Jews cannot be God's children but rather must have the devil as their father.

The second way the John 8:44 Satan passage links to Christology is through its connection with supersessionism and, specifically, the claim that Jesus, as God's Son, is now the one who mediates the covenantal relationship to the people Israel. To be related to God through this covenant requires faith in Jesus as the messiah and Son of God (cf. 20:30–31).

John 8:31–59 makes this argument in a detailed way by presenting a dispute between the Jews and Jesus as to the terms of God's covenant with God's people. The Jews' brief comments assert their covenantal relationship with God by emphasizing three key points: that Abraham is their father (8:33, 39), that they have never served or been enslaved to anyone or anything (8:33), and that they are children of God (8:41). In claiming to be children of Abraham, the Jews draw attention to Abraham's status as the patriarch of the Jewish people. As the first monotheist, Abraham is known in Jewish tradition as the first person to recognize the one God as the creator of the world.[16] The Jews are Abraham's children insofar as they too maintain a firm commitment to monotheism.

[14] Aristotle, *Generation of Animal, with an English Translation by A. L. Peck.*, ed. A. L. Peck (Cambridge, MA, 1953); A. J. Preus, "Science and Philosophy in Aristotle's Generation of Animals," *Journal of the History of Biology* 3 (1970), 1–52, in *Feminism and Ancient Philosophy*, ed. Julie K. Ward (New York, 1996), 30–50, 227–32.

[15] Adele Reinhartz, "'And the Word Was Begotten': Divine Epigenesis in the Gospel of John," *Semeia* 85 (1999), 83–103.

[16] See Jeffrey S. Siker, *Disinheriting the Jews: Abraham in Early Christian Controversy* (Louisville, KY, 1991). For detailed discussion of Abraham in John 8, see Ruth Sheridan, *The Figure of Abraham in John 8: Text and Intertext* (London, 2020).

The Jews' claim that they have never served or been enslaved to anyone is more ambiguous. In a literal sense, the Jews certainly were once enslaved, in Egypt under the Pharaohs. But the verb normally translated as "to be enslaved" has another, well-established meaning, namely, "to serve," as in, to serve many gods.[17] The Jews' boast that they have never "served" anyone or anything (8:33) is thus an expression of their devotion to the one God of Israel. Indeed, to serve another "divine" being – such as Jesus claims to be – would be tantamount to slavery.

Finally, the Jews' covenantal relationship with God bestows upon them the status of God's children. In Exodus 4:22–23, for example, God coaches Moses on what to say to the Pharaoh as he tries to secure Israel's release from slavery: "Then you shall say to Pharaoh, 'Thus says the LORD: Israel is my firstborn son.... Let my son go that he may worship me.'" Thus the Jews' three major claims – that they are children of Abraham, have never served any other beings, and are children of God – all make the same point: Jews are in an eternal covenantal relationship with God.

The Johannine Jesus, in turn, insists that the Jews can no longer lay claim to this special relationship. For Jesus, the Jews' rejection of his messiahship proves that they cannot be the children of Abraham. Whereas Abraham accepted God's messengers (cf. Genesis 18), the Jews try to kill God's son (8:40). Despite their boasts to the contrary, the Jews continue to be enslaved as long as they refuse to believe. In 8:34, Jesus proclaims: "Everyone who commits sin is a slave to sin. The slave does not have a permanent place in the household; the son has a place there forever. So if the Son makes you free, you will be free indeed." Finally, the Jews cannot be the children of God: "If God were your Father, you would love me, for I came from God and now I am here. I did not come on my own, but he sent me" (8:42).

By mounting this argument, the Fourth Gospel aims to persuade its audience of the supersessionist claim that the Jews' rejection of Jesus has ousted them from their covenantal relationship with God, and thereby revealed their true ancestry as children of the devil. The association of the Jews and Satan has a long history, continuing to the present day on antisemitic and white-supremacist websites. Its vituperative

---

[17] In the *Septuagint* (2nd-century BCE Greek translation of the Hebrew Bible), this verb is sometimes used to refer specifically to the worship of God or gods. In his letter to the Galatians, Paul uses this verb in a way that implies both worship and slavery (Gal. 4:9; cf. Jer. 5:19).

power carries on independently of the Gospel of John's covenantal argumentation, and of its deployment of Aristotle's theory of epigenesis.

THE DEICIDE CHARGE

All four canonical gospels hold the Jews and/or their leaders to blame for the process that leads to Jesus' crucifixion. (1 Thessalonians 2:14 also alludes to this, though many consider this passage to have been written by someone other than Paul.)[18] The Synoptic Gospels of Mark, Matthew, and Luke tell the same general story of this process in their last few chapters, usually referred to as the Passion Narrative. Judas betrays Jesus to the authorities; Jesus is cross-examined by the high priest and other leaders and convicted of blasphemy; he is then taken to Pilate, where he undergoes further questioning. Pilate is disinclined to follow through, but when he offers the release of a prisoner, the Jewish authorities clamour for Barabbas, an insurrectionist or "robber," rather than Jesus. Pilate reluctantly agrees to send Jesus for crucifixion.[19]

The Gospel of John sharpens the point by recounting an incident that is not paralleled in the other three canonical Gospels. In the aftermath of Lazarus's dramatic resurrection (John 11:38–44), many of the Jews who witnessed the miracle believed in Jesus. Others, however, went to report the event to the Pharisees (John 11:45–46). The chief priests and Pharisees called an emergency meeting of the Council, the Jewish leadership, exclaiming: "What are we to do? This man is performing many signs. If we let him go on like this, everyone will believe in him, and the Romans will come and destroy both our holy place and our nation" (11:47–48). At this point, Caiaphas the high priest says: "You know nothing at all! You do not understand that it is better for you to have one man die for the people than to have the whole nation destroyed" (11:49–50). And "from that day on they planned to put him to death" (11:53).

By recounting the Council meeting and decision, John's Gospel places the moral responsibility for Jesus' crucifixion squarely on the Jewish leadership. To ensure that Caiaphas's culpability remains in the front of the mind, the narrator later reminds us that "Caiaphas was the one who had advised the Jews that it was better to have one

---

[18] Carol J. Schlueter, *Filling up the Measure: Polemical Hyperbole in 1 Thessalonians 2:14–16* (Sheffield, 1994); Markus Bockmuehl, "1 Thessalonians 2:14–16 and the Church in Jerusalem," *Tyndale Bulletin* 52.1 (2001), 1–31.

[19] Matthew 26:30–27:66; Mark 14:26–15:47; Luke 22:39–23:56; and John 18:1–19:42.

person die for the people" (18:14). The blame is extended to "the Jews" and their leaders throughout the Passion Narrative. When Pilate attempts to remove himself from the situation – "Take him yourselves and judge him according to your law" (18:31a) – the Jews reply, "We are not permitted to put anyone to death" (18:31b). Later, the chief priests and police should "Crucify him! Crucify him!" Later, they cry out: "Away with him! Away with him! Crucify him!" (19:15). Pilate finally gives in and hands Jesus over to be crucified (19:16).

The Passion Narratives in all four canonical Gospels mark the Jews as guilty of deicide – killing God – even though Pilate was the one who ordered Jesus' crucifixion. They do so by showing Pilate to be reluctant to prosecute Jesus and depicting the Jewish crowds and leaders as eager for his death. The most damaging passage, however, is found in the Gospel of Matthew. As the Jews continued to shout for Jesus' crucifixion, Pilate feared that a riot was beginning (Matt. 27:24a). He then "took some water and washed his hands before the crowd, saying, 'I am innocent of this man's blood; see to it yourselves'" (Matt. 27:24b). The people – who are Jews – then responded, "His blood be on us and on our children!" (Matt. 27:25). "So, he released Barabbas for them; and after flogging Jesus, he handed him over to be crucified" (Matt. 27:26).

In Matthew 27:25, the Jews accept responsibility for Jesus' blood for themselves and future generations. It must be stressed that this statement, like John 8:44, is not a transcript of words actually spoken by historical individuals or groups but scripted by the author(s) of Matthew's Gospel. To their credit, many mainline Protestant and Catholic Churches have repudiated the deicide charge. The 1965 Vatican II document *Nostra aetate* states explicitly that while "the Jewish authorities and those who followed their lead pressed for the death of Christ; still, what happened in His passion cannot be charged against all the Jews, without distinction, then alive, nor against the Jews of today."[20] Like supersessionism and the association of Jews and Satan, however, the deicide charge has not entirely disappeared.[21]

---

[20] Unfortunately, *Nostra Aetate* did not address supersessionism; it continued to refer to the Church as the "new people of God." www.vatican.va/archive/hist_councils/ii_vatican_council/documents/vat-ii_decl_19651028_nostra-aetate_en.html.

[21] Amy-Jill Levine, "Christian Privilege, Christian Fragility, and the Gospel of John," in *The Gospel of John and Jewish-Christian Relations*, ed. Adele Reinhartz (Lanham, MD, 2018), 87–110.

EARLY CHRISTIAN RECEPTION

The New Testament themes of supersessionism, the association of Jews and Satan, and deicide continue in early Christian literature into the 2nd century, and beyond. *The Letter of Barnabas*, dated to the late 1st or early 2nd century, states that the Jews have been deceived by the "evil one" (8:7) into transgression and the false view that thinking that circumcision is still necessary for relationship with God.[22] In the *Dialogue with Trypho*, Justin Martyr tells Trypho the Jews that "[the gifts] formerly among your nation have been transferred to us ... The Scriptures are not yours, but ours. For we believe them; but you, though you read them, do not catch the spirit that is in them."[23] He also castigates the Jews for deicide: "You have slain the Just One, and his prophets before him; and now you reject those who hope in him ... cursing in your synagogues those that believe in Christ."[24] And the heading of Dialogue Chapter 16 reads: "Circumcision [was] given as a sign, that the Jews might be driven away for their evil deeds done to Christ and the Christians."[25] The lament of Melito of Sardis provides an apt summary of the anti-Jewish thread of early Christian thought:

What strange injustice have you done, O Israel?
> You have dishonored the one who honored you,
> you have disgraced the one who glorified you,
> you have denied the one who owned you,
> you have ignored the one who made you known,
> you have murdered the one who gave you life.[26]

---

[22] https://archive.org/stream/pdfy-p_dCmdKbL5O-r1Hf/The+General+Epistle+Of +Barnabas_djvu.txt. See also William Horbury, "Jewish-Christian Relations in Barnabas and Justin Martyr," in *Jews and Christians: The Parting of the Ways, A.D. 70 to 135: The Second Durham–Tübingen Research Symposium on Earliest Christianity and Judaism (Durham, September 1989)*, ed. James D. Dunn (1992), 315–45.

[23] Justin Martyr, *Dialogue with* Trypho, Chapter 29, in Alexander Roberts et al., eds., *Ante-Nicene Fathers: The Writings of the Fathers down to A.D. 325* (Peabody, MA, 1995), 209. www.earlychristianwritings.com/text/justinmartyr-dialoguetrypho.html.

[24] Justin Martyr, *Dialogue with Trypho*, Chapter 16, in Roberts et al., *Ante-Nicene Fathers*, 202. www.earlychristianwritings.com/text/justinmartyr-dialoguetrypho .html. See also Ruth Langer, *Cursing the Christians?: A History of the Birkat Haminim* (New York, 2011).

[25] Justin Martyr, *Dialogue with Trypho*, Chapter 16, in Roberts et al., *Ante-Nicene Fathers*, 202.

[26] Melito, *On Pascha: With the Fragments of Melito and Other Material Related to the Quartodecimans*, 2nd ed., St. Vladimir's Seminary Press Popular Patristics Series, no. 55 (Yonkers, NY, 2016), 57, paragraph 73.

The New Testament provided subsequent Christian theologians and leaders with plenty of fodder for what later became a widespread, though not universal, anti-Jewish agenda that went far beyond what New Testament authors would have envisaged or (I conjecture) desired.[27] In some cases, the statements that express, or that can be read as expressing, hostility towards non-Christ-confessing Jews point to the efforts by the Jesus movement to develop an identity that was distinct from Jewishness yet adopted many elements of Jewishness. For Paul and many post-New Testament authors, such differentiation was part of a polemical discourse targeted not so much at non-Christ-confessing Jews as at Jewish Christ-confessors. The tension between Christians of Jewish origin who retained Jewish practices such as circumcision and the dietary laws, and Gentile Christians who did not engage in such practices became more intense as the latter group grew in number and influence. When read, as they often were, without regard to the immediate historical and literary contexts, however, these statements became embedded in Christian theology, literature, and liturgy. Rosemary Ruether may well have been right that anti-Judaism is deeply embedded in Christology and Christian theology more generally. Understanding something of the historical context, along with other measures such as those undertaken by Vatican II, can help.

Further Reading

Bieringer, R., D. Pollefeyt, and F. Vandecasteele-Vanneuville, eds., *Anti-Judaism and the Fourth Gospel: Papers of the Leuven Colloquium, 2000* (Assen, 2001). The proceedings of a colloquium held in Leuven, Belgium, considering all aspects of the Gospel of John and anti-Judaism. Contributors include James Dunn, Judith Lieu, Alan Culpepper, C. K. Barrett, and many others.

Cohen, J., *Christ Killers: The Jews and the Passion, from the Bible to the Big Screen* (New York, 2007). A history of the deicide myth from the New Testament to the present, including patristic, medieval, and modern theology, as well as art, music, theatre, and film.

Donaldson, T. L., *Jews and Anti-Judaism in the New Testament: Decision Points and Divergent Interpretations* (Waco, TX, 2010). An introduction to diverse ways in which scholars have interpreted the New Testament in relation to anti-Judaism.

Fredriksen, P., and A. Reinhartz, eds. *Jesus, Judaism, and Christian Anti-Judaism: Reading the New Testament after the Holocaust* (Louisville, KY,

---

[27] Michael G. Azar, *Exegeting the Jews: The Early Reception of the Johannine Jews* (Leiden, 2016). See also Paula Fredriksen, *Augustine and the Jews: A Christian Defense of Jews and Judaism* (New York, 2008).

2002). A collection of essays, by P. Fredriksen, J. G. Gager, E. P. Sanders, A.-J. Levine, and A. Reinhartz, re-evaluating the historical figures and canonical texts that have fostered the negative characterizations of Jews and Judaism.

Levine, A.-J. et al., eds. *The Jewish Annotated New Testament*, 2nd ed. (New York, 2017). Introductions, annotations, and thematic essays, all by Jewish scholars.

Nirenberg, D., *Anti-Judaism: The Western Tradition* (New York, 2013). A comprehensive argument for the view that anti-Judaism is not a marginal phenomenon in western tradition, but foundational to western history and culture.

Reinhartz, A., *Cast Out of the Covenant: Jews and Anti-Judaism in the Gospel of John* (Lanham, MD, 2018). A book arguing that the Gospel's anti-Jewishness is evident both in the Gospel's hostile comments about the Jews and in its appropriation of Torah, Temple, and Covenant that were so central to 1st-century Jewish identity.

Ruether, R. R., *Faith and Fratricide: The Theological Roots of Anti-Semitism* (New York, 1974). A book arguing that anti-Judaism is intertwined with Christian theology and Christology from the New Testament to the present.

3 Anti-Judaism in Early Christian Writings

PIERLUIGI PIOVANELLI

MESSIANIC JEWS IN THE TURMOIL OF THE JEWISH—ROMAN WARS

From a sociohistorical perspective, until at least the destruction of Jerusalem by the Roman legions in 70 CE, the first Christians – the followers of a leader called Khristos, that is, the Greek equivalent to the Hebrew Mashiah – were but the members of a Jewish sectarian movement, albeit, as shown by their nickname, a strongly messianic one.[1] After the fall of the Second Temple, different Jewish religious groups reacted to that terrible shock, interpreting it in a variety of manners, with the narrator of the Passion story in the Gospel of Mark seeing in it a retrospective condemnation and punishment of the Jerusalem leaders involved in Jesus' trial and execution forty years earlier. Even if the target of such a polemical "myth of innocence"[2] was more the Jewish Christian leadership of the Jerusalem community than Judaism and the Jewish people themselves, its ideological consequences would soon become devastating for Jewish and Christian relations. As the pseudo-Paul of 1 Thessalonians 2:13–15 (a later addition to the original letter) would put it, "the Jews, who killed both the Lord Jesus and the prophets, ... displease God and oppose everyone ...; thus they have constantly been filling up the measure of their sins, but God's wrath has overtaken them at last."[3] Two and a half centuries later, the Church historian Eusebius of Caesarea will contend that the crucifixion of Jesus

---

[1] See, in general, Pierluigi Piovanelli, "Was There Sectarian Behavior before the Flourishing of Jewish Sects? A Long-Term Approach to the History and Sociology of Second Temple Sectarianism," in *Sectarianism in Early Judaism: Sociological Advances*, ed. David Chalcraft (London, 2007), 156–79.

[2] As Burton L. Mack, *A Myth of Innocence: Mark and Christian Origins* (Philadelphia, 1988), aptly puts it.

[3] English translations of the canonical texts are normally taken from the New Revised Standard Version.

was but the beginning of a protracted "process of divine punishment" of the Jews that culminated with the destruction of Jerusalem by Titus and ended with the Jewish banishment from Jerusalem in the aftermath of the Bar Kokhba's war.[4] The seeds of theological anti-Judaism were thus regrettably sown in the very soil of early Christian discourses and memories about Jesus' death.

This, however, was not the case for other early Christian authors who wrote about their experiences under their own names or chose to present them embedded in new midrashim about biblical prophets of old and/or Jesus and his disciples.[5] In what follows we are going to take into consideration the instances of, on the one hand, the Book of Revelation and the *Ascension of Isaiah*, and, on the other hand, Marcion and the anonymous authors of "gnostic" gospels, more specifically, the recently rediscovered *Gospel of Judas*.

JOHN OF PATMOS'S "FALSE" JEWS

The Book of Revelation relates the visions that the Christian prophet John had seen in the Greek island of Patmos. It was written sometime after Vesuvius's eruption (mentioned in Rev. 8:8–9) that completely obliterated the Campanian towns of Herculaneum, Oplontis, Pompeii, and Stabiae, in August or October 79, at the beginning of emperor Titus's short reign, most probably shortly after his sudden death two years later (evoked in Rev. 17:9–10), on September 13, 81. This was clearly an appropriate setting for an apocalyptic reaction to Titus's violent military repression of the Jewish revolt and the propaganda of the Flavian dynasty through the minting of the *Iudaea capta* coins,[6] not too different from the responses found in *4th Ezra*, *2nd Baruch*, and other Jewish apocalypses of the last two decades of the first century.[7]

---

[4] Bar Kokhba's messianic reputation was already a stumbling block to both the author of the *Apocalypse of Peter* (2:7–10) and Justin Martyr (*First Apology* 31:5–6), who claimed that the Jewish leader had persecuted local Christian Jews.

[5] Contrary to what is too hastily assumed for the *Gospel of Peter*, the *Ascension of Isaiah*, and the *Gospel of Thomas* by Bart D. Ehrman, *Forgery and Counterforgery: The Use of Literary Deceit in Early Christian Polemics* (Oxford, 2013), 323–44.

[6] See, most recently, G. Anthony Keddie, "*Iudaea Capta* vs. Mother Zion: The Flavian Discourse on Judaeans and Its Delegitimation in 4 Ezra," *Journal for the Study of Judaism* 49 (2018), 498–550.

[7] As convincingly demonstrated by John W. Marshall, *Parables of War: Reading John's Jewish Apocalypse* (Waterloo, Ont., 2001). On what follows, see also John D. Crossan, *God and Empire: Jesus against Rome, Then and Now* (New York, 2007); Shane J. Wood, *The Alter-Imperial Paradigm: Empire Studies and the Book of Revelation* (Leiden, 2016).

In this connection, it is appropriate to reconsider how John depicts certain individuals as Christian dissidents or (supposedly) Jewish opponents in the letters the "One like a son of man" orders him to write down and send to the seven *ekklēsiai* in Ephesus, Smyrna, Pergamum, Thyatira, Sardis, Philadelphia, and Laodicea (Rev. 1:9–20). Thus, in Ephesus some people falsely claim to be apostles (Rev. 2:2), while others belong to a group called "the Nicolaitans" (Rev. 2:6), perhaps the followers of the Hellenist deacon Nicolaus (a proselyte of Antioch mentioned in Acts of the Apostles 6:5). Other Nicolaitans are found in Pergamum (Rev. 2:15), alongside some "who hold to the teaching of Balaam ... so that they would eat food sacrificed to idols and practice fornication *(porneusai)*" (Rev. 2:14). The same accusations of "teaching and beguiling ... to practice fornication *(porneusai)* and to eat food sacrificed to idols" are made against a self-proclaimed prophetess from Thyatira who is derogatorily called "Jezebel" (Rev. 2:20). As for the communities in Smyrna and Philadelphia, they are victims of "the slander on the part of those who say that they are Jews and are not, but are a synagogue of Satan" (Rev. 2:9; 3:9). In the end, only Sardis and Laodicea are apparently free from any criticism.

Traditional exegeses identify the Nicolaitans and prophetess Jezebel with Christian heretics, preferably with "gnostic" enthusiasts, while those who are "a synagogue of Satan" are generally seen as the members of the local Jewish communities who denounced their Christian fellows to the Roman authorities. All this is well known, and having been repeated and interiorized for almost two thousand years, it is almost impossible for the majority of the readers of the Book of Revelation not to accept it as a self-evident truism.[8] Nonetheless, as Elaine Pagels has recently emphasized, such an interpretation is but the end of a long chain of preconceived ideas postulating that, on the one hand, the destruction of Jerusalem in 70 CE marked the definitive parting of the ways between Judaism and Christianity,[9] and that, on the other hand, for the Christian convert John of Patmos the only "true" Jews (in opposition to "false" Jews in Smyrna and Philadelphia) were the Messianic ones.

[8] See Steve J. Friesen, "Sarcasm in Revelation 2–3: Churches, Christians, True Jews, and Satanic Synagogues," and Paul B. Duff, "The 'Synagogue of Satan': Crisis Mongering and the Apocalypse of John," both in *The Reality of Apocalypse: Rhetoric and Politics in the Book of Revelation*, ed. David L. Barr (Leiden, 2006), 127–44 and 147–68, respectively,

[9] For a long-term perspective, see Daniel Boyarin, *Border Lines: The Partition of Judaeo-Christianity* (Philadelphia, 2004).

In the Book of Revelation, however, "Satan" is but a code name for Rome and, in John's eyes, those who are associated with Satan are but collaborators with the Roman Empire, not only the traitors ("those who say that they are Jews and are not") in Smyrna and Philadelphia, but also the enthusiasts in Ephesus, Smyrna, and Thyatira who did not comply with the laws of kashrut ("to eat food sacrificed to idols") and *niddah* ("to practice fornication"). In other words, it is highly probable that behind the mysterious Nicolaitans and prophetess Jezebel lie the non-Torah-observant members of some "proto-orthodox" Pauline communities. As for the profile of the implied author of the Book of Revelation, John of Patmos emerges as a philo-Judaic Christian, possibly one of the last survivors of the Messianic community of James, the brother of the Lord, in Jerusalem.[10]

THE CHRISTIAN MYSTICS OF THE ASCENSION OF ISAIAH

The *Ascension of Isaiah* is a pseudepigraphic text that tells the story of Isaiah's martyrdom at the hands of the evil king Manasseh (chapters 1–5) because of his prophecy about the coming of the Beloved, "the Messiah who will be called Jesus," he had witnessed at the end of his ascent through the seven heavens (chapters 6–11). It clearly belongs to a group of ancient Jewish (and Christian) ascent apocalypses like *1* and *2 Enoch*, the *Apocalypse of Abraham*, the *Apocalypse of Zephaniah*, *3 Baruch*, and the Book of Revelation that allow us to see, behind the shadows of their narrative conventions, the glimmers of visionary mystical activities.[11] The closest parallel, however, to the experiences described in the early 2nd-century *Ascension of Isaiah* is to be found in the late antique collection of the Hekhalot, or "Palaces" (referring to the seven palaces, one in each of the seven heavens, especially the last palace in the seventh heaven where the Merkavah, or divine chariot-throne, is located), a series of Jewish mystical texts, written mainly in Hebrew,[12] about two to six centuries after the *Ascension of Isaiah*, that is, between the 4th and 8th century.

---

[10] See John W. Marshall, "John's Jewish (Christian?) Apocalypse," in *Jewish Christianity Reconsidered: Rethinking Ancient Groups and Texts*, ed. Matt Jackson-McCabe (Minneapolis, MN, 2007), 233–56 and 328–31.

[11] See Pierluigi Piovanelli, "'A Door into an Alien World': Reading the *Ascension of Isaiah* as a Jewish Mystical Text," in *The Ascension of Isaiah*, ed. Jan N. Bremmer et al. (Leuven, 2016), 119–44.

[12] Now conveniently translated by James R. Davila, *Hekhalot Literature in Translation: Major Texts of Merkavah Mysticism* (Leiden, 2013).

There is a growing consensus among specialists that the *Ascension of Isaiah* is the product of a group of Christian prophets, perhaps still wandering, who experienced heavenly ascensions and carried out a charismatic exegesis of the Scriptures, especially the Book of Isaiah, thus meeting the opposition of the representatives of more routinized structures of authority, the "impious elders and shepherds unjust towards their sheep" (*Ascension of Isaiah* 3:24), to be identified with the priests and bishops of the region of Antioch.[13] Especially remarkable is the absence from the *Ascension of Isaiah* of explicitly supersessionist and/or anti-Jewish statements. Actually, it is rather anachronistic to perceive an anti-Jewish polemic[14] in the description of Isaiah and Jesus' persecutors among "the children of Israel," who acted in both cases at the instigation of Beliar/Sammael and "didn't know who (Jesus really) was" (*Ascension of Isaiah* 11:19). All these features, taken together, concur to recognize in the people behind the *Ascension of Isaiah* a group of Merkavah mystics very close to, if not identical with, the "Judaizers" repeatedly criticized by bishop Ignatius of Antioch, widely known for his anti-Jewish utterances.

MARCIONITE AND "GNOSTIC" ANTI-JUDAISM?

Marcion of Sinope was one of the first Christian thinkers to systematically contrast the Creator God of the Hebrew Bible with the Heavenly Father of the New Testament, thus laying down the premises for radical, ontological anti-Judaism. This is, at least, the reputation of the "deviator and destroyer of Judaism" (thus Tertullian of Carthage) that he has earned among the Church Fathers and the specialists of early Christianity, from Adolf von Harnack to Walter Bauer, as well. This is another traditional view against which a new generation of researchers has taken a robust stance.[15]

---

[13] On these and other issues, see Enrico Norelli, "The Political Issue of the *Ascension of Isaiah*: Some Remarks on Jonathan Knight's Thesis and Some Methodological Problems," in *Early Christian Voices in Texts, Traditions and Symbols: Essays in Honor of François Bovon*, ed. David H. Warren et al. (Leiden, 2003), 267–79; and Jonathan Knight, "The Political Issue of the *Ascension of Isaiah*: A Response to Enrico Norelli," *Journal for the Study of the New Testament* 35 (2013), 355–79.

[14] As does Greg Carey, "The *Ascension of Isaiah*: An Example of Early Christian Narrative Polemics," *Journal for the Study of the Pseudepigrapha* 17 (1998), 65–78.

[15] See, most recently, Heikki Räisänen, "Marcion and the Origins of Christian Anti-Judaism: A Reappraisal," *Temenos* 33 (1997), 121–35 (reprinted in H. Räisänen, *Challenges to Biblical Interpretation: Collected Essays 1991–2000* [Leiden, 2001], 191–205); Sebastian Moll, *The Arch-Heretic Marcion* (Tübingen, 2010); Marcus Vinzent, "Marcion the Jew," *Judaïsme ancien – Ancient Judaism* 1 (2013), 159–201.

According to this "New Perspective on Marcion," the author of the *Antitheses* distinguished between two Gods, two Messiahs,[16] two sets of Scriptures, two religions, the new one (Christianity) *not replacing* the old one (Judaism). As Markus Vinzent aptly puts it, "[t]he call to the gentiles, in Marcion, was a call to join the Christian antithetical Judaism, not a non-Jewish Christianity," that is, "an alter-Judaism ... modelled on its antithesis encompassing a strong monotheism, a Scripture-based revelation, a Messiah, a strict emphasis on ethics, food rules and regulations of relations."[17] From here to conclude that the historical Marcion conceived that both Judaism and Christian "alter-Judaism" could peacefully coexist side by side, in a non-antagonistic way, is a short step.

Be that as it may, this is precisely the perspective we can get from an unbiased reexamination of the Nag Hammadi and cognate "gnostic" texts, including the recently rediscovered *Gospel of Judas*. As is well known, its publication, in 2006–7, stirred up a great excitement among specialists of Coptic language and "gnostic" literature, with the result that an impressive number of articles and short monographs were hastily produced. The authors of this first wave of studies on the *Gospel of Judas* shared the basic conviction that the text conveys a positive image of the wayward disciple and that, simply put, it serves to rehabilitate him. A closer analysis of the Coptic text, however, has led other specialists to adopt a very different position which considers the protagonist of the *Gospel of Judas*, in April DeConick's words, to be "as evil as ever." As is usually the case, the truth is in the middle: the figure of the Iscariot does not really require, in the *Gospel of Judas*, any too polarized treatment for the excellent reason that its function is to provide a dramatic counterbalance to those of the Twelve, the founders of the Great Church, the real target of the narrator's criticism.[18]

---

[16] "The difference between two Christs was intended by the Creator for the regathering out of dispersion of the people [of Israel] and no others, whereas your Christ [i.e., Jesus] has been advanced by the supremely good God for the deliverance of the whole human race" (Tertullian, *Against Marcion* III 21:1, quoted by Vinzent, "Marcion the Jew," 186).

[17] Vinzent, "Marcion the Jew," 189.

[18] See Pierluigi Piovanelli, "Rabbi Yehuda versus Judas Iscariot: The *Gospel of Judas* and the Apocryphal Passion Stories," in *The Codex Judas Papers: Proceedings of the International Congress on the Tchacos Codex*, ed. April DeConick (Leiden, 2009), 223–39; and Joanna Brankaer, "Representations of Judaism in the *Gospel of Judas*: The Church of Judas, the Jew," in *The Apocryphal Gospels within the Context of Early Christian Theology*, ed. Jens Schröter (Leuven, 2013), 581–94.

Moreover, in contrast to other Christian narratives, "gnostic" writings display almost no animosity toward Judas and the Jewish characters involved in Jesus' passion. It is easy to understand how such hatred would have been a paradox for "gnostic" believers who belittled the theological relevance of the sufferings of a human Jesus left to die on the cross after the departure of the heavenly Christ. As the resurrected Jesus says to his spiritual brother in the *First Revelation of James*, "James, do not be concerned about the people [of Jerusalem, the Jewish people] or about me. For I am the one who preexists in me. For I have not suffered at all and I did not die, and this people has done no harm" (Al Minya Codex 2 18:4–11 // Nag Hammadi Codex V, 3 31:15–22).

Contrary to the commonly held opinion that the transformation of the God of the Hebrew Bible (the *Yotzer Bereshit*) into an arrogant and tyrannical lesser god was in the best case a heretical aberration, and in the worst case an anti-Jewish move (according to Hans Jonas, Gershom Scholem would have said that "gnosticism" is "the greatest case of metaphysical anti-Semitism"), in proceeding to such a value reversal "gnostics" were simply placing the Jewish heritage of Christianity in an unusual and more distant perspective.[19] As a consequence, "gnostic" Christianity was certainly less aggressive and supersessionist than the other branches of 2nd-century Christianity.

IN THE END, FROM PHILO- TO ALTER- AND ANTI-JUDAISM

At the end of this short survey, it appears that until the last decades of the 2nd century CE Christian authors adopted a variety of stances toward such key issues as the responsibility of the Jews in the death of Jesus and the meaning of the destruction of Jerusalem and its Temple by Titus's legions. The original attitude of John of Patmos could be qualified as openly philo-Jewish, and it is only at the price of a series of "orthodox" misinterpretations that the "synagogue of those false [Messianic] Jews who collaborate with Satan [i.e., Rome]" became the "synagogue of those Satanic Jews" *tout court* and the Book of Revelation another piece of anti-Jewish literature. The Christian practitioners of Merkavah mysticism who dared to rewrite a new Book of Isaiah, the *Ascension of Isaiah*, were

---

[19] In retrospect, one cannot but agree with the endeavor to de-essentialize the very category of "gnosticism" initiated by Michael A. Williams, *Rethinking "Gnosticism": An Argument for Dismantling a Dubious Category* (Princeton, NJ, 1996), and Karen L. King, *What Is Gnosticism?* (Cambridge, MA, 2003).

probably philo-Jewish too – in any case, definitively more sympathetic toward the Jewish roots of Christianity than their contemporary, the radically anti-Jewish bishop Ignatius of Antioch. As for Marcion of Sinope and the authors of "gnostic" gospels and revelations, the alter-Jewish way of life they promoted was clearly more tolerant and inclusive than the supersessionist one cherished by their ruthless critics Irenaeus of Lyon and Tertullian of Carthage.

The trajectories of philo-, alter-, and anti-Jewish attitudes in the Christian writings of the first two centuries are highly convoluted, not to say paradoxical. Ironically enough, those authors who most vocally claimed to endorse and defend the Jewish heritage of Christian religion were also those who gratified Judaism with the death kiss of true anti-Judaism. Let me be clear. Despite appearances and regardless of almost two thousand years of traditional exegesis, the Book of Revelation was primarily a powerful response to Roman oppression penned by a Messianic Jew, not an anti-Jewish tract written by a (Jewish) Christian author. As for the prophets who voiced their concerns through the *Ascension of Isaiah*, their foes were among the priests and the bishops of a Church in the process of becoming institutionalized, not their Jewish fellows at local synagogues. While in the case of Marcionite and "gnostic" Christians, their "metaphysical" anti-Judaism (if any) prevented them from making the extraordinary claim of being the "authentic Israel" (*verus Israel*), the true and only legitimate heirs of biblical Israel. Such a supersessionist claim was made by those who won, in the end, the competition for leadership and power inside and outside the Church. It is under their guidance that, in the course of the 4th century, the remains of early Christian philo- and alter-Jewish attitudes progressively disappeared, leaving regrettably the place to late antique anti-Jewish hatred, the ugly forefather of modern antisemitism.

Further Reading

Bibliowicz, A. M., *Jews and Gentiles in the Early Jesus Movement: An Unintended Journey* (New York, 2013). Extremely helpful at putting the sectarian polemics between different early Christian groups and main-stream ancient Judaism into historical perspective.

Chazan, R., *From Anti-Judaism to Anti-Semitism: Ancient and Medieval Christian Constructions of Jewish History* (Cambridge, 2016). A long-term approach to the history of Christian anti-Judaism.

Davies, A. T., ed., *Antisemitism and the Foundations of Christianity* (New York, 1979). Eleven specialists discuss and put into perspective R. Radford Ruether's main theses on the early Christian origins of antisemitism. It contains, among others, an important essay on patristic authors by D. P. Efroymson.

Gager, J. G., *The Origins of Anti-Semitism: Attitudes toward Judaism in Pagan and Christian Antiquity* (Oxford, 1983). An excellent synthesis written by one of the first proponents of the New Perspective on Paul.

Katz, S. T., ed., *The Cambridge History of Judaism*, vol. 4: *The Late Roman-Rabbinic Period* (Cambridge, 2006). Besides many valuable contributions, this volume contains well-informed overviews of early Christian anti-Judaism by P. Richardson, P. Fredriksen, and O. Irshai.

Lieu, J. M., *Neither Jew nor Greek? Constructing Early Christianity* (London, 2002). A useful collection of essays by one of the best specialists of the formation of early Christian identities.

Ruether R. R., *Faith and Fratricide: The Theological Roots of Anti-Semitism* (New York, 1974). The influential work of a feminist scholar who exposed the early Christian roots (the "other side of Christology") of what would later become modern antisemitism.

Schwartz, J., and P. J. Tomson, eds., *Jews and Christians in the First and Second Centuries: The Interbellum 70–132 CE* (Leiden, 2018). A collection of up-to-date studies on the critical period between the two Jewish-Roman Wars.

Simon, M., *Verus Israel: A Study of the Relations between Christians and Jews in the Roman Empire (135–425)*, trans. H. McKeating (Oxford, 1986). A true classic. Simon was among the first historians to argue that Judaism remained a living and active force even after the end of the Second Jewish-Roman War.

Taylor, M. S., *Anti-Judaism and Early Christian Identity: A Critique of the Scholarly Consensus* (Leiden, 1995). The author emphasizes the rhetorical, identity-building dimension of many early Christian anti-Jewish polemics.

Wilson, S. G., *Related Strangers: Jews and Christians 70–170 C.E.* (Minneapolis, MN, 1995). An extremely well-informed synthesis based on fresh examination of the primary sources.

Wilson, S. G., ed., *Anti-Judaism in Early Christianity*, vol. 2: *Separation and Polemic* (Waterloo, Ont., 1986). This volume provides an in-depth survey of 2nd-century Christian authors in relation to Judaism.

4 Church Fathers and Antisemitism from the 2nd Century through Augustine (end of 450 CE)

JOSHUA GARROWAY

> Blessed be the ashes of that humane theologian who was the first to declare that God was preserving us as a visible proof of the truth of the Nazarene religion. But for this lovely brainwave, we would have been exterminated long ago, humanly speaking.[1]

INTRODUCTION

The humane theologian to whom Moses Mendelssohn ironically referred in his 1769 exchange with Johann Kaspar Lavater was Saint Augustine (354–430), bishop of Hippo. The brainwave was Augustine's witness doctrine regarding the preservation of Jews and Judaism. Augustine, to be sure, was no friend of the Jews. Like other Christian thinkers, he saw in Jews a stubborn, carnal, accursed people who rejected and murdered the son of God. Augustine nonetheless diverged from his peers in that he viewed the ongoing presence of Jews, and their dispersal into Christian realms, as part of a divine plan to facilitate the ultimate triumph of Christianity. By clinging to the books and practices of the Old Testament, Jews would safeguard the scriptural witness to the truth of the New Testament and serve, as Mendelssohn put it, "as a visible proof of the truth of the Nazarene religion." By doing so in abased conditions, severed from their homeland and subservient to the religion that succeeded them, Jews at the same time would bear witness to the dreadful consequences of spurning Christ. Jews serve a decidedly Christian purpose, Augustine concluded, and as such Christians ought to tolerate their presence and encourage their continued observance of Jewish rites.

Lovely or not, Mendelssohn correctly observed that the survival of Jews in Christendom owed in part to Augustine's idea. The African bishop became a towering figure in medieval Christianity and his

---

[1] Marc Saperstein, *Moments of Crisis in Jewish-Christian Relations* (London, 1989), 11.

witness-people theology influenced policies of both church and state for nearly a millennium. It was even invoked on occasion to thwart popular violence against Jews, most famously by Bernard of Clairvaux (1090–1153) in response to the anti-Jewish riots accompanying the Second Crusade. The impact of Augustine is accentuated by the fact that his positive spin on the perseverance of the Jewish people hardly represented the inevitable culmination of three centuries of Christian thinking about Jews. While aspects of it appeared previously, his doctrine truly was a brainwave – an unforeseen flash of ingenuity, but for which history might have proceeded along an altogether different trajectory.

This essay explores the contribution of Augustine to the history of antisemitism, but it also asks what might have been, what might have happened had later Christian policy toward Jews reflected more so the thinking of Augustine's African predecessors, the Carthaginians Tertullian (c. 150–c. 220) and Cyprian (c. 200–258), or Augustine's mentor Ambrose (c. 340–397), the bishop of Milan, or perhaps even one of the Christian antagonists against whom these men inveighed, such as the Marcionites or Manichaeans.

TERTULLIAN, CYPRIAN, AND THE *ADVERSUS JUDAEOS* TRADITION

Augustine would ultimately achieve pride of place in Latin theology, but he was not its founder. Two centuries before Augustine flourished in Hippo Regius (modern-day Annaba, Algeria), the first Latin doctor of the church was busily articulating doctrines of Christianity, and defending it against adversaries, 300 kilometers to the east in the city Carthage (near modern-day Tunis). Septimius Tertullianus was not a priest. He was a convert to Christianity with a zealous devotion to his new faith. Tradition has it that he was a lawyer, though the veracity of that claim has been questioned. In either case, Tertullian wrote with the tenacity of a lawyer and the erudition of a man schooled in rhetoric and classical literature. His output was considerable, an array of important theological and apologetic works.

Perhaps most interesting about the course of Tertullian's Christian journey is the way it ended. He veered into an ascetic Christian renewal movement founded by the Phrygian prophet Montanus. The extent to which Tertullian's association with Montanism constituted a departure from the wider Christian community of Carthage remains a matter of debate; in the least, his legacy was not so tarnished that the leader of Carthaginian Christianity just two generations later avoided reading him. Jerome reports that Cyprian, the bishop of Carthage martyred in 258 during the persecutions under Valerian, read works of Tertullian daily and referred to him as "the master."[2]

Among the writings of Cyprian and Tertullian are two bearing similar titles: Cyprian's *To Quirinius: Testimonies against the Jews* and Tertullian's *Against the Jews*. As such, they were the principal Latin contributors to a body of early Christian literature called *Adversus Iudaeos*, "Against the Jews." This genre can be understood narrowly as referring to patristic works bearing that specific title, or more broadly to works that aim to demonstrate the inferiority of Judaism. Controversy with Judaism is not evident in the title of the *Epistle of Barnabas* (c. 130) or Melito's *On Easter* (c. 170) for example, but their subject matter is manifestly a polemic against Jews. Note the variety in form, too: *Barnabas* is a treatise posing as an epistle; *On Easter* is a homily. Other Christian writers took on Judaism using the form of a dialogue, most notably, Justin Martyr's *Dialogue with Trypho, the Jew* (c. 160). For their part, Tertullian's *Adversus Iudaeos* is an expository treatise, while Cyprian's is an anthology of scriptural citations, or "testimonies."

Despite this variety, Christian texts intended especially to disparage Jews and Judaism marshaled a standard assortment of arguments, among them the following: (1) Jews, from time immemorial, have been a nation of reprobates guilty of idolatry, depravity, murdering prophets, and, of course, rejecting God's messiah; (2) God, accordingly, rejected the Jewish people in favor of a new elect drawn from among the Gentiles, and allowed Jerusalem to be destroyed; (3) this replacement was foreseen in the Jews' own scripture, the Old Testament; (4) Jews are nonetheless blinded from a proper understanding of the Old Testament; and (5) Jews therefore fail to see that the Mosaic Law, as well as the Temple cult it prescribes, have been fulfilled spiritually in Christ, and therefore have been abrogated. These claims permeate the *Adversus Iudaeos* literature, even as each author forges his own unique case.

Significant scholarly debate has revolved around the root cause of *Adversus Iudaeos* literature. Some argue that it was largely a reaction to vigorous, at times violent, Christian competition with Jews over pagan souls. This view traces back to Marcel Simon, whose monumental *Verus Israel* (1964) bucked the trend of most prewar scholarship that saw Judaism after 70 CE as a lifeless fossil of a religion, unworthy of

---

[2] Jerome, *On Illustrious Men*, 53, trans. Thomas P. Halton, *The Fathers of the Church 100* (Washington, DC, 1999), 74.

attention from burgeoning Christianity.[3] Simon claimed in contrast that Judaism proved a formidable competitor to Christianity in the 2nd and 3rd centuries, and this struggle precipitated Christian invective against Jews. Simon and his successors have drawn a good deal of their evidence from Tertullian in particular. It was Tertullian who famously described synagogues as "fountains of persecution,"[4] and elsewhere told of a Jew who ambled through the streets of Rome heckling Christians by carrying a caricature of them as an ass dressed in a toga.[5] Simon conceded that such hostile descriptions need to be taken with a grain of salt, and that other evidence from Tertullian indicates that Jews at times offered Christians asylum from imperial persecution in their synagogues. Nonetheless, he concluded, the principal cause of Christian vilification of Jews was the animus stirred up by bitter competition against a robust foe. After all, Simon memorably asked with regard to the vitriol in *Adversus Iudaeos* literature, "do men rage so persistently against a corpse?"[6]

Critics of Simon's approach have said yes, indeed, they do. Not against a corpse per se, but people will rage against an idea they perceive as dead, especially if that idea threatens the theological integrity of their religion. More recent scholars have underscored the limited historical evidence for Jewish proselytism or persecution of Christians in the 2nd and 3rd centuries, arguing instead that *Adversus Iudaeos* rhetoric emerged from the theological threat posed by Judaism, a threat amplified by competing schools of thought within Christianity.

Here, again, Tertullian often plays an important role in the argument.[7] These historians note that Tertullian's most thoroughgoing condemnation of Judaism comes not in his *Adversus Iudaeos*, but in his *Adversus Marcionem*, "Against Marcion," a lengthy treatise intended to eviscerate the theological claims of the purported Christian heretic Marcion of Sinope. Marcion, who had flourished half a century earlier, promoted a version of Christianity that discarded the God and the scriptures of the Jews. Jesus, he argued, had been sent by a god superior to the vengeful God of the Hebrew Bible, which is why his

---

[3] Marcel Simon, *Verus Israel: A Study of the Relations between Christians and Jews in the Roman Empire, AD135–425*, trans. H. McKeating (Portland, OR, 1996).

[4] Tertullian, *Scorpiace* 10, trans. S. Thelwall, *Ante-Nicene Fathers* 3 (Peabody, MA, 1994), 643.

[5] Tertullian, *Ad Nationes* 1:14, trans. P. Holmes, *Ante-Nicene Fathers* 3, 123.

[6] Simon, *Verus Israel*, 140.

[7] David P. Efroymson, "The Patristic Connection," in *Antisemitism and the Foundations of Christianity*, ed. Alan Davies (New York, 1979), 98–117.

gospel message stood in such stark contrast to the Mosaic law. Marcion therefore assembled the earliest known Christian canon, a collection of Pauline epistles and a version of the Gospel of Luke purged of references to the Hebrew Bible. Put simply, Marcion and his followers aspired to a Christianity utterly denuded of Judaism.

Why, then, does anti-Judaism feature so prominently in Tertullian's five-volume repudiation of Marcionism? It was the inevitable consequence of his bid to preserve the God and the scriptures of the Jews as properly Christian. To thwart Marcion, Tertullian insisted that the God of the Jews was indeed the one, true, and fair God, and that the Jewish scriptures were necessary for a complete understanding of what God accomplished through Christ. All one needed, of course, was a correct Christian approach to the Old Testament that read it spiritually, allegorically, or typologically rather than literally. Whereas the Marcionite dualists – so-called because they posited a second god – accused Tertullian and his ilk of being "too Jewish" because they revered the God and the scriptures of Israel, Tertullian fired back the same charge: Marcionites are "too Jewish" because they read the scriptures literally, like Jews, and therefore fail, like Jews, to appreciate the unity of the old and the new. Jews and Marcionites share the same "poison," says Tertullian.[8] Jews and Judaism thus emerged as a theological category negotiated by polemicists when laying out the contours of one sort of Christianity over and against another. "Jewish" became the mud slung back and forth. Accordingly, some historians contend, the *Adversus Iudaeos* arguments about stubborn Jews, outmoded Judaism, and the like resulted not from historical encounters with actual Jews but from internal debates over Christian self-definition. As one notable historian has put it: "The image of Jews used in [Christian] polemics did not derive from these authors' observing and then describing their Jewish contemporaries, but from their deploying literary-rhetorical techniques in disputes over sacred texts."[9]

It is important to note that the debate over the origins of *Adversus Iudaeos* literature is not merely a historical one.[10] There are also ethical and theological implications that might affect the way one understands Christianity's relationship with Judaism beyond the confines of the

---

[8] Tertullian, *Adversus Marcionem* 3:8, trans. P. Holmes, *Ante-Nicene Fathers* 3, 327.

[9] Paula Fredriksen, *Augustine and the Jews: A Christian Defense of Jews and Judaism* (New Haven, CT, 2008), 226–27.

[10] Andrew S. Jacobs, "Jews and Christians," in *The Oxford Handbook of Early Christian Studies*, ed. Susan A. Harvey and David G. Hunter (Oxford, 2008), 169–72.

ancient world. The "conflict" theory of Simon and his successors revivi-
fied post-70 Judaism in Christian scholarship by depicting it as a robust
religious rival to Christianity, but this approach might also be viewed as
a rationalization, a pardon of sorts, for the viciousness that appears in
Adversus Iudaeos texts.[11] The alternative approach pins responsibility
for the malicious anti-Judaism squarely on the writers and communities
that produced it, but at the risk of re-concealing the real-life Jews who
may in fact be in its background to one degree or another. Moreover,
locating the origins of anti-Judaism within Christian discourse can lead
to the conclusion that anti-Judaism was, as a chief proponent of this
view has put it, "an intrinsic need of Christian self-affirmation."[12] The
extent to which Christianity was, and may still be, inescapably anti-
Jewish raises difficult questions for modern Christian theologians, as
well as Jews and Christians engaged in interreligious dialogue.

This ongoing challenge in Christian theology is part and parcel of
the triumph of Tertullian, Cyprian, and like-minded proto-Orthodox
thinkers in their contest with Marcion and the other dualist expressions
of Christianity. Identifying the God who sent Christ as the God of Israel
led naturally to the assumption that God had rejected the Jewish people,
especially in view of the fact that most Jews refused to accept the
Christian proclamation of Jesus as the messiah. By the same token,
declaring the Jewish scriptures to be properly Christian meant that
Jews must be misreading them. That the Christian truth in them was
so apparent could only mean that Jews had become blinded or obstinate
if they had not always been so. One can only wonder what Christianity
might have come to look like if history had gone the other way, if the
Christianity that ultimately gained preeminence was one that favored
severing the gospel from Jewish roots. With no common God or scriptures, might Christianity have ignored Judaism as something utterly
alien? Or might the lack of any theological kinship have led to an even
more hostile relationship? Again, there is no way to know. But imagining a Christianity without the God of Israel or the Old Testament brings
into bolder relief the ramifications of their preservation.

The Christianity that would come to predominate in the 4th and
5th centuries was bound to see Judaism as a perpetual competitor, if no
longer (or ever) as a real-life rival for souls or power, then as a theological

---

[11] See, e.g., Miriam Taylor, *Anti-Judaism and Early Christian Identity: A Critique of
the Scholarly Consensus* (Leiden, 1995).
[12] Rosemary R. Ruether, *Faith and Fratricide: The Theological Roots of Anti-Semitism*
(New York, 1974), 181.

rival over the meaning of shared scripture and the favor of a shared God. What changed in the 4th and 5th centuries was not only the triumph of orthodoxy, however. Indeed, that very triumph was partly the result of orthodoxy's endorsement by the imperial regime beginning with Constantine (306–37), and in the following centuries Christian deliberation over Jews and Judaism would become more than an exercise in theology, apologetics, or heresiology; it would shape the policies and practice of Christian political rulers in Europe until modernity. Given the tenor of the *Adversus Iudaeos* literature that had already emerged by the 4th century, it was unlikely that Christian thinkers would propose a magnanimous approach for dealing with so detested a religious minority. As we will see yet again, though, the direction in which the now politicized Christian anti-Judaism would proceed was no forgone conclusion. The two greatest western theologians after Tertullian, namely, Ambrose and Augustine, proposed very different approaches for dealing with Jews and Judaism.

AMBROSE

It is not as though Christian writers in the West ignored Judaism in the two centuries separating Tertullian from Ambrose. The 3rd-century Cyprian, as noted above, compiled scriptural testimonies to help Christians rebut Jewish claims, while his African contemporary, Novatian (d. 258), composed a treatise on Christian freedom from the Torah's food laws. Other Latin authors made disparaging observations about Judaism in passing or in works devoted principally to other topics – for example, the biblical commentaries of Hilary of Poitiers (d. 367), the pagan-Christian dialogue *Octavius* by Minucius Felix (d. c. 250), and the apologetic works, *Apotheosis* by the Roman poet Prudentius (d. c. 400) and *Divine Institutes* by the African Lactantius (d. c. 325).[13] The comments in these works by and large rehearse the general themes of the *Adversus Iudaeos* genre. With Ambrose, however, Christian anti-Judaism moved in a new direction.

Ambrose was born in Augusta Treverorum (modern-day Trier, Germany) around 340 into a well-connected family. By 370, he was

---

[13] See, e.g., Hilary of Poitiers, *Commentary on Matthew*, 13:12, trans. D. H. Williams, *The Fathers of the Church 125* (Washington, DC, 2012), 153–54; Minucius Felix, *Octavius* 10, ed. and trans. Gerald H. Rendall, LCL 250 (Cambridge, MA, 1984), 338–41; Prudentius, *Apotheosis* 321–25, trans. H. J. Thomson, LCL 387 (Cambridge, MA, 1949), 144–45; Lactantius, *The Divine Institutes*, 4:11, trans. William Fletcher, *Ante-Nicene Fathers* 7 (Grand Rapids, MI, 1985), 109–10.

residing in Milan as governor of Emilia and Liguria. When the bishop of Milan died in 374, Ambrose was elected to that office probably as a compromise candidate agreed to by competing Nicean and anti-Nicean factions. He would serve for twenty-five years.

Ambrose is widely recognized as a transitional figure in Christian thinking about violence and political power, which should come as no surprise given his time and place. Writing in the capital of the Western Empire two to three generations after Constantine when Nicene orthodoxy was consolidating its position as both the dominant Christianity and an imperial power, Ambrose thought extensively about Christianity as a state religion. Whereas earlier Christian writers had exhibited a pacifist orientation – stretching back to the instruction to "turn the other cheek" in the Gospel of Matthew – Ambrose initiated a transition toward the endorsement of just violence. He continued the praise of pacificism in the private life of Christians, urging them to refrain from returning blows in a struggle so as not to injure another, and he likewise expected men of the Christian cloth to avoid violence altogether. But matters of state were different. The 4th-century coalescence of church and state meant that for Ambrose "the defense of the empire coincided with the defense of the faith," as one historian puts it.[14] The struggle against Arian barbarians was a threat to Nicene orthodoxy no less than to the empire, and Ambrose saw the emperor's sword as the divine instrument for preserving both. Violence perpetrated by the state and/or the church against heretics should therefore be tolerated, even encouraged.

As for heretics, so for Jews, and this reality became apparent for Ambrose in a famous contretemps with emperor Theodosius in 388. A Christian mob in Callinicum, a city on the Euphrates in modern-day Syria, burned down a synagogue at the behest of the local bishop. The Roman administrator in Antioch was instructed by Theodosius to order the synagogue rebuilt at the expense of the bishop responsible for the malfeasance. To Theodosius, the emperor perhaps best remembered for making Christianity the official state religion, Christians were nonetheless bound by the law.

To Ambrose, however, the ruling was scandalous, and he communicated his disapproval in a letter to the emperor.[15] Some of the

---

[14] Roland H. Bainton, *Christian Attitudes toward War and Peace: A Survey and Critical Re-Evaluation* (New York, 1960), 90. See also Louis J. Swift, "St. Ambrose on Violence and War," *Transactions and Proceedings of the American Philological Association* 101 (1971): 533–43.

[15] Ambrose, *Epistula* 40, trans. Mary Melchior Beyenka, *The Fathers of the Church* 26, 6–19.

arguments Ambrose makes seem to acknowledge tacitly that the destruction of Jewish property was indeed an injustice, even if recompense was not in order. He notes, for example, that Jews were not ordered to rebuild Christian churches in Damascus that they helped to destroy during the reign of emperor Julian (361–363), and that Theodosius himself had forgone punishment when the episcopal residence in Constantinople was burned down during a riot. Elsewhere he plays up the potentially damaging political ramifications of making the local bishop a martyr should he refuse to pay up. More insidious are Ambrose's arguments to the effect that the destruction of the synagogue was no crime at all. On the contrary, it was the honorable Christian thing to do, so much so that Ambrose willingly takes credit for himself:

> I declare that I set fire to the synagogue, at least that I gave the orders, so that there would be no building in which Christ is denied. If the objection is raised that I did not burn the synagogue here, I answer that its burning was begun by God's judgment, and my work was at an end. If you want the truth, I was really remiss, for I did not think such a deed was to be punished.[16]

Ambrose suggests that he and other Christians are compelled to destroy edifices in which Christ is denied. A synagogue is, as he says later in the epistle, "an abode of unbelief, a house of impiety, a shelter of madness under the damnation of God Himself."[17] The only thing stopping him from destroying the synagogue in his own Milan is that it already had been ruined by a natural disaster, which he interprets literally as an act of God. While God's justice will destroy some synagogues, Ambrose intimates, Christians are deputized to carry out the deed when an earthquake, flood, or lightning strike does not manifest.[18]

In response to the potential objection that failing to discipline such hostility might compromise public order, Ambrose makes a remarkable claim: "Which is of more importance: a demonstration of discipline or the cause of religion? The maintenance of civil law should be secondary to religion."[19] The Christian commission to extirpate places in which (orthodox) Christianity is not espoused eclipses any legal protections that Jews might expect from the state. He makes the case even stronger

---

[16] Ibid., 10.
[17] Ibid., 12.
[18] Some historians wonder whether Ambrose really means to say that the synagogue in Milan was destroyed by a natural disaster. See, e.g., Neil B. McLynn, *Ambrose of Milan: Church and Court in a Christian Capital* (Berkeley, CA, 1994), 299.
[19] Ambrose, *Epistula 40*, trans. Beyenka, 11.

further on, arguing that Jews have no right whatsoever to expect justice from Roman laws because they – allegedly – do not consider themselves bound by such laws. Jews are the enemy of both Christianity and Rome, Ambrose insists, and as such they can expect no civil protection from the Christian empire.

As it turns out, Ambrose's letter was only partly effective. Although he agreed to finance the rebuilding of the synagogue himself, Theodosius still ordered the Christians in Callinicum to restore the property they had looted. That penalty, too, was canceled sometime later when Ambrose, bent on denying the Jews any restitution at all, confronted Theodosius at the cathedral of Milan. Following a sermon reprising many of the themes in the letter, Ambrose refused to continue the service until Theodosius relented. He did.[20]

It was not the last time Ambrose would speak to the subject of Jewish perfidy in the presence of Theodosius, however. Some six years later, in February of 395, Ambrose delivered the eulogy at a memorial service for Theodosius in Milan before the departure of the late emperor's remains for Constantinople. Toward the end of the oration, a mention of the family members and imperial predecessors awaiting Theodosius in heaven leads Ambrose on a digression about Helena, the mother of Constantine, and her alleged discovery of the true cross in Jerusalem. The unearthing of the cross, Ambrose concludes, marked the definitive triumph of Christianity over the Jews. A nail from the very cross of Christ now rested in the diadem upon the heads of emperors, Ambrose proclaimed, and thus Jews lament: "We thought we had conquered, but we confess that we ourselves are conquered! Christ has risen again, and princes acknowledge that He has risen. He who is not seen lives again."[21] As he does in his letter to Theodosius about the Callinicum affair, Ambrose sees Christianity locked in what one historian has called a "mortal struggle with its eternal enemy the Jew."[22] With the power of the state now at its disposal, Christianity could do more than just vanquish the arguments of the Jews; it could destroy their institutions.

It is important to note that Ambrose never explicitly ordered Christians to sack a synagogue, nor did he ever call for the expulsion

---

[20] The confrontation in Milan is reported in *Epistula* 41 (Beyenka, 385–98), a letter from Ambrose to his sister, Marcellina.

[21] Ambrose, *De Obitu Theodosii* 49, trans. Roy J. Deferrari, *The Fathers of the Church* 22, 329.

[22] David Nirenberg, *Anti-Judaism: The Western Tradition* (New York, 2013), 118–19.

of Jews from the empire or for harm to be inflicted on their persons. Even if it was only after the fact, his demand for the complete acquittal of the Christian perpetrators in Callinicum might nonetheless be understood as an endorsement of Christian violence against Jews, at least against the buildings in which Judaism was practiced. If a bishop would go so far as to defy an emperor in defense of unwarranted Christian violence, what was to stop Christians from destroying synagogues over and again? If the same bishop could assert that the cause of Christianity transcends civil law, and that Jews are Christianity's eternal enemy, what was to stop violence against the institutions of Judaism from becoming violence against Jews themselves?

Again, one can only wonder what might have happened had Ambrose become the benchmark on which later Christian rulers based their policy toward Jews. Jewish life in Christendom from the 5th century onward was no picnic, to be sure, but one can imagine Jews faring even worse if Christian mobs could routinely wreak violence on Jews with impunity. It would not take long for a different view to emerge, however; indeed, Ambrose himself would baptize the man from whose pen came the doctrine of Jewish preservation.

AUGUSTINE

When Ambrose baptized him in Milan during Easter Vigil in 387, the thirty-two-year-old Augustine was hardly a stranger to Christianity. He had been raised in Thagaste (modern-day Souk Ahras, Algeria) by a devoutly Catholic mother, Monica, and spent his twenties dabbling in Manichaeism, a beleaguered variety of Christianity founded a century earlier by the Persian prophet Mani. Of all the details in Augustine's well-documented life, this youthful dalliance might be the most important for understanding the theology of Judaism he ultimately fashioned. For it is in his lengthy refutation of Manichaeism that his unique contribution to the history of Christian anti-Judaism first emerges.

Manichaeism was a Christianity steeped in gnostic and dualistic ideas, what two leading scholars have called "a late avatar of the sorts of Christianities established by Marcion and [the gnostic] Valentinus."[23] Manichaeism postulated two gods and, like Marcionism, rejected the God, the people, and the scriptures of Israel. The Manichaean criticism

---

[23] Paula Fredriksen and Oded Irshai, "Christian Anti-Judaism: Polemics and Policies," in The Cambridge History of Judaism, vol. 4, ed. Steven T. Katz (Cambridge, 2006), 977–1034 (1013–14).

of the Old Testament evidently appealed to the young Augustine's own unease over its apparent absurdities and offensive descriptions. By the late 4th century, orthodox Christianity had at its disposal a tried-and-true method for dealing with difficulties in the Jewish scriptures. Tertullian and others, recall, salvaged the Old Testament by resort to spiritualized approaches that emphasized the distinction between letter and spirit. The Old Testament is only objectionable, they argued, when read literally and superficially, as it is by Jews and dualists. Proper Christians, by contrast, read spiritually. Over the course of the 3rd and 4th centuries, especially through the works of Origen of Alexandria (ca. 185–254) and his successors, Christianity carved out strategies for reading the Old Testament that eschewed the literal, "fleshly," "Jewish" approach. Allegory in particular proved effective. Indeed, it was the allegories he heard in the sermons of Ambrose in Milan that persuaded Augustine to accept the legitimacy of the Old Testament in Christianity. By Augustine's time, however, the increased abandonment of the literal level of meaning had begun to raise anxiety among the orthodox over the extent to which their own twofold approach to scripture was itself reflective of the dualism they opposed. Augustine, the Manichee turned Catholic, therefore found himself stuck between a rock and a hard place in negotiating the role of the Old Testament in his newfound Orthodoxy: he had to champion an approach that was sufficiently spiritual to distinguish Christianity from Judaism, but also literal enough to distinguish Orthodoxy from its dualistic counterparts. His solution to this conundrum would lead to a novel conceptualization of Jews and Judaism.

Augustine described this novel view for the first time around the year 400 in the *Contra Faustum*, a rebuttal of Manichaeism framed as a dialogue between himself and the illustrious Manichaean teacher Faustus of Mileum. Augustine's Faustus offers the standard array of dualist arguments against the Old Testament Law – for example, that circumcision and sacrifice are objectionable, the festivals are pointless, and the laws of the priesthood are bizarre; that Christ came to destroy the Law; and most importantly, that orthodox Christians are disingenuous when they praise the Old Testament while disregarding its statutes. In response, Augustine goes far beyond the usual rejoinder about reading spiritually and typologically. Even as the Old Testament is everywhere a prefiguration of Christ, he argues, it is also true on the literal level at which Jews read it; and moreover, God had intended from the beginning that the Law of the Old Testament should be observed in the carnal fashion. The Jews had been right to do so. Even circumcision in the flesh, the peculiar rite that so distinguished Jews from Christians and was so obviously a prefiguration of Christ, was meant originally to be observed literally. God intended for all the statutes of the Old Testament to be observed literally, so much so that Jesus himself observed the commandments meticulously and criticized others for not doing likewise.

With Jesus, however, everything changed. Once the event prefigured by the Old Testament had occurred, Augustine argues, observance of the commandments was no longer appropriate. The Law remains good, sacred, and praiseworthy, to be sure, but literal observance of it is no longer appropriate. The problem with Jews and Judaism, in other words, is not that they *were* wrong, but that they have become wrong by failing to appreciate the full impact of Christ on the Law. In Christ, fleshly observance of the Law has become obsolete.

Their outmoded observance of commandments hardly means that Jews are expendable, however, and it is here that Augustine truly innovated. Unlike Ambrose, who endorsed the destruction of a synagogue on the grounds "that there would be no building in which Christ is denied," Augustine insisted that Jewish communities were beneficial to Christianity. By clinging to their carnal observance of the Old Testament, especially in the face of Christianity's historical triumph, Jews had become *testes iniquitatis suae et veritatis nostrae*, "witnesses to their own iniquity and our truth," as Augustine would put it in a later work.[24] Living in humbled conditions, dispersed from their homeland, obliviously toiling away at the Law, Jews demonstrate to the world their error in rejecting Christ, while at the same time bearing testimony to the truth of Christianity by devoutly preserving the Old Testament:

> It is a great confirmation of our faith that such important testimony is borne by enemies. The believing Gentiles cannot suppose these testimonies to Christ to be recent forgeries; for they find them in books held sacred for so many ages by those who crucified Christ.... [The Jews] testify to the truth by their not understanding it. By not understanding the books which predict that they would not understand, they prove these books to be true.[25]

---

[24] Augustine, *Enarrationes in Psalmos* 58:22, trans. Maria Boulding, *Expositions of the Psalms 51–72. The Works of Saint Augustine* III/17 (Hyde Park, NY, 2000), 166.

[25] Augustine, *Contra Faustum* 16:21, trans. R. Stothert, *Reply to Faustus the Manichaean. Nicene and Post-Nicene Fathers* I/4 (Grand Rapids, MI, 1974), 227.

By continuing to practice the old rites of Judaism without appreciating the Christian direction in which they point, Jews serve as living proof of Christian claims. Jews are therefore like *scriniaria*, Augustine tells Faustus, guardians of a chest holding the books that display the evidence of Christianity. Elsewhere he uses similarly servile metaphors to depict Jews; they are book custodians, librarians.

In the Old Testament itself Augustine found an even more potent image to describe the present condition of Jews. They are like Cain, who offered worship unacceptable to God, murdered his younger sibling, and as a result was condemned to till the ground fruitlessly and wander for the remainder of his days. So, too, the Jews had failed to see that their obedience to the commandments, though commendable in its day, had become loathsome to God. They murdered their younger sibling, Christ, and as a result they wander the earth bemoaning the loss of their erstwhile kingdom while fruitlessly observing the Old Testament in a carnal manner. And just as Cain was given a mark of protection, so were the Jews:

> It is a most notable fact, that all the nations subjugated by Rome adopted the heathenish ceremonies of the Roman worship; while the Jewish nation, whether under Pagan or Christian monarchs, has never lost the sign of their law, by which they are distinguished from all other nations and peoples. No emperor or monarch who finds under his government the people with this mark kills them, that is, makes them cease to be Jews, and as Jews to be separate in their observances, and unlike the rest of the world.[26]

The Law, and their carnal observance of it, is the Jews' eternal mark of protection. So long as they toil away at the commandments in ignorance, thereby testifying to the truth of Christianity, they remain unmolested wherever they stray.

In time Augustine began referring to the biblical verse that would become so closely associated with his groundbreaking new conception of Judaism. Referring to Jews in *The City of God*, composed in the years following the sack of Rome in 410, Augustine draws upon Psalm 59:12, which in his Latin rendering says, "Slay them not, lest at any time they forget your law; scatter them in your might." Applying this verse to Jews was nothing new; already Tertullian had used the latter half to

---

[26] Augustine, *Contra Faustum* 12:13, 188.

account for the existence of the Jewish diaspora. For Augustine, however, both parts of the verse were crucial:

> It was not enough for the psalmist to say, "Do not slay them, lest at some time they forget your Law," without adding, "Scatter them." For if they lived with that testimony of the Scriptures only in their own land, and not everywhere, the obvious result would be that the Church, which is everywhere, would not have them available among all nations as witnesses to the prophecies which were given beforehand concerning Christ.[27]

Jews must be preserved, Augustine insists, and encouraged to observe the Law carnally as a testimony to Christian truth; no less importantly, he adds, they must accompany Christianity as it expands into new realms lest the purpose of Jewish preservation not be fulfilled.

Contemporary historians often emphasize that Augustine did not formulate his doctrine of Jewish witness as some sort of public policy proposal.[28] He was not advising future kings. Nor did he call for the protection of the Jewish way of life out of affection for Jews with whom he interacted in real life. The Jews in his writing are "rhetorical" or "hermeneutic," as leading scholars have described them.[29] Their value as witnesses emerges theoretically from Augustine's theological struggle to define orthodoxy within the Christian discourse prevailing at the turn of the 5th century. Whatever positive impact the doctrine of Jewish witness afforded in subsequent centuries was incidental. That said, the passage that closes Augustine's own treatise *Adversus Iudaeos*, composed near the end of his life, indicates that Augustine might have disapproved of the unduly harsh treatment Jews often experienced in medieval Europe. Following nine chapters in which he rehearses typical patristic arguments about the inferiority of Judaism, Augustine concludes the volume with a call for Christian humility. Referring to Paul's olive tree metaphor in Romans 11:17–24, he writes:

> Whether the Jews receive these divine testimonies with joy or with indignation, nevertheless, when we can, let us proclaim them with great love for the Jews. Let us not proudly glory against the broken branches; let us rather reflect by whose grace it is, and by much

---

[27] Augustine, *De civitate dei* 18:46, trans. H. Bettenson, *Concerning the City of God against the Pagans* (London, 1972), 828.

[28] Nirenberg, *Anti-Judaism*, 132.

[29] Fredriksen, *Augustine and the Jews*, 306; Jeremy Cohen, *Living Letters of the Law: Ideas of the Jew in Medieval Christianity* (Berkeley, CA, 1999), 2–3.

mercy, and on what root, we have been ingrafted. Then, not savoring of pride, but with a deep sense of humility, not insulting with presumption, but rejoicing with trembling, let us say: "Come ye and let us walk in the light of the Lord." (Isa. 2:5)[30]

Although he goes on to lament the ignorance of those Jews who will spurn this Christian invitation, Augustine does not withdraw his appeal to Christians to approach Jews "with a deep sense of humility, not insulting with presumption," ever aware of the Jewish root onto which Christians have been ingrafted.

CONCLUSION

Historians of medieval Europe can debate the extent to which Augustine's witness doctrine shaped Christian policy and affected Jewish endurance in subsequent centuries. This essay has endeavored to show that Augustine's ascription of Christian value to a Jewish diaspora, whatever its impact, was indeed a novel brainwave, as Mendelssohn remarked, and not the consummation of a trend in early Christian thought. Among Christian thinkers, in both the West and the East, the only such trend was the *Adversus Iudaeos* genre and its oft-repeated propositions, namely, that Jews are a rejected people who fail to read their own scriptures correctly. The likes of Marcion and Mani nonetheless disagreed, insisting that there is no appropriate Christian way to read the Old Testament, and even among the Orthodox the proper place of rejected Jews in a Christian realm could be understood in remarkably different ways. Ambrose deemed it a dereliction of Christian duty to tolerate the very existence of a synagogue, whereas Augustine saw the activity of the synagogue as a key ingredient in Christian expansion.

Further Reading

Barnes, T. D., *Tertullian: A Historical and Literary Study*, rev. ed. (New York, 1985). The place to begin serious study of Tertullian.
Cohen, J., *Living Letters of the Law: Ideas of the Jew in Medieval Christianity* (Berkeley, CA, 1999). An appraisal of Augustine's theology of Judaism and its influence on medieval Christianity, arguing that the witness doctrine reached maturity only late in Augustine's career.

---

[30] Augustine, *Adversus Iudaeos* 10, trans. Marie Liguori, The Fathers of the Church 27, 414.

Efroymson, D. P., "The Patristic Connection," in *Antisemitism and the Foundations of Christianity*, ed. A. Davies (New York, 1979). An early attempt to situate patristic anti-Judaism within debates over heresy, concentrating on Tertullian's response to Marcion.

Fredriksen, P., *Augustine and the Jews: A Christian Defense of Jews and Judaism* (New Haven, CT, 2010). The benchmark in recent appraisals of Augustine's positive estimation of Jews and Judaism shifted the focus of the field from Augustine's *Adversus Iudaeos* to his *Against Faustus*. A symposium dedicated to this book appears in *Augustinian Studies* 40, no. 2 (2009), 279–99.

Lee, G. W., "Israel between the Two Cities: Augustine's Theology of the Jews and Judaism." *Journal of Early Christian Studies* 24.4 (2016), 523–51. A recent treatment focusing on *The City of God* and arguing that Augustine's estimation of Jews and Judaism was not quite as positive as others have supposed.

Ruether, R. R., *Faith and Fratricide: The Theological Roots of Anti-Semitism* (New York, 1974). The influential study contending that anti-Judaism was an integral component in early Christian theology.

Simon, M., *Verus Israel: A Study of the Relations between Christians and Jews in the Roman Empire, AD 135–425*, trans. H. McKeating (Portland, OR, 1986). The *locus classicus* for the "conflict theory." Published in the wake of the Holocaust, Simon seeks to defang the *Adversus Iudaeos* tradition by locating its origin in Christian competition with a vibrant Judaism.

Stroumsa, G. G., "From Anti-Judaism to Antisemitism in Early Christianity?," in *Contra Judaeos: Ancient and Medieval Polemics between Christians and Jews*, ed. O. Limor and G. G. Stroumsa (Tübingen, 1996). An attempt to situate *Adversus Iudaeos* literature not in conflict or Christian discourse, but in the demise of paganism in the fourth century.

Swift, L. J., "St. Ambrose on Violence and War," *Transactions and Proceedings of the American Philological Association* 101 (1970), 533–43. A classic study that examines Ambrose's complicated view of violence, including analysis of the Callinicum affair.

Taylor, M., *Anti-Judaism and Early Christian Identity: A Critique of the Scholarly Consensus* (Leiden, 1995). A refutation of the "conflict theory" on both historical and ethical grounds.

Unterseher, L. A., *The Mark of Cain and the Jews: Augustine's Theology of Jews and Judaism* (Piscataway, NJ, 2009). An analysis of Augustine's witness doctrine with specific emphasis on the interpretation of Cain.

5 Christians, Jews, and Judaism in the Eastern Mediterranean and Near East, c. 150–400 CE

ANDREW S. JACOBS

INTRODUCTION: A SYNAGOGUE BURNS

In the year 388 CE, a gang of Christian monks went on a rampage in the Roman garrison town of Callinicum on the eastern fringes of the empire. They burned down a synagogue and destroyed a shrine supposedly belonging to a rival Christian group (Valentinians). The local magistrate ordered the Christian bishop to pay restitution to the Jewish community to rebuild their synagogue. At first the emperor Theodosius supported this measure, which conformed to laws against destruction of property. Under public pressure from Bishop Ambrose of Milan, however, Theodosius reversed course: first he exempted the bishop of Callinicum from any personal financial liability; ultimately, he rescinded any requirement for restitution.

Were the events surrounding this Christian destruction of a synagogue the result of an inexorable development of Christian anti-Judaism in the first centuries of the religion? What structures had to be in place for this violent act to transpire as it did, both the burning itself and the imperial approbation afterward? Do these forces, as they came together by the late 4th century, lay the seedbeds for what we in modernity might call "antisemitism"?

A quick survey of our evidence from these first four centuries might suggest that Christianity was, almost from the beginning, opposed to Jews and Judaism. It's difficult to find *any* extant Christian text from the eastern Mediterranean, from Egypt to Syria to Asia Minor, that does not speak about Jews and Judaism with some antipathy. Critiques of Jews and Judaism crystallized into a series of repetitive tropes, a remix of pre-Christian Greco-Roman prejudices and biblical motifs: Jews were superstitious, hard-hearted, and xenophobic; Judaism was Law-bound and punctilious; Jews as a people and Judaism as a religion were too "fleshly" (indicating both a lack of spirituality and a love of "this world"). The late 2nd-century Easter homily of Melito of Sardis (c. 175) portrayed Jews as deicides, eternally guilty for Christ's murder, a slur destined for a long and painful history. Scholars even speak of a genre of texts, *adversus Judaeos* ("against the Jews"), to capture this ubiquitous anti-Judaism. In many of these texts, Christians drew language from their sacred Scriptures. From their Old Testament (the Jews' own Bible) they could pluck passages from the prophets on the uselessness of sacrifice and the stiff-necked disobedience of Israel. In later centuries, when the texts originally generated in the Jewish matrix of the Jesus movement came to be understood as the "New Testament," Christians could reread lines of internal polemic as wholesale divine condemnation of Jews and Judaism: Paul's rejection of "the Law" in Galatians, Jesus' rejection of the Jews as children of "the Devil" in the Gospel of John, and the Jews' own seeming confession of deicide in the haunting words of Matthew 27:25: "His blood be on us and our children."

In considering the seeming ubiquity of these critiques, we should, however, keep two points in mind. First: almost all of our sources for this period are literary texts, meaning our historical window is very narrow; it's difficult to know with any certainty what the "Christian on the street" might have thought about Jews and Judaism. Second: the texts that do survive were kept and recopied by later Christians for whom Christianity was self-evidently opposed to Judaism. Our Christian evidence from the 2nd and 3rd centuries is a product of 4th- and 5th-century processes of selection and preservation.

We must attempt to resituate our surviving evidence in its original contexts before asking how it was later used to produce the anti-Jewish Christian culture that resulted in the legally sanctioned destruction of the synagogue of Callinicum. In order to peel back these historical layers, I lay out three crucial contexts for Jews and Christians in the East: the institutional, the social, and the theological. I begin by looking at major institutional developments in this period resulting in the imposition of an imperial, episcopal orthodox framework for Christianity. I then turn to three social contexts in which Jewish–Christian interaction – whether actual or imagined – created space for Christians to naturalize Jewish–Christian difference: in theological dialogue, in scriptural interpretation, and in ritual and festival celebration. Having laid out how Jewish–Christian social interactions became an area of concern within particular segments of orthodox Christianity, I explore the key role that Jewish affiliations and temptations played in the imaginative division of Christianity into "orthodox" (correct) and "heretical" (deviant) forms. I conclude by zeroing in on the rich borderlands of Syria to think through the consequences of Jews becoming the quintessential "other" of imperial orthodox Christianity.

INSTITUTIONS: BISHOPS, EMPERORS, AND ORTHODOXY

Much of what we know about the first three centuries of Christianity is distorted by the determined efforts of Christian writers of the 4th and 5th centuries to tell a specific story about the triumphant rise of a holy, unified, apostolic Church. According to that later story the Church resisted persecution, first from Jews, then from pagan emperors. It built up organized churches and beat back the deviance of heretics. It converted the emperor Constantine, the first of a series of imperial patrons. This narrative, refined by Eusebius of Caesarea (d. 339 CE), obscures Christian diversity behind a screen of teleological unity.

Writers such as Eusebius projected backward a uniformity which, even in Eusebius's own day, was far from universal. The ecclesiastical mascot of this aspirational uniformity was the urban bishop, the singular spiritual leader of each city's Christian community (the so-called monepiscopacy: one bishop per city). The title "bishop" (episkopos) appeared already in letters written by and ascribed to the apostle Paul (d. c. 60 CE), where it signaled some nebulous leadership position (literally, "supervisor"). The 2nd century brought concerted efforts to assert the supremacy of single bishops over discrete urban communities. The letters of Ignatius of Antioch (d. c. 112) insisted on the absolute authority of the bishop; the pseudepigraphic letter *1 Clement* linked this episcopal authority to the chain of apostolic succession, a point repeated in the 3rd century and enshrined by Eusebius's inclusion in his *Church History* of episcopal succession lists reaching back to the apostles.

This insistence on the universal authority of bishops smacks of apologetic: writers from Ignatius to Eusebius would not have to insist on the unique authority of bishops if all Christians, in all times and places, acknowledged the monepiscopacy. (Imagine if major US newspapers kept publishing op-eds defending the office of *governor* or *mayor*.) Diverse Christian organizational structures existed in these centuries, from disciples of charismatic figures to students in philosophical circles. The monepiscopacy became the normative form of Christian authority by the 4th century (bolstered by its earlier boosters) because it allowed for a centralized, uniform model of communal identity. The authority of a bishop also channeled the violence prevalent in urban centers in the service of this Christian uniformity and normativity. Those cities with strong episcopal traditions by the 4th century – such as Rome, Alexandria, and Antioch – were also the sites of violent struggle between Christians and non-Christians as well as among competing Christian groups.

The bishop became the internal symbol of Christian institutional uniformity; after Constantine (d. 337) the emperor became the external guarantor of that uniformity. The two worked in tandem. Christian sources from the 2nd and 3rd centuries portrayed non-Christian emperors as, at best, persuadable allies and, at worst, bloodthirsty persecutors. Apologetic 2nd-century authors, such as Justin Martyr or Athenagoras, appealed to the reasonableness of emperors to extend clemency to beleaguered Christians, who were suffering unofficial and at times official sanction for their unusual religious beliefs and actions. Martyr texts viewed the Roman state as antithetical to Christianity, driven by demonic forces to torture and kill brave Christian martyrs.

Eusebius, both in his *Church History* and in his *Life of Constantine*, sanitized the image of the emperor as the benevolent patron of Christianity. How and why Constantine became a patron of Christians, after the official anti-Christian policies of his predecessors, remains one of history's great mysteries. Whether sincere or cynical, Constantine's patronage allowed some Christians (although not all) to accept that Roman emperors were, and should be, staunch defenders and promoters of Christianity. (The one exception, Constantine's great-nephew Julian, who renounced Christianity and reigned as the last pagan emperor in 361–363, became the exception that proved the rule.) This acceptance of Christian empire was not merely pragmatic but ideological, working in tandem with the promotion of the monepiscopacy: the tools of an absolutist form of Christian truth determined to enforce the boundaries between Christians and outside "others" – Jews and pagans – as well as between right-thinking Christians (orthodoxy) and deviants (heresy).

This totalizing Christianity developing into the 4th century was not eliminationist; that is, we do not see calls for the eradication of pagans, Jews, and heretics or even for their forced conversion. (This attitude would change in later centuries.) Instead, bishops and emperors used traditional, Roman tools of political and social management of "others": disabling laws, economic favoritism, the occasional use of violence as a disciplinary tool of terror. The imperial management of difference that had characterized Roman rule for centuries provided this episcopal-imperial orthodoxy with the tools to create the uniformity it imagined. Beginning with the Council of Nicaea (325 CE) the emperor convened "ecumenical" (i.e., "worldwide") councils at which bishops issued creeds (uniform statements of belief) and canons (universal rules for church discipline). Together, emperors and bishops enforced a singular orthodoxy, "right belief," which necessitated identifying and disciplining "wrong belief."

When these institutional threads of episcopacy, empire, and orthodoxy came together in the later 4th century they reworked earlier discourses of difference into their totalizing worldview, including discourses about Jews. That is not to say that we can trace a linear development from 150 to 400 CE: anti-Judaism, like most sociocultural phenomena, is never linear. Rather, earlier sources, selected and interpreted, provided the materials from which later, 4th-century Christians might fabricate their orthodox Christian empire. I turn now to two contexts in the first Christian centuries that would become, in the late 4th century, resources for this imperial orthodoxy: discussions of Jewish–Christian interaction and heresiological formulations of Judaism. As much as possible I try both to disentangle these earlier sources from their later incorporation into an imperial orthodox framework and to trace that later incorporation.

INTERACTIONS: JEWS AND CHRISTIANS IN DIALOGUE AND CONFLICT

To speak of "Jewish–Christian interaction" in the 2nd through 4th centuries is already to concede a key plank of late 4th-century imperial Christianity orthodoxy: that Jews and Christians were, by definition, socially and theologically distinct. Yet even sources that think about Jewish–Christian difference were not necessarily thinking in the same absolutist terms as later imperial Christians. Sources I address in this section on "interaction" became valuable for later theorists of imperial Christian identity because they *could* be understood as assuming the mutual distinctiveness of Judaism and Christianity. In their own context, however, these sources reveal a sense that religious boundaries were tentative and provisional.

Scripture and Debate

Although writing in Greek in the city of Rome, where he had settled as a philosophical teacher of Christianity, Justin Martyr (d. c. 165), originally from Samaria, set his longest and most complex work in the eastern Mediterranean city of Ephesus. There, he reported in his *Dialogue with Trypho the Jew*, he encountered a group of Jewish refugees who had fled the unsuccessful Bar Kokhba's revolt in the 130s. Their leader, Trypho, recognized Justin's philosophical cloak and sought to engage him in a discussion of God and truth. When Justin revealed that he was a Christian, and that his interpretation of the Jewish Scriptures was superior to Trypho's, a two-day discussion ensued during which Justin set out to prove that the Hebrew Bible predicted the messiahship of Jesus and that Jews who still obeyed its literal precepts were in error. At the end Trypho departed amiably, unconvinced.

Scholars still debate whether such a dialogue ever took place and, if it did, how accurately Justin reported its contents at some temporal and geographic remove. (One motive of scholars who defend the *Dialogue*'s historicity is the recovery of a rare Jewish voice from the mid-2nd century CE in the person of Trypho.) Earlier Jewish–Christian dialogues existed but do not survive and the genre continued in later centuries, in Latin, Greek, and Syriac. The *Dialogue with Trypho* is notable, however, for how it staged a form of Jewish–Christian interaction grounded simultaneously in sameness and difference. The entire debate is structured around what Justin and Trypho had in common: veneration of the Scriptures as divine revelation from the one Creator God. They differed in their interpretation: Trypho saw a covenantal blueprint for Israel and a future Jewish messiah, while Justin saw predictions of Christ's advent and the calling of the gentiles. For Justin Christian truth came out of dialogue *with* Jewish others, not wholesale rejection of Jews and Judaism. (A form of Christianity that did totally reject Jews, Judaism, and the Old Testament emerged some time before Justin's career, ascribed to an eastern Christian named Marcion; Marcionite Christianity survived for several centuries in the East.)

The shared intelligibility of Scriptures became an even more complex marker of commonality and difference in the 3rd century, exemplified by the textual scholar Origen (c. 184–253). Origen left rafts of commentaries and homilies on the books of the Christian Bible in which he insisted that the Scriptures must be understood allegorically: beneath its literal stories of floods, patriarchs, kings, exiles, and fishermen lay a metaphysical story about God, human souls, and cosmic redemption. Often Origen's allegorical interpretation of the Bible is read as supersessionist; he harped on Jews' interpretation of their Scriptures (his Old Testament) as lamentably "fleshly" in contrast with his "spiritual" understanding. Nonetheless, Origen viewed Christian engagement with Scripture as another area in which Christian truth emerged through Jewish encounter.

Origen also turned to Hebrew texts of the Old Testament in order to amend his received Greek translation (the Septuagint). He compiled a costly and elaborate reference guide in six columns ("Hexapla"): his Greek text sat in the middle, surrounded by the Hebrew, Greek transliteration of the Hebrew, and three other Greek translations. Writing, teaching, and preaching first in his native Alexandria and later in Palestinian Caesarea, Origen relied on not only Jewish texts but Jewish teachers. He refers several times to "the Hebrew master," a source who was likely a Jewish convert to Christianity from whom he drew occasional insight into Jewish interpretation.

Origen also referred to Scriptural debates between Christians and Jews in which Christians could deploy the biblical expertise derived *from* Jews in order to argue *against* Jews and Jewish interpretation. Writing to another learned Christian, Julius Africanus, Origen defended his reliance on Jewish texts and sources as a tool for "when we are in debates with the Jews," a situation he also evoked in his anti-pagan apologetic treatise *Against Celsus*. Whether Origen participated in or witnessed such debates, in public or private settings, or whether he was familiar with their literary forms (like Justin's *Dialogue with Trypho* or earlier examples), the larger cultural world constructed in the 3rd century was one in which Jews and Christians engaged in a shared, albeit at times competitive endeavor: deriving truth from God's revealed words. Such Scriptural debate, of course, also thrived *within* Christian and Jewish communities, where it could be viewed as a normative form of religious truth-seeking. By the 4th century, such Scriptural "debate" between Jews and Christians would come to be understood as a mechanism of exclusion and "othering." In the world of pre-Constantinian Christianity we might imagine the situation otherwise, more analogous to rival political parties than warring nation-states.

Ritual and Contact

Justin and Origen also discussed ritual contact between Jews and Christians. Justin conceded to Trypho that a Jew could follow ritual laws (circumcision, the Sabbath, and dietary restrictions) *and* believe in Jesus as Messiah, as long as that Jew did not try to force his ritual observances onto other Christians. (Justin also noted that not all gentile Christians agreed with his viewpoint.) Origen, when preaching in Caesarea, a city with a prosperous and learned Jewish population, expressed concern that his congregants might understand the Jewish commandments in a literal fashion and indulge in fasting on the Day of Atonement, eating unleavened bread during Passover, or avoiding bathhouses on the Sabbath (since the last prohibition is not biblical, modern scholars see it as evidence for Origen's firsthand knowledge of post-biblical Jewish custom). Origen's warning might have been hypothetical or even metaphorical. Yet other contemporary sources, such as the *Didascalia apostolorum* ("Teaching of the Apostles"), a pseudepigraphic work composed in 3rd-century Syria in Greek but surviving in a 4th-century Syriac translation, also admonished Christians who practiced Jewish rituals, perhaps with Jews or former Jews or without making such distinctions.

When Justin, Origen, and the *Didascalia* imagined Christian attraction to Jewish ritual they articulated another domain, like Scripture, in which distinction emerged from common endeavor. From the 2nd through 5th centuries CE this ritual communion was most evident in the calculation of the date of Easter. Christian communities throughout the East kept the observance of Christ's death and resurrection calendrically linked to the Jewish Passover (during which festival the commemorated events occurred). Since Passover is observed according to a luni-solar calendar, ritual coordination of Easter and Passover required consultation between churches and synagogues, which set the date of Passover annually. Of course, such coordination did not guarantee positive feeling: Melito's vitriolic Easter homily accusing "Israel" of deicide was almost certainly preached on a Sunday during the local Jewish Passover observance.

Still we should not ignore the fact of calendrical cooperation even in the face of such vitriol. (The analogy of rival political parties, at times even bloodthirsty in their opposition, may again be apposite.) Some Christians thought this calendrical coordination crossed a line and even gave it a heretical label: Christians who placed Easter on the Sunday following 14 Nisan (the date of Passover) were labeled "Fourteeners" (*quartodecimani* in Latin, *tessareskaidekatitai* in Greek). Yet despite repeated condemnations well into the 5th century, it continued to make sense to many Christians that their festivals and the festivals of Jews existed in the same divine economy, just as their Scriptures did. Even as Christians sought boundaries and distinction, they did so through connection and affinity with Jews and Judaism.

In the late 4th century, John Chrysostom, a preacher in Antioch (who later became bishop of the capital city of Constantinople), delivered a blistering series of homilies "against Judaizing Christians" (manuscripts often refer to these sermons more economically and accurately as "against Jews"). The precipitating incident was, as in Origen's day, Christian attendance at synagogues and participation in Jewish ritual.

John chastised Christians who frequented a house of "demons" as if it had anything to do with God. Antioch was a religiously and culturally diverse city, sitting at multiple geographic, linguistic, and political crossroads. Was John raging against a kind of religious promiscuity common in major urban centers, in which cultic activity was open to all comers, sincere believers along with the curious? Were the synagogue-friendly practices of these Christians part of a long tradition among Jewish and Christian communities of the East, or were these Antiochene Christians innovating new boundary-crossing rituals? The evidence of our 2nd- and 3rd-century authors suggests that, even if the specific practices condemned by John were novel – such as marching in Jewish parades or swearing oaths on the Torah scrolls of the synagogue – the impulse behind them to see commonality and cooperation before or alongside difference and distinction was not.

What was new, in John's day, was the authority of clerical and political institutions to clamp down on difference sought through commonality. By John's day, as the institutional forces of bishops and emperors colluded to tighten up the boundaries of Christian identity, new tools were brought to bear to portray meaningful Christian engagement as not just distasteful or inadvisable but punishable. The most creative and successful way that these institutions could sanction the desire for Jewish–Christian interaction was by incorporating Jews into the burgeoning Christian discourse of orthodoxy and heresy, making Jews not just socially distinct but theologically dangerous.

THEOLOGIES: JUDAIZING CHRISTIANS AND CHRISTIAN JEWS

Heresy comes from a Greek word meaning *choice*; it was used of rival Hellenistic philosophical schools that were not necessarily antagonistic or mutually exclusive. By the late 2nd century, some Christians had adapted the term to disparage what they viewed as deviant malformations of apostolic truth. Irenaeus of Lyon (c. 180) wrote a treatise, "Against Knowledge Falsely So-Called," calling out "gnostic" (esoteric and mythopoetic) forms of Christian thought as twisted and demonic. Justin Martyr, too, wrote a more general treatise "against all heresies" as did the shadowy 3rd-century figure Hippolytus. Whether we can map these rhetorical and polemical treatises onto actual groups of Christians – whether, on the ground, "Valentinians" were distinct from "Marcionites" or "orthodox" Christian groups – remains unknown. As in the realm of Jewish–Christian interaction, what is significant in the 2nd and 3rd centuries is the power of *imagining* intra-Christian difference as the boundary between singular, eternal, apostolic Christian orthodoxy and fractured, immoral, and diabolical Christian heresies. In the specific case of Christian anti-Judaism, what is significant in later centuries are the uses to which such rhetoric was put by imperializing orthodoxy.

Early in the 2nd century some Christians viewed the attraction of Judaism as part of a nascent heresiological discourse. Ignatius of Antioch, the bishop who wrote in defense of the monepiscopate, also warned against the dangers of "Judaizing" and the dangerous appeal of "the Jewish Law." What this term "Judaizing" (*ioudaizein*) might mean is unclear; it appears in Paul's letter to the Galatians, where it refers to gentiles "acting like" Jews. For Ignatius, too, as well as later authors like Clement of Alexandria (c. 200) and Origen, it indicates non-Jews acting like Jews through practices such as Sabbath observance, dietary restrictions, and male circumcision. Needless to say, for those authors for whom Christianity was, by definition, not-Judaism, "acting Jewish" was at best ill-advised, at worst unacceptable deviance.

These early imprecations against "Judaizing" took two paths into the 4th century and the age of imperial orthodoxy. The first path consists of an array of what modern scholars call "Jewish-Christianities," putatively emerging in the 2nd century, if not earlier, and elaborated throughout late antiquity. The second saw the accusation of "Judaizing" attached to diverse theological errors, such that *Jew* could become a smear broadly synonymous with *heretic*. This "hereticizing" of Jews transformed Judaism into a theological "other" embedded in a distinctive (non-Jewish and anti-Jewish) Christian framework.

Jewish-Christianities

We have already seen how Justin Martyr referred to Jews who both believed in the messiahship of Jesus and persisted in observing the Jewish Law. Later in the 2nd century Irenaeus framed the most extreme Judaizing Christ-followers as heretics he called *Ebionites*. According to Irenaeus, Ebionites used only the Gospel of Matthew (Irenaeus was an early proponent of a four-fold gospel canon), rejected Paul as an "apostate from the Law," were circumcised and followed customs which adhere to a "Jewish mode of life," venerated Jerusalem, denied the Virgin Birth, and said Joseph was Jesus' father. *Ebionite* comes from the Hebrew/Aramaic word for "poor" (*'evyon*), as Origen attested; the 4th-century heresiologist Epiphanius of Cyprus (c. 377) reported that the Ebionites derived their name from the voluntary poverty of the apostles as recounted in Acts 4. We have little evidence that any Christians,

"Judaizing" or otherwise, used these labels themselves: it was standard heresiological practice for defenders of orthodoxy to apply sectarian labels to their opponents in order to delegitimize them.

Self-styled defenders of Christian orthodoxy in the centuries that followed elaborated Irenaeus's brief notice. Origen lamented the "poverty of thinking" (a play on the meaning of *'evyon*) displayed by Ebionites, both in their deficient appreciation of Jesus' divinity (since many denied the Virgin Birth) and in their literal reading of Scripture (such that they continued to follow the defunct Law of Moses). Eusebius recapitulated the charges of Irenaeus and Origen, adding that even those who acknowledged the Virgin Birth refused to confess that Christ was also God.

The must fulsome attack on the Ebionites came from Epiphanius. In his compendious heresiological treatise the *Panarion* he imagined a founder named Ebion, a "many-headed monster" who combined all the worst traits of Judaism with other heresies. Epiphanius quoted with distaste from their "Gospel of the Hebrews" (which they claimed was an original form of the Gospel of Matthew), inveighed against their perversion of Jewish customs (they practiced circumcision but also vegetarianism), and mocked their incoherent ideas about Christ (some thought he was just a man, some thought he was a ninety-six-mile tall angel). Epiphanius wrote against other "Judaizing" heresies (the Cerinthians and Nazoreans), but the Ebionites encapsulated for Epiphanius the deep *wrongness* of combining Judaism and Christianity: the result was poorer versions of both. The Ebionites erred in both their Christianity (with their ninety-six-mile Christ) and their Judaism (with their vegetarianism). That Epiphanius was able to correct them on both counts shows how imperializing orthodox Christianity came to value knowledge about, and over, Jews and Judaism. It also shows how central Judaism had become to Christian heresiological thinking. Epiphanius could even include "Judaism" as one of the "mother-heresies" of Christian error in an early chapter of the *Panarion*.

That Christians continued to conjure up a Jewish (per)version of their orthodoxy against which to fulminate shows that anxieties about and attraction to Jewishness had a powerful hold on the orthodox Christian imagination. To be sure, evidence does survive of Christ-followers who aligned the covenant of Israel with saving faith in Christ. In addition to Justin's cautious report and the later heresiologists' polemical, if not fanciful, refutations, we possess a body of texts known as the "Pseudo-Clementine" writings, composed in Greek but surviving in Greek, Syriac, and Latin versions from the 4th century.

Set in a fanciful apostolic age ("Clement," the hero of the narratives, was a protégé of Peter, who became the bishop of Rome), these texts united "Israel" and "Christ" against "Hellenism" and assumed that the Law of Moses remained valid, especially ritual and dietary laws (the villain of the tales, Simon Magus, preached the end of the Law and may have been a cipher for the apostle Paul).

Were such texts used as foundational for a real community of Judaizing Christians (like Acts of the Apostles became foundational for the orthodox)? Were they an exercise in theological and historical imagination, untethered to community practice? Posing the question this way places too much emphasis on a kind of lived reality that is inaccessible to us centuries later. What the Pseudo-Clementine writings do demonstrate, along with the neutral and polemical "evidence" for Jewish-Christians, is the ongoing attraction of Jewishness *within* Christianity even after the rise of imperial, episcopal Christian orthodoxy. The allure of a "Jewish-Christianity" – among possible adherents, certain opponents, and hopeful scholars who seek to recover a "primitive" form of Christianity – is evidence for the theological attachment of Christianity to a Jewish "other" constellating on its borders

"New Jews"

By the early 4th century, for some Christians seeking to naturalize the edifice of imperial, episcopal orthodoxy, the term "Judaizing" and its attendant anxieties and attachments took a different theological turn: no longer about *doing* the wrong (Jewish) thing, "Judaizing" signaled *believing* the wrong things, principally about Christ and the Trinity. The major theological conflict of the 4th century concerned the nature of the relationship between the Father, Son (incarnate in the God-man Jesus), and Holy Spirit. This Trinitarian conflict was central because it was taken up with vigor (and violence) by the bishops and emperors so set on securing a unified, totalizing Christian polity. Creeds and councils, endorsed by bishops and enforced by emperors, became the institutional tools of orthodox enforcement. Christians defending the absolute equality of the Father, Son, and Holy Spirit against other theological understandings of God accused their opponents of "Judaizing" because they diminished the glory of the Son of God. The logic, evident already in the messianic dispute between Justin and Trypho in the 2nd century, was that the refusal to grant Christ fully divine status indicated that one held Jewish sympathies. "Denying the Son" was something Jews would (and did) do.

The city of Alexandria in Egypt was a hotbed of Trinitarian conflict, a site where bishops early on sought to create unified Christianity through theological control. In the early 4th century, Bishop Alexander of Alexandria declared that the "heretical priest" Arius and his fellow theological deviants "cobbled together a Christ-fighting gang like Jews." His successor Athanasius took up this rhetoric of heretics-as-Jews with vigor in numerous polemical tracts throughout the 4th century. Drawing on the image of Jews as "Christ-killers," Athanasius wrote of the violent tactics of his theological opponents: "This new Jewish heresy not only rejects the Lord, but has learned how to murder." These "new Jews," he wrote, "from Jews of old have learned" stubborn disbelief, even in the face of miracles. That Alexander and Athanasius could deploy "Jew" as a theological slur against their Christian opponents shows the theological force the opposition between "Jew" and "Christian" had acquired by the late 4th century, at least in some Christian circles.

A contemporary of Athanasius, a deacon named Ephrem living in the Syrian borderlands with Persia, elaborated this theological anti-Judaism in treatises and hymns written for his Christian congregations. Ephrem composed in Syriac, an eastern dialect of Aramaic that was the lingua franca of this region for centuries. In addition to deploying anti-Jewish rhetoric familiar from other parts of the ancient Mediterranean world – Jews were foolish, deranged, defiling deicides – Ephrem also conflated the errors of the Jews with the theological faults of Trinitarian heretics. Ephrem picked up on the theme of contentious disputation, common to the inquisitorial Pharisees of the gospels and the sophistic hair-splitters among the heretics. The aim of both Pharisees then and heretics now was the same: to attack God in the person of Christ. Like his Alexandrian contemporaries, Ephrem's expansive and even slippery use of anti-Jewish language against Christian heretics shows how firmly lodged in a particular imperial orthodox consciousness the "Jewish other" had become by the late 4th century.

CONCLUSIONS: OTHER BORDERS

We began our story in the eastern borderlands of the Roman Empire, in the garrison town of Callinicum where a burning synagogue emblematized imperial Christian intolerance. We have also seen how much textual evidence for both virulent anti-Judaism and "Jewish-Christianity" comes from these Syrian borderlands. The "Judaizing" Pseudo-Clementine writings were probably composed in Syria and survive in a fulsome Syriac translation. Likewise, the *Didascalia apostolorum*, which admonishes its readers against attraction to Judaizing practices, is thought to have emerged in Syria. Ignatius, who in the early 2nd century warned against "Judaizing," came from Antioch, a major Syrian metropolis, as did John Chrysostom, who issued even more dire warnings in the 4th century. To these we might add an earlier 4th-century (c. 345) author writing in Syriac on the Persian side of the border (where both Christians and Jews were minorities): Aphrahat, or "the Persian Sage." Among his twenty-three theological *Demonstrations* are several anti-Jewish tracts framed as polemical responses to an anonymous Jewish "sage" (reminiscent of Justin Martyr refuting Trypho) and designed to warn Christians away from Judaism. Aphrahat's dogged attention to dangerous Judaism adds one more compelling voice to the chorus of Syrian and Syriac sources fixated – positively and negatively – on Judaism. By way of conclusion I want to dig a bit into this borderlands anti-Judaism and ask how it has been framed by modern scholarship, and how that framing speaks to the larger place of eastern early Christian thought in histories of "anti-Judaism" and "antisemitism."

Some scholars have, since the 19th century, considered this preponderance of Christian anti-Judaism and Jewish-Christianity from the Syrian borderlands as evidence of a persistent contact and mutual influence between Jews and Christians, a mingling and crossing which became intolerable with the rise of an imperially sanctioned episcopal orthodoxy. These fulminations against and flirtations with Judaizing are read either as remnants of a primitive Aramaic Jesus-movement fossilized before its Hellenization or as evidence of continued mingling of Christ-fellowship and Jewish covenant that calls into question any secure "parting of the ways" between Jews and Christians even into the 4th century. The burning of the synagogue at Callinicum, then, could be read either as the stamping-out of the last embers of a 1st-century relic or as the fury of an imperial Christian orthodoxy against centuries of boundary-crossing.

Both of these readings of an alleged Christian Syrian predilection for Jews and Judaism cast Judaism as the Ur-heresy of "real" Christianity, the tempting other that either never went away or keeps coming back, again and again, to lead orthodoxy astray. These readings also locate that Ur-heresy in the imperial borderlands of Syria and so literally marginalize this Jewish archetypal heresy, partitioning it off away from the imperial center. Here we must remember our initial caution: that our surviving sources are the end result of ideological process of selection and preservation, not only in antiquity but up to the modern day. It suited the purposes of an imperializing orthodoxy to locate the dangerous Judaizing other in the margins; it has also suited modern students of ancient Christianity and Judaism, still so indebted to and entangled in our disciplines' European Protestant roots.

Yet we have seen the Christian fascination with the Jewish other across the chronological and geographical spread of our sources. Justin the Samaritan wrote of his encounter of a Jew in Ephesus while teaching in Rome. Origen contemplated the authoritative Jewish texts of the Bible, misread by his Jewish contemporaries, in Egypt and Palestine. Athanasius and Epiphanius pondered the dangers of "Judaizing heresy" as fulsomely as Ephrem and Aphrahat. The "border" between Jews and Christians cannot be contained in the physical borders of the Roman Empire, but rather shimmers continually across the Christian East. The omnipresence of this boundary required technologies of comprehension and refutation that kept the otherness of Judaism paradoxically at the forefront of non- and anti-Jewish Christian cultural consciousness.

This desire to comprehend Judaism as the confrontable, containable, and knowable other – occasionally subject to the disciplining violence of the state – was the work of an imperial, episcopal orthodoxy that was neither inevitable nor sustainable. Its particular strategies and discourses reworked earlier instances of contact and communication into models of confrontation and rejection. The result was the naturalization of violence – rhetorical and material – against Jews and Judaism that would continue to escalate throughout the 5th, 6th, and 7th centuries, well after the advent of Islam.

Was this late ancient "othering" of Jews the seedbed of what would bloom into "antisemitism" in the modern period? Historians will usually make important distinctions between the anti-Judaism of late antiquity and the antisemitism of modernity, particularly the constellation of race, nation, and capitalism that created the conditions for 20th-century antisemitism. Yet there are important overlaps, as well: the centering of Christianity as a dominant political identity, the incremental transformation of "contact" into "conflict," and the framing of Jews as a dangerous other constellating too close to the Christian self, a threatening reminder of a past origins that can never be forgotten. Finally, we must consider the ethical concerns raised by any comparative study of anti-Judaism, which so often imagines that robust Jewish presence might in some way have "provoked" violent Christian opposition.

Further Reading

Becker, A. J., and A. Y. Reed, *The Ways That Never Parted: Jews and Christians in Late Antiquity and the Early Middle Ages* (Minneapolis, MN, 2007). A collection of essays dealing with the so-called parting of the ways between Christianity and Judaism from diverse theoretical perspectives and engaging with a variety of Jewish and Christian materials; Becker and Reed's programmatic introduction is an especially useful guide to a fraught but tenacious historical idea.

Drake, S., *Slandering the Jew: Sexuality and Difference in Early Christian Texts* (Philadelphia, 2013). This book examines the ways embodiment and sexuality were marshaled in anti-Jewish texts (or texts that were later read as anti-Jewish, such as Paul's letters) from the 2nd through 4th century with special attention to Origen and John Chrysostom.

Koltun-Fromm, N., *Jewish-Christian Conversation in Fourth-Century Mesopotamia* (Piscataway, NJ, 2011). This study of Aphrahat's *Demonstrations* places him in conversation with roughly contemporary rabbinic sources to argue for sustained contact and conversation among Christian and Jewish communities in the Sasanian Persian empire.

Lieu J., *Image and Reality: The Jews in the World of the Christians in the Second Century* (London, 1996). A detailed engagement with the earliest explicitly non-Jewish Christian sources (Ignatius, Justin Martyr, Melito of Sardis, and other apologetic and martyr texts) that attempts to discern what, if any, is their historical value and what is heightened rhetoric in the service of Christian self-definition.

Neusner, J., *Aphrahat and Judaism: The Christian-Jewish Argument in Fourth-Century Iran* (Leiden, 1971). Although somewhat out of date (see Koltun-Fromm above) Neusner's volume contains English translations of Aphrahat's "anti-Jewish" *Demonstrations* along with accompanying essays that place Aphrahat in the context of both Sasanian Persia and early Christian writings about Jews and Judaism.

Reed, A. Y., *Jewish-Christianity and the History of Judaism: Collected Essays* (Tübingen, 2018). Several essays in this collection explore the so-called Pseudo-Clementine writings which seem to envision social and theological compatibility between Christ-veneration and the Israelite covenant. Equally important are Reed's historiographic essays, which explore the deeply embedded European Protestant roots that drive scholarship on Jewish–Christian difference.

Shepardson, C., *Anti-Judaism and Christian Orthodoxy: Ephrem's Hymns in Fourth-Century Syria* (Washington, DC, 2008). This study of Ephrem's writings against Jews and heretics argues that anti-Judaism supplies Ephrem with much of his heresiological vocabulary and frameworks; Shepardson also provides a robust comparison with Athanasius's contemporary anti-Jewish heresiology in Alexandria.

Simon, M., *Verus Israel: A Study of the Relations between Jews and Christians in the Roman Empire, 135–425* (Oxford, 1986). Originally published in French in 1948, expanded in 1964, and translated into English in 1986, this classic work posits that Christian anti-Jewish texts provide evidence for robust Jewish life throughout the Roman Empire during the period in question, including competing attempts by Jews and Christians to convert pagans. Simon was working to countermand earlier theories that post-Temple Judaism was essentially lifeless and dormant during the rise of Christianity.

Taylor, M., *Anti-Judaism and Early Christian Identity: A Critique of the Scholarly Consensus* (Leiden, 1994). The "consensus" that Taylor is critiquing is that established by Simon (see above) that, as Taylor argues, functionally blamed Jews for provoking Christian anti-Judaism. For Taylor this argument sets a dangerous precedent by blaming victims of intolerance for violence against them.

Wilken, R., *John Chrysostom and the Jews: Rhetoric and Reality in the Late 4th Century* (Berkeley, CA, 1983). A classic work that tries to make sense of John Chrysostom's *Homilies against Judaizing Christians* by reconstructing both the robust Jewish community of 4th-century Antioch and the oratorical conventions of the day employed by John.

Williams, A. L., *Adversus Judaeos: A Bird's-Eye View of Christian Apologiae until the Renaissance* (Cambridge, 1935). Written by a Christian theologian with missionizing ideals, this outdated volume remains one of the only English-language compendia of Christian texts about (usually, as the title suggests "against") Jews and Judaism. The introductions and comments may usually be skipped.

6 Christianizing the Roman Empire: Jews and the Law from Constantine to Justinian, 300–600 CE

ANDREW S. JACOBS

INTRODUCTION: CHRISTIANIZATION AND THE LAW

The term *Christianization* can sound inevitable, as if the process by which the Roman Empire became enmeshed with Christian interests and institutions was an evolutionary process analogous to the rise of mammals in the Cenozoic Era. *Christianization* also often connotes judgment, as if the "triumph of Christianity" led either to the redemption of a pagan culture or to the "fall" of a classical one. When I speak of Christianization in this essay, I mean neither an inevitable, linear process nor an utter change in the character of Mediterranean society (for better or worse). By *Christianization* I mean the increasing availability of "Christian" as a legible, flexible, and meaningful frame of identity for oneself or others.

In order to assess how imperial institutions enabled and encouraged Christianization I focus on Christian Roman law. Roman law was not just a mechanism of criminal and civic enforcement but was how "Romanness" was projected and experienced across the vastness of the empire. The imperial center was materially present through markers like coinage and statuary. But for most inhabitants of the Roman Empire the law was how they came to understand the largely invisible *imperium* that ruled over them and how they interacted with that *imperium*. Rome's authority was like a shadow that occasionally obscured the sun of local life. The form that shadow took was the irregular and often capricious enforcement of Roman law by local officials invested with imperial authority. Laws issued under Christian Roman emperors, then, point both to specific contexts and to larger ideologies of imperial Christianization.

I focus here on the crucial period from the reign of Constantine (r. 306–337) to that of Justinian (r. 527–565). It is easy, and not inaccurate, to view this as the period during which Rome became more Christian and Christianized Rome became more anti-Jewish. But both of these easy assertions obscure important complexities. After a quick overview of the first point (that Rome became more Christian during this period) I turn to the second point (that Christianized Rome became more anti-Jewish) by looking at Jews and Judaism at the intersection of Christianization and the law.

The several dozen extant laws addressing Jews and Judaism demonstrate the Christian Roman Empire's sustained attention to Jewish life, frequently with a tone of exasperation and censure. On the one hand, it is clear that Roman Christians are (to borrow once more Claude Lévi-Strauss's well-worn phrase) using Jews "to think with," as "others" through which to chart the blurry frontiers of Christianity and Christianizing. On the other hand, these laws suggest a desire on the part of the Christian Roman Empire to make sense of Jews *within* that Christianizing space. Legal imagination sought to constrain the possibilities of Jewish life in an ideally Christianized world. At the same time, that legal imagination left critical space for Jews to exist, survive, and even flourish as an uncanny "other" in that world.

CHRISTIANIZING EMPERORS

Constantine was the son of Constantius, one of four co-emperors whose joint rule of the Roman Empire emerged out of a period of imperial reorganization and reformation. This period of reform lasted from the 280s, when Diocletian became emperor and formed the first tetrarchy, to the 320s, when Constantine defeated his last co-emperor Licinius to become sole ruler of the Roman Empire. Reform, reorganization, and dynastic struggle continued to characterize his imperial rule. Constantine built a new capital city on the site of ancient Byzantium and named it after himself: Constantinople. In reality the "capital" of the empire was wherever an emperor and his army were in residence. But the dedication of a "New Rome," complete with its own new senatorial class, cemented the political and cultural divide between "eastern" and "western" Roman Empire that would continue through the reign of Justinian, when much of the "West" would slip away forever from Roman rule.

Among Constantine's many reforms during his long reign was, perhaps most famously, his patronage of Christianity. The tetrarchs had effectively outlawed Christianity in 303 through property confiscation and compulsory sacrifice to the traditional gods; these laws were unevenly applied and already losing steam by the time Constantine defeated his rival emperor Maxentius at Rome in 312. The religious toleration enacted the next year by Constantine and Licinius (remembered as the Edict of Milan) singled out Christianity as legitimate within a general grant of freedom of worship. Although Constantine was not baptized until he was dying, during his reign he established himself as a patron of Christianity.

While historians will continue to debate the sincerity of Constantine's "conversion," its effects on public life are undeniable: Christianity became public and monumentalized, raising the cultural "volume" of Christianity and so raising the value of Christianizing. Every Roman emperor after Constantine, with one important exception, was not just a Christian but a public patron of Christianity. Constantine modeled the Christian ruler wielding his absolute authority for "the Church" (and using that authority to police the boundaries of "the Church"). When Constantine's great-nephew Julian came to power in 361 he announced that he was not a Christian, as he had been raised, but was an ardent devotee of the traditional Greek and Roman gods. His religious about-face sent a shockwave through an empire growing accustomed to Christianizing. Julian's reign was brief (only eighteen months) but the shockwave rippled for centuries: a Christian sixty years later felt the need to write a refutation of Julian's sneering anti-Christian treatise, *Against the Galileans*.

The horror of Julian's brief anti-Christian reign reinforced the need for "new Constantines," emperors who were not only Christian but who worked to enable Christianization. More buildings went up as churches took on the distinctive look of imperial halls (the literal meaning of "basilica"). More legal and economic advantages were provided to Christian clergy as the monepiscopacy – the institution of a single bishop in charge of the ecclesiastical life of a city – was mapped along provincial boundaries. Emperors retained their traditional roles as guardians of public piety, but now that meant intervening in theological conflicts, convoking councils of bishops, and choosing sides among Christian factions. Orthodoxy, the establishment of a single correct mode of Christian belief, was subject to political enforcement.

In 380 the co-emperors Gratian, Valentinian, and Theodosius I issued an edict known by its incipit, *Cunctos populos* ("all peoples"). This law established a single form of Christianity as legitimate and all others as illegal. *Cunctos populos* is sometimes mistakenly described as establishing Christianity as the "official" religion of the Roman Empire; while it forged a tight bond between imperial power and singular Christian orthodoxy, it did not outlaw non-Christian religions. "Christianization" in the Roman Empire would be accomplished not by fiat but rather by a gradual shift in atmosphere. The long-lasting Theodosian dynasty, enduring well into the 5th century, promoted episcopal Christian orthodoxy through legal acts and munificence while removing privileges from non-Christians and imposing sanctions on "heretical" Christians.

The 5th century brought tectonic shifts in the political structure of the Roman Empire. Historians disagree on how best to narrate the incremental disintegration of Roman rule in the western Mediterranean over the course of the century: as a cataclysmic "fall" or a gradual transition. Germanic tribes had served as military support for Roman emperors since the late 3rd century, migrating westward into Roman territory from Asia. While some Germanic elites integrated into the Roman aristocracy, most settlements remained confined to the frontiers until, by the late 4th century, their leaders began to seize territory in the heart of the empire. In 410 the Visigothic king Alaric led his troops down into the Italian peninsula and sacked the city of Rome, a symbolic blow to the historic heart of a thousand-year-old empire. (Although the city of Rome had not served as an imperial base for decades, it was still the home of the hereditary senatorial class.)

Further economic, military, and political disruptions led to the direct rule of non-Roman Germanic tribes over what been the western half of the Roman Empire: Britain, Spain, France, Italy, North Africa. Sometimes these rulers styled themselves as successors to the Roman Emperors, cementing formal ties with the emperors in Constantinople; sometimes they established self-consciously "post-Roman" kingdoms. Almost all of these Germanic kingdoms were Christian, although many of them had embraced a Christian confession at odds with the official orthodoxy of Rome and Constantinople.

While the West transitioned (or fell) the eastern Empire was more successful in fighting off "barbarian" incursions from the north and south. The Sassanid Persian empire to the East remained a major political and military foe until the rise of Islam. Emperors throughout the 5th and 6th centuries continued massive building projects (particularly, sponsorship of dazzling churches), promoted economic and military reorganization, and engaged in heavy-handed oversight of the episcopal orthodox network. Justinian I rose to power in 527; during his nearly forty-year reign in Constantinople he transformed the civic, cultural, and religious landscape.

Justinian's reign was turbulently constructive. His enforcement of orthodoxy among rival Christological schools led to the fragmentation of multiple "orthodox" Christian denominations which survive today in Egypt, Greece, Armenia, and Syria. Urban unrest early in his reign led to the destruction of Constantine's basilica to Holy Wisdom ("Hagia Sophia"); in its place Justinian built the domed wonder which stands in Istanbul today. He unleashed talented generals on the West who engineered a brief reunification of the Roman territories in Italy, North Africa, and Spain under Justinian's rule; ultimately, imperial resources were stretched too thin and much of this territory once more fell out of Roman rule for good.

Justinian's reign encapsulates the efforts of Christianizing emperors to reimagine their world as irrevocably Christian: orthodox, unified, pious, and obedient. That those efforts failed as much as they succeeded demonstrates how impossible it was to fully Christianize a space so vast and diverse as the Roman Empire. Orthodoxy could never outpace heresy, unity could never erase division, and piety and obedience required rigid and constant enforcement. Even the most autocratic and long-reigning Christian emperor could only create an atmosphere in which Christianizing acts were encouraged and rewarded; he could not make them natural and inevitable.

Did these efforts at Christianizing create a concomitant atmosphere of anti-Judaism? As I explained in my earlier contribution to this volume, the institutional nexus of imperial-episcopal orthodoxy during this period made concerted efforts to bound off Jews and Judaism from their ideal of Christian identity and community. Pre-Christian Romans had not been disposed to think warmly about Jews: two failed revolts in the province of Judea (ending in 73 and 135 CE) led to additional taxes levied against Jews as well as the renaming of the Jews' ancestral province *Judaea* as *Syria Palaestina*. Latin and Greek authors marveled at the physical and cultural peculiarities of the Jews. Whether Jews were any more reviled than other provincial populations subject to demeaning stereotypes is unclear.

We have very limited direct evidence from Jews themselves as to how they fared under a Christian Roman Empire. Scholars have sought to deduce veiled references to Christians and Christianity from rabbinic texts; in addition to being ambiguous (since they are veiled) these texts also speak to the experience of a very limited number of Jews, primarily in Palestine. Ross Shepard Kraemer has recently tried to discern the fate of diaspora Jews using literary evidence, archaeological remains (synagogues and inscriptions), and legal texts. The literary evidence mostly comes from Christian histories, hagiographies, treatises, letters, and sermons and is difficult to disentangle from the ideological presuppositions of their authors. If future historians were to try to decipher the habits and customs of Texas oilmen by watching episodes of the night-time soap opera *Dallas* they might glean some accurate information but are much more likely to learn about the tastes and interests of the show's producers and viewers. From Christian literary sources we learn information either banal and unilluminating (Jews engaged in commerce, politics, and cultural events with their non-Jewish neighbors) or antagonistic and inflammatory (Jews conspired with Rome's enemies, plotted against Christians, committed bloody and impious atrocities). Archaeological evidence may be less overtly ideological but is still open to divergent interpretation, particularly because its survival is so spotty and unpredictable. Christian writings and material remains leave no doubt that Jews continued to live in the Christian Roman Empire and even thrive in some places. But were their lives more constrained than under pagan emperors?

To explore this question I turn to the third body of evidence that Kraemer treats: the law. As I noted above, the law is not merely a technology of civic and criminal discipline but a way of theorizing and even fantasizing about an idealized polity. Imperial laws might be responses to specific legal queries; they might also issue forth unprompted if an emperor (or his aides) wanted to send a message about what was right, proper, and Roman. Dissemination and awareness of specific laws was haphazard. Professional jurists in the 2nd and 3rd centuries had attempted to create systematic treatises on Roman jurisprudence, and Christian emperors in the 4th and 6th centuries commissioned two massive compendia of official legal rulings: the *Codex Theodosianus* and the *Corpus juris civilis*.

Theodosius II (r. 402–450) reigned in Constantinople for most of his life (he was declared co-emperor with his father and uncle when he was an infant). An ardent Christian in the mold of Constantine and his grandfather Theodosius I, he was also, like them, a reformer. In the 420s he conceived a plan to produce a systematic collection of all Roman laws issued under the Christian emperors since Constantine (laws issued by Julian were not included). In 438 the result, the *Codex Theodosianus* ("Theodosian Code"), was presented to the senates in Rome and Constantinople. Thousands of laws, divided into sixteen books, preserved the rulings of over a century of emperors.

A century later, Justinian – always seeking to outdo his predecessors in scale – commissioned an even more ambitious legal collection, encompassing not only the Theodosian Code and laws issued after its publication (*novellae*, or "new laws"), but laws and legal treatises produced in the earlier centuries of the empire. Known to modern scholars as the *Corpus juris civilis* ("Body of Civic Law"), what Justinian's jurists produced in the 520s and 530s was a multipart attempt at a total legal curriculum: a code of laws (*Codex Justinianus*, modeled on and incorporating much of the *Codex Theodosianus*), a collection of short legal rulings dating to the 2nd century (*Digesta*), a textbook for jurists (*Institutiones*), and laws issued under Justinian (more *Novellae*). If we view Justinian's inclusion of pre-Christian law as signaling a more ecumenical understanding of Rome as more than a Christian Empire, we misread Justinian's ambitions. His goal was to subsume all of Rome's authority under the aegis of the Christian Empire. The first law in Justinian's Code is *Cunctos populos*, the declaration of imperial orthodoxy found in the last book of the Theodosian Code.

Roman magistrates under these emperors, and later Byzantine and post-Roman Germanic courts, used these collections as legal precedents. But these codes were more than mere reference works: they aimed to shape the political, social, cultural, and religious environment in which law expressed Roman *imperium*. Through selection, editing, and organization these Codes imagined the totalizing space within which Christian Roman power might operate: the outer limits of Christianization. As we turn to these sources, then, we can ask two questions. First: What insight do the particular circumstances of a law, or set of laws, give us into Jewish life under a Christian Roman Empire? Second: How does a totalizing vision of Christian Roman Empire emerge in these laws, and how are Jews and Judaism imagined therein?

JEWS AND JUDAISM UNDER THE LAW

It is a historical commonplace to note that Judaism in the Roman Empire was a *religio licita* ("a legal religion"), but this was not a real designation in Roman law. The phrase was used by the Christian Tertullian in the early 3rd century in his defense of Christianity. Tertullian was inventively playing with judicial language as means of grappling with the antagonistic relation of Christians to the Roman state. Jews appear as a distinct category in pre-Constantinian laws as a particular population requiring special consideration in laws concerning public service, property rights, and legal obligations. Jews are described in these laws as a *religio* (probably best understood not as our "religion" but perhaps a "community of obligation"), a *superstitio* (an especially scrupulous and idiosyncratic *religio*), and as a *natio* (again, not our "nation" but "a community of common birth").

Christian emperors retain this language marking out Jews as a distinct body under Roman Law: they are a *secta* ("subgroup," once even a *feralis secta*, "beastly subgroup") as well as a *superstitio*, a *religio*, and a *natio*. Some Christian laws deal with typical legal issues, such as property and status. Others treat the religious issues unique to Jews and Judaism. I turn now to examine these three topics in turn and ask how Christian law imagines Jews as economic, social, and religious subjects in order to glimpse some of the possibilities of Jewish life under Christian Roman law.

Economic Jews

Christian law treats Jews as both individual and corporate economic subjects. One place we see the individual economic status of Jews is in laws concerning the decurionate. The decurionate, or curial class, comprised the wealthy elites of municipalities and regions who were expected to provide for the local economy by paying for building projects (including temples), public works, games, and festivals. Decurions were also responsible for collecting imperial taxes in their region and making up any shortfall. In return for their financial beneficence the members of the curial class received formal and informal recognition of status (civic offices as well public honor). As the imperial infrastructure grew throughout late antiquity, and wealthy families were granted imperial aristocratic status that pulled them out of the decurionate, the financial obligations of the curial class grew more burdensome. In addition, Christian emperors from Constantine onward granted curial exemptions to members of the Christian clergy, which drew increasingly from the aristocratic classes.

Wealthy Jews served as decurions at least from the 3rd century; a partial law preserved in Justinian's *Digests* exempts curial Jews from participating in activities that "offend against their *superstitio*" (such as repairing pagan temples or sponsoring pagan rituals). One of Constantine's earliest laws curtails these exemptions, out of financial need for more curial participation or to signal less respect for Jewish *superstitio* or both. Later Constantine offered "all those who serve in synagogues" the same curial exemption available to Christian bishops, an exemption which was repealed, reasserted, and repealed again in the last decades of the 4th century.

At the very least we can infer from these laws that Jews enjoyed the wealth and status that accompanied curial obligations. But the fact that all of these conflicting laws are preserved in the Theodosian Code makes clear that the Code is not just establishing precedent but also conveying anxiety about Jewish financial authority. Do wealthy Jews have the same responsibilities, and do they receive the same honors as wealthy Christians and pagans? Does their religious scrupulosity (as *superstitio* implies) require accommodation or not? Are their "heads of synagogues" analogous to Christian bishops? (Indeed, are their synagogues analogous to churches?) There is clear discomfort with Jewish privilege. In the 6th century Justinian settled the matter by declaring that Jews bore the financial responsibilities of the decurionate but should receive none of its accompanying honors.

Similar concern for the economic status of individual Jews appears in laws about Jewish ownership of enslaved non-Jews. A law surviving from the 3rd century threatens any Jewish person who circumcises an enslaved non-Jew with banishment or capital punishment. Christian law focuses on Jewish enslavement of Christians. A Constantinian law bans Jews from circumcising enslaved Christians. Later laws construe such circumcision as forcing Christians to participate in Jewish rituals (or even forcing them to become Jews). Given that, in the Roman Empire, enslavers had more or less full control over the bodies of those enslaved to them, this singling-out of Jews and circumcision is a noteworthy exception. The prohibition expands: by the late 4th century Jews are prohibited from owning enslaved Christians at all. Then, in the 5th century, Jews are allowed to keep enslaved Christians as long as the enslaved can keep "their own *religio*." A few years later comes another about-face, a recapitulation of a ban on enslaved Christians in Jewish households. In the 6th century, Justinian issues several laws reiterating this ban.

As a window into Jewish social history these laws are not especially revelatory: wealthy Jews, like all propertied elites in the Roman world, participated in the dehumanizing commerce of enslaved people vital to the empire's economy. But what do we make of the repeated ban on Jews circumcising enslaved men? Did some Jews interpret the Bible (e.g., Gen. 17:13) as requiring the incorporation of enslaved men into Israel? Or do these laws reflect deep suspicion of and anxiety about Jewish circumcision that predated and persisted well into the Christian Roman period? Much like the inconsistent laws on Jewish decurions, this centuries-long spate of laws tells a complex story about the limits of Jewish economic subjectivity under the law, constrained by considerations of religious difference. It would have been typical to require enslaved people to participate in the household religion of their enslavers; that Jews are repeatedly denied this privilege, even as they are imagined to desire it, diminishes their economic autonomy.

That emperors felt the need to reiterate this prohibition over 200 years may show that Jews continue to own enslaved Christians; it may also show that anxiety over Jewish economic superiority continued to trouble the Christian Empire.

Jewish economic subjectivity is also addressed on a corporate level in multiple laws about synagogues. Pre-Christian Roman law recognizes these buildings as the communal property of Jewish communities and thus exempt from burdens placed on individual households as, for example, in one law, the compulsory quartering of soldiers. Christian law also recognizes synagogues as "places of *religio*" and grants them protections analogous to Christian churches. Several laws prohibit damage to synagogues that was done "in the name of the Christian religion." One law even requires that Jewish communities be compensated for destroyed and damaged synagogues, and, if their synagogue has been consecrated as a church (one imagines against their will), they must be compensated for the loss of the building.

Emperors' repeated imprecations against synagogue destruction indicate that Christians were, out of piety or brutality or both, targeting synagogues for damage and destruction. We know of one very famous case of a synagogue burned down by Christian monks in the late 4th century in the eastern garrison town of Callinicum; despite the laws punishing such acts, Emperor Theodosius I, under pressure from Bishop Ambrose of Milan, declined to penalize the arsonists or enforce the required compensation. But are we to imagine waves of synagogue arsons throughout the 4th, 5th, and 6th centuries? Given that we know of quite large and lavish synagogues being expanded and adorned into the 5th century, as at Sardis and Aphrodisias, it is difficult to imagine synagogues under constant threat. (If John Chrysostom is to be believed, the synagogue of Antioch was rather too popular with Christians in the 380s.)

Christians derived some satisfaction imagining Jewish synagogues in danger of destruction, lightly restrained by imperial sanction. Synagogues created cognitive dissonance in the Christianizing city landscape where, by contrast, public performance of pagan rituals was gradually outlawed by the 5th century. It is unsurprising, then, that the same laws prohibiting Christian destruction of synagogues and requiring compensation for damages also prohibit Jews from building new synagogues or repairing damaged ones. Christian law imagines synagogues crumbling and disappearing on their own, Jewish presence fading away naturally to make way for Christianization.

A *novella* of Justinian hints at imperial impatience with this gradual disappearance. The law, issued in the reconquered provinces of North

Africa, reiterates the ban on Jews owning enslaved Christians and on Jews circumcising unbaptized enslaved Christians; the emperor then abruptly orders Jewish synagogues to be seized and rebuilt as churches. The contemporary historian Procopius reports a similar order in reconquered territory east of Carthage, adding that Justinian "managed" to get the Jews to "become" Christians. Procopius might mean that Justinian forced Jews to be baptized (as would happen in the 7th century under the emperor Heraclius in the same area) or that the seizure of the Jews' synagogue accomplished the same effect. Notably, Justinian issued these extreme laws in a newly reconquered and tenuously held territory and not, say, in his own backyard; also, notably, he included this legal ruling, and its fantasy of a landscape swept clean of Jews and Judaism, in his legal compendium to preserve and disseminate that fantasy in his capital city.

Social Jews

Laws about social relations – family, dress, class, professional status – are always entangled in economics. Laws about Jews and the decurionate try to disentangle financial obligation from social prestige. Laws concerning Jewish ownership of enslaved Christians may have been as much about social relations as economic autonomy. Recent scholarship has highlighted the sexual vulnerability of enslaved men and women; the repeated attention to Jewish ownership of Christian bodies may evoke fears expressed by Christian orators and writers about Jews' dangerous and uncontrolled sexuality.

Social and economic concerns may also be linked in a law forbidding Jews from engaging in *consortium* (business? sexual relations? marriage? the term could mean any or all three) with (non-Jewish?) women employed in the imperial weaving factories. A more straightforward law from 388 prohibits marriage between Jews and Christians entirely. The penalty for intermarriage was the same as that for adultery: obligatory dissolution of the marriage and referral to the courts for possible capital punishment. Marriage laws are about social regulation but they are also about economics, as legal *matrimonium* was a mechanism for the intergenerational transfer of wealth within families. Likewise, a late 4th-century law prohibiting Jewish "marriage custom," specifically polygyny, may be as much about moral regulation as the smooth transfer of property within families.

Unlike later medieval laws, we see little restriction of Jewish professional status except in appointment to offices where Jews might issue legal judgments against Christians. A law of 425 includes among its proscriptions a decree that "Jews and pagans" cannot serve in legal or municipal offices in which they might rule against Christians. A *novella* of Theodosius II affirms this expulsion of Jews (and Samaritans) from any office from which they might wield the law against Christians. Justinian, predictably, pushes these laws even further and forbids Jews, except in very limited circumstances, from even testifying against Christians in the courts.

Laws concerning the social status of Jewish leaders in Palestine raise questions about how Jews could fit within the Christianizing social landscape of the Roman Empire. A late 4th-century law speaks of "primates ... noble and illustrious patriarchs," who have the sole right to determine who is included and excluded from Jewish communities. Other laws assert that these "illustrious patriarchs" are legally protected from "public insult" and must be accorded all of the "privileges" due their status. Other epistolary and literary sources give us some insight into the patriarchate. This hereditary office in Palestine, which had some social connection to the nascent circle of rabbis there, enjoyed high status among Jews and non-Jews throughout the Roman Empire.

The status of the patriarch among diaspora Jews is affirmed by references in Roman law to an annual collection of "gold and silver" sent by diaspora synagogues to support the patriarch. The patriarch's imperial prestige is clear from the titles employed in these laws: *clarissimus*, *illustris*, and *spectabilis* were all titles conferred to men with imperial aristocratic status, accompanied by varied formal and informal privileges. When the patriarch begins appearing in Roman laws in the late 4th century, this status seems already to be an issue. First, the collection of "gold and silver" is halted, and any funds are redirected from the patriarch's agents into the imperial treasury. Less than a decade later, this annual collection is restored. Ten years after that, the emperors strip the patriarch Gamaliel of his honorary imperial status; in 429 Theodosius II redirects any annual collection of funds that might have gone to the patriarch to the imperial treasury. Justinian edited this law into his own code, effectively transforming it into a special tax on Jewish communities.

Much like the back-and-forth laws about enslavement and synagogues, these laws about the patriarch, his privileges, and his eventual demotion give us hints of social history and insight into Christian Roman ideology. From a social historical perspective, we can track the rise and fall of a high-status provincial family leveraging the (perhaps) unique situation of a network of affinity-based meeting-houses (synagogues) to build a social network of prestige and parlay that network into financial support and imperial status. If other empire-wide affinity groups established similar hereditary networks, they remain invisible to us, at least in the legal record; by contrast, the patriarchate is an object of ongoing judicial concern. The legal attention to the patriarchate reveals, from an ideological perspective, the anxiety over Jewish social status on an imperial scale. Eventually, the only way to resolve the cognitive dissonance of *Jews with power* was to remove the patriarch's status while leaving in place the financial and social Jewish network, now directed at the emperor and his treasury. That is, much as with the laws about Jewish decurions, Jews remain a collective object of imperial attention and financial obligation without any concomitant access to social status or prestige. Christian Roman law expresses repeated concern that Jews might gain status over Christians, whether through enslavement, marriage, or imperial privilege.

Religious Jews

Speaking of "religion" as a discrete category in this period risks anachronism, but it is clearly the case that Christian law identifies groups of legal subjects according to their mode of religious worship apart from any ethnic or geographic identity: pagans, "orthodox," heretics, Samaritans, "heaven-worshipers," and Jews. Some have argued that legal compendia like the Theodosian Code may be one place where we see something like our concept of *religion* coming into being. Not only are groups singled out for special treatment based on their religion, but the practices we might identify as *religious* are identified and subject to legal regulation. The final book of the Theodosian Code and the first book of Justinian's Code both treat topics we would call *religious*.

Christian Roman law grants Jews certain forms of religious autonomy, such as the ability to adjudicate their own religious conflicts and have these religious judgments enforced by Roman authorities. Like the laws about clerical tax exemption and synagogue protection, the legal logic at work is an implicit analogy between Christian and Jewish religious privilege: during this same period we see the rise of "episcopal courts" that were granted the right to adjudicate legal matters between Christians. Several laws acknowledge the sanctity of Jewish holy days by protecting Jews from being summoned to conduct legal or financial business on the Sabbath or other holy days. This protection, issued in the 5th century and affirmed by Justinian in the 6th, again envisions Jewish religious protections as analogous to those granted to Christians, for whom Sunday and other holy days were similarly protected.

Once the law puts into place the analogous categories of *Jew* and *Christian* it creates the possibility of legal subjects moving from one category to the other through conversion. Throughout this period Christian law fretted over ex-Jewish Christians and ex-Christian Jews. As for the latter – Christians who have become Jews – the law was unequivocal: a law of Constantius II (Constantine's son) in 353 threatens Christians who join the "sacrilegious meetings" of Jews with imperial confiscation of property. According to a later law, Christians who attend Jewish rituals (or pagan or Manichean rites) lose their right to transmit property to their heirs. Finally, a law of 409 condemns those who "force" Christians to be "tainted by Jewish perversity alien to the Roman Empire." The message of these laws is clear: to move from Christian truth to Jewish falsehood is to cede one's social, economic, and even political status.

Laws about Jews converting to Christianity are more ambiguous. A law issued by Constantine that prohibited the Jewish circumcision of enslaved Christians also issues sanctions against Jews who "attack" or "injure" Jews who "choose to be Christian." Two later laws also hint at retribution against Jewish converts to Christianity: laws issued in 426 and 527 forbid Jews from disinheriting children or grandchildren who become Christian, even if these descendants have been found guilty of crimes that would otherwise allow for disinheritance. Two additional laws from the 4th and 5th centuries speculate that Jews might be converting to Christianity in order to wriggle out of pending civil or criminal actions (although what mechanism conversion would provide for such legal relief is unstated). The latter law, from 416, even goes so far as to empower judges to ascertain the sincerity of a Jew's conversion and, if it is found lacking, to "allow them to return to their own law," that is, to revert.

From a social historical perspective we might learn, unsurprisingly, that sometimes Jews became Christians and Christians became Jews. (The penalties for conversion to Judaism were irrelevant for most imperial subjects, who lacked property and did not write wills.) What is more revealing in these laws are their ideological assumptions, transformed into legal realities. First is the very notion of conversion, that one must be either a Jew or a Christian: participating in the festivals and rituals of a religion takes on an ontological status rather than allowing for a more fluid, situational approach to religious life. Second is the notion that conversion is socially disruptive: the law imagines families disrupted, violence against converts, obligations evaded. Most surprising to modern readers may be that Christian Roman law does not encourage

Jewish conversion to Christianity. Instead, the law reiterates the social and ideological troublesomeness of the ex-Jewish Christian.

These laws on conversion also show Christian Rome's eagerness to regulate the specifics of Jewish religious customs and rites. One 5th-century law (which I address below) forbids Jews from setting fire to effigies of Haman during the festival of Purim. Our most detailed intervention into the religious practices of Jews comes from a *novella* of Justinian near the end of our historical period, probably issued in 553. Ostensibly written in response to Jewish "petitions," the *novella* issues several commands about synagogue rites. First, the law permits reading of "holy books" (the Bible) in Greek or Latin; for Greek the synagogues must use the Septuagint (favored by Christians) or, in a pinch, the post-Septuagint Greek translation of Aquila, which some Jewish communities may have already used. Jews are also forbidden from adding "supplements" to their readings of the Bible; this term, *deuterōseis*, has occasioned much commentary among historians of Judaism since the Greek word may refer to the Mishnah (both mean "repetition"). The law continues by compelling the expulsion from synagogues of those who deny the resurrection, angels, last judgment, or God's creation, all of which were probably well accepted among most Jews. Finally the law hopes that, by hearing the Bible in Greek, Jews will move away from the "bare letter" and embrace Scripture's deeper, spiritual meaning.

Were Jews arguing over whether the Bible might be read in Greek or Latin in synagogues? (If so, where? In Constantinople? Throughout the empire?) Did they appeal to the emperor for a definitive ruling on the matter? Does Justinian (or his legislator) betray knowledge of rabbinic influence by banning *deuterōseis*? Is the goal of the law merely regulation of Jewish religious custom or, as the final clause might hint, a subtle push toward Jewish acceptance of Christian truth? More accessible are the ideological underpinnings and possible effects of such a law. Roman law Christianizes Jewish ritual practice by subordinating it to Christian interests: the insistence on Greek, the list of required beliefs, the hope for spiritual enlightenment are all Christian impositions on Jews and Judaism. What's more, the law portrays Jews as seeking out this Christian judicial intervention. Here we arrive perhaps at the ideological goal of Christian laws on Jews and Judaism in this period: not elimination, not coercion, not conversion, but total legal subjection of Jews *as Jews* to Christian Rome. Only through such subjection and legal constraint can Jews be imagined into a Christianizing world.

CONCLUSIONS: RIOTS AT PURIM

Is it possible to imagine how Jews positioned themselves in this Christianizing world? To gauge the possibilities I turn to a law I mentioned above, from 408, included in both the Theodosian Code and Justinian's Code. It reads:

> Governors of the provinces shall prohibit Jews, at a particular commemoration of a festival, from setting fire to Haman (as a memorial of his erstwhile punishment) and from burning an image made to look like the holy cross in disdain for Christian faith with a sacrilegious intent, so they may not mix up the symbol of our faith with their frivolities; but let them maintain their rituals without disdain for Christian law; for without doubt they are going to lose what up to now has been permitted to them if they don't refrain from what is illegal.
>
> (*Codex Theodosianus* 16.8.18; *Codex Justinianus* 1.9.11)

Christians may have witnessed ritual immolations of Haman on the gallows (see Esth. 7:10) and misread the hanging figure as a crucified one. Jews may have folded anti-Christian sentiment into their commemoration of a historic instance of persecution and redemption (celebrated roughly one month before Passover and Easter). Both may have been true in different times and places. Scholars often point to a horrifying story in the 5th-century *Church History* of Socrates Scholasticus (d. c. 440). Some Jews drunkenly enjoying "frivolous pastimes" were "making fun of the cross"; they got carried away, kidnapped a Christian child (or an enslaved Christian; the Greek term *paidion* could mean either), lashed him to a cross, mocked him, and killed him. Socrates does not specify the incident took place at Purim; rather, the law from 408, the drunkenness, and the cross for some modern interpreters place this early version of a blood libel at that festival.

I do not take Socrates as evidence for a real Jewish act; likewise, I do not take the law as clear evidence for Jewish activities (burning Haman) or intentions (mocking the crucifixion of Christ). The obvious ideological framing of both lines up with what we see in other literary and legal contexts: the marginalization of Jewish life and Judaism in the service of normalizing Christian life and Christianization. On the one hand, Jews and Judaism are so utterly other to the Christian world around them they can be imagined as bloodthirsty monsters. On the other hand, Jews are so subjected they can be contained by the stern warning of the imperial legislator that they will "lose what up to now has been permitted to them," an ominous but vague threat of, perhaps, extermination.

When it comes to Jews and Judaism in the late Roman Empire, Christianization was not the imposition of a singular Christian framework on all subjects; it was a way of viewing and integrating the Jewish "other" into Christian Rome, of making Jews and Judaism into one more opportunity for Christianizing acts of legal and social subjection. In this imagined state the fearsome otherness of Jews was constrained in the margins by legal handicaps and vague threats. Legal imagination can place limits of material existence. I do not doubt that Jewish life suffered in the face of legislative Christianizing. But we must also allow ourselves to imagine Jews creating a new kind of life precisely by inhabiting those fearsome margins, engaging in "frivolities" right up to those legal limits – or, on occasion, beyond those limits. Did Jews really imagine the face of Christ, or the Roman emperor, on the effigy of Haman, even after the law forbade "burning" the effigy? After the issuance of this law, surely some must have despite and because of the prohibition. Legal imagination may desire constraint, but it cannot help but conjure up even small moments of joy and resistance.

Further Reading

Bonfil, R., et al., eds., *Jews in Byzantium: Dialectics of Minority and Majority Cultures* (Leiden, 2011). While many of the essays extend beyond our period, several treat the early Byzantine period, including an essay by Amnon Linder (see below) on "The Legal Status of Jews in the Byzantine Empire."

Horowitz, E. S., *Reckless Rites: Purim and the Legacy of Jewish Violence* (Princeton, NJ, 2006). A study of the long tradition of imputing violence to Jewish celebrations of Purim, including the long history of the Jewish law of 408 and Socrates Scholasticus's account.

Humfress, C., *Orthodoxy and the Courts in Late Antiquity* (Oxford, 2007). A detailed and lucid explanation of how law worked in the late Roman Empire, with particular attention to the "forensic" rhetoric that shaped Christian discourses of orthodoxy and heresy.

Kraemer, R. S., *The Mediterranean Diaspora in Late Antiquity: What Christianity Cost the Jews* (New York, 2020). A careful sifting of the literary, documentary, and material evidence for Jewish life under the Christian Roman Empire which surveys the transformations and survivals dimly visible to us.

Linder, A., *Jews in Roman Imperial Legislation* (Detroit, MI, 1987). A collection of all extant Roman laws pertaining to Jews and Judaism in their original languages and English translation with introductions, copious notes, and bibliography.

Monnickendam, Y., "Late Antique Christian Law in the Eastern Roman Empire: Toward a New Paradigm," *Studies in Late Antiquity* 2 (2018), 40–83. An important essay on comparative legal history bringing together Greek, Jewish, Christian, and Roman legal texts and theories.

Tolan, J., et al., eds., *Jews in Early Christian Law: Byzantium and the Latin West, 6th–11th Centuries* (Turnhout, 2014). "Law" in these essays encompasses state law (under Rome, the successor states, and Byzantium) as well as canon law and other religious regulations. Of particular importance for this period is the lucid contribution of R. W. Mathisen, "The Citizenship and Legal Status of Jews in Roman Law during Late Antiquity (ca. 300–540 CE)."

7 Antisemitism in Byzantium, 4th–7th Centuries

STEVEN B. BOWMAN

"Anti-Semitism" (now more commonly written as antisemitism) was a 19th-century term coined by a German, Wilhelm Marr, in 1879 on the basis of the ethnic rivalry discovered by earlier German philologists in 2 Maccabees of the second century BCE. This rivalry between Hellenes and Jews – Hellenismos and Joudaismos in the language of the ancient source – was now updated to a perceived rivalry between contemporary Germans and Jews. The opposition between Deutschtum and Judenthum was generated in the attempt to replace the abolition of the Holy Roman Empire in 1806 by the new French emperor Napoleon Bonaparte with the novel identity of "nationalism," inspired by the US, French, and later Greek revolutions. Since the Jews had been perceived and treated as the excluded Other by Christian Europe for the past two millennia, they had now become the natural other, "chosen" to reify the opposition to a new German national identity, hence "Antisemitism" or, more commonly, "antisemitism." The question is whether such a modern term as "antisemitism" can be properly applied to the complicated religious and political situation in the Christian Roman Empire of the 4th–7th centuries.

The Christianization of the Roman Empire during the 4th–7th centuries made official the animosity for Jews and Judaism already initiated in the Gospels and early Church Fathers. The 4th century initiated the period of Late Antiquity, according to Peter Brown, while the Islamization of the Middle East in the 7th century is a more reliable marker for the emergence of the Middle Ages. The term "Byzantine" is now commonly accepted to begin with the reign of Heraclius in the 7th century. The overused term "anti-Semitism or "antisemitism" is somewhat anachronistic applied to the Empire and Church for the period 4th–7th century when animosity for the Jews and Judaism was reified into the very structure of the new Christian civilization.

After several centuries of persecution, torture, and occasional massacre of Christians, the new imperator Constantine, having just reunited the Mediterranean wide empire, issued the Edict of Milan in 313 CE that proclaimed the Christians to be members of a *religio licita*, a legal collegium parallel to that of the Jews who had enjoyed that status since the last days of the Roman Republic, traditionally traceable to Julius Caesar. The 3rd-century persecutions of Christians by Decius and Diocletian were now at an end with Constantine's new policy to unite his empire based on a widely dispersed urban revolutionary religious group which proved to be quite loyal in the wake of the emperor's edict. Constantine went further and called a colloquium of bishops from throughout the empire to Nicaea in 325, where he ordered them to "hammer" out a common or "orthodox" credo to unite the various interpretations of the newly legalized religion. This the bishops did in raucous sessions during which each, supported by his aggressive monastic retinue, presented his understanding of the phenomenon of Jesus as the Christ and his relationship to the God who made the heaven and earth (cf. LXX 1, 1). The result of the colloquium presided over by the emperor himself made successive emperors the head of the new religion defined by the Nicaean Creed, the developing definition of Orthodoxy ("the correct opinion") obligatory on all Christians. Those who refused to agree were labeled as heterodox ("other or wrong opinion") and their bishops were anathematized and some banished from the empire, for example, Arius, who went north through the Balkans to the Germanic wandering tribes and converted them to his "opinion" with subsequent important ramifications for the Jews in the territories they conquered. The rival opinions (i.e., heresies) continued, however, to harass the empire and cause civic unrest that manifested in periodic attacks on Jews, their religion, and their synagogues.

The ecclesia, as the body of worshippers of the crucified messiah of the Jews was now called, engaged in a tripartite war: against the polytheists who constituted the vast majority of the population of the empire with their myriad of gods and goddesses, each with its coterie of priests and temples supported by the public treasury; against the Jewish monotheists who rejected the claim of the Christians to be the True Israel (*Verus Israel*); and against the heretics who had developed a wide variety of versions of Christianity, ranging from Jews who accepted Jesus as their long-awaited messianic redeemer to former polytheists (now called "pagans," meaning "country bumpkins") who accepted Paul's message.

The main gods of the polytheists were Isis and Serapis of Egypt, Mithra of the armies, the old Olympian gods and goddesses, the new imperial divine rulers deified after death (and in some cases even before), and a host of tribal and ethnic divinities, among others.

The polytheists maintained the tolerance of the ancient world save for the Manicheans, the dualist reincarnation of Zoroastrianism which was to haunt the ecclesia (hence Church) as it influenced for a millennium its emerging theology.

The Jews (also known as Hebrews, Judaeans, Israelites, and by other designations) constituted a widespread diaspora led by the Patriarch of the Jews whose administrative center was in the Galilee region of Palaestina Secunda (north-central Israel). He was the chief tax collector for Rome from the widespread Jewish diaspora out of which profits he trained administrators in Greek and Roman law as well as Jewish law. The latter had been codified in the late 2nd century by the Pharisees, who had survived the great revolt against Rome in the 1st century during which the central Temple in Jerusalem and the capital itself were destroyed. The Pharisees in their colloquium c. 90 CE canonized the Hebrew Scriptures – the Tanakh – which became the central identifying text of the Jews, and during the 2nd century they codified the Mishnah (i.e., "repetition"), which taught Jews how to live as Jews and regulated their communities. The Patriarch also controlled the Jewish calendar which imposed a practicing unity among the far-flung diaspora from Spain to Persia and England to Arabia. The Jewish diaspora flourished mostly in the urban centers of the empire as well as in agricultural settlements in the provinces of Palaestina Prima and Secunda (save for Jerusalem and its environs, from which they were legally banned). Their population is estimated at about 10 percent of the empire's population, perhaps an equal amount to that of the Christians before the increasing conversions to the latter in the 4th–6th centuries.

The Jews were in fact a nation, albeit conquered by Rome, allowed to live according to their own law (*Torah* or *dat*) and recognized by Roman law as a special entity. Christians too recognized the Jews' special status as keepers of the ancient promise of God to be a special people. Yet once Christians appropriated this special status themselves through their acceptance of Jesus as the descendant of David, hence the Messiah, as their own god, they pressured the Jews to convert in order to bring about the return of the messiah (Christ in Greek), who would initiate the End of Days as prophesized in both Jewish and Christian Scriptures. This eschatology was increasingly pursued from the reign of Justinian through that of Heraclius. Manichaean influence, based on Zoroastrian beliefs in the battle between Good and Evil, was Christianized into the competition between Jesus and the Devil, with the Jews now identified as the acolytes of Satan. The preaching of this message to the masses stirred them in their riots against the state and the pagan majority to also attack Jews, destroy their synagogues, and occasionally baptize them for the ultimate glory of their religion and their salvation.

The highly diverse range of heresies in the empire had to be curtailed in order for Constantine's new political base to be effective in his plan to reunite the empire, a policy pursued by emperors throughout the medieval empire and later by the Orthodox Church. The emperor was represented in the new imperial iconography as the representative of the sun (cf. Sol Invictus), an ancient tradition by the Egyptians and the Hellenes who often used local theophoric names. In addition to imperial laws, the Church was encouraged to continue to call local and regional councils to designate how to be a Christian and what to believe as well as how to avoid Jews and Jewish practices. The imperial laws were the first stage; the Nicaean Creed was the beginning of the second stage. Already in the Council of Elvira (in Spain c. 300) Christians were warned to avoid Jews, not to receive presents at Purim, and not to have rabbis bless their fields. Bishops were constantly warned against fraternizing with Jews and to be aware of Judaizing tendencies among their flocks. Bishops scoured the LXX translation of the Tanakh for prophetic castigations of the Jews, while preachers culled the gospels for the admonishments of Jesus against the Jews and the evangelical diatribes against the Scribes and Pharisees. This policy of insult and negativity toward practicing Jews instilled in the new Christian populaces an antipathy that turned to hatred over the years and indeed still continues, particularly at Easter when the Jews are accused of deicide (*theoktonoi* in Greek) and the murder of the prophets. So vile had the language devolved that heretics (in particular, Nestorians) were called "Jews," and so-called Judaizers were named in ecclesiastical treatises – along with Jews – as enemies of the Church, of Christians, of Jesus, and of God. The Septuagint, a Hellenistic translation of what was originally a Hebraic polemic against the polytheistic fertility religions of the ancient Near East, soon became a Christianized diatribe against the Jews. Jerome's 4th-century Latin translation of the Tanakh and intertestamental literature (apocrypha) added new sources for the preachers of the western, Latin-speaking part of the empire.

At the same time as the Christianization of the Hebrew Scriptures via Greek translations and the emerging canonization of the New Testament literature took place, other elements of Judaism were Christianized. The Books of Maccabees, for example, with their description of persecutions and martyrdom, as well as the Maccabees themselves, were sanctified as models of Christian saints (later to be joined by Philo and Josephus). Similarly, the Maccabean sites in Antioch – highly revered by the Jews – as well as Palaestina as a whole did not escape this process of absorption: a third province was carved out of the southern homeland of the Jews – Palaestina Tertia – and a wave of pilgrimages initiated by St. Helena, the mother of Constantine, himself soon to become a saint despite never being baptized (except perhaps on his deathbed). Monastic individuals flooded the deserts around the Dead Sea, and monasteries and churches dotted the pilgrim routes to provide hospitality and guides to salvation of worshippers. All sites mentioned in the Jewish and Christian testaments were claimed by the Church and land was ceded by the emperor; Church ownership of these sites has been in the main respected by subsequent governments to the present day. Helena's archaeological pilgrimage supposedly found the cross of the crucifixion and other relics, which initiated the great relic treasuries of Constantinople and Jerusalem. The Church of the Resurrection (later the Crusader Church of the Holy Sepulcher) in Jerusalem was soon built to enclose Golgotha, the hill of the crucifixion; the liturgy of the clergy that emerged in it became the most virulently anti-Jewish of the Orthodox Church. The immolation of Judas, the loyal apostle who, following his teacher's command, handed Jesus over to the Temple police, became an Easter tradition in the Orthodox and Latin Churches, and Judas became the bête noir of Christianity as well as the unpopular icon of Jews (Judaeans) and Judaism. The Holy Land was now a Christian bastion and in the process of a dejudaization that spewed anti-Jewish propaganda and polemic to the myriads of pilgrims that came to the land to worship their savior, the high point of their religious life. Jewish (and Samaritan) revolts in the Galilee (and Mount Grizim, respectively), where their population predominated, were frequent during the 4th to 7th centuries especially following the dissolution by Theodosius II of the office of the Patriarch of the Jews in 429 and the subsequent dismemberment of his administration and academies.

The 4th–7th centuries were characterized by periodic waves of persecution of the Jews that included occasional forced baptisms in Carthage, Spain, France, southern Italy, and elsewhere. The Jewish communities suffered Christian attempts to unify the Empire and degrade Jews in the expectation of converting them. From 313 CE, Christians gloried in their domination of Jerusalem and attempted to Christianize the former capital of the Jews. Constantine strengthened Hadrian's ban on Jewish settlement in Jerusalem and its environs and turned the Temple Mount into the city's garbage dump, a process highly praised by St. Jerome. For three centuries Christian menstrual rags were shipped to Jerusalem and covered the sacred stone (*sakhra*) in the Holy of Holies of the Temple. In the wake of the Arab Muslim liberation of the city in 638, Arabs and a few Jews cleaned the *sakhra* and Jews were allowed to return to the city to clean and tend the Temple Mount. Construction rubble had all but obliterated any trace of the Temple save for the annual pilgrimage of Jews on the 9th of Ab to circumambulate the walls of the city, point out its memorials, and weep over its destruction. The local Christians and pilgrims rejoiced at their misery and perversely named the western surviving wall of Herod's expansion of the Temple plateau the "Wailing Wall," an insult that continues to characterize the *Kotel* to this day. Justinian built the huge Ta Nea Church overlooking the Temple Mount which he claimed outdid Solomon's Temple (now under a parking lot in the Jewish Quarter) and Heraclius restored the "True Cross" after defeating the Sassanians, who had taken it as a trophy when they conquered Jerusalem. The "True Cross" has been fragmented into myriads of slivers and dispersed as relics throughout the Christian world.

Meanwhile, legal restrictions on the polytheistic clergy proceeded apace with the Christianization or destruction of their temples; the clergy was removed from public treasury support, which left many unemployed. Many undoubtedly found refuge in the Church or joined Arius and Nestorius in their missionary wanderings. It was not until the reign of Justinian that the philosophical schools in Athens were closed in 529. Many of the unemployed likely joined the Church or migrated to more hospitable environs, for example, Persia. With the failure of the Emperor Julian (361–362) to revive the ancient gods and even sponsoring the rebuilding of the Jewish Temple in Jerusalem, the polytheists (now pejoratively called Hellenes) continued to decline until their final rebellion c. 395, which dates the end of the polytheistic threat, although not their ubiquitous survival, to resume cult and power.

Despite the vicissitudes of the Jews as increasingly second-class citizens, their fate was assuredly better than the deteriorating status of heretics and pagans. Roman law was increasingly Christianized to the Orthodox Credo and pressures on the Jews to become Orthodox were mounted in two stages under aggressive emperors: Constantine to Theodosius in 4th–5th centuries and Justinian in the 6th, leading to Heraclius's persecutions in the 7th. The majority of Jewry laws in the Theodosian and Justinian codes (*Codex theodosianus* and *Coden Justinianus*) were ostensibly meant to protect Christians from any control or interference by Jews. Heretics could be salvaged if they converted, but many chose to emigrate or die. Pagans went underground. Jews in the main took a low profile or were rewarded should they convert; their legal scholars used the toleration implicit in Roman law, as well as the messianic hopes of the Christian clergy, to survive the periodic laws (many of which were observed in the breach) and pogroms stimulated by zealous bishops and fanatic monks.

Theodosius I in 383 made Orthodoxy the official religion of the Empire; his namesake Theodosius II issued in 438 the first official Roman law code, which incorporated the first section of Jewry law, a collection of Roman laws referring to Jews dating back to Julius Caesar. The laws were ad hoc responses to various local developments through the intervening centuries and had become more restrictive of Jewish rights as citizens since 212, when the emperor Caracalla extended the rights of citizenship to every free man in the empire. Such laws restricted the political, military, legal, and financial rights of Jews; restricted ownership of slaves; and forbade intermarriage with the women workers in the imperial textile factories (a kind of industrial theft) on pain of death (Jews for religious purposes had to produce kosher clothing, an industry that existed since their first settlements among the Hellenes). Finally, in 429 Theodosius recognized the absence of a successor to Gamliel VI, the Patriarch of the Jews, so that the office remained unfilled until its disappearance. The leadership status of the descendants of David was a major tension between Christians and Jews and was connected with the interpretation of Genesis 49:10, namely, who was the expected messiah and who is his legitimate successor as representative in the meantime: Was it the Roman Emperor, whether Heraclius or even Charlemagne, the Pope in Rome, the Patriarch of the Jews in Palaestina, or the Exilarch in Babylonia? Along with the tripartite division of Palaestina, this law ended the universal leadership of the Jews in the Roman Empire, ended the income for the training of religious and fiscal administrators, and ended the salaries of the scholars who worked on the expanding commentary to the Mishnah (the Talmud of the Land of Israel, also known as the Talmud of Tiberius). These individuals now dispersed among the leaderless communities of the empire, contributing to the decentralization of the Jews hampered by the restrictive laws of the Theodosian Code.

This political pressure on the Jews and the subsequent polemics by the emerging ecclesiastical spokesmen no doubt contributed through conversion to the demographic decline of the Jewish populations of their diaspora for the next millennium. The new literature of the

Church had proliferated from the collected memories of Jesus' disciples in the wake of his martyrdom and the vastly influential propaganda of a Pharisee called Saul turned disciple as Paul (whose prolific travels and letters predate the four gospels of Jesus' life and career). The Orthodox gospels were compiled in the wake of the violent war with Rome (66–73 CE) and reflect the developing animosity to the defeated Jews following the major revolts under Trajan and Hadrian. The Gospels of Mark, Matthew, Luke, and John along with the sophisticated letters of Paul gradually replaced the plethora of gospels and theological tracts of the emerging Christian literature as the official doctrines of Constantine's imperial religion. This codification in Greek, later translated to Latin by St. Jerome, was due to the prodigious efforts of Eusebius Bishop of Caesarea, the father of Christian historiography, "archaeology" of the Holy Land, and his major defenses of the new Orthodoxy: *Praeperatio evangelica* and *Demonstratio evangelica*. Even so, a continuing literature of apocryphal gospels and treatises survived and proliferated with the translations of various apocalyptic oriental treatises that served to illuminate the impending end of this world with the reappearance of the messiah Jesus. The Book of Revelations served as a centrifugal source that radiated through the heresies and sects of the emerging religion.

While polemics against the Hellenes (also called "pagans") continued, polemics against Jews proliferated in an attempt to separate Christians from Jews. Constantine had already decreed that Pasxa (Easter) was not to follow the Jewish Pesax (Passover); Justinian reissued this decree in the mid-6th century. However, this attitude toward Jews and Judaism in a way hampered Christians' struggle for their own survival and ultimate conquest of the empire. From the perspective of Christian doxa, Jews had to continue to exist since they represented the authentic descendants of Abraham, David, the prophets, and Jesus himself, who was born, lived, and died as a Jew, as did the authors of the Gospels (save for Luke) and nearly all of the heroes of the emerging New Testament. Gregory of Tours, in one of his many letters, advised that "Just as it is permitted to the Jews according to the law [*Codex theodosianus*] this much is allowed and no more," thus defending their legitimate status. Second, the Jews were the authors and guardians of the Sacred Scriptures even if they misinterpreted them to the detriment of Christianity. Augustine Bishop of Hippo commented on Psalm 59:11 – "Slay them not [the Jews] lest my people [the Christians] forget" – in the wake of continued attacks by Christians against Jews, particularly in Alexandria and Antioch as well as continued revolts in Palaestina. The fiery Easter sermons of St. John Chrysostom against Christians who celebrated Passover with Jews and attended synagogues stirred up anti-Jewish sentiments and provoked riots. Christianity thus held a two-pronged attitude to the Jews: they must disappear or be converted to Christianity, so that the long-awaited messiah Jesus might return to usher in the Kingdom of Heaven. The survival of the stiff-necked Jews prevented that salvation even as they persisted since "antiquity" – a highly respected concept among the ancient Greeks and a major theme in Eusebius's historical enterprise. Similarly, Origen's great effort to establish a polyglot anthology of Bible texts was indebted to Jewish scriptural efforts through the centuries, as was Eusebius's great project to Christianize a world history based on a biblical vision.

The dream of converting all the Jews was pursued through legal harassment and outright violence by the great mob of Christian masses led by the new monastic movement. The higher clergy mostly condemned the attacks, especially the consecration of synagogues, for example, Callinicum, which Ambrose condoned, although not the consecration of pagan temples by monks, even though both groups – Jews and Hellenes – were still legal religious groups in the 4th century. Even so, polemics proliferated. An anonymous scholar of Latin rhetoric about the time of Emperor Julian penned a treatise that – based on Josephus's seminal apologetic study and memoir of the Jewish War with Rome – castigated the Jews for their responsibility in the death of the Christian messiah (Jesus Christos), declaring that the destruction of Jerusalem and the Temple was God's punishment in fulfillment of Jesus' prophecy that the Temple would be destroyed. This text later designated as Hegesippus or Pseudo Hegesippus – a variant of Josephus – would not be answered until the 9th–10th century by an anonymous Jewish scholar in southern Italy in a more nationalistic apologia for Judaism (Sepher Yosippon).

Christian polemics ranged from abolition of the Hebrew Scriptures by Marcion (2nd century) whose teachings – although rejected by the official church – did survive unofficially in the emerging Christian Bible which included the Hebrew Scriptures (TaNaKh; later designated the [superseded] Old Testament by Eusebius compared with the New Testament). The ancient emphasis of the Christian polemic was the Jewish guilt in the death of Jesus and the Jews' eternal curse, which justified their continued downfall. Christian literature considered the Jews as troublemakers politically and socially and as religious tempters of Christians. This emphasis on the Jewish danger became the sustained ingredient in the developing Christian literature leading to the reign of Justinian as Roman emperor in the 6th century. Justinian's code of Roman law became the basis for the subsequent law codes of the Roman Christians and the western portion of the empire until the proclamation of the Napoleonic Code of the 19th century, and in the eastern Christian world until the Russian Revolution of the 20th century. Justinian's code earned him the epithet of Great, but he was the bane of the Jews. His code curtailed outdated laws and updated the Theodosian collection of Jewry laws in a decidedly hostile manner to the Jews, in derogatory and restricting language. His near destructions of the Samaritan branch of the Jewish ethnos after their rebellion was matched by his designation of Judaism as a "superstition" and heresy which bordered on a criminal charge. His most egregious interference in the Jewish fate is contained in his Novella 146, issued in 553 in response to a controversy in an unidentified community (presumably Constantinople) over whether the regular readings of the Torah be recited in Hebrew or in Greek. He sanctioned the reading of Scriptures in any language, preferring that of the Septuagint, which had become the sacred text authenticating and authorizing Christianity. He prohibited the "deuterosis" – either the mishnaic law code or the entire oral tradition of midrash and Halakhah which defined the Jewish religion; he also threatened the death penalty for the political and religious leaders who rejected "resurrection, 'judgement,' the work of God, or that angels are part of creation." In this Novella then, Justinian, in his capacity as Pontifex Maximus, that is, head of Orthodoxy, interfered directly with Judaism, heretofore a *religio licita*, and curtailed its further development in the empire. At the same time, Romanos, the great Melodist of the Byzantine Church, more than likely of Syrian Jewish origin, was creating his memorable *kontakia* (hymns), which contained numerous attacks on the Jews alongside his intricate summary of New Testament themes. Their effect would only strengthen anti-Jewish sentiments, particularly during their Easter recital. His melodic creativity is contemporaneous with the flourishing of the Palestinian Jewish *piyyut* (from Greek *poesia*), which further influenced the Jewish tradition castigated and prohibited by the emperor; however, the synagogue service was not affected. Yannai, the well-known poet in Palaestina, it is recently suggested, composed at the time of the Samaritan (and Jewish) revolts in Palaestina (555–556). His intricate compositions are replete with messianic allusions and warnings against potential rebellion to anticipate a divine redemption.

The emperors continued to recognize the legal status of the Jews even as they restricted their legal rights and interfered with Judaism as a *religio licita*. Constantine had already decreed that Pasxa (Easter) was not to follow the Jewish Pesax; Justinian reissued this decree in the mid-6th century. Zeno issued a law against the celebration of Purim (*Codex theodosianus* 16.18.18) in 408 which involved the immolation of Haman on a cross and was considered an anti-Christian icon. The higher clergy protected Jewish rights even though some of them produced virulent polemics and riot-inciting sermons that attacked Jews and their synagogues. Antioch and Alexandria were the two main ancient centers of Christianity that differed over their theological interpretations of Jesus: Was he God or man or the Christ of the Bible; did he have One Will or Two? Each opinion had its overzealous clergy: Cyril in Alexandria, who banished the Jews, and Chrysostom in Antioch, who railed against the synagogues and proudly orated, "I hate the Jews." Already Jews were accused of being in league with Satan and being Satan's acolytes in this world. A second disturbing factor was the popularity of the circus factions – the Greens and the Blues, named after the colors worn by their favorite chariot racers. They frequently rioted and theology fueled the animosity between them. In late 5th-century Antioch the Greens fought the Blues and massacred the Jews, who were well established in the city since antiquity. During the reign of Zeno, riots in the hippodrome saw the Greens attacking the Blues and their allies the Jews, whom they killed. An earlier synagogue there named for the Maccabees had been turned into a church in the late 4th century. A further attack followed, instigated by a fanatic monk, and the Greens burned a major synagogue in the southern section of Antioch. They desecrated the graveyard and burned the bodies. Zeno angrily commented that the Greens should have burned the live Jews instead.

Attacks on Jews and synagogues induced emperors to issue laws protecting their Jewish citizens despite Christian mobs and ecclesiastical protest, for example, Ambrose versus Theodosius I in 388 regarding the destruction of the synagogue in Callinicum. Ambrose argued that Christian piety superseded Roman law and the destruction was justified recompense for Jewish attacks on Christian churches during Julian's reign twenty-five years earlier. Theodosius II later rejected this argument and delicately emphasized that the rule of law should be applied even as he warned the Jews against committing any irreverence toward the Christian religion. Justinian reissued two of the laws in the *Codex theodosianus* but reduced the compensation for damages by half to only twice the value of the damage.

The ecclesiastical canons against the Jews were mostly concerned with creating barriers between Christians and Jews through fear of Judaizing influences. This was the main concern of the Church that was expressed in increasingly vituperative terms, echoing, and even surpassing, the biblical prophetic polemics against pagan polytheists. Such weekly attacks, especially on holidays like Easter, inflamed the congregations (as they still do in various Christian and Muslim settings), resulting in occasional riots and attacks paralleling the violence that accompanied the circus races wherein Jews were active participants and occasional rioters. In the apocryphal Canons of the Apostles that appeared in the late 4th century, four of its eighty-five rules prohibit clerical contact with Jews. This pattern was already established with the Council of Elvira c. 300 and continued in subsequent councils through the Quinisect (in Trullo) Council of 691.

Justinian (527–565) was both Imperator and Pontifex Maximus. As imperator he was in charge of the army and the state administration, both of which he used to authorize his new code (*Corpus juris civilis* of 529) that became the basis for all subsequent law codes in Byzantium and beyond. He ordered his armies to reconquer the areas lost to the Germanic invasions during the previous century, for example, parts of Italy, Spain, and North Africa. He had to deal with effects of the outbreak of the devastating plague (perhaps bubonic) that Procopius described in the words of Thucydides's account of the great plague during the Athens–Sparta 30 Years' War. Justinian, with the strong support of the empress Theodora, also had to deal with the Nike riots in his own capital in which Jews are cited as participating. As Pontifex Maximus he was also head of the Church and dealt with its internal heresies, in particular, that of the Monophysites centered primarily in Egypt, home of his wife Theodora. He proposed a compromise between the Monophysites and the Nicaean Orthodox which produced the Melkite Church. His Novella 146 of 553 interfered with the beliefs and practice of Judaism in response to an internal struggle among Jews who applied to Justinian for a decision, as discussed above. Jewish officials had to accept these innovations in practice or suffer the death penalty. Twentieth-century scholars, influenced by Nazi actions, treated Justinian's policies toward the Jews as antisemitic. More recent scholarship sees his actions as a continuation of the Christianizing policies of the empire, while still protecting the status and legality of Jews as Roman citizens.

On the popular level, the homilies of Leontius, a presbyter during Justinian's reign, describe the preacher's attitude toward Jews for his congregants of workers, artisans, and the poor. A lively and popular preacher, he did not ignore heretics, pagans, and Jews, referring to the latter as impious Jews, fashioning the cross to crucify Jesus at the devil's instigation, the devil being their father and they his accomplices. He blamed them for hostility to Christians, described them as painted black and bloodthirsty, practicing magic and juggling, demons, spiritually blind, and so on. The homilies give us a picture of the capital from the perspective of the lower classes. With respect to the Jews, however, it differs little from that of the higher clergy. The ecclesiastical literature was paralleled by the intellectuals, themselves Orthodox trained, who wrote the histories and chronicles during the 4th–9th centuries, mainly for the upper and literate classes. Their themes, accompanying the few references to the Jews in their treatises, repeated traditional anti-Jewish tropes: crucifiers of Jesus, attackers of Christians and Christianity, instigators of heresy (e.g., Nestorius, Paulicians, iconoclasts), rioters, and rebels against the divinely sanctioned authority of the Empire. The paucity of references to the Jews in these texts may be deliberate, that is, a downplaying of their existence in a world now officially Christian in which the Jews were an accursed minority. The development of antisemitic roots in the earliest Christian writings may just be traced to the programs preached to the mobs who enacted them and to the scholars who recorded them.

The 7th century witnessed both better times and the worst of times since the disastrous revolts of the 1st and 2nd centuries. During the chaos of the reign of Phocas (602–610) the emperor ordered the Jews baptized, likely in response to the Jews reported rioting in the East and attacking Christians, before his overthrow and murder by Heraclius in 610. Renewing their attacks of the 6th century, the Persian Empire invaded the Byzantine East in 607–608, which led to the conquest of Syria, Egypt, and Palestine. The capture of Jerusalem in 613 humiliated Byzantium, especially the loss of the "True Cross." Jews rallied to the Persian conquest and occupation, jubilant that the onerous burden of Christian antisemitism was lifted even if only briefly (until 628). The revolution of Heraclius and his subsequent reorganization of the army (and, by extension, of the empire) issued in the period of "Byzantium" as the modern designation of the period which superseded the traditional Roman empire, now divided among its Eastern Orthodox sphere and a bevy of barbarian kingdoms subject to the influence if not authority of the papacy in Rome.

Heraclius led his army to victory reclaiming Egypt, overrunning Syria and Palestine, retaking Jerusalem, defeating the Sassanians at the Battle of Nineveh, and burning the environs of Ctesiphon (like Alexander), finally bringing to an end the ten-century-long conflict between Greece and Persia and its recent four-century-long Sassanian interlude. Christian jubilation was rampant. Polemics and disputations flourished among all branches of Orthodoxy. Revenge on the Jews for their participation in the

Persian occupation and administration of Jerusalem was demanded amid stories of atrocities, a common feature of contemporary propaganda in the East through the ages. Heraclius's punishment of the Jews was welcomed amid the reports of Christian martyrdoms at the hands of Jews. The many sources cited by modern scholars and their interpretations reflect the complicated situation of the period. The hysteria and euphoria of the sources ranging from chronicles to sermons to apocalypses and eschatological revelries were matched by massacres and forced baptisms of Jews both locally and among the western kingdoms of Dagobert's France and Visigothic Spain, even apparently in southern Italy, instigated by Heraclius's forced baptism of 632. Yuri Stoyanov, Fred Astren, and other scholars have argued that this Byzantine polemical propaganda adversely affected the status of the Jews in the West and influenced the later Muslim accounts of the conquests in Spain. The decade of Heraclius's victory (628–638) witnessed his emerging identity as David (as well as Alexander and Constantine), evidenced in the newly commissioned silver plate that updated the biblical story. He revived the ancient Hellenic title of Basileus to indicate his unique status of emperor with no equal now that his rival Shahanshah was defeated and the western kinglets were his recently Christianized juniors. After the death of Heraclius and the loss of the eastern provinces of the empire, polemics continued: for example, Anathasios the Sinaitic (c. 665–700), penned his "Against the Jews," and Bishop Leontios of Neapolis, Cyprus (c. 625–668), wrote one against the Jews denouncing the use of images. Maximus the Confessor (d. 662), a Palestinian monk and sometime student of Sophronius, fulminated against Jews, "[t]his people who are the masters of falsehood, the agent of crime, the enemy of truth, the savage persecutor of truth ... a cruel and alien nation authorized to raise its hand against the Divine inheritance ... who announce by their actions the presence of the Antichrist since they ignored that of the divine savior." For Maximus the Jews were a fifth column, "most ready to welcome hostile forces." As Robert Hoyland put it: "the Arabs are simply extras in the eschatological drama with the Jews occupying the leading role. They effectively became the Christians' punch bag; it is through hitting out against them that the Christians worked out their frustration, and through derogating them that they salvaged some measure of self-esteem."[1] The scapegoating of the Jews as arch-enemy and cause of Christianity's and Empire's troubles was continually updated.

---

[1] Robert Hoyland, *Seeing Islam as Others Saw It* (Princeton, NJ, 1977), 78.

In 634 the Muslim Arabs rode out of Arabia and with the help of the local Arab tribes, former allies of the Byzantines, defeated the Byzantine army. In 638 they accepted the surrender of Jerusalem from its Bishop Sophronius, who demanded the continued ban on Jews living in Jerusalem, in accordance with the Roman laws that were recognized as part of the surrender treaty. Nevertheless, after the Jews demanded the right to return to Jerusalem, Caliph Umar negotiated a deal with the bishop, and seventy Jewish families were permitted to return to their ancient capital. Thus, Jews returned and helped the Muslims find the *sakhra* on which Abraham supposedly offered up to God his son Isaac and from which Muhammed visited heaven according to Muslim tradition, his horse's hoofprint still visible to pilgrims to this day. Jews flourished in Jerusalem, albeit still subject to prior Roman restrictions (now extended to Christian *dhimmi* as well), and today they share it with most branches of Christianity and sects of Islam as they had throughout the Muslim occupation of the city (638–1918).

In sum, "the problem with *the* Jews . . . is that they aren't allied with *anyone*."[2] This is true in one sense, although individual Jews occasionally joined different factions in any fractured society and rioted with non-Jews, for example, in Antioch, Alexandria, Thessalonica, and Constantinople. They were recognized, however, as a dangerous and disruptive element in Christian society during the violent troubles both internal and external of the 5th, 6th, and 7th centuries. Still, the Jews usually pursued their own minority interests and kept a low profile; the infrequent excesses suggest that they lived out their lives pursuing their social and economic interests and celebrating their customs and rites alongside their Christian neighbors who bordered on their own neighborhoods (Judaiki, Hebraiki, Ovraiki). Archaeological data from excavated churches and synagogues of the Byzantine period suggest a largely peaceful coexistence and sociocultural exchange between the Jewish and Christian communities in Palestine. During the 4th–7th centuries, on the other hand, the majority Christian leadership, while recognizing the continuity of Jews' legal status as Roman citizens, supported the Christianization of any and all minorities and heresies with policies of population transfer and various tactics of persecution. Their polemics reflected the vicissitudes of their own times, usually expressed in the highly developed literature inherited and updated from the 1st through the 7th centuries.

---

[2] Mark Helprin, *A Soldier of the Great War* (New York, 1991), 131.

Further Reading

Alexander, S. S., "Heraclius, Byzantine Imperial Ideology and the David Plates." *Speculum* 52 (1977), 217–237.

Bonfil, R., et al., eds., *Jews in Byzantium. Dialectics of Minority and Majority Cultures* (Leiden, 2012).

Cameron, A., "Blaming the Jews: The Seventh-Century Invasions of Palestine in Context." *Traveaux et Memoires* 14 (2002), 57–78.

De Lange, N. "Jews in the Age of Justinian," in *The Cambridge Companion to the Age of Justinian*, ed. M. Maas (Cambridge, 2005), 401–426.

Haldon, J., *Byzantium in the Seventh Century: The Transformation of a Culture*, 2nd rev. ed. (Cambridge, 1997).

"The Reign of Heraclius: A Context for Change?," in *The Reign of Heraclius (610–641): Crisis and Confrontation*, ed. G. J. Reinink and B. H. Stolte (Leuven, 2003), 1–16.

Hoyland, R. G., *Seeing Islam as Others Saw It: A Survey and Evaluation of Christians, Jews, and Zoroastrian Writings on Early Islam* (Princeton, NJ, 1977).

Krauss, S., and W. Horbury, *The Jewish-Christian Controversy from the Earliest Times to 1789* (Tübingen, 1996).

Lindner, A., "The Legal Status of Jews in the Byzantine Empire," in *Jews in Byzantium*, 2012, 149–217.

Mathison, R. W., "The Citizenship and Legal Status of Jews in Roman Law during Late Antiquity," in *Jews and Early Christian Law: Byzantium and the Latin West*, ed. John Tolan et al. (Turnhout, 2014), 35–54.

Parkes, J., *The Conflict of the Church and Synagogue: A Study in the Origins of Antisemitism* (New York, 1969).

Simon, M., *Verus Israel*, trans. H. McKeating (Oxford, 1996).

Starr, J., *Jews in the Byzantine Empire, 641–1204* (Athens, 1939).

Stoyanov, Y., "Apocalypticizing Warfare from Political Theology to Imperial Eschatology in Seventh and Early Eighth-Century Byzantium," in *The Armenian Apocalyptic Tradition*, ed. K. B. Bardakjian and S. La Porta (Leiden, 2014), 379–433. Gives further analysis of propaganda during Zoroastrian and Muslim invasions.

Van Bekkum, W., "Jewish Messianic Expectations in the Age of Heraclius," in *The Reign of Heraclius (610–641)*, 95–112.

Part II

Medieval Times

8 The Medieval Islamic World and the Jews

REUVEN FIRESTONE

The Muslim world expanded quickly from its origin in Arabia, westward to Spain and Mauritania and eastward to Indonesia and China. It soon consisted of many thousands of language communities and cultures that were unified by little more than a common religious consciousness. This extraordinary diversity expressed itself in a substantial variety of Islamic expression in ritual, literature, art, thought and law. The medieval period spans roughly from the emergence of Islam in the 7th century to the Renaissance sometime around the 15th century. "Medieval" means "middle age" (from *medium aevum*) and is a Western category that does not apply well to Islam, for it places the beginning of Islam "in the middle." The majority of the world's Jewish population during the Middle Ages lived in the Muslim world.

This essay appears in a collection that treats antisemitism as it originated and developed in the West – meaning the Greco-Roman world until its mantle passed to Europe. There has never been agreement over the meaning of "antisemitism," even among scholars of antisemitism, let alone the public at large, and it often serves in the popular press as a vehicle for particular political or religious positions that tend to be reductive and essentializing. While it is true that Jews suffered as a minority community in the Muslim world just as they did elsewhere, it is not clear how that suffering relates to something that could be called "antisemitism." It is not particularly useful to use the term in relation to the medieval Muslim world, though it is relevant in the modern period when antisemitism enters Muslim discourse with the rise of Western colonial power and influence.

For these reasons, it is best to leave the term aside when considering the treatment of Jews under medieval (or classical) Islam. This is not to suggest that there was not prejudice directed against Jews in the premodern Muslim world or that Jews did not suffer there *as* Jews. How and why this occurred will be explored in some detail in what follows. This essay treats the position of Jews in the world of Islam in relation to other minorities and majority power from before the origin of Islam until the rise of the modern Western powers that challenged many of the established assumptions associated with traditional Muslim identity and thought. Muslims responded to the rise of the West in a variety of ways, including in their attitude and behavior toward Jewish and Christian minorities living in their midst. This chapter treats the period before these changes.

Because of the vastly different contexts in which the Jews of premodern Islam lived in terms of both period and setting, they experienced a wide range of treatment in the many Muslim communities among whom they lived. Their status was fluid and could change as circumstances changed around them, though always within certain parameters established by Islamic law and culture. The great variety of treatment cannot be treated fully here, but one must nevertheless take care not to essentialize this complex situation by ignoring its variety.[1] In order to avoid the errors of "getting lost in the weeds" of detail, on the one hand, and offering a reductive analysis based on limited examples, on the other, I concentrate on foundational narratives in the emergence of Islam that have served to establish patterns of Muslim perspective and behavior toward Jews. This will then be followed by a brief appraisal of how later Muslims responded to those foundational narratives. What follows here will concentrate on the earliest phase of Islam because it is during this period that the paradigms of perspective which became more or less standardized in later years were established. Finally, because the worldviews of early Islam were profoundly influenced by the context into which Islam was born, we need to begin with the image and position of Jews in that birth environment.

JEWS IN ARABIA BEFORE ISLAM

Jews had lived in the Arabian Peninsula for many centuries before the emergence of Islam. This should not seem surprising, since the land in which the ancient Israelites dwelt was adjacent to Arabia and is geographically part of that peninsula on its far northwestern flank. People defined as Arabs are a part of biblical history, the most obvious example being "Geshem the Arab" (*geshem ha'arvi*), who is also referred to according to the Arabian pronunciation of his name, *gashmu*

---

[1] The recently published *Encyclopedia of Jews in the Islamic World*, edited by Norman Stillman (Leiden, 2010), is an excellent resource for treating detail in this regard.

(Nehemia 2:19, 6:1, 6:6). Several other characters throughout the biblical corpus from Genesis to Chronicles are identified as Arab by the nature of their names and the socioeconomic *realia* associated with their portrayals.[2]

There is as of yet no physical evidence for settled Israelite communities in Arabia during the biblical period, though several legends from Jewish and other traditions place Jewish travelers, traders and even significant communities there.[3] By the time of the Roman destruction of Jerusalem in 70 CE, large communities of Jews had spread through many parts of the Middle East and North Africa. A large community lived in Egypt, Jewish traders regularly traveled in Arabia, and Jewish communities eventually settled in the northern areas around the region of al-ʿUlā in the northern Ḥijāz and in the east in Dilmūn, the area along the Persian (or Arabian) Gulf known today as Baḥrayn and Qatar. Several other religious communities also lived in Arabia (in addition to the traditional Arabian communities practicing indigenous forms of Arabian religion), including Christian groups from the Greco-Roman world, Persian Zoroastrians (known as *Majūs* in Arabic textual history), Ethiopian Christians and others of East African origin.

A powerful Jewish kingdom emerged in southern Arabia during the late 4th century CE in Ḥimyar, a region in what is today Yemen. Ḥimyar is known already from the late Second Temple period, but it was polytheist until the last decade or two of the 4th century when it, along with much of South Arabia, transformed its worship practices from venerating a pantheon of deities to a single deity called "Lord of Heaven" or *Raḥmānān*, meaning "the Merciful."[4] A generation earlier, the powerful rival kingdom of Aksum across the Red Sea in what is today Ethiopia and Eritrea had converted to Christianity. The Ḥimyarite kingdom took on Jewish practices partly in order to assert an independent position from the competing Christian Aksumites. This competition would eventually cause the demise of Jewish Ḥimyar. Christians also lived in southern Arabia and periodically engaged in proselytizing efforts that were opposed by Jewish Ḥimyarite kings, sometimes with violence.

---

[2] Reuven Firestone, "Muslim-Jewish Relations," *Oxford Research Encyclopedia of Religion* (Oxford, 2016), DOI: 10.1093/acrefore/9780199340378.013.17.

[3] Gordon N. Newby, *A History of the Jews of Arabia: From Ancient Times to their Eclipse under Islam* (Columbia, SC, 2009).

[4] Norbert Nebes, "The Martyrs of Najrān and End of the Ḥimyar: On the Political History of South Arabia in the Early Sixth Century," in Angelika Neuwirth et al., eds., *The Qur'ān in Context: Historical and Literary Investigations into the Qur'ānic Mileiu* (Leiden, 2011), 27–60.

The Jewish kingdom of Ḥimyar succeeded in controlling a large swath of territory not only in southern Arabia but also in the central regions, and the tension between Christian Aksum and Jewish Ḥimyar mirrored in part the competition much farther north between the Christian Byzantine Empire and the Zoroastrian Sassanian Persian Empire. Both endeavored to use the southern kingdoms of Aksum and Ḥimyar as political proxies to benefit from the incense and spice trade and to access markets. Most important for our purpose, Jews represented a significant and sizable community in southern Arabia before the rise of Islam. They held political power, had a formidable military, and exercised sovereignty over a substantial area.

Aksum (Ethiopia) intervened twice militarily in southern Arabia during the first half of the 6th century. These occurred during the rule of the Jewish Ḥimyarite king Yūsuf As`ar Yath`ar, also known as Dhū Nuwās, meaning "the one with the (side?) curls." Dhū Nuwās responded to the first intervention by attacking Ethiopians in the capital Ẓafār, about eighty miles south of today's Sana`a. According to Ḥimyarite epigraphic sources, Dhū Nuwās burned down the Ethiopian church in Ẓafār and killed the priests.[5] He then moved against Ethiopian military units and Christian tribes allied with them in various parts of the region, and he blockaded the harbors on the Red Sea to prevent the arrival of reinforcements. The attacks against Christians included the destruction of churches, the most famous and significant occurring in 523 at Najrān, a town north of today's border between Yemen and Saudi Arabia. Most of the information about this episode comes from Christian sources written in Christian Aramaic or Syriac, but even with their inherent pro-Christian bias, respected historians accept the basic accuracy of the depiction even if some details may have been exaggerated. The city of Najrān was put to siege and, according to the Christian accounts, despite the personal guarantee of Dhū Nuwās sworn before rabbis on the Torah and Ark of the Covenant that the Christians would not be harmed if they surrendered, hundreds or thousands of Christians were massacred, and the bones of priests exhumed and desecrated.

The massacre was publicized throughout eastern Christianity, not only in Yemen and Ethiopia but also in Byzantium. It provided justification for the Aksumite king, Kaleb Ella Aṣbeḥa, to invade with a large force with support from the Byzantines, resulting in the killing of Dhū Nuwās and the collapse and destruction of the Jewish kingdom of

---

[5] Nebes, "The Martyrs of Najrān and End of the Ḥimyar," 45–46.

Ḥimyar. South Arabia then came under the rule of Christian Aksum for the next fifty years until it became a Persian province in 575, shortly after the birth of Muhammad in Mecca some 500 miles north of Najran.

The story of the rise and demise of Jewish Ḥimyar is important for a number of reasons. It indicates that Arabia had a strong Jewish presence in the period just before the rise of Islam. Jews had power in Arabia, and like those who hold power everywhere, they used it against their rivals, often violently. The story of Jewish persecution and massacre of Christians became a part of Arabian lore and tradition. That in itself would not be surprising, for oppression and even massacres of enemies occasionally occurred at that time and place, and such events perpetrated by various individuals and communities were remembered in traditional Arabian lore. As a result, the legend of Jewish power, violence and persecution entered into later Muslim lore and can be found in the classic Muslim sources. For example, Ibn Hishām's (d. 833) edited version of Ibn Isḥāq's (d. 767) classic biography of Muhammad depicts Dhū Nuwās as attacking the Najrāni Christians simply in order to convert them forcibly to Judaism.[6] Al-Ṭabarī's (d. 923) citation of the same source (which probably follows the more complete original) includes the larger context of the wars between Aksum and Ḥimyar and does not portray it as forced conversion.[7] Several renderings of the story associate it with an obscure verse of the Qur'an in 85:4: "The companions of the trench (aṣḥāb al-ukhdūd) perished."[8] According to these traditions, the Jewish Dhū Nuwās had the Christian martyrs burned in a trench (ukhdūd), thus explaining the puzzling qur'anic reference. The association between the Jewish massacre of Najrani Christians and the qur'anic reference to the "Companions of the Trench" became standardized through the repeated appearance of the story in popular Qur'an commentaries. As a result, an old pre-Islamic memory of Jewish persecution of Christians became established later in Islamic lore and tradition, which served to generate an image or archetype of Jewish power and violence directed against competing monotheists in the classic Muslim sources. This story, however, was not unique. It occurs alongside many ancient stories of brutality that were remembered in the Muslim sources, whether perpetrated by Jews, Christians or Arabs practicing indigenous religions.

[6] Alfred Guillaume, The Life of Muhammad: A Translation of Ibn Ishaq's Sirat Rasul Allah (Oxford, 1955), 17, henceforth referred to as Ibn Isḥāq.
[7] Al-Ṭabarī, History of al-Ṭabarī, trans. C. E. Bosworth (Albany, NY, 1999), vol. 5, 202–205.
[8] Ibn Kathīr, Ismā'īl, Tafsīr Ibn Kathīr, 9 vols. (Beirut, 1980/1405), 8:258–260.

MUHAMMAD AND THE JEWS OF THE ḤIJĀZ

There is no evidence of a permanent Jewish settlement in Muhammad's birthplace of Mecca, but Jews were a powerful and influential community in the oasis settlement of Yathrib, some 200 miles to the north. According to legend, it was two rabbis from Yathrib who convinced the Ḥimyarite king As'ad abū Karīb to become Jewish, which resulted in bringing most of the population of today's Yemen into Judaism some two centuries before Muhammad's birth.[9]

The Jews of Yathrib were well established by the time that Muhammad made his *hijra* or emigration there from Mecca in 622. Yathrib would soon be called *medīnat al-nabī* ("City of the Prophet"), or Medina for short. The Jewish population of Yathrib/Medina was organized into three distinct Jewish clans or tribes, along with a significant but unknown number of Jews who belonged to kinship communities not recognized specifically as Jewish. A great deal has been written about the relations between Muhammad and the Jews of Medina, and it has become a point of great controversy. Space here allows for only an overview of this epochal chapter, with reference to the sources in translation for the reader interested in greater depth. The sources all derive from later Muslim tradition that was transmitted orally for generations until it was written down in several differing versions well over a hundred years after the events.[10] I refer to the relations between Muhammad and the Jews as a chapter because it is constructed from many short oral stories that were collected generations after the occasions they purport to describe. Some written collections of these narrations include several sometimes contradictory perspectives transmitted by different sources. They may not reflect actual history, but whether or not they convey true facts about what actually occurred, they have become an authoritative basis for

[9] Al-Ṭabari (Bosworth) 145, 164; Ibn Isḥāq 7–12. For more on Jewish Ḥimyar, see G. W. Bowersock, *Empires in Collision in Late Antiquity* (Waltham, MA, 2012; G. W. Bowersock, *Throne of Adulis: Red Sea Wars on the Eve of Islam* (Oxford, 2013).

[10] In addition to Ibn Isḥāq via the edition of Ibn Hishām (d. 833) and al-Ṭabarī (d. 923) mentioned above, is found in Muhammad b. 'Umar al-Wāqidī (d. 823; *Kitāb al-Maghāzī*; English trans. Rizwi Faizer, *The Life of Muḥammad; Al-Wāqidī's Kitāb al-Maghāzī* [London, 2011]), Muḥammad ibn Sa'd (d. 845; *Kitāb al-Tabaqāt al-Kabīr*; trans. S. Moinul Haq [New Delhi, n.d.]), and the much later Ismā'īl b. 'Umar Ibn Kathīr (d. 1373; *Al-bidāya wal-nihāya*, trans. Trevor Le Gassick, *The Life of the Prophet Muḥammad: Al-Sīra al-Nabawiyya* [Reading, 1998]).

constructing normative points of view in Islamic tradition. The following is my reading of the story as derived from those sources.

Muhammad knew about Jews long before he left his hometown of Mecca for Medina. As noted above, Jews had been living in Yemen for centuries before Muhammad's birth, and Jews came to Mecca regularly to trade. He undoubtedly interacted with Jews at one level or another for years. When Muhammad began to proclaim his prophethood, some Meccans who were wary of his claims sent emissaries to Medina to invite learned Jews living there to come and test his prophetic assertions. Jews were well respected in Arabia for their monotheism and their learning, to such an extent that some legends even tell of Jews predicting the future birth of Muhammad, who would become a great prophet. When Muhammad later moved to Medina, the Jews living there knew about him. In any case his visit was not a surprise, for he had been invited to Medina for the purpose of mediating an intractable and violent conflict between two non-Jewish tribal clans living there.

Muhammad organized his mediation through a form of "binding arbitration," for which both sides of the conflict had to agree *ab initio* to abide by Muhammad's adjudication even before his arrival. They agreed, and he succeeded, not only in resolving that particular dispute but also in keeping the peace in general between the fractious clans of Medina. He did this by assigning himself as a neutral leader to whom the parties continued to be required to appeal in order to resolve future disputes. Something like a formal "rules of engagement" between all the parties of Medina was then written in a document known today as the Pact of Medina.[11] The original document does not survive, but it is recorded in a number of sources and believed by scholars to be authentic. The Jews of Medina appear in the document several times, and they are afforded the same basic privileges as Muhammad's followers and other members of the Medinan population as long as they follow the authority established by Muhammad: "Those Jews who obey us will have aid and equality without being oppressed, nor will any help be given against them." Several Jewish clan groups are specifically named in the document, and they are accepted as part of the political community (*umma*) along with the followers of Muhammad. The Jews, in turn, were required to share the common expenses of war, and all those who would break the treaty, whether Jewish or not, would suffer the consequences along with their families.

[11] It is also referred to as the "Covenant," "Constitution," or "Charter" of Medina. See Ibn Isḥāq 231–233; Ibn Kathīr 2:212–214.

The document was written early on in Muhammad's stay in Medina. It recognizes the Jews as full members of the newly organized Medinan community and affords them equal rights as long as they submit to his overall leadership. They could continue to follow their own religious and cultural traditions and their own leaders on internal matters, and they were not required to convert to Islam. The arrangement seems fair, and there is no evidence that the Jewish clans of Medina resisted it. Things would change, however, as Muhammad's status and authority in Medina increased, his retinue grew, and he became recognized increasingly as "the messenger of God" (rasūl Allāh).

As noted previously, the Jews of Arabia were respected as an ancient and wise community in possession of a divine scripture and ancient tradition; they were consulted several times by non-Jewish Arabs about whether Muhammad was an authentic prophet.[12] When Muhammad arrived in Medina, some Jews immediately recognized his claim to prophethood and abandoned their community and religion to follow him. The overwhelming majority, however, did not. This is exemplified in the story of Abdullah Ibn Salām, a Jewish scholar who recognized Muhammad as a prophet right away; he also warned him that the Jews were a stubborn and deceitful people who would certainly undermine him.[13]

The story of Abdullah Ibn Salām conveys something of the predicament facing both Muhammad and the Jews. Because of the Jews' status and authority as well-established monotheists, Muhammad would gain greatly if they would recognize his prophethood. Their refusal as a community to do so was problematic for him. The Jews, on the other hand, came under increasing pressure to recognize his religious claims as his power and prestige increased. The Jews could accept him as a civic leader; the problem from the Jewish perspective was Muhammad's authority as prophet of God. According to normative Jewish tradition, prophethood had already ceased in ancient times. The Hebrew Bible had been canonized, and with the finality of canonization there can henceforth be no new prophets and revelation.[14] Muhammad's prophetic assertion became a threat to the Jews' own religious integrity, and his rhetoric included censure of the Jews for

[12] Ibn Isḥāq 197–198; Ibn Kathīr 2:114–115, 118.
[13] Ibn Isḥāq 240–241; Ibn Kathīr 2:194–197.
[14] Reuven Firestone, "The Problematic of Prophecy," Presidential Keynote Address, International Qur'anic Studies Association Conference, Atlanta, GA, November 20, 2015. https://iqsaweb.files.wordpress.com/2013/05/atlanta2015_keynote_rf2.pdf. *Journal of the International Qur'anic Studies Association* 1 (2016), 11–22.

refusing to recognize him, along with other Jewish faults and short-comings that were to be corrected by the religious dispensation that he claimed God was offering through him.[15] As Muhammad's prophetic fame spread and as he succeeded in amassing greater power and authority in Medina, the situation for the Jews became increasingly difficult. Consequently, the Jews found themselves in a serious dilemma. The Constitution of Medina, to which they evidently signed on, required their obedience to Muhammad as the leader of the overall community. Meanwhile, he was known increasingly as the Prophet of God, an authority which Jews were forbidden to recognize. As the power differential changed increasingly in Muhammad's favor, the circumstances of the Jews in Medina became increasingly threatened.

Consequently, while the Jewish community of Medina initially accepted Muhammad on good faith, they ultimately had to oppose him. And as their relative position declined and their disapproval of his status became increasingly unsafe, they became increasingly surrep-titious in their opposition. The situation ended up becoming dangerous for both parties as the stakes were raised. Muhammad eventually suc-ceeded in dividing, outmaneuvering and ultimately defeating the Jewish community over the first five years of his residence in Medina. Two of the three major tribes were exiled (the Banū Qaynuqā` and the Banū Naḍīr); the men of the third and largest Jewish tribe, the Banū Qurayẓa, were killed and the women and children taken by Muhammad and his community as spoil.[16]

The violence and killing associated with the destruction of Medina's Jews has been a subject of much controversy, and polar pos-itions have developed between two partisan groups, each of which decisively condemns the another. According to most on the partisan "Jewish side," Muhammad cruelly and gratuitously exiled and then massacred an innocent Jewish community that was not threatening him. According to most on the partisan "Muslim side," the Jews had undermined Muhammad for years, tried to murder him, and then treacherously broke the Pact of Medina by siding with the enemy in the Battle of the Trench (a fierce battle at which many lives were lost), thus getting what they deserved. As is clear from the number of pages

[15] Such critiques can be found in the Qur'an. See, for example, Q.2:91, 105; 3:70–71, 78, 93–94; 4:155; 5:15, 57–59; 62:5–7, etc. Cf. Firestone, "Qur'anic Anti-Jewish Polemics," in G. H. van Kooten and J. van Ruiten, eds., *Intolerance, Polemics, and Debate in Antiquity* (Leiden, 2019), 443–462.
[16] Ibn Isḥāq 363–482; Al-Ṭabarī (Watt), VII:85–161, (Fishbein) VIII:1–41; Ibn Kathīr III:2–174.

cited in note 10 above referencing the sources, anyone interested in drawing their own conclusion must read and analyze hundreds of pages of material. The situation was exceedingly complicated, and the tension and conflict built up over a number of years. All the information derives from Muslim oral reports, which include a variety of witnesses with somewhat different angles on what occurred and were only put into writing more than a century after the events. There are no Jewish sources for any of these events.

One can draw several conclusions depending on one's reading of the sources, but they clearly depict the Medinan Jewish tribes trying to undermine Muhammad verbally and physically and refusing to fight and defend their fellow Muslim members of the Pact at the Battle of the Trench. The evidence is strong that they indeed "aided and abetted" the enemy. The "Jewish side" argues that the accusations are false because Jews do not behave in such an underhanded manner; they were falsely accused, and pretexts were fabricated in order to destroy them. But it is likely that the portrayals are accurate on the whole. The Jews of Arabia shared a common martial culture with their non-Jewish neighbors, as the militancy of the Arabian Jewish kingdom of Ḥimyar demonstrates. A wide range of Arabic sources treating unrelated topics, for example, notes in passing that Jews carried weapons and could and did use them.

The Jews and the Muslims of Medina slid, perhaps inescapably, into a conflict situation. Both sides were jockeying over status, authority, economic position and power – and ultimately for survival. It seems clear from the sources that they were all functioning according to the same cultural assumptions or, put differently, "playing by the same rules." In fact, the horrific treatment meted out to the Jewish Banū Qurayẓa, the tribe whose men were massacred and whose women and children were taken as booty, seems virtually identical with the "rules of engagement" established for Israelite conquest of neighboring tribes in Deuteronomy 20:10–14. This seems to be not a case of gratuitous Muslim violence directed against an innocent and defenseless community, but rather a conventional situation in which two competing communities were engaged in brutal but culturally acceptable violence against one another.

The larger of the two Jewish tribes exiled from Medina found refuge in the Jewish oasis town of Kaybar, situated about ninety miles to the north. They, along with the Khaybaris, were attacked and defeated by Muhammad and his followers some two years later. It was a long and bloody battle with significant loss of life on both sides, but it resulted in no massacre of unarmed Jews as in Medina. The Jews continued to live in Khaybar, with the condition that they pay half of their produce to the Muslim victors.[17] The tension between Muhammad and the Jews of the region persisted until he defeated them decisively. It is important to note, however, that Muhammad's relationship with and treatment of the Jewish opposition does not appear to differ significantly from that of other groups that threatened the status and growth of his community.

An important story is found within the Khaybar episode that conveys a great deal about the historical and cultural context. It appears in all the relevant historical sources and a number of authoritative Hadith collections as well.[18] According to the story, a Jewish woman named Zaynab bt. Al-Ḥārith lost her husband, brothers, and other members of her family in the fighting. In order to exact revenge, she cooked up what she learned was Muhammad's favorite food (a lamb or, in some versions, a goat) and thoroughly poisoned it, especially the shoulder, which was Muhammad's favorite cut. She then offered it to him as a gift. The several versions of the story differ over details, but the gist of the story is that Muhammad took a bite about the same time that his friend and fellow warrior Bishr b. Barā'. Bishr was stricken by the poison, but Muhammad spat his out in time to be saved from certain death. According to Ibn Hishām's recension of Ibn Isḥāq, "Then he called for the woman and she confessed, and when he asked her what had induced her to do this she answered: 'You know what you have done to my people. I said to myself, if he is a king I shall ease myself of him and if he is a prophet he will be informed (of what I have done).' So the apostle let her off. Bishr b. al-Barā' died from what he had eaten."[19]

Zaynab's logic was entirely acceptable to Muhammad, who did not punish her for her attempt to kill him. The story becomes even more surprising at its conclusion, for when Muhammad eventually dies some three years later after complaining of an extremely painful headache, he announces that his death is a result of the residual effect of the poison: "The Messenger of God said during the illness from which he died – the mother of of Bishr b. al-Barā' ... had come in to visit him – 'Um Bishr ('Mother of Bishr'), at this very moment I feel my aorta being severed because of the food I ate with your son at Khaybar.'"[20]

[17] Ibn Isḥāq 510–523; Al-Wāqidī 311–341; Ibn Saʿd II:131–146; Ibn Kathīr III:265–278.

[18] Ibn Isḥāq 516; Al-Wāqidī 333–334; Ibn Saʿd II:133, 143–144, 250–252; Al-Ṭabarī VIII:123–124; Ibn Kathir III:283–287; Al-Bukhārī III:475, IV:261–262, VII:449.

[19] Ibn Isḥāq, 516.

[20] "my aorta being severed ..." (qataʿa abharahu) is an idiom expressing excruciating pain. Al-Ṭabarī VIII: 124. See also Ibn Kathīr III:386, Al-Bukhārī V:509–510.

Muslims had a famous precedent for considering this episode as justification for institutionalizing the hatred of Jews. That precedent is the well-known Christian libel of Jewish deicide, that "the Jews" killed God by killing Christ. This pernicious slander resulted in centuries of persecution and mass murders of Jews by Christians during the Crusades, the Spanish Inquisition, in pogroms in Eastern Europe and, finally, the Holocaust. Yet despite the charge in the name of Muhammad himself that his death was a result of his having been poisoned by a Jew, traditional Islam has no charge of Jewish "propheticide."

JEWS IN THE QUR'AN

The Qur'an uses a wide variety of terms to refer to Jews: "Children of Israel" (banū isrā'īl), which appears forty-three times and often refers to the ancient Israelites in stories with clear parallels from the Hebrew Bible; "the people of Moses" (qawm mūsā, three times); "those who have Judaized" (al-ladhīna hādū, ten times); "Jews" (al-yahūd, eight times); and "Jew" or "Jewish" (yahūdī). [21] The last three words constructed from yahūdī seem to refer to Jews contemporary with Muhammad. Another common term is various forms of "People of the Book" (ahlū al-kitāb), which occurs thirty-three times: "[those] who have been given the Book" (nineteen times), "[those] whom We[22] have given the Book" (six times), "[those] who have been given a portion of the Book" (three times), and occasionally other labels such as "[those] who have read/recited the Book," "successors who have inherited the Book" and "People of the Reminder" ("Reminder" can be a synonym for scripture). These designations refer in general to people who are in possession of pre-Qur'anic scripture, so they actually refer to both Jews and Christians. Sometimes ahlū al-kitāb refers only to Jews, sometimes only to Christians, and sometimes to both simultaneously. But the contexts in which they appear most often reflect reference specifically to Jews.

The Qur'an uses still other terms, such as "[those] who have been given the Knowledge beforehand" (17:107) and the collective "those

---

[21] Significant portions of this section are taken from my "Qur'anic Anti-Jewish Polemics," in van Kooten and van Ruiten, eds., *Intolerance, Polemics, and Debate in Antiquity*, 443–462.

[22] God is usually, but not always, represented in the "plural of majesty" (*pluralis majestatis*) form.

who have knowledge of the Book" (13:43), which probably refers not only to Jews and Christians but also to followers of Muhammad. Other appellations include "People of Abraham" (āl ibrāhīm, 4:54), who were given "the Book and the wisdom and ... a great kingdom," and "the tribes" (al-asbāṭ), that is, the tribes of Israel, which always (four times) occurs in the expression, "Abraham, Ishmael, Isaac, Jacob and the tribes." The Qur'an also refers to two additional categories within the community of Jews. One refers to rabbis – rabbāniyūn (3:79; 5:44, 63) and perhaps rabbiyyūn (3:14), and the other to scholar-colleagues – aḥbār (sing., ḥabr 5:44, 63; 9:34).[23]

The large number and variety of references to Jews show how significant Jews and Judaism were in 7th-century Arabia. The Qur'an calls on skeptics to consult with the "People of the Reminder" to learn the truth about revelation and scripture (16:43–44), and even instructs the Prophet, "If you are in doubt about what We have sent down to you, ask those who have been reciting the Book before you" (10:94). It would be natural for Jewish opinions and practices to appear within the Qur'an, just as they appear also in the New Testament, because as we have observed above, Jews were important actors in the emergence of Islam. And as in the New Testament, most Jewish opinions, practices and behaviors found in the Qur'an are criticized because they represent a respected religious community that refused to accept the authority of the new religious leader. The Jews' refusal to accept Muhammad and the Qur'an is often noted, but one must keep in mind that the Qur'an also criticizes Christians and practitioners of traditional Arabian polytheism for their refusal to join the program.

The following qur'anic references treat specific aspects of what is considered to be Jewish intransigence. Q 2:105; 5:59; 61:6 complain that the Jews refuse to accept Muhammad's prophetic status and the revelation he was given. Jews wish to turn (Muslim) believers into disbelievers and lead them astray (2:109; 3:98; 5:77). Jews (and Christians) will never accept anyone who does not follow their creed (2:120, 135; 3:69), nor will they ever accept the leadership of Muhammad or believe the revelations he received, even though they recognize their validity and truth (2:145–146; 3:98). They mix truth

---

[23] The latter category is known in the Talmud as ḥaver – learned Jews with a status somewhat below rabbis. See Marcus Jastrow, A Dictionary of the Targumim, the Talmud Babli and Yerushalmi, and the Midrashic Literature (London, 1903), pp. 421–422; Michael Sokoloff, A Dictionary of Jewish Babylonian Aramaic of Talmudic and Geonic Periods (Ramat Gan: Bar Ilan University, 2002), pp. 428–429.

with falsehood and conceal the truth (3:71). They demand that the prophet bring down a book from the sky to prove the authenticity of his mission (4:153). Of all the opponents of the prophet, the Jews (along with the idolaters) are among the most violent in their enmity (5:82).[24] The Qur'an argues further that the Jews' stubbornness often angered God long before Muhammad was born: "Certainly Moses brought you the clear signs, [but] then you took the calf [i.e., the "Golden Calf" of Exodus 32] after him [when Moses was away], and you were evildoers" (2:92). Some Jews refused even to accept their own Torah (62:5). Israelites/Jews disbelieved the divine signs, disobeyed God and killed their own prophets (2:61, 91). They did not accept God's revelation given through Jesus (3:52) nor the new revelation given through Muhammad (4:153). Because of their refusal, most Jews are not true believers (3:110; 26:67).

These texts reflect a good deal of anger. The high emotion signals not only the real threat of Jewish opposition but also the universal conflict between emergent religion and established religion. Members of established religions always oppose the emergence of new religions, which represent competition and existential threat.[25] Jews, for example, could not accept the emergence of Christianity as a valid religion because such an acceptance would acknowledge that their own religion was lacking or incomplete. Otherwise, why would God send another prophet with another divine message, and one that contradicts their own scripture at that? And neither Jews nor Christians could accept the emergence of Islam without undermining their own faith.

The Qur'an recognizes that not all Jews (or not all Jews and Christians) are alike. Some are believers and behave properly by doing good deeds and acting righteously (2:62; 3:113, 199; 4:54, 155; 5:69; 22:17; 28:52–55). Such references may refer to those Jews who recognize the prophethood of Muhammad and accept his revelation (3:199; 4:162), but the Qur'an also contains material that seems to reflect positively on Jews in general – not simply on those few who go against the grain of normative Jewish practice or belief to accept the new prophet and the revelation he brought. These texts are quite pluralistic and express an

[24] "The closest ... in affection to the believers are those who say, 'We are Christians'" (5:82).

[25] Think of religious "cults" in this generation, which are simply attempts to form new religions. The formation of new religious movements (read cult, sect, heresy, heterodoxy) has existed since the emergence of religion itself.

openness to other monotheists: "Surely those who believe [a reference to followers of Muhammad], and those who are Jews, and the Christians, and the Sabians – whoever believes in God and the Last Day, and does righteousness – they have their reward with their Lord. [There will be] no fear on them, nor will they sorrow" (2:62, repeated in 5:69). It appears, therefore, that at least in some Qur'anic layers, People of the Book who remain Jews or Christians may hold the same status as Believers, meaning followers of Muhammad and his revelation.

The Qur'an allows Believers to eat the food and marry the virtuous women of those who have been given the Book (5:5). Likewise, the requirement for fasting is introduced as a requirement upon the Believers just as it was required for those – presumably Jews – before them (2:183). Synagogues as well as churches, mosques and other places "in which the name of God is mentioned often" are to be respected and protected (22:40). Some of the People of the Book are very pious and "recite the verses of God during the hours of the night and prostrate themselves" (3:113). One reference to the revelation of the Qur'an contains a comparative note, that "those who have been given the Knowledge beforehand, when it is recited to them they fall down on their faces in prostration and say, 'Glory to our Lord! Surely the promise of our Lord has been fulfilled!'" (17:107–108).

The very large number of references to Jews in the Qur'an reflect the Jews' importance in the earliest period of Islam. Some references are neutral or positive, but as would be expected during the period of religious emergence, most criticize Jews along with all communities that opposed the status and authority of Muhammad and his movement. Because the Jews were one of the more threatening oppositional communities, the Qur'an directs relatively more negative rhetoric toward them. The greatest opponents of the Muhammad and his community, however, were those Arabs who practiced traditional Arabian polytheism, and they are condemned much more often and more violently in the Qur'an than are Jews. Another category that is criticized incessantly by the Qur'an are the so-called hypocrites (munāfiqūn), meaning those who profess to be Muslims but are nevertheless critical of the movement or its ideals, goals or aspirations. The Qur'an, like the Hebrew Bible, New Testament, and other sacred texts believed by their devotees to be divinely authored or inspired, includes a significant amount of negative rhetoric directed against all the communities it considers threatening. Jews are not singled out for this role in the Qur'an. They do not represent any kind of archetype for evil nor are they portrayed as inherently treacherous or diabolical.

JEWS IN THE ḤADĪTH

The Ḥadīth, the most sacred literature in Islam after the Qur'an, is a genre of tradition literature in which is collected the *sunna* (the speech and behavior) of Muhammad. Similar in both value and style to significant parts of Rabbinic literature, it is made up of thousands of short citations and descriptions of Muhammad's deeds and communications, each prefaced with a list of people through whom the tradition was conveyed from Muhammad or a witness who observed him down to the moment the tradition was reduced to writing. It is therefore a particularly important body of literature for Muslims, and it is vast in size and scope. Traditional Muslim scholars have always been aware that many statements attributed to Muhammad were inauthentic, forged in order to authorize certain opinions or practices that had developed, so techniques were developed to evaluate the quality of rectitude associated with them. Six collections in the Sunnī world are considered canonical, and among them, the most important are the collections assembled by Muhammad al-Bukhārī (d. 870) and Muslim b. al-Ḥajjāj (d. 875). I restrict my references in what follows to these most respected collections.

The relative volume of references to Jews in the Ḥadīth is far less than in the Qur'an, but like the Qur'an it contains a range of views spanning from positive to negative. On the positive side, there is a considerable amount of material reflecting the view that Jews were privy to extraordinary wisdom, much of it esoteric wisdom. In one typical example, "Abd al-Malik b. Shu'ayb b. al-Layth related a tradition based on a chain of authority going back to Abū Saʿīd al-Khudrī: The Apostle of God [i.e., Muhammad] said: On the Day of Resurrection, the earth will be a single [loaf] of bread, the Almighty turning it in His hand just as you would turn a loaf on a journey as food for the people of the Garden. [Abū Saʿīd] said: Then a Jewish man came and said: May the Merciful bless you O Abūl-Qāsim [another name for Muhammad], shall I tell you about the feasting for the people of the Garden on the Day of Resurrection? He said: Of course! He went on: The earth will be one loaf. [Abū Saʿīd] said: So the Apostle of God looked at him. Then he laughed so much that his molars showed. [The Jew] went on, shall I tell you about what they will eat with it?[26] He said: Of course! He said: It is *balām* and fish [*nūn*]. They [the Prophet's companions?] asked: What is [*balām*]? He answered: Ox and fish, the leftovers from whose livers

---

[26] *Idām* – whatever food is eaten with bread.

would feed seventy thousand. Yaḥyā b. Ḥabīb al-Ḥarithī ... Abū Hurayra: The Prophet said: If ten Jews would follow me, no Jew would remain that would not embrace Islam!"[27]

In another chain of tradition going back to Muhammad's wife 'Ā'isha, she said:

> The Apostle of God came to me [once] when a Jewish woman was with me and [the Jewish woman] said: Did you know that you will be tested in the grave? ['Ā'isha] said: The Apostle of God was frightened [in response] and said: It is the Jews who will be tested! 'Ā'isha said: We stayed together some nights, and then the Apostle of God said: Did you know that I was given a revelation that you will be tested in the grave? 'Ā'isha said: Thereafter I heard the Apostle of God seeking refuge from the torment of the grave.[28]

In another tradition that reveals a great deal about how Jewish lore remained competitive in relation to Muhammad, one of Muhammad's companions (Ibn `Abbās) is purported to have said: "How can you ask the people of Scripture about their books, when you have the Book of God, the most recent of revelations covenanted by God, which you read unadulterated and unspoiled?"[29] Muhammad is even quoted as saying, "Follow the *sunna* of who was before you inch by inch and span by span, such that if they entered into the burrow of a lizard, you would follow them. We said: O Apostle of God, the Jews and Christians? He answered: Who else?"[30]

On the other hand, Jews are portrayed as asking Muhammad annoying questions and disrespecting him.[31] They lie and cover the actual verse of the Torah that requires stoning for adultery.[32] They practice magic and succeed even in bewitching Muhammad until he is cured by an angel.[33] Muhammad is recorded as having said that he would rather go to Hell than be a Jew or a Christian.[34]

---

[27] Muslim (all references are to the English translation of Ṣiddīqī), 4:1463.

[28] Muslim 1:290 #1212–1214). See also Bukhārī (all references are to the English translation of Kazi), 2:256.

[29] Bukhārī 9:460–461 #613, 614.

[30] Bukhārī 9:314–315 #421–422.

[31] Bukhārī 9:295 #400; Muslim 4:1464, 4:1265 #5853ff.

[32] Bukhārī 8:530, 550; see also 4:532 #829 for another version. This famous tradition is found repeatedly in the sources and reflects the restrictions that rabbinic law added to the biblical requirement of capital punishment for adultery to make it almost impossible to enforce.

[33] Al-Nasā'ī 7:112–113; Cf. Muslim Ṣiddīqī 3:1192-3.

[34] Muslim, 1:30 #68.

In some traditions Muhammad recommends following certain Jewish practices.[35] In others he forbids it.[36]

In short, the Ḥadīth contains a range of views about Jews and Judaism. Some scholars have considered it to be more antagonistic to Jews than the Qur'an, but I believe that remains an open question. The one tradition that people point to most often in order to argue that the Ḥadīth is violently anti-Jewish is one that treats the fate of the Jews at the Endtime, found in both of the most authoritative Ḥadīth collections of Bukhāri and Muslim and given in the name of Muhammad: "The Jews will fight with you, and you will be given victory over them so that a stone will say, 'O Muslim! There is a Jew behind me; kill him!'"[37] This tradition has loomed large in current polemical rhetoric between Jews and Muslims and Israelis and Palestinians. In one rendering of this tradition found only in the collection of Muslim b. al-Ḥajjāj, it is slightly extended: "The last hour would not come unless the Muslims will fight against the Jews and the Muslims would kill them until the Jews would hide themselves behind a stone or a tree and a stone or a tree would say: Muslim, or the servant of Allah, there is a Jew behind me; come and kill him; but the tree Gharqad would not say, for it is the tree of the Jews."[38] That tradition has taken a life of its own in the Israel–Palestine conflict, with each side vilifying the other over various implications drawn from it.[39]

MUSLIM RESPONSES TO THE CLASSIC ARTICULATIONS

In sum, the view of Jews in the Ḥadīth is as mixed as it is in the Qur'an. Jews represent an "other" that remained stubborn in its refusal to recognize the prophetic status of Muhammad and the divine origin of the Qur'an. As a result of their stubbornness and refusal to accept the true status of Muhammad, it was concluded that their status in relation to Muslims must be subordinate and inferior. That lower status became codified in the legal tradition of Islam, but the Jews were not unique. Other minorities such as Christians had the same status. Jews, therefore, are not singled out as "other" in Islam, but rather take their place alongside a number of other "others," ranging from Christians to certain

[35] Bukhārī 7:525; Muslim 2:550–552 #2518–2523, 2528.
[36] Bukhārī 4:442 #668. See also Muslim 3:1156 #5245, 1:268 #1079–1080.
[37] Bukhārī 4:110 #176, 177; 4:509 #791; Muslim 4:1510, #6981–6984.
[38] Muslim 4:1510 #6985.
[39] Anne Marie Oliver and Paul Steinberg, *The Road to Martyrs' Square: A Journey in the World of the Suicide Bomber* (Oxford, 2005), 19–24.

Muslim sectarian communities and even non-monotheists such as Zoroastrians, Hindus and others.

How, exactly, did Muslims in the Middle Ages read the range of positions regarding Jews in the sources? It would be easy for Muslims to construct a permanent portrait of Jews as evil by cherry-picking only the negative sources, of which there were plenty. That, however, rarely happened. Jews were seldom a threat to Muslim power anywhere in the Muslim world during the Middle Ages, while Christians often were. So when there was interest in constructing a negative portrait of a religious minority in the Muslim world, it tended to be directed against Christians. Jews were rarely scapegoated alone as religious minorities, but rather suffered along with other minorities. There were some rare cases, however, in which a Muslim leader or intellectual might feel personally threatened by a Jew or the local Jewish community. This seems to have occurred with an important Muslim intellectual and scholar named `Ali ibn Hazm (Muslim Spain, d. 1064), who was a contemporary of the famed Jewish scholar Isma`il ibn Nagrila (Shmuel HaNagid). Due to a series of historical events and simple bad luck, Ibn Hazm was unable to realize what he believed to be his rightful status as Muslim leader-scholar, while he watched as his Jewish colleague managed to realize "a glorious career at the court of the Berber king of Granada, who appointed him vizier."[40] This seems to have infuriated him, and he wrote a number of works attacking Jews, which became fodder for later antisemitic writings that emerged in the Muslim world during the modern period.

LEGAL AND SOCIAL STATUS

Jews were defined as *dhimmī* people, meaning that they were protected by law despite the fact that they were not Muslims. Jews, along with Christians and sometimes other non-Muslim communities, held legal citizenship in the Muslim world, a status that Jews lost entirely by the high middle ages in the Christian world. The term *dhimmī* derives from the Arabic root *dh.m.m.*, which conveys a sense of blame or fault. A person protected as a *dhimmī*, therefore, is both protected and labeled as in some way blameworthy. This ambivalence is reflected in the treatment of *dhimmī* communities over the centuries. They had legal rights, but at a reduced level than Muslims. They could serve as

---

[40] Camilla Adang, *Muslim Writers on Judaism and the Hebrew Bible* (Leiden, 1996), 68.

witnesses in court, but at half the level of Muslims. They also suffered under sumptuary laws that limited their social rank and privilege in the larger society, sometimes restricting their professions and otherwise humiliating them through certain customs such as wearing distinguishing clothing, dismounting when in the presence of a Muslim pedestrian or not riding horses altogether. *Dhimmīs* were also required to pay a special tax from which Muslims were exempt.[41]

Jews suffered as a second-class minority in the Muslim world, and they sometimes suffered greatly. That was the fate of most minorities in the Middle Ages. The legal and social status of Jews in the Muslim world was no different qualitatively than that of Christians and other protected non-Muslim communities; and it should be added that Muslim non-majoritarian communities could also suffer similarly from their minority status. Jews suffered humiliation and deprivation at times, and they also suffered from occasional violence, even massacres. Jews endured many hardships living among Muslims in the Middle Ages, but they were not referred to as a pariah community relentlessly and unavoidably stamped for evil and slandered as having been totally rejected by God, as occurred to them in the Christian world. In some situations, the legal restrictions imposed on them by law and culture were not enforced or were enforced only partially. Life was good enough materially and spiritually in some places to enable them to produce great literary, legal, artistic and scientific advances that benefited both the Jews and the people living among them. But their legal and social status was always as an underclass. Such was the reality for Jews in the pre-modern world. It was a situation that cannot possibly be compared positively with the treatment of minorities in modern, functional democracies today. Whether or not the comparison is meaningful, the position of Jews (and Christians) under Muslim rule was considerably better than the position of Jews under Christian rule. They were rarely singled out, nor were they demonized in the medieval Muslim world, though this would indeed occur later, in the modern period. Their lot was to be a minority religious community, and minority communities were always susceptible to the possibility of abuse. As the famous Arabic proverb says (cited by all speakers of Arabic, whether Muslim or not), *al-dunya badal: yom ʿasal, yom baṣal* – "Life alternates: one day, honey; another day, onions."

---

[41] Norman Stillman, *The Jews of Arab Lands: A History and Source Book* (Philadelphia, 1979); and Mark Cohen, *Under Crescent and Cross: The Jews in the Middle Ages* (Princeton, NJ, 1994).

Further Reading

Cohen, M., *Under Crescent and Cross: The Jews in the Middle Ages* (Princeton, NJ, 1994). An analytic, comparative study of the treatment of Jews under Christian and Muslim rule.

Firestone, R., "Muhammad, the Jews of Medina, and the Composition of the Qur'an: Sacred History and Counter-History," in Mehnaz Afridi, ed., Special Issue: "Remembering Jewish-Muslim Encounters: Challenges and Cooperation." *Religions* 2019, 10, 63: DOI: 10.3390/rel10010063. www .mdpi.com/2077-1444/10/1/63. A focused study on relations between Muhammad and the Jews of his time according to traditional Muslim and Jewish narratives.

"Muslim-Jewish Dialogue," in C. Cornille, ed., *Blackwell Companion to Interreligious Dialogue* (Oxford, 2013), 224–243. A study of religious discussion and intellectual interchange between Jews and Muslims from the time of Muhammad to the present.

"Muslim-Jewish Relations," in *Oxford Research Encyclopedia of Religion*. DOI: 10.1093/acrefore/9780199340378.013.17. An investigation of religious and political relations between Jews and Arabs/Muslims from before the emergence of Islam to the 21st century.

Who Are the Real Chosen People? The Meaning of Chosenness in Judaism, Christianity and Islam (Woodstock, VT, 2008). An examination of the notion of divine election in Jewish, Christian and Muslim scriptures and tradition.

Goitein, S. D., *Jews and Arabs: A Concise History of Their Social and Cultural Relations* (New York, 1955; reprinted multiple times). A broad study of cultural relations and reciprocal influence between Jews and Muslims from earliest times to the 20th century.

Lewis, B., *The Jews of Islam* (Princeton, NJ, 1984). A longitudinal review of mutual influence and learning between Jews and Muslims in the Muslim world.

Meddeb, A., and B. Stora, eds., *Encyclopedia of Jewish-Muslim Relations from the Origins to the Present Day* (Princeton, NJ, 2013). French edition: *Histoire des relations entre juifs et musulmans des origines à nos jours* (Paris, 2013). A very large collection of original articles on virtually all aspects of relations between Jews and Muslims: ethnic, cultural historical, liturgical, literary, military, etc.

Stillman, N., *The Jews of Arab Lands: A History and Source Book* (Philadelphia, 1979). A history of Jewish life in the Arab world based on Jewish and Muslim sources, with many original writings in translation.

Zeitman, K., and M. Elsanousi, eds., *Sharing the Well: A Resource Guide for Jewish-Muslim Engagement*, www.jtsa.edu/stuff/contentmgr/files/0/4ba8adb270fb8b873ab22fdf33ae9b0f/misc/sharing_the_well.pdf. A "how-to" manual that offers not only information about parallels but also programs and ideas for establishing ties and improving relations between Jews and Muslims in North America.

9 Medieval Western Christendom

ROBERT CHAZAN

The term "Middle Ages" was coined by Renaissance thinkers disdainful of the culture of the medieval period. For these Renaissance thinkers, the centuries they termed the Middle Ages were characterized – perhaps "stigmatized" is better – by the centrality of Christian and Muslim monotheism to every aspect of western life. This monotheistically dominated civilization constituted for the Renaissance thinkers a middle period – that is to say, a period of serious decline – in the history of the West. The decline from antiquity to the Middle Ages involved abandonment of the robust naturalism and empiricism of the Greco-Roman world in favor of the supernaturalism of Christianity and Islam. This middle period of decline was – for the Renaissance thinkers – already showing signs of replacement by a newly invigorated naturalism and empiricism. Thus, the supernaturalism of Christianity and Islam constituted a middle and lamentable segment of western history, sandwiched between the glories of Greco-Roman antiquity and the anticipated achievements of modernity.

While the harsh evaluation of the Renaissance thinkers with respect to the medieval centuries has been softened somewhat with the passage of time, their fundamental definition of these centuries in terms of domination by Christian and Muslim monotheism has remained the core perception of the Middle Ages. Precise dating of this medieval period is not agreed upon, but the central features of this civilization have remained relatively clear in scholarly discourse and popular perception. During what was roughly the millennium from the 6th through the 16th century, all aspects of life in most of the West were dominated by Christianity and Islam – religious sensibilities, cultic praxis, governance, societal structuring, and public and private culture.

In order to understand the imagery of Jews and the actions toward them that evolved in medieval western Christendom, it is certainly important to acknowledge the centrality of the Roman Church during the Middle Ages. However, there are other important aspects of this civilization, its majority structures, and its Jewish minority that must be borne fully in mind as well. Perhaps most important is awareness that, despite the popular perception of the Middle Ages as a period of stagnation, western Christendom changed radically during this period. Rapid and radical change was especially prominent during the second half of the Middle Ages, the 11th–15th centuries.

During this period, western Christendom emerged from profound weakness vis-à-vis its rivals – the Islamic world and eastern Christendom – into a position of strength, indeed, a position of dominance. A major factor in this shift from European weakness to European strength lay in the vitalization of Northern Europe, which was transformed from a backward hinterland to the Mediterranean south into the center of power in western Christendom and in fact throughout the West in its entirety.[1] The development of Northern Europe resulted, *inter alia*, in the emergence of a new branch of the Jewish people, usually designated Ashkenazic Jewry.[2] Just as Northern Europe came to dominate the West, so too did Northern European Jewry come to dominate world Jewry – in numbers, economic strength, political influence, and cultural creativity.

All through late antiquity, Jews inhabited the southern sectors of Europe. This set of Jewish communities is sometimes attributed to a purported Roman expulsion of the Jews from Palestine in the wake of the failed Jewish rebellion of 66–70. In fact, there was no such expulsion; indeed, Jewish settlement across Southern Europe much preceded the rebellion against Rome.[3] The creation of the western Jewish diaspora simply reflects the general tendency toward movement across the Mediterranean Basin throughout late antiquity. Roman control of the entire Mediterranean littoral very much facilitated the movement of people, including Jews, across the length and breadth of this great sea.

The antiquity of the Jewish settlements across Southern Europe meant that, by the beginning of the Middle Ages, these Southern European Jews were well integrated into their environment. As long-time inhabitants of the area, their economic activities were diversified,

---

[1] The changing position of western Christendom and the invigoration of northern Europe are treated in all major surveys of the European Middle Ages. For two major formulations of this invigoration, see R. W. Southern, *The Making of the Middle Ages* (New Haven, CT, 1953), and Johannes Fried, *The Middle Ages* (Cambridge, MA, 2015).

[2] For discussion of the emergence and development of this Northern European Jewry, see Robert Chazan, *Refugees or Migrants: Pre-Modern Jewish Population Movement* (New Haven, CT, 2018), chaps. 8–10.

[3] Ibid., 83–87.

their political status was well established, and their social relations with non-Jews were comfortable.[4] As Europe became increasingly Christian in population and governance, Jews became a community of obvious religious dissidents. Given the backdrop of early Christian–Jewish relations and the residual negativity toward Judaism and Jews embedded in the New Testament, the Church and the Christian populace harbored an inherently negative view of this Jewish minority. However, the early Church had softened the negativity considerably. Major Church Fathers, especially the authoritative Augustine, had pointed to the importance of the Jews in bringing the one true God into human society, which constituted a major contribution to humanity. These Church Fathers also embraced the Pauline conviction that the Jews would eventually recognize their error and embrace Christian truth. In light of past Jewish greatness and future Jewish embrace of truth, Jews had to be preserved and protected within Christian societies.[5] Thus, across Southern Europe of late antiquity and the early Middle Ages, those in the well-established Jewish communities were treated as dissidents who had to be tolerated and to an extent respected, but of course not emulated.

During late antiquity and the first half of the Middle Ages, Jewish traders occasionally made their way across Northern Europe for business purposes. There was, however, no incentive for Jewish settlement in the north, given its obvious backwardness. Jews well ensconced across Southern Europe could hardly take seriously the thought of transplanting themselves to the barren areas of Northern Europe, so clearly deficient in every respect to their present habitation across the south.

In ways still not fully understood, toward the end of the first half of the Middle Ages Northern Europe began a process of vitalization that transformed it from the backward appendage of the weakest of the three major religio-political blocs of the West into the power central of western Christendom, which was becoming the strongest of the three blocs. Indeed, it was precisely the vitalization of Northern Europe that lay at the core of the newfound strength of western Christendom. The once primitive areas that evolved into the powerful monarchies of England

---

[4] On medieval Southern European Jewry, see Chazan, *The Jews of Medieval Western Christendom* (Cambridge, 2006); *Cambridge Medieval Textbooks*, chap. 3.

[5] For the authoritative formulation of these views by Augustine, see Jeremy Cohen, *Living Letters of the Law: Ideas of the Jews in Medieval Christianity* (Berkeley, 1999), chap. 1; Paula Fredriksen, *Augustine and the Jews: A Christian Defense of Jews and Judaism* (New York, 2008); Chazan, *From Anti-Judaism to Anti-Semitism: Ancient and Medieval Constructions of Jewish History* (New York, 2016), chap. 4.

and France and the German principalities came to dominate the West overall. The explanation for the onset of this remarkable vitalization at the midpoint of the Middle Ages has eluded the scholarly world, but the elements in the vitalization have been fully depicted. Enormous progress in economic activity, in political organization, and in cultural creativity transformed the once primitive territories of Northern Europe. In the process, an area long bereft of Jewish population came to harbor the largest portion of worldwide Jewry.

From antiquity onward, the Israelites/Jews were a remarkably mobile people. The potential for mobility was created by the core Israelite conviction of one and only one God in the universe. This one God could be obeyed and worshipped anywhere that Israelites/Jews might find themselves.[6] To be sure, there was special sanctity attached to Canaan/Palestine, which was viewed as the point of origin of Israel and the site promised by God to Israel as its home. Nonetheless, after being expelled by their Babylonian overlords in the wake of their failed uprising against imperial rule, the Judeans of the 6th pre-Christian century settled well into their new environment and quickly picked up the thread of religious creativity, adding new elements and themes to their prior legacy. Indeed, when permitted by their new Persian overlords to return to Canaan, the majority of Judeans elected to remain in Mesopotamia, thus solidifying an eastern diaspora fated to last for millennia.[7] As noted, a parallel western diaspora was created around the Mediterranean Basin as well.

All through late antiquity, Jews were settled across the vast southerly area that stretched from Mesopotamia in the east to the Atlantic Ocean in the west. The configuration of Jewish settlement included an eastern diaspora, a centrally located homeland, and a western diaspora. By the end of the first half of the Middle Ages, the centrally located Jewish community in Palestine had lost its demographic and religious dominance, with the eastern diaspora Jewry – now under the rule of Islam – emerging as the largest and most authoritative of the Jewries. No one at the time could have imagined altered demographic and religious patterns of Jewish life, but in fact such new patterns emerged by the end of the Middle Ages.

The earliest migration of Jews northward in Europe involved two factors: Jewish awareness of the vitalization taking place across

---

[6] For this general mobility, see Chazan, *Refugees or Migrants*.

[7] Limited but useful insight into the early evolution of this eastern diaspora Jewry is provided by the biblical books of Ezra and Nehemiah.

northwestern and north-central Europe and the interest of some of the rulers of this developing area in attracting urban settlers into their domains. As noted, the well-rooted Jewries of Southern Europe were economically diversified. Many of the economic subgroups of southern Jews were locked into place, with their economic activities grounded in their sites of habitation; one economic subgroup, however, was especially mobile: those Jews involved in trade. Such Jews gained firsthand awareness of the developments taking place across the north and fairly quickly opted to take advantage of these developments. Both the Jewish and non-Jewish sources that have survived from the 11th and early 12th centuries indicate that the early Jewish settlers across Northern Europe were predominantly involved in trade and business.

The second factor in the movement northward was the support of many of the rulers in this rapidly developing area. One of the features of the vitalization of Northern Europe – indeed, one of the major factors in this vitalization – was the emergence of a group of dynamic and insightful rulers committed to advancing the development of their domains. These rulers understood the importance of the expansion of urban centers and the economic and governmental role these urban centers might play. Key to the expansion of the urban centers was the attracting of urban settlers from the better-developed areas of the south. The rulers of Northern Europe made strenuous efforts to attract urban settlers, including Jewish urban settlers. This governmental support was the second major factor in stimulating Jewish settlement during the earliest stages of Jewish migration northward.

An unusually valuable set of sources for the establishment of a new Jewish settlement in the Rhineland town of Speyer illuminates the role of supportive rulers and clarifies at the same time the other forces at work for and against Jewish immigration. In the year 1084, the ruling authority in Speyer – Bishop Rudiger, the local bishop – exploited unusual circumstances to invite Jews to settle for the first time in his town. Two sources for this event have survived – one in Hebrew composed by slightly later Speyer Jews and the second composed in Latin in 1084 by Bishop Rudiger himself.[8]

The Hebrew report was composed a few decades after 1084, on a celebratory occasion. The Jews of early 12th-century Speyer recalled the circumstances of the founding of their community. They were aware that the origins of their community lay in the neighboring Rhineland

---

[8] For these two documents, see Chazan, ed., *Church, State, and Jew in the Middle Ages* (New York, 1980), 57–59.

town of Mainz. That older Jewish community was distressed by a pair of untoward developments. First, a fire broke out in the Jewish neighborhood of Mainz and spread beyond it. The damage caused by this fire infuriated the Christian burghers of Mainz, deeply discomfiting the Mainz Jews. At the same time, a visiting Jewish merchant carrying a precious book was murdered as part of an effort at plunder. The combination of these two events frightened many Mainz Jews, and their fears convinced the bishop of nearby Speyer that he might lure them to his town. The role of the bishop in the establishment of the Jewish community of Speyer is emphasized in the Hebrew narrative. "The bishop of Speyer greeted us warmly, sending his ministers and troops after us. He gave us a place in the town and expressed his intention to build about us a wall to protect us from our enemies, to afford us fortification. He pitied us as a man pities his child."[9] Later Speyer Jews expressed deep appreciation and high praise.

Fortunately, history has provided for us the charter that Bishop Rudiger extended to the frightened Mainz Jews. While this charter does not include information on the Mainz Jews whose situation occasioned the invitation to Speyer, it does corroborate the later Speyer Jewish sense of the central role of Bishop Rudiger and provides much greater detail on his thinking and on the terms of his invitation. The bishop indicates that his motivation was improvement of the town over which he ruled. "When I wished to make a city out of the village of Speyer, I Rudiger surnamed Huozmann, bishop of Speyer, thought that the glory of our town would be augmented a thousandfold if I were to bring Jews."[10] This is a striking preamble to a charter of invitation to new Jewish settlers. The bishop does not point to religious or moral obligation; his focus lies clearly with the material development of his town of Speyer. The contribution of the Jewish settlers to the glory of Speyer surely lay in the economic contribution they would make to their new abode. It seems clear that many Northern European rulers shared this sense of the contribution that Jewish settlers might make to their domains.

The protections that Bishop Rudiger details out are illuminating. The very first involves physical safety. As noted in the Jewish recollection and spelled out in the charter of invitation, Bishop Rudiger provided for the new Jewish settlers a separate neighborhood and encircled that area with a wall, intended to provide safety. The charter of invitation and the later Jewish recollection agree on these details.

[9] Ibid., 59.
[10] Ibid., 58.

Next, Bishop Rudiger provided the immigrating Jews with the right to carry on their trading freely. Litigation involving these Jews was to be conducted by internal Jewish courts; disputes that could not be addressed internally would be adjudicated by the bishop himself; these Jews would not be subjected to the authority of the municipal burgher court. Finally, these Jews were not to be burdened by a number of traditional ecclesiastical limitations. The set of protections and rights granted to the Mainz Jews settling in Speyer was comprehensive and surely appealing.

The combined sources for the founding of the Jewish community of Speyer highlight the role played by the political authorities in the settlement of Jews across Northern Europe during the second half of the Middle Ages. They also indicate that, beyond the political authorities, there were two additional societal elements in Northern Europe that impacted Jewish settlement: the powerful Roman Church and the burgher population. We shall follow the evolution of the stances of the three majority societal elements that shaped Jewish life across rapidly developing and changing Northern Europe.

In our Speyer sources, the urban Christian populace appears as negative from the outset to the immigrating Jews. To return briefly to our Speyer material, we saw that the urban Christian populace played a major and negative role. We recall the outbreak of burgher antipathy as a result of the fire in the Jewish neighborhood of Mainz and the role of that burgher hostility in stimulating many – but by no means all – Mainz Jews to uproot themselves. Bishop Rudiger put burgher animosity – expressed in Mainz and anticipated in Speyer – front and center in his charter, providing the new Jewish settlers with an area of the town all their own and surrounding that area with a wall. The sources of burgher opposition to the new Jewish settlers in Northern Europe are not difficult to reconstruct. Like all indigenous groups, the burghers of Mainz, Speyer, and other Northern European towns resented the intrusion of newcomers. This is a tendency by no means confined to medieval Northern Europe; it is a ubiquitous human reaction. Additionally, since business was a mainstay of the developing urban economy of Northern Europe, the newly settling Jewish merchants constituted economic competitors to the indigenous Christian burghers, indeed, competitors enjoying the advantage of the bishop's support.

In addition to the normal human resentment of newcomers and competitors, there was a specifically Christian factor as well. The Gospel portraits of Jesus' Palestinian Jewish contemporaries are extremely harsh. Jesus was, to be sure, crucified by the Romans, but the Gospel authors were anxious to indicate that the Romans in fact had no quarrel whatsoever with him. Rather, according to the Gospel accounts, it was the relentless, misguided, and groundless Jewish enmity toward Jesus that moved the Romans to condemn and crucify him. Jewish celebration of the crucifixion of Jesus further deepens the negativity of the Gospel portraits of these first-century Palestinian Jews.

We have noted that the Church softened considerably the harsh Gospel portrait, which resulted in the eventual consolidation of the balanced Church policy we have cited – the combination of protection and limitation of Jews in Christian societies. However, the rank-and-file Christian populace had very limited grasp of – or indeed little interest in – the intricacies of Church doctrine and policy. Most medieval Christians knew little of the Church view of a brilliant early Jewish history or little of the Church conviction of eventual Jewish acceptance of Christian truth.

What the Christian populace at large knew in detail was the extremely negative Gospel portraits of the Jews who opposed and perse-cuted the entirely innocent Jesus, essentially out of Jews' misguided and heartless hatred of him and the truth he brought to the world. This imagery of hateful and heartless Jews was a key element in the founding story of Christianity, and everyday Christians were confronted with this story from birth through death. The story of the Crucifixion was pre-sented movingly in every possible art form. Indeed, one of the two major events of the Christian calendar – Easter – focused on the Crucifixion and thus inevitably brought to the fore the dastardly Jews responsible for the tragic aspects of Easter. Celebration of Easter and engagement with the inevitably related imagery of Jewish hatred and hatefulness constituted central and recurring experiences in the lives of the Christian populace of Northern Europe. The anti-Jewish sentiment evoked by the Gospel portrayal of Jesus' Jewish contemporaries exacer-bated the normal human antipathy toward newcomers.

The impact of this Gospel portrait and its broad societal embrace is clearly reflected in the first incident of broad anti-Jewish violence unleashed against the Jews of Northern Europe: the assaults on a number of Northern European Jewish communities triggered by the First Crusade.[11] The First Crusade was called by Pope Urban II in late 1095, and crusading militias began to organize almost immediately. The First Crusade reflects accurately the religious aggressiveness of rapidly developing western Christendom. Earlier in the 11th century, the

---

[11] For an overview of these assaults, see Chazan, *European Jewry and the First Crusade* (Berkeley, CA, 1987).

militias of western Christendom began a protracted effort to conquer areas of the Iberian Peninsula wrested from Christian control many centuries earlier. This campaign lasted until 1492, at which point the final Muslim stronghold fell into Christian hands. The achievements on the Iberian Peninsula in conjunction with the voyage of Columbus in that same year are key factors in the common dating of the close of the Middle Ages at the end of the 15th century. The Iberian enemy against which invigorated western Christendom mobilized was Islam, and the same is true of the newer campaign called by Pope Urban in 1095.

The First Crusade constituted a brilliant, albeit short-lived achievement for western Christendom. Major barons organized effective militias that battled their way eastward through hostile territory – land controlled by the Byzantine Greeks and a variety of Muslim rulers. During the summer of 1099, a number of these effective militias besieged Jerusalem and conquered it, to the joy of western Christendom in its entirety. The successes of these militias were widely chronicled, and the extensive narratives report engagement with only Muslim forces. Attacks on Jews do not make an appearance in these narratives, which reflects the broad sense that the pope had in no way suggested a conflict with Jews.

While Pope Urban II was essentially interested in the effective fighting forces that coalesced under baronial leadership and conquered Jerusalem, the campaign he launched galvanized a far larger swath of European Christians. In addition to the experienced warriors that Urban sought to mobilize, popular preachers and minor barons reacted with enthusiasm and excitement. These popular preachers and minor barons in turn attracted large crowds of followers. The end result was the unleashing of unruly forces, involving a very high likelihood of the explosion of dangerous popular sentiment, and this is precisely what happened in certain areas of Northern Europe, where the new Jewish settlers were deeply resented by their Christian neighbors.

While the well-organized and successful crusading militias are not reported to have expanded their mission against the Muslims holding Jerusalem into anti-Jewish violence, the popular bands that coalesced across Northern Europe, on the other hand, actually achieved nothing against the Muslim enemy but deflected their sense of mission into attacking a number of the new Jewish communities of the north. These attacks are documented in both Jewish and Christian sources, which by and large agree with each other. The grounds for the assaults lay clearly in the Gospel imagery we have highlighted. The exhilarated attackers made the following argument for attacking the Jewish communities of

Northern Europe. The campaign to which they had committed themselves involved attacking Muslims in the East. However, beginning the campaign by attacking Jews in Northern Europe made more sense, for two reasons. First, Muslims merely failed to acknowledge Jesus; Jews were clearly far worse, since they were responsible for the death of Jesus. Second, the Muslim enemy was far off in the East, while the more heinous Jewish enemy was right here at home. The obviously more sensible path was to first annihilate the Jewish enemy and then proceed eastward to assault the Muslim enemy.[12]

This view of the crusade was obviously not promulgated by Pope Urban II; it was utterly incompatible with the traditional Church doctrine we have noted; and it was quickly denounced by the leadership of the Church as the succeeding crusades developed. Additionally, the political leadership of Northern Europe intervened in 1096 and thereafter to protect Jews endangered by the unwarranted spillover of crusading fervor. The assaults of 1096 are sometimes portrayed as a turning point in the history of Northern European Jewry and a major milestone in the history of anti-Jewish imagery and behavior. Both evaluations are misguided. While two major Jewish communities – Mainz and Worms – were destroyed, they were quickly rebuilt. The rest of Northern European Jewry was largely unscathed and continued its remarkable growth. Given the subsequent repudiation of the extreme and unusual anti-Jewish crusading slogan, it is difficult to see these limited attacks as a milestone in either anti-Jewish thinking or behavior. What the assaults of 1096 do reveal is the intense level of anti-Jewish sentiment within the Christian populace of Northern Europe.

Further intensification of burgher animosity resulted from important Church policies, both general and addressed specifically to the issue of the Jews. By the end of the first Christian millennium, the Church had articulated clear doctrine vis-à-vis Jewish presence in Christian societies and had adumbrated policies designed to ensure that these doctrines were operative. The core Church doctrine proclaimed the initial contribution that early Jews had made to humanity by bringing the one true God into human society. This virtue was to an extent offset by the historical error of the Jews of Palestine in rejecting Jesus, indeed, in occasioning his death. The Church, however, embraced the Pauline conviction that the Jews would ultimately recognize religious truth and accept Christianity. The virtues of the Jewish past and the assurance of the Jewish future

---

[12] For a version of this argument reported in an early Hebrew source, see ibid., 225.

meant that Jews deserved a safe and secure place in Christian society. Violence against Jews grounded in their religious dissidence was forbidden. To be sure, the Church did not have the means of enforcing this policy, but it could insist that the secular authorities provide the requisite protection, which they by and large did.

While insisting on the Jewish right to safe and secure existence in Christian societies, the Church was also concerned with potential harm that Jews might inflict on the Christian societies that hosted them. What forms might such harm take? The most direct harm involved denigration of the ruling faith. Medieval Christians were well aware of the lengthy history of Christian–Jewish religious polemic, beginning with the exchanges between Jesus and the Jews of Palestine recorded in the Gospels. They knew that their leaders had over the ages forged further arguments for the superiority of Christianity over Judaism. To an extent, these arguments involved the virtues of Christianity; inevitably, however, they also contrasted the virtues of Christianity with the shortcomings of its Jewish rival. Aware of this tendency toward religious contrast, medieval Christians understood that their Jewish contemporaries drew parallel contrasts between the positives of their faith and the negatives of Christianity. Indeed, the Gospels themselves show the Jews of 1st-century Palestine leveling harsh criticisms against Jesus, criticisms portrayed in the Gospels as specious but criticism, nonetheless. Aware of Jewish critiques of Christianity, the Church forbade public expression of such critiques, and the political authorities bore the obligation of enforcing this important prohibition.

There was a second Church concern with the harm that Jews might inflict on their Christian contemporaries. Given the common grounding of the two religions in the Hebrew Bible, the Church feared that Jews might quietly argue to Christian associates the superiority of their faith and thus seduce Christians from Christianity to Judaism. This concern manifested itself early in the maturation of the Church. The very first steps taken to reduce this possibility involved prohibiting relationships in which Jews might exercise authority over Christians. Thus, the Church prohibited Jews from owning Christian slaves, from marrying Christians, or from occupying positions of political power. In all these situations, a Jewish position of power might well eventuate in Jewish religious influence and infringement on Christian religious identity. This early Church concern was maintained through the ages.

As western Christendom became increasingly well organized and powerful during the second half of the Middle Ages, the Church became better organized as well and was thus in a position to intensify its strictures against public criticism of Christianity and against private efforts to sway individual Christians out of their faith and broadened its perception of the harm that Jews might inflict on their Christian neighbors. The increasingly powerful Church of the latter centuries of the Middle Ages moved beyond the prohibition of Jews occupying positions of power toward an effort to limit Christian–Jewish contact far more drastically. Indeed, the range of Church concerns with the Jews was expanded markedly.

With the passage of time, medieval Jews were forced into separate neighborhoods. We recall Bishop Rudiger's creation of a separate Jewish neighborhood in order to protect the immigrating Jewish settlers of Speyer. The new Church initiative was oriented in a completely different direction. These later separate neighborhoods – increasingly identified as ghettoes – were not at all intended as protective; rather, they were intended to reduce the likelihood of Christian–Jewish contact and thus the potential for Jewish influence on Christian believers. The most radical innovation in this direction was the 1215 Church decree ordering that Jews wear distinguishing garb that would make them readily identifiable under all circumstances.[13] Once again, the Church could enjoin, but it was up to the political authorities to enforce the ecclesiastical decrees.

Entirely new Church concerns with Jews emerged during the second half of the Middle Ages. Because of the popular antipathy already noted, opportunities for the new Jewish settlers across Northern Europe to diversify economically were impeded. The new Jewish immigrants were rescued from economic limitation and potential economic disaster in an unexpected way, through a new Church initiative. Increasingly powerful and aggressive, the 12th-century Roman Church sought to revive and enforce energetically long-neglected traditional prohibitions. One such traditional prohibition that was newly emphasized involved the taking of interest on loans by Christians from Christians.

Such taking of interest by Christians from Christians was prohibited in Deuteronomy, and the prohibition was embraced early on by the Church.[14] It was not, however, vigorously enforced until the 12th century. The new enforcement was especially problematic in Northern Europe, given the rapidly expanding economy of that area during the

[13] Solomon Grayzel and Kenneth R. Stow, eds. and trans., *The Church and the Jews in the XIIIth Century*, 2 vols. (Philadelphia, 1933–1989), vol. 1, 308–309.
[14] Deut. 23:20–21.

12th century. The new Church effort and the widespread need for the
exchange of funds opened a window of opportunity for the new Jewish
settlers in the north, who were encountering serious economic competition and limitation on the part of the indigenous burghers. While Jews
were forbidden from taking interest from fellow-Jews, there was no
prohibition of their taking interest from Christians. Thus, Jews were
available to fill the newly created gap in the Northern European money
trade, and they did so. Moneylending became a central facet of Jewish
economic activity across Northern Europe, to the advantage of the Jews
themselves, of the general economy, and of the rulers who could readily
tax burgeoning Jewish wealth.

By the early 13th century, Jewish involvement in moneylending had
reached the point of evoking considerable Church concern. Scattered
ecclesiastical voices argued that Jewish moneylending was inherently
illegitimate, but these voices were in the minority and failed to impact
Church policy. Jewish moneylending remained permitted; however,
abuses were identified by the Church and zealously opposed. These
abuses began with the depositing of sacred ecclesiastical vessels as
pawns with Jewish lenders. The fate of such pawns aroused fears among
churchmen. What might Jews do with such sacred objects in their
possession? The possibilities seemed frightening, and churchmen
insisted on governmental limitation of the range of objects that might
be deposited with Jewish lenders.

There were far broader Church concerns elicited by Jewish
moneylending. The Church from early in its history assumed the role
of protector of the disadvantaged in society. This role came to involve
protection for the poorer class in Northern Europe forced by dire
necessity to turn to Jewish lenders. Churchmen were deeply concerned over maltreatment of these poor and unfortunate Christian
borrowers and sought to provide as many safeguards as possible.
Such safeguards included limitations on the amount of interest
charged by Jewish lenders, prohibition of compounded interest that
could quickly escalate indebtedness, limitations on those who might
borrow from Jews, and limitations on the items that might be
deposited as pawns, in order to ensure, for example, that poor borrowers not leave their winter garb with Jews and thus expose themselves
to the cold and that they not leave with Jews the implements with
which they supported themselves. Eventually, many churches established lending institutions of their own with arrangements extremely
favorable to impoverished borrowers, in order to provide indigent
Christians with safe alternatives to the Jewish lenders. Once again,

the Church could demand, but it required the secular authorities to enforce, which they often did.[15]

The Jewish turn to moneylending added further fuel to the animosity of the populace already noted. While the money trade has always been critical to societal success, it has never been appreciated. Those involved in banking and moneylending have always been deeply resented. Jewish gravitation to the money trade was triggered by the Church's 12th-century assault on Christian taking of usury from fellow-Christians and was valuable to the burgeoning economy of Northern Europe, but it reinforced the initial resistance of the Northern European populace to the new Jewish settlers. It enhanced the traditional Christian imagery of Jewish enmity to Jesus by portraying Jews as profoundly hostile to contemporary Christianity and Christians.

Over the course of the 12th century, this conviction gave rise to imagery of Jews gratuitously killing innocent Christian contemporaries, especially blameless and defenseless children. These charges of gratuitous murder were in mid-century embellished with the claim that Jews sometimes committed their killing by crucifying the young victims. During the 13th century, this imagery gave way to the allegation that Jews murdered Christian youngsters in order to use their blood for Passover rituals. The repeated efforts on the part of the leadership of both church and state to rebut these stereotypes were largely unsuccessful. The new imagery became embedded in the cultural folklore of western Christendom and did incalculable harm to Jews over the ensuing centuries.[16]

The rulers of medieval Christendom were located within a complicated context that included the following: important material considerations involving both general economic development and the immediate fiscal needs of the ruling class; the Church with its balanced policies vis-à-vis Jews, and the hostile populace of the rapidly developing northern sectors of Europe. Once again, there was evolution and change. To an extent, the ruling class overall impacted the Jews of western Christendom in positive ways; to an extent, the impact was negative.

We have already seen the positive role played by the rulers of Northern Europe in the initial settlement of Jews across their territories. The thinking of these rulers seems to have largely involved general

---

[15] For a set of responses of 13th-century French monarchs to ecclesiastical demands, see Chazan, *Church, State, and Jew*, 205–217.

[16] For an overview of this new imagery, see Chazan, *Medieval Stereotypes and Modern Antisemitism* (Berkeley, CA, 1997).

economic stimulation of their domains, as reflected in the charter of
Bishop Rudiger of Speyer. Stimulation of the general economy played an
important role in governmental encouragement and protection of the
young Jewry of northwestern and north-central Europe during the 11th
and 12th centuries; the same considerations emerged during the closing
centuries of the Middle Ages across northeastern Europe. As these
backward areas sought to emulate the successes of their more westerly
neighbors, attracting Jewish settlers became a governmental policy
across northeastern Europe, whose rulers offered potential Jewish immigrants charters that provided multiple inducements to settlement.[17]

With the passage of time, another material factor in governmental
protection of Jewish clients emerged into prominence, and that involved
governmental revenue derived from the Jews. During the second half of
the Middle Ages as the rulers of western Christendom became increasingly ambitious, their aspirations were restricted by the limited financial resources at their disposal. Innovative taxation to enable expansive
new governmental projects lay in the future. Under these circumstances, a deeply dependent group like the new Jewish settlers of
Northern Europe – and eventually the Jews of the older southern areas
of Jewish settlement in western Christendom as well – proved invaluable. Such dependent Jews could not oppose or evade tax imposts, as
heavy as they might be. On occasion, taxation gave way to outright
confiscation. The Jews came to constitute a major revenue source for
the rulers of medieval western Christendom. This aspect of governmental benefit from the Jews bore serious dangers. In some instances, Jewish
communities were in effect taxed out of existence, as their holdings
were taxed to the point of total depletion of Jewish economic resources;
in other instances, one of the motivations for expulsion of Jews was
confiscation of Jewish holdings in their entirety.

The rulers of medieval western Christendom could and did predi-
cate their actions vis-à-vis the Jews in terms of the economic benefits
for their domains and/or themselves. Besides their assessments of
material gains to be derived from their Jewish clients through steps
helpful or harmful to these Jews, the rulers of medieval western
Christendom had to relate to the two further forces on the European
scene: the Roman Church and the populace at large. As noted, the
Middle Ages have been defined as a period during which Christianity
and Islam dominated the behavior and thinking of the West. In medieval

[17] For two of these charters, see ibid., 84–93.

western Christendom, this dominance was reflected in the societal power exercised by the organized Church centered in Rome. The prevailing imagery projected the Church as the soul of western Christendom, orienting that society in proper directions, and the state as the body of western Christendom, carrying out the dictates of the soul. While this is an oversimplification of the complex relations between the medieval church and state, there is no question as to the power exercised by the Roman Church throughout medieval Europe.

The Church demanded physical protection of the Jews, and the ruling class concurred with this necessity. Governmental stances toward the limitations demanded by the Church involved considerable ambivalence. Often these demands impinged seriously on governmental profit generated from the Jews, thus moving the rulers of western Christendom to oppose or at least neglect Church demands.[18] Overall, however, consistent opposition or neglect of Church demands vis-à-vis the Jews was difficult. Conversely, some independently conceived governmental policies were intended *inter alia* to curry favor with the Church.

In addition, the rulers of medieval western Christendom had to relate to the populace at large, which across Northern Europe was by and large hostile to the new Jewish settlers. Considerations of governmental needs and of Church policy enabled the rulers of western Christendom to consistently and readily oppose popular anti-Jewish violence. At the same time, here too some governmental initiatives were intended to win favor with the populace at large. Prominent among such initiatives was the innovative step of expelling Jews from local domains or even entire kingdoms. Not surprisingly, this innovation first appeared across Northern Europe, where Jewish presence was new and much resented. Eventually, the innovation made its way southward into the older areas of Jewish settlement. The most stunning expulsions of the Middle Ages involved the Jews of the Iberian Peninsula, whose origins lay far back in antiquity. These expulsions shook the Jewish world of the late 15th and the 16th centuries to its core.

While expulsion of Jews was an important element in Jewish experience in antiquity, the medieval expulsions differed so radically that it is appropriate to identify them as innovations and indeed important innovations, which were to have significant impact on late medieval and early modern Jewish life. The two major expulsions of antiquity involved Jewish polities in Canaan, which were accurately perceived by

---

[18] For interesting instances of rulers rejecting Church demands, see Chazan, *Church, State, and Jew in the Middle Ages*, 179–183.

imperial overlords – Assyria and Babylonia – as challenging their domination. There was nothing uniquely anti-Israelite or anti-Judean in
these expulsions. Expulsion was the standard imperial strategy for
responding to perceived opposition on the part of subject peoples and
has been widely documented throughout the Ancient Near East.[19]

The circumstances of the medieval expulsions were radically different. They did not involve Jews as a political unit in their homeland and
did not reflect political issues. Rather, the medieval expulsions involved
the Jews as a dissident religious community within Christian society.
This dissident religious minority enjoyed the right to a safe and secure
existence in Christian society; at the same time, it was limited in some
of its actions that would have been detrimental to the Christian majority. Thus, the formal grounds for expulsion were not political opposition
as in antiquity, but rather Jewish religious misbehavior. In the early
sequence of expulsions from northwestern and north-central Europe,
the Jewish misbehavior regularly involved Jewish usury; in the late
medieval expulsions from Iberia, the Jewish misbehavior allegedly
involved religious influence on Christian contemporaries.

Our analysis of the complexities of the Jewish situation in medieval
western Christendom suggests that there was much more than simple
enforcement of the rules for Jewish life in these medieval expulsions. In
some cases, there was clearly a desire on the part of the rulers for
material gain. Expulsions always involved confiscation of much if not
all of the resources of the expelled Jews. Further, in many cases, the
expulsions were intended to curry favor with the Christian populace at
large, which across Northern Europe tended to be hostile to the new
Jewish settlers. Rationalizations of expulsions of the Jews were focused
on Jewish breach of the rules governing Jewish life; motivations for
expulsions were considerably more complicated.

The stances of the three majority elements that shaped Jewish life
across Northern Europe during the second half of the Middle Ages – the
populace, the Church, and the ruling class – tended toward greater
negativity during the second half of the Middle Ages. The urban burghers were from the outset of Jewish immigration negative, and their
negativity became more pronounced over the centuries. The Church's
moderate position of protection and limitation came to focus increasingly on limitation. The rulers, who tended to be supportive at the
outset, became increasingly harsh, eventually expelling their Jews from

---

[19] See Bustenay Oded, *Mass Deportations and Deportees in the Neo-Assyrian Empire*
(Wiesbaden, 1979).

the most advanced areas of Northern Europe. Strikingly, these Jews found new homes in the more backward regions of Northern Europe, opting to stay within the new ambience of Northern Europe and to pursue the growth and development that would eventually make them the dominant element in worldwide Jewry.

Further Reading

Baer, Y., *A History of the Jews in Christian Spain*, trans. Louis Schoffman et al., 2 vols. (Philadelphia, 1961–1966). The authoritative reconstruction of Jewish life in Spain subsequent to its reintegration into western Christendom.

Chazan, R., ed., *Church, State, and Jew in the Middle Ages* (New York, 1980). A collection of useful source materials for studying the history of the Jews in medieval western Christendom during the second half of the Middle Ages.

Chazan, R., *The Jews of Medieval Western Christendom 1000–1500* (Cambridge, 2006). A broad overview of Jewish life in medieval western Christendom during the second half of the Middle Ages.

Reassessing Jewish Life in Medieval Europe (Cambridge, 2010). An examination and explanation of the ways in which the preceding overview of medieval European Jewish life differs from the prevailing views.

Cluse, C., ed.. *The Jews of Europe in the Middle Ages (Tenth to Fifteenth Centuries)* (Turnhout, 2004). Valuable essays on Jewish life in medieval western Christendom during the second half of the Middle Ages.

Jordan, W. C., *The French Monarchy and the Jews: From Philip Augustus to the Last of the Capetians* (Philadelphia, 1989). Careful reconstruction of Jewish life and royal policy toward the Jews in medieval France.

Kisch, G., *The Jews in Medieval Germany: A Study of Their Legal and Social Status* (New York, 1970). A broad overview of the history of the Jews in the diverse German principalities by a distinguished legal scholar.

Moore, R. I., *The Formation of a Persecuting Society* (Oxford, 1987). A pathbreaking study of the enhanced marginalization of a number of medieval minority groups, including the Jews.

Richardson, H. G., *The English Jewry under Angevin Kings* (London, 1960). A study of medieval English Jewry by a distinguished scholar of medieval England.

Stow, K. R. *Alienated Minority: The Jews of Medieval Latin Europe* (Cambridge, MA, 1992). Another valuable overview of the history of the Jews in medieval western Christendom.

10 Christian Theology and Papal Policy in the Middle Ages

JEREMY COHEN

Few would dispute that medieval Christianity and the popes who stood at the head of the medieval Catholic Church contributed roundly to the history of anti-Judaism. But historians have disagreed extensively as to change and development in theological attitudes toward the Jews during the Middle Ages and the ways in which theology conditioned ecclesiastical policy. Surely, the papacy championed the rights of Jews to live securely and practice their religion in European Christendom, perhaps more than any other medieval institution. At the same time, however, doctrinal principles also underlay its efforts to ensure that the social, economic, and political status of the Jews would not impinge on the interests of the church or the welfare of Christians. While other chapters in this volume address important dimensions of Christian–Jewish relations in medieval Europe, here we focus on the impact of doctrine on papal policy.

As with so many other issues, the great church father Augustine of Hippo (354–c. 430) laid the doctrinal foundations for medieval Christian attitudes toward Jews and Judaism, in their case in his acclaimed doctrine of Jewish witness. Over the last several decades, Augustinian teaching concerning the Jews has offered fertile ground for scholarly investigation – and debate – and here we shall suffice with a brief summary that highlights its essential components and ramifications in the legacy bequeathed to Augustine's medieval.

One might well term this Augustinian doctrine balanced, ambivalent, or both. It found its best-known expression in Augustine's understanding of God's instructions for dealing with his enemies in Psalm 59:12 (Psalm 58 in the Vulgate): "God shall let me see over my enemies: slay them not, lest at any time my people forget. Scatter them by thy power; and bring them down." On the one hand, Jews and Judaism still had a vital role to play in Christendom, notwithstanding their rejection of Jesus and their complicity in his crucifixion. God had preserved them and their biblical books as witnesses to the truth of Christianity that the

Old Testament embodied and prefigured, even if the Jews remained blind to their scripture's meaning. Providing this testimony depended on their survival, both physical and cultic: Jews and their biblical religion had a necessary, rightful place in the proper Christian world order.

> That same nation, even after being conquered and subjugated ..., persisted in the old law, so that within it [the Jewish people] there would be witness of the Scriptures throughout the world, wherever the church would be established.... Therefore "slay them not"; do not destroy the name of that nation, "lest at any time they forget your law" – which would surely happen if, having been forced to observe the rites and ceremonies of the gentiles, they would not retain their own religious identity at all.[1]

On the other hand, Augustine explained, it was inadequate for God to say, "'Slay them not, lest at any time they forget your law,' without adding 'scatter them.' For if they were not everywhere, but solely in their own land with this testimony of the scriptures, the church, which is everywhere, could surely not have them among all the nations as witnesses to the prophecies given previously regarding Christ."[2] Just as it mandated their survival, the testimony that the church sought from Jews and Judaism required their dispersion and subjugation in exile, the loss of their temple and political autonomy in Jerusalem, and their subjugation for the benefit of the church. One needed not only their testimony but also living proof that the church had vanquished the synagogue, that Christianity had superseded Judaism as sole legitimate expression of God's covenant with Israel.

Augustine had constructed a theological Jew, a "hermeneutical Jew" as I have suggested elsewhere,[3] to serve the needs of the church in authenticating the legitimacy of Christianity in his day. These needs, rather than familiarity with contemporary Jews or Judaism, determined the constitution and character of this Jew, and the services provided by the hermeneutical Jew underlay the mandate to preserve him. The assumption that the Jews in Christendom were, in fact, the Jews as Augustine imagined them lay at the theological basis of subsequent ecclesiastical policy, to which Augustinian teaching made a fourfold

---

[1] Augustine, *Epistulae* 149.9, CSEL 44:356.

[2] Augustine, *De civitate Dei* 18.46, CCSL 48:644–645.

[3] Jeremy Cohen, *Living Letters of the Law: Ideas of the Jew in Medieval Christianity* (Berkeley, 1999), pt. 1. I have drawn repeatedly from this study throughout the present essay.

contribution: (1) the recognition of a definite need for the Jews (appropriately dispersed and subjugated) within Christian society; (2) a polemical imperative of *Adversus Judaeos* – negating the Jewish understanding of Hebrew Scripture as a means of asserting Christianity; (3) the direction of such scripturally focused polemic to Christian and pagan – but not to Jewish – audiences; and (4) a lack of concern with postbiblical Judaism. Why polemicize and missionize among the Jews if Christendom required their presence? Why concern oneself with postbiblical Judaism if the Jews, as Augustine construed them, preserved and embodied the law of Moses and if the development of Judaism effectively stopped on the day of Jesus' crucifixion, when the Old Testament gave way to the New? Many have appraised Augustine's doctrine of Jewish witness as essentially benign in its stance vis-à-vis Jews and Judaism. As one expert has written, it proffered "a brilliant and novel defense" of Jews and Judaism, safeguarding Jewish lives for centuries.[4] As we shall see, however, the doctrine came to have a menacing dimension and made a lasting mark on the history of antisemitism.

Did that doctrine undergo transformation during the Middle Ages? Some have argued that it remained essentially unchanged, from the 5th and 6th centuries until the 15th and 16th. Others have maintained that "during the Middle Ages two schools of thought emerged, each with its own program – the first emphasizing exclusively the negative, and the second both the positive and negative aspects of Paul's writings on the Jews."[5] The first of these schools of thought found expression in the virulent anti-Jewish sermons of John Chrysostom in 4th-century Antioch and found a medieval proponent of the 9th-century bishop Agobard of Lyons; the second in the Pauline prophecy that all Israel would ultimately be saved and in the Augustinian instruction that sought to temper toleration with subordination and enslavement. Subsequent churchmen tended toward one of these outlooks or the other in dealing with the Jews, often trying to strike an appropriate balance between them. Still other historians, the present writer included, have discerned important shifts in Christian attitudes toward Jews and Judaism, in the 12th and 13th centuries above all, when the church's awakening to the reality of a still evolving, postbiblical

---

[4] Paula Fredriksen, *Augustine and the Jews: A Christian Defense of Jews and Judaism* (New York, 2008), 211.

[5] Kenneth R. Stow, "Hatred of the Jews or Love of the Church: Papal Policy toward the Jews in the Middle Ages," in *Antisemitism through the Ages*, ed. Shmuel Almog, trans. Nathan H. Reisner (Oxford, 1988), 71–72.

rabbinic Judaism threatened the basis for preserving Jews as witnesses to ancient biblical tradition. Disqualification of Talmudic Judaism as having no place in a properly ordered Christian society may certainly have influenced ecclesiastical policy, both in obvious and in subtle fashion, undermining the security of the Jews in the domains of the medieval Catholic Church.

Presenting a meaningful overview of our subject proves more difficult still, owing to the problematic relationship between theological principle and papal policy. All of the theological stances regarding the Jews and Judaism to which we have alluded were rife with ambivalence, and various factors broadened the gap between theory and practice. Doctrine alone rarely dictated the decrees and declarations of medieval popes concerning the Jews, but social, political, and, perhaps most important, economic issues played their part as well. Understandably, historians have debated the extent to which papal policy itself remained constant during the Middle Ages, some arguing that it did, others that one cannot discern a common strategy in the varying policies of individual popes. Nonetheless, most would agree that by the end of the medieval period papal policy toward the Jews had grown more hostile and oppressive. As one of leading authorities on our subject concluded, "the attempt of the papacy to steer a middle course between the conflicting demands of the Augustinian formula had finally ended in failure."[6]

When did this happen, and why? The pages that follow consider three stages in the medieval history of ecclesiastical and papal pronouncements concerning Jews and Judaism. Without attempting here to resolve any of the scholarly debates that we have mentioned, we hope to highlight the complexities and ambivalence that characterize the relation between theology and papal policy.

GREGORY THE GREAT AND THE FORMULA OF *SICUT JUDAEIS*

If Augustine stood on the precipice overlooking the end of late antiquity, Pope Gregory the Great, more than any other single individual, led the Latin West into the Middle Ages. In the history of Christianity, Gregory's literary career and pontificate (590–604) heralded the end of the patristic period and the entry of Roman Catholicism and its church into a patently different phase in their development.

---

[6] Shlomo Simonsohn, *The Apostolic See and the Jews: Documents* (Toronto, 1991), 38.

Gregory's role as a trailblazer extends to our story as well. As one historian of the papacy has affirmed, "With respect to the Jews, as with everything else Pope Gregory touched, he is a founder of papal tradition, one of those great men who work for the future as they respond to the turmoil of the present collapse."[7] In the unfolding history of Jewish–Christian relations, Gregory blended Augustinian theology and principles of Roman law into policies that figured significantly in medieval canon law for centuries to come. At the same time, Gregory's theological and exegetical works – perhaps his commentary (Moralia) on Job above all – often veered in a different direction, giving expression to traditional messages and motifs of patristic Adversus Iudaeos doctrine but comporting neither with the singular features of Augustinian teaching nor with the norms of his own administrative policy. As such, Gregory's career and literary legacy exemplify the frequently recurring dissonance between theology and policy in the medieval church's attitudes toward Jews and Judaism.

During the years of his pontificate, Gregory addressed the subject of the Jews and their communities in more than two dozen letters, which divide readily among several chief concerns. Although many scholars have reviewed the specific circumstances and legal ramifications of Gregory's decrees, we adduce them here for their ideological underpinnings – that is, for their perceptions of the Jewish condition and purpose in Christian society. Responding to the complaints of Jews, Gregory intervened on at least six occasions to prevent violence against Jews, their synagogues, and their religious practices. In March 591, a Jew named Joseph complained to the pope that Bishop Peter of Terracina had repeatedly expelled the Jews of that town from their places of worship. Gregory admonished the bishop that "they should be allowed to convene, as they used to do, in the place that (as we have said) they obtained with your knowledge in order to congregate there. It is necessary to join to the unity of the faith people who differ from the Christian religion through gentleness, friendliness, exhortation, and persuasion, but not with physical compulsion."[8]

---

[7] Edward A. Synan, The Popes and the Jews in the Middle Ages (New York, 1965), 35. On Gregory and the Jews, see also the recent essays of Bruno Judic, "Grégoire le Grand et les juifs, pratiques juridiques et enjeux théologiques," in Jews in Early Christian Law Byzantium and the Latin West, 6th–11th Centuries, ed. John Tolan et al. (Turnhout, 2014), 95–117; Rodrigo L. Cohen, "Theological Anti-Judaism in Gregory the Great," Sefarad 75 (2015), 225–252; and other studies cited therein.

[8] Gregory, Epistulae 1.34, in Simonsohn, The Apostolic See and the Jews, 3; Amnon Linder, ed., The Jews in the Legal Sources of the Early Middle Ages (Detroit, MI, 1997), 418. I have followed the numeration of Gregory's letters appearing in Dag Norberg, ed., Sancti Gregorii Magni Registrum Epistularum, CCSL 140–140A.

Gregory evinced determination to redress the injustice done the Jews, and several months later he appointed two other bishops to join with Peter in assuring the Jews a house of worship and putting their complaint to rest. "We forbid that the said Hebrews be aggrieved or harassed contrary to reason. But as they are permitted to live by the Roman laws, justice allows that they should manage their affairs as they see fit, without any obstruction."[9] In the same year, a report from southern France elicited similar instruction to the bishops of Arles and Marseilles: "Many of the Jews dwelling in that region are led to the baptismal font by force rather than through preaching." Praiseworthy motivations notwithstanding, "I fear that this very intention ... either should not produce the labor's reward or should even result (God forbid) almost in the loss of the souls we want to save."[10]

Later in the decade, when a Jewish convert to Christianity brought a crucifix into the synagogue of Cagliari, seeking to prevent Jewish worship, Gregory cited the Roman statute permitting Jews to maintain their old synagogues despite their inability to build new ones. Even if Christian missionaries should claim to act out of zeal for the faith, they should deal with the Jews in moderation, so "that they should be attracted [to convert] willingly rather than led unwillingly."[11] In 602, similarly minded Christian zealots in Naples received more outspoken condemnation: "Those who desire in a sincere effort to bring aliens to the Christian religion – to the right faith – should strive toward it with allurements, not harshness, lest those whose mind should be attracted by clear reason should be driven away by hostility." Christians who violently distance Jews "from the accustomed observation of their rite, prove that they are acting for themselves and not for the sake of God."[12] In 598, with words that would have critical impact on ecclesiastical policy toward the Jews centuries hence, Gregory encapsulated the rationale for these various rulings in a letter to the bishop of Palermo, against whom the Jews had also lodged a complaint with the pope. "Just as the Jews should not [*Sicut Judaeis non* ...] have the freedom to presume anything in their synagogues beyond what is permitted by law, in the same way they should not suffer any prejudice in those matters which were granted them."[13]

---

[9] Ibid. 2.45, ed. Simonsohn, 7; Linder, *The Jews in the Legal Sources*, 423.
[10] Ibid. 1.45; Simonsohn, 4–5; Linder, *The Jews in the Legal Sources*, 419.
[11] Ibid. 9.196; Simonsohn, 19–20; Linder, *The Jews in the Legal Sources*, 439.
[12] Ibid. 13.13; Simonsohn, 23–24; Linder, *The Jews in the Legal Sources*, 433.
[13] Ibid. 8.25, Simonsohn, 15–16; Linder, *The Jews in the Legal Sources*, 434.

Although Gregory's opposition to baptizing the Jews under duress acknowledges the rightfulness of their presence in his Christian society, one finds little evidence that he deemed that presence a necessity. On the contrary, Gregory's correspondence also alludes to an additional priority of his policy, no less important: undermining that presence through the conversion of the Jews to Christianity. In his letter quoted above, Gregory did not merely command his bishops to desist from anti-Jewish violence; he directly instructed them to preach to the Jews and thus win their souls for the church. He frequently prescribed that baptized Jews receive special protection and financial rewards, because "we should, with reasonable moderation, aid those whom our Redeemer deems worthy to convert from the Jewish perdition to himself."[14] Nor did the danger of insincere conversion, which informed Gregory's insistence that Jews not be baptized against their will, militate otherwise in this case. As he wrote to a Sicilian deacon in 594, at least the souls of subsequent generations would be protected: "We do not act in vain when we lead them to Christ's grace through the alleviation of *pensio*, for even if they themselves come with but small faith, their children after them will be baptized with greater faith. We shall gain either them or their sons."[15] Gregory's apocalyptic expectations rendered the task of converting the Jews an urgent one, and he therefore proposed to dispense with the normally required period of the catechumenate for prospective proselytes, "for time impels us now to delay their wishes no longer on account of the raging plague."[16]

If the exigencies of history motivated Gregory to relax ecclesiastical rules and expedite the conversion of Jews, how much the more so did he stand by the restrictive half of his *Sicut Judaeis* formula and endeavor to prevent encroachments of Jews and Judaism on Christianity. He objected to the sin (*nefas*) of the sale of sacred objects to a Jew, ordering the vessels restored, and he responded vehemently to reports of Judaizing among Christians. Romans who advocated refraining from work on the Jewish Sabbath Gregory labeled "preachers of Antichrist," who, at the end of days, will observe both Saturday and Sunday as days of rest. Because the Antichrist "feigns his death and resurrection from the grave, he wishes Sunday to be kept holy; and, because he compels the people to Judaize – in order to restore the exterior observance of the law and subordinate the perfidy of the Jews to himself – he wishes

---

[14] Ibid. 4.31; Simonsohn, 10–11.
[15] Ibid. 5.7; Simonsohn, 11–12; Linder, *The Jews in the Legal Sources*, 429.
[16] Ibid. 8.23; Simonsohn, 4–15; Linder, *The Jews in the Legal Sources*, 33.

Saturday to be observed."¹⁷ Repeatedly, Gregory's letters prohibit
Jewish ownership of Christian slaves, "lest, God forbid, the Christian
religion should be polluted by its subjection to Jews."¹⁸ Once again, the
pope took care that his decrees complied with the protective provisions
of Roman law, and he upheld the rights of Jews to sell slaves acquired
expressly for resale and to retain Christian serfs on their estates. Yet, as
he explained to the kings and queen of the Franks, the ownership of
Christian slaves by Jews subverted the very integrity of Christ and his
church: "For what are all Christians but members of Christ? We all
know their head, for you honor it faithfully. But what a difference, let
your Excellence judge, between honoring the head and permitting his
enemies to tread down his members."¹⁹

Even though Gregory might have sounded more avidly anti-Jewish
in his theological and exegetical works, even though he never cited
Augustine's exegesis of Psalm 59:12, and even though his commitment
to proselytizing among the Jews may have strayed from the logic of
Augustinian witness doctrine, he still played a role in transmitting the
Augustinian legacy. Given the administrative context in which Gregory
had regulated the status of what he still perceived as Roman Jewry, one
can readily discern the logic in his translation of theology into papal
policy. If Augustine had understood Roman rule over the Jews to fulfill
biblical prophecy, it behooved Gregory, head of the Roman Church, to
maintain that aspect of imperial policy and govern his subjects accordingly. Gregory claimed justification for his Jewish policy in terms of
Roman legal precedent, both in the application of the Theodosian Code
to the protection of synagogues and to the restriction on Jewish slave-
holding as well as in a recurring appeal to the general import of Roman
legislation. Inasmuch as the Jews "are permitted to live by the Roman
laws, justice allows that they should manage their affairs as they see fit,
without any obstruction." His principle of *Sicut Judaeis* invokes a
similar rationale, limiting Jewish rights to that which is "permitted by
law [*permissum est lege*]." Furthermore, the recurring emphasis on the
public rituals of the Jews – their holy days, their celebrations, their
communal worship and its venue – in Gregory's protective edicts
bespeaks the Augustinian notion that the divine mandate of "slay them
not" entails the perpetuation of their Judaism, the *forma Iudaeorum*,
and not merely the preservation of their lives. As we have seen, Gregory

¹⁷ Ibid. 13.1; Simonsohn, 8–9.
¹⁸ Ibid. 3.37; Simonsohn, 4–5; Linder, *The Jews in the Legal Sources*, 425.
¹⁹ Ibid. 9:214, 9:216; Simonsohn, 20–21; Linder, *The Jews in the Legal Sources*, 440.

acknowledged the didactic purpose of Jewish survival in a dispersed, subjugated state. He reaffirmed Augustinian instruction that the blindness of the Jews in Jesus' day resulted in their persecution of him and that such blindness, then and now, constitutes divine punishment for their sin. Gregory's aforecited rationale for preaching to contemporary Jews despite their intransigence reads much like the directive of Augustine's *Tractatus adversus Iudaeos*: "Testimonies should be taken from the holy scriptures, whose authority is very great among them, too; if they refuse to be restored by the benefit which they offer, they can be convicted [*convinci*] by their blatant truth."[20] No wonder historians have frequently grouped the two churchmen together in laying the groundwork, both theological and legal, for papal protection of – and discrimination against – the Jews during the Middle Ages.

INNOCENT III AND THE PLENITUDE OF PAPAL POWER

The massacres of Northern European Jews that accompanied the launch of the First Crusade in 1096, even if such violence contravened the norms established by the papacy, initiated a century of developments that would prove critical in the history of European Jewry. Anti-Jewish violence that stemmed from the fervor of the crusade did not, as some may have thought, express a conscious repudiation of Augustinian doctrine of Jewish witness or a reversal in medieval Jewish policy that marked the "beginning of the end" for the Jews of the Middle Ages. In virtually every respect (demographic, economic, social, and cultural), the medieval civilization of Western European Jews followed the lead of the majority, Christian experience, and it reached the peak of its achievement only during the 12th and 13th centuries. Nevertheless, the unlicensed violence of 1096, although not within the mandate of the crusaders, undoubtedly awakened Christian society to the anomaly of the Jews' position: enemies/killers of Christ whose lives and errant religion God had protected for the greater good of Christendom. Yet such an awakening transpired in a rapidly changing Christian Europe. New interaction with Muslims, Islam, and Muslim culture; the continuing renewal of commerce and urban life; the rise of schools, universities, and Scholasticism; and the emergence of a stronger, more assertive papacy and ecclesiastical bureaucracy – all these nourished a

[20] Augustine, *Tractatus adversus Judaeos* 1:2, PL 42:51–52; see also 6:8 (col. 56), "sive consentiant sive dissentiant," and 10:15 (cols. 63–64), "sive gratanter, sive indignanter audiant Judaei."

new "discourse of otherness" that understandably wrestled afresh with the Jews and Judaism, scrutinizing and classifying them along with everything else in the Christian experience. The crusaders' disorderly departure from the norm of "slay them not" only fueled the urgency to define the proper place of the Jews in the new Christian order of things. What Jaroslav Pelikan once termed the age-old and "ineluctable demand that the church make sense of Judaism and clarify its relation to the ancient people of God"[21] now assumed new importance, as R. I. Moore has argued forcefully:

> The entire movement for the reinvigoration of the Church, the revival of learning, and the reassertion of royal authority ... was founded on the conviction that the laws, customs, and standards of antiquity must be restored, both in religious and in secular matters.... Such a programme was bound to heighten awareness of the patristic account of the position of Jews in Christian society, to be preserved securely but miserably as a reminder to Christians of the death of their Saviour.[22]

Though he was not the first 12th-century pope to reflect this awareness, the pontificate of Innocent III (1198–1216), when Innocent's personality and policies helped bring the medieval papacy to the peak of its power and influence, gave it its most forceful expression. His policies reflect a papal ideology and a program for implementing an ideal order in Christian society, and they testify to the successes of a reform papacy as medieval Christendom flourished in its expansion and prosperity – soon to give way to entrenchment, regimentation, fragmentation, and, ultimately, decline.

Innocent's pontificate marked an important stage in European Jewish history, as over thirty of his extant letters and canons 67–70 of the Fourth Lateran Council – truly one of his crowning achievements – concern the Jews, most of them marked by a fervently hostile, even zealous tone. They bespeak a determination to eliminate perceived abuses of the limited toleration and harsh restrictions mandated for the Jews of Christendom in canon law and patristic theology – abuses whereby Jews enjoyed superiority over Christians in everyday life and, more infuriating still, flaunted their thankless contempt for Christianity and the

---

[21] Jaroslav Pelikan, *The Christian Tradition: A History of the Development of Doctrine*, 5 vols. (Chicago, 1971–1989), 3:34.

[22] R. I. Moore, "Anti-Semitism and the Birth of Europe," in *Christianity and Judaism*, ed. Diana Wood (Oxford, 1992), 37.

Catholic Church to whom, Innocent emphasized, they owed their survival. Some historians have actually labeled Innocent's bulls and conciliar canons a noteworthy turning point in the history of medieval Jewry,
although these judgments may have exaggerated. In their tone,
Innocent's correspondence and legislation surely display an uncompromising impatience that might at times have approached the fanatical. In
their substance, however, they reaffirm a commitment to the
Augustinian doctrine of Jewish witness and the Gregorian legal principle
of *Sicut Judaeis*: Innocent seeks not to eliminate the presence of Jews and
Judaism from Christendom but rather to assert the "plenitude" of his
papal power in enforcing their inferior, subjugated, and enslaved status.

The following examples from among letters and decrees give
instructive expression to Innocent's concerns.

- Innocent numbers among a series of 12th- and 13th-century popes
  to issue the "Constitution on Behalf of the Jews," the famous *Sicut
  Judaeis* bull of the Middle Ages, that used this principle of Gregory
  the Great to enumerate the protections extended to the Jews by the
  Church. Christians may not convert the Jews to Christianity by
  force, subject them to physical violence, rob them, damage their
  synagogues and cemeteries, or interfere with the lawful practice of
  their religion. Innocent prefaced his version of the bull with a
  blatantly Augustinian rationalization:

  > Although the Jewish perfidy is in every way worthy of
  > condemnation, nevertheless, because through them the truth
  > of our own faith is proved, they are not to be severely oppressed
  > by the faithful. Thus the prophet says, "Slay them not, lest at
  > any time they forget your law, or more clearly stated, you shall
  > not destroy the Jews completely, so that the Christians should
  > never by any chance be able to forget your law, which, though
  > they themselves fail to understand it, they display in their
  > books to those who do understand."[23]

- No less emphatically, Innocent concluded his bull with the following
  proviso: "We wish, however, to place under the protection of this
  decree only those who have not presumed to plot against the
  Christian faith." And one understandably wonders how many Jews

---

[23] Simonsohn, *The Apostolic See and the Jews*, 74–75; Solomon Grayzel, ed., *The
Church and the Jews in the XIIIth Century*, rev. ed. (New York, 1966), 93, 95, with
minor changes.

Innocent would have classified as plotting or not plotting against the Christian faith.

- Indeed, in a series of letters to prelates and princes during the years that followed,[24] Innocent railed against abuses of this ecclesiastical policy, as if the Jews and their Christian patrons had upset the necessary balance: demeaning Christianity, they kept Christian servants and nursemaids in their homes. Their usurious money-lending oppressed vulnerable Christians and, owing to foreclosures, deprived the church of rightful tithes. They kept the better parts of meat, cheese, and wine that they produced for themselves, selling the rest to Christians. They blasphemed, abetted Christian criminals, and benefited from undue privileges in legal disputes with Christians. All this, as some have suggested, violated the quasi-contractual terms of *Sicut Judaeis*,[25] inasmuch as the guilt of the Jews in the rejection (and crucifixion) of Jesus has confined them "to perpetual servitude," Innocent wrote a pair of French bishops in his *Etsi Judeos* bull of 1205.[26] In the same year (in *Etsi non displiceat*) he denounced Christian rulers "who prefer the sons of crucifiers ... to the heirs of the crucified Christ and who prefer the Jewish slavery to the freedom of those whom the Son freed."[27] In his 1208 letter (*Ut esset Cain*) to a French count, Innocent likened the Jews to Cain, whom God surely protected with his mark. "Although they ought not to be killed, lest the Christian people forget the divine law, yet as wanderers ought they to remain upon the earth, until their countenance be filled with shame and they seek the name of the Lord Jesus Christ."[28]

- Convened in November of 1215, the Fourth Lateran Council "in many ways represents the culmination of Innocent's efforts to take control of the Church and to reform it: and also to 'protect' Christians from the potential harmful influences of schismatics, heretics, Jews and Muslims."[29] Innocent sought to define, consolidate, and enhance the

---

[24] On these bulls as a threesome, see, among others, Simonsohn, *The Apostolic See*, 19–21; John Tolan, "Of Milk and Blood: Innocent III and the Jews, Revisited," in *Jews and Christians in Thirteenth-Century France*, ed. Elisheva Baumgarten and Judah D. Galinsky (New York, 2015), 139–149, and "Introduction," in *Jews and Muslims under the Fourth Lateran Council*, ed. Marie-Thérèse Champagne and Irven M. Resnick (Turnhout, 2018), 15–18.

[25] Stow, "Hatred of the Jews or Love of the Church," 8off.

[26] Simonsohn, *The Apostolic See*, 86–87.

[27] Ibid., 82–83; Grayzel, *The Church and the Jews*, 107.

[28] Simonsohn, *The Apostolic See*, 92–94; Grayzel, *The Church and the Jews*, 127.

[29] Tolan, "Introduction," 12; and see the other essays in pt. 1 of the same volume.

power of the Roman Church both within and beyond the geographical limits of European Christendom, and several of its decrees
addressed the Jewish and Muslim minorities living under Christian
rule. At Innocent's initiative, the council sought to prevent Jewish
moneylenders from extorting "oppressive and excessive interest"
from their Christian borrowers. Since "it would be too absurd for a
blasphemer of Christ to exercise power over Christians," it banned
Jews from holding public office. It forbade baptized Jews from
reverting to their previous religious rites. And, in the decree that
European Jews found especially dangerous to their safety, it decreed
that – in order to obviate sexual relations with unknowing
Christians – Jews and Saracens must wear distinguishing marks on
their clothing and must avoid appearing in public from Holy
Thursday through Easter Sunday.[30]

His zeal in discriminating against the Jews notwithstanding, while
Innocent bemoaned the damages and insults that they cause Christians,
he refrained from meddling in their inner religious lives, and he did not
indict contemporary Talmudic Judaism as a postbiblical heresy as his
successors would do two to three decades later. Similarly, he did not call
for organized, ecclesiastically sponsored efforts to convert the Jews to
Christianity; this too would ensue years hence, after the legitimacy of
contemporary European Jewry had been undermined. Scrutinizing the
realities of Jewish–Christian interaction and displaying zero tolerance
for divergence from patristic or canonical norms, Innocent surely
planted seeds for such developments that would soon transpire. For
the moment, however, Innocent appeared determined to enforce the
balances mandated in existing papal policy, albeit with greater strin-
gency and less permissiveness.

THE ATTACK ON THE TALMUD AND
CONTEMPORARY JUDAISM

Innocent's aggressive posture and his zealous scrutiny of contemporary
interactions between Jews and Christians may well have laid the
groundwork for changes in papal policy that he himself did not institute
but that transpired within decades after his death – above all in the
condemnation of the Talmud and in the promotion of missionary efforts

---

[30] Tolan, *Jews and Muslims under the Fourth Lateran Council*, 223–233; cf. also
Grayzel, *The Church and the Jews*, 308–313.

to convert the Jews. Pope Gregory IX heard the Talmud denounced by Nicholas Donin, an embittered Jewish apostate, in 1236. Three years later Gregory issued a series of condemnatory bulls, ordering rulers and prelates of Christian Europe to impound the Talmud and other Jewish writings on the first Sabbath during Lent in 1240 and to submit the books to ecclesiastical authorities for inspection. Only King Louis IX of France complied; he confiscated rabbinic texts, summoned leading French rabbis to his court in 1240 to defend the Talmud against Donin's charges, and, after an ecclesiastical commission passed judgment, proceeded to burn the Talmud in Paris in 1242. Soon after ascending the papal throne, Innocent IV renewed Gregory's decrees in 1244. Yet this time the Jews protested directly to the papal curia, and in 1247 Innocent ordered King Louis to refrain from moving against the Talmud until a new investigation conducted by the papal legate Odo of Chateauroux should render a verdict. Odo and his colleagues reaffirmed the earlier condemnations and urged not to return confiscated Talmudic texts to their Jewish owners. A number of subsequent popes followed suit in condemning the Talmud, which was confiscated, censored, and/or burned under ecclesiastical direction on several additional occasions during the following centuries.[31] And, as the 13th century progressed, popes required the Jews to submit to the proselytizing sermons of Dominican and Franciscan friars.[32]

The attack on the Talmud constituted an unprecedented ecclesiastical offensive against contemporary rabbinic Judaism. Talmudic Judaism, ran the argument, amounted to Jewish heresy, inasmuch as it allegedly replaced the biblical covenant between God and Israel with a new law fabricated by the rabbis who understood that the Bible properly led to an acceptance of Christianity. Concerning the Jews, Pope Gregory wrote,

> not content with the Old Law which God gave in writing through Moses, and even ignoring it completely, they affirm that God gave them another Law which is called the Talmud, that is teaching.

---

[31] Numerous historians have told and retold this story; recently, see Chazan, "Trial, Condemnation, and Censorship: The Talmud in Medieval Europe," in John Friedman et al., *The Trial of the Talmud: Paris, 1240* (Toronto, 2012), 1–92, and the sources and other studies cited therein.

[32] Among others, see Simonsohn, *The Apostolic See*, 228ff., 313ff., and elsewhere; Cohen, *The Friars and the Jews: The Evolution of Medieval Anti-Judaism* (Ithaca, NY, 1982), esp. chap. 4; Chazan, *Daggers of Faith: Thirteenth-Century Christian Missionizing and Jewish Response* (Berkeley, 1989), esp. chaps. 1–3.

They lie to the effect that it was handed down to Moses orally and implanted in their minds, and was preserved unwritten for a long time until there arrived those whom they call sages and scribes, who reduced it to writing so that it not be forgotten from people's minds. Its written version exceeds the text of the Bible in size.[33]

When the Jews pleaded with Innocent IV not to take renewed action against the Talmud, they evinced an awareness of Augustinian doctrine and argued that without it "they are incapable of understanding the Bible and the other statutes of their law in keeping with their religion." For his part, Pope Innocent acknowledged: "We who, in keeping with the divine injunction, are obligated to tolerate them in the observance of that law ... do not want to deprive them of their books unjustly, if, in so doing, we should deprive them of the observance of their law." Yet the papal commission ruled that the Jews had lied in their assertion, and the campaign against the Talmud continued. Thus did Innocent IV, in his own commentary on Gregory IX's code of canon law, the *Decretales*, explain his actions:

The pope can judge the Jews if they violate the moral precepts of their law and their own prelates do not punish them, and likewise if they invent heresies against their own law. Impelled by this latter reason [*hac ratione*], Pope Gregory and Pope Innocent ordered the books of the Talmud, in which many heresies are contained, to be burned.[34]

Some historians have maintained that the concern of the popes soon shifted from alleged heresy to anti-Christian blasphemy and hatred in the Talmud, as "the question of false, extra scriptural traditions was being astutely swept aside,"[35] and that confiscation and censorship replaced burning as the disciplinary measure of choice. Nonetheless, however one gauges the relative weight of the accusations against rabbinic literature, one can hardly deny that they signal a new focus. No longer does papal policy suffice with addressing the interactions of Christians and Jews, seeking to ensure that Jews enjoy no more than the

[33] Simonsohn, *The Apostolic See*, 172; Grayzel, *The Church and the Jews*, 127 (with modification).
[34] Innocent IV, *Commentaria ... super libros quinque decretalium* ad X.3.34.8, re-edited in Benjamin Z. Kedar, "Canon Law and the Burning of the Talmud," *Bulletin of Medieval Canon Law* 9 (1979), 80–81.
[35] Stow, *Alienated Minority: The Jews of Medieval Latin Europe* (Cambridge, MA, 1992), 258–259.

"perpetual servitude" accorded them in the pronouncements of Augustine, Gregory the Great, and others. Now the church asserted that the plenitude of papal power extends to the religion of the Jews as well; for the Talmud and the contemporary rabbinic Judaism that it nourished, fraught with anti-Christian hostility, marked a departure from the stagnant biblical Judaism whose scripture and whose observance underlay the mandate to preserve them. Popes now took action against the Talmud, and they called for active efforts to undermine the Jewish presence in Christendom and to induce Jews to convert. Popes continued to oppose forced baptisms and repeatedly sought to defend Jews against violence sparked by ritual murder accusations and blood libels. Yet what else remained of the spirit of *Sicut Judaeis*? As Solomon Grayzel responded over forty years ago, "little more was left than that living Jews, when all was peaceful around them, could not be compelled to accept baptism, and that dead Jews might remain in their cemeteries undisturbed."[36]

* * *

Evidently, the grounding of papal policy in the teaching of Augustine proved more complicated than one might have supposed. Although it expressly forbade such violence, guaranteed the Jews the right to continue living as Jews in Christendom, and minimized the urgency in the church's mission to the Jews, Augustine's doctrine of Jewish witness eventually contributed to the darker side of the subsequent history of Christian anti-Judaism. Building on the teachings of Paul, it too enshrined the place of the Jews as quintessential "other" in the process of Christian self-definition and mandated that Jews be "convicted" of their error as a means of validating the tenets of Christian doctrine. More important still, it grounded the protection of Jews and Judaism in their embodiment of the character and images that Augustine (and other church fathers) had constructed for them, with little or no basis in the realia of contemporary Jewish life. In due course, the medieval church awakened to the reality that the Jews of Christendom had not remained fossilized or "stationary in useless antiquity" as Augustine postulated they had; they no longer embodied and testified to the Christian truth of Hebrew Scripture.

---

[36] Grayzel, "Popes, Jews and Inquisition from 'Sicut' to 'Turbato,'" in *Essays on the Occasion of the Seventieth Anniversary of the Dropsie University*, ed. Abraham I. Katsch and Leon Nemoy (Philadelphia, 1979), 167.

Some churchmen thus began to conclude that, owing to the gap between rhetoric and reality, the logic and protection of "slay them not" no longer extended to the Jews of their own day. Augustine's witness doctrine – and the realization that it might no longer have applied to postbiblical Jewry – ultimately aggravated the processes that led to the destruction of Jewish books, the persecution of Jews and Judaism, and the expulsions of the Jews in late medieval Europe. When European kings and princes did expel the Jews from their domains during the last centuries of the Middle Ages, the papacy evinced no meaningful opposition.[37]

Further Reading

Champagne, M.-T., and I. M. Resnick, eds., *Jews and Muslims under the Fourth Lateran Council* (Turnhout, 2018). A recent collection of essays on the decrees of the Fourth Lateran Council (1215) concerning non-Christians in Christendom.

Chazan, R., *Daggers of Faith: Thirteenth-Century Christian Missionizing and Jewish Response* (Berkeley, CA, 1989). A study of 13th-century interreligious polemics against the background of unprecedented ecclesiastical efforts to convert Jews to Christianity.

Cohen, J., *The Friars and the Jews: The Evolution of Medieval Anti-Judaism* (Ithaca, NY, 1982). A study of the new Christian assault on contemporary postbiblical Judaism in the 13th and 14th century, and the role of Dominican and Franciscan friars in implementing it.

Living Letters of the Law: Ideas of the Jew in Medieval Christianity (Berkeley, CA, 1999). The career of Christianity's "hermeneutical Jew," the Jew constructed to meet the needs of Catholic theology, from Augustine to the 13th century.

Grayzel, S., *The Church and the Jews in the XIIIth Century*, 2 vols. (New York, 1966–1989). First published in 1933, the classic collection of papal and conciliar decrees, in their Latin original and English translation, summaries, and/or notes. Vol. 1 is prefaced by Grayzel's still valuable historical overview, vol. 2 contains Grayzel's important study of 13th-century ecclesiastical policy, "Popes, Jews and Inquisition from 'Sicut' to 'Turbato.'"

"The Papal Bull *Sicut Judaeis*," in *Studies and Essays in Honor of Abraham A. Neuman*, ed. Meir Ben-Horin et al. (Leiden, 1962), 243–248. Grayzel's foundational essay on the standard papal constitution on behalf of the Jews, protecting their rights to live unharmed under Christian rule.

Linder, A., ed., *The Jews in the Legal Sources of the Early Middle Ages* (Detroit, MI, 1997). Documents of early medieval legislation concerning the Jews, in their Latin original with Linder's notes and translation. Pts. 3–5 contain ecclesiastical sources.

---

[37] Cf. Simonsohn, *The Apostolic See and the Jews*, 37.

Pakter, W., *Medieval Canon Law and the Jews* (Ebelsbach, 1988). A topically organized legal-historical study of the Jews in ecclesiastical legislation and jurisprudence, through the 13th century.

Rist, R., *Popes and Jews, 1095–1291* (Oxford, 2016). A fresh reevaluation of high medieval papal policy, stressing the specific concerns and contexts of individual popes and decrees.

Simonsohn, S., *The Apostolic See and the Jews*, 7 vols. (Toronto, 1988–1991). A monumental collection of papal letters concerning the Jews through the mid-16th century: six volumes of documents followed by a broad, topically organized historical overview.

Stow, K. R., "Hatred of the Jews or Love of the Church: Papal Policy toward the Jews in the Middle Ages," in *Antisemitism through the Ages*, ed. S. Almog, trans. N. H. Reisner (Oxford, 1988), 71–89. An engaging presentation of the author's understanding of constancy and development in medieval papal Jewry policy.

11 Crusades, Blood Libels, and Popular Violence

EMILY M. ROSE

When Jews in Northern Europe heard the hoofbeats of horses pounding the ground and signaling the advance of crusaders headed to Jerusalem, they were terrified. Jews rounded up their families, buried their valuables, and raced to safety in the nearest fortification or lord's castle*. The arrival of armed Christian pilgrims often spelled disaster for Jews as crusaders rushed through towns searching for coins, metal, treasures, anything that could be carried off or exchanged for necessary equipment, clothing, supplies and food to venture across continental Europe toward the Holy Land. Inflamed by eloquent preachers, crusaders were a brotherhood of sworn compatriots energized by their families and neighbors. Conscious of the serious commitment they were making and the costs it entailed, these armed bands charged across the landscape. Jewish communities in Northern Europe were often their first target.

Crusaders knew that many Jews were urban dwellers, moneylenders and coin dealers who kept pawned objects, cash and valuable merchandise in their houses. Crusader attacks on Jewish homes were pragmatic because they thought "that's where the money is." But it was not mere practicality or the heightened emotions of the time and place that drew them to assault Jews, offer them the choice of baptism at the point of a sword or hack them to death without waiting for a response.[1] Many of those who had taken vows and were "signed by the cross" (*crucesignatus*) were also inspired by stories they heard of Jewish treachery. As well as seeking valuable loot, crusaders were aroused to violence against Jews by religious tales and horrific rumors about Jews that first began to circulate precisely in this era. The worldly benefits they received, the

---

* The author would like to thank Joshua Franklin, Jordan Goldson, James Marrow, Irven Resnick, Vasily Rudich, Gabriel Spiegel and Froma Zeitlin for helpful comments.
[1] David Malkiel "Destruction or Conversion. Intention and Reaction, Crusaders and Jews, in 1096," *Jewish History* 15.3 (2001), 257–280; and in his *Reconstructing Ashkenaz: The Human Face of Franco-German Jewry, 1000–1250* (Stanford, CA, 2009).

booty, the destruction of the records of their debts, merely confirmed the righteousness of the soldiers' cause.

The violence of the crusader attacks is one of the sorriest aspects of Jewish history in Western Europe. Antisemitism of the High Middle Ages was once understood as a straightforward narrative with a clear beginning and end. The periodization was simple: toleration for centuries, outbreaks of frenzy against Jews and Jewish communities during and in the immediate wake of the Crusades, followed by a gradual diminishment of targeted violence during the early modern era. But this is vastly oversimplified. Violence against Jews and Jewish communities differed significantly according to time and place, even during the heyday of medieval Jew hatred. And far from disappearing, with the emergence of print, myths about Jews that first took hold in the Middle Ages were increasingly and widely disseminated and became institutionalized and entrenched in popular culture.

Changing attitudes have to be understood, moreover, in relation both to long-term forces and to immediate conditions rooted in local financial, political and religious affairs. Against this backdrop, the Crusades to the Holy Land were an important spur to attacks on Jews but were only one factor in the growth of popular antisemitism during this period. Other more insidious developments discussed here, such as stories told about Jews, accusations made against them and observations of their behavior, had significant impacts on the shape, the intensity and the lasting power of popular Jew hatred, even if they frequently appear much less dramatic in the sources. This essay will outline major developments of the period in roughly chronological order and consider many factors that contributed most significantly to the growth and power of popular animosity against Jews. All these elements reinforced negative ideas about the role of Jews and how they should be treated, even as they were modified by local circumstances.

The first crusader massacres in 1096, apparently unprecedented, have long been considered a turning point in the history of Jewish–Christian relations following centuries of relative toleration.[2] For hundreds of years after the fall of the Roman Empire Jews and Christians had lived together in relative peace and stability. But when Pope Urban II preached the First Crusade, rousing knights to head across Europe to protect Christian pilgrims and to liberate Jerusalem from its recent

---

[2] David Nirenberg, "The Rhineland Massacres of Jews in the First Crusade: Memories Medieval and Modern," in *Medieval Concepts of the Past: Ritual, Memory, Historiography*, ed. G. Althoff, J. Fried and P. J. Geary (Cambridge, 2002), 279–310.

conquest by Muslim rulers, crusaders attacked Jews along their path, most notably in Speyer, Worms and Mainz, old Roman cities along the Rhine River.[3] Jews were closer at hand and more readily coerced than distant Muslims.

As they stormed through Jewish quarters, crusading knights – together with townsmen and peasants who joined the fray for their own purposes – accosted those they considered perfidious unbelievers. Jews were tormented and slain in town after town in England, France, and Germany, in small hamlets and large cities where they been established for centuries as well as in places where they had settled only recently. Their goods were seized, their financial records torched, and religious books confiscated. Circular letters were sometimes sent ahead to warn Jewish communities of the impending danger, but often there was little warning. Trapped in places where they had sought refuge and faced with the prospect of immediate death, some Northern European Jews chose to take their own lives and those of their family members in front of their enemies, an act they termed Sanctifying the Name of God (*Kiddush hashem*).[4] Afterward, Jewish victims were celebrated in the communal memory in the obituaries (*memorbuchen*), poetry (*piyyutim*) and penitential verses (*selichot*) composed by guilt-stricken survivors. Hebrew and Latin chronicles recorded the events in the following generations.[5]

Popes and leading churchmen regularly inveighed against violence against Jews and instructed the devout that such behavior was not to be condoned, that Jews in their midst were not to be persecuted.[6] But as a result of the failure to prosecute those responsible for the attacks, some Jews observed that "we doubt not that there will be many future imitators of [a murderer's] audacity, and indeed, that worse will follow."[7] Modern accounts of crusade violence nonetheless pit sympathetic

---

[3] Shmuel Shepkaru, "The Preaching of the First Crusade and the Persecutions of the Jews," *Medieval Encounters* 18.1 (2012), 93–135.

[4] Simha Goldin, "The Socialization for *Kiddush ha-Shem* among Medieval Jews," *Journal of Medieval History* 23.2 (1997), 117–138. See also Jeremy Cohen, *Sanctifying the Name of God: Jewish Martyrs and Jewish Memories of the First Crusade* (Philadelphia, 2004).

[5] Shlomo Eidelberg, *The Jews and the Crusaders: The Hebrew Chronicles of the First and Second Crusades* (Madison, WI, 1977). Robert Chazan, *European Jewry and the First Crusade*, has translations of the Hebrew chronicles in the appendices (Berkeley, CA, 1996).

[6] Rebecca Rist, "Papal Protection and the Jews in the Context of Crusading, 1198–1245," *Medieval Encounters* 13.2 (2007), 281–309.

[7] These Jewish statements were reported by the monk Thomas of Monmouth, *Vita* II, xiv, 67.

authorities against murderous mobs. Thus the saintly Bernard, abbot of the Cistercian abbey of Clairvaux, who preached the Second Crusade in 1148, has been held up as a case in point.[8] He tracked down and chastised the unauthorized crusade preacher Radulph, who crossed France and Germany urging his listeners "to destroy, slay, annihilate them [the Jews] just as wicked Haman had attempted to do." Radulph, however, was no renegade, as he has been described, but an influential cleric, and it took months to silence him.

It is difficult to reconcile images of Jewish children torn from their mothers, young people tossed into rivers and purposefully drowned, and Jewish bodies burned in makeshift cemeteries with descriptions of crusading as "an act of love." But that is how the crusades were promoted to the participants who were told that they were defending Christ's honor.[9]

In popular imagination, "medieval antisemitism" has come to represent senseless hatred of an illiterate population fueled by emotion, whipped up by demagogues and resulting in bloodshed unanticipated by authorities who were eager but unable to manage social unrest. The violence perpetrated on defenseless Jews is regarded as typical of the brutal era in which they lived, and a far cry from the economic or racial antisemitism of later periods.[10]

PERIODIZATION

The interpretive framework offered for understanding medieval popular antisemitism was a simple one: that of ignorant thugs let loose in a violent time fueled by religious extremism after centuries of relatively serene coexistence, followed by periods of greater toleration after the ebbing of the crusades and the "desacralization" of Europe.

In retrospect, not all was calm and peaceful beforehand: there are hints in the few surviving records of attacks, expulsions and anti-Jewish legislation in preceding centuries, such as in the Visigothic kingdom of Spain in the 7th century, or in France in the 11th century against a

---

[8] Jeremy Cohen, "'Witnesses of Our Redemption': The Jews in the Crusading Theology of Bernard of Clairvaux," in *Medieval Studies in Honour of Avrom Saltman*, ed. Albert Bat-Sheva, Yvonne Friedman and Simon Schwarzfuchs (Ramat-Gan, 1995), 67–81.

[9] Jonathan Riley-Smith, "Crusading as an Act of Love," *History* 65 (1980), 177–192.

[10] Gavin I. Langmuir, *History, Religion and Antisemitism* (Berkeley, CA, 1990).

backdrop of millenarian expectations of the coming apocalypse.[11] And shortly after the First Crusade, in the first half of the 12th century, Jewish communities in Northern Europe quickly rebuilt.

The life of Jews in medieval Christian Europe is not simply a tearful history of suffering and constant attacks, as sometimes written. In many times and places during this period Jews flourished, their communities multiplied and expanded, and scholarship blossomed.[12] Many Western European Jews enjoyed a vibrant religious, social and cultural life. Jews can be found in a wide variety of occupations other than finance, including medicine, specialized agriculture, trade, royal and princely administration and real estate. They found the time, opportunity and support to write Talmud commentary, create refined works of art and compose poetry of lasting beauty. Unconstrained in many cases as to where they lived and worked, many benefited from close interaction with their neighbors and on occasion debated freely. In many places they also enjoyed legal protections and benefited from a firm theological defense in canon law and papal pronouncements. The routine aggressions they often suffered did not always spell utter disaster or increasing hostility but were taken in stride.[13] Rabbi Solomon ben Isaac (Rashi), his grandson rabbi Jacob ben Meir (Jacob Tam the *Tosafist* commentator), Judah the Pious (Judah *heHasid*) and rabbi Jacob of Lunel are among the famous scholars who worked in the shadow of the crusades. Dragged out to a field, Tam was able to enlist the aid of a passing nobleman when French crusaders robbed and attacked him, tore a Torah scroll, stole his horse and inflicted five cuts on him in emulation of Christ's wounds.[14]

It has been traditional, therefore, to regard the uncontrolled mob violence of the crusaders and townsmen as separate and distinct

---

[11] Rachel L. Stocking, "Early Medieval Christian Identity and Anti-Judaism: The Case of the Visigothic Kingdom," *Religion Compass* 2.4 (2008), 642–658; Richard Landes, "The Massacres of 1010: On the Origins of Popular Anti-Jewish Violence in Western Europe," in *From Witness to Witchcraft: Jews and Judaism in Medieval Christian Thought*, ed. Jeremy Cohen (Wiesbaden, 1996), 79–112.

[12] For especially positive accounts, see Robert Chazan, *The Jews of Medieval Western Christendom, 1000–1500* (Cambridge, 2006), and Jonathan M. Elukin, *Living Together, Living Apart: Rethinking Jewish-Christian Relations in the Middle Ages* (Princeton, NJ, 2007).

[13] David Nirenberg, *Communities of Violence: Persecution of Minorities in the Middle Ages* (Princeton, NJ, 1996).

[14] Norman Golb, "The Rabbinic Master Jacob Tam and Events of the Second Crusade at Reims," *Crusades* 9 (2010), 57–67.

from the considered, thoughtful actions of the educated elite. We are told that the secular rulers and political authorities who valued Jews as merchants, doctors and moneylenders and the influential clerics who relied on Jewish teachers and translators were far removed from the uneducated and ruthless peasants wielding cudgels or knights brandishing their swords. The theologians, after all, followed the teachings of Augustine of Hippo, who insisted "slay them not," arguing that Jews ought to be preserved within medieval Christian society as witnesses to the antiquity and veracity of holy texts.

Irrational and superstitious medieval Jew hatred has also been held up as categorically different from modern, racially based *antisemitism*, a term concocted only in the late 19th century. The hatred of Jews and Judaism that invigorated the crusader attacks was characterized as a frenzied expression of the rabble; the bloodcurdling myths that underpinned their actions were long considered bizarre and fantastical, psychological projections of inner turmoil. Jewish–Christian relations expressed in those terms became part of the overarching narrative of a Dark Ages that was distant and fairly incomprehensible. The vicious crusaders were dismissed as motivated by greed and credulous ignorance that punctuated and interrupted an otherwise fairly tranquil and predictable engagement between adherents of different faiths.

A better understanding today of popular movements of the medieval period suggests that it is not always easy to disentangle common myths and savagery of the masses from state-sanctioned brutality and popular theology. Rulers and local communities often benefited from outrages inflicted on Jews and were reluctant to condemn with any force those regarded as local heroes. Even when Jews were the victims of murderous thugs dressed as courtly knights in shining armor, the conventional story line of the period portrayed the Church as victim and the Jew as perpetrator. Indeed, the very image of *the Jew* developed as a result. The purported victims of Jewish aggression were regarded as miracle-workers and heralded as saints, reinforcing the notion of Jewish enmity in contrast to Christian innocence.

The myths about Jews that arose were for the most part based not on the texts of the Gospels themselves but on new interpretations of scripture that spread from the 12th century onward, compiled in the *glossa ordinaria*. These were short excerpts of biblical commentaries put together and widely circulated that gradually offered a standard explanation of biblical texts. These refashioned and aggressive interpretations informed preaching to crusaders and their families.[15]

Vicious attacks on Jews were often the result of purposeful instruction and at least tacit endorsement at the highest levels of society. Leaders of the crusades regularly extorted money from Jews before their followers attacked them: butchery often followed bullying. In luxury manuscripts made for the royal court in the early 13th century, the king of France, for example, proudly depicted himself observing Jews burned to death. Slanders did not, in fact, spread quickly among the masses during the high Middle Ages, but only gradually infused thinking and behavior at all levels of society. The myths, legends and folklore about Jews that were assumed eventually to have dissipated and weakened in fact laid the groundwork for the judicial torture, riots and expulsions of later periods. Long-standing distinctions between judicial violence and popular hostility, law and literature, art and life, the easy separation of high and low culture, as well as the standard periodization of Jewish–Christian relations are worthy of reconsideration. Perceptions of Jewish malevolence and of a need to counter it with firm action permeated all arenas of medieval life and can be seen as a coherent program rather than a marginal and intermittent phenomenon.

Legends and tall tales that circulated about medieval Jews were often rooted in apocryphal stories based on the Gospels, rather than in Gospel texts. They asserted that Jews were blind, had a bad odor, were devilish, suffered from leprosy and were a stateless people doomed to wander. These myths reinforced the notion that Jews were determined to destroy and threaten Christ, his mother Mary and, by association, all of Christendom. Such stories were promulgated to and by crusaders who were taught that Christ was their feudal lord to whom they owed homage. Even as Jesus was portrayed in terms that emphasized his human nature, represented in his youth and innocence, Jews were increasingly dehumanized, depicted as animalistic, demonic and malevolent. The art, literature, economics and theology of the period (treated in detail elsewhere in this volume) have their own histories, but they all contributed to inform the crusaders and others of the possibilities that Jews could and would inflict harm on Christians and Christian society. Some people therefore considered attacks on Jews as just

---

[15] Michael A. Signer, "The *Glossa ordinaria* and the Transmission of Medieval Anti-Judaism," in *A Distinct Voice: Medieval Studies in Honor of Leonard E. Boyle, O.P.*, ed. Jacqueline Brown and William P. Stoneman (Notre Dame, IN, 1997), 591–605.

revenge and proactive defense. The deeds of the crusaders should not be considered separately from the broader cultural environment that informed their conduct. Rarely were they grounded in a personal knowledge of living Jews.

THEMES

Crusaders came to believe that Jews were suspect for their financial dealings, their physical weaknesses and their desire to inflict harm on their Christian neighbors. Some Jews engaged in moneylending and pawnbroking because they were effectively prohibited from many other occupations and their loans were given state sanction. They were not, however, the only moneylenders, and their role in this profession has been greatly exaggerated – at least for the early period before they were increasingly pushed into that activity.[16] Nonetheless, negative associations of Jews and money were based less on knowledge of Jewish activities in the realm of finance than on the account of Christ's expulsion of the moneylenders from the Temple, and Christian teachings against "usury." The discourse of Jews as congenitally and permanently different in their bodies as well as in their beliefs also blossomed in this period and were not based on observations of daily life. These powerful themes and metaphors ("tropes") established in the medieval period were adapted, secularized and rationalized over centuries, and had – indeed still have – remarkable and enduring power. It was such characterizations of Jews in medieval teaching that encouraged the crusaders to target Jews on their way to the Holy Land. The violence they perpetrated echoed the violence they heard in miracle stories and Saints' Lives and witnessed in art and performance. A study of medieval behaviors can no longer be separated from the art, literature and theology of the period.

BLOOD LIBEL

The most powerful, malicious and enduring anti-Jewish myth of all was that of ritual murder, the accusation that Jews kidnapped and killed Christian boys in mockery of Christ and, later, that they collected the blood of these innocent children to consume or use for various purposes. This charge, which became known as the *blood libel*, is often described as bizarre and peculiar, yet its existence was

---

[16] Julie Mell, *The Myth of the Medieval Jewish Moneylender* (New York, 2017).

gradually accepted by a majority of the population. Although strongly challenged when it was first promulgated, by the late Middle Ages the notion that Jews required Christian blood for their religious rituals was widely accepted, even though it was known that Jewish law prohibits the consumption of blood.

The first recorded charge was concocted in the immediate aftermath of the Second Crusade when Jews were blamed for the death of little William of Norwich, England (1150).[17] Far more important was the later accusation of child murder laid against the Jews of Blois in central France (1171), as a result of which the count of Blois ordered the public burning of the entire local Jewish community.[18] The count of Blois related the story to his nephew the king of France, so that in the same generation the purported murder of another Christian child, Richard of Pontoise, outside Paris, was said to be occasion for the expulsion of Jews from the French capital in 1180. Richard's shrine in the Church of the Holy Innocents, which received significant royal patronage, endured until the French Revolution. The first case that specifically mentions Jewish need of Christian blood "as a remedy" concerned five children of a miller who were said to have been burned by Jews of Fulda in central Germany on Christmas Day 1235. In a case of "popular justice," more than thirty of the alleged Jewish perpetrators were killed by participants passing through Fulda on their return from crusade. The demands of local residents who carried the bodies of the children to the emperor sparked an investigation and denunciation of the charge by the Holy Roman Emperor Frederick II. Having consulted with other rulers and having called upon Jewish converts to Christianity to advise him, he issued an edict which absolved Jews of the crime, but with little effect.

One of the best-known purported victims was little Hugh of Lincoln, said to have been cast into a well and drowned in 1255, whose story was recalled by Chaucer in the *Canterbury Tales*. In punishment, King Henry III of England executed a young Jew on the spot, and eighteen more Jews were sentenced to be drawn by horses and hanged a month later after they requested a jury composed of Christians and Jews. Another one hundred Jews were locked in the Tower of London until they converted to Christianity or paid heavy fines for their release. A generation later saw the enthusiastic veneration of Werner of Oberwesel on the Rhine (1287) despite the halfhearted attempt of Emperor Rudolph to prohibit

---

[17] E. M. Rose, *The Murder of William of Norwich: The Origins of the Blood Libel in Medieval Europe* (Oxford, 2015).
[18] "Blois," in ibid., 151–185.

the establishment of a cult of this supposed child martyr. Just as, centuries later, William of Norwich became patron saint of leather-workers, so Werner (St. Vernier) was later adopted as a patron saint of French winegrowers. Shrines and memorials to these purported child martyrs dot the European countryside and were objects of pilgrimage and tourism for centuries.

The master narrative of the blood libel was a simple story that could be elaborated, adapted and localized in each generation. It had well-defined characters and familiar settings. A young boy went missing, his distraught mother frantically searched for him while he was enticed to a Jewish space, held for some period of time, bled and tortured to the point of death. Eventually, he was found, and his body was regarded as sanctified for his suffering. These accounts were modeled in part on the story from the New Testament of young Jesus getting lost and his mother Mary finding him in the Temple, among the Jewish doctors of the Law (Luke 2:41–52). Medieval children said to have been murdered by Jews were conflated as well with the Holy Innocents, the children of Bethlehem described in the Gospel of Matthew (Matt. 2:16–18) who were killed by Herod's soldiers in place of the Christ child. Although the Massacre of the Innocents was a story of murdered Jewish children, in the high Middle Ages these *innocenti* were often understood as Christian infants murdered by order of a Jew.

TYPOLOGY

A basis for this kind of reversal was the medieval habit of "typological reading," that is, understanding events in the past, especially those in the Hebrew Bible (the Christian "Old Testament") as foreshadowing or anticipating ("prefiguring") events in Christ's life recounted in the New Testament. For example, the inconsolable Jewish matriarch Rachel mourning for the Children of Israel (Jer. 31:15) was viewed as a prefiguration of Mary weeping over Christ's body. This merging of the past and present into one often resulted in a failure to distinguish Jews of antiquity who were blamed for crucifying Jesus from contemporary Jews who lived in Europe more than a thousand years later; both were deemed enemies of Christendom.

HOST DESECRATION

In the late 13th century, on the back of the blood libel or ritual murder accusation, another equally flexible and horrifying charge arose, claiming that Jews attacked the wafer used in holy communion (the eucharistic host). The charge of "host desecration" was easier to invoke than outright homicide (it required no corpse of a victim) and was widely disseminated after a famous case said to have occurred in Paris in 1290.[19] It was claimed that Jews stole or bribed someone to give them a consecrated wafer and they repeatedly stabbed it; because of the doctrine of transubstantiation, an attack on the host was understood as the equivalent of stabbing Christ himself. Accounts of the alleged profanation of the host prompted riots and pillaging. Frequently, such accusations were invoked to threaten Jews and extort money from them, especially by city officials and local worthies. Miraculous wafers became the object of numerous blood cults and famous pilgrimage sites in the later Middle Ages. Many stories, such as those of Werner and the "Holy Infant of LaGuardia" (1490), combined ritual murder and host desecration in a single gruesome narrative. Events such as the killing of Jews in the Rintfleisch massacres (1298) and other regional riots triggered by accusations of host desecration cannot be separated from the fictional stories that circulated in literature. Imaginative actions and real-world behaviors were intimately related.

BODILY WEAKNESS

During this period Jews were increasingly associated with malefactors of the Old and New Testaments: they were likened to the murderous Cain, the resentful Esau, the mad Herod and the treacherous Judas; they took on their attributes and were denigrated in similar terms: as perfidious, faithless and disloyal. Contemporary Jews were said to suffer a bloody flux that was apparently based on their affiliation with Judas; this "fact" was included in influential medical texts that remained in print well into the 17th century. The explanation offered for this link was the cry "his blood be upon us" (Matt. 25:27) in which Jews were held responsible for the Crucifixion and were therefore permanently stained with blood, not just metaphorically, but with an infirmity passed down through the generations. Jews were regarded as spiritually and physically blind, inheriting weak eyes, and they were also said to suffer skin diseases.[20] Grounded in scriptural stories and earlier ancient Egyptian traditions,

---

[19] Miri Rubin, *Gentile Tales: The Narrative Assault on Late Medieval Jews* (New Haven, CT, 1999).

[20] Irven M. Resnick, *Marks of Distinction: Christian Perceptions of Jews in the High Middle Ages* (Washington, DC, 2012), addresses a number of these slanders.

Jews were accused of having leprosy, later understood as any skin disease. Jews were also said to endure hemorrhoids, a fact which became proverbial in early modern Eastern Europe. The smell (*foetor judaicus*) from which they were said to have suffered (like the farts of the devil) was purposefully contrasted to the sweet odor of sanctity attributed to saints. The nomadic existence of many Jews likewise originated in the legend of the Wandering Jew who had cursed Jesus and was condemned to endure an itinerant life until the Second Coming.

CLOSE RELATIONSHIPS

These ideas did not spread immediately; it took some time for them to percolate through society. During the high Middle Ages, Jews and Christians still encountered each other on the street and in the marketplace; some Jews stored their valuables in churches; they arranged financing for monasteries, studied holy texts together with Christians and went about their daily business, living cheek by jowl next door to one another. Some traveled together, joked together and attended celebratory family occasions; other Christians and Jews hired the same masons and artists for their domestic and religious works.

Indeed, it was close relationships between Christians and Jews that many clerics denounced. They demanded that Jews wear a distinctive sign on their clothes to make sure that they were distinguished from Christians who otherwise might not know them for the threat they posed. Enunciated in the Fourth Lateran Council (1215) this requirement took some time to enforce. Even earlier, Christian wet nurses were forbidden from working in Jewish households where they might be subject to undue Jewish influence. Threats from medieval Jews were portrayed as a growing menace, so Jews were increasingly confined and their behavior, dress and employment were proscribed. Christians were taught to view Jews as physically different, and when they did not appear so, Jews were required to conform to those expectations by wearing distinctive garb such as a pointed hat, yellow dress or bright badge on the outside of their clothing. Jews were likewise depicted with a hooked nose, red hair and swarthy skin, which like other traits attributed to medieval Jews, were not typical of them, but presumed to be true. People saw what they expected to see. As Jews were increasingly isolated, marginalized and made to stand out from the general population, their physical safety could not be assured.

MONKS AND FRIARS

Questions about the status of Jews in Christian society took on new urgency with the arrival of the mendicant friars, Dominicans and Franciscans, the preaching orders established in the early 13th century, whose popularity spread far and wide in just a few decades. These brothers sworn to poverty went out into the world to minister to the growing number of new urban residents. As did their affiliated sisters, they embraced a simpler life than that of the Benedictine monks in their elaborately adorned monasteries who had first endorsed the blood libel. The friars were particularly charged with listening to confessions and to administering the Inquisition to target heretics. Accustomed to speaking to the layman on the street and highly mobile, they also were employed to travel and preach later crusades.

For some historians, the advent of the friars and their confrontational stance spelled a great change in Christian–Jewish relations.[21] Dominicans (*domini canes*, the hounds of the lord) studied Jewish texts to better oppose the intellectual challenge of Judaism and required Jews to engage in public disputations. Franciscans sought to limit Jewish moneylending and were in the forefront of advocating the expulsion of Jews from communities when this was not possible. Together, these new orders had momentous effects on Jewish life – both in the northern kingdoms and in Southern Europe, which had generally been considered more urbane and diverse. The friars played a part in a number of accusations of ritual murder and are often found lurking in the background of such accounts. It was in this period that Jews began to be treated as heretics and subject to the same penalties, which sometimes included being burned alive. Claiming the Talmud was blasphemous, the friars organized the burning of books as well as people. In 1242 in Paris, at the urging of a Jewish convert, twenty-four wagonloads of Hebrew books were burned. Those responsible for the conflagration thought that without their rabbinical books it would be easier to persuade Jews of the truth of Christianity. On the commission that condemned the Talmud were university professors and scholars, another indication that harsh attitudes toward Jews did not stem primarily from the ignorant masses.

---

[21] Jeremy Cohen, *The Friars and the Jews: The Evolution of Medieval Anti-Judaism* (Ithaca, NY, 1983), and Susan E. Myers and Steven J. McMichael, eds., *Friars and Jews in the Middle Ages and Renaissance* (Leiden, 2004).

THE PLAGUE

Anti-Jewish feelings sharpened considerably at the onset of the Black Death c. 1348–1350 when Jews were accused of spreading plague far and wide. Jews were charged with poisoning well water, engaging in magic and dealing in blood.[22] The plague hysteria resulted in extensive looting and pogroms and the permanent destruction of numerous communities. The penitential processions which assailed Jews were denounced by popes but continued nonetheless; some justified their attacks by claiming that killing Jews would stop the spread of the plague. The discovery of Jewish family heirlooms in the wall of a pharmacy in Colmar, France, recently put on display, speaks to the rich lives some Jews enjoyed, but also how quickly they were destroyed.[23] In Cologne, western Germany, a rumor spread that Jews had poisoned the wells, resulting in outbreak of violence that forced Jews to flee the city. Although some later returned, they were not guaranteed protection and by 1424 all were expelled. In 1349 a massacre in Erfurt in central Germany coincided with riots and looting and the death of perhaps 3,000 Jews; the bishop pardoned the city the following year. A Jewish family treasure of jugs, goblets, coins, fashionable belt ornaments and a finely crafted Jewish wedding ring was discovered under the wall of a cellar there in 1998; an Erfurt mikveh was unearthed only in 2007.[24] In Regensburg the Jews were protected during the Black Death, but later assaulted and expelled; a jar of gold coins, one of the largest such treasures ever found, was buried in the Jewish area near the synagogue that was turned into a church.[25] Surviving vestiges of material culture hint at how little the official accounts – either Jewish or Christian – tell us about Jewish life in medieval Europe until it came to an end.

Many Jewish communities are known to historians only through accounts of their destruction, which suggests that there may have been others not recorded. But far more has been attributed to fear of the plague than is warranted. Recent scholarship indicates that many

---

[22] Tzfrir Barzilay, "Early Accusations of Well Poisoning against Jews: Medieval Reality or Historiographical Fiction?," *Medieval Encounters* 22.5 (2016), 517–539, emphasizes the novelty of the 14th-century accusations.

[23] Barbara D. Boehm, *The Colmar Treasure: A Medieval Jewish Legacy* (London, 2020).

[24] "Erfurt: Jewish Treasures from Medieval Ashkenaz" (New York, Yeshiva University Museum, September 2008–February 9, 2009).

[25] Silvia Codreanu-Windauer, "Regensburg: The Archaeology of the Medieval Jewish Quarter," in *The Jews of Europe in the Middle Ages (Tenth to Fifteenth Centuries)*, ed. Christoph Cluse (Turnhout, 2004), 391–403.

attacks on Jews in the mid-14th century were the carefully planned and executed work of local governments.[26] This challenges previous narratives that such riots were spontaneous affairs rooted in emotion rather than deliberately calculated efforts initiated by jealous civic authorities.

Provocations to violence were in many cases closely linked to the religious calendar and competitive holidays, so reinforced on a weekly and monthly basis. It was well known that when Passover and Easter coincided in late spring, conflicts between Christians and Jews often ensued. But such conflicts occurred throughout the year: in late winter with Purim and Carnival just before the beginning of Lent; in early summer when Jews celebrated Shavuot, which overlapped with feast days of important Christian saints and Pentecost (Whitsunday); and in mid-August when the Christian commemoration of the Destruction of Jerusalem coincided with the Jewish commemoration of the Destruction of the Temple (*Tisha B'Av*). Crusaders also chose such feast days in the spring to gather and set forth together toward the East. These Christian feasts often provided occasions to raise charges of ritual murder and host desecration, especially dangerous when towns swarmed with armed forces. Annual events such as the performance of the Stoning of the Jews at Easter also grew significantly more dangerous and menacing.[27]

Historians now pay attention not just to the outcome of the libels and slanders but also to how they were spread and to whom. They were disseminated especially in persuasive and memorable stories told to children. Jews were demonized in tales that were neither the exclusive province of the ignorant nor the texts of the educated, but somewhere in between, simplified for the faithful. It is such stories that lay the groundwork and justified the inhumane treatment of Jews in the high and late Middle Ages, of which the most publicized incident was the alleged murder of little Simon of Trent (1475).

SIMON OF TRENT

The case of the child Simon of Trent is widely regarded as a significant turning point in Christian–Jewish relations at the very end of the

[26] I. Ritzmann, "The Black Death as a Cause of the Massacres of Jews: A Myth of Medical History?" (in German), *Medizin, Gesellschaft, und Geschichte* 17 (1998), 101–130.
[27] Cecil Roth, "The Eastertide Stoning of the Jews and Its Liturgical Echoes," *Jewish Quarterly Review* 35.4 (1945), 361–370.

Middle Ages. As a result of this accusation of ritual murder, fifteen Jewish men who had confessed under torture were burnt at the stake after a formal legal trial. The accusation and trial combined much of what has been considered as characteristic of medieval antisemitism: they were provoked by the preaching of a charismatic Franciscan, Bernardino da Feltre, against the Jewish community; the alleged event occurred at Easter, which also coincided with one of the great feasts of St. Mary (the Annunciation, March 25); and Simon was said to have been not only kidnapped but also drained of blood, as revealed by an investigation of the corpse by medical professionals brought in by the city. Carefully engineered by the prince-bishop of Trent, the cult of little Simon became the subject of an extraordinary media campaign that spread far and wide thanks to the new technology of print. After hearing the news of Simon of Trent, near the Italian–German border, other towns soon manufactured their own stories. Many of the purported incidents of medieval ritual murder were apparently invented only in the early modern period but were said to have occurred much earlier. Images of Simon of Trent, now widely reproduced as the quintessential example of the medieval blood libel, reflect the concerns of the late 15th century. This case can be said with some justification to have produced the first and most enduring antisemitic memes.

END OF AN ERA

With Simon of Trent, we come to the culmination of medieval popular antisemitism. National expulsions from England in 1290, France repeatedly until the final one in 1394, Spain in 1492, Portugal in 1497 and from many cities on the Italian peninsula throughout the 15th century effectively brought an end to communal Jewish life in Western Europe. The petering-out of the crusades reduced the militarization of religious partisans as well. In the wake of momentous technological, religious and social developments, the place of Jews in civic society took a dramatically different turn.

By then, medieval attitudes were deeply entrenched, albeit not always with recognition of where and how they originated. Many of the same techniques employed to promote the blood libel are those used today by modern advertising to create brand awareness – repetition, association, specific claims and active involvement. Belief in the blood libel was sustained by reenactments, repeated visual impressions and dramatic sensory accompaniments. These practices were overtly peda-gogical. The accounts and images placed Christians – especially younger

Christians – within schemes of salvation history and associated them closely with the Christ child and his mother Mary.

It has long been argued that antisemitism in general – and the blood libel in particular – was a bottom-up phenomenon, spread by rumors among the uneducated masses and punctuated by outbreaks of irrational mob violence, especially provoked by the crusades. Alternatively, it has been said that it was a top-down phenomenon spread in Latin texts by the educated elite and prompted primarily by theological or financial concerns. But there is a third possibility: that many such beliefs originated and were promulgated from the center – not by the highly educated or uneducated but by the semi-educated. They were spread not by studious written texts nor vague oral traditions, but by action, ritual and instruction. The conscious destruction of loan records as a rational response to heavy debts incurred by local townsmen and the murderous rampages by armed crusaders passing through different European territories stemmed from similar and overlapping impulses.

Extravagant tales once dismissed as utter nonsense have now been subject to renewed scrutiny. In the modern era people have tried to find reasonable, even scientific, explanations for myths that were spread about the Jews – that they had horns, that they had a special smell, that they suffered monthly bleeding like women. Other explanations assume accusations against Jews arose from linguistic confusion or had some basis in Jewish practice.[28] But many such accusations can be traced back to stories of biblical characters with which they were associated.

LASTING EFFECTS

Over the course of the Middle Ages Judaism was increasingly seen as ineradicable. It was more than a belief, more than a cultural or ethnic choice; it was a permanent stain exemplified in the term "baptized Jew," which became a late medieval commonplace. The term signified that even after conversion to Christianity, a Jew remained an identifiable outsider rather than being integrated into the community of Christ. Medieval imagery of anti-Jewish slander was called upon by the Nazis to reenforce their ideology. More recently, white supremacists have used imagery from the crusading era and its anti-Jewish attitudes to advocate

---

[28] Israel J. Yuval, *Two Nations in Your Womb: Perceptions of Jews and Christians in Late Antiquity and the Middle Ages* (Berkeley, CA, 2006), suggests that the blood libel arose from observation by Christians of Jewish martyrdom during the First Crusade, but Yuval's controversial argument has been widely challenged.

for their exclusionary platform. They too often combine hate speech with calls to armed action.

The accumulation of accusations made against Jews and Judaism through the centuries, the repetitions and layering of assertions of Jewish perfidy and threat, and the ease with which allegations of Jewish misdeeds and guilt could be repurposed at different times and places were and are responsible for one of the sadder chapters of human history.

The era of the crusades and their aftermath (the 12th–15th centuries) played an important part in contributing to the elaboration of this sorry history of anti-Jewish malice, ranging from the violence visited on Jewish households and communities by armies of would-be liberators of the Holy Land and the rabble that accompanied or joined them as they marched across Europe to the invention and widespread circulation of wild tales of Jewish malevolence. These myths included the alleged kidnapping and killing of Christian children in mockery of Christ and the Crucifixion (the blood libel), the host desecration, the use of Christian blood in Jewish rituals, the spread of the plague and the poisoning of wells, to name only the most prominent. These accusations and events aroused fierce enmity between Christians and Jews, heightening notions of Jews and Jewish communities as a threat to individuals, families and all of Christendom. No matter how unjustified, contrived or fanciful, or how often opposed by Church leaders, these and other eruptions of anti-Jewish animosity and accusations became part of lived or remembered history, embedded in long-term communal memory. It is the breadth and depth of this history and the ease with which it can be recalled and recycled that gave and still gives it continued force and life.

Further Reading

Abulafia, A. S., *Christian Jewish Relations 1000–1300: Jews in the Service of Medieval Christendom* (New York, 2011). In this clear survey Abulafia draws together much of her decades of focused scholarship to emphasize theology and pragmatism in considering how the crusades and anti-Jewish libels affected those relations.

Bronstein, J., "The Crusades and the Jews: Some Reflections on the 1096 Massacre," *History Compass* 5.4 (2007), 1268–1279. Offers an overview of historiography on the First Crusade.

Chazan, R., *Medieval Stereotypes and Modern Antisemitism* (Berkeley, CA, 1997). The author makes an early argument for continuities rather than a sharp break between medieval and modern Jew-hatred.

Franke, D. P., "The Crusades and Medieval Anti-Judaism: Cause or Consequence?," in *Seven Myths of the Crusades*, ed. Alfred Andrea and

Andrew Holt (Cambridge, MA, 2015), 48–69. This essay succinctly lays out questions for classroom discussion, while offering evidence that the Crusades were not a decisive event in Christian–Jewish relations and finding no link between Crusade ideology and Nazi Germany.

Kaplan, L. *Figuring Racism in Medieval Christianity* (New York, 2019). This work skillfully addresses notions of hereditary inferiority and the Christian doctrine of Jewish perpetual servitude.

Lasker, D. J., "The Impact of the Crusades on the Jewish-Christian Debate," *Jewish History* 13.2 (1999), 23–36. This study explicitly addresses the issue of whether the crusades were a sharp break or part of an incremental transformation in relations between Christians and Jews.

Malkiel, D., "Destruction or Conversion: Intention and Reaction, Crusaders and Jews, in 1096," *Jewish History* 15.3 (2001), 257–280. Based on a close reading of the sources, this article questions whether Jews were actually offered the choice of baptism during the mayhem of the crusades.

Resnick, I. M., *Marks of Distinction: Christian Perceptions of Jews in the High Middle Ages* (Washington, DC, 2012). This book examines accusations of physical deformities, leprosy and food, sexual and planetary influences that helped define Jewish otherness. It draws on a wide range of sources including medical texts, encyclopedias, chronicles, exempla collections, sermons, polemical treatises and Bible commentaries.

Rose, E. M., *The Murder of William of Norwich: The Origins of Blood Libel in Medieval Europe* (New York, 2015). This suspenseful unraveling of a medieval trial reexamines the first accusations of the blood libel beginning in 1150. It then looks at "copycat" allegations (Gloucester 1168, Blois 1171, Bury 1180 and Paris 1180) to explain how the blood libel managed to take hold.

Rubin, M., *Gentile Tales: The Narrative Assault on Late Medieval Jews* (New Haven, CT, 1999). This offers a thorough and readable examination of the host desecration accusation, the rhetoric that was used and the violence it frequently produced.

12 Jews and Money: The Medieval Origins of a Modern Stereotype

JULIE MELL

The trope of the Jewish moneylender has taken different forms over the centuries: the Jewish "usurers" of medieval England and France, the "Shylocks" of Renaissance Italy, "Jud Süss" and the Court Jews of Central Europe, and the "Rothschilds" of 19th-century international banking. There is little empirical evidence for Jewish preeminence in moneylending.[1] Yet the association of Jews with money has been pervasive, figuring in anti-Jewish accusations from medieval expulsions to *The Protocols of the Elders of Zion*, from the Holocaust to Le Happy Merchant memes. This essay will trace the emergence of the stereotype in medieval Europe.

The trope of the Jewish moneylender also has its philosemitic versions. For well over a century, liberal historians, sociologists, and political economists have described medieval Jews as modernizers fulfilling a special economic function: Jews provided credit – the ingredient necessary for economic development – at a time when Christians could not or would not. Jews, in consequence, suffered a tragic antisemitic backlash. The liberal-economic narrative counters antisemitic economic stereotypes by inverting them, making the "Jewish predilection for money-making" a contribution to the nation. Antisemitic or philosemitic, the assumption of an association between Jews and money remains a dangerous trope, a stereotype disconnected from economic realities.

Jews were neither medieval Europe's chief moneylenders nor the credit engine for emergent commercial capitalism. Jews *did* loan money, but the majority of professional moneylenders, money changers,

---

[1] Julie Mell, *The Myth of the Medieval Jewish Moneylender*, 2 vols. (New York, 2017–18), esp. chaps. 4–6, documents this fallacy for medieval Europe based on England as the *locus classicus* for medieval Jewish moneylending. Tax records and loan documents from 13th-century England reveal that professional moneylending was limited to a small elite and only of moderate significance for English economic life. The distribution of wealth in the Jewish community closely mirrored that of urban Christians.

bankers, and merchants were Christian. *A few* Jews were wealthy moneylenders and merchants, but most Jews – like most Christians – were too poor to have been members of this urban elite. Credit was used widely throughout Europe in the 12th and 13th centuries, and most of it did not pass through Jewish hands. From peasants to popes, Christians of all social and religious statuses supplied credit and relied on it.

Credit stood at the heart of the medieval commercial revolution: Merchants received investments from sleeping partners, peasants borrowed to carry themselves from one harvest to the next, and when they had a bit of extra income, they invested it in a consumptive loan or commercial venture, as did townsfolk. Italian merchant-bankers attached to the papal court transferred tithes to Rome, exchanged money for the papal administration, and served as a bank for its deposits and loans. Christian military orders such as the Hospitallers and Templars similarly served popes and kings, often funding wars and crusades. Cistercians were "business monks" and mendicant friars set up loan and pawn shops. Italian families invested in dowry funds for young daughters which would grow with interest until their marriage. Local merchants, moneychangers, and bankers were found in every corner of Europe, along with foreigners working in trade and the money trade.[2]

This essay approaches the discourse on medieval Jewish usurers as an antisemitic stereotype rooted in religious difference, not as a warped reflection of a minority's economic niche. Between the 12th and 16th centuries, European Jews were first collectively labeled, then criminalized as "usurers" when engaged in the same economic activities as Christian merchants who came to be regarded as contributing to the common good. Ironically, this new social labeling originated with a religious movement to reform *Christian usury*. In the mid-12th century, legislation on lay Christian usury was decreed for the first time by church councils. By the late 13th century, the charge of usury was leveled against Jewish communities and used by secular rulers to justify mass expulsions. By the 16th century, to be a Jew was to be a usurer; to be a merchant was to be an upright member of the civic and Christian community. This dualism was immortalized in the characters of

---

[2] The former paragraphs, with the kind permission of the Jewish Museum London, draw from my piece commissioned for the catalogue accompanying the Museum's exhibition "Jews, Money, Myth" (March 19–October 17, 2019); Mell, "The Myth of the Medieval Jewish Moneylender," in *Jews, Money, Myth*, ed. Joanne Rosenthal and Marc Volovoci (London, 2019), 39–41.

Shylock, the Jewish moneylender, and Anthony, the Christian merchant, in Shakespeare's *Merchant of Venice*.

The persistence of erroneous assumptions about Jewish moneylending is due in part to modern antisemitic politics and in part to a poor
understanding of medieval economic history and economic thought.
The term "usury" in particular has given rise to much confusion. We
have the tendency to read it as a pejorative, pre-modern term for "interest." But usury referred (as it still does today) to exploitive and illegal
profit as defined by custom, culture, and law. In probing the ethical and
legal limits of just profit, medieval religious authorities – Jewish,
Christian, and Muslim – all developed sophisticated economic thought
on markets and prices, contracts, loans, interest, currency exchange,
and commercial investment. Ethical concerns did not obstruct economic growth. Rather, they simultaneously produced more precise
definitions of usury and more expansive permissions on profit. Both
were driven by the religious aim to fulfill divine law. For example, our
term "interest" was created by medieval Christian theologians and
canon lawyers to define *permissible* profit on a loan due to loss, damage,
or injury. And investment loans were permitted by Jewish, Christian,
and Muslim law when the investor shared risks as well as profits. In
short, the religious law of all Abrahamic religions defined, and simultaneously refined, which contractual obligations would be considered as
"usury" and which as licit profit.

Neither Jews nor Christians were free from legal restrictions on
usury. Rabbinic law had developed extensive prohibitions on usury
long before the western church developed legal decrees and theological
tracts on the subject. The rulings of the church roughly paralleled
those of the rabbis (with one exception), for both were grounded in
shared biblical texts (Exod. 22:24–26; Lev. 25:36–37; Deut. 23:20–21,
24:10–13; Ps. 15:5, Prov. 28:8; Ezek. 18:7; 2 Kings 4:1–7; Hab. 2:6; Neh.
5:1–11). Secular and canonical laws on Jewish lending mirrored limits
set on Christian lending in medieval Europe: the church stretched its
canon law on Christian usury to cover Jews; secular rulers and towns
set interest rates on loans by Christians and Jews; at other times they
regulated Jewish loans or prohibited them altogether. One reason we
have such excellent records on Jewish loans is because they were
closely regulated out of fear of Jewish deceit.

The following pages trace how and why the labels "usurer" and
"usury" came to be particularly, but not exclusively, linked to
Jewishness and Judaism in the high middle ages. The new discourse on
Jewish usury developed in three waves over the 12th and 13th centuries.

In the 1140s, Jews and Judaism were labeled as usurious in the wake of the Church's revival of late antique concerns with Christian usury. Beginning around 1200 the papacy made Jewish usury the object of secular regulation and administrative surveillance. In the late 1280s and 1290s, secular rulers used the charge of usury to justify mass expulsions across Western Europe.

Two Christian religious movements rooted in the 11th-century reform movement are essential for understanding why the stereotype emerged: the crusades and the Church's campaign against *Christian* usury. In theory, neither should have affected medieval Jewish life, but the opposite was true. The crusades were directed against Muslims in the Middle East, North Africa, and Islamic Europe; against non-orthodox Christians (i.e., heretics); and against European pagans – but never officially against Jews, despite the violence crusaders wreaked on European Jewish communities. The papacy protected the right of Jews to live and practice Judaism within European Christendom. Church doctrine was based on Augustine of Hippo's interpretation of Psalm 59:12 (Vulg. 58:12): "Slay them not, lest my people forget; scatter them and bring them down."[3] Augustine read it as a command from God, saying "slay not" the Jews, lest they and their scriptures be forgotten, because Jews and the Jewish scriptures testify to Christ and Christianity.[4] In their exile, Jewish scriptures have been spread to all lands where Jews have been "scattered," and the visible subjugation of the Synagogue to the Church provides proof that God's favor has been transferred to Christians. In keeping with this doctrine, the church recognized the authority of rabbinic law over the Jewish community, even where Jewish religious practice differed from that of Christians as in the laws governing divorce, kashrut, and usury. However, the crusades led to a radical change of emphasis in Augustine's doctrine. Writing in the late Roman Empire, Augustine emphasized the scriptures' ongoing role in the drama of Christian salvation to counter Manicheans who advocated abolishing Jewish scriptures. Writing during the crusades, medieval religious leaders emphasized Jewish exile and subjugation as punishment for killing Christ to counter Christians who advocated slaughtering European Jews.

---

[3] See Jeremy Cohen's chapter in this volume and his *Living Letters of the Law* (Berkeley, CA, 1999), 23–71.

[4] Paula Fredriksen, *Augustine and the Jews: A Christian Defense of Jews and Judaism* (New Haven, CT, 2010), 290.

PHASE I: NAMING JEWS AS USURERS

In the late 1130s and 1140s, a new ecclesiastical campaign against lay Christian usury and a new crusade (the Second Crusade) served to highlight the dissonance between rabbinical and canonical laws on usury, related to Deuteronomy 23:20–21 (Vulg. 23:19–20). The campaign against usury burst on the scene in 1139 at the Second Lateran Council with the first canonical decree against lay Christian usury. "Usury" was a catchall term for economic acts defined by their doers' sinful or wicked intent: greed, fraud, injustice.[5] During the 1140s, it became a keyword in the newest textbook for the study of canon law, the *Decretum*. When Pope Eugenius III granted a new privilege to crusaders, it became intertwined with crusading, too. The Pope absolved indebted crusaders of paying usury and placed a moratorium on lawsuits involving their property until their return or confirmed death. The campaign against usury would escalate over the next 150 years, as the growing body of canons show. It did not apply to Jews, at least in theory, inasmuch as canon law applies only to members of the Latin Church. But Jewish religious difference became increasingly intolerable in the religious climate of the 12th and 13th centuries. As doctrinal variants and new forms of Christianity were labeled heretical, especially when they offered resistance to the hierarchical authority of the church, crusading fed Christian fantasies of Jews as enemies of Christ and Christians, and a new Jewish stereotype was born: the Jewish usurer.

The earliest references to Jewish usury are provided by three of the greatest spiritual and intellectual figures of the mid-12th century: the theologian, philosopher, and logician Peter Abelard; the head of the Cistercian order, Bernard of Clairvaux; and the head of the Benedictine house of Cluny, Peter of Montboissier (also known as Peter the Venerable) – and by a fourth, the late 12th-century theologian Peter the Chanter. Contrary to what historians once thought, their works do not provide historical descriptions of Jews' concentration in moneylending.[6] Rather, they point to a theological difference between rabbinic and canon law in the interpretation of Deuteronomy 23:20–21 (Vulg. 23:19–20):

---

[5] Gratian, *Decretum*, D.46.c.8–10, D.47.c.1–5; C.14.q.3–12 in Aemilius Friedberg, ed., *Corpus iuris canonici*, 2 vols. (Leipzig, 1879).

[6] Constant Mews, "Abelard and Heloise on Jews and *Hebraica Veritas*," in *Christian Attitudes toward the Jews in the Middle Ages*, ed. Michael Frassetto (New York, 2007), 83–108, esp. 84–87; Yvonne Friedman, "Anatomy of Anti-Semitism: Peter the Venerable's Letter to Louis VII, King of France (1146)," *Bar-Ilan Studies in History* (1978), 87–102, esp. 95–101.

"You shall not lend upon interest to your brother (אח), interest on money, interest on food, or interest on anything that is lent for interest. To a stranger (נוכרי) you may lend on interest, but to your brother you shall not lend upon interest, so that the Lord, your God, will bless you in all you undertake in the land which you are about to enter and possess."[7] Interpretations of this passage vary widely in the Talmud. But medieval rabbinic commentators largely agreed that it gave European Jews permission to give and take usury from Christians.[8] Medieval Christians in later polemical literature sharply disagreed, arguing that Deuteronomy 23 was trumped by Psalm 15 and that Christians should be regarded as "brothers."

The Christian texts discussed below all refer to the theological difference over Deuteronomy 23:20–21 and place it within the larger framework of Augustine's vision of salvation history. They reveal a range of responses to this theological difference, from indifference (Abelard) to deprecation of Christian usurers as worse than Jews (Bernard and Peter the Chanter) to deprecation of Jews as stealing from Christians (Peter of Montboissier). The theological framework reveals the association of Jews and money to be emerging from religious difference, not from Jewish moneylending.

In a "Dialogue between a Philosopher, a Jew, and a Christian" (c. 1130–42), Abelard's Jew, like Shakespeare's Shylock, laments the difficulties of Jewish life in a long monologue: we are persecuted for having killed the Christians' God. We are in exile, and in constant fear for our lives and livelihood. Nowhere may we find rest. We are ground down and oppressed. The whole world conspires against us. It is a miracle that we are allowed to live. We have no fields, no vineyards, no land, because no one can or will protect them for us. "So, the only way we can maintain our miserable existence is by making a profit (*lucrum*) on loans to strangers (*alienigenis fenerantes*). And this makes us hateful to all."[9] Abelard's Latin terms *lucrum*, *alienigenis*, and *fenerantes* evoke the new canon against lay Christian usury, as well as the rabbinic interpretation of Deuteronomy

---

[7] My translation remains close to that of the JPS Hebrew-English Tanakh (Philadelphia, 1999) and the Revised Standard. More traditional Jewish interpretations understand the phrase "you shall not lend" as a causative, i.e., "you shall not cause your brother to lend on interest."

[8] BT *Bava Metzia* 70b and 71a.

[9] My paraphrase of Peter Abelard, *Collationes*, ed. and trans. John Marenbon and Giovanni Orlandi (Oxford, 2001), 16–21.

23:20–21 (Vulg. 23:19–20).[10] By having a Jewish character complain about the misery of exile, Abelard seems sympathetic to the Jewish plight, but his portrait remains squarely within an Augustinian theological framework with its medieval emphases on Jewish exile and servitude as punishment for killing Christ. In the process, the Jew as a practitioner of rabbinic law emerges from Christian theology as a moneylender, without any empirical reference to economic practice.

In 1146, Bernard of Clairvaux and Peter of Montboissier wrote letters enlisting support for the Second Crusade (1147–49). Violence against Jews was threatening to break out again as it had during the First Crusade (1096–99), and both endeavor to contain it. Peter of Montboissier describes contemporary Christian thinking like this: "Why should we pursue the enemies of the Christian faith in a far and distant land while vile blasphemers far worse than any Saracens – namely, the Jews – are not far away from us, but live in our midst, blaspheme, abuse, and trample on Christ and the Christian Sacraments so freely, insolently, and with impunity?"[11]

The ideas behind crusader violence against Jews have altered drastically between the First and Second Crusades. Jews are not merely the descendants of Christ's historical enemies, as they were fifty years earlier, but living enemies of Christ: they hate Christ and Christians and seek to blaspheme and abuse Christ through the vessels which hold the sacraments of his body and blood. "Perhaps the most accurate gauge for the development of these new stereotypes is the rapid emergence and spread of the accusation" of ritual murder, which coincided with the Second Crusade.[12] Both Bernard of Clairvaux and Peter of Montboissier hold the line on the Augustinian doctrine: "slay them not."[13] But they have divergent ideas about how the Jews should be treated, which go to the heart of their responses to Jewish usury.

---

[10] Deut. 23:19–20 in the Vulgate reads: "Non fenerabis fratri tuo ad usuram pecuniam ... sed alieno." See below for Lateran II.

[11] Giles Constable, ed., *The Letters of Peter the Venerable*, 2 vols. (Cambridge, MA, 1967), 1:327–330, cit. 328. My translation alters slightly that of Friedman, "Anatomy of Anti-Semitism," 93.

[12] Robert Chazan, "From the First Crusade to the Second: Evolving Perceptions of Christian-Jewish Conflict," in *Jews and Christians in Twelfth-Century Europe*, ed. Michael Signer and John Van Engen (Notre Dame, 2001), 46–62, cit. 50. On ritual murder and other libels against medieval Jews, see the chapter by Emily Rose in this volume.

[13] Cohen, *Living Letters*, 219–70.

Bernard of Clairvaux insists that Jews "must not be persecuted, slaughtered, or driven away."[14] Jews, having been exiled, subjugated, and scattered among the nations, he argues, have *already* paid "a just penalty" for "the crime of killing Christ." They are undergoing a "hard captivity to Christian princes," but "when the time comes, all Israel will be saved." While laying out this drama of salvation history, Bernard evokes the difference between the rabbinic and canonical interpretation of Deuteronomy 23:20–21 (Vulg. 23:19–20) in an aside: "I pass over in silence that wherever Jews are wanting, we are sorry to say that Christian lenders Judaize worse (*peius iudaizare dolemus christianos feneratores*) – if they should be called Christians and not baptized Jews."[15] The Latin phrase *christianos feneratores* links this statement directly to the canon made at the Second Lateran Council of 1139 denouncing Christian lenders' greed.[16] But "Judaize" is a strange term to use here. Christian discourse, since late antiquity, has used "Judaizing" to refer to the adoption of Jewish *religious practices*, never to economic practices. In what way, then, were the Christian lenders following Jewish religious practice? By receiving usury from Christians as Jewish law permits based on Deuteronomy 23:20–21! Bernard of Clairvaux, in short, is playing on the term "Judaize" to suggest that Christian lenders are practicing Judaism. The stereotype of the Jewish usurer who, following rabbinic law, treats Christians as "strangers" is implied, but Bernard does not condemn (or even mention) Jewish moneylending or rabbinic law. His main rhetorical point is that Christian lenders act worse than Jews: they loan to their brothers, which is forbidden by Jewish law.

Peter of Montboissier suggested a harsher treatment of Jews. Writing to Louis VII, King of France, Peter of Montboissier asserted that in retribution for the "crime of spilling Christ's blood," Jews have been spared by God for "a life worse than death" – like Cain. Consequently, he counsels the king to spare their lives, but "plunder" them for the glory of God.[17] "What is a more appropriate way for those impious ones to be punished than that by which both iniquity is condemned and charity is sustained?" Jewish riches "wickedly acquired for the sake of growing fat" shall be carried away "for the sake of the Christian army

---

[14] Bernhard von Clairvaux, Epistola 363 in *Sämtliche Werke*, 10 vols., (Innsbruck, 1990–99), 3:311–17, cit. 316.

[15] Berhnard von Clairvaux, *Sämtliche Werke*, 3:316.

[16] Norman Tanner, ed., *Decrees of the Ecumenical Councils*, 2 vols. (Washington, DC, 1990), 1:200.

[17] Constable, ed., *Letters of Peter the Venerable*, 1:329. The Latin verb *auferre*, which he uses, can mean "carry off," "seize," or "rob."

assaulting the Saracens." Without ever mentioning moneylending, he charges the Jews with usury:

> What is more just than that these who fraudulently have made a profit, shall be left destitute; those who wickedly have stolen like thieves, and what is worse with audacity and impunity, shall be stolen from? What I say has been noted by all. For it is not by simple farming, nor lawful military service, nor by any other honest and useful occupation that [Jews] have filled their barns with crops, their cellars with wine, their purses with coins, their chests with gold and silver as much as, as I reported, by cunningly taking them from Christians, by stealthily buying from thieves [and] acquiring at a cheap price what is high-priced.[18]

Usury is writ large here in the charges of fraudulent profit, stealing with audacity, dishonest and cunning means of acquisition. Jewish conduct is usurious and, therefore, associated with theft.[19] In retribution, Peter of Montboissier proposes Christian theft.

But Peter of Montboissier goes further: he presents Jews' usury as a form of religious desecration. He invents a false scenario in which Christian thieves sell to Jews sacred vessels, such as chalices or ciboriums used for communion. The greatest atrocity here is not the theft of sacramental objects by the false Christian, but their purchase by Jews "who killed the body and poured out the blood of Christ" when he dwelt on earth. Just as then Jews "insulted and injured Christ," so too today do they "abuse Christ" and use these "sacred vessels" in ways that are "horrible to contemplate."[20] Peter of Montboissier may argue against slaughtering Jews, but he fully agrees with Christians who advocate genocide that Jews "blaspheme, abuse, and trample on Christ and the Christian sacraments freely, insolently, and with impunity."[21] Their crime is being Jewish. Any Jewish economic activity is usurious because it is done by Jews. The rhetoric on Jewish usury is the product of theology, not the other way around.

Over the next forty years, the papacy would forward the campaign against Christian usury, but not all clergy supported it. At the Third

---

[18] Ibid.

[19] Giacomo Todeschini, "The Origins of a Medieval Anti-Jewish Stereotype: The Jews as Receivers of Stolen Goods (Twelfth to Thirteenth Centuries)," in *The Jewish-Christian Encounter in Medieval Preaching*, ed. J. Adams and J. Hanska (New York, 2015), 240–52.

[20] Constable, ed., *Letters of Peter the Venerable*, 1:329.

[21] Ibid., 1:328.

Lateran Council (1179), Pope Alexander III proposed a new canon on lay Christian usury, but as the theologian Peter the Chanter reported, some prelates took the sting out of the legislation by limiting it to "infamous usurers," that is, ones who publicly advertised as moneylenders.[22] Peter the Chanter further complained that "moneybags" and "horseleeches" are promoting their sons to positions in the church with money made through usury. "Such ones," he bemoaned, "even have adopted the name of Jews!"

> For, princes who protect them do not allow them to be accused of any crime, saying, "Such ones are our Jews." But, on the contrary, they are worse than Jews! Because a Jew, according to the prescription of the law, "shall not lend to his brother (Deut. 23)," but only to [one who is] a stranger from the promise [to Israel]. But these [Christians], however, lend both to those closest [to them] and to foreigners, contrary to the precepts of the Lord.[23]

Like Bernard of Clairvaux, Peter the Chanter argues that Christian usurers, because they lend to their own "brothers," are worse than Jews who observe Deuteronomy 23:20–21. But Peter the Chanter's testimony reveals something new. The Christian elite around 1190 deploy the label "Jew" as a legal strategy for protecting Christian usurers from prosecution in ecclesiastical courts, because Jews are subject only to secular law.

PHASE 2: REGULATING JEWS AS USURERS

At the turn of the 13th century, the students of Peter the Chanter stood at the center of a new phase in the construction of the Jew as usurer. The Chanter and his students championed a new practical theology aimed at the moral reform of Christian life through preaching and penance.[24] Usury was a central concern for the movement, and some of the Chanter's students, such as Robert de Courçon and Thomas de Chobham, composed extensive tracts on usury, considered the first medieval works in economic thought.[25] Under Innocent III, a member

---

[22] Tanner, ed., *Decrees of Ecumenical Councils*, 1:223.

[23] Petrus Cantor, *Verbum abbreviatum textus conflatus*, Corpus Christianorum. Continuatio Medievalis (Turnhout, 2004), 196:324–25, and *Verbum abbreviatum textus prior*, Corpus Christianorum. Continuatio Medievalis (Turnhout, 2012), 196A:292–93.

[24] John Baldwin, *Masters, Princes, and Merchants: The Social Views of Peter the Chanter and His Circle*, 2 vols. (Princeton, NJ, 1970), 3–59, 261–311.

[25] Odd Langholm, *Economics in the Medieval Schools* (Leiden, 1992), 37–62, esp. 37.

of this circle, the concept of crusading was transformed by making its success contingent on the moral reform of European Christendom. Innocent III appointed many in the Chanter's circle to positions of ecclesiastical power as papal legates, bishops, and cardinals. Using this network, he launched preaching campaigns for the twin purposes of crusade and moral reform. Preaching against usury, consequently, became closely tied to crusade recruitment.[26]

Christian usury remained the central focus of the reform movement, but we find growing references to Jewish usury in the circle's theological writings and increasing efforts to regulate Jewish usury in papal bulls and conciliar legislation. Some secular rulers created systems of royal surveillance. Loan chests, systems of seals, and royal registries began to be used to monitor Jewish loans and protect Christian borrowers. Innocent III, when elected to the papal seat in 1198, urged recalcitrant rulers to regulate Jewish lending. And in his calls for the Fourth Crusade (1202–4) and the Fifth Crusade (1217–29), Innocent III ordered the remission of Jewish usury on crusaders' loans – an act taken on Christian usury in earlier crusades.[27]

A letter to the French king, Philip Augustus, illustrates well how Innocent III regarded Jewish usury in 1205. Like the 12th-century spiritual leaders, we have seen, Innocent III too uses the Augustinian doctrine to frame his argument. He emphasizes the doctrine's negative medieval aspects: Jews as crucifiers of Christ, Jews as kin of Cain, Jews as the enslaved subjugated to the free children of Christ. Here he uses it to chide the king into regulating Jewish usury and repressing other Jewish practices.

> the Jewish Dispersion should live ... under Christian princes ... nevertheless, Princes who prefer the sons of the crucifiers ... to the heirs of the Crucified Christ, and who prefer the Jewish slavery to the freedom of those whom the Son freed are exceedingly offensive in the eyes of God.... Know then that the news has reached us ... that in the French kingdom the Jews have become so insolent that by means of their vicious usury, even usury on usury, *they appropriate ecclesiastical goods and Christian possessions.*[28]

---

[26] Jessalynn Bird, "Reform or Crusade? Anti-Usury and Crusade Preaching during the Pontificate of Innocent III," in *Pope Innocent III and his World*, ed. John Moore (Aldershot, 1999), 165–85.

[27] Jessalynn Bird, Edward Peters, and James Powell, eds., *Crusade and Christendom: Annotated Documents* (Philadelphia, 2013), 28–37, 107–12, 124–29.

[28] Solomon Grayzel, *The Church and the Jews* (Philadelphia, 1933), 1:104–9, cit. 1:104–7. Emphasis mine.

For Innocent III, as for Peter of Montboissier, the principal offense is that Jews possess ecclesiastical goods and Christian wealth, thereby inverting "the slave" and "the free." But usury is not disassociated from other religious transgressions. Innocent III goes on to list a whole set of "Jewish outrages," from hiring Christian servants to blaspheming to receiving stolen goods and murdering Christian hosts at "every wicked opportunity." If Philip Augustus "restrains the Jews from their presumptuous conduct in these and similar matters," Innocent III promises him a crusader privilege – remission of sins. A year and a half later, Philip Augustus made the first ordinance on Jewish loans, establishing a rate of interest, limiting compound interest, and setting up a new system of seals on Jewish loans.

The struggle against usury now became focused on regulation of moneylending, but its religious framing was stronger than ever: it was now part of the moral crusade for the reform of Christendom. Yet another shift was beginning to take place in the early 13th century: rulers from England and France to the Holy Roman Empire began spouting a new political ideology of "Jewish serfdom," adapted from the Church's theology of "Jewish servitude."[29] Secular rulers laid claim to legal and fiscal authority over "their Jews," just as the Church began extending canon law over Jews, albeit in cases restricted to the protection of Christianity and Christians.

By tying the success of the crusades to the moral reform of Christendom, the Chanter's circle effectively sacralized Christian Europe. The first step in this direction had already been taken in the mid-12th century when crusaders' possessions had been taken under the Church's wing and protected from usury and legal suits. A further step was taken at the Fourth Lateran Council (1215), when Innocent III prohibited Jews from exacting heavy usury from *all Christians*, not just crusaders.

> The more the Christian religion (*religio*) is restrained from usurious exactions, that much more oppressive grows the treachery (*perfidia*) of the Jews in such. So that, in a short time

---

[29] Kenneth Stow, "Papal and Royal Attitudes toward Jewish Lending in the Thirteenth Century," *AJS Review* 6 (1981), 161–84; Mell, *Myth of the Medieval Jewish Moneylender*, chaps. 5 and 6; Robert Stacey, "The Massacres of 1189–90 and the Origins of the Jewish Exchequer, 1186–1226," in *Christians and Jews in Angevin England* (York, 2013); Gavin Langmuir, "'Tanquam Servi': The Change in Jewish Status in French Law about 1200," in his *Toward a Definition of Antisemitism* (Berkeley, CA, 1990), 167–94.

the Jews exhaust the resources of Christians. Therefore, in our desire to protect Christians in this matter, from being excessively oppressed by Jews, we order by synodal decree, that when in the future under any pretext, Jews extort oppressive and excessive usuries from Christians, association with Christians shall be denied to them, until they shall have made sufficient amends for their exorbitant exactions.[30]

The hostility to Jews and Judaism is evident in the canon's contrast between the "Christian religion" and "Jewish treachery." As in the 1205 letter to Philip Augustus, the claim that Jews "exhaust the resources of Christians" goes hand in hand with the notion of Jews as subjugated to the Church and as enemies of Christ. A change has taken place between 1140 and 1215: in the 12th century, Jews had been collectively categorized as usurers, but Christian responses to this interpretive difference varied. Now the overriding presumption was that Jews, as enemies of Christ, his church, and the church's Christians, will use usury to injure the Church, its crusaders, and Christendom.

The new tracts on usury from the Chanter's school explain how Christian usury and Jews as usurers threaten the stability and prosperity of Christian society. Central to these fears was a narrowing of the concept of usury. Whereas Gratian's *Decretum* presented usury as an *immoral desire* for "more than was given," the 13th-century theologians limited it to a particular *type of legal contract* – a loan of money defined as a *mutuum* in Roman law.[31] Thirteenth-century theologians shifted the locus of sin from the actor's desire (for "more than was given") to the act itself, the contract. They thereby freed from suspicion many types of contracts, thus facilitating a more fluid credit market, but they also created new problems. An example from Robert de Courçon's early 13th-century tract on usury will help explain how the new, narrower definition of usury resulted in an increased sense of social threat.

A prince collected taxes and dues from usurers, gave instructions to make new coins from the bullion, and had them circulated in the market among merchants and moneychangers, so that he could make a profit. Can goods in this market, Robert de Courçon asks, be legally acquired? No – ownership passes from one person to another either through a contract (a loan, purchase, or sale) or through a freely given gift.

---

[30] Tanner, ed., *Decrees of Ecumenical Councils*, 1:265–66. Translation my own.
[31] Langholm, *Economics in Medieval Schools*, 45–46.

But by none of these means can he who holds this money transfer ownership of it to you. For he is not able to sell [it, in other words, he cannot] say: "I give you a loan (*mutuum*) from this money; I make mine (*meo*) yours (*tuum*)." Nor can he rightfully say: "This is mine." [And] since it is not his, he is not able to transfer that to you by any type of contract or by any kind of gift, when the rightful owner protests.[32]

Using an invented etymology for *mutuum*, Robert de Courçon argues that since money made through usury has not been legally acquired, it cannot effect a transfer of ownership. All subsequent exchanges become invalid, and the market collapses.

Just as coins made from usurious money cannot transfer ownership, so, too, money given by a Jew who "has nothing except what he has from usury" cannot rightfully transfer ownership.

When for instance the Jew says to someone to whom he is going to make a loan: "I give to you a loan (*mutuum*), that is, I make mine (*meo*) yours (*tuum*)," he himself speaks falsely, because it is another's property which he gives in a loan or in a contract or in a gift; and you know this with certainty; therefore knowing [this] and being prudent, you ought not receive from a Jew any kind of loan, either in a contract or as a gift.[33]

Ownership cannot be transferred where one does not have a proper right to ownership, and Jews as usurers do not have one. Money circulating in the market dissolves the legitimacy of market exchange when tainted by Christian usury or handled by a Jew (whose money, our theologian assumes, comes from usury). Consequently, rulers who take taxes from such monies risk the prosperity of their realms, particularly as the emerging doctrine of restitution makes them responsible for returning usurious funds to the rightful party.

Over the 13th century, secular rulers' policies on Jews came to be shaped by the theological category of the Jew "who has nothing except what he acquired from usury." In the late 1230s, Louis IX, years after he had forbidden Jewish usury, was haunted by the specter of monies tainted by usury, Christian and Jewish. Pope Gregory IX gave him an "out" by directing him to put these funds toward "pious causes" – ones

---

[32] Robert de Courçon, *Le Traité "De usura,"* edited by Georges Lefèvre (Lille, 1902), 50–51.
[33] De Courçon, *De usura*, 52–53.

connected with crusading.[34] In 1270, Margaret of Constantinople, Countess of Flanders, sought Thomas Aquinas's guidance on whether it was permissible to tax Jews in her realm. Aquinas replied, yes, on the basis of both the medieval Church's Augustinian doctrine and the political ideology of Jewish serfdom: "the Jews because of their guilt are in perpetuity bound in slavery, and thus their property belongs to the earthly lord to take as his own. Still this servitude should be moderated" so that Jews can survive.[35] Aquinas surmised, however, that the real cause of her doubt was the situation envisioned by Robert de Courçon where Jews seem "to have nothing but what they have acquired through the depravity of usuries (*usurariam pravitatem*)." Aquinas's solution: if a ruler cannot find those to whom restitution should be made, the ruler can use the money for pious purposes "or even for the common benefit (*communem utilitatem*) of the land, if poverty threatens it or utility demands it." Aquinas uses a new economic concept, the "common good," which will come to play a decisive role in the third phase of the Jewish usurer. The concept arose with the new religious orders of Franciscans and Dominicans (Aquinas belonged to the latter), whose commitment to voluntary poverty led to innovative thinking about ownership, property use, and communal wealth.

PHASE 3: EXPELLING JEWS AS USURERS

By the end of the 13th century, kings and counts advised by Franciscans and Dominicans sought to eradicate Jewish usury through the expulsion of their Jewish subjects, going beyond papal directives. This was a reversal of the dynamic at the beginning of the 13th century, when the papacy prodded rulers to regulate Jewish loans. The University of Paris and its theologians remained central across the century – first with the school of Peter the Chanter and their penitential tracts on usury, then with the friars and their debates over poverty and property.

A wave of mass expulsions first took place during the 1280s and 1290s, all in Western Europe: Edward I of England expelled the Jews from his French province of Gascony in 1287 and from England in 1290. Charles II, King of Naples, expelled the Jews from his French

---

[34] Michael Lower, *The Tunis Crusade of 1270* (Oxford, 2018), 157.

[35] Thomas Aquinas, "Epistola ad ducissam Brabantiae," in *Opera Omnia* (Rome, 1979), 42:374–78. On the identification of the addressee, see Leonard Boyle, "Thomas Aquinas and the Duchess of Brabant," in *Facing History: A Different Thomas of Aquinas* (Louvain-La-Neuve, 2000), 107–21.

territories of Maine and Anjou in 1289. The Count of Nevers expelled
the Jews in 1294. In 1291, Philip IV expelled Jews newly arrived from
England and renewed his father's order expelling Jews from villages
and small towns. In 1306, Philip IV expelled the Jews from all royal
domains (though this expulsion would become final only in 1394 under
Charles VI, and Provence was added only in 1501). More localized
expulsions would occur across Central Europe and the Italian
Peninsula in the 14th and 15th centuries, and the final mass expulsions in Western Europe would occur in Spain in 1492 and Portugal in
1496 (with forced conversion in 1497).

In the documents from the 1280s and 1290s, usury is used as a
justification for expulsion. But it continues to be framed by the theology
elucidated in the preceding 150 years. The Anjou and Maine order – our
oldest full expulsion document – describes Jews as the "enemies" of all
Christians, responsible for "crimes odious to God" and "abhorrent to
Christianity," despoiling Christians "of their movable and immovable
goods by their devious deceits and by the endless abyss of usury."[36] The
circumstances under which Edward I decreed expulsion in 1287 are
telling: recovering from illness in Gascony, he took an oath to undertake a new crusade and ordered the expulsion of Gascon Jewry.[37] In
England, Edward I had prohibited Jewish usury in 1275 when he
returned from the Tunis crusade. Historians have judged the Jewish
move from lending to commerce in response as successful – but to no
avail. Edward I claimed that Anglo-Jews cunningly invented a new kind
of usury, which justified their expulsion as traitors.[38]

> In the third year of our reign, We, moved by solicitude for the honour
> of God and the wellbeing of the people of our realm, did ordain and
> decree that no Jew should thenceforth lend to any Christian at
> usury ... and whereas the said Jews did thereafter wickedly conspire
> and contrive a new species of usury ... to the abasement of our said
> people.... We, in requital of their crimes and for the honour of the
> Crucified, have banished them [from] our realm as traitors.[39]

Edward I voices a similar theological ideology to that of Charles II of
Naples: Jews as killers of Christ, Jews as enemies of Christ and

---

[36] Robert Chazan, ed., *Church, State, and Jew*, 314–17.
[37] Robin Mundill, *England's Jewish Solution* (Cambridge, 1998), 269–70.
[38] Ibid., 108–45.
[39] J. M. Rigg, *Select Pleas, Starrs, and Other Records from the Rolls of the Exchequer of the Jews, A.D. 1220–1284* (London, 1902), xli.

Christians, Jewish usury as a means of injuring Christians and dishonoring God. By expelling their Jewish subjects, these rulers went beyond the bounds of the Augustinian doctrine – something no pope ever did (or will do). They criminalized Jews by coupling the traditional emphasis on Jewish servitude as punishment for killing Christ with claims of usury extracted in defiance of royal decrees.

Further research is needed to clarify why a wave of mass expulsions took place precisely in the late 1280s and 1290s. One key element seems to have been the alignment of the economic market with the concepts of the common good and public use, propelled in part by political contests of the 1290s.[40] When adopted by civic institutions, the Franciscan idea of the "common good" legitimated both political power and credit institutions. The common good (*communem utilitatem*) and public use (*utilitas publica, utilitas populi*) came to be contrasted with personal gain and personal use. The common good was civic, communal, and Christian, and associated with Christian charity and fidelity. Personal good was individual, self-interested, and associated with un-Christian greed and infidelity.[41] In the Italian civic centers was born the duality of the Christian merchant and the Jewish usurer, to which Shakespeare would give voice. The merchant of Venice circulated his wealth out of charity, aiding the common Christian good, but the Jewish Shylock lent out of malevolent religious hatred and private vengeance, despoiling and injuring the Christian merchant and his society.

CONCLUSION

The association of Jews with money originated in medieval Western Europe during the 12th and 13th centuries. A new stereotype portraying Jews as usurers emerged in three phases. In the 1140s, when the papacy initiated a campaign against lay Christian usury, Jews were collectively labeled as usurers on account of their adherence to rabbinic law, specifically, their interpretation of Deuteronomy 23:20-21 (Vulg. 23:19-20). Jews were deemed usurers whether they were involved in moneylending or not. Beginning in 1200, the theological school of Peter the Chanter intensified the campaign against lay Christian usury, initiated economic-theological

[40] Matthew Kempshall, *The Common Good in Late Medieval Political Thought* (Oxford, 1999), 6-25.
[41] Giacomo Todeschini, *Franciscan Wealth: From Voluntary Poverty to Market Society* (Saint Bonaventure, NY, 2009), 105-96.

thought, and transformed the crusades by tying their success to the reform of Christendom. Pope Innocent III, a member of this circle, encouraged rulers to regulate Jewish loans and issued a canon against Jewish usury at Lateran IV, which mirrored that against Christian usury at Lateran III. The rulers of England and France began regulating Jewish loans through seals, chests, and inquests. They also began protecting their authority over Jewish populations from incursions by the papacy through politicizing the theological ideology of Jewish servitude as "Jewish serfdom." In the mid- to late 13th century, rulers in France and England disallowed Jewish lending as a pious act to protect their Christian subjects and to protect their realms from the contamination of usury. By the 1280s and 1290s, kings and counts of France and England expelled Jews en masse, accusing them of being Christ-killers, Christian haters, and usurers. These secular rulers, often radicalized in the Seventh Crusade, were advised by Franciscans and Dominicans and influenced by the new political-economic concept of the common good.

The primary conditions for the creation of the stereotype, I have argued, were the campaign against lay Christian usury and the escalation of crusading with its hostility toward Jews and Judaism. In conclusion, I'd like to set these in a broader religious context that helps explain why these propelled forward a new antisemitic stereotype. Crusading and the anti-usury campaign were bound up with larger religious movements known to medieval historians as the 11th-century reform movement and the medieval reformation. The 11th-century reform movement (which continued long after the 11th century) was led by popes and prelates who sought to free the Church and its property from lay control, to reform the clergy (and later laity), and to launch crusades. The medieval reformation refers to an evangelical awakening of laypersons that resulted in new religious movements, some adopted by the church as religious orders, others denounced as heresies often because they challenged the hierarchical authority of the church. Jewish religious difference reverberated in this climate as blasphemy, challenging church authority. These two religious movements were central in the growth of anti-Judaism, antisemitism, and the suppression of Jewish difference. Their aims and instruments included ecumenical councils, canon law, crusade preaching, moral reform and penance, suppression of heresy, economic thought on poverty and property, and the imagined fantasies of Jews as present-day killers of Christ and Christians. The medieval category "usurer" was fundamentally a theological category (or more precisely a theological-economic category). The collective labeling of Jews as usurers, originally based on a theological difference, became inextricably bound up with a Christian ideology of Jewish subjugation to prelates and princes, and with a Christian animosity to Judaism imagined as "blasphemy" and to Jews as "Christ-haters" and "Christian-killers."

Further Reading

Gamoran, H., *Jewish Law in Transition: How Economic Forces Overcame the Prohibition against Lending* (Cincinnati, OH, 2008). Surveys the rabbinic discussions of five types of business agreements related to usury from the Bible and Talmud to medieval and early modern rabbinic commentators.

Karp, J., *The Politics of Jewish Commerce: Economic Thought and Emancipation in Europe, 1638–1848* (Cambridge, 2008). Traces economic aspects of the debates over Jewish status in Western Europe from 1638 to 1848, giving attention both to Jewish and non-Jewish voices.

Kobrin, R., and A. Teller, eds., *Purchasing Power: The Economics of Modern Jewish History* (Philadelphia, 2015). A collection of articles that explore how Jews' economic choices and practices shaped their place in the global economy of the early modern and modern world.

Mell, J., *The Myth of the Medieval Jewish Moneylender*, 2 vols. (New York, 2017–18). Traces the modern construction of the historical narrative of a Jewish economic function as moneylenders in medieval Europe, challenges it empirically with tax and loan documents from medieval England, and explores the consequences of this revision for European history more broadly.

Penslar, D., *Shylock's Children: Economics and Jewish Identity in Modern Europe* (Berkeley, CA, 2001). Tells the history of how modern Jews have perceived and responded to claims of Jews' economic distinctiveness in commerce and credit.

Rosenthal, J., and M. Volovici, eds., *Jews, Money, Myth* (London, 2019). A collection of short scholarly essays published in conjunction with the exhibit of the same name at the Jewish Museum London in 2019. Essays cover topics related to money in Jewish tradition, moneylenders in medieval Europe, Shakespeare's Shylock, and modern philanthropy and fortune.

Satlow, M., *Judaism and the Economy: A Sourcebook* (London, 2019). Provides ancient, medieval, and modern sources related to Jewish economic life and thought.

Schraer, M., *A Stake in the Ground: Jews and Property Investment in the Medieval Crown of Aragon* (Leiden, 2019). Challenges the view of medieval Jews as primarily moneylenders and merchants by documenting Jewish property ownership in medieval Aragon.

Toch, M., *The Economic History of European Jews: Late Antiquity and Early Middle Ages* (Leiden, 2012). Describes the breadth and diversity of Jewish economic life from late antiquity to the central middle ages.

Todeschini, G., *Franciscan Wealth: From Voluntary Poverty to Market Society* (Saint Bonaventure, NY, 2009). Traces the development of Franciscan economic thought which led to a binary split between the Christian merchant and the Jewish usurer when the marketplace was legitimized by identification with a Christian civic common good.

13 Jews and Anti-Judaism in Christian Religious Literature*

MIRI RUBIN

Jews were a very small minority in medieval Europe. Around the year 1000, Jews lived around the Mediterranean, in the Christian cities of southern France, Italy, and northern Iberia, and in Muslim polities in that peninsula and in North Africa. In fewer numbers they were also known in Northern European cities, but their numbers there grew significantly over following centuries. With economic growth and urbanisation, rulers – ranging from kings to bishops – encouraged the settlement of Jews as agents of prosperity and fiscal sophistication. Jews received charters and privileges of protection through which they became an embedded and familiar presence in large towns and cities for long periods of time. They lived within urban communities, where they worked and even flourished, but where they were also vulnerable. This vulnerability was caused by the fact that Jews did not possess full rights of citizenship and political representation, and by their dependence on the goodwill – and whimsy – of rulers. It was enhanced by the Christian religious culture of their societies, a culture which had a great deal to say about Jews. The narratives about Jews in their literary expression are the subject of this chapter.

Jews were few in number, but they loomed very large in the narratives created by medieval Christian writers across Europe, both in Latin and in local, vernacular languages. These narratives reached diverse audiences, even in communities that had never known a Jew. The effect of such narratives was to create a set of associations, between Jews and certain behaviours, tendencies, feelings. The variety and inventiveness of these narratives were inspired by their themes that interested Christian writers and their audiences. Jews were central to the story of

---

* This chapter was written during the lockdown in response to Covid-19. I was able to discuss it with the virtual group of medievalists at Queen Mary which assembled during that period: Eliot Benbow, Matthew Champion, Rosa Vidal Doval, Annabel Hancock, David Harrap, Kati Ihnat, Amanda Langley, and Claire Trenery.

salvation not only because Jesus had been born a Jew, but also due to the belief that Jews were implicated – some would say fully to blame – in the Crucifixion. This belief was expressed most precisely, in texts and images, and was emphasised in preaching and teaching with particular intensity from the 12th century.

I use the word "narrative" here, since it allows us to consider – as we ought – a whole range of genres and situations where anti-Jewish ideas were explored. The Christian gospels told of Jesus' life and ministry, death and resurrection. They offered the core narratives which were conveyed in turn through worship: in parish churches or cathedrals, in biblical readings and sermons for Sundays and feast days. Narrative was embedded in drama on liturgical themes, as well as in the vernacular religious chants sung at pilgrimage sites or during processions. Such performances unfolded within meaningful urban spaces, were accompanied by sounds and enhanced by props. Think, for example, of the enactments of Christ's entry into Jerusalem on Palm Sunday, which combined biblical readings, chant, and the use of greenery representing the palm branches, and was accompanied by an edifying sermon.[1] In this performance Jews were presented as welcoming Jesus on his entry to Jerusalem, but it also pointed to their complicity in his death, remembered on the following Good Friday.

Jews were considered by Christian thinkers as privileged guardians of the Hebrew Bible – what Christians called the Old Testament – who were blind to the meaning of its prophecies in foretelling the coming of Jesus. Augustine (354–530), bishop of Hippo in North Africa, influenced thinking about Jews very strongly, with his own version of their usefulness to Christians. He saw Jews as "book carriers," whose unique affinity to the Bible set them apart from other people. Yet in their very existence, outside the Christian faith, Jews offered "evidence of truth" (testimonium veritatis) to the events told in the Christian gospels. Their exile and state of disenfranchisement in the Christian world was testimony to their error, their failure to see the truth.[2] Jews had been God's chosen, hence possessed traditions regarding the Bible, which could be useful too. They also had a role to play in Christian history, looking into the apocalyptic future, when they would convert. At the same time, early medieval traditions, especially those associated with the Holy Land, imputed to Jews

---

[1] Eyal Poleg, *Approaching the Bible in Medieval England* (Manchester, 2016), chap. 1.
[2] Paula Fredriksen, *Augustine and the Jews. A Christian Defence of Jews and Judaism* (New York, 2008).

"local" knowledge about holy places and relics, knowledge they some-times offered only grudgingly, another sign of their obduracy. Such was their mention in the traditions of the Invention (Finding) of the Holy Cross,[3] and those associated with the transfer of the Virgin Mary's robe. Some narrative contexts were strongly polemical in tone, like the narratives about the end of Mary's life, where the Jews were cast as cruel disrupters of her funeral procession.[4]

The Jew as witness offered fascinating literary possibilities, for who was more compelling than a Jew led to acknowledge Christian truth? Hence Jews were often present in accounts of miracles and martyrdoms. By the 7th and 8th centuries the Iberian accounts of the suffering unto death of Eulalia, Vincent, Sabina, and Cristete have Jews as witnesses to their suffering. To this role as witness, which prevailed during the first millennium, was added a new emphasis at the beginning of the second: Jews were considered to be the cruel torturers of Christ – a theme to develop even more powerfully in the 13th century in the sermons and devotional writings of Franciscan friars in particular.

Jews thus appear – singly and in groups – in a variety of situations within Christian narratives. There were the Jewish patriarchs and prophets whose lives were interpreted by Christians as foretelling the coming of Christ. They were treated with reverence and conceived quite apart from the Jews of the gospel story, or indeed who were their neighbours. For the "Jew" portrayed by medieval intellectuals as they developed narratives for much wider telling are usefully captured in Jeremy Cohen's term "the hermeneutical Jew,"[5] that is to say, the Jew imagined for purposes of interpreting and exploring Christianity. Such a Jew was not bound by criteria of realism or probability. It was a creature made up of a rich Christian culture, combined with the emphases of particular places and times.

This hermeneutical Jew could be quite different from any Jew encountered in the course of life in medieval communities. It was almost always a male adult, and it was one who was not only blind to Christian truth, but obstinate in his blindness. Certain writers associated this Jew with age-old tendencies and traditions, passed on as it were across the generations, as was the case in the child murder narrative we shall

---

[3] Barbara Baert, *A Heritage of Holy Wood: The Legend of the True Cross in Text and Image*, trans. Lee Preedy (Leiden, 2004).

[4] Miri Rubin, *Mother of God: A History of the Virgin Mary* (London, 2009), 53–57.

[5] Jeremy Cohen, *Living Letters of the Law: Ideas of the Jew in Medieval Christianity* (Berkeley, CA, 1999).

discuss below, born in mid-12th-century England. There was also a long-term process of associating the Jew with the devil, both acting to the detriment of good Christians. Across the period we discuss here, the Jew is imagined as acting with purpose, across regions, and with the deployment of economic power.[6] And alongside the written narratives in this period, a visual language for depicting Jews developed too, with distinctive characteristics that have been used and reused over the centuries.[7]

These narratives were Christian stories, gentile tales. They expressed the preoccupations of Christian writers and served ends which Christian intellectuals and leaders sought to achieve. There was a voluminous body of theological preoccupation which will not be the subject of our discussion here; alongside it developed literary production aimed at edifying and engaging wide and diverse audiences. The theological engagement with Jews and Judaism was especially lively and innovative from the later 11th century, often associated with the growth of cathedral schools, and in the next century with new directions in monastic life and thought. Between 1100 and 1200 monks of all colours innovated in imagining the Jew through genres old and new. The "dialogue" with a Jew was an interesting way of exploiting in narrative the reality of encounter and contiguity with Jews that many religious now experienced. The Jew – sometimes named – posed hard questions, which the Christian then triumphantly answered. Such was the dialogue on Original Sin the Incarnation between Odo, bishop of Tournai, and a Jew, "Leo."[8] Here was a way of thinking the unthinkable, by making the Jew counter, even ridicule, Christian beliefs. Such texts were theological narratives, playful in their dialogic form, but which left no one in doubt as to the appropriate final score – Christian triumph.

In the course of the 12th and 13th centuries, an ambitious system of religious instruction spread across Europe, often associated with the directives of the Third and Fourth Lateran Councils of 1179 and 1215, which emphasised better standards for the clergy and so also better education for the laity. The religious education of the laity took place in the parish, and usually by the parish priest. At the core was conveying the theology of the sacraments, the channel of grace

---

[6] Giacomo Todeschini, *Franciscan Wealth: From Voluntary Poverty to Market Society*, trans. Donatella Melucci (New York, 2009), chap. 4.

[7] Sara Lipton, *Dark Mirror. The Medieval Origins of Anti-Jewish Iconography* (New York, 2014).

[8] Odo of Tournai, *On Original Sin and A Disputation with the Jew, Leo, Concerning the Advent of Christ, the Son of God: Two Theological Treatises*, trans. and ed. Irven M. Resnick (Philadelphia, 1994).

necessary for salvation. People were taught that grace came to the world with Christ's Incarnation in the flesh, and was realised in his saving Crucifixion, and ultimate Resurrection. These concepts were embedded in biblical narratives communicated in the course of preaching, and enacted in the liturgy, especially on major feast days. And preaching was often enlivened with short illustrative tales called *exempla*, which did just that – exemplify. Such tales were meant to adorn the sermon with dramatic or somewhat comic moments in the course of which human folly – expressed in the rejection of Christian truth – was exposed and corrected. The *exempla* often used morally ambiguous figures – women, heretics, rural people, and Jews – to enact error, but also as the recipient of illumination and correction. For Jews in these roles the story usually ended in conversion.

The language and genre used by each writer offer us a good sense of the intended audience they had in mind. Yet the lie of any work is not determined by its author alone; texts written for an exclusive group might reach far beyond through subsequent processes of translation, excerption, and dramatization. So, for example, the stories collected for the use of monks in their devotions into the vastly successful Latin *Miracles of the Virgin Mary* (*Miraculae Virginis Mariae*) by the mid-12th century in English monasteries like Evesham and Bury St Edmunds were subsequently used by a monk in northern France, Gautier de Coinci (1177–1236) as the basis for his *Miracles de Nostre Dame*. This collection in French verse was offered in rhyme and aimed at an aristocratic lay audience.[9] The matter in question included some of the best-known and much-repeated stories of Mary's power to convert hearts, including those of Jews.

This very creativity in styles and genre of religious literary production reworked old narratives, but also – occasionally – gave rise to something new. As we shall see below, stories that involved Jews and children within the world of Marian tale ultimately allowed a monk of Norwich to invent the narrative of Jewish child murder around 1150. By the end of the 13th century another offence was imagined in narrative, the attack of Jews on the most precious and symbolically laden material which linked Christians to their God: Corpus Christi, Christ's body, the consecrated Eucharistic bread.

---

[9] Kati Ihnat, *Mother of Mercy, Bane of the Jews: Devotion to the Virgin Mary in Anglo-Norman England* (Princeton, NJ, 2016); Anna Roussakoff, *Imagining the Miraculous: Miraculous Images of the Virgin Mary in French Illuminated Manuscripts, ca. 1250–c. 1450* (Toronto, 2019), chaps. 1 and 2.

THE JEWISH BOY: BETWEEN WITNESS AND CRUELTY

One of the oldest and best-known narratives about non-biblical Jews involves a Jewish family; this is the story of the Jewish Boy.[10] Its origins are in early medieval Byzantium and in Greek, but it became known in Europe following its incorporation into the *Glory of Martyrs*, a much-used collection of miracle tales compiled by Gregory, Bishop of Tours (538–594), a prolific and influential writer. The story dwells on the intuitive attraction of a Jewish child to Christian ritual. In Constantinople, so the story goes, the son of a Jewish glazier entered a church with a group of his Christian schoolmates, where he partook in communion, receiving "bread and blood." On his return home, the boy told his parents where he had been and what he had done. The father, enraged, promised to take revenge and threw his son into the open oven (a glazier always had a fire going), while the boy's mother cried in anguish.[11] When Christians gathered around the wailing mother, with her they found the boy unscathed; he even told those assembled that a woman had protected him in the fire. The boy and his mother converted, while the father was thrown into the fire.

The story of the Jewish boy was copied and elaborated by several important writers even before the year 1000, and was much used and reworked thereafter, as we shall see. It contains several themes which were to recur in narratives about Jews, above all, that the quintessential Jew is male and is perverse, acting against natural paternal sentiment. The Jewish father acts in a cruel manner towards his son, the eponymous Jewish Boy, as no father should, while the mother displays the tenderness and emotion associated with women, and with mothers above all. Like the child, she was blameless, and like him she was easily convinced of Christian truth, when she witnessed the miraculous saving of her son; with her son, she converted and became a good Christian. Within the Jewish family, the father alone portrayed "Jewishness," while the mother and child responded to the manifestation of Christian ritual and grace. The adult male was the quintessential Jew, and he alone was punished.

By the 12th century, a time when polemical engagement with Jews and Judaism had become more pointed and frequent, the story of the Jewish boy was inserted more regularly into sermons. And so, when

---

[10] Ihnat, *Mother of Mercy, Bane of the Jews*, 148–54; Miri Rubin, *Gentile Tales: The Narrative Assault on Late Medieval Jews* (New Haven, CT, 1999), 7–28.

[11] *De Gloria Martyrum*, lib. 1, c. 10; see Rubin, *Gentile Tales*, 8–9.

the bishop of the recently founded cathedral at Norwich, Herbert of
Losinga (d. 1119), prepared a Christmas sermon, he naturally paid attention to the Virgin Mary, and included a tale which demonstrated her
power, but also cast the Jew as a determined adversary. Herbert's version
magnifies the ending with the death of all the Jews: "Forthwith there
followed a most just vengeance on the heads of the Jews; and they who
would not believe in the incarnate word were all alike burned in the
aforesaid furnace."[12] It expressed the Marian meaning of Christmas, as
the moment of the Incarnation within a Jewish woman's body, the very
belief Jews rejected. The Boy's experience in the church was a Marian
one, seeing the Virgin at the altar. This early medieval story had become
a monastic favourite. An imagined Jewish family thus became part of the
Christian story for the community of Norwich monks.

Alongside the story of the Jewish Boy, other narratives involved
Jewish protagonists, who in turn abuse the image of the Virgin or are
moved by miraculous action by her.[13] By the end of the century this
body of narratives was translated into Anglo-Norman, and in the 13th
century into other vernacular languages, alongside the northern
French we have already encountered. In these, acts of disbelief, desecration, and cruelty by Jewish men were contrasted to the Virgin's
mercy, which is shown extending even to Jewish women and children.
Jews were not the only groups punished in the Marian tales – there
were heretics, and lazy priests, and careless lay people too – but the
Jews' presence in this popular genre made them a frequent presence in
the life of instruction and devotion.

Through translation, these Marian miracles with Jews at their heart
reached new audiences. Let us return to the movement of a monastic
text into the lay sphere. The monk Gautier of Coinci (1177–1236), prior
of the abbey at Vic-sur-Aisne, did just so, when he began in 1218 work
on the miracles of the Virgin. This project continued throughout his
lifetime, and produced two books, including fifty-eight miracles and
seven songs. Gautier was inspired by a manuscript he had found at the
monastery of St Médard of Soissons, where he had been educated, and to
which he returned later in life. But to the Latin miracles he found
therein, he also added some local tales. In turn, Gautier's *Miracles of
Our Lady (Miracles de Nostre Dame)* inspired the intellectually and

---

[12] Edward Meyrick Goulburn and Henry Symonds, eds., *The Life, Letters, and Sermons
of Bishop Herbert de Losinga (b. circ. A.D. 1050, d. 1119)*, 2nd ed. (Oxford, 1878,),
65–66.
[13] Ihnat, *Mother of Mercy*, chap. 4.

devotionally curious King Alfonso X of Castile (1221–1284) to commission a collection in Galician-Portuguese, the preferred language of Iberian poetry, of Marian miracles. This vast collection of 419 poems, *The Songs of St Mary* (*Cantigas de Santa Maria*), incorporated the French miracles, but many others too, including some monastic milieu, from Gonzalo de Berceo's *Milagros de Nuestra Señora*, composed between 1245 and 1260 for the use of pilgrims.

The *Songs of Holy Mary* included Marian miracles which had been circulation in the Latin for about a century, but also added ones that were of particular interest to Iberian aristocratic readers. For its stories of Marian recognition and conversion included those with Jewish protagonists, but many involve Muslims. In terms of their function in these narratives, there is some equivalence between Jews and Muslims. As they were shown to recognise the Virgin and, through her, Christian faith, readers and audiences gained strength and comfort in their own religion.

The move into the vernacular enabled stories to reach wider social locations and contexts for use. And so, as the story of the Jewish Boy entered into prayer books, it was occasionally accompanied by illumination. The narrative of the Jewish Boy, one among several Marian miracles, adorned the books of prayer used by grand patrons. Images depicting the narrative accompany Psalm 142 in the Carew-Poyntz Book of Hours, made c. 1350–60, which was created for an aristocratic woman.[14] On the lower margin of folio 188v, the Jewish Boy is seen not just entering a church (as the earlier versions of the story had indicated), but kneeling to receive communion with other, Christian boys. The story continues on the next folio, where the Virgin stands by the burning oven, facing the child's father, the boy between them, as in a tug-of-war. A decade or so later, in an English Book of Hours (Danish National Library, *Thott* 547), the lower margin is again used as a space for three adjacent scenes: that of communion to a group of boys in the presence of the Virgin, another of the furious father throwing the Boy into the fire as the mother and other Jews recoil in horror, and the scene of the Boy's protection in the hands of the Virgin Mary, who removes him from the fire. The Jewish Boy, who suffered at the hands of his father, thus became an aid to devotion of those able to support their religious experiences with well-adorned books.

The narrative of the Jewish Boy was also depicted in more public settings, such as the mid-13th-century stained-glass windows of both

---

[14] Fitzwilliam Museum.

Bourges and Lincoln cathedrals.[15] Aloft in spaces which were often somewhat obscure, their presence indicates an interesting choice, but we cannot be sure that those present in the cathedral would have fully appreciated the narrative depicted. More effectively didactic is the depiction of the story on church walls, at a level which allowed engagement by viewers. Such was the inclusion of the story, not in a Marian context, but as a story about the power of the Eucharist. In the Chapel of Orvieto cathedral, dedicated to the memory of a famous Eucharistic miracle, around 1330, a series of wall paintings included the story of the Jewish Boy among such miracles. We have already seen that the ancient tale had been transformed into one about a young and pure Jew savouring the Body of Christ in form of bread. Yet most commonly the Marian association prevailed, as it did in a series of wall paintings of the later 15th century in the Chapel at Eton College, as well as in Winchester Cathedral. The Jews had been expelled from England in 1290, but stories about them – cruel fathers, willing mothers and children – still remained interesting, especially as manifestations of the power of the Virgin Mary.

THE LIBEL: JEWS AS MURDERERS OF CHILDREN

Setting a child protagonist at the heart of a narrative – as in the case of the Jewish Boy – raised the level of pathos and engagement, but also the power of the resolution offered by the Virgin's mercy and the Jews' conversion. Danger to children invariably raised anxiety in individuals and communities, together with the desire to apportion guilt, and narratives helped people make sense of events when children seemed to be in danger. One of the most powerful narratives about Jews with a child at its heart emerged in the city of Norwich in southeast England. Its author was a monk of Norwich Cathedral Priory, Thomas of Monmouth, who created c. 1150 a narrative that cast Jews as the murderers of a twelve-year-old Christian boy during Holy Week, a time when Passover and Easter coincided.[16] Like all narratives, this too, built on pre-existing materials in several genres: on hagiography, scripture, polemical literature, and the ever-present liturgy. But what Thomas of

---

[15] Meredith P. Lillich, "Gothic Glaziers: Monks, Jews, Taxpayers, Bretons, Women," *Journal of Glass Studies* 27 (1985), 79–92.

[16] For the text in translation and an introduction to it, see Thomas of Monmouth, *The Life and Passion of William of Norwich*, trans. Miri Rubin (London, 2014), esp. the introduction, vii–l. For further context, see E. M. Rose, *The Murder of William of Norwich: The Origins of the Blood Libel in Medieval Europe* (New York, 2015).

Monmouth created was new: a powerful story of Jewish cruel intent, which also invited Christians to remember the boy and support his emergent cult in Norwich Cathedral.

How did Thomas of Monmouth create this new tale about Jews? While setting the scene of the boy-victim's life in a rural household, he used all the tropes of hagiography – the familiar genre by which the biography of a saint or martyr was told – to set the scene: the boy's mother received a message in a dream about the impending birth of a most worthy son, that boy performed miracles already in infancy, and grew up precocious in religion, work, and learning. The encounter between William and the Jews was set on the streets of Norwich, where William was sent to learn the skinner's craft. Away from his family, the boy was in a danger zone that allowed the Jews of Norwich to get to know him and choose him as their victim for an alleged annual ritual of child-killing.

In making his tale, Thomas borrowed from some of the newest polemical writings about Jews, imputing to them the need to kill a Christian boy at every Passover. As was often the case, Passover and Holy Week coincided, so Thomas could easily draw parallels between the story of the Crucifixion and his own newly invented fiction. He also turned to other literary and rhetorical devices in constructing his story. He imputed to the Jews an elaborate ruse whereby they tempted the boy away from his widowed mother's home in Holy Week, on the pretext of employment in the city. The mother was cast as a traitor of sorts, for despite her premonitions of danger, she relinquished her son to a suspect stranger in return for a handful of silver coins. Having used the narrative to place the unsuspecting boy in the Jews' house, Thomas moved on to the heart of the tale: the torture and killing of the boy William.

The narrative describes the cruelty with which the boy's tender body was tied with a rope and pierced, and finally hung between the doorposts and unto death. While this was not a crucifixion, the scene borrowed heavily from elements of the Passion story: the boy was like a lamb led to the slaughter, and the boy's torturers were cruel and full of purpose. A knotted rope encircled the boy's head, placed carefully so as to cause pain by pressure on five tender spots: the temples, the nape, the forehead, the neck. Thomas was an inventive writer indeed: the five painful spots reminding every Christian who heard the story of the five wounds of Christ.

To the best of our knowledge, the narrative born in Norwich did not cause reprisals against Jews in that city. But it did have future effects. In the later decades of the 12th century, it appeared on occasion in the

annals of English monasteries: an accusation recorded in the chronicle
of St Peter's abbey in Gloucester and as a local cult around the boy
Robert of Bury (St Edmunds), which still had some adherents in the 15th
century.[17] The sole city where the story unfolded as a social drama was
Lincoln, in 1255. The disappearance of a child – Hugh – promoted an
accusation against the substantial local Jewish community, even before
the child's body was found. A legal response began in the city, but soon
the case was moved to London, as were the accused Jews, of which
eighteen were found guilty and executed.[18] The case of Lincoln in turn
prompted further literary creativity, as the cause célèbre inspired the
composition of verse vernacular versions. It was sufficiently well
known even in the 14th century, a century after the expulsion of the
Jews in 1290, for Geoffrey Chaucer to refer to the case of Lincoln, at the
end of the Prioress' Tale.[19]

The story born in Norwich soon became known outside England. By
1171 the Jews of Blois were accused of murder in Holy Week, and at
least one chronicler associated with the case of Norwich. By the mid-
13th century it was familiar in the Holy Roman Empire, where so many
Jewish communities flourished. There it was elaborated in new ways,
soon to be associated with imagined bloody ritual purposes. The story
remained a literary resource. It was rarely enacted as a social drama, but
it contributed to the hostile environment that could develop around
Jews in difficult times.

The later 15th century saw a spate of enactments of the child
murder narrative, elaborated and cast anew. At the end of a century
that saw expulsions in tens of cities of the Holy Roman Empire, limitations of Jewish labour and settlement in Italian cities, and outbursts of
violence, which led in Iberian cities to conversions of Jews in the tens of
thousands, a number of spectacular accusations were made against
Jews. Large numbers of Jews were accused, in trials led by trained
inquisitors, who helped produce elaborate protocols that have survived
for our study. These enactments of the ritual murder narratives also

---

[17] Joe Hillaby, "The Ritual-Child-Murder Accusation: Its Dissemination and Harold of
Gloucester," *Transactions of the Jewish Historical Society of England* 34 (1996),
69–109; Anthony Bale, *The Jew in the Medieval Book: English Antisemitisms,
1350–1550* (Cambridge, 2006), chap. 4.

[18] Gavin I. Langmuir, "The Knight's Tale of Young Hugh of Lincoln," *Speculum* 47
(1972), 459–72.

[19] Roger Dahood, "The Punishment of the Jews, Hugh of Lincoln, and the Question of
Satire in Chaucer's Prioress's Tale," *Viator* 36 (2005), 465–91; Bale, *The Jew in the
Medieval Book*, chap. 3, esp. 81–103.

benefitted from the recent development of print media – woodcuts, engravings – and genres that combined word and image in new ways. Hence news of them travelled faster and wider than had been the case in the earlier centuries.[20] In the following century, the 16th, the ritual murder lost some of its currency in Protestant lands, but was established and enacted in Catholic ones, and especially in areas of large Jewish settlement, such as Poland-Lithuania.[21]

JEWS AND THE BODY OF CHRIST

Narratives about Jews developed and emerged within dynamic literary and religious cultures, hence they reflect the concerns – old and new – of those who participated in them. An excellent example is the emergence of a new narrative at the end of the 13th century: the host desecration narrative.

In the course of the 13th century the recently codified theological tenet – that after the consecration at the mass, the Eucharistic wafer (host) was *transubstantiated* into Christ's historic body and blood – became a required belief. People were taught this in their parishes as children and preaching continued to bolster the claim with edifying arguments and exemplary narratives over their lifetimes. Annual communion – the reception of the Body of Christ, Corpus Christi – was received once a year, at Easter, to every man and woman who had confessed their sins and made penance for them. The belief was not an easy one – and it was easy to ridicule – so writers and preachers invested a great deal of effort in supporting the belief in transubstantiation with accounts of miracles. These habitually involved the improper use of the consecrated bread, as in its use in magic, or trespasses by Christians, who were miraculously chastised and put right in their belief.[22]

Even more intriguing was the dangerous idea that a Jew might harbour ill intent towards God in the shape of the eucharistic wafer. While a Christian might be careless or greedy in their abuse of the fragile bread that was God, Jews rejected the very belief in an incarnate God, and might approach his Body with derision, disrespect, and even

---

[20] Ronnie Po-chia Hsia, *Trent 1475: Stories of a Ritual Murder Trial* (New Haven, CT, 1996); Ronnie Po-chia Hsia, *The Myth of Ritual Murder: Jews and Magic in Reformation Germany* (New Haven, CT, 1988), 58–61.

[21] Magda Teter, *Blood Libel: On the Trail of an Antisemitic Myth* (Cambridge, MA, 2020).

[22] On the use of exemplary tales, *exempla*, for teaching the Eucharist, see Miri Rubin, *Corpus Christi: The Eucharist in Late Medieval Culture* (Cambridge, 1991), 108–26.

violence. The earliest known telling of such a host desecration tale was in Paris. On Easter 1290 in the parish of St Jean en Grève, on the right bank of the Seine, a Jewish moneylender, Jonathan, acquired from a Christian debtor the Eucharistic bread she had received that day. He had released for her use some pawned garments that she wished to wear to church on that holy day, in return for the consecrated host. Jonathan then "tested" the bread claimed as Christ's body in various ways, finally by piercing it with a small knife, only to see it bleed. He next tried to hammer a nail into it, only to find the host whole and bleeding. Finally, he threw it into a cauldron of boiling water, and it still remained whole and bleeding. A Christian woman finally found out the culprit; the host became a precious relic, as did the small knife. The Jew was arrested, tried, and executed.[23] The story was recounted in the royal French chronicles, in Latin and French, and gained vast notoriety. Within a decade it was mentioned in sermons in Tuscany. Accusations against Jews in Franconia in 1298 may have been inspired by knowledge of the case of Paris. Accusations against Jews in Franconia in 1298, also known as the Rintfleisch massacres, may have been inspired by knowledge of the case of Paris. These massacres in turn led to the making of new narratives, collected by a Dominican preacher, Rudolph of Schlettstadt, c. 1300, for future use in preaching.

By the 13th century every handbook for preachers, and many devotional works for the use of literate lay people, included miracle stories which recounted Jewish offences against all that Christians held dear, and the subsequent miraculous manifestations that revealed the culprits and punished them.

LITERARY THEMES ASSOCIATED WITH JEWS

We have so far considered some of the most established anti-Jewish narratives, ones that cast Jews as dangerous enemies to Christians. The role of the Jews in scripture was much elaborated, and turned the Jews into cruel and knowing enemies of Christ and all Christians.[24] This founding narrative allowed others to grow. And since the Passion of Christ was taught as an act always alive and re-enacted in liturgy as well as in Christian lives, the Jews of medieval Europe were cast as still bearing the guilt and sharing the desire of their biblical forebears.

---

[23] Rubin, *Gentile Tales*, 40–46.
[24] William C. Jordan, "The Last Tormentor of Christ: An Image of the Jew in Ancient and Medieval Exegesis, Art, and Drama," *Jewish Quarterly Review* 78 (1987), 21–47.

Jews thus appeared wherever the Passion was retold and re-enacted. The liturgy itself was understood as a dramatic re-enactment, with the priest as actor.[25] Dramatic performance accompanied the liturgy in Holy Week,[26] and when the Passion was performed, the Jews were represented. Yet Jews were a diverse group for Christians, including both virtuous patriarchs as well as those who according to scripture attended – and were increasingly seen as the cause of – the Crucifixion. In turn, Passion Plays became the basis of later medieval biblical play cycles, performed in the summer months in cities across Europe.[27]

A logic of repetition linked biblical past with the here and now, and so Jewish neighbours were imagined as re-enacting that primal act – the Passion – on an innocent child, or on the body of Christ in its Eucharistic form.[28] These narratives did not convince everyone, nor were they known everywhere, but they became current – in word and image – especially in urban communities where preaching was frequent and lively, and where patronage of the visual arts produced public display of religious narratives. And Christ's enemies were not Jews alone, but Christians who acted *as Jews*: cursing "as a Jew" was tantamount to wounding Christ's body again, as Jews had done at the foot of the Cross.

Jews also made occasional appearances in less well-known and less deadly literary situations. While we have noted that Jewish women rarely appeared as perpetrators, and often were shown as repelled by the actions of their menfolk, they were sometimes considered as objects of desire. In Iberian cities, where large communities of Jews lived alongside Christians and Muslims, love poetry expressed the yearning of Christian men for beautiful – forbidden – Jewish women.[29] Jews were also imagined as welcome converts, and one unique and early

---

[25] See the example discussed in Rachel Fulton, *From Judgment to Passion: Devotion to Christ and the Virgin Mary, 800–1200* (New York, 2002), 265–68.

[26] Susan Boynton, "The Bible and the Liturgy," in *The Practice of the Bible in the Middle Ages: Production, Reception, and Performance in Western Christianity*, ed. Susan Boynton and Diane J. Reilly (New York, 2011), 10–33.

[27] See, for example, the link between Passion plays and the N-Town cycle from 15th-century England in Penelope Granger, *The N-Town Play: Drama and Liturgy in Medieval East Anglia* (Cambridge, 2009), 85–86.

[28] For several examples of such repetition, see Anthony Bale, *Feeling Persecuted: Christians, Jews and Images of Violence in the Middle Age* (London, 2010), esp. chap. 2.

[29] Carsten Wilke, "Jewish Erotic Encounters with Christians and Muslims in Late Medieval Iberia: Testing Ibn Verga's Hypothesis," in *Intricate Interfaith Networks in the Middle Ages: Quotidian Jewish–Christian Contacts*, ed. Ephraim Shoham-Steiner (Turnhout, 2016), 193–230.

conversion narrative of the 12th century is cast as autobiography. The intent is implicitly anti-Jewish inasmuch as it traces the journey of a young Jewish man, through travel to the archiepiscopal city of Cologne on family business, towards appreciation of Christianity through an encounter with its rituals and aesthetic.[30]

* * *

Anti-Jewish narratives – their production, performance, and dissemination – and the ways they affected Jewish lives must be understood as dynamic historical phenomena. As we have seen, alongside the biblical narrative, and early medieval account of miracles, there developed early in the second millennium new narratives which imputed to Jews regular and knowing acts of disrespect and violence against Christian children and Christ's own body as contained in the Eucharistic host consecrated at the mass. We have also seen that tales could be transformed through translation to the vernacular and repurposing as sermon or drama.

Another process must be acknowledged as we trace these narratives, and this is their spread and effect in visual form. Sometimes illustrative of a text, but often in stand-alone situations, visual versions of the narratives we have encountered were sometimes painted over sequences of several scenes. Some have accompanying inscriptions, but other did not. This must mean that their makers assumed the prior knowledge of the narratives, or a didactic situation which had images explained: like a chaplain discussing an illuminated prayer book, or a preacher using a wall painting as an aid in instruction.

The visualisation of narratives into performance became more common over the period we have examined here. There were enactments of biblical or apocryphal narratives involving Jews, sometimes associated with the liturgy, and other times with feast days. Here the historic-literary subjects – the Jews – interacted in an unstable and sometimes dangerous fashion with the living Jews of the urban communities where such performances were staged. These occasions illustrate for us yet again the danger which arose for Jews from the confusion between the Jew next door and the hermeneutical Jew of scripture, theology, and exegesis. Most of the time, most people could tell them apart. But when the two merged, this spelt out the deadliest of danger.

---

[30] Jean-Claude Schmitt, *The Conversion of Herman the Jew: Autobiography, History, and Fiction in the Twelfth Century*, trans. Alex J. Novikoff (Philadelphia, 2010).

JEWS AND ANTI-JUDAISM   247

Further Reading

Abulafia, A. S., *Christian-Jewish Relations 1000–1300: Jews in the Service of Medieval Christendom* (New York, 2011). A survey and analysis of the theological concept of Jewish "servitude" and of the ways it informed policies towards Jews in medieval Europe.

Bale, A., *The Jew in the Medieval Book: English Antisemitisms, 1350–1550* (Cambridge, 2006). An analysis of the narratives involving Jews within English literature, in Latin and the vernacular, before and after the expulsion of 1290.

Cohen, J., *Christ Killers: Jews and the Passion from the Bible to the Big Screen,* (Oxford, 2007). This book explores the long history of representation of Jews in association with the Crucifixion, and points to intensification in text and image of the active role of the Jews in the Crucifixion, leaving a powerful legacy to Europe and the world.

Living Letters of the Law: Ideas of the Jew in Medieval Christianity (Berkeley, CA, 1999). This book introduces the theology which underpinned the relations between Judaism and Christianity, and which also influenced the attitudes towards Jews within medieval polities.

Lipton, S., *Dark Mirror: The Medieval Origins of Anti-Jewish Iconography* (New York, 2014). The development of the visual representation of the Jew is traced here with great care, and with attention to new developments in the course of the 12th century.

Images of Intolerance: The Representation of Jews and Judaism in the Bible Moralisée (Berkeley, CA, 1999). A luxurious new type of illustrated bible was created in the early 13th century, and it offered a polemical interpretation of the relation between the Old and New Testaments, through word and image.

Odo of Tournai, *On Original Sin and A Disputation with the Jew, Leo, Concerning the Advent of Christ, the Son of God: Two Theological Treatises*, trans. and ed. Irven M. Resnick (Philadelphia, 1994).

Rubin, M., *Gentile Tales: The Narrative Assault on Late Medieval Jews* (London, 1999).

Mother of God: A History of the Virgin Mary (London, 2009). This study of ideas and practices associated with the Virgin Mary pays attention throughout to ideas about Jews and Judaism embedded in the theology and devotions associated with Mary.

Thomas of Monmouth, *The Life and Passion of William of Norwich*, trans. Miri Rubin (London, 2014). This is a translation of the sole manuscript (c. 1200) of the first known version of the child murder narrative against Jews, which was developed by a monk of Norwich Cathedral Priory in the 1150s.

14 Antisemitism in Medieval Art

DEBRA HIGGS STRICKLAND

Ugly or beautiful, simple or complex, pictures can express ideas beyond words. This is true of antisemitic images produced during any age, but it is especially true of the ones created by medieval Christian artists, whose grotesquely stereotyped representations of Jews attacking Jesus or engaging in other nefarious activities were consumed by the educated elite as well as a broad and largely illiterate public for whom works of art were important anchors for lessons learned from sermons and other audio-visual experiences. This chapter surveys major antisemitic themes in pictorial works of art produced between the 12th and 15th centuries in England, France, and Germany, because it was during this period and in these places that such image-making was the most wide-spread and intensely hostile. I exclude artworks created in southern Europe, such as Spain and Italy, because they emerged here in distinct cultural circumstances and in comparatively less virulent forms.[1] A focus on Northern art clarifies how medieval artists helped shape a hostile cultural climate in which Jews were impoverished, persecuted, murdered, and expelled from Christian lands. The story of antisemitic medieval art is thus a case study of the power of images to defame targeted groups and to incite violence against them.

Jews living in medieval Christian towns and cities were a very small minority but a significant cultural presence. They were considered suspect for following the "wrong" religion, speaking a foreign language (Hebrew), and adopting unfamiliar dress and ritual practices. Some Christians believed Jews had horns and tails, and that Jewish men suffered a perpetual haemorrhage as punishment for shedding the blood of Jesus.[2]

---

[1] Pamela A. Patton, *Art of Estrangement: Redefining Jews in Reconquest Spain* (University Park, PA, 2012); Dana E. Katz, *The Jew in the Art of the Italian Renaissance* (Philadelphia, 2008).

[2] Joshua Trachtenberg, *The Devil and the Jews: The Medieval Conception of the Jew and Its Relation to Modern Antisemitism* (New Haven, CT, 1993), 44–53.

Such beliefs likely influenced reception of the artistic figure of the horned Moses and frequent use of the colour red for the hair, skin, and costumes of Jewish figures. In urban environments, Jews lived in separate sections of town but had daily social and business interactions with Christians that ranged from intimate to hostile.[3] In medieval art, hostile attitudes towards Jewish moneylenders are referenced by the attribute of the moneybag, which ultimately linked medieval Jews to the despised figure of Judas (Matt. 26:15). From the early 13th century, Jews living in Christian societies were required to wear distinctive identifiers which took the form of hats and badges; similarly, hats are often distinctive markers of Jews in medieval art: the attribute of the "Jewish hat" or *Judenhut* (pl. *Judenhüte*) varies in form from a knobbed or soft-folded Phrygian cap to a spikey "inverted funnel."[4] Badges, far less frequently depicted, are rendered in French and German art as small yellow rings or discs, and in English art, shaped like the twin tablets of the Law, reflecting the different forms of badges legally mandated in these regions.[5]

Persecutory legislation, high levels of taxation, property confiscation, physical attacks, and incarceration on trumped-up charges characterized a deteriorating situation that culminated in wholesale expulsions of Jewish communities, first from England in 1290, and subsequently from France, Germany, and other Western European countries over the course of the 14th and 15th centuries.[6] Negative pictorial images of Jews produced in tandem with fake news accounts of anti-Christian conspiracies helped pave the way for expulsion, and equally negative, post-expulsion imagery helped keep Jews "virtually" present in places they no longer resided for Christian devotional and ideological purposes.[7] The consistently stereotyped nature of Jewish figures demonstrates that in medieval art, "Jews" were a constructed imaginary rather than reflective of living reality. The types of images discussed in this chapter therefore tell us next to nothing about medieval Jews, but they reveal a great deal about the preoccupations of medieval Christian image-makers.

[3] Miri Rubin, *Cities of Strangers: Making Lives in Medieval Europe* (Cambridge, 2020), 50–70.

[4] Sara Lipton, *Dark Mirror: The Medieval Origins of Anti-Jewish Iconography* (New York, 2014), 16–54.

[5] Nicholas Vincent, "Two Papal Letters on the Wearing of the Jewish Badge, 1221 and 1239," *Jewish Historical Studies* 34 (1994–96), 209–24.

[6] Sophia Menache, "Faith, Myth, and Politics: The Stereotype of the Jews and Their Expulsion from England and France," *The Jewish Quarterly Review* 75 (1985), 351–74.

[7] Miramne A. Krummel, *Crafting Jewishness in Medieval England: Legally Absent, Virtually Present* (New York, 2011).

CHRIST-KILLING

Christian hostility towards Jews was ostensibly grounded in the belief that Jews murdered Jesus Christ, and that the guilt for this unforgiveable act of deicide must be borne by all Jews, for all time.[8] This is why narrative images of the Passion – the events surrounding Jesus' crucifixion – emerged as a primary arena for antisemitic invention. In Passion scenes, all of Jesus' persecutors are cast as Jews, and even the Roman official, Pontius Pilate, is rendered according to the stereotype to maintain a consistent focus on Jewish guilt.[9] This stereotype consists of grotesque physiognomy, featuring an enlarged or hooked nose, scraggly beard, large eyes, and wide mouth or grimace. Profile positioning, ruddy or dark skin, red hair, and a malformed body are additional somatic features.[10] Tight-fitting, parti-coloured, or otherwise outlandish or immodest garments function as negative intensifiers, especially with the addition of the colours red or yellow.[11] The attention-commanding brightness of these two colours facilitates associations of red with blood, evocative of Christ-killing and other murderous accusations levelled against Jews; and yellow with stigmatizing identity badges. Costume details, especially hats, complete the stereotype and most importantly, wordlessly conflate New Testament Jews with medieval ones as confirmation of perpetual "Jewish guilt."

The virulence of this stereotype varies by degrees, but even if it was not used at all, medieval Christian viewers would have still identified Jesus' tormenters and crucifiers as Jewish as a matter of fundamental belief. For this reason, medieval Passion images must be understood collectively as antisemitic. Equally, it is important to understand that pointed hats, use of red and yellow, tight-fitting costumes, and grotesque profiles do not *automatically* signal a Jewish figure, as these same elements are deployed in medieval representations of other types of negative figures: context is key.

Beyond somatic features, Jewish figures are often signalled by the objects they hold and the company they keep. The *Judenhut* remains

[8] Jeremy Cohen, *Christ Killers: The Jews and the Passion from the Bible to the Big Screen* (Oxford, 2007), 9–36.
[9] Colum Hourihane, *Pontius Pilate, Anti-Semitism, and the Passion in Medieval Art* (Princeton, NJ, 2009), 227–95.
[10] Debra Higgs Strickland, *Saracens, Demons, and Jews: Making Monsters in Medieval Art* (Princeton, NJ, 2003), 105–22.
[11] Ruth Mellinkoff, *Outcasts: Signs of Otherness in Northern European Art of the Late Middle Ages*, 2 vols. (Berkeley, 1993), vol. 1, 41–43, 147–59.

the most ubiquitous identifier, but the attribute of a moneybag runs a close second as a sign of Jewish avarice rooted in the legacy of Judas viewed against the medieval backdrop of moneylending, as mentioned above. Other negative attributes include other types of headgear (hoods, turbans, winged caps) and banners emblazoned with hats, dragons, or scorpions.[12] A popular German motif is the "spikeblock," an imaginary torture instrument supposedly affixed by Jews to Jesus' robes to pierce his legs as he carried the cross.[13] Companion cats, dogs, goats, pigs, asses, toads, and other ill-regarded animals symbolically visualized alleged Jewish traits of ignorance, lust, and evil.[14]

Representative Passion images in English art that deploy the negative stereotype include the Despenser Retable, an altarpiece commissioned in 1382 by Henry le Despenser, Bishop of Norwich, for installation in Norwich Cathedral; the late 13th-century Salvin Hours (Fig. 14.1);[15] and the 14th-century Holkham Bible, whose narrative miniatures feature exceptionally sadistic Jewish figures whipping Jesus and nailing him to the cross.[16] In French art, the lavishly illustrated, 13th-century moralized bibles (Bibles moralisées) made for members of the Capetian monarchy include an expansive range of images directed against Jews and Judaism that rely more on negative attributes, such as hats and animals, than on physiognomical distortion.[17] Representative of a more complex strategy are numerous small, 14th-century ivory altarpieces intricately carved in Parisian workshops and decorated with elegant, restrained Passion imagery that mitigates the brutality of Jewish tortures described in contemporary devotional literature.[18] In Germany, an eight-scene Passion cycle carved around 1250 on the choir screen of Naumburg Cathedral is organized around angrily aggressive Jewish figures wearing exaggerated spiked hats; among the figures

[12] Mellinkoff, Outcasts, vol. 1, 59–94.
[13] Phillip Jeffrey Guilbeau, "Iuxta iter scandalum: The 'Wayside Stumbling-Block' in Late Medieval Passion Imagery," Studies in Iconography 27 (2006), 77–102.
[14] Mellinkoff, "One Is Good, Two Are Better: The Twice-Appearing Ass in a Thirteenth-Century English Nativity," in New Offerings, Ancient Treasures: Studies in Medieval Art for George Henderson, ed. Paul Binski and William Noel (Stroud, 2001), 325–42.
[15] Anthony Bale, Feeling Persecuted: Christians, Jews, and Images of Violence in the Middle Ages (London, 2010), 70–75.
[16] London, British Library, Add. MS 47682, fols. 29–39v; see Michelle Brown, The Holkham Bible Picture Book (London, 2007), 73–77.
[17] Sara Lipton, Images of Intolerance: The Representation of Jews and Judaism in the Bibles moralisées (Berkeley, CA, 1999).
[18] Nina Rowe, "Pocket Crucifixions: Jesus, Jews, and Ownership in Fourteenth-Century Ivories," Studies in Iconography 32 (2011), 81–120.

Fig. 14.1 Jesus before Caiaphas, in the Salvin Hours, England (Oxford?), c. 1275. London, British Library, Add. MS 48985, fol. 29 (detail). (Photo: British Library, London, UK © British Library Board. All Rights Reserved/ Bridgeman Images.)

carved on a late 13th-century baptismal font installed in the Marian church (*Marienkirche*) in Rostock is a Jewish hat–wearing Pilate. A panel attributed to the Master of the Coburg Roundels, *Flagellation of Christ and Crowning with Thorns* (c. 1490), presents Pilate as a grotesque Jewish stereotype surrounded by similar figures, garbed in red and yellow, engaged in the savage abuse of a forlorn Jesus.[19]

The virulence of images like these can make it difficult for modern viewers to understand their devotional significance, yet this must be borne in mind when assessing their full range of meanings. From this perspective, the primary purpose of the stereotyped Jewish villains in Passion scenes was not to condemn or defame Jews but rather to vividly evoke Jesus's protracted suffering to enhance the viewer's affective experiences and, by identifying with his tormentors, facilitate a state of penitence.[20] However, the devotional dimension of Passion scenes did not diminish their power to defame, ratchet up social tensions, or even

---

[19] Mainz, Landesmuseum; Mellinkoff, *Outcasts*, vol. 2, fig. IX.22.
[20] Caroline Walker Bynum, "Violent Imagery in Late Medieval Piety," *Bulletin of the German Historical Institute* 30 (2002), 1–36; Bale, *Feeling Persecuted*, 7–29.

incite the violence emblematized with chilling economy in a commentary image from the Abingdon Apocalypse (c. 1265–1270), in which a sword-wielding king and two bishops depicted barring grotesque, dark-skinned, hunchbacked, hat-wearing Jews from entering heaven reference the rejection and destruction of 13th-century English Jews.[21]

A non-narrative Passion genre known as the *arma Christi* (weapons of Christ) provided an abstracted, mnemonic guide to the "Jewish tortures" inflicted on the body of Jesus. In these depictions, the weapons are organized inside individually framed compartments or made to "float" surrealistically around a central image of Christ, Man of Sorrows. Typically, they include the ropes, the column, the scourge, the crown of thorns, the nails, the lance, the side wound, the sponge, the dice, the divided cloak, the crowing cock, and the empty tomb.[22] A disembodied slapping "Jewish hand" and the heads of Pontius Pilate, Caiaphas (the Jewish high priest), and a "spitting Jew" also counted among the weapons.[23] The aggregate thus presented Jesus' Passion ordeals one by one as a series of Jewish crimes, as did the accompanying text, which also circulated independently to provide a meditative, blow-by-blow account of the corporeal damage inflicted by each weapon.[24]

Like other types of Passion imagery, the *arma Christi* were rendered in all artistic media. Examples include a full-page miniature in the 14th-century English illuminated encyclopaedia, *Omne bonum* ("All Good Things"), featuring a Jewish figure spitting at the Man of Sorrows,[25] the small, framed image series that surrounds all sides of the Passion panels of the Despenser Reredos, mentioned above; and a full-page miniature in the Boucicaut Hours, produced in Paris around 1408.[26] A tiny devotional booklet made of ivory, probably in Cologne around 1330–40, includes a series of *arma Christi* panels, one of which presents a half-length Jewish figure pushing Jesus and a disembodied slapping Jewish

[21] Suzanne Lewis, "Giles de Bridport and the Abingdon Apocalypse," in *England in the Thirteenth Century*, ed. W. M. Ormrod (Woodbridge, 1986), 107–19, 116–18.

[22] Lisa H. Cooper and Andrea Denny-Brown, eds., *The Arma Christi in Medieval and Early Modern Material Culture* (Farnham, 2014).

[23] Bale, *Feeling Persecuted*, 90–117.

[24] Bale, *The Jew in the Medieval Book: English Antisemitisms, 1350–1500* (Cambridge, 2006), 145–68, 177–81.

[25] London, British Library, MS Royal 6.E.VI, fol. 15; Lucy Freeman Sandler, *Omne bonum: A Fourteenth Century Encyclopedia of Universal Knowledge*, 2 vols. (London, 1996), vol. 1, 94, 127.

[26] Paris, Musée Jacquemart-André, MS 2, fol. 242.

Fig. 14.2 *Arma Christi* panels, Devotional Booklet, Germany (Cologne?), c. 1330–1340. London, Victoria and Albert Museum (11-1872). (Photo: © Victoria and Albert Museum, London.)

hand (Fig. 14.2).[27] A 15th-century Flemish tapestry depicts a "spitting Jew" and Jewish hand on a monumental scale,[28] and a late 15th-century devotional woodcut designed in Ulm shows a full-length Man of Sorrows bleeding into a chalice, flanked by the head of Judas wearing a moneybag necklace, kissing Jesus' head; and a Jewish head wearing a beard and knobbed hat, turned in left profile while spitting large red droplets at the level of Jesus' loincloth.[29]

[27] London, Victoria and Albert Museum; Paul Williamson and Glyn Davies, *Medieval Ivory Carvings, 1200–1550*, 2 vols. (London, 2014), vol. 1, 352–57.
[28] New York, Met Cloisters; Adolfo Salvatore Cavallo, *Medieval Tapestries in the Metropolitan Museum of Art* (New York, 1993), 250–53.
[29] Nuremberg, Germanisches Nationalmuseum; Peter Parshall and Rainer Schoch, *Origins of European Printmaking: Fifteenth-Century Woodcuts and Their Public* (Washington, DC, 2005), 240–50.

SPIRITUAL BLINDNESS

According to the earliest Christian theologians, Jews did not recognize Jesus as the Messiah and so remained ignorant, or "blind," to the True Faith.[30] During the middle ages, this idea was expressed across Northern Europe in the paired figures of *Synagoga* and *Ecclesia*, female personifications of Judaism and Christianity, respectively.[31] Typically, *Ecclesia* stands tall, crowned, and alert, holding a chalice in one hand and a cross staff in the other; while a blindfolded *Synagoga* lowers her head in defeat as her crown falls from her head, her staff snaps into pieces, and the twin Tablets of the Law slip from her hand. Together, the figures signal the redundancy of Judaism in the wake of Christianity's triumph.

The blind *Synagoga*'s message of defeat was especially potent on urban church exteriors visually accessible to medieval Jews as well as Christians.[32] Nearly life-size sculpted examples of *Synagoga* are paired with *Ecclesia* on the façades of Reims Cathedral, Strasbourg Cathedral (Fig. 14.3), the abbey church of St-Giles-du-Gard (where *Synagoga* wears a crown rendered as the Dome of the Rock), and Bamberg Cathedral.[33] In England, a tiny but intensely aggressive figure of a blindfolded *Synagoga* stabbing the Lamb of God was carved on the 12th-century Cloisters Cross, originally carried in procession and displayed inside the (now destroyed) abbey of Bury-St-Edmunds.[34] A monumental, blindfolded *Synagoga* painted on an oak panel recovered from the wooden vault of the York Cathedral chapter house was originally paired with another panel depicting *Ecclesia*.[35] The dedication miniature in a manuscript copy of *The Mirror of Man's Salvation*, illuminated in Bruges in 1455 for Philip the Good, Duke of Burgundy, features a blindfolded *Synagoga* gaudily dressed in a tight-fitting blue bodice and bright red

[30] Sara Lipton, "Unfeigned Witness: Jews, Matter, and Vision in Twelfth-Century Christian Art," in *Judaism and Christian Art: Aesthetic Anxieties from the Catacombs to Colonialism*, ed. Herbert L. Kessler and David Nirenberg (Philadelphia, 2011), 45–73.

[31] Miri Rubin, "*Ecclesia* and *Synagoga*: The Changing Meanings of a Powerful Pairing," in *Conflict and Religious Conversation in Latin Christendom: Studies in Honour of Ora Limor*, ed. Israel Jacob Yuval and Ram Ben-Shalom (Turnhout, 2014), 55–86.

[32] Nina Rowe, *The Jew, the Cathedral and the Medieval City: Synagoga and Ecclesia in the Thirteenth Century* (Cambridge, 2011).

[33] Rowe, *The Jew, the Cathedral*, 86–139 (Reims); 191–37 (Strasbourg); 74–76 (St-Giles-du-Gard); 140–90 (Bamberg).

[34] Rowe, "Other," *Studies in Iconography* 33 (2012), 131–44.

[35] J. G. Alexander and Paul Binski, eds., *Age of Chivalry: Art in Plantagenet England 1200–1400* (London, 1987), 346–47.

Fig. 14.3 *Synagoga*, c. 1230, from the south transept double portal, Strasbourg Cathedral. Musée de l'Oeuvre, Strasbourg. (replaced by replica on the south transept). (Photo: Suren Manvelyan/Alamy Stock Photo.)

skirt with yellow trim standing beside a triumphant and crowned *Ecclesia* wearing the modest black-and-white dress of a beguine.[36]

The visual economy of *Synagoga* made her one of the most popular antisemitic motifs in medieval Christian art and also one of the earliest, with examples dating from the 9th century onward, well before the invention of the grotesque Jewish stereotype. By contrast, *Synagoga* is consistently rendered as a beautiful woman to suggest a positive perception of Judaism as a worthy precursor to Christianity. The worthiness of Judaism is an idea equally relevant to Old Testament illustrations populated with neutral renderings of the ancient Israelites (albeit often wearing various forms of the *Judenhut*).[37] *Synagoga* is also one of the few medieval Christian artistic figures of Jewish women, who otherwise are limited to Old Testament characters and supporting actors in antisemitic narrative scenes in which Jewish men or boys play the main negative roles.[38]

The concept of "Jewish blindness" was expressed more indirectly in artistic representations of Jewish idolatry and denial of God.[39] The idolatry accusation was rooted in the Hebrew Bible account of the back-sliding Israelites who fashioned and subsequently worshipped a golden idol in the form of a calf (Exod. 32), a story that was "updated" in a 15th-century stained glass panel installed in St Lawrence Church in Nuremberg. On a panel dedicated to the Second Commandment (Exod. 20:4), which proscribes the making of a graven image, Israelites garbed in contemporary German dress, including yellow *Judenhüte*, dance around the Golden Calf.[40] In England, a more complex update of this episode may be found in a detail prominently positioned on the Hereford World Map (c. 1300). Positioned just below a horned Moses receiving the Law on Mount Sinai, a group of grotesquely stereotyped

[36] Glasgow University Library, MS Hunter 60, fol. 1; Nigel Thorp, *The Glory of the Page: Medieval and Renaissance Illuminated Manuscripts from Glasgow University Library* (London, 1987), 178–79; Rubin, "*Ecclesia* and *Synagoga*," 77–78.

[37] Mellinkoff, "The Round, Cap-Shaped Hats Depicted on Jews in BM Cotton Claudius B.IV," *Anglo-Saxon England* 2 (1973), 155–67.

[38] Miri Rubin, *Gentile Tales: The Narrative Assault on Late Medieval Jews* (New Haven, CT, 1999), 73–77; Sara Lipton, "The Temple Is My Body: Gender, Carnality, and Synagoga in the *Bible Moralisée*," in *Imagining the Self, Imagining the Other: Visual Representation and Jewish-Christian Dynamics in the Middle Ages and Early Modern Period*, ed. Eva Frojmovic (Leiden, 2002), 129–54; Lipton, *Dark Mirror*, 203–37.

[39] Michael Camille, *The Gothic Idol: Ideology and Image-Making in Medieval Art* (Cambridge, 1989), 129–60.

[40] Strickland, *Saracens*, 109–10.

Jews kneel before an animated idol defecating coins.[41] The idol's inscribed reference to Islam (*mahun*) is a reminder that like Jews, medieval Muslims were accused of idolatry, which gave rise to shared patterns of pejorative representation in medieval Christian art.[42]

The ultimate manifestation of Jewish blindness – denial of God – was sometimes the subject of prayerbook illustrations to Psalm 52, which begins, "The fool said in his heart: There is no God." In a French prayerbook created in Paris before 1349 for Bonne of Luxembourg, Duchess of Normandy, this psalm is matched to a miniature depicting a pair of stereotyped Jewish fools (Fig. 14.4).[43] The first stands in profile to emphasize his long beard and large nose as he drinks from a green chalice, while the second, hooded and wearing a money bag at his waist, tugs on his friend's hood while threatening him with a red flail. Jewish denial of God is brought up to date in narrative scenes of stereotyped figures turning away from monks or bishops to avoid hearing the Word of God, as in some of the commentary images included in the Gulbenkian Apocalypse, made during the late 13th century for an English bishop with a conversionist agenda.[44]

DEMONIC ALLEGIANCE

Grotesquely stereotyped figures of Jews in medieval art are sometimes further intensified by dark skin, which carried symbolic associations with sin and evil; and as noted above, the figure of Moses is frequently horned.[45] That hooked noses, scraggly beards, hateful grimaces, dark skin, and horns are also key elements of medieval representations of demons is not a coincidence but rather a wordless way of linking Jews to the Devil. New Testament references to Jews as the "synagogue of Satan" (Apoc. 2:9, 3:9), among other derisory metaphors, authorized

---

[41] Strickland, "Edward I, Exodus, and England on the Hereford World Map," *Speculum* 93 (April 2018), 420–69.

[42] Strickland, *Saracens*, 157–209; Debra Higgs Strickland, "Meanings of Muhammad in Later Medieval Art," in *The Image of the Prophet between Ideal and Ideology: A Scholarly Investigation*, ed. Christiane J. Gruber and Avinoam Shalem (Berlin, 2014), 147–63.

[43] Jean le Noir (attr.), *Prayerbook of Bonne of Luxembourg*, fol. 83v (New York, Metropolitan Museum of Art, Cloisters Collection); Annette Lermack, "The Pivotal Role of the Two Fools Miniature in the Psalter of Bonne of Luxembourg's Prayerbook," *Gesta* 47 (2008), 79–98; Lipton, *Dark Mirror*, 172–75, 186–99.

[44] Suzanne Lewis, "*Tractatus adversus Judeos* in the Gulbenkian Apocalypse," *Art Bulletin* 68 (1986), 543–66.

[45] Strickland, *Saracens*, 61–93; Mellinkoff, *The Horned Moses in Medieval Art and Thought* (Berkeley, CA, 1970); Stephen Bertman, "The Antisemitic Origins of Michelangelo's Horned Moses," *Shofar* 27 (2009), 95–106.

Fig. 14.4 Jean le Noir (attr.), Two fools, Prayerbook of Bonne of Luxembourg, fol. 83v (detail), Paris, before 1349. New York, Cloisters Collection. (Photo: The Cloisters Collection, 1969.)

medieval claims that Jews were allied with the Devil and his minions.[46] Thus, the 13th-century *Bibles moralisées* include

---

[46] Robert Bonfil, "The Devil and the Jews in the Christian Consciousness of the Middle Ages," in *Antisemitism through the Ages*, ed. Shmuel Almog, trans. Nathan H. Reisner (Oxford, 1988), 91–98.

Fig. 14.5 Isaac of Norwich, demons, and associates; Exchequer Receipt Roll, London, 1233. (Photo: London, The National Archives E 401/1565 M1.)

numerous commentary illustrations of Jews worshipping and other-wise engaging with the Devil and Antichrist.[47] Images of hell popu-lated with Jewish figures wearing hats and/or money bags not only imply close relationships between Jews and demons but also corrobor-ate the belief that Jewish souls are damned.[48] The full-page, multi-level image of hell copied from the late 12th-century *Hortus deliciarum* ("Garden of Delights") compiled by Abbess Herrad for the sisters of Hohenburg Abbey in Alsace features a flaming cauldron inscribed *Judei* (Jews), into which dark, grimacing demons gleefully toss Jewish men – young and old, bearded and clean-shaven – wearing nothing but tall, white hats.[49] An especially striking family resem-blance between demons and Jews survives in the top margin of the London Exchequer Receipt Roll for the year 1233 in a famous drawing that mocks the successful Jewish financier Isaac of Norwich (c. 1170–c. 1235) (Fig. 14.5). Isaac is the central, three-faced, crowned figure towering above his nefarious Jewish associates, Moses and Abigail, whose long noses, emphasized by their profile positioning, mimic the

[47] Lipton, *Images of Intolerance*, 113–42.
[48] Strickland, *Saracens*, 122–30.
[49] *Hortus deliciarum*, fol. 255 (19th-century copy of the 12th-century lost original); Rosalie Green et al., *The "Hortus deliciarum" of Herrad of Hohenbourg*, 2 vols. (London, 1979) (facsimile).

ones exhibited by the demons positioned between and around them. This complex image and its references to Jewish avarice require more nuanced interpretation, but the visual connection between Jews and demons is fundamental to its messages.[50]

Jewish allegiance to the Devil was a recurring theme in late medieval miracle stories in which the Virgin Mary comes to the aid of Christians victimized by the Devil, Jews, or both working together.[51] The most popular of these tales is the one about Theophilus, who with the assistance of a Jewish magician entered into a pact with the Devil to renounce Jesus and Mary in exchange for wealth and power. When he came to regret his decision, Theophilus implored Mary, who annulled the pact and saved his soul. The Theophilus story and other antisemitic Marian tales were illustrated in devotional manuscripts and church art, such as a 13th-century glass panel installed in the north choir of Laon Cathedral (Fig. 14.6).[52] The artist's treatment of the Jewish magician, brandishing the contract behind Theophilus as he swears fealty to the Devil, emphasizes the Jewish-demonic connection and fuelled the belief that Jews still practiced black magic.[53] Although the magician's rendering is physically neutral, his Jewish identity is signalled by his beard, bright red knobbed hat and gown, yellow stockings, and yellow cloak clasp that doubles as the stigmatizing Jewish badge. Here as in so many other medieval images, costume details collapse the distinction between the Jewish-demonic allegiances of the distant past and those alleged to be ongoing in the (medieval) present.

CONSPIRACY

From the twin convictions that Jews were enemies of Jesus and friends of the Devil grew fears that they were actively plotting against Christendom, either working alone or with other rejected groups, such as Muslims, known pejoratively as "Saracens."[54] The raft of conspiratorial accusations

---

[50] Sara Lipton, "Isaac and Antichrist in the Archives," *Past & Present* 232 (2016), 3–44.

[51] Denise L. Despres, "Immaculate Flesh and the Social Body: Mary and the Jews," *Jewish History* 12 (1998), 47–69; Adrienne W. Boyarin, *Miracles of the Virgin in Medieval England: Law and Jewishness in Marian Legends* (Cambridge, 2010).

[52] Strickland, *Saracens*, 122–23; Pamela A. Patton, "Constructing the Inimical Jew in the *Cantigas de Santa Maria*: Theophilus's Magician in Text and Image," in *Beyond the Yellow Badge: Anti-Judaism and Antisemitism in Medieval and Early Modern Visual Culture*, ed. Mitchell B. Merback (Leiden, 2007), 233–56.

[53] Trachtenberg, *Devil*, 57–96.

[54] Strickland, *Saracens*, 211–39.

Fig. 14.6 Theophilus, the Devil, and the Jewish magician; stained glass panel, early 13th century, Cathedral of Notre-Dame, Laon (choir, bay 1, panel 12). (Photo: © Centre André Chastel.)

levelled against Jews during this period included well-poisoning, image and host desecration, and the ritual murder of Christian children, all of which were endorsed by medieval artists in illuminated manuscripts, stained glass, wall painting, early printed books, and on at least one monumental world map.[55] An 8th-century story about Jews desecrating an image of the Crucifixion during a dinner party, known as the Beirut

---

[55] Rubin, *Gentile Tales*, 7–39; Strickland, *Saracens*, 211–39; Asa Simon Mittman, "Gates, Hats, and Naked Jews: Sorting out the Nubian Guards on the Ebstorf Map," *FKW: Zeitschrift für Geschlechterforschung und visuelle Kultur* (2013), 89–101.

Legend, was rarely depicted in the North,[56] but other stories were widely illustrated, for example, the widely circulating Nuremberg Chronicle, which includes a woodcut of a Jew assaulting a crucifix, two scenes of Jews ritual murdering Christian boys, and a three-times repeated image of hatted, screaming Jewish men burning on a bonfire as retribution for the Black Death and other anti-Christian conspiracies.[57]

To medieval Christians, host desecration was an especially grave "Jewish crime" because violence enacted upon the consecrated Eucharistic wafer, understood as the body of Christ, was tantamount to crucifixion. This point is clarified in the early 15th-century Lovell Lectionary, on a folio that pairs a scene of a bishop carrying a host-bearing monstrance in a Corpus Christi procession with a lower marginal image of two Jews plunging large daggers into a profusely bleeding host (Fig. 14.7).[58] More journalistic are the series of six stained glass panels originally installed in the mid-16th century church of St-Eloi in Rouen, which depict how the Jew, Jonathan, procured a host, took it to the synagogue, and stabbed and abused it.[59] Beyond defaming Jews, such images had added value for Christian audiences as affirmations of the "truth" of transubstantiation.[60]

The most virulent picture of Jewish conspiracy emerges from the medieval Antichrist legend, which forecast the imminent, end-of-time attempt by Christ's archenemy to destroy Christendom. The legend took nascent shape in 10th-century Germany with the prophecy that Antichrist will be born a Jew of the tribe of Dan and welcomed by the world's Jews as their Messiah.[61] In later medieval art and literature, therefore, Antichrist, his henchmen, and followers were routinely cast as Jews.[62] In the c. 1420 German Wellcome Apocalypse, hat-wearing Jews

---

[56] Michele Bacci, "The Berardenga Antependium and the *Passio Ymaginis* Office," *Journal of the Warburg and Courtauld Institutes* 61 (1998), 1–16.

[57] Debra Higgs Strickland, "Foreign Bodies in the Nuremberg Chronicle," *Bulletin of the John Rylands Library* 95 (2019), 19–42; Samuel J. Cohn, Jr., "The Black Death and the Burning of Jews," *Past and Present* 196 (2007), 3–36.

[58] London, BL, MS Harley 7026/1 (probably Glastonbury, c. 1400–c.1410); Rubin, *Gentile Tales*, 19, 27–39; Strickland, *Saracens*, 116–17.

[59] Rouen, Musée des Antiquités.

[60] Rubin, "Imagining the Jew: The Late Medieval Eucharistic Discourse," in *In and Out of the Ghetto: Jewish-Gentile Relations in Late Medieval and Early Modern Germany*, ed. R. Po-chia Hsia and Hartmut Lehmann (Cambridge, 1995), 177–208.

[61] John Wright (trans.), *The Play of Antichrist* (Toronto, 1967); Andrew Gow, "The Jewish Antichrist in Medieval and Early Modern Germany," *Medieval Encounters* 2 (1996), 249–85.

[62] Debra Higgs Strickland, "Antichrist and the Jews in Medieval Christian Art and Protestant Propaganda," *Studies in Iconography* 32 (2011), 1–50.

Fig. 14.7 Two Jews desecrating the Host, Lovell Lectionary, S. England (probably Glastonbury), c. 1400–c. 1410. London, British Library, MS Harley 7026/1, fol. 13 (detail). (Photo: British Library, London, UK © British Library Board. All Rights Reserved/Bridgeman Images.)

rebuild the Temple at Antichrist's command and also round up, torture, and mass-murder the Christian resistance.[63] The Gulbenkian and Abingdon Apocalypses pair Apocalypse scenes with commentary images in which Antichrist and his wicked henchmen are rendered as grotesque Jewish stereotypes carrying out violent attacks on Christians while engaging in the full range of nefarious activities imputed to 13th-century Jews, including idolatry, sexual perversity, and denial of God.[64] These two English manuscripts rank among the most antisemitic treatments of the Apocalypse, both for the virulence of their imagery and for their projection of the medieval Christian attack on Jews into the eschatological future, where it is to end, predictably, in Christian triumph.

The most bizarre imaginary Jewish conspiracy is the focus of another eschatological tradition, that of the Red Jews. Although rarely illustrated, the Red Jews deserve mention because they enlarge the profile of evil, bloodthirsty Jews by capitalizing on the association between Jews and the colour red, which, in middle High German (*rot*) had secondary meanings of duplicitous, wicked, faithless, and

---

[63] London, Wellcome Institute Library, MS 49.
[64] Lewis, "*Tractatus adversus Judaeos*"; Lewis, "Giles de Bridport"; Nigel Morgan et al., *Apocalipsis Gulbenkian*, 2 vols. (Barcelona, 2002).

cunning.[65] Known exclusively in German-speaking regions, the Red Jews are a group of supernatural, cannibalistic Jews, imprisoned for the time being in the Caspian Mountains by Alexander the Great, but scheduled to break free at the end of time to destroy Christendom, assisted by the world's Jews, with whom they secretly communicate in Hebrew. A rare, full-page miniature of Red Jews included in a German weapons book (*Wappenbuch*) exploits the antisemitic connotations of yellow and red with the emphatically repeated motifs of the figures' yellow Jewish hats and open mouths dripping (human) blood.[66] A convoluted mash-up of the Alexander romance, the Ten Lost Tribes, and Gog and Magog traditions, the legend of the Red Jews thus represents the nadir of conspiracy theories propagated for centuries by medieval Christian accusers.

ANIMALITY

The manticore as described in medieval bestiaries is a hybrid creature with a leonine body, a scorpion's tail, and the face of a man. Like the Red Jews, manticores enjoy eating human flesh.[67] Medieval artists who rendered manticores with leonine bodies, red colouring, and grotesque, bearded Jewish heads wearing hats and devouring human flesh, as in the 13th-century Bodley 764 bestiary, went beyond the bestiary text to conceptually link monsters, Jews, and animals (Fig. 14.8).[68] As the manticores attest, the medieval bestiaries were yet another breeding ground for antisemitic imagery. Often lavishly illustrated, they anthropomorphize the behaviours of a variety of beasts, birds, and other creatures for purposes of Christian moral instruction.[69] Illuminated bestiary manuscripts were popular throughout Western Europe, especially in England, and the imagery also circulated independently in all artistic media.

While the christological allegories of the pelican, unicorn, and lion are well known, the bestiary's antisemitic dimension has been largely

---

[65] Andrew Gow, *The Red Jews: Antisemitism in an Apocalyptic Age 1200–1600* (Leiden, 1995), 67.

[66] Strickland, *Saracens*, 233–35.

[67] *The Book of Beasts: Being a Translation from a Latin Bestiary of the Twelfth Century*, trans. T. H. White (New York, 1984), 51–52.

[68] Oxford, Bodleian Library, MS 764, fol. 25; Christopher de Hamel, *Book of Beasts: A Facsimile of Ms. Bodley 764* (Oxford, 2008).

[69] Debra Hassig [Debra Higgs Strickland], *Medieval Bestiaries: Text, Image, Ideology* (Cambridge, 1995).

Fig. 14.8 Manticore, Bestiary, England (Salisbury?), c. 1240–1250. Oxford, Bodleian Library, MS Bodley 764, fol. 25 (detail). (Photo: Bodleian Libraries.)

overlooked.[70] According to the bestiarists, the owl loves the night and shuns the day, just as the Jews reject the light of Christ and prefer the darkness of ignorance.[71] The duplicitous hyena, who feeds on corpses and changes sex from male to female and back again, is compared to the "idolatrous Jews," who first worshipped the true God but were later given over to idolatry.[72] The caladrius, an all-white bird, prognosticates the death of a sick king by turning away from him, just as Christ turns away

---

[70] Debra Higgs Strickland, "The Jews, Leviticus, and the Unclean in Medieval English Bestiaries," in Merback, ed., *Beyond the Yellow Badge*, 203–32.

[71] *Book of Beasts*, 134.

[72] Ibid., 30–32; Hassig, *Medieval Bestiaries*, 145–55.

from the Jews because they deny him.[73] The sweet-breathing panther symbolizes Jesus Christ, whose tortures by the bestial Jews are described as "Jewish mockeries."[74] These and other bestiary entries demonstrated to Christian reader-viewers that prooftexts for their beliefs about Jews were written across Creation by the very finger of God.

Bestiary illustrations operate differently from other types of antisemitic medieval imagery because their pejorative force is activated by knowledge of the texts rather than by the images themselves, which can otherwise "pass" as neutral animal illustrations. However, medieval artists sometimes visualized antisemitic meanings, for example, by rendering the owl's beak as long and hooked,[75] by endowing the hyena with a circumcised penis,[76] or by rendering the driver of the elephant, a bestiary symbol of Jesus, as a hatted Jew beating the animal with a flail, as in the 13th-century Cambridge Bestiary.[77] The prominent church that forms the backdrop of the Ashmole Bestiary hyena illustration transforms the scene into a church graveyard to emphasize Jewish "contamination" of Christians figured by the corpse-violating hyena. Pairing the bestiary owl, a symbol of the Jews, with the pelican, a sacrificial figure of Jesus, recreates the Christ-killer narrative. Less subtle was the approach taken in a late 13th-century English manuscript copy of the French metrical *Bestiaire* composed by Guillaume le Clerc (fl. c. 1210–1238), which pairs each small animal image with a larger illustration of that animal's Christian moralization.[78] The moralization image for the hyena is predictably antisemitic: a horned Moses and hat-wearing Jews kneel before the face of Christ (!) in the Burning Bush in the upper register, while below, back-sliding, bearded Jews wearing hats kneel in left profile before an image of the Golden Calf, while other Jews, also wearing hats, are put to the sword.[79] Beyond the

[73] *Book of Beasts*, 115–16.

[74] Ibid., 14–17; Hassig, *Medieval Bestiaries*, 156–66.

[75] Mariko Miyazaki, "Misericord Owls and Medieval Anti-Semitism," in *The Mark of the Beast: The Medieval Bestiary in Art, Life, and Literature*, ed. Debra Hassig [Debra Higgs Strickland] (New York, 1999), 23–43.

[76] Emma Campbell, "Visualizing the Trans-Animal Body: The Hyena in Medieval Bestiaries," in *Trans Historical: Gender Plurality before the Modern Era*, ed. Anna Kłosowska, Masha Raskolnikov, and Greta LaFleur (Ithaca, NY, forthcoming). I thank the author for pre-publication access to her study.

[77] Cambridge, University Library, MS Ii.4.26, fol. 7.

[78] Paris, Bibliothèque Nationale de France, MS fr. 14969 (London or Oxford, c. 1265–70); *The Bestiary of Guillaume le Clerc*, trans. George Druce (Ashford [Kent], 1936), 49.

[79] Strickland, "Jews, Leviticus," 209–10.

hyena's stated allegorical meanings, this last detail soberly references the forced conversion of Jews, on pain of death, ongoing in England at the time and place this manuscript was produced.[80]

The most shockingly offensive medieval animal motif did not originate with the bestiarists and had no pretence to a moralistic function; its singular purpose was to mock and insult the Jewish communities at which it was directly aimed. The *Judensau* (Jewish sow), popular in German-speaking cities, associated Jews with the gluttony, lust, and ignorance imputed to an especially reviled animal.[81] The motif consists of one or more small, hat-wearing, stereotyped Jewish figures suckling or otherwise obscenely engaging with a large, ugly sow or, less often, a goat. Besides accusing Jews of bestiality, the *Judensau* weaponized the Jewish ban on pork. Graphic examples, such as a widely distributed, single-sheet woodcut produced in mid-15th-century Breisach, incorporate texts that detail the lewd acts depicted.[82] Like *Synagoga*, monumental images of the *Judensau* were popular in urban environments with sizeable Jewish communities. Today, sculpted examples disgrace the exteriors of Colmar Cathedral, the church of St Sebald in Nuremberg, and the collegiate church of St Peter in Bad Wimpfen, among other places, where they were – and still are – encountered daily by church visitors and passers-by.[83]

* * *

The images discussed in this chapter raise important questions about medieval artistic contributions to historical antisemitism. Their defamatory power is self-evident, but beyond this: How did medieval Jews respond to this imagery? To what extent were antisemitic images expressive of medieval *Christian* identity? What other outgroups or concepts were figured as "Jews" in medieval Christian art? Did medieval artistic traditions influence the visual propaganda of the Holocaust? How might understanding of pejorative medieval image-

---

[80] Robert C. Stacey, "The Conversion of Jews to Christianity in Thirteenth-Century England," *Speculum* 67 (1992), 263–83.
[81] Isaiah Shachar, *The Judensau: A Medieval Anti-Jewish Motif and Its History* (London, 1974); Claudine Fabre-Vassas, *The Singular Beast: Jews, Christians, and the Pig* (New York, 1997).
[82] Munich, Staatsliche Graphische Sammlung; Mellinkoff, *Outcasts*, vol. 1, 93, 108; vol. 2, fig. IV.24.
[83] Caroline Walker Bynum, "The Presence of Objects: Medieval Anti-Judaism in Modern Germany," *Common Knowledge* 10 (2004), 1–32, esp. 12–14 (on the *Judensau*).

making inform current debates around racism? Antisemitic medieval art will always make for difficult viewing, but towards answering these and other questions, as well as gaining a fuller understanding of the medieval period itself, they deserve continued scholarly study.

Further Reading

Bale, A., *Feeling Persecuted: Christians, Jews, and Images of Violence in the Middle Ages* (London, 2010). Argues that images of violent Jewish aggressors reinforced medieval Christians' identities as victims, and thus justified their own violent attitudes towards the Jews living in their midst. Chapters 3 and 4 are especially valuable for art historians.

Camille, M., *The Gothic Idol: Ideology and Image-Making in Medieval Art* (Cambridge, 1989). This highly influential study was the first to position antisemitic imagery and pejorative representations of other outgroups, including women and Muslims, at the heart of Gothic image-making.

Lipton, S., *Dark Mirror: The Medieval Origins of Anti-Semitism* (New York, 2014). Traces the emergence of medieval antisemitic iconography, tracking the shift in artistic treatment of Jews from benign figures of wisdom to increasingly sinister figures designed to provoke fear and hostility in their Christian viewers.

Images of Intolerance: The Representation of Jews and Judaism in the Bible moralisée (Berkeley, CA, 1999). Analyzes representations of Jews in two Parisian 13th-century copies of the *Bible moralisée* as figures of sin relevant to changing French social, political, and economic concerns.

Mellinkoff, R., *Outcasts: Signs of Otherness in Northern European Art of the Late Middle Ages*, 2 vols. (Berkeley, CA, 1993). This lavishly illustrated work identifies the negative visual signs of cultural outsiders, especially Jews, in late medieval Christian art produced in Northern Europe.

Patton, P. A., *Art of Estrangement: Redefining Jews in Reconquest Spain* (University Park, PA, 2012). Analyzes relationships between Northern and Southern European antisemitic traditions through examination of a wide range of medieval Spanish artworks produced from the 12th through the 14th centuries.

Reider, J., "Jews in Medieval Art," in *Essays on Antisemitism*, ed. K. S. Pinson (New York, 1942), 45–56. Included in a volume on antisemitism published during the Second World War, this study was one of the earliest to argue that antisemitic works of art were constructed by the Church to poison public attitudes towards Jews.

Rowe, N., *The Jew, the Cathedral and the Medieval City: Synagoga and Ecclesia in the Thirteenth Century* (Cambridge, 2011). Demonstrates the potency of the *Ecclesia* and *Synagoga* motif in the 13th-century North with three case studies of monumental sculptural pairs analyzed in relation to local antisemitic attitudes and policies in their respective cathedral town locations.

Rubin, M., *Gentile Tales: The Narrative Assault on Late Medieval Jews* (New Haven, CT, 1999). A historical account of the circulation across late medieval Europe, especially Germany, of antisemitic stories and images that helped shape multiple communities of violence.

Schreckenberg, H., *The Jews in Christian Art: An Illustrated History*, trans. John Bowden (London, 1996). A valuable compendium of over 1,000 antisemitic medieval artworks representative of all media, organized by theme and chronology.

Strickland, D. H., *Saracens, Demons, and Jews: Making Monsters in Medieval Art* (Princeton, NJ, 2003). Influential study of pejorative representations of Jews, Muslims, Asians, and Black Africans in medieval Christian art that links them conceptually to principles of monstrosity inherited from Classical traditions.

Part III

The Modern Era

15 Martin Luther and the Reformation

DEBRA KAPLAN

In a 1543 treatise, Martin Luther described a statue on the outside of the church in Wittenberg where he frequently preached. Likely erected in the early 14th century, it depicted "a sow carved in stone. Under her, young piglets and Jews lie sucking. Behind the sow stands a rabbi who lifts the sow's right leg and with his left hand he pulls the rear over himself."[1] Vulgar images of Jews and pigs, in which one or more Jews suckled from a pig, ate its feces, or peered into its bottom, were known as *Judensau* (literally, a Jewish pig), and were constructed on a number of late medieval churches in German-speaking lands.[2] Luther offered a new and offensive interpretation of the "rabbi's" actions, claiming that he "bends down and looks most studiously under her rear at the Talmud inside."[3] Approximately 200 years later, Luther's boorish comparison of the Talmud to a pig's rectum was literally carved into stone in Wittenberg, when the word "Rabini" (rabbi) and the title of Luther's treatise, *Von Schem Mephoras (On the Ineffable Name of God)*, were inscribed above the *Judensau*.[4] Debate over this statue continues until today. In the 1980s, a memorial for those murdered in the Holocaust was built on the ground beneath the statue.[5] In 2019, a German Jew brought a court case before the German court, in an unsuccessful attempt to have the *Judensau* removed from the church.[6]

---

[1] For the translation, see Brooks Schramm and Kirsi I. Stjerna, *Martin Luther, the Bible, and the Jewish People: A Reader* (Minneapolis, MN, 2012), 179. Wherever possible I have cited only English translations and secondary literature.

[2] Isaiah Shachar, *The Judensau: A Medieval Anti-Jewish Motif and Its History* (London, 1974).

[3] Schramm and Stjerna, *Luther*, 179.

[4] Shachar, *Judensau*, 31.

[5] Schramm and Stjerna, *Luther*, 178.

[6] www.theguardian.com/world/2020/feb/04/german-court-rules-antisemitic-carving-can-stay-on-church-wall. Accessed 10 June 2020.

The Wittenberg *Judensau* is in many ways emblematic of Luther's antisemitism. It was rooted in medieval stereotypes, while reflecting Luther's particular theology, expressed in the harsh and crude metaphors for which he was renowned.[7] Like the statue, which was embellished further in the 17th century and still stands at Wittenberg, the impact of Luther's antisemitism was felt from the early modern period through the 19th and 20th centuries. Luther's antisemitism remains a topic of contemporary discussion and was the focus of multiple conferences marking the 500th anniversary of the Ninety-Five Theses in 2017.

Luther's antisemitic writings generated intense scholarly debate because Luther is such a towering historical figure. His theology transformed Christian practices and beliefs across Europe and beyond. In addition, Luther came to be viewed as a pivotal figure in German national history. His influence as a Christian leader, and more specifically as a German theologian whose antisemitic writings were cited by the Nazis in the 20th century, render his antisemitism a widely studied and hotly debated issue.

Moreover, Luther was an extremely prolific and popular writer. Many of his writings deal with Jews, albeit in different genres and to different ends. His sermons and biblical interpretations often reference Jews and Judaism in a theological context, while additional compositions include explicit polemics advocating concrete policies regarding the local Jewish population. David Nirenberg has claimed that Luther represents a turning point in the history of anti-Judaism precisely because he both wrote about theology and attempted to convince others to translate his ideas into political action.[8]

Theologians and historians have applied different methodological approaches when examining Luther's antisemitic writings, analyzing various elements of his vast literary corpus in order to interpret his attitudes toward the Jews. The specific texts scholars choose to study shape their interpretation of what Luther thought about the Jews, and when and why his perspective evolved. In this essay, I will present a broad view of Luther's writings about the Jews, including different genres of his writing as well as different scholarly approaches to those texts. The impact of these texts in both Christians and Jewish circles in the early modern period will be considered.

[7] Heiko A. Oberman, *Luther: Man between God and the Devil*, trans. Eileen Walliser-Schwarzbart (New York, 1992), 106–9.
[8] David Nirenberg, *Anti-Judaism: The Western Tradition* (New York, 2014), 264–66.

LUTHER THE AUTHOR

Born in Eisleben in 1483, Luther went on to study theology and entered the Augustinian order, eventually serving as faculty at the University of Wittenberg. His Ninety-Five Theses, posted and disseminated in 1517, questioned many teachings of the Catholic church, including the primacy of the papacy. Luther's ideas drew the ire of the church, and he was excommunicated in 1521. Protected by his powerful patron, Friedrich, the Elector of Saxony, Luther found shelter and wrote prolifically. During the 1520s, his ideas and those of other reformers spread widely, and multiple cities in the Holy Roman Empire and the Swiss Confederation adopted reformed preaching and theology. In 1530, many imperial cities officially adopted Lutheranism. Following wars between confessions and futile attempts by church leaders to heal the rift between Catholics and Protestants, the 1555 Peace of Augsburg in the Holy Roman Empire officially permitted territorial authorities to determine the confession practiced in their area of jurisdiction. European Christendom was irrevocably rendered multi-confessional.[9]

From his early years in Wittenberg until his death in 1546, Luther continually composed treatises, exegetical works, and sermons. Stories of what was said around his table were also preserved in what is known as Luther's Table Talk, and his correspondence with various reformers, theologians, and political leaders is preserved as well.[10] Luther was renowned as a best-selling author, although some of his writings were far more popular than others; his German treatises were far more accessible than his Latin compositions. Some of his teachings were printed as pamphlets or broadsides, illustrated by Luther's friend and neighbor Lucas Cranach. The juxtaposition of short, sometimes rhymed German texts with simple woodcuts brought Luther's message to a wider, often illiterate population. Thus, for example, a pamphlet with paired images comparing the life of Jesus with the decadence of the pope created a vivid and accessible picture of Luther's criticism of the papacy.[11] Other Lutheran ideas were spread through the sermons of local clerics and through hymns sung by

---

[9] For an overview of the Reformation, see Euan Cameron, *The European Reformation* (Oxford, 2012).

[10] For Table Talk, see Martin Luther, Helmut T. Lehmann, and Theodore G. Tappert, *Luther's Works*, vol. 54 (Philadelphia, 1983).

[11] Martin Luther, *Passional Christi und Antichristi* (Wittenberg, 1521).

parishioners.[12] The vastness of Luther's corpus – from ribald remarks at dinner to poems accompanied by grotesque images to complex theological interpretations of seemingly opaque biblical verses – renders the task of understanding Luther a lifelong enterprise. Therefore, scholars have tended to focus on one or another specific segment of his work, which in turn has shaped their respective inter-pretations of his antisemitism.

LUTHER'S THEOLOGICAL STANCE TOWARD THE JEWS

In Wittenberg, Luther taught and wrote about the Old Testament exten-sively. The hermeneutical Jew – not a real person, but a theoretical figure diametrically opposed to the teachings of the church – was there-fore present in many of Luther's writings about the Bible. Luther was deeply rooted in the medieval tradition of interpreting the Bible chris-tologically, and for him, the Old and New Testaments were interwoven and inseparable texts. The New Testament was the fulfillment of the prophecies of the Old Testament, and at their center was the truth that Jesus was the messiah. The Jews' rejection of Jesus was incomprehen-sible to Luther, and they therefore symbolized the antithesis of a good Christian.[13] Even in his early lectures on the Psalms in Wittenberg, the Jew appears in this vein. Luther's exegesis of Psalms 1:1, "Blessed is the man who has not walked in the counsel of the ungodly," interprets the word "ungodly" as referring to the Jews: "He did not consent to the designs of the Jews, who afterwards crucified him."[14] The Jews thus epitomized all that was ungodly and opposed to Jesus.

Moreover, Luther considered the political realities of the Jews for the past 1,500 years as evidence of their rejection by God. Having suffered the destruction of the temple in Jerusalem, exile, a lack of autonomy, and, in Luther's own lifetime, expulsions from major German cities, it was impossible that the Jews still be considered the chosen people.[15] This claim was a major refrain in Luther's writings about the Bible more generally, and about the Jews specifically.[16]

---

[12] Robert Scribner, "Oral Culture and the Diffusion of Reformation Ideas," *History of European Ideas* 5.3 (1984), 237–56. On music, see Rebecca Wagner Oettinger, *Music as Propaganda in the German Reformation* (Aldershot, 2001).

[13] Schramm and Stjerna, *Luther*, 12–13.

[14] Martin Luther, First Lectures on Psalms, 1513–15, in Schramm and Stjerna, *Luther*, 42.

[15] Schramm and Stjerna, *Luther*, 5–6.

[16] See, for example, Luther's *Against the Sabbatarians*, below.

The argument that the Jews had rejected the messiah and that their current historical situation was the result of a punishment for that sin was by no means unique to Luther. His stance against Judaism echoed that of his forebears, some from ancient times, others from the Middle Ages.[17] Indeed, given his background as an Augustinian monk and the fact that in his early years he set out to reform rather than rupture the church, it is not surprising that Luther's theology toward the Jews was firmly rooted in medieval anti-Judaism.[18] Luther, however, intensified the argument against the Jews, claiming that the Jews must be linked to God's adversary, the devil. How else could a people so stubbornly and willfully ignore the messiah and the divine message which their own historical circumstances reflected?

The devil played a particularly central and fearsome role in Luther's personal theology. Terrified of sin, fearful he was being tricked by the devil, persuaded the pope was the antichrist, and convinced that the end of times was nigh, Luther has been dubbed by the scholar Heiko A. Oberman as a man caught "between God and the devil."[19] Thus, while the link between the Jews and the devil did not originate with Luther,[20] casting the Jews as satanic had a deeper meaning given Luther's preoccupation with the devil.

As Luther's theology developed, the Jews also became a trope through which he could polemicize against the Catholic church. One recurring theme in his work is the carnal nature of the Jews (an idea expressed already by Paul), which was exemplified by the Jewish observance of commandments. For Luther, as for centuries of Christian thinkers, there was no need to observe the strictures of the Old Testament once the messiah had arrived. Yet Luther used the example of Jewish observance to vilify the Catholic belief in justification by works. In Luther's theology, humans were saved through faith alone – *sola fidei* – by the grace of God. This was a rejection of Catholic theology, which claimed that both faith and good works, such as charity, led to salvation. Luther connected the Jews with the "papists" in various texts, mocking both for performing actions for heavenly merit.

---

[17] For a medieval precedent and a Jewish response, see David Berger, *The Jewish-Christian Debate in the Middle Ages: A Critical Edition of the Nizzahon Vetus* (Philadelphia, 1979), 226–27.

[18] Heiko Augustinus Oberman, *The Roots of Anti-Semitism in the Age of Renaissance and Reformation* (Philadelphia, 1984).

[19] Oberman, *Luther*.

[20] Joshua Trachtenberg, *The Devil and the Jews: The Medieval Conception of the Jew and Its Relation to Modern Antisemitism* (Philadelphia, 2015).

For Luther, while such behavior might be the mark of a good Christian, it could not possibly earn salvation.[21]

Furthermore, in his earlier years, Luther hoped that his teachings would entice the Jews to convert to Christianity. Convinced of the truth of his message and of the errors of the Catholic church, Luther explained the Jews' resistance to earlier attempts to convert them as the result of faulty Catholic theology. He believed, in the 1520s, that his truth would convince the Jews otherwise.

THAT JESUS CHRIST WAS BORN A JEW

It was in his 1523 treatise, *That Jesus Christ Was Born a Jew*, that Luther made the latter claim. Initially published in German, followed by a Latin translation intended for an international audience, the bulk of the treatise was a defense against Catholic claims that Luther did not believe in doctrines such as the virgin birth or the presence of the body of Christ in the Eucharist. Luther defended himself in the treatise, demonstrating how Old Testament prophecies indeed heralded the virgin birth.

Yet the treatise also had a secondary purpose, namely, to convert the Jews.[22] Luther sharply critiqued Catholic treatment of the Jews, stating that the Catholics "have dealt with the Jews as if they were dogs rather than human beings."[23] He further argued that misguided Catholic teachings had prevented the Jews from converting:

> When the Jews then see that Christianity has become a mere babble without reliance on Scripture, how can they possible compose themselves and become right good Christians?... I hope that if one deals with them in a kindly way and instructs them carefully from Holy Scripture, many of them will become right good Christians.[24]

Luther explained that had he been a Jew, he would never have converted to Christianity, and advocated for a concrete policy change toward the Jews, one that he hoped would attract them to convert. During the

---

[21] See, for example, Luther's lectures on Galatians 4:21–31, in Schramm and Stjerna, *Luther*, 60–66.

[22] Thomas Kaufmann, *Luther's Jews: A Journey into Anti-Semitism* (Oxford, 2017), 55. The Latin version of the treatise includes a letter mentioning the conversion of Bernhard, a Jew who converted to Lutheran Christianity and who lived near Luther's Wittenberg.

[23] Luther, *That Jesus Christ Was Born a Jew*, in Schramm and Stjerna, *Luther*, 78.

[24] Ibid.

16th century, Jews were limited in where they could live and in which professions they could hold in the Holy Roman Empire. Luther encouraged allowing the Jews greater freedom, to the specific end of enticing them to convert.[25]

In the decades following, Luther's hopes that the truth of his message would be confirmed by mass Jewish conversion were dashed. This is, perhaps, one of the major reasons for what many scholars have seen as a turn in Luther's attitudes toward the Jews. While in 1523, Luther advocated for more benevolent policies toward the Jews, by the late 1530s, and certainly by the 1540s, his recommendations had changed.

Luther voiced his reluctance to help the Jews in a letter he wrote to Josel of Rosheim, the leader of German Jewry. The Elector of Saxony forbade Jews access to his lands, whether as residents or as travelers, in 1536. Josel turned to Luther, hoping the latter might exert his influence and convince the Elector to reinstate the right for Jewish safe passage. Luther refused:

> For my heart has been, and still is, that one should treat the Jews kindly, out of the conviction that God might now graciously consider them and bring them to their Messiah; but not out of the conviction that through my benevolence and influence they should be strengthened in their error and become worse.[26]

Luther elucidated that his recommendations in 1523 had been based solely in the hope that they would convert, not out of any kindness toward Jews, and certainly not toward Judaism. Luther hardly interacted with Jews, if at all, and his report of having met with three learned Jews resulted not in their conversion but, rather, in him being exposed to their aversion to Christian interpretations.[27] By the 1530s, the Jews still had not converted en masse, and Luther had despaired of converting them.

LUTHER AND THE JEWS: THE LATER YEARS

In 1537, Luther penned *Against the Sabbatarians*. Nominally an invective against a Christian sect observing the Sabbath on Saturday, his wrath was directed against the Jews, whom he blamed for luring

---

[25] Luther urged allowing the Jews "to trade and work with us, to associate with us, and hear our Christian teaching." Luther, *That Jesus Christ Was Born a Jew*, in Schramm and Stjerna, *Luther*, 82.

[26] Luther, "Letter to Josel of Rosheim," in Schramm and Stjerna, *Luther*, 127.

[27] See the relevant texts describing the encounter in Schramm and Stjerna, *Luther*, 105.

Christians into erroneous practices.[28] The text of *Against the Sabbatarians* is an attack on Jewish practice, in line with the theological arguments against Judaism described above. Luther castigated the Jews for their continued observance of the commandments and ridiculed the notion that the messiah had not yet come.

At the conclusion of *Against the Sabbatarians*, Luther promised to follow up with additional thoughts on the Jews. He then dedicated three extremely harsh treatises to the topic of the Jews, all published in 1543: *On the Jews and Their Lies*, *On the Ineffable Name of God*, and *On the Last Words of David*. The treatises termed the Jews blasphemers and usurers, attacking Jewish theology and ritual practice. Luther summed up his position by explaining, "They are the Devil's children damned to hell."[29]

Though the theology was not new, the language was harsher and more vulgar than in his earlier writings. It was in the second treatise that Luther linked the Talmud to the Wittenberg *Judensau*. Moreover, in *On the Jews and Their Lies*, Luther recommended setting "fire to their synagogues or schools and to bury and cover with dirt whatever will not burn, so that no man will ever see a stone or cinder of them again."[30] He advocated that Jewish homes be "razed and destroyed," claiming they were loci for Jewish sins, and counseled confiscating all Jewish books and banning Jewish prayer and teaching.[31] Luther urged denying Jews safe conducts for travel, remarking, "Let them stay at home." Calling to abolish usury, Luther suggested forcing them into manual labor. Citing the biblical verse punishing Adam with labor as a means to obtain food, Luther also drew on stereotypes of the lazy, Jewish usurer:

> For it is not fitting that they should let us Goyim toil in the sweat of our faces, while they, the holy people, idle away their time behind the stove, feasting and farting, and on top of all, boasting blasphemously of their lordship over Christians by means of our sweat.[32]

Should the local Christian populace fear the Jews, however, Luther advocated expelling them, "ejecting them forever from this country."[33]

---

[28] Kaufmann, *Luther's Jews*, 90.

[29] Luther, *Von Schem Mephoras*, in Schramm and Stjerna, *Luther*, 179.

[30] Luther, *On the Jews and Their Lies*, in *Luther's Works*, vol. 47: *Christian in Society IV*, ed. Franklin Sherman and Helmut T. Lehmann (Saint Louis, MO, 1971), 268.

[31] Ibid., 269, 286.

[32] Ibid., 272.

[33] Ibid.

INTERPRETING LUTHER'S ATTITUDE TOWARD JEWS

The vitriol in *On the Jews and Their Lies* is all the more shocking when compared with the earlier policies advocated by Luther twenty years earlier. The attempt to understand Luther's attitude toward the Jews, particularly this apparent shift over time, has therefore attracted much scholarly attention.

One view, promoted in particular by theologians, is that Luther's position vis-à-vis the Jews was fundamentally consistent over the course of his life. The classic articulation of this position is seen in Wilhelm Maurer's scholarship. Maurer argues that Luther's attitude toward the Jews was based entirely on his theology and did not shift from his early writings on the Psalms until his later writings in 1543. He insists that the primary motive of Luther's 1543 treatises was how to read the Old Testament properly, with Jewish practice and exegesis exemplifying that which was antithetical to the truth. He highlights that this was consistent with Luther's earlier writings, in which Luther stated that Jewish opposition to and antagonism toward Christ had earned them divine wrath. Maurer argues that Luther's later policy recommendations were rooted in his existing theological view that Jews were blasphemous; it was due to his desire to root out blasphemy from Christian society that he called for burning synagogues and destroying Jewish books.[34] Maurer separates himself from those policy recommendations by explaining these as anachronistic and rooted in erroneous ideas of the Middle Ages.

Maurer's position has been critiqued by Mark U. Edwards, who views the former's perspective as ahistorical. Edwards argues that theologians such as Maurer are motivated to detach Luther's theology from his "anachronistic" policies as this permits modern Lutherans to retain the former while rejecting the latter.[35] Edwards further notes that many of these scholars go on to highlight the fact that Luther's antisemitism was rooted in religious rather than in racial categories, facilitating an important distinction between the early modern Luther and the modern Nazis, whose hatred of Jews was racially based.

Edwards maintains that historians must apply a historical lens to Luther, analyzing all of his writings in the context of the 16th century.[36] Edwards focused, therefore, not solely on Luther's anti-Jewish

---

[34] Wilhelm Maurer, "Die Zeit der Reformation," in *Kirche und Synagoge*, ed. Karl-Heinrich Rengstorf and Siegfried von Kortzfleisch (Stuttgart, 1968), vol. 1, 363–452.

[35] Mark U. Edwards, *Luther's Last Battles: Politics and Polemics, 1531–1546* (Ithaca, NY, 1986), 139.

[36] Ibid., 142.

writings but, rather, on all of Luther's writings in his later years. Edwards points to parallels between Luther's writings against the Turks, Catholics, Jews, and even in internecine battles between Protestants. Throughout these texts, Luther utilized bestial and scatological language to vilify his opponents (and as noted above, sometimes with accompanying illustrations).[37]

Various scholars have sought to identify a specific catalyst that led to Luther's harsher attitudes later in life. Some have looked to developments in his personal life, pointing to physical illnesses that plagued Luther in later years.[38] Other scholars have taken a more psychohistorical approach, claiming that Luther suffered from mental illness and melancholy.[39] Some scholars have argued that he suffered because of concrete personal events, such as the death of his daughter, which led him to question whether he was in fact being punished by the devil.[40] As mentioned above, Luther's belief that the Last Judgment was approaching shaped his core beliefs and writings; this too likely intensified in later years.[41]

Some scholars have pointed to historical, rather than personal, catalysts to analyze Luther's later writings. As mentioned above, Luther's failure to convert the Jews has been regarded as a factor that resulted in the policies in the later treatises. Thomas Kaufmann, who tends to argue that Luther's views toward the Jews were theologically consistent, claims that Luther's 1523 treatise reflects his willingness to reserve judgment on the Jews, waiting to see whether they would indeed convert.[42] When they did not, he followed through with policy recommendations that were, for a 16th-century theologian, the logical extension of his long-held theological position toward the Jews.[43]

Kaufmann points to an additional adversary against whom Luther was writing in *On the Jews and Their Lies*, one from within his own community: Christian Hebraists. Many of Luther's colleagues had been trained as Renaissance humanists, and as part of their quest to understand the Old Testament in its original Hebrew, had studied Hebrew

---

[37] Ibid., 203–8.
[38] Edwards, *Luther's Last Battles*, 9–15.
[39] Ibid., 15–19.
[40] Kaufmann, *Luther's Jews*, 94–95.
[41] Oberman, *Roots of Anti-Semitism*.
[42] Kaufmann, *Luther's Jews*, 97–98.
[43] Schramm and Stjerna also contend that Luther held a consistently negative theology about Jews, while recognizing that his hostility toward them intensified in his later years. See Schramm and Stjerna, *Luther*, 3.

and Jewish rabbinic commentaries.[44] While all theology students studied Hebrew, Luther did not master the language as well as many of his contemporaries, and his knowledge of Jewish interpretations rested largely on the writings of his predecessors, such as the medieval Nicholas of Lyra,[45] and on the polemical writings of contemporary converts from Judaism to Christianity, such as Antonius Margaritha.[46] Luther was troubled by the extensive use of rabbinic materials employed by Christian Hebraists, angered by their reliance on Jewish interpretations. Luther in fact argued that the Hebraists' reliance on Jewish materials was deeply misguided.[47] "Since Jews repudiate this Christ," Luther explained, "they cannot know or understand what Moses, the prophets, and the psalms are saying, what true faith is, what the Ten Commandments purport, what tradition and story teach and prove."[48] The later treatises therefore constituted an attack on the Hebraist approach, as well as on the Jews themselves.[49]

CONTEMPORARY REFORMERS AND THEOLOGIANS

The historical approach to understanding Luther's antisemitism mandates examining him alongside his contemporaries. Luther was by no means the only Christian theologian of his time to write against the Jews. Hebraists who studied and collaborated with Jews frequently used anti-Jewish language to mock Jewish beliefs and practices as superstitious, often as a means of distancing themselves from charges of Judaizing despite their reliance on Jewish interpretations.[50] Even reformers such as Andreas Osiander, who defended the Jews against accusations of ritual murder, wrote against them using pejorative language.[51] Tolerance in the 16th century did not include accepting

[44] Allison Coudert and Jeffrey S Shoulson, eds., *Hebraica Veritas?: Christian Hebraists and the Study of Judaism in Early Modern Europe* (Philadelphia, 2004).
[45] Deeanna Copeland Klepper, *The Insight of Unbelievers: Nicholas of Lyra and Christian Reading of Jewish Text in the Later Middle Ages* (Philadelphia, 2008).
[46] Maria Diemling, "Anthonius Margaritha on the 'Whole Jewish Faith:' A Sixteenth-Century Convert from Judaism and His Depiction of the Jewish Religion," in *Jews, Judaism, and the Reformation in Sixteenth-Century Germany*, ed. Dean Phillip Bell and Stephen G. Burnett (Leiden, 2006), 303–34.
[47] Kaufmann, *Luther's Jews*, 102.
[48] Martin Luther, *On the Last Words of David*, in Schramm and Stjerna, *Luther*, 190.
[49] Edwards, *Luther's Last Battles*, 142; Kaufmann, *Luther's Jews*, 123–24.
[50] Debra Kaplan, *Beyond Expulsion: Jews, Christians, and Reformation Strasbourg*, (Stanford, CA, 2011), 120–21.
[51] Joy Kammerling, "Andreas Osiander, the Jews, and Judaism," in Bell and Burnett, eds., *Jews, Judaism, and the Reformation*, 219–48.

that others held diverse beliefs. Moreover, the sincerity of some Jews who had converted to Christianity and joined the clergy was doubted long after their conversion. Consequently, some found a spiritual home in neither the Catholic nor the Protestant church, despite having migrated from one to the other. As Elisheva Carlebach has shown, baptismal water was not always enough to remove the stain of having been born a Jew.[52]

Like Luther, many other reformers' interpretations of the Old Testament referred to Jews, who, according to Christian theology, had once been chosen, but who were chosen no longer. Theologians such as Philip Melanchton, Luther's right-hand man, and John Calvin, therefore, wrote about Jews and Judaism as quintessentially anti-Christian, yet their words were not as harsh as Luther's.[53]

Such attitudes were not limited to Protestants. Sixteenth-century Catholics, such as Johann Eck, Luther's nemesis, wrote against the Jews in language that paralleled Luther's in its charges and contempt.[54] While he did not issue policy recommendations as Luther did, it should nevertheless be noted that in papal Rome and elsewhere in Italy, the 16th century witnessed the construction of ghettos to which Jews were forced to move. Open during the day but locked at night, the ghettos enclosed and confined the Jewish minority population.[55] Such enclosure of the other, intended to keep the majority society free of impure influences, was typical of 16th-century Europe.[56]

The desire to maintain a pure society is also prominent in the writings of reformer Martin Bucer. Bucer consulted to Philipp, Landgrave of Hesse, who, when the privilege extended to Jews resided in his lands was set to expire in 1538, sought advice about the proper status for Jews. The Jews also wrote to Philipp with their own suggestions regarding the renewal of their privileges.[57] Philipp rejected Bucer's

---

[52] Elisheva Carlebach, *Divided Souls: Converts from Judaism in Germany, 1500–1750* (New Haven, CT, 2001), 60–62.

[53] Timothy J. Wengert, "Philip Melanchton and the Jews: A Reappraisal," in Bell and Burnett, eds., *Jews, Judaism, and the Reformation*, 105–36; Aachim Detmers, "Calvin, the Jews, and Judaism," in ibid., 197–219.

[54] Edwards, *Luther's Last Battles*, 119–20.

[55] See, for example, Robert C. Davis and Benjamin C. Ravid, *The Jews of Early Modern Venice* (Baltimore, MD, 2001).

[56] Nicholas Terpstra, *Religious Refugees in the Early Modern World: An Alternative History of the Reformation* (New York, 2015).

[57] Hasting Eels, "Bucer's Plan for the Jews," *Church History* 6 (1937), 127–136; Carl Cohen, "Martin Bucer and His Influence on the Jewish Situation," *Leo Baeck Institute Yearbook* 12 (1968), 93–101.

advice, and subsequently, Bucer's initial advice to Philipp and its rejection were published. The publication of the rejection spurred Bucer to pen a new, even harsher letter about the Jews, in which he called for a Protestant city devoid of Jewish influence. Bucer further recommended that the Talmud be confiscated, that Jews be forced to listen to Christian sermons, and that their synagogues be burned.[58]

LUTHER'S TREATISES IN THE EYES OF HIS CONTEMPORARIES

Thus, while Luther was by no means alone among Christian theologians in viewing the Jews as Christ's enemies, and Judaism as irrational practice, the harshness of his words and the specific policies he advocated set him apart from most of his contemporaries. It should not be surprising then that Luther's later works were not as popular as his other writings. Mark Edwards has shown that only fifteen editions were published of all of the four later treatises. This stands in sharp contrast to *That Jesus Christ Was Born a Jew*, which was reprinted thirteen times.[59]

Both Catholics and Protestants were highly critical of the later treatises. *On the Ineffable Name of God* was termed "hateful" and "cruel" by Catholics in 1545.[60] Luther's colleagues in Zurich termed the book "swinish" and "filthy."[61] Even closer colleagues such as Melanchton and Osiander may have distanced themselves from the work.[62]

That something about Luther's 1543 works was deemed extreme is best captured by a negotiation between Josel of Rosheim and the magistrates of Strasbourg. A native Alsatian Jew, Josel was in frequent contact with the city magistrates over matters both personal and communal.[63] After the publication of *On the Jews and Their Lies*, Josel turned to the magistrates, beseeching that they censor publication of the treatise in Strasbourg, a major center of print and Protestantism. The magistrates agreed, presumably because they were convinced by Josel's arguments that

---

[58] Martin Bucer, *Judenratschlag*; Martin Bucer, *Von der Juden: Brief an einen guten Freund*, in *Martin Bucers Deutsche Schriften*, vol. 7, ed. Robert Stupperich (Gütersloh, 1964).

[59] Edwards, *Luther's Last Battles*, 136.

[60] Ibid., 134.

[61] Ibid., 135. On Heinrich Bullinger, see Kaufmann, *Luther's Jews*, 122.

[62] Edwards, *Luther's Last Battles*, 135.

[63] Debra Kaplan, "Entangled Negotiations: Josel of Rosheim and the Peasants' Rebellion of 1525," *AJS Review* 40.1 (2016), 125–43.

the contents were liable to lead to violence and unrest.[64] That Protestant magistrates would censor the publications of a writer as influential as Luther demonstrates that Luther's later works were clearly seen by some as beyond the pale.

Contemporary Jews, too, saw Luther and Bucer as antisemitic. Jews in the 16th century were subject to various restrictions. They had been expelled from most cities in the Empire by the second decade of the 16th century. In those cities where they were permitted to live, they were confined to a *Judengasse*, a street locked at night and open during the day. In smaller towns and villages they were subject to quotas, requiring special residence permits that expired and were not always renewed. Jews could not participate in guilds and paid special taxes that were levied only on their community.[65] The policies for which Bucer and Luther advocated would have destroyed whatever degree of stability these Jews had achieved; even rescinding their right to travel would wreak havoc on their daily lives.

It is not surprising that contemporary Jews condemned these two reformers, and Luther in particular. Josel of Rosheim blamed Luther and Bucer for not helping the Jews in Hesse and Saxony, respectively. While Josel praised Strasbourg's magistrates and one of its reformers, Wolfgang Capito, in glowing terms, he criticized Bucer and Luther as heretics. For Josel, it was their refusal to help the Jews, and not their Protestant beliefs, that was problematic. A different anonymous Hebrew polemic referred to the "bitterness" that Luther had brought on the Jews.[66]

By examining 16th-century responses to Luther in the broad context of both Jewish and Christian circles, a more nuanced picture emerges. Luther was by no means alone in his attitudes toward Jews, as negative ideas about Jews and Judaism abounded among theologians and lay-people alike. And yet, even in the context of the 16th century, in which a de facto "tolerance" of the Jews nevertheless included significant restrictions on their daily activities, Jews and some Christians viewed Luther's antisemitism as extreme.

---

[64] Chava Fraenkel-Goldschmidt and Adam Shear, eds., *The Historical Writings of Joseph of Rosheim: Leader of Jewry in Early Modern Germany*, trans. Naomi Schendowich (Leiden, 2006), 400–417.

[65] Michael Toch, "The Formation of a Diaspora: The Settlement of Jews in the Medieval German Reich," *Aschkenas* 7.1 (1997), 55–78.

[66] On the polemic, see Kaplan, "Sharing Conversations: A Jewish Polemic against Martin Luther," *Archiv für Reformationsgeschichte* 103.1 (2012), 41–63.

THE IMPACT OF LUTHER'S TREATISES

Despite some initial opposition to Luther's later tracts, it was not long before they were quoted at length. Already by the 1570s, theologians such as Nikolaus Selnecker of Leipzig and Georg Nigrinus of Hesse quoted extensively from the tracts.[67] In the 17th century, Johann Müller of Hamburg consulted with Strasbourg's theologians, who cited long verbatim passages from *On the Jews and Their Lies* mere decades after the text had been banned.[68] Luther's ideas disseminated on a more popular level as well. Depictions of the Wittenberg *Judensau* were printed, available for viewing well beyond that city.[69] In Strasbourg in 1574, a broadsheet depicting a Jewish woman giving birth to twin piglets – a motif of the *Judensau* – was accompanied by text based on Luther's read connecting the pig, Jewish blindness, and the Talmud.[70]

The antisemitism in broadsheets and in theological writings was also expressed in more tangible ways that affected the local Jewish population of the Empire. In the 16th century, a Jew blamed Luther explicitly for the expulsion of the Jews in his native Braunschweig.[71] The Elector of Saxony revoked some of the privileges of Jews, openly citing Luther's treatises. Philipp of Hesse tightened restrictions on the Jews, as did the Margrave of Neumark.[72] In Strasbourg, relations between Christians and neighboring Jews had been positive in the early years of the Reformation. Jews had entered the city to work, adjudicated at court, and taught reformers Hebrew. Josel of Rosheim had collaborated with Strasbourg's leaders on more than one occasion.[73] Yet by 1570, when the city became increasingly orthodox, Strasbourg also enacted harsher policies excluding Jews, and publication of antisemitic texts resumed.[74] In 17th-century Hamburg, Lutheran sermons led to unrest for the local Jewish population.[75]

[67] Kaufmann, *Luther's Jews*, 129.
[68] Kaplan, *Beyond Expulsion: Jews, Christians, and Reformation Strasbourg*, 64–65.
[69] Kaufmann, *Luther's Jews*, 120.
[70] Kaplan, *Beyond Expulsion: Jews, Christians, and Reformation Strasbourg*, 112–15.
[71] Haim Hillel Ben-Sasson, "The Reformation in Contemporary Jewish Eyes," *Proceedings of the Israel Academy of Sciences and Humanities* 4 (1971), 239–326.
[72] Edwards, *Luther's Last Battles*, 136.
[73] Kaplan, "Entangled Negotiations."
[74] Kaplan, *Beyond Expulsion: Jews, Christians, and Reformation Strasbourg*, 98, 118.
[75] Jutta Braden, *Hamburger Judenpolitik im Zeitalter Lutherischer Orthodoxie, 1590–1710* (Hamburg, 2001).

Although some Lutheran theologians, particularly the Pietists, high-lighted Luther's earlier treatises, this was done in an effort to missio-nize among Jews.[76]

As Kaufmann describes in detail, Luther's impact was most deeply felt in the 19th and 20th centuries, when multiple editions of Luther's later treatises were published by individuals associated with racial antisemitism in Germany; one of these editions sold over 300,000 copies.[77] The reception of Luther's work in the 19th and 20th centuries leaves little doubt about how his ideas were later employed. The leading Protestant bishop of Thuringia published 100,000 copies of a pamphlet in 1938, in which he linked Kristallnacht to Luther's birth-day, applauding Luther as a prophet and lauding him as "the greatest anti-Semite of his age."[78]

While the reception history of Luther's writings includes their popularity in Nazi Germany, it is nevertheless ahistorical to refract the 16th century through the lens of the 20th. Although Luther was avidly cited by proponents of Nazi propaganda, his own writings did not include a call for extermination. Luther's odious call to deprive Jews of their livelihood and to destroy Jewish religious institutions must be seen in the context of the early modern period. His recom-mendations, although perceived by Christian contemporaries as some-what extreme, nevertheless reflected certain cultural, theological, and political understandings which can be found in elite contemporary thought and popular culture.

Moreover, an evaluation of the influence wielded by Luther's anti-semitic writings must include not only reactions of Christian audi-ences. It is imperative to consider contemporary Jewish perceptions of their impact. Luther's policy recommendations were never imple-mented on a grand scale, nor could they be in the politically fragmented and religiously divided Empire. They did nevertheless impact policies in a number of regions, upending the rhythms of daily life for Jews. More importantly, Luther's ideas spread in print, sermons, and artwork. For the Jews of early modern German lands, Luther's words endangered their already precarious position.

---

[76] Kaufmann, *Luther's Jews*, 130–32; Debra Kaplan, "'Adopt This Person So Totally Born Again': Elias Schadeus and the Conversion of the Jews," in *Jewish Culture in Early Modern Europe: Essays in Honor of David B. Ruderman*, ed. Richard I. Cohen et al. (Philadelphia, 2014), 193–204.

[77] Kaufmann, *Luther's Jews*, 137–48, esp. 142.

[78] As cited in ibid., 148.

Further Reading

Bell, D. P., and S. G. Burnett, eds., *Jews, Judaism, and the Reformation in Sixteenth Century Germany* (Leiden, 2006). An anthology comprising a wide range of scholarship about Jews and Christians during the Reformation, including articles about specific reformers, Jewish life, and Christian–Jewish polemics during the Reformation.

Ben-Sasson, Ḥ. H., "The Reformation in Contemporary Jewish Eyes," *Proceedings of the Israel Academy of Sciences and Humanities* 4.12 (1971), 239–326. Ben-Sasson discusses Jewish reactions to the Reformation from the Ottoman Empire to the Holy Roman Empire. He includes the theological and messianic interest that the Reformation sparked among some Jewish thinkers as well as the conservative approach of Jews residing in German lands.

Burnett, S. G., "Jews and Judaism," in *Luther in Context*, ed. D. M. Whitford (Cambridge, 2018), 179–86. A brief and useful overview of Jews in Germany during Luther's lifetime, and a discussion of Luther and the Jews.

Edwards, M. U., *Luther's Last Battles: Politics and Polemics, 1531–46* (Ithaca, NY, 1982). Edwards analyzes Luther's works over the last years of his life, arguing that his writings in his later years were increasingly hostile toward Jews and others, providing a wider context to the issue of Luther's antisemitism.

Gershon, ben J., Ch. Fraenkel-Goldschmidt, and A. Shear, eds., *The Historical Writings of Joseph of Rosheim: Leader of Jewry in Early Modern Germany* (Leiden, 2006). An English translation of Josel of Rosheim's writings, including sources and an excellent introduction to Josel's interactions with Luther and other Protestant figures.

Hsia, R. P., and H. Lehmann, eds., *In and Out of the Ghetto: Jewish-Gentile Relations in Late Medieval and Early Modern Germany* (Cambridge, 2002). An anthology of Jewish–Christian relations in Germany, including in the Reformation period. Provides important examples of such interactions from the perspective of intellectual and social history.

Kaplan, D., *Beyond Expulsion: Jews, Christians, and Reformation Strasbourg* (Stanford, CA, 2011). A case study of Jewish–Christian relations in Strasbourg, a Protestant city from which Jews were expelled. Kaplan argues that Jews were very much a fabric of early modern European life and that they influenced and were impacted by the Protestant Reformation.

Kaufmann, T., *Luther's Jews: A Journey into Anti-Semitism*, trans. Lesley Sharpe and Jeremy Noakes (Oxford, 2017). Kaufmann discusses the development of Luther's attitudes toward the Jews, arguing that they firmly reflected attitudes held by his contemporaries in the 16th century. He also traces the reception of Luther's antisemitic writings into the 20th century, arguing that how a book was received is an undeniable part of its legacy.

Oberman, H. A., *The Roots of Antisemitism in the Age of Renaissance and Reformation* (Philadelphia, 1984). Oberman traces the development of anti-semitism in the 16th century, examining Erasmus, Reuchlin, and Luther. He highlights the influence of Luther's apocalyptic thinking on his antisemitic writings.

Schramm, B., and K. I. Stjerna, *Martin Luther, the Bible, and the Jewish People* (Minneapolis, MN, 2012). An anthology of Luther's texts about Jews and the Old Testament presenting Luther's theology and Jews' place in his biblical exegesis and teachings. The introduction provides vital context for understanding Luther and the Jews.

16 The Enlightenment and Its Negative Consequences

ALLAN ARKUSH

In the ears of readers unfamiliar with the subject, the phrase "Enlightened antisemitism" probably has an oxymoronic ring to it. To be enlightened, it would seem, should mean being free of anti-Semitic prejudice. The Enlightenment was, after all, an effort to step out of what its proponents considered to be the dark shadow of the Middle Ages, to leave behind the irrational, theologically based conceptions that had previously governed the world, and to build a new society based on reason and humane principles. Shouldn't that have entailed the replacement of the anti-Jewish beliefs that had always pervaded Christendom with a fresh, rational, and perhaps even benevolent reassessment of the Jewish people and their religion?

To some extent, this is what happened. There is a bright side to the story of the relationship between the Enlightenment and the Jews. But there is another, disturbing side as well. For a number of reasons, many of the 18th century's leading avatars of rationalism remained deeply hostile to the Jewish religion and harsh in their judgment of the Jewish people. These thinkers' anti-Jewish utterances were for the most part not specifically designed to impede the "emancipation" of the Jews in the post-Enlightenment years, nor did they usually do so, but they definitely had long-term effects. Precisely how much influence they had on the subsequent course of events is another question that remains a matter of ongoing scholarly discussion.

POSITIVE VOICES

Let's look at the bright side first, if only briefly. The question of when the Enlightenment began is a thorny one, but we do not have to address it in order to identify the first of the major thinkers associated with the movement who had something positive to say with respect to the Jews. The great British philosopher John Locke (1632–1704) takes pride of place, even though his comments on this subject were brief and incidental. In his *Letter on Toleration* (1689), he argued that "Neither Pagan nor Mahometan nor Jew ought to be excluded from the civil rights of the commonwealth because of his religion."[1] Locke was apparently not deterred from making such a pronouncement by the fact that the Jews continued to adhere to a religion that was, in his opinion, fundamentally theocratic and therefore intrinsically at odds with the liberal order that he outlined in his enormously influential political works.[2]

The Irish-born Deist John Toland (1670–1722), who was briefly connected with Locke and in some respects influenced by him, discussed the Jews much more explicitly, extensively, and enthusiastically. His point of departure, however, in calling for better treatment of them in Great Britain, was not the need to grant the Jews their natural rights but the Jews' merits, proven in antiquity and equally manifest in the present, and his interest in advancing his own country's welfare by welcoming more of them.[3]

In France, the great political philosopher Charles-Louis de Secondat Montesquieu (1689–1755) had a lot more to say about the Jews than Locke did, and much of it was favorable. He evidently had a low opinion of the Jewish religion, but that did not prevent him from denouncing the persecution of its practitioners. In Book XXV of *The Spirit of the Laws* he voices through the mouth of a fictional Jewish figure a "very humble" but actually quite fierce and compelling "remonstrance to the Inquisitors of Spain and Portugal."[4] Elsewhere in the same work, Montesquieu highlights the contribution of the Jews to the rise of modern capitalism through their invention of the bill of exchange.[5]

Montesquieu was not the only Enlightenment thinker who denounced the Inquisition's merciless persecution of crypto-Jews. Even in the writings of Voltaire (1694–1778), who evinced more hostility toward the Jews than any other writer of the era, we can find expressions of similar sentiments. Unlike Montesquieu, however, Voltaire pointed to no positive contribution to civilization on the part of the Jews.

[1] John Locke, *Epistola de Tolerantia: A Letter on Toleration*, ed. Raymond Klibansky, trans. J. W. Gough, (Oxford, 1968), 145.
[2] Adam Sutcliffe, *Judaism and Enlightenment* (Cambridge, 2003), 219.
[3] Jonathan Karp, *The Politics of Jewish Commerce: Economic Thought and Emancipation in Europe, 1638–1848* (Cambridge, 2012), 43–66.
[4] Charles de Montesquieu, *The Spirit of the Laws* (Cambridge, 1989), Book V, chapter 13, 490.
[5] Montesquieu, *The Spirit of the Laws*, Book XXI, Chapter 20, in *The Promise and Peril of Credit: What a Forgotten Legend about Jews and Finance Tells Us about the Making of European Commercial Society* (Princeton, NJ, 2019). Francesca Trivellato has demonstrated how mistaken Montesquieu was on this score.

Jean-Jacques Rousseau (1712–1788), the third member, along with Montesquieu and Voltaire, of what Jeremy Popkin in his new history of the French Revolution has called "the French Enlightenment's trinity of celebrities," had much less to say concerning the Jews than the other two, and what he did say was largely favorable. As Ronald Schechter has observed, Rousseau "lavished the biblical legislator with praise." In his *Considerations on the Government of Poland* he wrote that "Moses dared to make a free people" out of the "errant and servile gang" that left Egypt, "and gave them that durable institution, which withstood the force of time, of fate and of conquerors, which five thousand years could neither destroy nor even alter, and which survives still today in all its power." The Law of Moses had its downside, to be sure, in that it separated the Jews so greatly from their neighbors – but this, too, was by no means without its advantages. It is this that enabled this "singular nation" to preserve itself "to our days."[6]

No representatives of the Enlightenment in Great Britain or France had a more benevolent attitude toward the Jews than the German playwright, essayist, art critic, and theological writer Gotthold Ephraim Lessing (1729–1781). In two plays, one nearly forgotten (*The Jews*, 1749) and another that remains famous as a call for tolerance (*Nathan the Wise*, 1779), Lessing depicted Jews as men of outstanding virtue. His assessment of Judaism as a religion gave it its due, to some degree, but culminated in *The Education of the Human Race* (1780), in an account of the reasons for its obsolescence already in antiquity.

Even the quickest review of the positive side of the Enlightenment has to include mention, finally, of a much less significant writer than anyone we have mentioned so far, a man whose work nevertheless had a great impact on subsequent Jewish history: Christian Wilhelm von Dohm (1751–1820). A Prussian bureaucrat, Dohm was the author of *On the Civic Improvement of the Jews* (1781), the book that launched the discussion of the extension of equal rights to Europe's Jews. Neither a friend of the Jewish religion nor an enemy, Dohm based his argument in support of Jewish rights on the fact that "the Jew is a man more than a Jew."[7] Whatever moral or intellectual flaws disfigured the Jews, Dohm insisted, were due not to their nature or to their beliefs but to the

---

[6] Ronald Schechter, *Obstinate Hebrews: Representations of Jews in France, 1715–1815* (Berkeley, CA, 2003), 54–55.

[7] Christian Wilhelm von Dohm, *Concerning the Amelioration of the Civil Status of the Jews*, in Paul Mendes-Flohr and Jehuda Reinharz, eds., *The Jew in the Modern World, a Documentary History* (New York, 2011), 28.

discriminatory treatment that they had long been accorded. The Jews would rapidly improve their ways if it were terminated.

This is by no means a full summary of what we might call the philosemitic dimension of the Enlightenment, but it is enough to show that the Enlightenment was, at least to some extent, what one would have expected it to be, as far as the Jews were concerned. But what about the other side of the ledger?

DEIST CRITICS

If we return to Great Britain, we see that John Toland's positive assessment of the Jews and his favorable disposition toward them were not matched by those of his fellow Deists. In these rationalist thinkers' struggle against the revealed religion they wished to undermine or completely transform, as Jacob Katz has written, "Judaism came under attack simply because its lowest stratum, Biblical literature, was also the basis of Christianity."[8] And a number of them extended their critiques from biblical religion to rabbinic Judaism and present-day Jews as well.

John Toland himself was by no means an unequivocal admirer of Judaism. While he portrayed Moses as a sophisticated philosopher and a wise legislator, he believed that his work had been corrupted by later generations' narrow emphasis on ritualism. Other Deists, such as Thomas Morgan (d. 1743) and Matthew Tindal (1657–1733), regarded Mosaic law as deeply flawed from the outset. Echoing Spinoza's 17th-century critique of Judaism (like most of the other Deists), Morgan described it as having been "a most intolerable Yoke, or cruel Bondage," imposed on a people that "could scarce be parallel'd, by any other Nation upon Earth, for their gross Ignorance, Superstition and moral Wickedness." Nor did the Jews, in his estimation, ever get any better. In Tindal's eyes, the Old Testament represented a descent from the previously existing natural religion into superstition, slavish ritual, and the supremacy of priests.[9]

For all of their animus toward Judaism, however, the other Deists did not conclude, contrary to Toland, that the Jews of their own day were unworthy of equal rights. "It is a fact," writes Jacob Katz, "that criticism of the Bible by the Deists was not accompanied by hostile

---

[8] Jacob Katz, *From Prejudice to Destruction, Anti-Semitism 1700–1933* (Cambridge, MA, 1980), 29–30.

[9] Diego Lucci, "Judaism and the Jews in the British Deists' Attacks on Revealed Religion," *Hebraic Political Studies* 3.2 (2008), 210–214.

expressions toward the Jews and found no place in contemporary anti-Jewish propaganda." But what did not happen in the Deists' own home-land did take place, Katz concludes, when their doctrine was translated from English into French – by Voltaire.[10]

VOLTAIRE

No figure is more emblematic of the Enlightenment as a whole than the poet, philosopher, playwright, historian, and polemicist universally known by the pen name of Voltaire, François-Marie Arouet. No Enlightenment thinker is more closely associated with the struggle for religious tolerance than the man who issued the call *écrasez l'infâme* (crush the infamy) in his battle against the oppression exercised by the Catholic Church. And – for Jewish historians, at least – no representative of the Enlightenment stands out as a more vociferous detractor of the Jews.

Some scholars, to be sure, have seen Voltaire as a thinker who was no more centrally concerned with the Jews than were the English Deists from whom he borrowed so much. According to Peter Gay, an outstand-ing 20th-century historian of the Enlightenment, Voltaire, like his Deist teachers, "struck at the Jews to strike at the Christians," and his "anti-Jewish remarks are a partly unconscious, partly conscious cloak for his anti-Christian statements."[11] No one disputes this. In the years since Gay wrote, however, there have been a number of efforts to demonstrate that Voltaire's antisemitism went much deeper than that.

Voltaire's voluminous writings on the Jews and Judaism rely heavily not only on the Deists but on the work of Pierre Bayle (1647–1706) and other French critics of revealed religion and focus mainly on the biblical period. But if Voltaire was lacking in originality he made up for that by his extremism. He insulted the Jews more memorably than anyone else. Over a period of many years, Voltaire, who was not a systematic thinker, nevertheless painted a coherent, derogatory portrait of the Jews that fit neatly into a comprehensive worldview.

In his pioneering effort to write a universal history, Voltaire com-pletely abandoned any theological perspective. He reduced the Jews from one of the seminal forces in the development of human civiliza-tion to a small, culturally backward subdivision of the Arabs. To their own account of their early history, in the Bible, he gave little credence, relying instead on what Greek, Roman, and even Egyptian sources said

---

[10] Katz, *From Prejudice to Destruction*, 33.
[11] Peter Gay, *Voltaire's Politics: The Poet as Realist* (Princeton, NJ, 1959), 353.

with regard to that subject. Casting into doubt the very existence of Moses, he was more inclined to accept ancient non-Jewish authors' mocking accounts of the exodus from Egypt than the one contained in the Pentateuch.

Despite his low estimation of the Bible's reliability, Voltaire was happy to mine it for evidence of the Jews' inferiority on all scores. By his Scriptures-based account, they fell short of true monotheism insofar as they believed in the actual existence of other people's gods. They lacked any conception of the immortality of the soul, which Voltaire himself did not affirm but still regarded as an indispensable curb on secret crime. Their religion was replete with irrational and superstitious rituals. "Is it really agreeable to the Being of all Beings," he asked facetiously, "to burn on a stone the intestines and the feet of animals? What could result from this but an insupportable stench?"[12] They sacrificed not only beasts but humans, as the example of Jepthah and his daughter demonstrates (or so he claimed).

Voltaire frequently characterized the Jews as a people who had deceived themselves into believing that they had been specially selected by God and treated all others with great cruelty. The crime with which he most frequently charged them was their expropriation of Canaan and their ruthless extermination of its previous denizens. "The Jewish people was a pretty barbarous people. It butchered without pity all the inhabitants of an unfortunate little country to which it had no more right than it did to Paris or London."[13]

Despite their success in conquering Canaan, the Jews' inability to hold on to their land over the long run amply demonstrated their lack of political acumen. They were always more skilled in commerce than in war and diplomacy. In other terrestrial affairs, however, they did not distinguish themselves at all. Their attainments in philosophy and science were nugatory and they had to rely on their neighbors for technological assistance. They needed Hiram of Tyre, for instance, in order to build their Temple in Jerusalem. All in all, as Jacob Katz has observed, "the image of the Jews that arises from Voltaire's description of Biblical times is that of a people inferior from every point of view, culturally, religiously, ethically, socially, and politically."[14]

---

[12] *Profession de Foi des Théistes*, in *Oeuvres Complètes de Voltaire* (Paris, 1885), vol. 27, 59.

[13] Voltaire, *Philosophical Dictionary*, "Toleration," trans. and introduction by Peter Gay (New York, 1962), 483.

[14] Katz, *From Prejudice to Destruction*, 41.

If Voltaire's sole purpose in targeting the Jews and Judaism had been to weaken the foundations of Christianity, he could have ignored post-biblical Jewry altogether. But the Jews of later times did not escape his attention, and he did not assess them any more favorably than he did their ancestors. He mocked the sectarianism and strife that character-ized the Jewish world during the Second Temple period. And echoing the anti-Jewish writings of Cicero and Tacitus, he placed the following epitome of classical antisemitism in the mouth of a Roman character in one of his later works: "They are, all of them, born with raging fanati-cism in their hearts, just as the Bretons and the Germans are born with blond hair. I would not be surprised if these people would not someday become deadly to the human race."[15] Speaking in his own name, Voltaire characterized the Jews of his own day as "nothing but an ignorant and barbarous people, who have long combined the most sordid avarice with the most detestable superstition, and the most invincible hatred for all peoples who tolerated and enriched them."[16] Elsewhere he characterized them as "a nation opposed in everything to all others," people "who serve the nations with avarice, detesting them fanatically, to make usury their sacred duty."[17]

Voltaire's unvarying denunciations of the Jews evoked a spirited if qualified defense on the part of Isaac de Pinto (1717–1787), a Dutch Jewish businessman who had distinguished himself as a writer on economic matters. In an "Apology for the Jewish Nation," de Pinto complained that Voltaire had "melted" all Jews "down to the same substance" and given his readers a "shocking picture" of them. He upbraided him for failing to recognize that the dispersed Portuguese community to which he himself belonged did not "deserve those epithets which M. Voltaire lavishes" on the Jews as a whole.[18] In what Adam Sutcliffe has termed a "deftly ambiguous" response, Voltaire half-heartedly gestured toward an apology while simultaneously asserting and denying that de Pinto, as a Jew, could also be a philoso-pher. To be accepted as one, de Pinto would have to "transcend and disavow an identity that Voltaire himself seems determined to pin back on to him."[19]

---

[15] Voltaire, *Ouevres complètes*, vol. 28, 439–40.

[16] Voltaire, "Jews," in *Philosophical Dictionary*. He followed this up, to be sure, with some words of caution: "Nevertheless, it is not necessary to burn them."

[17] Voltaire, *Essai sur les moeurs*, 2:64.

[18] Isaac de Pinto, "An Apology for the Jewish Nation," in Mendes-Flohr and Reinharz, eds., *The Jew in the Modern World*, 281.

[19] Sutcliffe, *Judaism and Enlightenment*, 244–45.

INTERPRETATIONS OF VOLTAIRE

At the very least, Voltaire was less than fully ready to acknowledge that an individual Jew could rise above his origins and become a full participant in an advanced civilization. He certainly showed no willingness to exempt any tribe of this pernicious people, at any time, from the condemnation he heaped upon the Jews in their entirety. The depth of his hostility toward the Jews has consequently led historians to attempt to determine what it was, beyond his unmistakable desire to undermine Christianity, that prompted him to focus on them so relentlessly.

Some have suggested that even after his renunciation of Christianity he could not break free of the anti-Jewish prejudices that his earlier education had inculcated in him. Others have noted that Voltaire had suffered financially from his dealings with unsavory Jewish moneylenders both in London and in Berlin, experiences that only nurtured his prejudices. The explanation that has received the most attention, however, over the past half-century is the one offered by Arthur Hertzberg in his ground-breaking book *The French Enlightenment and the Jews*.

According to Hertzberg, Voltaire considered the Jews to be a hopelessly alien people, one which had for a very long time exercised a harmful influence on the course of European civilization and continued to constitute a menace to it. The Jews, he believed, entered into Europe and subverted the normative, Greek-inspired culture disseminated there by the Romans, not by propagating their own religion but by spreading a variant of it. "Christianity," according to Voltaire, "is the Jewish religion superimposed on people of a different world, both ethnically and culturally." It is, however, "somewhat better than Judaism because it has been affected by the nature of those who have adopted it and by their earlier, healthier tradition."

After reviewing his diagnosis of the situation, Hertzberg describes what Voltaire believed to be the necessary remedy: "European men can be freed effectively of Christianity because Christianity is here a long-standing infection; it is not one of the foundations of the European spirit, deriving from its character." Things are different, however, with the Jews themselves. "Being born a Jew and the obnoxiousness of the Jewish outlook are indissoluble; it is mostly unlikely that 'enlightened' Jews can escape their innate character.... Cure them of their religion and their inborn character remains."[20] According to Hertzberg, Voltaire believed that the Jews remained the same innately corrupt people they

---

[20] Arthur Hertzberg, *The French Enlightenment and the Jews* (New York, 1968), 307.

had always been and that they were still capable of doing additional, large-scale harm to the Europeans among whom they lived.

Hertzberg was incorrect, however, in his claim that Voltaire saw Christianity as constituting, in essence, merely a sort of Judaism for the Gentiles. While Voltaire did, of course, recognize its Jewish roots, he also highlighted the respects in which it departed decisively from its parent religion. It was indeed this departure that accounted for what he considered to be the worst aspects of Christianity: its dogmatism, its intolerance, and its urge to dominate the world. The crucial event in the history of the Christian religion that saddled it with these deficiencies, Voltaire believed, was the encounter in the 1st century between the members of a small Jewish sect from Palestine and Jews of a Platonizing bent in Alexandria.

What Jesus' followers discovered in that city was a world in which the philosophers, including Jews like Philo, propounded the doctrines presented in Plato's *Timaeus*. They spoke incessantly of the *logos*, the demiurge through which God had created the universe. Under the influence of these Platonists, the Christians elevated Jesus to a new supramundane status; they started calling him "the word."[21] For them, Jesus ceased to be merely a man, and "little by little became a God engendered centuries earlier by another God and incarnated at the present time." It is thus apparent that "it was the philosophy of Plato that made Christianity." This new religion may have preserved the books of Judaism and some of its trappings, but it was nevertheless something "totally different in spirit."[22] It developed dogmas "absolutely different from those of Jesus himself."[23]

The ambitious sectarians who adopted these irrational doctrines, and fought over their precise interpretation, sought to convert the world to their new religion. When they did so, they became a far greater menace to humanity than the Jews had ever been. For the Jews in the Roman Empire "didn't cross land and sea to make proselytes but thought only of making money. It is undeniable, however, that the Christians wanted their religion to be the dominant one. The Jews didn't want the statue of Jupiter in Jerusalem; but the Christians didn't want it in the Capitol."[24] Its eventual removal marked only the beginning of the "infamy."

[21] *Dieu et les hommes*, 223.
[22] *Histoire de l'établissement du christianisme*, 72.
[23] *Dieu et les hommes*, 225.
[24] *Philosophical Dictionary*.

Voltaire did not, then, regard the Jews as having once been the great world-historical enemy of the West, as Hertzberg maintains, nor is there any real evidence that he saw them as a continuing menace of major proportions.[25] Whatever warnings he may have placed in the mouth of an ancient Roman, he saw them, in his day, not as an existential threat but as a contemptible crew, destined to assimilate, for the most part, into the rabble of other nations. Why, then, did he devote so much attention to them?

Adam Sutcliffe sees Voltaire's preoccupation with the Jews primarily in the light of his overall intellectual strategy. Like others, Sutcliffe notes that Voltaire rarely attempted a thorough exposition of his philosophy and that his project was in large measure a destructive one. He stood for reason, justice, and tolerance, but he was "unable to define the meaning of these concepts in positive terms." He chose instead to engage in "destructive polemic directed against their designated antitheses." For Voltaire, "Judaism was the ideal target for this destructive energy, because it was centrally associated with a cluster of the most troublesome issues in Enlightenment thought: the nature of myth, the problem of origins and the formation of group identity."[26]

Ronald Schechter draws a somewhat similar conclusion with respect not only to Voltaire but to French Enlightenment discourse in general. Borrowing a term from Claude Lévi-Strauss, he states that the Jews were "good to think with." Enlightenment authors consequently invoked them when they "wished to discuss the following ideas: fanaticism and tolerance; carnality and spirituality; the 'natural' role of ceremony and dogma in religious belief and practice; the proper relationship between religion and morality"; and an assortment of other questions.[27]

Sutcliffe and Schechter do not emphasize precisely the same things, but they concur in regarding the disproportionately large presence of the Jews in French Enlightenment literature not as a manifestation of a "clash of civilizations" or as merely a reflection of anti-Christian animus, but in large part as the outcome of purely intellectual imperatives. This seems like the best path to pursue in an attempt to understand the abundant and unfriendly preoccupation with the Jews on the part of writers who lived at a time and in a place where they were barely present.

---

[25] For further discussion of these matters, see Allan Arkush, "Voltaire on Judaism and Christianity," *AJS Review* 18.2 (1993), 223–243.

[26] Sutcliffe, *Judaism and Enlightenment*, 239–240.

[27] Schechter, *Obstinate Hebrews*, 36–37.

IMMANUEL KANT

The Jews in Germany greatly outnumbered those in France in the 18th century and consequently provided non-Jewish thinkers with much greater cause for reflection. Lessing's positive depiction of Jewish characters and Dohm's call for improving their condition met with significant opposition from critics who took their bearings from religious doctrines as well as others whose reasoning was essentially secular. A review of antisemitism on the part of Enlightenment thinkers during this period probably has to take note of someone like the biblical scholar Johann David Michaelis (1717–1791), who took issue with what both Lessing and Dohm had to say about the Jews. After reading Lessing's *The Jews*, Michaelis scoffed at the idea that there could be a Jew as good as the play's Jewish hero, and decades later he rejected Dohm's call for extending greater rights to the Jews on the grounds of their corrupt nature and their adherence to a religion that bred disloyalty. But Michaelis was not a figure of sufficient historical importance for us to dwell on him here.[28]

In the German Enlightenment, which was far more positively oriented toward religion than the French Enlightenment, Voltaire had no true counterpart. There was no thinker of comparable stature who attempted to undermine Christianity and targeted Judaism in part as a means of doing so. But there was a great rationalist whose attempt to transform Christianity entailed extensive discussion of Judaism in a manner that has led many scholars to identify him as an antisemite: Immanuel Kant (1724–1804). Does this charge have a basis in fact?

We would not even ask this question if Kant had died before 1789, the year conventionally regarded as the end point of the Enlightenment and the beginning of a new revolutionary era. By that time Kant had already published his most earthshaking books, including the *Critique of Pure Reason*, and he had also compiled a record of statements pertaining to the Jews and Judaism, but he had not yet written the works that have led some to include him in the ranks of the antisemites. Of these the most important were *Religion within the Limits of Reason Alone* (1791) and his *Anthropology from a Pragmatic Point of View* (1798). Published slightly past most historians' demarcation point for the Enlightenment, they must still be seen as products of it.

[28] For a different assessment of Michaelis, see Jonathan Hess, "Johann D. Michaelis and the Colonial Imaginary: Orientalism and the Emergence of Racial Antisemitism in Eighteenth Century Germany," *Jewish Social Studies* 6.2 (Winter 2000), 56–101.

In *Religion within the Limits of Reason Alone*, Kant defines religion in a way that excludes Judaism from consideration on the grounds that it is not imbued with a true spirit of morality. Following in the footsteps of Spinoza and Moses Mendelssohn, but with intentions of his own, he described it purely in political terms. "Judaism is not a religion at all," he wrote, "but simply the union of a number of individuals who, since they belonged to a particular stock, established themselves into a community under purely political laws, hence not into a church." The Jews' legislation is not truly religious because "all its commands are of the kind which even a political organization can uphold and lay down as coercive laws, since they deal only with external actions." They are concerned only with outer conduct and "are given with no claim at all on the *moral disposition* in following them (whereas Christianity later placed the chief work in this)."[29] Thus, as Paul Lawrence Rose has put it, "Judaism completely lacked moral content, being based on obedience to an externally imposed law that testified to the absence of an inner moral imperative – that is to say, of 'freedom.'"[30]

The Jews were just as devoid of morality as their religion, Kant explains in his *Anthropology*. "The Palestinians who live among us," he wrote (with irony that only his latter-day readers can appreciate), owe their not undeserved reputation for cheating (at least the majority of them) to their spirit of usury which has possessed them ever since their exile." It would be vain, he says, to try to make this bunch of dishonest traders into moral people. In short, as Rose puts it: "Judaism is an *immoral* and *obsolete* religion; the Jews are an *alien* nation; the Jews are a nation of *traders* devoted to *money*." They represent the opposite of "the Kantian revolutionary idea of moral freedom."[31]

Michael Mack deepens Rose's analysis, explaining how Kant's "pseudotheology," that is, his "secularized and politicized Christian theology," adopts old Christian notions of Judaism and transposes them into a new realm. "Kant in fact saw in the Jews," he writes, "the opposite of reason's purity: they embodied the impurity of empirical reality, of 'matter.'"[32] Adhering to laws that negated their autonomy, desiring nothing but the consumption of material goods, they represented the opposite of

---

[29] Immanuel Kant, *Religion within the Boundaries of Mere Reason and Other Writings*, ed. Allen Wood and George di Giovanni (Cambridge, 1998), 130–131.

[30] Paul Lawrence Rose, *German Question/Jewish Question: Revolutionary Antisemitism from Kant to Wagner* (Princeton, NJ, 1990), 94.

[31] Ibid., 96–97.

[32] Michel Mack, *German Idealism and the Jew: The Inner Anti-Semitism of Philosophy and German Jewish Responses* (Chicago, IL, 2003), 3.

"an idealist type of body politic" and therefore merited exclusion from it.[33] This disqualification was not temporary. While he did not hold any pseudoscientific belief that the Jews were different by nature, "according to Kant's anti-Semitic fantasy, it was the religion of the Jews that positioned them as the immutable other of a body politic based on the transcendental indifference to empirical objects."[34]

Unlike Voltaire, Kant had Jewish friends – most famously, the philosopher Moses Mendelssohn, but also a considerable number of other Jewish associates and disciples (which at the very least indicates the limits to whatever antisemitism may be attributed to him). What he did not have was a Jewish challenger who stood up to him and defended Judaism or the Jews in anything like the manner that Isaac de Pinto had responded to Voltaire. Instead, he had, in Germany and elsewhere, generations of Jewish followers who did their best to demonstrate that he had been right about religion but wrong about Judaism, which was, properly understood, the quintessential "religion within the boundaries of reason alone." They also did their best to ignore his disparaging remarks about their people.

REPERCUSSIONS

That the Enlightenment contained an unhealthy dose of antisemitism is evident enough. This does not alter the fact that in the short run, at least, it led to very substantial improvement in the Jews' circumstances. As a result of the spread of its core ideas, the Jews in the Western world were indeed, as Locke, Lessing, Dohm, and others had advocated, acknowledged to be men more than they were Jews and granted far more extensive – if not always equal – rights. But what about the longer run? To what extent did ideas broached by leading Enlightenment thinkers contribute to the antisemitism that flourished in Europe in the 19th and 20th centuries? Did the avatars of Enlightenment perhaps play as much of a part in the dissemination of antisemitism as its enemies did?

That they in fact did so was the most provocative claim made by Arthur Hertzberg in *The French Enlightenment and the Jews*. As he wrote in the book's introduction, "modern secular anti-Semitism was fashioned not as a reaction to the Enlightenment and the Revolution,

---

[33] Ibid., 9.
[34] Ibid., 40–41.

but within the Enlightenment and the Revolution themselves."[35]
More specifically:

> An analysis of everything that Voltaire wrote about the Jews
> throughout his life establishes the proposition that he is the major
> link in Western intellectual history between the anti-Semitism of
> classic paganism and the modern age. In his favorite pose of Cicero
> reborn he ruled the Jew to be outside society and to be hopelessly
> alien even to the future age of enlightened men.[36]

Hertzberg himself did not substantiate these assertions in any detailed
fashion, but merely gestured toward Jacobin antisemites and figures
such as "Charles Fourier and even Karl Marx" as proof of Voltaire's
influence. But was he, even if he was not thorough, perhaps correct? In
the half-century that has elapsed since the publication of *The French
Enlightenment and the Jews*, many have echoed his claims, but no one
has written the intellectual history that would uphold them.

Jacob Katz has made a much less sweeping but more persuasive
assessment of Voltaire's impact on subsequent antisemitism. His
"abandonment of Christian theology," he writes, "destroyed the justification for the existence of the Jewish nation as a testimony to the truth
of Christianity. Likewise, it eliminated the basis for the hope that the
Jews would eventually recognize this truth and accept Christianity.
A new solution to the problem of the future of the Jews had to replace
the Christian expectation of their conversion."[37] For those who agreed
with Voltaire that the Jews were an utterly worthless people, the range
of available options was both narrow and ominous. Even as it undermined old prejudices, secularization removed old restraints and placed
the Jews in greater danger. Katz's use of the word "solution" in this
context seems to telegraph what was on his mind.

Paul Lawrence Rose identifies Voltaire as the man who engineered
"the transition from Christian to enlightened antisemitism" and credits
him, with a nod to Hertzberg, as having drawn "on the ancient pagan
testimonies to the evil national character of the Jews as enemies of
humanity and reason."[38] In his elaborate "genealogy of modern antisemitism," however, Voltaire plays no major part. He assigns the

---

[35] Hertzberg, *The French Enlightenment and the Jews*, 7.
[36] Ibid., 10.
[37] Katz, *From Prejudice to Destruction*, 46–47.
[38] Rose, *German Question/Jewish Question*, 9.

THE ENLIGHTENMENT AND ITS NEGATIVE CONSEQUENCES 305

pivotal role to Immanuel Kant, whom he regards, as we have seen, as the thinker who inspired what he calls "revolutionary antisemitism."

Rose traces this concept from Kant to Fichte, who relied on "Kant's a priori definition of the Jew as the negation of freedom and morality" when he constructed "a *political* definition of the Jew as being inherently unsuitable for citizenship and civil rights."[39] In the writings of Jakob Fries he locates "the first extensive working-out of the classic principles of moral and revolutionary antisemitism set down by Kant and Fichte."[40] Richard Wagner, Rose writes, presented "in socialist revolutionary language the kernel of Kant's critique of Judaism," articulating in numerous works the "fundamental anti-Semitic principle that Judaism is the enemy of revolution."[41] From Wagner, Rose moves on – omitting any mention of the next, very full generation of antisemites – directly to Hitler, who knowingly echoed "Wagner's revolutionism."[42]

Michael Mack likewise traces the influence of Kant's anti-Jewish ruminations on German thinkers, stretching from his own day to Richard Wagner. Following in his footsteps, he explains, Hegel, Feuerbach, Schopenhauer, and Wagner all focused "on the Jews as the empirical impediment to the construction of an idealist type of body politic."[43] But Mack does not stop with Wagner and leap from there to Hitler. He seeks to show how late 19th-century German antisemites such as the historian Heinrich von Treitschke (1834–1896) and the racist immigrant from Great Britain, Houston Stewart Chamberlain (1855–1927), framed their discourse around a divide between materialism and idealism, assigning the Jews by then their familiar, inferior role. Their work reflects the ways in which "pseudoscientific antisemitism at the end of the nineteenth and the beginning of the twentieth century was informed by the German idealist fantasy of an immutable tie between Jehovah and his people."[44] And from Chamberlain to Hitler the road is very short.

Rose's and Mack's genealogies are bound to disappoint readers who would like intellectual history to be clearly marked, with rationalist defenders of the Jews lined up on one side and antirationalist antisemites on the other. It is singularly disturbing, for instance, to see Mack describe Houston Stewart Chamberlain, one of Hitler's main inspirations, as not

[39] Ibid., 121.
[40] Ibid., 129.
[41] Ibid., 361.
[42] Ibid., 378.
[43] Mack, *German Idealism and the Jew*, 63.
[44] Ibid., 12.

only a Wagnerian but a Kantian.[45] But Rose's and Mack's work – debatable as it may be on some points – shows that things are by no means as simple and straightforward as one would like them to be. The German Enlightenment, like the French Enlightenment, definitely opened many doors for the Jews, but it also provided their 19th- and 20th-century enemies with ammunition to use against them, and thus not only benefited them but cast a dark shadow over their future.

Further Reading

Gay, P., *Voltaire's Politics: The Poet as Realist* (Princeton, NJ, 1959). A readable and engaging portrayal of Voltaire.

Hertzberg, A., *The French Enlightenment and the Jews* (New York, 1968). A pioneering study that situates the French Enlightenment's assessment of the Jews in the context of 18th-century French-Jewish history.

Karp, J., *The Politics of Jewish Commerce: Economic Thought and Emancipation in Europe, 1638–1848* (Cambridge, 2012). Includes a thorough exposition of the thinking of Christian Wilhelm von Dohm with regard to the Jews.

Mack, M., *German Idealism and the Jew: The Inner Anti-Semitism of Philosophy and German Jewish Responses* (Chicago, IL, 2013). A searching account of German philosophical antisemitism from the Enlightenment onward.

Marks, J. D., "Rousseau's Use of the Jewish Example," *The Review of Politics* 72.3 (Summer 2010), 463–481. A careful analysis of the philosopher's positive assessment of the Jews.

Mitchell, H., *Voltaire's Jews and Modern Jewish Identity* (London, 2014). A recent reassessment of Voltaire's stance toward the Jews and Judaism.

Rose, P. L., *German Question/Jewish Question: Revolutionary Antisemitism from Kant to Wagner* (Princeton, NJ, 1990). Develops a theory concerning the negative impact of Kant's portrayal of the Jews and Judaism.

Schechter, R., *Obstinate Hebrews: Representations of Jews in France, 1715–1815* (Berkeley, CA, 2003). A nuanced treatment of the thinking of Voltaire and other French Enlightenment figures with regard to the Jews and their impact in revolutionary France.

Shell, S. M., *Kant and the Limits of Autonomy* (Cambridge, MA, 2009). Chapter 8 analyzes Kant's relationships with his Jewish friends.

Sutcliffe, A., *Judaism and Enlightenment* (Cambridge, 2003). Extensively explores non-Jewish thinkers' writings on the Jews from the pre-Enlightenment period through the Enlightenment.

---

[45] Ibid., 103.

17 Modern Antisemitism in Western Europe: Romantic Nationalism, Racism and Racial Fantasies

SHULAMIT VOLKOV

The term *"modern* antisemitism" entered the historiographical dis-course at the end of the Second World War. As the dimensions of the National Socialists' crimes against the Jews became known, a growing interest in the sources of their obsessive antisemitism was to be expected. While generations of historians before them had conceived of antisemitism as "an eternal hatred," with roots going back to pre-Christian antiquity, this paradigm seemed inadequate now for explain-ing the National Socialists' uncompromising *war against the Jews*.[1] Even describing the history of antisemitism in terms of a spiral devel-opment, moving from milder to extreme forms seemed no more than a simplification. After all, most of the German-born historians at the time, in exile either in Britain or in the United states, Jews and non-Jews alike, came from a country in which Jews were on the whole genuinely assimilated, an integral part of non-Jewish society, active in all spheres of life.

Anti-Jewish sentiments, though always there to some extent, had been normally considered a remnant of old prejudices or an appendage to extreme nationalism, sometimes joined with imperial aspirations and often with a generalized fear of modernity. Thus, as one sought to investigate the novelty of antisemitism, the focus was either on the late 1870s, with the establishment of antisemitic political parties and the emergence of pseudo-scientific racial the-ories together with racial fantasies and paranoias, or – more com-pellingly indeed – on the late Enlightenment and the start of the Jewish route to emancipation. As the status of Jews in society and state gradually changed, so did the content and character of antisemitism.

---

[1] See the book under this title by Lucy S. Dawidowicz (New York, 1975).

DURING THE CONTROVERSY OVER EMANCIPATION

To be sure, *old* prejudices did not suddenly disappear. During the French Revolution, in debates at the National Assembly, some still described the Jews as "a tribe with different habits," complete strangers of no "utility" to the state or the nation.[2] Nevertheless, after some delays and hesitation, the Assembly – having passed the Declaration of the Rights of Man, announcing that "all men are born and remain free and equal in rights" – completed its legislation with regard to the Jews and on September 28, 1791, granted them full equality.

A few decades earlier, in 1753, a Jewish Naturalization Bill, allowing the settlement of foreign Jews, had been passed by the English Parliament. It was, indeed, soon repealed under pressure from the Tory opposition and widespread popular protest, but the status of the small Jewish local community did not change much as a result of this debacle. Meanwhile, during the following decades, its members were made repeatedly and ever more explicitly aware of their role as representing "Jewry" in general and of standing for "*the* Jew" – an abstract figure, a danger to Christianity, demonic and treacherous.[3] In the end, "Judo-phobia" may have been "minor" in Britain, but it was surely keenly felt, both socially and culturally.[4]

In Germany, things took yet another route. Enlightened discourse on toleration in that country had often been contradictory and ambivalent, while old restrictive legislation was everywhere still in force. Finally, a full-blown controversy on the pro and contra of emancipation surfaced in response to the 1781 publication of Christian Wilhelm Dohm's book *On the Civil Betterment of the Jews.*[5] Dohm did not deny what he saw as Jewish "repugnant characteristics," but stressed that they were, nevertheless, "more human than Jewish" and that they would become useful citizens if and when they would be more fairly treated. Unexpectedly, his book aroused great interest. It was everywhere hotly debated and soon translated into several European languages. At the same time, Kaiser Joseph II in Vienna promulgated his Toleration Acts, granting Jews in his various lands some, though by no

[2] For further details and the quotes, see Paula E. Heyman, *The Jews of Modern France* (Berkeley, CA, 1998), 27–28.
[3] See Anthony Julius, *Trials of the Diaspora: A History of Anti-Semitism in England* (Oxford 2010), 242–54.
[4] Ibid., 242.
[5] (Berlin, 1781). A further edition, including responses to various critiques and interventions, was published in 1783.

means all, civil rights. Clearly, their formal status was almost everywhere in flux even before the French Revolution.

Still, anti-Jewish sentiments continued to find various expressions – old and new – in all European countries. In England, where old and new were never so neatly separated, neither by a violent revolution, as in France, nor by a protracted war, as on the continent, antisemitism was mainly manifested in culture. In theater, the English "fourth estate," the Jew became a regular figure now. Shylock appeared in new disguises, and contemporary Jewish characters, though sometimes wise and benevolent, were still seen as the "crucifiers," "professed enemies of Christianity."[6] They were associated in the minds of the "English multitude," as one review stated in May 1814, "with roguery ... malignant villainy [and] contemptible meanness."[7] In a 1794 play by Richard Cumberland, a sad figure of a Jew, Sheva, turns out to be "pathetic and disempowered," without friends or family,[8] reminiscent of Nathan in Lessing's "Nathan the Wise" of a decade earlier in Berlin, who at the end also stood alone and abandoned despite his wisdom and kindness. In more openly anti-Jewish productions, it was commonly the Jew's "damned dialect" and his presumably typical physical characteristics that made it so difficult for him to "pass."

"Passing" was difficult for Jews in Germany too, despite their energetic efforts at acculturation. As in Britain, now gradually being constituted of various so-called nations, nascent German nationalism also made good use of presenting Jews as foreigners, frequently as hated foreigners. In responding to Dohm, Johann David Michaelis, a theologian at the University of Göttingen, explained that Jews, formed as a tribe under the hot sun of the Middle Eastern deserts, could by no means become members of the German *Volk*. Even Herder, impressed by the biblical poetry of the ancient Hebrews, did not overcome his distaste of contemporary Jewry.[9] Interestingly, in France too, Jewish loyalty and their true belonging to the grand nation had frequently been called in question. And finally, this is what Johann Gottlieb Fichte, originally a great supporter of the French and the French Revolution, wrote in his 1793 anonymously published *Contributions to Correcting the Views of*

---

[6] See, in addition to Julius, 251, Michael Ragussis, "Jews and Other 'Outlandish Englishmen': Ethnic Performance and the Invention of British Identity under the Georges," *Critical Inquiry* 26.4 (Summer 2000), 773–97.

[7] Ragussis, "Jews and Other 'Outlandish Englishmen,'" 790.

[8] Ibid., 792.

[9] For details on these examples, see Ofri Ilani, *In Search of the Hebrew People: Bible and Nation in the German Enlightenment* (Bloomington, IN, 2018).

the Public Concerning the French Revolution: "I see no other means of
giving them [the Jews] civil rights than to chop off their heads in one
night and replace them with new ones, containing not even one Jewish
idea."[10] This caused much acrimony at the time, and a year later, Saul
Ascher compared the respected philosopher in his *Eisenmenger the
Second* to this well-known antisemitic author of a hundred years
earlier, placing him firmly within the antisemitic tradition.

To be sure, a new stress on the value of one's belonging to a large,
ethnically inclusive "national" community – sometimes indeed only an
"imagined" community – was already widespread, especially in literary
formulations, in earlier periods and then increasingly toward the end of
the 18th century.[11] It was, however, the French Revolution that introduced the nation into politics, conceived as an important aspect of the
individual's identity, central within its list of human rights. For some
hundred years, until the last quarter of the 19th century, it was an
inherent part of liberalism, joined to other values of the Enlightenment.
Gradually, however, the potential for xenophobia, inherent in nationalism, could also be perceived, and it turned out not to be entirely inimical
to antisemitism. Employed by anti-Semites, it was used as the basis for an
argument that Jews were a separate nation, a nation with its own character, values and traditions. Accordingly, Jews could not be members of
their own nation while also seeking to become members of other
national entities.

Almost parallel to the growth of nationalism, though this time with
an explicit anti-Enlightenment tone, the so-called Romantic movement
had slowly emerged. Essentially a literary phenomenon, it soon
developed a political flank, not always conservative but often turning
to the past, stressing the emotional, nonrational or even mystical side of
man, admiring the medieval social order and the original spirit of the
Volk with their special folktales and music, while at the same time
turning back to religion. For the Romantics, the elemental spirit of a
people was revealed by the peasants on farms and in villages, not by
intellectuals in large cities and universities. Each community possessed
its own unique "spirit" that came from its historical experience. Thus,
people like Jacob and Wilhelm Grimm began to collect folk tales, to
create national dictionaries and to emphasize ancient mythologies such
as those found later on in the operas of Richard Wagner.

---

[10] Quoted from his *Sämtliche Werke* (Berlin, 1845), vol. 6, 149–50.
[11] See Benedict R. Anderson, *Imagined Communities: Reflections on the Origins and
Spread of Nationalism*, rev. and extended ed. (London, 2010).

The Jews, it was argued from this perspective, had their own past, their own specific character, that explained their alterity and foreignness. Thus, antisemitism – first in England and Germany and then also in France – became rather contagious within the aristocratic milieu of Romantic intellectuals. The new Christian-German Table Society, which met in Berlin, closed its doors not only to lower-class men and to women of all classes, but also to all Jews – even to the converted. Clemens von Brentano and Ludwig Achim von Arnim, the outstanding figures in this context, conceived and propagated the essentialist contrast between Germans, not Christians, and Jews, between Germanness and Judaism, and this remained a powerful constant in the political culture of Germany for decades. They presented it in satirical pamphlets and essays, as well as in their literary fiction, influencing contemporary politics too, especially during the years immediately before and after Hardenberg's emancipatory legislation of 1812.

Arnim was particularly outspoken about antisemitism. In a number of dramas and novellas, with a stark anti-Enlightenment tone, his Jewish characters appeared selfish, disloyal, corrupt and physically degenerated. Finally, he concluded that "[t]he Jew creates evil even when he wants Good."[12] For Adam Heinrich Müller, like other Romantics who stressed Christianity as an indispensable aspect of German identity, there was likewise no way of integrating the Jews into the nation. He rejected their claim to become Germans, a claim – he felt – that was inherent in the project of their emancipation and turned it into a dangerous experiment.

In fact, already under French rule, other social elements in Germany fiercely objected to emancipation, using an openly antisemitic language in the service of their ideology. It was particularly citizens of the three northern Hanseatic port cities and Frankfurt am Main who felt endangered by the open-door policy of the French, and as soon as the French were defeated, they took every possible measure to revoke Jewish rights. Pressure from below was stronger even than the intervention of both Hardenberg and Metternich to treat Jews "in keeping with the demands of the time, of humanity and of the paternal ruling-system they had always enjoyed," as the latter wrote to his business representative in Hamburg.[13]

---

[12] See Katja Garloff, "Figures of Love in Romantic Antisemitism: Achim von Arnim," *The German Quarterly* 80.4 (Fall 2007), 427–48.

[13] Quoted in Salo Baron, *Die Judenfrage auf dem Wiener Kongress* (Vienna, 1920), 92–93.

Then, in the summer of 1819, while the Bavarian parliament was debating new regulations concerning the Jews, they were violently assaulted – first in the city of Würzburg, where the mob raged for a number of days, and then throughout Bavaria. The Riots, rather inexplicably called "Hep-Hep," extended to Frankfurt, to various locations in the Duchy of Baden and the Rhineland, and finally to Hamburg, Breslau, Danzig and Königsberg.[14]

Particularly effective in spurring men to action was the hostile propaganda against the Jews disseminated by various speakers and writers, who popularized the more sophisticated antisemitic literature of the day. Outstanding among them were two anti-Jewish works by Friedrich Christian Rühs, a historian at the University of Berlin, published in 1816, entitled *On Jewish Claims to Acquire German Civil Rights* and *The Rights of Christianity and the German Volk against the Claims of the Jews and Their Advocates*. An enthusiastic review by Jakob Friedrich Fries, *On Endangering the Well-Being and Character of the Germans by the Jews*, took up the same themes with even greater vehemence. Fries, like Rühs, was a respected university professor, but he was also known as an outspoken liberal and his pamphlet stood out in its radicalism and callousness. The Jews had no interest to "better" themselves, he stated. They constituted a "State within a State" – a repeated claim, earlier used by Fichte too – and therefore ought to be considered *Volksschädlinge* – a term that would be reapplied by the Nazis. They ought to be banished, he insisted, if they do not renounce their religion and the "indecent" patterns of behavior contingent on it.[15]

Antisemitism was rampant among national-liberal youths, too. It was already manifested during the festivities at the Wartburg in 1817, when – among other books – some printed Jewish replies to their detractors were set to fire. Famously, this brought Heinrich Heine to prophesize that "[t]his was a prelude only. There, where books are burned, in the end people will be burned, too."[16]

Less aggressively but no less significantly, anti-Jewish sentiments were sounded in the emancipation debate by more established liberal spokesmen. Jews were repeatedly required to "improve" themselves;

[14] See Stefan Rohrbacher, "The 'Hep-Hep' Riots of 1819: Anti-Jewish Ideology, Agitation and Violence," in *Exclusionary Violence: Antisemitic Riots in Modern German History*, ed. C. Hoffmann, W. Bergmann and H. W. Smith (Ann Arbor, MI, 2002), 23–42.
[15] See Jacob Katz, *From Prejudice to Destruction: Anti-Semitism 1700–1933* (Boston, 1982), 82–83.
[16] From his tragedy *Almansor*, verse 243f.

their alterity was considered an obstacle to their belonging; and equality was being offered them in exchange for the abandonment of their history and sense of nation.[17] Indeed, cultural diversity was problematic even for Liberals and not only in Germany but also in France, as the Republicans were trying to define the meaning of citizenship and the boundaries of their own nationality.[18]

The last series of physical attacks on Jews in Western or Central Europe came with the Revolution of 1848. It began in Alsace, where some 70 percent of all French Jews still resided. Despite Napoleon's suspicion of their loyalty and despite his so-called *Décre infâme* of 1808, Jews – everywhere in France – continued to enjoy civil equality and were even strengthening their inner solidarity and self-consciousness. But by 1848, pre-revolutionary violence drove many of them to leave their villages, and some even fled across the Rhine River. Soon, the riots spread to Germany too, where noblemen, tax-collectors and especially well-off Jews were brutally attacked. By March 1848, violence spread to over thirty localities in the south and southwestern parts of the country, and then all the way to Westphalia, Upper Silesia, Posen, Bohemia, Moravia and Hungary. Attacks on Jews were clearly everywhere part of riotous peasants' uprisings against the establishment as a whole, but they also sometimes appeared as familiar old-style anti-Jewish pogroms.[19]

In France, the Jewish issue did not come up again during the 1848 revolution. In England, during the 1850s, as Lionel de Rothschild was elected to represent the City of London in Parliament for the fifth time and the problem of admitting him finally had to be solved, hostility toward the small community of Jews, settled mostly in London, became noticeable again. By then, full formal equality had gradually been achieved, but both Rothschild and prime minister Benjamin Disraeli, a converted Jew, were repeatedly vilified, the latter as "our modern Shylock," "Asiatic" and "traitorous."[20] Finally in Germany, the

---

[17] For all that, see the important work of the German historian Reinhard Rürup, mostly in German. In English, see his article, "The Torturous and Thorny Road to Legal Equality, 'Jew Laws' and Emancipatory Legislation from the late Eighteenth Century," *Leo Baeck Institute Yearbook* 31 (1986), 3–33.

[18] On France, see Julie Kalman, *Rethinking Antisemitism in Nineteenth Century France* (New York, 2010).

[19] See the English-language summary of the research on these riots in Manfred Gailus, "Anti-Jewish Emotion and Violence in the 1848 Crisis of German Society," in Hoffmann et al., eds., *Exclusionary Violence*, 43–66.

[20] See Julius, *Trials of the Diaspora*, 258–59 and 263–68 (quotes from 264 n. 107.

revolution first assured equality to all citizens regardless of their confession, and although this was not made the law of the land, Jewish
equality was legislated in one German state after another between
1862 and 1871, when it was anchored in the constitution of the newly
established German Empire.

RACISM AND RACIAL FANTASIES

Meanwhile, the seeds for the development of new forms of antisemitism were planted. In 1851, Richard Wagner, a disillusioned revolutionary, published – at first anonymously – his *Judaism in Music*, insisting
on the foreignness of the Jews again and on their dangerous, parasitic
existence within German culture. The somewhat vague meaning of this
foreignness in earlier nationalist writings received here a more concrete
and sinister meaning. But for a full development of racism, additional
elements were needed. Between 1853 and 1855 Arthur de Gobineau
published his extensive *Essai sur l'inégalité des races humaines* in four
volumes, the first attempt at presenting a systematic race theory.
According to this theory, "race" not only is a biological matter – that
is, whether one is tall or short, has black or white skin, blond or black
hair – but also determines the values of both individuals and communities. The creativity of a group, its moral qualities, its acquisition of
political power, are all determined by "race," and those who are "pure
blooded" possess the most powerful characteristics. "Race" thus not
only has aesthetic implications but, in an ultimate sense, defines the
rise and fall of nations. It is therefore not surprising that to his race-
based division between aristocracy and commoners, and to his separation of the world population into white, black and yellow races, de
Gobineau also introduced gradations within "white humanity,"
crowning the Aryans as a superior race and identifying it with
Germany and the Germans. Unsurprisingly, his book found enthusiastic
readership in that country, and Wagner, who first met Gobineau only in
1876, was deeply impressed.

     To be sure, fragmented racial theories were known in Germany
earlier, too. Partly relying on the theories of physiognomy – popular
and well-respected during the second half of the 18th century – Johann
Friedrich Blumenbach was the first to divide humanity into five races
and attach to each of them specific physical and mental characteristics. In one form or another, moreover, some such theories were not
uncommon in all European countries in that age of colonialism.
Fantasies of homogeneity and national purification combined with

visions of world historical mission. Moreover, strict definition of enemies from within and from without had always been part of the nationalist vision, to which racial theories with a strong biological component were now added. Finally, a combination of traditional antipathy toward Jews as members of another religious faith with nationalism and one or another form of nascent racism became increasingly common, especially in Germany.

While the theological faculty in Göttingen of the 18th century had produced the anti-egalitarian and anti-Jewish vision of Michaelis, another luminary Orientalist at the same university, Paul de Lagarde, published almost exactly 100 years later his *Deutsche Schriften*, in which the same combination could be found. Jews ought to give up "Moses' laws," as he put it, "since this law and the fierce arrogance that emanates from it preserves them as a foreign race."[21] Religion, nationalism, and the use of racialist language, if not really of full-scale racial argumentation, are all apparent in Lagarde's texts, and it was this mixture that made him a venerated figure, a "prophet of national revival," even as late as the First World War. This also remained the hallmark of antisemitism in Germany later on. Racism as a theory did not simply replace older notions of Jew-hating – surely not at this stage – but was an important added layer in the *Weltanschauung* associated with it. Somewhat later it gave new meaning to the notion of improvement along racial principles, as in eugenics, pointing out the presumed danger of race-mixing and of miscegenation. Most importantly, racial theory held that, insofar as "blood" was determinative, one could not escape one's racial situation. No conversion, as was available in Christianity, no assimilation as envisioned by modern liberals, was possible. A person and a people are what they are by virtue of their genetic inheritance. Race was destiny.

The third quarter of the 19th century was everywhere a time of rapid and ground-breaking modernization. The role of the Jews in this process may have been overestimated for the first half of the century, but it was now clear to all that they were not only active in propelling it onward but also among those who always stood to gain from it. Jews seemed to be better prepared to deal with its influences, and their success – economic, social and cultural – was seen as dependent on it. Soon, envy was added to old and new reasons for hating them. Historian Götz Aly underlined this envy most particularly in his interpretation of

---

[21] Paul de Lagarde, *Deutsche Schriften* (Göttingen, 1878), 296, quoted by Wolfgang Benz, *Antisemitismus: Präsenz und Tradition eines Ressentiments* (Schwalbach, 2015), 43.

Jewish life in Germany.[22] Still, general mistrust and aversion of modernity was probably more important. As the connection of Jews and modernity became clearer, so was the link between them and the sorrows of modernity, too. "The social question is the Jewish question," proclaimed Otto Glagau, a journalist of previous liberal attachments, in writing about the misfortunes of artisans and the lower middle-class under the presumed yoke of capitalist "Manchesterism." An old fear and hatred of the Jews as financiers and moneylenders, together with vague notions concerning their role in modernization and their alliance with both economic and political liberalism, were all made considerably more concrete by this indefatigable antisemite and an army of other like-minded publicists.[23]

Significantly, these were years of drastic political change as well. The post-1867 reorganization of the Habsburg monarchy, even before the stock-exchange crash of 1873, was detested by conservatives of all shades, including aristocratic landlords and the lower *Mittelstand*. In Austria, Catholic anti-Jewish propaganda grew especially in opposition to the triumphant liberalism there. By the third quarter of the 19th century, the church felt enclosed by a united, liberal Italy, and the solidly Catholic empire to the north was now split into two, equally anticlerical parts. In Germany, Constantin Frantz was the most vocal anti-Jewish voice within the Catholic anti-liberal milieu, objecting to Bismarck's project of a united Germany as well as to all of his by then mainly liberal allies. He made a name for himself with his book *National-Liberalism and the Rule of the Jews*, in which the theme of Jewish dominance was paramount, a novel contention, though by no means his original invention. Beyond the border, in Austria, it was August Rohling's pamphlet of some seventy pages, *Der Talmudjude*, that managed to reawaken old religious and social anti-Jewish claims á la Eisenmenger and combine them with deep resentment toward emancipation, fears of the "Golden International" and predictions of Jewish world supremacy. Becoming a professor of Old and New Testaments at the university in Prague, Rohling attempted to serve as an expert witness in a blood-libel court proceeding in the Hungarian town of Tisza-Eszlár, and although he was then disclosed as a complete fraud, this did not diminish his popularity.[24]

---

[22] See Götz Aly, *Why the Germans? Why the Jews? Envy, Race Hatred, and the Prehistory of the Holocaust* (New York, 2014).

[23] For more details, see Shulamit Volkov, "Antisemitism as a Cultural Code," *Leo Baeck Institute Yearbook* 23 (1978), 25–45.

[24] For antisemitism in Austria, see Peter Pulzer, *The Rise of Political Anti-Semitism in Germany and Austria*, rev. ed. (London, 1988).

But the classical seat of Catholic antisemitism was doubtlessly France, not Germany or Austria. In the aftermath of the Damascus affair, in which the French consul publicly supported blood-libel accusations against a group of local Jews, anti-Jewish attacks mixed with anti-capitalism, until then mostly sounded by early socialists such as Blanqui and Proudhon, began to be overhauled by the Ultramontane Catholics. As early as 1843, Louis Veuillot, a lay exponent of this extreme Catholicism, was made editor of the Catholic journal *L'Univers* and began publishing anti-Jewish articles, defaming Jews mainly by using traditional Christian tropes. By 1882, the financial scandal that involved the Catholic bank *Union Générale* helped join these with resentment against presumably ruthless Jewish financiers, especially the Rothschilds. In England too, hostility to this banking house surfaced repeatedly, combining old prejudices and new fears. It was only some-what later that the publication of Edouard Drumont's *La France Juive*, in 1886, managed to firmly connect counterrevolutionary Catholic antise-mitism to socialist anti-capitalism and to an emerging "scientific" racism, thus heralding a truly modern antisemitism in France.

New sorts of anti-Jewish rhetoric were now appearing in Germany, too. Following the financial crash of 1873, Otto Glagau published two pamphlets about it and about the apparent political bankruptcy of national liberalism associated with it. For both kinds of collapse he blamed the Jews, whose devious manipulations, according to him, lay behind them. In essence, Glagau's tirades were not so different from those of another onetime liberal publicist at the time, Wilhelm Marr. A productive publicist and a known agitator against the Jews, Marr finally published his opus magnum in 1879: *The Victory of Judaism over German-ness*. In it he moved away from traditional anti-Jewish argumentation by defining Jews as Semites, rejecting hate against them on religious grounds, applying racial cri-teria to prove their immutable evil, while prophesizing their approaching victory over German civilization. Marr was since then credited – probably incorrectly – with inventing the term "antisemit-ism." It appeared to be a significant novelty and had soon replaced all other synonymous terms for Jew-hating – past and present. It clearly served an important function at the time. The Jews as targets of hate were made less concrete, and hostility toward them received an unex-pected scientific aura.[25]

---

[25] For Marr, see Moshe Zimmermann, *Wilhelm Marr: The Patriarch of Anti-Semitism* (Oxford, 1986).

Eugen Dühring must also be added to the gallery of new anti-Jewish propagandists presented here. Like Marr, he too was toying with fragments of racism, while in his case this was roughly combined not with anti-liberalism but with his presumed socialism. An economist at the University of Berlin, Dühring had a certain reputation, and his book *The Jewish Question as a Racial, Moral and Cultural Question* was widely read for its scientific and intellectual pretensions. In effect, Dühring – like other publicists at this time – used "race" interchangeably with "people," "nation" and "culture." His frequent application of the term *Judenhaftigkeit*, which characterizes non-Jews who behaved like Jews, made it impossible for him to adhere to strictly racial arguments. Nevertheless, the mixture he presented was effective enough, and his writings, partly also due to Friedrich Engel's sharp-tongued response in his *Anti-Dühring*, were reprinted in large editions and read even across the borders of the Reich.

POLITICAL PARTIES, SOCIAL ORGANIZATIONS AND CONSPIRACY THEORIES

In the spring of 1878, Adolf Stöcker, the Protestant court preacher in the Prussian capital, began an aggressive campaign, intent on regrouping the working-class of Berlin away from social democracy and under the banner of church and crown. Soon he had to admit defeat. His audience was apparently not really made up of the proletariat but instead of various lower *Mittelstand* elements. They were enthusiastic to hear his message, and while they were apparently less attracted by his attacks on liberalism, which many of them supported in previous years, they responded better to his attacks on the Jews – at first rather cautious, to be sure, and then ever more radical. The latter no longer constituted a religious community, he insisted, and his was not a religious hatred. Moreover, he did not reject liberalism as such but only its "rotten branch," dominated by the Jews; not the "system" as a whole but its destroyers; not even the Jews personally but their arrogance, intolerance and will to power. Stöcker was running for a seat in parliament at the head of his Christian-Social Workers' Party, and was seeking the right tone with which to attract as many voters as he could. It is instructive that he thought antisemitism would be the best tool for achieving his purpose. In fact, this was also the stand taken by another antisemitic leader at the time, the conservative Liebermann von Sonnenberg, who had once shocked even his staunchest supporters in a street-side café in Berlin by remarking:

"First we want to become a political power; then we shall seek the scientific evidence for antisemitism."[26]

Within a few years there were a number of so-called antisemitic political parties in Germany. Some of them were led by conservatives of various shades; some by ex-liberals of a more radical temperament; some in Berlin and others in various – especially Prussian – districts; some of Protestant leaning, others with mainly Catholic followings; all with more than antisemitism in their programs. In the end, all were short-lived, often acting against each other, achieving little if any success at the polls, but having other indirect and far-reaching consequences.

The year 1879 was a turning point in German history. During that year Bismarck was finally convinced to abandon his liberal allies and reform his politics to fit the interests and perhaps also the principles of the conservatives, and when needed even of the Catholic forces in Germany. At the University of Berlin, the distinguished historian Heinrich von Treitschke, Reichstag delegate for the National-Liberal party, and – as a consistent admirer of Bismarck – active on its right wing, chose a unique way of expressing his own further turn to the right. While his idol in the seat of power and even the Kaiser himself were suspicious of antisemitism as a political movement, Treitschke took the opposite route. On November 15 of that year he published an extensive article in the pages of the *Preussische Jahrbücher*, in which he openly supported this movement, though he too deplored its vulgarity. Under his pen antisemitism became respectable (*salonfähig*). Treitschke resented the influence of Jewish journalists, "manufacturing" public opinion in Germany, and what he saw as the disproportional Jewish share in the financial, economic and cultural life of the nation. He then set out to attack Jewish immigration, coming into Germany now from the East, a new theme that would later become ever more important; all these "ambitious trouser-selling Jews whose children and children's children one day will dominate Germany's stock exchange and newspapers," to use his own words. And although Treitschke realized that emancipation could not be reversed, he shared – to the horror of some of his Jewish and non-Jewish admirers – some of the racial fantasies of the most primitive antisemites. "The Jews are our misfortune," he summarily announced, coining one of the most hateful and dangerous slogans of his time, later used as a matter of course by National Socialism.[27]

---

[26] Hellmut von Gerlach, *Vom Rechts nach Links* (Zürich, 1937), 112.

[27] Quotes from Treitschke's, "Unsere Aussichten," reprinted in his *Deutsche Kämpfe: Schriften zur Tagespolitik* (Leipzig, 1896), 1–28.

Treitschke's intervention in the contemporary controversy over the "Jewish Question" on the side of the antisemites came as a shock for many Jews and was a source of concern for many of his non-Jewish colleagues. Theodor Mommsen, the illustrious historian of Rome, responded with indignation. Nevertheless, one could not restrain Treitschke's influence, who was for fifteen years a much-respected university lecturer and a widely read historian in his own right.

In the meantime, antisemitism spread from the radical antisemitic political parties to the more established ones, especially to the conservatives, who in 1892 added an unadorned antisemitic clause to their so-called Tivoli Program. The Catholic Center party was at least more reserved, and the liberals usually positioned themselves on the other side of this front line. Social democracy, now for the first time confronting Karl Marx's until then forgotton essay of 1844, "On the Jewish Question," was at first somewhat equivocal. With time, they realized that antisemitism usually stood for everything they always opposed and served as a cultural code for loyalty to nationalism, the autocratic monarchy and imperialism. They finally took a clear side, not only for emancipation but also against antisemitism, denounced now by their leader, August Bebel, as "Socialism of the fools."

In the long run no less important than the anti-Jewish organized political parties was the anti-Jewish atmosphere, creeping into the academic world and into the social milieu of the educated bourgeoisie. Antisemitism then regained the respectability that had been mostly lost during the age of liberalism. During the last two decades of the 19th century, antisemitism spilled over into students' corporations, some professional associations and some political interest groups. Such were the German Association of Commercial Employees, established in 1893, for example, or the Pan-German League, whose leader Heinrich Class later became known for his vehemence on this matter.

In other countries too, antisemitism gained in influence during these years. The long-triumphant liberals in the Austrian parliament, operating with what seemed like a secure liberal majority since 1867, began to lose voters as the economic crisis of 1873 gave a death blow to their dominance, and by 1879 were completely under siege. Economic hardship drove artisans and small shopkeepers to take an outspoken anti-liberal line. They were organizing in order to defend their interests and sometimes joined the demand for a more democratic voting system, usually coming from the left, which would allow them to change the inner-political course of the land. At the same time, German nationalists in Austria, frustrated at their exclusion from the German Empire, were agitating in similar directions, leaning more specifically on students' corporations in Vienna and consistently using antisemitic arguments to buttress their case.

Catholic ultraconservatives were vocal in Austria even earlier. Karl Freiherr von Vogelsang, since 1870 the editor of their main organ, *Das Vaterland*, was a social reformer and radical antisemite. His and similar publications poisoned the famous open atmosphere of the Habsburg capital. And then, during the 1880s, party political organizations of the antisemitic persuasion sprang up elsewhere in the monarchy, too. The Tisza-Eszlár blood-libel case of 1882, mentioned above, was a sufficient indication of the radical antisemitism in Hungary. In 1881, a backbencher liberal, Gyöyö Istóczy, was invited to the First International Anti-Jewish Congress in Chemnitz and came with his "manifesto to the governments and peoples threatened by Judaism," which was unanimously adopted by his like-minded colleagues in Germany. He then founded the National Antisemitic Party, which won seventeen seats in the 1884 parliamentary elections, more than all such parties ever had in the German Reichstag prior to 1914. Meanwhile in Vienna, Georg Ritter von Schönerer – an outspoken racist – adding the championship of Austrian peasants to his platform of German nationalism, revised its so-called Linz Program in 1885, by demanding "the removal of Jewish influence from all areas of public life."[28] At the end of the decade, the Christian Social Party, headed by Karl Lueger, included in its program demands for restrictions on immigration as well as the call for "de-Judaization" of the civil service, the judiciary, the officer corps and the professions. Lueger's political ambitions, however, centered on achieving control over the Viennese city council, and in 1895, using his by-now perfected oratorical skill, he did indeed win the elections for the city mayor at the head of his antisemitic faction. This was a sensation, and the fact that the Kaiser refused to confirm him in this post, once and again, made it even more pronounced. By April 1897 the government surrendered, and Vienna gained an antisemitic mayor for twelve years. As far as the Jews were concerned, a long era of relative tolerance was clearly at an end, though surprisingly, this hardly impinged on Jewish success there, both in all branches of the modern economy and – more than anywhere else – in the city's vivid cultural life.

In England too, anti-Jewish feelings, sometimes seen as only one version of a more general anti-alienism, ran suddenly high as increasingly

[28] Pulzer, *The Rise of Political Anti-Semitism*, 153.

larger numbers of Jewish immigrants, fleeing the pogroms in Tsarist Russia, were reaching its shores. And in France, the Dreyfus affair shook the Republic and brought out a wave of radical antisemitism.

Convicted of treason in December 1894, Captain Alfred Dreyfus, a Jewish artillery officer, was sentenced to life imprisonment and sent to Devil's Island in French Guiana. Soon, however, it became clear that this was a miscarriage of justice and that his indictment for espionage had been fabricated. When the military then prevented a revision, the affair turned into a battle between Dreyfusards and anti-Dreyfusards, in fact, into a moral battle on the character of the Third Republic, "a political battle for the soul of France."[29] In the meantime, the newly established Ligue antisémitique française gained considerable popularity and aggressively promoted its candidates in various municipal and national elections. The group of antisemitic delegates eventually sent to the chamber was loud enough, no doubt, though in the end not very effective. Still, by January and February of 1898, the Ligue managed to incite over sixty anti-Jewish riots throughout France, developing into real pogroms in Algeria and thoroughly intimidating the entire Jewish population everywhere in France.[30] The country was flooded with antisemitic caricatures, postcards and comic strips, showing Jewish foreignness "in speech, appearance and sensibility."[31] Then, following a second conviction, Dreyfus was pardoned, released and exonerated. The affair receded into the background, although it continued to echo in and out of France, alarming all who had believed in the end of antisemitism.

At the same time, during the late 19th century, yet another layer had been added to the repertoire of anti-Jewish accusations. Historian Saul Friedländer named it "redemptive antisemitism" and identified its self-appointed prophets in the Bayreuth circle of Richard Wagner's admirers.[32] The apocalyptic tone was already unmistakable in the master's operatic world, Friedländer explains, but the real momentum was given by one of his staunchest admirers, later to become his son-in-law too, the Englishman Houston Stewart Chamberlain, in a

---

[29] Hyman, *The Jews in Modern France*, 106.

[30] See Pierre Birnbaum, *The Anti-Semitic Moment: A Tour of France in 1898* (Chicago, IL, 1998), and particularly on Algeria, Sophie B. Roberts, *Citizenship and Antisemitism in Algeria, 1870–1962* (New York, 2017).

[31] Hyman, *The Jews in Modern France*, 106.

[32] See his *Nazi Germany and the Jews*, vol. 1: *The Years of Persecution, 1933–1939* (New York, 1997), 87–95.

two-volume book, *The Foundations of the Nineteenth Century*. Here the dualistic view of the world, which divided it between good and evil, between Aryans and Jews – an image that had appeared in previous antisemitic works, too – received a particularly fantastic and paranoid character, next to a call for a racially purified Christianity that would lead to redemption. Until 1915, the book had sold more than 100,000 copies and was widely cited and reviewed.

Then, following war and revolution, another antisemitic bestseller replaced it, namely, *The Protocols of the Elders of Zion*. This fabricated text apparently originated in the ranks of the Russian secret service as early as the mid-1890s and received its final form through the work of Serge Nilus in 1903, funded in secret by the Czar. It described in detail the presumed once-in-a-century meetings of representatives of some fictitious twelve Jewish tribes, conspiring to take over the world. Of course, plans of the so-called world Jewry plotting to take over European civilization played on older antisemitic paranoia, while simplifying modern political and economic circumstances. It now turned antisemitic racism into a vicious nightmare. By the second decade of the 20th century, this elaborated version of previous fantasies became known across Europe and soon held sway over the minds of antisemites everywhere. Later on, indeed, it often guided the hands of the Nazi perpetrators.

* * *

Despite all that, at least up to the First World War, Jews continued to enjoy the fruits of their emancipation. On the whole, they managed to uphold a viable Jewish identity, often by way of reforming and modernizing their religious practices, despite widespread acculturation and progressing social integration. Above all, their success in the economic sphere and especially their prominence in the cultural life of their respective countries seemed to drive into the shadow the menacing omens of antisemitism. In most cases, these could be considered the stuff bred in reactionary circles, associated with one or another form of conservatism, loyalty to monarchism and hopes for imperial grandeur. These were likewise associated with anti-modernism, the creed of those who saw themselves as the inevitable losers in the process of modernization, dreading its unforeseen consequences. Most Jews in these parts of Europe felt they were on the winning side of this ongoing process. The fierce antisemitic onslaught that still awaited them could not yet be anticipated.

Further Reading

Arendt, H., *The Origins of Totalitarianism* (New York, 1951). The first part of
  this book treats antisemitism since the rise of the modern state, especially
  in Germany and France. It stresses the Jews' special function in the age of
  modernity and the effects of what the author sees as their resistance to full
  assimilation.
Birnbaum, P., *The Anti-Semitic Moment: A Tour of France in 1898* (Chicago, IL,
  1998). Analyzes the antisemitic mood in France during a year of rising
  tension around the Dreyfus Affair.
Frankel, J., *The Damascus Affair: Ritual Murder and the Jews in 1840* (New
  York, 1997). This is a detailed description of this event in 1840, far away in
  the Middle East, and the various reactions to it throughout Europe, at a time
  when Jews were in the midst of fighting for emancipation.
Hyman, P. E., *The Jews in Modern France* (Berkeley, CA, 1998). A full overview
  of Jewish history in France with extensive sections on antisemitism as well
  as on the fight against it from before the French Revolution until the later
  part of the 20th century.
Julius, A., *Trials of the Diaspora: A History of Anti-Semitism in England* (Oxford,
  2010). A book reviewing antisemitism in England from the Middle Ages and
  into the second half of the 20th century, describing its presence in that
  country in modern times as mild, often hidden and implicit.
Katz, J., *From Prejudice to Destruction: Anti-Semitism 1700–1933* (Cambridge,
  MA, 1980). By now a classic book on this topic with emphasis on the 19th
  century, mixing the history of ideas and social history, stressing continuities with earlier periods and pointing out the road to the Holocaust.
Mosse, G. L., *Towards the Final Solution: A History of European Racism* (New
  York, 1978). An illuminating and as yet unsurpassed exposition of the
  development of racial thinking from the Enlightenment to National
  Socialism.
Pulzer, P., *The Rise of Political Anti-Semitism in Germany and Austria,
  1879–1933* (New York, 1964). A short but nevertheless detailed and precise
  description of antisemitism in Germany and Austria, with emphasis on the
  new political parties that led the fight against Jews and Jewish emancipation
  in central Europe, from the 1870s to the rise of Nazism.
Schechter, R., *Obstinate Hebrews: Representations of Jews in France,
  1715–1815* (Berkeley, CA, 2003). A well-balanced analysis of attitudes
  toward Jews and the Jewish religion, positive and negative, during the age
  of enlightenment in France.
Smith, H. W., *The Butcher's Tale: Murder and Anti-Semitism in a German
  Town* (New York, 2002). A micro-history, using a blood-libel case in a small
  East Prussian town in 1900, showing the depth of Jew-hatred but also the
  strength of the forces acting against such prejudices at the time.
Volkov, S., *Germans, Jews, and Antisemites: Trials in Emancipation*
  (Cambridge, 2006). A book summarizing the research results of various
  smaller projects, with focus on the process of Jewish emancipation and the
  hurdles it has had to overcome in modern Germany from the late 18th
  century onward.

18 Antisemitism in Late Imperial Russia and Eastern Europe through 1920

LAURA ENGELSTEIN

At the end of the 18th century, the Polish-Lithuanian Commonwealth, home to the vast majority of European Jews, was partitioned by Prussia, Austria, and Russia, which acquired the largest share. In the territories now under Austrian and Russian rule, Jews constituted at least 10 percent of the general population and a greater proportion in many cities and towns. At its founding in 1867, the Austro-Hungarian dual monarchy granted them civil and political rights. The Russian Empire, by contrast, recognized no universal principle of citizenship. In a social hierarchy built on privileges, burdens, and exemptions, the Jews occupied a contradictory place. By legal category, they were classified as "aliens," a status shared by various Siberian and Central Asian peoples, yet Judaism was acknowledged as a legitimate religion, along with the other so-called foreign faiths. The Jews were incorporated into existing social estates yet restricted in ways that marked them as potentially harmful.

Over time, tsarist policy reinforced the Jews' separate identity and impeded their movement into mainstream society.[1] The basic institution that both embodied and symbolized the limits on Jewish integration was the so-called Pale of Settlement, the region in which most Jews were legally compelled to reside. Established in embryo in the wake of the partitions, it was formalized in 1835 to include the fifteen provinces in what are today's Lithuania, Belarus, Ukraine, and Moldova. Its inhabitants were permitted to move back and forth between the Pale and the ten Polish provinces also under Russian rule, then known as the Kingdom of Poland. Within the Pale, restrictions on occupation, property rights, and residence were designed to control and shape the Jewish

---

[1] Michael Stanislawski, "Russian Jewry, the Russian State, and the Dynamics of Jewish Emancipation," in *Paths of Emancipation: Jews, States, and Citizenship*, ed. Pierre Birnbaum and Ira Katznelson (Princeton, NJ, 1995), 262–283; Benjamin Nathans, *Beyond the Pale: The Jewish Encounter with Late Imperial Russia* (Berkeley, CA, 2002); Hans Rogger, "Introduction," in Hans Rogger, *Jewish Policies and Right-Wing Politics in Imperial Russia* (Berkeley, CA, 1986), 1–24.

population.[2] By the end of the century, its number had swelled to over five million, not counting the three million who emigrated.

Despite the obstacles to Jewish integration, the gradual transformation of imperial Russian society, as railroads spread, cities grew, and education and public life expanded, allowed many Jews to transcend them. Progress nevertheless posed dangers of its own. As popular unrest began to challenge the basis of traditional authority, a new kind of antisemitism appeared, here as in the West, "as a distinctly modern phenomenon, inseparable from the emergence of mass politics."[3] This activist antisemitism was, however, as much a danger to the regime it purported to defend as the monarchy's outright opponents, a paradox of which some antisemites in high places were all too well aware. Populist antisemitism was also a useful tool in the hands of nationalist leaders challenging imperial domination.

The regime never relinquished the techniques of administrative antisemitism, but its policies shifted over time. Some relaxation in official constraints occurred in the 1860s, in connection with the Great Reforms under Alexander II, when individual Jews in categories deemed socially useful were permitted to reside in the Russian interior.[4] The decade was also, however, a period of increasing opposition to the autocracy, particularly among educated youth, inspired by socialist ideas coming from Europe. Though few were of Jewish background, the conservative press, newly empowered by the loosening of censorship, nevertheless blamed the radicalism on Jewish involvement.[5] The Polish rebellion of 1863, in which Polish Jews played an active role, reinforced official distrust of the western region and of the Jews as a subversive force.

By the end of the decade, animosity toward the Jews had begun to acquire systematic form. In 1879, German journalist Wilhelm Marr put the term "antisemitism" into circulation.[6] His intervention became part of a debate over the character of post-unification German nationalism, a controversy well covered in the Russian press. In Russia, the

---

[2] Hans Rogger, "Government, Jews, Peasants and Land after the Liberation of the Serfs," in Rogger, *Jewish Policies*, 116–118.

[3] Robert Nemes and Daniel Unowsky, "Introduction," in *Sites of European Antisemitism in the Age of Mass Politics, 1880–1918*, ed. Robert Nemes and Daniel Unowsky, afterword Hillel J. Kieval (Waltham, MA, 2014), 5.

[4] Rogger, "Introduction," 16; David Sorkin, *Jewish Emancipation: A History across Five Centuries* (Princeton, NJ, 2019), 196–197.

[5] John Doyle Klier, *Imperial Russia's Jewish Question 1855–1881* (Cambridge, 1995), 396–401.

[6] Shulamit Volkov, *Germans, Jews, and Antisemites: Trials in Emancipation* (Cambridge, 2006), 82–83.

discourse hostile to the Jews also acquired a more political direction. The focus, however, was not on defining the nation or rejecting a liberal order that here did not exist, but on finding an alternative to German-style ethnic identity, one better suited to the empire's multifaceted profile and dominant culture.

What became the classic expression of nativist antisemitism in its Russian form was the work of a Belorussian Jewish convert to Orthodoxy named Jacob Brafman. His two influential tracts, published by government presses in 1869 and often reprinted, identified the traditional Jewish council, the *kahal*, as the center of a Jewish plot devoted to the destruction of Orthodox Christianity.[7] A Polish translation reached Catholic antisemites in Austrian Galicia, who combined it for local use with German-language "authorities" on Jewish beliefs.[8] Other Russian publications in the 1870s peddled images of the Jews as economic predators, accountable in addition for the murder of Christians "out of religious fanaticism, for ritual purposes," the so-called blood libel.[9] Ideas concerning the global power allegedly exercised through Jewish control of finance and the press were not confined to scurrilous pamphlets. They influenced the thinking of leading neo-Slavophiles and inspired the ruminations of Fyodor Dostoevsky, for whom the Jews represented the dangers of Western-style modernity.[10]

Western-style modernity was nevertheless making itself felt, not least in the spread of the new agitational antisemitism. Its intrusion into Russian public life accelerated with successive moments of political crisis. The first milestone was the Russo-Turkish War (1877–1878), prompting accusations of Jewish draft evasion and charges of corruption and profiteering aimed at Jewish purveyors to the imperial army.[11] The assassination of Alexander II in March 1881 by a handful of populist terrorists provided another, more powerful, flash point. Though only

---

[7] Yohanan Petrovsky-Shtern, "Iakov Aleksandrovich Brafman" (2010), in *Yivo Encyclopedia of Jews in Eastern Europe*, https://yivoencyclopedia.org/article.aspx/ Brafman_Iakov_Aleksandrovich (accessed July 20, 2020).

[8] Theodore R. Weeks, *From Assimilation to Antisemitism: The "Jewish Question" in Poland, 1850–1914* (DeKalb, IL, 2006), 82; Daniel Unowsky, "Local Violence, Regional Politics, and State Crisis: The 1898 Anti-Jewish Riots in Habsburg Galicia," in Nemes and Unowsky, eds., *Sites of European Antisemitism*, 17.

[9] Quoted in Harriet Murav, "The Beilis Murder Trial and the Culture of Apocalypse," *Cardozo Studies in Law and Literature* 12.2 (2000), 243; John D. Klier, "German Anti-Semitism and Russian Judeophobia in the 1880s," *Jahrbücher für Geschichte Osteuropas* 37.4 (1989), 530.

[10] Klier, *Imperial Russia's Jewish Question*, 411–413.

[11] Ibid., 391–393.

one of the bomb-throwers had an identifiably Jewish family name, right-wing journalists blamed the murder on the Jews.

In spring and summer 1881, the assassination spawned an outbreak of intimate local aggressions. At least 250 anti-Jewish attacks, known as pogroms, from the root "to smash or destroy," struck over 200 towns and villages in over half the provinces of the Pale. The year was capped by a prolonged episode that began in Warsaw on Christmas Day; a few other incidents followed in 1883 and 1884. Altogether, forty Jews were murdered, many humiliated and beaten, women routinely raped, property plundered and destroyed. Odessa had previously experienced pogrom-type assaults, the latest in 1871, but those that began on the tenth anniversary of the 1871 attack were distinguished by their ferocity and scope.[12]

The Jews' pariah status in the eyes of the law encouraged both victims and perpetrators to believe the attacks had been authorized at the highest levels. Rumors suggested that Alexander III, who succeeded his father on the throne, had called for revenge. Local officials often enabled the outbreaks or failed to curtail them. The tsar indeed saw the pogroms as a justified response to Jewish rapacity, but he did not endorse popular violence.[13] Rather, the stream of anti-Jewish invective in the right-wing press, the implication of the Jews in the murder of the tsar, and rumors of impending Jewish riots all contributed to an atmosphere of anti-Jewish excitation, encouraging attackers to feel they were responding to Jewish provocation.

The impetus to violence was a symptom not of backwardness but of change. The pogroms were not the work of benighted peasants in remote villages but spread along railway lines from the larger towns.[14] In the Belorussian provinces, where industry was undeveloped and traditional social relations largely intact, there were notably fewer pogroms.[15] The Lithuanian region, still mostly agrarian, was also

---

[12] I. Michael Aronson, "The Anti-Jewish Pogroms in Russia in 1881," in *Pogroms: Anti-Jewish Violence in Modern Russian History*, ed. John D. Klier and Shlomo Lambroza (Cambridge, 1992), 47; John D. Klier, "The Pogrom Paradigm in Russian History," in ibid., 15, 21–22; I. Michael Aronson, *Troubled Waters: The Origins of the 1881 Anti-Jewish Pogroms in Russia* (Pittsburgh, PA, 1990), 61, 67–71.

[13] Aronson, "The Anti-Jewish Pogroms in Russia in 1881," 51; I. Michael Aronson, "The Attitudes of Russian Officials in the 1880s toward Jewish Assimilation and Emigration," *Slavic Review* 34.1 (1975), 3.

[14] Aronson, "The Anti-Jewish Pogroms in Russia in 1881," 47.

[15] Claire Le Foll, "The Missing Pogroms of Belorussia, 1881–1882: Conditions and Motives of an Absence of Violence," in *Anti-Jewish Violence: Rethinking the Pogrom in East European History*, ed. Jonathan Dekel-Chen, David Gaunt, Natan M. Meir, and Israel Bartal (Bloomington, IN, 2011), 164.

relatively calm.[16] In the Ukrainian provinces, at the center of the vortex, manufacture and commercialized agriculture had already made inroads. There, the main perpetrators were unskilled contract laborers, many of them recent migrants to the cities or factory centers, many laid off in the economic downturn, often joined by railroad workers and local townspeople.[17]

The shock of the pogroms was immediate. In the long term, the effect of the tsar's assassination was to halt the progress toward integration initiated in the era of reform. The so-called May Laws of 1882 tightened existing residence restrictions and further curtailed Jewish economic activity within the Pale. Other measures narrowed access to education, the professions, the military, and the civil service.[18] Officials now tended to view converts to Orthodoxy with increasing suspicion. In 1891 Jewish artisans residing illegally in Moscow were expelled en masse from the city.[19]

The official conservatism of the 1880s marked a reassertion of bureaucratic containment. At the same time, antisemitic populism was gaining a foothold on the ethnic periphery. In Russian-ruled Poland, an array of Polish intellectuals, from Catholics to progressives, articulated a nationalist antisemitism, which only intensified in coming years. In 1892 a pogrom broke out in the textile-manufacturing powerhouse of Łódź, where Jews were a major presence.[20] Across the border, the Polish Catholic elite in West Galicia took advantage of an expanded franchise to form peasant-oriented political parties, which flooded the countryside with tirades against Jewish exploitation, inspiring a massive wave of pogroms that tore through the villages in 1898.[21] In East Galicia, Ukrainian nationalists denounced the Jews as allies of the

---

[16] Klaus Richter, "'Horrible Were the Avengers, but the Jews Were Horrible, Too': Anti-Jewish Riots in Rural Lithuania in 1905," in Nemes and Unowsky, eds., *Sites of European Antisemitism*, 214; Darius Staliūnas, *Enemies for a Day: Antisemitism and Anti-Jewish Violence in Lithuania under the Tsars* (Budapest, 2015).

[17] David Gaunt, Jonathan Dekel-Chen, Natan M. Meir, and Israel Bartal, "Introduction," in Dekel-Chen et al., eds., *Anti-Jewish Violence*, 1–2, 7; David Engel, "What's in a Pogrom? European Jews in the Age of Violence," in ibid., 32; Aronson, "The Anti-Jewish Pogroms in Russia in 1881," 51.

[18] Hans Rogger, "The Jewish Policy of Late Tsarism: A Reappraisal," in Rogger, *Jewish Policies*, 36; Nathans, *Beyond the Pale*, 203.

[19] Eugene M. Avrutin, *Jews and the Imperial State: Identification Politics in Tsarist Russia* (Ithaca, NY, 2010), 98–101, 119–120; Eugene M. Avrutin, "Racial Categories and the Politics of (Jewish) Difference in Late Imperial Russia," *Kritika* 8.1 (2007), 34–35.

[20] Weeks, *From Assimilation to Antisemitism*, 89, 92–108, 113–114.

[21] Unowsky, "Local Violence, Regional Politics, and State Crisis."

Polish nobility, adding a political dimension to economic tensions between peasants and Jews.[22]

In 1894, Nicholas II had ascended the throne in the wake of a widespread famine, only to confront an economic slump, rising tensions in factories and villages, and the mobilization of respectable educated society, demanding civil rights and political representation. Antisemitism too picked up steam. In the 1890s, political parties were still illegal and even public associations were suspect, but antisemitic ideologues gained a platform in the mainstream press and the military authorities spread antisemitic propaganda in the ranks. The first public organization with an antisemitic profile formed in St. Petersburg in 1900, with an official seal of approval.[23]

The return to violence was not long in coming. In 1902, a pogrom broke out in the pilgrimage town of Częstochowa, in Russian Poland.[24] It was quickly overshadowed, however, by one that began on Easter Sunday, 1903, in the Bessarabian capital of Kishinev. The Kishinev events combined the essential elements of what became a recognizable pogrom scenario. First, the timing in connection with Orthodox Easter. Second, the blood libel accusation. Third, the role of rumors and inflammatory rhetoric in the press. Fourth, the failure of provincial officials to stop the mob. After two days of looting and violence, forty-nine Jews had been murdered, a shocking number at the time, and over 200 wounded, hundreds of Jewish houses burned, and shops pillaged. Kishinev was followed before the end of the year by another outburst, this time in the Belorussian city of Gomel.[25] Officials accused the Jews of provoking them both.

The Kishinev pogrom aroused widespread international protests; Leo Tolstoy and other Russian writers also expressed their outrage. The Gomel perpetrators – and some of the Jews who had fought back – were brought to trial in late 1904, inspiring a vigorous defense by Jewish

---

[22] John-Paul Himka, "Ukrainian-Jewish Antagonism in the Galician Countryside during the Late Nineteenth Century," in *Ukrainian-Jewish Relations in Historical Perspective*, ed. Peter J. Potichnyi and Howard Aster (Edmonton, 1990), 111–158.

[23] Hans Rogger, "The Formation of the Russian Right, 1900–1906," in Rogger, *Jewish Policies*, 191–193; Don C. Rawson, *Russian Rightists and the Revolution of 1905* (New York, 1995), 47–55.

[24] Theodore R. Weeks, "Polish-Jewish Relations 1903–1914: The View from the Chancellery," *Canadian Slavonic Papers* 40.3–4 (1998), 240.

[25] Shlomo Lambroza, "The Pogroms of 1903–1906," in Klier and Lambroza, eds., *Pogroms: Anti-Jewish Violence*, 195–247; Edward H. Judge, *Easter in Kishinev: Anatomy of a Pogrom* (New York, 1992), 16; Steven J. Zipperstein, *Pogrom: Kishinev and the Tilt of History* (New York, 2018).

lawyers. By then, Russia was embroiled in a war with Japan, and another wave of pogroms, beginning in the town of Bendery, not far from Kishinev, had engulfed the provinces of the Pale. Many were the work of army recruits, who turned their resentment of the draft against the Jews, accused by the antisemitic press of avoiding military service. In total, the pogroms of 1903 and 1904 resulted in the deaths of ninety-three Jews and thousands injured.[26]

Despite its intensity, the violence in Kishinev was nevertheless local; the pogroms accompanying the Russo-Japanese War were bypro-ducts of the traditional draft riot. The full-scale revolution that began in January 1905, by contrast, marked a dramatic shift in the character and political meaning of anti-Jewish violence. Distinguished by its unprecedented scale and virulence, the onslaught of pogroms the crisis unleashed reflected the breakdown in imperial authority, as well as the formal constitution of an empire-wide antisemitic movement.

Populist mobilization on behalf of absolute power was a contradiction in terms. Its proponents nevertheless founded a series of organizations, including a Patriotic (or Fatherland) Union, a Monarchist Party, and the Union of Russian People (Soiuz Russkikh Liudei, SRL), devoted to just that. The Union of the Russian Folk (Soiuz Russkogo Naroda, SRN) appeared later in the year with covert police backing. It relied on religious symbolism for its mass appeal, but its demagogic methods were modern.[27] These methods also entailed the creation of vigilante groups known as the Black Hundreds, a designation evoking militias formed during the dynastic crisis of the early 17th century to defend the principle of sovereignty.

The proclamation in October 1905 of a manifesto establishing an elected assembly, the State Duma, and promising the extension of civil liberties constituted a major turning point in right-radical mobilization. The SRN was not yet strong enough to have organized the wave of violence that followed the manifesto, but the Black Hundreds were heavily involved. Altogether, over 600 pogroms hit the Pale in 1905 and 1906. A particularly vicious pogrom shook the Polish city of Białystok in June 1906, leaving 200 Jews dead and hundreds

---

[26] Lambroza, "The Pogroms of 1903–1906," 214–218.
[27] Rogger, "The Formation of the Russian Right," 195–200, 204–207; Hans Rogger, "Was There a Russian Fascism?," in Rogger, *Jewish Policies*, 213, 220, 227; Rawson, *Russian Rightists*, 34–41, 56–69; Heinz-Dietrich Löwe, "Political Symbols and Rituals of the Russian Radical Right, 1900–1914," *Slavonic and East European Review* 76.3 (1998), 456–457, 462–463.

injured.[28] Across the cities of the Pale at least 3,000 Jews were murdered, including many women, and over 15,000 were seriously injured. Many Jewish children were orphaned, property damage was extensive, synagogues were not spared.[29]

The pogroms were a feature of the broader political turmoil. Radicalized workers targeted factory owners or foremen, peasants and artisans assailed landlords or masters, but Jews or anyone perceived as Jewish were also targets. In practice, socialism and antisemitism, as mobilizing devices, were not mutually exclusive. Both expressed hostility to the powers controlling the lives of ordinary people, in the shape of capitalists, shop owners, bankers, or humble moneylenders. Both authorized violence. Striking workers sometimes engaged in pogroms; rioters occasionally combined the red flag of revolution with portraits of the tsar.[30]

Yet, despite the possible convergence, contemporaries interpreted the pogroms as a defense of the old order threatened by the incursions of modernity, a threat personified in "the Jew," the face of commerce and of revolution. The patriotic version of Russia for the Russians and the unity of tsar and (Russian) people against the enemy in their midst echoed the tenor of official policy. Indeed, the events of 1905 confirmed the belief of many diaspora Jews that the regime used "massacre as an instrument of government."[31] There was in fact no "pogrom policy" issuing from St. Petersburg, which never ceased to fear the volatility of mass violence, but officials down the line, and even some high-ranking figures, were free to enable or promote what was formally condemned.[32]

Many officials at every level, whatever their relation to the pogroms, nevertheless accepted the basic postulates of the antisemitic worldview, which identified an enemy known as "the Jew," allegedly engaged in a conspiracy to dominate the Christian world through the power of finance and occult ritual practices. This was the vision encapsulated in *The Protocols of the Elders of Zion*, a fabrication first

---

[28] Lambroza, "The Pogroms of 1903–1906," 225–227, 229, 237; Theodore R. Weeks, "1905 as a Watershed in Polish-Jewish Relations," in *The Revolution of 1905 and Russia's Jews*, ed. Stefani Hoffman and Ezra Mendelsohn (Philadelphia, PA, 2008), 129.

[29] Lambroza, "The Pogroms of 1903–1906," 231.

[30] Charters Wynn, *Workers, Strikes, and Pogroms: The Donbass-Dnepr Bend in Late Imperial Russia, 1870–1905* (Princeton, NJ, 1992), 201–207, 212–216, 218–219, 226.

[31] Lucien Wolf, "Introduction," in E. Séménoff, *The Russian Government and the Massacres: A Page of the Russian Counter-Revolution* (London, 1907), xi.

[32] Lambroza, "The Pogroms of 1903–1906," 238–242; Rogger, "The Formation of the Russian Right," 210.

published during the pogrom year of 1903 in a newspaper financed by the ministry of the interior. This installment and a series of editions appearing before 1917 were based on similar forgeries produced in Europe, revised for Russian consumption by one or more authors whose identity remains a matter of dispute.[33]

The increasing prominence of antisemitism on the public stage cannot, however, be attributed to the influence of the *Protocols*, which elaborated on views already in wide circulation. It was the revolution and its aftermath that cemented the link between antisemitism and political action, both for imperial Russian patriots and for anti-Russian nationalists, as in the case of Poland. By 1910 even Polish liberals had come to see the Jews as a foreign element, advancing Russian influence or their own communal interests over those of the aspiring Polish nation. In 1912, an ever more strident press promoted the boycott of Jewish businesses initiated by Roman Dmowski and the programmatically antisemitic National Democratic Party.[34]

In the wake of the revolution, meanwhile, Russian right-radicals pursued an agenda of their own. The SRN failed in the attempt to assassinate Prime Minister Sergei Witte, whom it blamed for the tsar's constitutional concessions and considered soft on the Jews, but in 1906 and 1907 its agents succeeded in murdering two Jewish Duma deputies, one a Christian convert.[35] In the Duma, antisemites faced off against liberals who defended Jewish rights and in 1910 introduced a proposal to abolish the Pale.[36] In courts of law, activist antisemites promoted the blood-libel legend. A first such trial in 1902 ended in the defendant's acquittal, thanks to the efforts of Jewish lawyers and their gentile allies.[37]

[33] Lucien Wolf, *The Myth of the Jewish Menace in World Affairs, or The Truth about the Forged Protocols of the Elders of Zion* (New York, 1921), 5–32; Faith Hillis, "The 'Franco-Russian Marseillaise': International Exchange and the Making of Antiliberal Politics in Fin de Siècle France," *Journal of Modern History* 89 (March 2017), 75–77; Michael Hagemeister, "The Protocols of the Elders of Zion: Between History and Fiction," *New German Critique* 35.1 (2008), 83–95; Zipperstein, *Pogrom*, 146, 148, 171; Richard S. Levy, "Setting the Record Straight: Regarding *The Protocols of the Elders of Zion*: A Fool's Errand," in *Nexus: Essays in German Jewish Studies*, ed. William Collins Donahue and Marthe B. Helfer, vol. 2 (Rochester, NY, 2014), 43–62.
[34] Weeks, "1905 as a Watershed," 132–135, 166.
[35] Rawson, *Russian Rightists*, 128–136.
[36] Laura Engelstein, *The Resistible Rise of Antisemitism: Exemplary Cases from Russia, Ukraine, and Poland* (Waltham, MA, 2020), 43–44.
[37] Ibid., 29, 47; Christoph Gassenschmidt, *Jewish Liberal Politics in Tsarist Russia, 1900–1914* (New York, 1995), 7–9.

Of greater notoriety was the case of Mendel Beilis, the manager of a Kiev brick factory arrested in 1911 and indicted on the same grounds. The case against Beilis was brought by the minister of justice, supported by the aggressively reactionary minister of the interior, on the initiative of a right-radical group in Kiev. Not all ministers approved, but the spectacle was seen, at home and abroad, as a verdict on the monarchy as a whole.[38] Beilis's defense enlisted the cream of the Russian bar, Jewish and gentile, whose efforts were bankrolled by a Russian Jewish industrialist from Minsk. The SRN supplied the lawyers for the prosecution. Ultimately, Beilis was acquitted by a jury of ordinary men that cleared him of guilt but accepted the plausibility of the charges.[39]

The heart of the matter in the Beilis case was a seemingly archaic belief, still not entirely extinct even in Europe, which was suffused with religious symbolism.[40] Even some antisemites denounced it as absurd, but few in Russia were ready to embrace the racialized antisemitism then gaining traction in the West. Ideologues and officials came to see even converts to Orthodoxy as untrustworthy, but many were in fact able to advance in professional and official careers. Most highly placed bureaucrats considered assimilation the preferred solution to the so-called Jewish question.[41] Time to debate the issue was, however, running out.

In 1913, the Beilis trial came to a close; the Romanov dynasty celebrated its centenary. In summer 1914, Russia went to war. The official

[38] Engelstein, *Resistible Rise*, 44–47; Jonathan Dekel-Chen, "A Half-Full Cup? Transnational Responses to the Beilis Affair," in *Ritual Murder in Russia, Eastern Europe, and Beyond: New Histories of an Old Accusation*, ed. Eugene M. Avrutin, Jonathan Dekel-Chen, and Robert Weinberg (Bloomington, IN, 2017), 185–203; Hans Rogger, "The Beilis Case: Anti-Semitism and Politics in the Reign of Nicholas II," in Rogger, *Jewish Policies*, 52; Robert Weinberg, "Introduction: A Murder without a Mystery," in Robert Weinberg, *Blood Libel in Late Imperial Russia* (Bloomington, IN, 2013), 12–13.

[39] Robert Weinberg, "The Trial of Mendel Beilis: The Sources of 'Blood Libel' in Late Imperial Russia," in *Russia's Century of Revolutions: Parties, People, Places*, ed. Michael Melancon and Donald Raleigh (Bloomington, IN, 2012), 20.

[40] Hillel J. Kieval, "*Yahrzeits*, Condolences, and Other Close Encounters: Neighborly Relations and Ritual Murder Trials in Germany and Austria-Hungary," in Avrutin et al., eds., *Ritual Murder in Russia*, 111–112; Robert Weinberg, "Connecting the Dots: Jewish Mysticism, Ritual Murder, and the Trial of Mendel Beilis," in ibid., 175; Weinberg, "Introduction," 7.

[41] Avrutin, "Racial Categories," 13–40; Eli Weinerman, "Racism, Racial Prejudice, and Jews in Late Imperial Russia," *Ethnic and Racial Studies* 17.3 (1994), 442–495; Vera Tolz, "Discourses of Race in Imperial Russia (1830–1914)," in *The Invention of Race: Scientific and Popular Representations*, ed. Nicolas Bancel, Thomas David, and Dominic Thomas (New York, 2014), 130–144.

campaign against "civilian enemy aliens" targeted domestic groups with ties across national borders: subjects of German origin, Poles, and Jews, the latter denounced as cowards and traitors. The Army High Command, with final authority in the region encompassing the Pale, ordered the deportation of the local population into the Russian interior. By late 1915 as many as a million Jews had been uprooted.[42] The methods used to empty the area amounted to officially executed pogroms. In occupied Galicia, the army's treatment of the Jewish inhabitants included hostage-taking, plunder, the destruction of synagogues, murder, and rape.[43] The cabinet ministers, no friends of the Jews, rightly feared the policy in both cases was self-defeating.

The Great War had a decisive impact on the fate of the Jews in Eastern Europe. In connection with heightened nationalism and xenophobia, it amplified the power of antisemitic propaganda. The violence against civilian populations perpetrated by all belligerent parties, in defiance of international law, habituated fighting men to practices that carried over into smaller conflicts after 1918.[44] The war was also largely responsible for destabilizing the Russian Empire, which collapsed in February 1917, leaving the Jewish population of the borderlands in the eye of the coming storm.[45]

With the tsar's abdication, a committee of liberal Duma deputies formed the so-called Provisional Government, which ended legal discrimination on the basis of nationality or religion. The Pale had been dismantled de facto during the war; it was now legally abolished. When the Bolsheviks seized Petrograd in October, they accepted Jews in positions of power and authority. The barriers to Jewish equality seemed to have fallen, but the coup unleashed a civil war, in which various

---

[42] Laura Engelstein, *Russia in Flames, War, Revolution, Civil War, 1914–1921* (New York, 2018), 58, 60–61; Peter Gatrell, *A Whole Empire Walking: Refugees in Russia during World War I* (Bloomington, IN, 1999), 145–150 and passim; Eric Lohr, *Nationalizing the Russian Empire: The Campaign against Enemy Aliens during World War I* (Cambridge, MA, 2003), 140–142.

[43] Engelstein, *Russia in Flames*, 62–63; Alexander Victor Prusin, *Nationalizing a Borderland: War, Ethnicity, and Anti-Jewish Violence in East Galicia, 1914–1920* (Tuscaloosa, AL, 2005), chap. 2; Peter Holquist, "The Role of Personality in the First (1914–1915) Russian Occupation of Galicia and Bukovina," in Dekel-Chen et al., eds., *Anti-Jewish Violence*, 52–73.

[44] Eric Lohr, "1915 and the War Pogrom Paradigm," in Dekel-Chen et al., eds., *Anti-Jewish Violence*, 41–51.

[45] Piotr Wróbel, "The Seeds of Violence: The Brutalization of an Eastern European Region, 1917–1921," *Journal of Modern European History* 1.1 (2003), 124–149; Jochen Böhler, "Enduring Violence: The Post-War Struggles in East-Central Europe 1917–1921," *Journal of Contemporary History* 50.1 (2015), 58–77.

contenders embraced antisemitism in pursuit of different, often opposing, political goals.

It is not surprising that Jews should have been caught in the cross-
hairs of the civil war. Some of the most brutal fighting in a brutal
struggle occurred on the lands of the former Pale, where no stable
authority was able to survive and which, despite the wartime exodus,
was still the center of Jewish habitation. Between 1918 and 1920, this
area was the site of murderous pogroms, resulting in somewhere
between 60,000 and over 100,000 deaths.[46]

The ferocity of anti-Jewish violence, the magnitude of the casualties
inflicted, and the scale of destruction visited on Jewish communities
suggest a mode of surgical terror later associated with the annihilation
of the Jews in World War II. Yet as deadly as the civil war pogroms
proved to be, their purpose was not the total – or even partial – elimination of the Jewish population. Antisemitism in this context tapped into
a reservoir of violence that easily escaped control. It did not constitute a
political program in its own right.

Pogromists now included men in uniform, as well as local mobs. All
the hastily assembled armies and paramilitary formations drew from
the same peasant communities and depended on the countryside for
food and supplies. Hungry recruits needed no excuse to loot and pillage.
Assailed by competing ideologues, the ill-disciplined armed men and
their local leaders often switched allegiances, but they carried their
distrust of the Jews along with them. Jews were attacked not only for
their possessions but for what they represented: the rapacious merchant
or profiteer; the wartime traitor; the armed provocateur, as in the myths
of earlier pogroms; or the Bolshevik fanatic.

Slogans from all sides encouraged these associations. The former
imperial officers in the White Volunteer Army were traditional old-
regime antisemites who now equated Bolshevism with the Jewish threat
to Russian statehood. Commanders urged their men to "Beat the Jews
and Save Russia."[47] The Jews were no more congenial, however, to the
nationalists who opposed the Whites' neo-imperial ambitions. The
founding architects of Ukrainian nationhood, the most consequential of
these threats, had built an identity on ethnic exclusion.[48] Simon Petliura,

[46] Engelstein, *Resistible Rise*, 88.
[47] Peter Kenez, "Pogroms and White Ideology in the Russian Civil War," in Klier and
Lambroza, eds., *Pogroms: Anti-Jewish Violence*, 302.
[48] Faith Hillis, *Children of Rus': Right-Bank Ukraine and the Invention of a Russian
Nation* (Ithaca, NY, 2013).

leader of the short-lived Ukrainian People's Republic, in homage to his socialist roots and with an eye to foreign opinion, denounced antisemitism and courted Jewish support, but he relied on commanders who fostered a level of anti-Jewish violence that tarnished his name.[49]

Among Polish leaders, Roman Dmowski was less equivocal, insisting the resurgent nation must be free of its Jews.[50] Józef Piłsudski, independent Poland's first head of state, did not adopt antisemitic rhetoric, but the dawn of independence in November 1918 was marked by a powerful pogrom in the Galician city of Lwów/Lemberg (Lviv). Pogroms continued in 1919 and 1920, during the war with Soviet Russia.[51] Poles considered the minority rights treaty imposed by the Great Powers in 1919 an infringement on sovereignty. The creation at the same time of Greater Romania, which included formerly Russian Bessarabia and its "Russian" Jews, was similarly accompanied by the obligation to acknowledge minority rights, a condition resented by Romanian leaders who had long refused to embrace the nation's Jewish population.[52]

When it came to pogroms, the Volunteer Army and the various freebooters tied to the Polish and Ukrainian campaigns were the worst offenders, but the Red Army was not exempt. Despite the prominence of Leon Trotsky, a prime target of antisemitic invective, as commissar of war, Red commanders could not prevent their troops from laying waste to Jewish settlements. Not unlike Petliura, the Bolsheviks condemned antisemitism as a matter of principle. Their appeals were not framed in ethnic or national terms, but the language of class warfare (targeting "bourgeois speculators"), like the language of Ukrainian nationalism (targeting "enemies of Ukraine"), was easy to interpret as an endorsement of anti-Jewish violence.[53] The connection was often explicit.

---

[49] Engelstein, *Resistible Rise*, chap. 2.

[50] Grzegorz Krzywiec, "Eliminationist Anti-Semitism at Home and Abroad: Polish Nationalism, the Jewish Question and Eastern European Right-Wing Mass Politics," in *The New Nationalism and the First World War*, ed. Lawrence Rosenthal and Vesna Rodic (Houndmills, 2015), 65–91.

[51] William W. Hagen, "The Moral Economy of Ethnic Violence: The Pogrom in Lwów, November 1918," *Geschichte und Gesellschaft* 31.2 (2005), 203–226; Prusin, *Nationalizing a Borderland*, chaps. 4 and 5; Engelstein, *Russia in Flames*, 536–539.

[52] William Brustein and Amy Ronnkvist, "The Roots of Anti-Semitism: Romania before the Holocaust," *Journal of Genocide Research* 4.2 (2002), 223 and passim.

[53] Engelstein, *Russia in Flames*, 511–540; Brendan McGeever, *Antisemitism and the Russian Revolution* (Cambridge, 2019); Oleg Budnitskii, *Russian Jews between the Reds and the Whites, 1917–1920*, trans. Timothy J. Portice (Philadelphia, 2012).

Among the many conflicts that constituted the greater civil war, the war against the Jews, waged directly or indirectly from many sides, was a major component. The Jew of antisemitic lore represented the intimate enemy or traitor. In the absence of political authority, when loyalties were always in question, the myth provided a stable point of reference: the Jew was by definition suspect. Antisemitism provided an idiom, moreover, that easily shifted gear. It could endorse authority – as in the case of imperial patriots before and after 1917 – but could just as well defy it. When the workers, peasants, and soldiers who had welcomed Bolshevik power rebelled against requisitions, conscription, and repression, they often denounced the "Yid-Commissars" for betraying the revolution.

In its early days, this revolution had seemed to many Jews, though far from most, the best defense against hatred and a chance to take action against it. Their involvement only reinforced the association between Jews and Communism that animated forces on the European as well as Russian right.[54] It was left to Joseph Stalin to remobilize antisemitism on behalf of the Soviet regime, confounding the myth and betraying Jewish hopes of political salvation. The fate of Eastern European Jews was decided, however, not in Moscow but in Berlin.

Further Reading

Blobaum, R., ed., *Antisemitism and Its Opponents in Modern Poland* (Ithaca, NY, 2005). Leading scholars treat a range of issues from the mid-19th century to post–World War II.

Budnitskii, O., *Russian Jews between the Reds and the Whites, 1917–1920*, trans. T. J. Portice (Philadelphia, 2012). Comprehensive treatment of complex issues in the Russian Civil War by a leading Moscow-based scholar.

Dekel-Chen, J., et al., eds., *Anti-Jewish Violence: Rethinking the Pogrom in East European History* (Bloomington, IN, 2011). Overview, plus regional studies, from 1881 to 1940.

Engelstein, L., *The Resistible Rise of Antisemitism: Exemplary Cases from Russia, Ukraine, and Poland* (Waltham, MA, 2020). Twentieth-century Jewish challenges put antisemites on the defensive.

Klier, J. D., *Russians, Jews, and the Pogrom Crisis of 1881–1882* (Cambridge, 2011). Leading scholar treats a key episode in the escalation of anti-Jewish violence.

Klier, J. D., and S. Lambroza, eds., *Pogroms: Anti-Jewish Violence in Modern Russian History* (Cambridge, 1992). Studies on the years 1881–1906, with an essay on the civil war and several overviews.

---

[54] Paul Hanebrink, *A Specter Haunting Europe: The Myth of Judeo-Bolshevism* (Cambridge, MA, 2018).

Löwe, H.-D., *The Tsars and the Jews: Reform, Reaction and Anti-Semitism in Imperial Russia, 1771–1917* (Chur, 1993). Useful study of imperial policy by a German scholar, which interprets antisemitism as a form of anticapitalist resistance.

Nathans, B., *Beyond the Pale: The Jewish Encounter with Late Imperial Russia* (Berkeley, CA, 2002). This study of "selective integration" examines how Jews entered and influenced Russian public life.

Prusin, A. V., *Nationalizing a Borderland: War, Ethnicity, and Anti-Jewish Violence in East Galicia, 1914–1920* (Tuscaloosa, AL, 2005). Covers Russian military occupation and the Polish-Jewish conflict in Austrian Galicia during World War I.

Rogger, H., *Jewish Policies and Right-Wing Politics in Imperial Russia* (Berkeley, CA, 1986). Unsurpassed classic essays with interpretations that have shaped the field.

Staliūnas, D., *Enemies for a Day: Antisemitism and Anti-Jewish Violence in Lithuania under the Tsars* (Budapest, 2015). Studies the cultural and sociological aspects of ethnic relations.

Weeks, T. R., *From Assimilation to Antisemitism: The "Jewish Question" in Poland, 1850–1914* (DeKalb, IL, 2006). Examines the emergence of antisemitism as a modern political movement in Russian-ruled Poland.

19 Marxism, Socialism, and Antisemitism

JACK JACOBS

The socialist movement does not have and has never had a unified approach to antisemitism. Indeed, socialists have displayed a variety of attitudes toward Jews and Jewry, on the one hand, and toward antisemitism, on the other. Individuals associated with socialist movements, including leading figures in such movements, have, in some instances, manifested prejudiced attitudes. The most prominent representatives of the major socialist parties of the late 19th century and of the 20th century, on the other hand, were often critical of explicitly antisemitic political parties.

The early French utopian socialist Claude Henri de Saint-Simon did not have any particular interest in the Jews of his day. However, he attracted a small but notable number of Jewish supporters, such as Benjamin Olinde Rodrigues and Leon Halevy, who played highly conspicuous roles among the Saint-Simonians, particularly after the death, in 1825, of Saint-Simon himself. Neither Rodrigues nor Halevy can fairly be said to have held anti-Jewish views – but the same cannot be said of all of their political opponents. Indeed, in the wake of Saint-Simon's demise, the Saint-Simonians were regarded (inaccurately and misleadingly) by certain of their political enemies as a movement overly influenced by Jews.

This critique of the Saint-Simonians was evident, for example, among the followers of Charles Fourier, who, like Saint-Simon, was both French and a utopian socialist. Fourier (1772–1837) clearly held anti-Jewish predilections. He mentioned Jews rather often in his denunciations of usurers and bankers, maintained that Jews avoided productive positions, suggested that Jews were parasitical, and suggested that the political emancipation of French Jewry had been too rapid.

But the most important figures of the Marxist movement in France, which came into being in the latter decades of the 19th century, long after the death of Fourier, did not support such views. The leader of the French Workers' Party, Jules Guesde, insisted that the enemies of the working class were the capitalists, not the Jews, and that those who focused undue attention on those members of the bourgeoisie who were Jewish were misleading the proletariat (though he did sign on, in 1898, to a Manifesto of the Socialist Group of the French Parliament which suggested that many members of the petty bourgeoisie who opposed Jewish businessmen were thereby fighting capital, and thus were socialists in the making). Like Guesde, Paul Lafargue, another major figure among the French Marxists – and the son-in-law of Karl Marx – was completely unsympathetic to political antisemitism and spoke out against it. The French Marxists tended to believe that the Dreyfus Affair was best understood as a disagreement among wings of the bourgeoisie, and thus was not a matter in which socialists should unduly intervene. This view, however, was not motivated by a general animosity toward Jews per se.

Unlike the Marxists of France, Jean Jaurès, a non-Marxist socialist and the leader of the French Socialist Party in the period leading up to the First World War, ultimately became a very prominent defender of Dreyfus. Particularly after 1898, he tended to condemn political antisemitism as a fake which, he believed, was intended to deceive and divert workers.

Leon Blum, who was a Jew, became a major figure among French Socialists between the two world wars, and became Prime Minister of France in the mid-1930s. He pointedly underscored his Jewish identity in the face of attacks by French antisemites and, in 1938, delivered a widely noted speech to the International League against Antisemitism.

* * *

Socialist ideas began to attract adherents somewhat later in Germany than in France. A similar spectrum of positions on antisemitism, however, existed among German-speaking socialists in the second half of the 19th century as had manifested itself in France.

Ferdinand Lassalle, who established the General Union of German Workingmen in 1863, a year before his death, was of Jewish origin, but, as an adult, did not publish any works focused on Jewry or on antisemitism. On the other hand, in a private letter to a woman he was trying to impress, he revealed that he generally detested Jews and believed them to have taken on the characteristics of slaves.

The newspaper of the Lassallean General Union in the early 1870s published articles containing antisemitic phrases, particularly in attacks by the newspaper on German socialists who were not Lassalleans. Nevertheless, antisemitism did not play a major role in the political program of the Lassallean movement. Moreover, traces of antisemitism in the party's newspaper generally diminished after 1873.

There was never a point at which antisemitism was a central plank in the program of the Social Democratic Party of Germany (SPD) – the largest and most important socialist party in the German-speaking lands – which contained both Lassalleans and Marxists. The SPD's stance on antisemitism generally had more in common with pronouncements of Marx's coauthor and close collaborator Friedrich Engels than with any statements made by Marx himself.

Both of Marx's parents were born Jews. However, Marx's father was baptized before Marx was born, and Karl Marx himself was baptized in an Evangelical church when he was six years old. It is therefore altogether unsurprising that Marx did not receive a Jewish education.

In 1841, a draft law was circulated which was intended to exclude Prussian Jews from military service, public offices, and positions of honor. It was, in other words, intended to oppose granting equal civil rights to Prussian Jewry. In the wake of the circulation of this draft law, a journalist, Carl Heinrich Hermes, who was among those who opposed granting full civil rights to Jews, wrote several pieces in the *Kölnische Zeitung*. Marx, in turn, wrote to his friend Arnold Ruge, in 1842, that he found Hermes to be ignorant and trivial.

While Marx was studying at the University of Berlin, he had become friends with Bruno Bauer, and took a course taught by Bauer on the prophet Isaiah. Bauer, who was very eager to state his opinion on contemporary controversies, published several articles on the Jewish question in 1843. Given Marx's preexisting ties to Bauer, and Marx's comments on Hermes, one can understand why Marx read Bauer's articles on Jewish matters closely, and why he ultimately published responses to these works.

Bauer insisted that civil emancipation pure and simple would not suffice to make Jews free. From Bauer's perspective, Jews needed to recognize that their religious beliefs were hindering their liberation, and thus needed to reject those beliefs in order to move toward freedom. Bauer, in other words, maintained that Jews would have to give up Judaism before they could be free.

Marx did not accept Bauer's views on this subject. As early as March 1843, Marx wrote to Ruge that the head of the Jewish community of Cologne had requested that Marx write a petition on behalf of the

Jewish community to the provincial diet, and that he wanted to do so. Marx also informed Ruge that Bauer's views on Jews seemed to him to be too abstract.

Marx's most famous reply to Bauer, "On the Jewish Question," which appeared in print in 1844, has been interpreted by some scholars as an antisemitic work. However, Marx, unlike Bauer, favored the political emancipation of the Jewish community, and thus held a sharply different view on this critically important matter than did the overwhelming bulk of those who held anti-Jewish views at that time. Indeed, Marx's position on the question of civil emancipation for Prussian Jews had more in common with that of Bauer's Jewish critics, including Philippson, Hirsch, and Riesser, than with the position staked out by Bauer himself.

Marx insisted that there was a distinction between political emancipation – formal, legal political equality – on the one hand, and human emancipation, on the other, and that Jews were entitled to the former even if they had not yet obtained the latter. In *The Holy Family*, which appeared roughly a year after Marx's "On the Jewish Question," Marx (and Friedrich Engels, who cowrote *The Holy Family*) went significantly further, and suggested that the modernity of a state could be judged by the extent to which Jews had been granted equal political rights within it.

Marx's support for the political emancipation of the Jews, however, was not accompanied by sympathy for Jews as such, for Judaism, or for Jewry. In the same letter in which Marx informed Ruge that he intended to accede to the request that he intervene on behalf of the Jewish community of Cologne, Marx also proclaimed that he found the Jewish faith to be repugnant (*widerlich*). Moreover, in the second portion of "On the Jewish Question," having made his political and philosophical argument against Bauer, Marx goes on to pose a series of rhetorical questions: "What is the secular basis of Judaism? *Practical* need, self-interest. What is the worldly cult of the Jew? *Huckstering* [*Schacher*]. What is his worldly God? Money ... Contempt for theory, art, history, and for man as an end in himself, which is contained in an abstract form in the Jewish religion, is the real, conscious standpoint, the virtue of the man of money.... The *chimerical* nationality of the Jew is the nationality of the merchant." Marx's harshly critical attitude toward Judaism, his political position on civil emancipation notwithstanding, is manifest in these and similar passages.

In the decades following the publication of "On the Jewish Question" and *The Holy Family* Marx did not devote sustained attention to the Jewish question. It should be noted, however, that he

344   JACK JACOBS

continued to make use, both in his published work and in his correspondence, of deplorable, anti-Jewish slurs, and regularly described individuals of Jewish origin using highly distasteful epithets. Nevertheless,
since Marx's writings of the 1840s are his only extended pieces focused
on the Jewish question, and since the position taken by Marx on civil
emancipation in these pieces – one which favored political equality for
Prussian Jewry – was both shared by leading contemporary German Jews
and rejected by the Jew-haters of his day, the allegation that Marx was
an antisemite ought not be upheld.

To be sure, Marx never did publicly condemn antisemitism. Engels,
on the other hand, did. In *Anti-Dühring*, which was published in
1877–1878, Engels conducted a frontal attack on the antisemitism of
E. Dühring, a lecturer at Berlin University who had a considerable
following among German socialists. In this work, Engels refers to popular
prejudice against Jews as inherited from the bigotry of the Middle Ages.
Moreover, in a famous letter written in 1890 to an obscure Austrian bank
employee, Isidor Ehrenfreund, and repeatedly published in various periodicals, Engels stressed that antisemitism was a characteristic feature of a
backward culture, and nothing but a reactionary movement of decaying,
medieval, social groups against modern society. Though it had a socialis-
tic disguise, Engels added, antisemitism served only reactionary purposes
and was a movement from which socialists ought to stay away. Engels
made it clear that his opinion of antisemitism had been influenced by
contact he had had with socialists of Jewish origin and notes in his letter
that one conservative weekly had claimed that Engels was himself
Jewish. Though that was not in fact the case, Engels added, if he had to
choose, he would rather be a Jew than a "Herr von."

Around 1890, Engels is known to have written not only the letter to
Ehrenfreund described above but also an introduction for a Yiddish
translation of the *Communist Manifesto*. In this introduction, which
Engels sent to Jewish socialists living in New York, he noted that the
fact that the *Manifesto* was being translated into Yiddish was itself a
good answer to antisemitic contentions that Jews were merely exploiters, not workers.

Engels continued to make use of unflattering expressions when
describing individual Jews even in the period during which he condemned political antisemitism. He attributed unattractive features to
Jews, parodied Jewish speech patterns, and described Polish Jews in an
unsavory, stereotyped, manner. It ought to be added, however, that he
was quite supportive of the Jewish socialist and labor movements that
came into being in the last quarter of the 19th century.

August Bebel, a very prominent leader of the SPD from the time that that party was established until his death in 1913, first became aware of Engel's letter to Ehrenfreund in 1892, and promptly crafted a resolution on antisemitism that was similar in spirit to Engel's letter. Antisemitism, Bebel's resolution said, arose from discordance within bourgeois society. As Bebel saw it, antisemitism was reactionary and had to be struggled against. Bebel's resolution was endorsed by SPD party congresses on several occasions.

Personal prejudice on the part of specific German Social Democrats, including prominent and powerful members of the Party, was certainly not unknown in imperial Germany. But the SPD itself was committed to the view propounded in Bebel's resolution for many years thereafter.

The three leading ideologists of German Social Democracy in the early years of the 20th century – Rosa Luxemburg, who ultimately became the key theoretician of the Party's left wing; Eduard Bernstein, who was the foremost theoretician of the Revisionists (the right wing of the Party); and Karl Kautsky, a defender of orthodox Marxism (and, as such, the ideologue of the Party's centrists) – differed sharply from one another in their writings on many subjects, including various matters related to Jewry. They ultimately disagreed, for example, in their approaches to Zionism (toward which Bernstein displayed considerable sympathy, and Luxemburg displayed disdain). However, none of them ever endorsed political antisemitism. The SPD maintained its "anti-antisemitism," during the late 1920s and early 1930s, even when it might have been politically advantageous for the Party to have adopted a rather different position.

The SPD's record of consistent opposition to Nazism and to antisemitism compares favorably to that of all other important political parties in Weimar Germany, including the occasionally opportunistic Communist Party of Germany (KPD). In 1923, at which point the KPD was in favor of a rapprochement between German nationalism and Communism, Ruth Fischer, a German Communist leader of Jewish origin, told a KPD-sponsored meeting in Berlin that they were right to oppose Jewish capital, and urged them to trample Jewish capitalists under foot and to hang these capitalists from the streetlamps. In 1930, the KPD revived the approach that had apparently motivated Fischer's remark, and once again made use of antisemitism in an attempt to attract right-wing nationalists.

* * *

Antisemitic sentiment was widespread in the (non-Marxist) Russian populist movement during the pogroms of the 1880s. In August 1881, the Executive Committee of the populist People's Will party proclaimed that the Jews were the greatest exploiters of the people of the Ukraine and encouraged the peasantry to rise up against the Jews. There were populists, in other words, who welcomed the pogroms. But the Marxist-oriented Russian Social Democratic Workers' Party (RSDRP) opposed political antisemitism and condemned pogroms.

Jewish socialists in the Russian Empire formed several different parties of their own. The first and most important of these parties, the General Jewish Workers' Bund, was created in Vilna in 1897, and played a major role, in 1898, in organizing the RSDRP. The Bund – which was strongly influenced by Marxist ideas and which ultimately developed an anti-Zionist orientation – staunchly confronted antisemites. The Bund argued that the struggle against antisemitism was part and parcel of the struggle against capitalism and autocracy. Antisemitism was used by the ruling class as a means by which to divide and thereby weaken the proletariat. Antisemitism among non-Jewish workers was, in other words, attributable, according to the Bund, to a lack of sufficient class consciousness on the part of those workers. The Bund's position implicitly suggested that it was only in the socialist society of the future that antisemitism could be fully eliminated. But the Bund did not by any means maintain that there was nothing to be done in the present. On the contrary: beginning in 1902, Bundists called for armed self-defense against violent antisemitic attacks. The Bund asked its local committees to organize and to lead defense efforts. In specific cases, the self-defense groups organized under Bundist auspices succeeded in protecting Jews confronted with violent antisemitic mobs, including not only Jews associated with the Bund but other Jews victimized by pogromists. These self-defense groups functioned, when needed, for years thereafter.

Vladimir Lenin was sharply critical of the national program of the Bund – a program that demanded national cultural autonomy for the Jewish people of the Czarist Empire. He was also deeply opposed to ideas of the Zionist movement. His critique of both the anti-Zionist Bund and Zionism, however, was not motivated by antisemitism. Indeed, Lenin noted that antisemitism served the interests of the bourgeoisie, not those of the proletariat. He condemned the 1906 pogrom in Bialystok as a maneuver instigated by the Czarist regime, supported draft legislation intended to combat antisemitic discrimination in 1914, endorsed a decree opposing the antisemitic movement in 1918, and, in March 1919, gave a speech (a recording of which was played at workplaces, demonstrations, and elsewhere) in which he explicitly condemned antisemitic slander. To be sure, later in 1919, Lenin also began to argue that the Bolsheviks ought to display more sensitivity to Ukrainian national sentiments and drafted a document in which he advised that the Party keep Jews in Ukraine on a tight leash, transfer them to the front, and not allow them into positions in government agencies. But these wrong-headed and crudely worded arguments were apparently intended by Lenin to fight antisemitism (by countering the slur that there were not enough Jews fighting, and too many Jews in the government), not to encourage it.

There was not substantial disagreement within the RSDRP with Lenin's opposition to political antisemitism in the years leading up to the Bolshevik Revolution. Neither Georgii Valentinovich Plekhanov, the founding father of Russian Marxism, nor those who eventually formed the leadership of the Menshevik faction of the RSDRP displayed sympathy for antisemitism. Plekhanov's approach to the Dreyfus Affair was similar to that of the French Marxists.

Russian Marxists were concerned first and foremost with revolution, not first and foremost with antisemitism. When, in 1903, Bundists accused some prominent Russian socialists of fighting harder against Zionism than against antisemitism (the Bundists' own staunch opposition to Zionism notwithstanding), L. Martov, a leading member of the RSDRP who was himself of Jewish origin, replied that this was not only true but justified. He insisted that Zionism had to be fought even more vigorously than antisemitism because Zionists wooed members of the Jewish proletariat (who might otherwise become members of the RSDRP), while the antisemites lured only backward and undesirable elements of the population. Martov, however, most definitively intended not to endorse antisemitism but rather to make a point about political priorities. Pavel Axelrod, who was Jewish and who, like Martov, eventually became a prominent anti-Leninist Russian Marxist, was troubled by the Beilis blood-libel trial of 1913. He publicly condemned antisemitism in forthright language in 1917 (and also expressed sympathy at that time for Zionist goals).

The tradition of consistent opposition to antisemitism manifest in the RSDRP in the era before the Russian Revolution of 1917, however, was not carried over unaltered into the Communist era. Though the Bolshevik leadership opposed antisemitism in principle, there were Red Guards who perpetrated anti-Jewish violence in the spring of 1918, and units of the Red Army that engaged in pogrom-like activity in Ukraine in 1919. The Red Army was certainly less prone to such activity than were its opponents. However, there was in fact antisemitic sentiment in the rank-and-file of pro-Bolshevik forces in the era of the Russian Civil War.

It is true that the Party undertook a campaign opposing antisemitism in 1926 and that Stalin explicitly and forcefully condemned antisemitism in 1927 and 1931. But Stalin and those who supported him also made use of antisemitic innuendo when struggling to consolidate power, notably in attacks on Leon Trotsky and other members of the Opposition. Stalin's tactics apparently fanned antisemitism within the rank and file, and undermined support for Stalin's opponents.

Trotsky, born in 1879 to a Jewish family, was proudly internationalist in his worldview and, like Lenin, a consistent opponent of both Bundism and Zionism. His opposition to these movements, it should be underscored, was rooted not in prejudice against Jews but rather in his belief that the Bundist and Zionist movements were nationalistic. Early in his career, a prominent leader of the Bund accused Russian Social Democrats of having consistently neglected the task of confronting antisemitism, which, the Bundist argued, was a serious shortcoming that had to be avoided in the future. Trotsky retorted, first of all, that Russian Social Democrats had in fact fought antisemitism, but also argued that it was not necessary for Marxists to fight against antisemitism in particular, because, once the masses achieved a requisite degree of consciousness, antisemitism would simply fade away. Thus, Trotsky maintained in the first years of the 20th century, it was superfluous to make Jews a special subject of discussion among the masses. In later eras, he changed his mind.

Trotsky explicitly called out the antisemitism of the Stalinists in the late 1930s, in an article entitled "Thermidor and Anti-Semitism," and, late in 1938, presciently warned that the victory of fascism would signify the physical extermination of the Jews. In the face of virulent antisemitism, however, Trotsky continued to insist that the fate of Jews – including their physical survival – was contingent on their linking themselves to the revolutionary struggles of the proletariat, which, he believed, alone could stop the wave of fascism that was inundating the world. As the danger of fascism grew larger, Trotsky proclaimed that disclosure of the roots of antisemitism ought to become part and parcel of the daily work of all sections of the Fourth International (the grouping of revolutionary socialist and communist parties, founded in 1938, with which he and his supporters were associated).

Antisemitism was manifest in the Soviet Union not only in the era of Stalin but also in later years. While Khrushchev was in power, there were efforts made to limit the number of Jews holding prominent positions in specific sectors of Soviet society. Later still, viciously anti-semitic tropes and images were repeatedly used in purportedly anti-Zionist writings and cartoons published in the USSR. Indeed, there can be no question that, though antisemitism and anti-Zionism are most definitively conceptually distinct, the campaigns against Israel undertaken by the Soviet Union, particularly after 1967, regularly made use not only of anti-Zionist argumentation but also of clearly antisemitic sentiments.

The same can be said about campaigns in a number of Soviet satellites. In 1968, Polish Jews who had no connections of any kind to the Zionist movement or to Israel were drummed out of positions – including but not limited to academic positions, positions in hospitals, and administrative jobs – on the spurious grounds that they were con-spiring with Zionists against the interests of the Polish People's Republic and were slandering Poland itself. Those persecuted included many individuals who were only partially of Jewish descent. It was, however, precisely their descent that explains the treatment to which they were subjected.

* * *

Marxists and Marxist-influenced intellectuals produced several ana-lyses of antisemitism during the middle decades of the 20th century. One such study, Otto Heller's *Der Untergang des Judentums*, was published in 1931 and, attempting to explain antisemitism from the perspective of historical materialism, argued that the forms of Jew-hatred in different eras were linked to the dominant ideologies of the societies in which they arose. Race, he underscored, was an indispens-able element of contemporary imperialistic politics of oppression. Thus, in contemporary bourgeois society, the religious element of antisemitic argumentation had retreated, and a racialist element had come to the fore. The author, born a Jew, had been a founding member of the Communist Party of Czechoslovakia but had been booted out of that party in the mid-1920s. He noted in his book that racial antisemitism was a weapon of fascist reactionaries in his era. Heller believed, how-ever, that the proletarian revolution would ultimately eliminate the social preconditions on which antisemitism rested. Heller himself died while being held captive by the Nazi regime in 1945.

Der Jud ist Schuld ...?, published in 1932, shortly before Hitler was appointed Chancellor of Germany, contains articles written from a variety of political perspectives, including a piece by an anonymous member of the KPD entitled "Kommunismus und Judenfrage." This essay, the only substantial document produced by the KPD during the Weimar era in which a representative of the Party attempts to grapple with antisemitism, asserted that contemporary fascism was making use of animosity toward Jews in order to mask class antagonisms. Racial hatred, this author noted, was one of the most dangerous weapons of the bourgeoisie in the era of imperialism. The author thus insisted that Communists see it as their task to struggle against the ideology of fascism and that the struggle to exterminate antisemitic demagoguery was essential to that task.

The revolutionary socialist Abram Leon, born in Warsaw to a Jewish family, became a major activist in the Trotskyist movement in Belgium following Trotsky's murder in 1940. He completed *The Jewish Question: A Marxist Interpretation* at the end of 1942, while living in Nazi-occupied Belgium. The book was published, posthumously, in 1946. Antisemitism, Leon stressed, was not a residue of the feudal era (as Engels, among others, had earlier suggested) but rather a typical manifestation of the era of imperialism. Jews had become scapegoats of the economic contradictions inherent in the society in which they lived. Thus, antisemitism was analyzed by Leon as a tool that allowed the high bourgeoisie to turn radicalized petty bourgeois elements who had been impacted negatively by economic crises against the Jews rather than against those responsible for these crises.

The studies of antisemitism written by thinkers associated with the Frankfurt School were far more sophisticated than were those of figures like Heller or Leon and are among the most significant attempts to grapple with antisemitism from a socialist-inflected perspective. The single most important such analysis was written by Max Horkheimer (the long-term director of the Institute of Social Research, within which the Frankfurt School crystallized), who was Jewish, and by his colleague Theodor W. Adorno (who was partially of Jewish origin). In their coauthored book *Dialectic of Enlightenment*, written while the authors were in exile in the United States, Horkheimer and Adorno asserted that the rise of antisemitism was a crucial indicator of contemporary barbarism, both explained by the history of civilization and a means through which to explain that history. The most important chapter in this book, for our present purposes, was entitled "Elements of Antisemitism" and was written primarily in 1943 (though *Dialectic of Enlightenment* was not published until four years later). "Elements" illuminated antisemitism by delineating a series of linked theses. The first of these suggested that fascism emerged from the womb of liberalism and that both the liberal and the fascist understandings of antisemitism were very problematic. A second thesis notes that antisemitism cannot be explained, or combatted, solely by rational argumentation. The third, in turn, explores links between changes in the means of production and contemporary antisemitism. As the economic roles traditionally played by Jews in Europe became less important, Jews themselves, long blamed for economic injustices of the capitalist class, were pushed to the margins of the class with which they were associated.

The next thesis examines religious origins of antisemitism and argues that the long-standing animosity of Christians toward Jews had by no means been extinguished in the modern world, but rather incorporated into it. The last of the original theses explores the connection between antisemitism and mimesis and points out that the Nazis made ritualized use of mimetic behaviors. At later points in time, two additional theses were composed – one arguing that antisemitism is based on false projection, in the course of which antisemites attribute to Jews desires located within themselves, and a final thesis explaining that antisemitism had become a plank in a broader fascist perspective. The ideas inherent in "Elements of Antisemitism," a work which has Marxist roots, and which is also influenced by Freudian, Nietzschean, and other perspectives, have been widely debated and discussed, both in earlier eras and in the present, and remain influential.

* * *

Several significant analyses touching on matters related to antisemitism and written from socialist or Marxist perspectives were produced in the decades following the Holocaust and the establishment of the State of Israel. Maxime Rodinson, born in Paris during the First World War into a secular, assimilationist, and anti-Zionist Russian Jewish family, joined the French Communist Party in 1937, but was expelled from that party some two decades later. Rodinson (who had a fluent command of a number of languages, including Arabic and Hebrew, and who wrote scholarly studies of Muhammad, of Islam, and of Marxism in the Muslim world) asserted that antisemitism had not been a major problem in the Arabic-speaking lands before the creation of the State of Israel, and that it was precisely the establishment of the State that had led to a fanning of anti-Jewish attitudes among Arabs. From Rodinson's perspective, Israel was a colonial state.

Isaac Deutscher, born in 1907 and raised in a Hasidic home in a town near Cracow, was in the Polish Communist Party in the late 1920s and early 1930s, and was later active in Trotskyist circles in pre–World War II Poland. In the 1950s and 1960s, he wrote a number of essays on matters related to Jews or to Israel, of which the most famous is a piece entitled "The Non-Jewish Jew," first delivered as a lecture to a meeting of the World Jewish Congress in 1958. He comments in this essay that the (profoundly tragic) Nazi massacre of six million European Jews had actually not made much of an impression on other Europeans and explains the fact that this was the case by pointing to the economic roles that Jews had played in the pre–World War II European economy as traders, businesspeople, and moneylenders. Deutscher contends that when, in the first half of the 20th century, the peoples of Europe turned against capitalism, they tended to attack not capitalism's core but rather its trappings and suggests that this explained the antisemitism of the Nazi era.

To Deutscher, the rise of Israel was paradoxical: Jews were embracing a nation-state of their own at precisely the moment when, from Deutscher's perspective, nation-states were becoming anachronisms. Deutscher, who lived in England from the late 1930s onward, proclaimed in the 1950s that he had abandoned his pre-Holocaust anti-Zionism, and he seemed to regret, during that era, that he had not urged European Jews to go to Palestine in the 1920s or 1930s. But, as he made crystal clear in an essay entitled "Who is a Jew?" and in other works, it was Deutscher's belief that neither the Holocaust nor the creation of the State of Israel made it necessary to revise the classic Marxist analysis of antisemitism. Though a Marxist, an atheist, and an internationalist, he continued to insist that he was a Jew throughout his life, because he felt the tragedy of the Jews to be his own, and because, while living in a world in which antisemitism was by no means a phenomenon solely of the past, he was committed to doing whatever he could to assure the security of other Jews.

Horkheimer and Adorno also displayed continued concern with antisemitism in the decades following the Holocaust. In "The Meaning of Working Through the Past," for example, a piece written by Adorno and first presented as a talk in 1959, Adorno argued that the survival of Nazism within democracy was potentially more menacing than the continuation of fascist tendencies against democracy and discussed both methods that might help grapple with continued antisemitism and tactics that would be unlikely to help. The old method of underscoring the great achievements and contributions of particular Jews, for example, Adorno believed, would not be useful, nor would organized encounters between Jews and non-Jews (because, Adorno continued to believe, antisemitism was rooted not in experiences that antisemites have with Jews but rather in the needs of the antisemites themselves). In order to work through the past, the causes of past events would have to be eliminated. In another piece, dating from 1962 and devoted directly to the topic of combatting contemporary antisemitism, Adorno described antisemitism as a medium which manipulated unconscious conflicts. He linked antisemitic attitudes to an authoritarian character structure and recommended that educators encountering antisemitism in young children try to undermine it by providing such children with the warmth and understanding that they were likely not getting from their parents.

Herbert Marcuse, who, like Rodinson and Deutscher, was of Jewish origin and who, like these other writers, was born in Europe long before the Nazi era but succeeded in living through that era, did not have much to say about antisemitism per se, and never did attempt to grapple with the significance of the Holocaust. However, Marcuse, who was widely admired by those associated with the New Left, did comment directly on antisemitism in an interview conducted in 1977. When asked whether he believed that antisemitism was a matter of real concern for Jews around the world, including in the United States (which was where Marcuse lived in the latter half of his life), he asserted that antisemitism was rampant in all states and that it might assume more aggressive forms under certain circumstances – suggesting though not explicitly stating that, for example, a dramatic economic collapse could lead to an upsurge in antisemitism in some contexts.

* * *

One of the geographic areas in which the relationship between socialism and antisemitism has become a hotly contentious issue in recent years is the United Kingdom. British Jewry did not tend to think of the British left as intrinsically antisemitic in the past. However, some of the leading voices of the established Jewish community of Great Britain have charged that that is the case in the 21st century.

Robert Owen, a prominent British utopian socialist who wrote primarily in the first half of the 19th century, made a handful of comments about Jews. His comments suggest that he did not see any particular reason to discriminate against them. Owen was in favor of the emancipation of British Jewry. Moreover, he hoped to bring into being a new world in which there would be no persecution. The Chartists, a movement devoted to obtaining political rights for workers

in the middle of the 19th century, likewise, advocated Jewish emancipation and are known to have protested against mistreatment of Jews.

In the 1920s and 1930s, an era in which a substantial part of the
Jewish population of Britain was made up of poor and working-class
immigrants of East European origin, and the progeny of such immigrants,
many British Jews voted for the British Labour Party. Accenting the
support granted by much of British Jewry in the middle of the 20th
century to the political left is not meant to suggest that there was not a
degree of antisemitism apparent within the British left before, during, and
after that era – there certainly was. Sidney Webb, to take a particularly
prominent example, is alleged to have made anti-Jewish comments. The
antisemitism of figures like Webb notwithstanding, however, much of
the British Jewish population ultimately began to identify rather closely
with the Labour Party. This was true not only in the era of the Great
Depression but also in the decades immediately following the end of the
Second World War. One significant factor here was doubtless that, however much antisemitism there may have been within Labour, antisemitism appears to have been far more widespread among the Tories. British
Jewry in the early and middle parts of the 20th century regularly perceived the Conservative Party as a cold and unwelcoming place and had
good reason for this perception. Over time, however, as, among other
matters, the socioeconomic demographics of British Jewry began to
change, the links between British Jews and Labour weakened.

This is evident by examination of the era during which Ed Miliband –
who was raised in a non-religious Jewish home – was Leader of Labour,
from 2010 to 2015. The leadership of the organized Jewish community of
Britain was clearly skeptical of Miliband's stances on matters related to
Israel from the beginning of his tenure as leader onward. It was not
explicit antisemitism on the part of Labour (or of Miliband) that led many
British Jews to decline to support Miliband in the elections of 2015. Deep
dissatisfaction by some Jews with Miliband's position on matters related
to Israel and Palestine, on the other hand, seems very likely to have
played a role in their voting decisions.

The period during which Jeremy Corbyn rose to become leader of
Labour, and the years during which he served as leader, raised serious
questions about antisemitism in Labour's ranks. Throughout his years in
Parliament, it ought to be noted, Corbyn supported motions condemning
antisemitism. At one and the same time, Corbyn also strongly supported
Palestinian causes and movements. This latter fact apparently contributed to anxiety about Corbyn in some sectors of the Jewish community,
his forthright opposition to antisemitism notwithstanding.

A series of incidents led some to accuse Corbyn of harboring anti-semitic views. In 2012, prior to becoming Leader of Labour, Corbyn commented via social media about a controversy involving a mural in East London which depicted a group of prosperous-looking white men, some of whom were painted with stereotypically Jewish facial features, playing a Monopoly-like game on a board resting on the backs of a number of dark-skinned men. The mayor of the neighborhood where the mural was located asserted that the image perpetuated antisemitic tropes about Jewish domination of financial institutions and advocated having the mural painted over. When, however, the artist complained via Facebook about the fact that his work was going to be destroyed imminently and included an image of his mural with his complaint, Corbyn posted a sympathetic reply pointing out that, in 1934, a mural by Diego Rivera that had included a picture of Lenin had been destroyed in New York, and explicitly proclaiming that the artist of the London mural was in good company.

A second incident widely used as evidence to support the contention that Corbyn has (or had) antisemitic views took place in 2013. In the course of remarks made at a meeting convened by the Palestinian Return Centre, Corbyn referred to a speech made by Manuel Hassassian, the Palestinian Authority's diplomatic representative to the United Kingdom, about the history of Palestine. Corbyn noted that the speech had been recorded by individuals whom Corbyn described as Zionists who were in the audience on that occasion, and who berated Hassassian for his remarks. Corbyn then added that these "Zionists" had two problems. The first, Corbyn asserted, was that they (purportedly) did not want to study history. The second, he added, was that, though they had lived in the United Kingdom for a very long time, probably for their entire lives, they (supposedly) did not understand English irony.

In these comments, by suggesting that British Zionists were somehow foreign, regardless of how long they may have lived in the United Kingdom, Corbyn has been alleged to have made use of a slur associated with those who hold anti-Jewish prejudices.

Corbyn, to be sure, denied that he had made an antisemitic remark, insisting that he had spoken of Zionists, not Jews, and that the distinction was a crucial one. He consistently denies holding antisemitic views. He thinks of himself as proudly antiracist, and also thinks that opposition to antisemitism is part and parcel of a consistent antiracist approach. But it is not out of the question that Corbyn holds certain prejudices or accepts specific stereotypes without even being aware of them. In any event, the issue of antisemitism in Labour is one which manifestly goes well beyond the views of Jeremy Corbyn. The question of whether or not there is a culture of antisemitism in Labour is currently being officially investigated and continues to be hotly debated.

* * *

The meaning, the uses, and the function of antisemitism have been rather varied, among socialists as on other points on the political spectrum. Specific socialists and radicals, including but not limited to French utopian socialists, Lassalleans, and Russian Populists, made use of antisemitic rhetoric or made statements making it clear that they held negative feelings about Jews or Jewry. Major Marxist-influenced social democratic parties (as distinguished from Communist parties), on the other hand, while by no means wholly immune to antisemitic sentiment, were regularly opposed to political antisemitism in the late 19th century and in the century that followed. Although individual Marxists – including, notably, Karl Marx – certainly made use of anti-Jewish slurs, the most important social democratic parties have tended, by and large, to perceive political antisemitism as reactionary and have argued against it in many different contexts. And yet the question of the relationship of socialism to antisemitism has been a perennial one, discussed over a period of generations and in many lands, and remains a sensitive topic.

Further Reading

Carlebach, J., *Karl Marx and the Radical Critique of Judaism* (Littman Library of Jewish Civilization) (London, 1978). The most thorough analysis of Marx's relationship to antisemitism. Includes an extensive, annotated bibliography.
Fischer, L., *The Socialist Response to Antisemitism in Imperial Germany* (Cambridge, 2007). An impressive study on the relationships of German Social Democrats toward antisemitism at the end of the 19th century and the beginning of the 20th.
Linfield, S., *The Lions' Den: Zionism and the Left from Hannah Arendt to Noam Chomsky* (New Haven, CT, 2019). Explores the attitudes of 20th-century left-wing intellectuals, including Maxime Rodinson, Isaac Deutscher, Albert Memmi, and Noam Chomsky.
McGeever, B., *Antisemitism and the Russian Revolution* (Cambridge, 2019). An excellent study of the relationships between the Bolsheviks and antisemitism in the era of the Russian Revolution and of the Russian Civil War.
Mendelsohn, E., ed., *Essential Papers on Jews and the Left* (New York, 1997). Reprints of classic pieces by prominent scholars such as Edmund Silberner, Shlomo Avineri, and Jonathan Frankel.
Nedava, J., *Trotsky and the Jews* (Philadelphia, 1972). An extended analysis, including discussion of the roles of antisemitism in Trotsky's life, and the changes in his ideas over the course of his career.

Niewyk, D. L., *Socialist, Anti-Semite, and Jew: German Social Democracy Confronts the Problem of Anti-Semitism, 1918–1933* (Baton Rouge, LA, 1971). A compelling analysis of the positions of the German Social Democratic Party on matters related to antisemitism in the era of the Weimar Republic.

Rich, D., *The Left's Jewish Problem: Jeremy Corbyn, Israel and Antisemitism* (London, 2018). A thorough investigation of contemporary attitudes toward antisemitism in the British Labour Party.

Silberner, E., "British Socialism and the Jews," *Historia Judaica* 14 (1952), 27–52. An important source on Owen, the Chartists, the Webbs, and early British Social Democrats.

"French Socialism and the Jewish Question, 1865–1914," *Historia Judaica* 16 (1954), 3–38. Surveys opinions of French leftists, with special attention devoted to the range of perspectives expressed in the era of the Dreyfus Affair.

Traverso, E., *The Marxists and the Jewish Question: The History of a Debate (1843–1943)*, trans. B. Gibbons (Atlantic Highlands, NJ, 1994). A sensitive examination of the attitudes of such figures as Marx, Engels, Lenin, Trotsky, Stalin, and Gramsci and of the relevant policies of both socialist and communist movements.

Wistrich, R. S., *Revolutionary Jews from Marx to Trotsky* (London, 1976). Contains chapters on the ideas of a number of leading socialists of Jewish origin in Germany, Austria-Hungary, France, and Russia.

20A Antisemitism in Modern Literature and Theater: French Literature

MAURICE SAMUELS

Although Jews have never made up more than 1 percent of the French population, they have played an outsized role in the French literary imagination, offering a pretext for discussions about national and cultural identity. Jewish characters in French literature have served to focus debates over what it means to be modern and over the effects of the political and economic revolutions that transformed French society so radically, beginning in the late 18th century. They have also allowed the French to debate the meaning of their universalist tradition, the degree to which all citizens can claim equality before the law. And while many of these depictions of Jews can be considered antisemitic, others present a far more nuanced vision. The ambivalence surrounding Jews in modern French literature reflects the larger French ambivalence toward the issues and ideas that Jews represent.

Prior to the late 18th century, French writers showed little interest in Jews. While it is true that some of the classics of the early modern French canon focused on Jewish characters – such as Racine's plays *Bérénice* (1670) and *Esther* (1689) – it was figures from the Old Testament and from ancient Jewish history that sparked literary interest, not actual, living Jews. This stands to reason given how small and marginal were the Jewish communities in France at the time. At the time of the Revolution of 1789, there were fewer than 40,000 Jews in a country of more than 25 million people, mostly concentrated in the far eastern provinces of Alsace and Lorraine.

And yet, despite these small numbers, the philosophers of the French Enlightenment began to take a greater interest in Jews. They did so primarily for humanitarian reasons. Intent on refashioning society on the basis of reason, certain 18th-century writers saw the persecution of Jews by the Catholic Church as the ultimate symbol of the intolerance, injustice, and irrational superstition they were seeking to eradicate. In *The Spirit of the Laws* (1748), Montesquieu compared the Inquisition's persecution of Jews to the persecution of Christians in the far East.

Voltaire also condemned the persecution of Jews by the Inquisition, although he blamed the Jewish religion for providing the basis for Christianity, the irrationality of which he abhorred. In his *Philosophical Thoughts* (1746), Denis Diderot likewise attacked the religion of the Old Testament as the very opposite of his ideal of enlightened reason.[1]

When they reflected on modern Jews, the writers of the French Enlightenment tended to see them as every bit as backward as their ancient forebears. Although Voltaire made an exception for certain more acculturated Sephardic Jews, he denounced the poor, religiously observant, Yiddish-speaking Ashkenazic Jews for holding on to their "ancient mass of superstitions," as he put it in his epic poem *La Henriade* (1723). In his highly influential *Essay on the Manners of Nations* (1756), Voltaire denounced the fanaticism and greed of ancient Jews and mocked their scorn for the Romans who conquered them.[2] "They made usury into a sacred duty," Voltaire wrote, underlining the connection between ancient Jews and their modern descendants, many of whom, especially in Alsace and Lorraine, were engaged in small-scale moneylending because most other trades and professions were barred to them.[3]

Given that the Jews were denounced as the most backward and unmodern of peoples in the 18th century, it is ironic that in the 1830s writers began to identify them with the modernizing forces that were transforming France. After France became the first country to grant the Jews full civil rights – during the French Revolution, in 1790–1791 – many Jews began to settle in Paris, which had previously been forbidden to them, and began to participate actively in the economic, political, and cultural life of the nation. In the 19th century, Jews moved from the margins to the very center of French national life. And they moved to the center of French literature as well. Between 1830 and 1880, almost every major French writer in the French canon devoted at least some attention to Jews. Jews also became a major preoccupation on the French stage during this period. The opera "The Jewess" (1835), with music by Fromenthal Halévy and a libretto by Eugène Scribe, about a medieval Jewish woman who prefers to be boiled alive rather than convert to Christianity, was one of the most popular works of the era.

Many novels from this period feature a Jewish banker figure, at a time when actual Jewish bankers – such as the Rothschilds – were rising to prominence. There is a fantastically rich banker's son named Thaler

---

[1] Arthur Hertzberg, *The French Enlightenment and the Jews* (New York, 1968), 282.
[2] Ibid., 272, 284.
[3] Ibid., 302–303.

(after the European coin) in Stendhal's *The Red and the Black* (1831), who vies unsuccessfully for the affections of the aristocratic heroine. Examples of scheming and greedy Jews can be found in works by most mid-19th-century French authors, including Honoré de Balzac, George Sand, Victor Hugo, and Théophile Gautier. A particularly repugnant variant on this stereotype of the crass Jewish capitalist is the figure of the Jewish art dealer found in novels by Balzac, Henri Murger, and many others. During the Romantic period, when art itself became a kind of religion, the Jewish art dealer served as an antichrist, corrupting culture by monetizing it. It is notable that the real-life model for Jacques Arnoux, the founder of an aptly named journal called *Industrial Art* in Flaubert's novel *Sentimental Education* (1869) was Jewish, even though the character is not described as such. Flaubert, however, was hardly free of antisemitic prejudice: in his letters to George Sand, he referred to their common publisher, Michel Lévy, in extremely antisemitic terms.

Balzac stands out among 19th-century French writers both for the variety of his Jewish characters and for their complexity. There are many Jewish characters in Balzac's *Human Comedy*, the vast cycle of works he completed between 1830 and 1850. These include central figures like Gobseck, an enigmatic usurer whose sharp practices conceal a fundamental probity, as well as more minor characters, such as the Jew who teaches the Christian miser in *Eugénie Grandet* (1833) how to get what he wants in financial transactions by feigning stupidity. Of all Balzac's Jewish characters, however, it is Baron Nucingen, a prominent banker, who epitomizes Balzac's ambivalent relationship both to Jews and to the culture of capitalist modernity they represent.

Nucingen was partly modeled on James de Rothschild, and the character figures in a number of novels, including *Old Goriot* (1834) and the eponymous *The Firm of Nucingen* (1838), which describes the Jew's unsavory financial manipulations in great detail. *A Harlot High and Low* (1838–1847), a major novel in the Balzacian canon, centers on Nucingen's romantic obsession with a beautiful prostitute, who offers to sleep with him in exchange for a million francs that she will then pass on to her real lover, a handsome non-Jewish poet. Throughout the novel, Nucingen's greed and immoral business practices are described in terms that come straight out of the antisemitic anticapitalist tracts of the period by the likes of Karl Marx: "That man is a Stock Exchange swindler," one character remarks of Nucingen to justify the prostitute's actions; "He has shown pity to no one; he has grown rich off the fortunes of widows and orphans. You will be their Vengeance!" The plot against Nucingen is described as a way to redeem not just the Jew's ill-gotten gains but modernity itself from the contamination of a kind of capitalist greed that is seen as fundamentally Jewish.

What sets *A Harlot High and Low* apart from other negative portrayals of Jewish financiers, however, is that the prostitute who seduces him – Esther van Gobseck – is also described as Jewish: she is none other than the niece of the usurer Gobseck from other novels in the *Human Comedy*. And while the novel depicts the Jewish Nucingen as the emblem of all that is negative about capitalism, it presents Esther's Jewishness in a much more positive light: "Esther came from the homeland of the human race, the land of beauty: her mother was Jewish," the narrator informs us. Balzac was hardly the first writer to split his image of the Jew along gender lines. From Shakespeare's *The Merchant of Venice* (1598) to Walter Scott's *Ivanhoe* (1819), the Jewish moneylender was often shown to have a beautiful daughter free of the Semitic sin of greed. Balzac updated this topos for the modern era, showing how the same economic forces he makes an elaborate show of denouncing in the form of Nucingen can have their own seductive charms. He thereby reveals his desire for the very economic forces he criticizes. By linking his greedy banker and his beautiful prostitute through their Jewishness, Balzac expresses his ambivalent feelings toward the capitalist system they both represent.

Esther is hardly the only Jewish prostitute in modern French literature. Indeed, numerous 19th-century novelists and poets depicted Jewish women who sell their bodies, whether as common streetwalkers or as high-class courtesans. From the glamorous actress Josépha in Balzac's novel *Cousin Bette* (1846), whose deadly charms destroy respectable families, to the cadaverous whore in Charles Baudelaire's poem "One Night When I Lay beside a Frightful Jewess" (1857), the bordellos of French literature are filled with Jewish prostitutes. And the majority of these Jewish whores lack the redeeming qualities – the proverbial "heart of gold" – of Balzac's Esther. They are man-devouring harpies who destroy love by commercializing it. In one of the more insidious variations of this topos, the eponymous Jewish heroine of the Goncourt brothers' novel *Manette Salomon* (1867) is an artist's model – a career dominated by Jewish women that was often considered a form of prostitution – whose corrupting materialism crushes the spirit of her painter lover.[4]

[4] Maurice Samuels, "Metaphors of Modernity: Prostitutes, Bankers, and Other Jews in Balzac's *Splendeurs et misères des courtisanes*," *Romanic Review* 97.2 (March 2006), 169–184.

The last two decades of the 19th century saw a dramatic increase in antisemitism in France, fueled by a sensationalist press. Following the publication of Édouard Drumont's best-selling antisemitic screed *Jewish France* (1886), a thousand-page denunciation of the supposed takeover of the nation by Jews, overt antisemitism became commonplace in French literature. Alongside the popular novels of writers like Gyp (pseudonym of Sibylle-Gabrielle Marie-Antoinette de Riqueti de Mirabeau), which were filled with degrading antisemitic stereotypes, more high-brow writers continued to use the figure of the Jew for more nuanced explorations of the meaning of modernity. Guy de Maupassant's novels – such as *Bel-Ami* (1885) and *Mont-Oriol* (1886) – display scorn as well as a bit of grudging admiration for the dynamism of their Jewish characters, capitalist power-brokers who leave scruples behind in their drive to get ahead.

Zola's novel *Money* (1890), set at the Paris Stock Exchange, depicts capitalism as a game at which only Jews can win and contains numerous unflattering portraits of Jewish financiers. A few years later, however, the writer would temper his views. After recognizing the danger posed by the new political antisemitism of Drumont and his acolytes, Zola penned "J'Accuse" (1898), a powerful defense of Alfred Dreyfus, the Jewish army officer falsely accused of treason in a case that would divide French society. Zola's final novel, *Truth* (1902), a fictional transposition of the Dreyfus Affair, denounces antisemitism as a social and political scourge, but imagines a future in which Jews have intermarried with their Christian persecutors. Antisemitism ceases to exist in Zola's well-meaning but nevertheless disturbing utopia because Jews have also ceased to exist.

Marcel Proust offered a far more probing analysis of antisemitism in his modernist masterpiece *In Search of Lost Time* (1913–1927). Half-Jewish on his mother's side, Proust filled his sprawling novel with Jewish characters, from the worldly art critic and society swell Charles Swann to the pretentious arriviste Bloch to the prostitute-turned-actress Rachel. Several of these depictions might seem to trade in negative stereotypes of Jews, but Proust's view of the dynamics of Jewish assimilation in fin-de-siècle France was ultimately that of an "insider" and can be understood within the tradition of Jewish self-critique. He was fascinated by the sociology of antisemitism – the way it altered the landscape of Parisian high society during the Dreyfus Affair – but he was equally attentive to the psychological complexities of Jew-hatred, examining both the psycho-sexual motivations of its perpetrators (in characters like the Baron de Charlus) and the personality-shaping effects on its victims (such as Swann and Bloch).

After ebbing somewhat in the aftermath of the Dreyfus Affair, anti-semitism came roaring back in the 1920s and '30s, a period that saw the Jewish population of France double as a result of immigration from Eastern and Central Europe. Critics have accused Irène Némirovsky, a Russian-born Jewish author who would die in Auschwitz, of "Jewish self-hatred" for her extremely harsh portrayals of immigrant Jewish financiers and their families in novels like *David Golder* (1929). But her negative portrayals of Jews – which like those of Proust, bear the hallmark of Jewish self-critique – pale in comparison to the violently antisemitic diatribes of her contemporaries, such as Louis-Ferdinand Céline.

Known for his energetic, slang-inflected portrayals of lower middle-class France in novels such as *Journey to the End of the Night* (1932), which was not antisemitic, Céline also penned a series of pamphlets in the late 1930s, such as *Trifles for a Massacre* (1937), that denounced the "Jewification" of France in hyperbolic terms. For the Céline of the pamphlets, all the corruption and stagnation of modern life is the fault of the Jews, whom he says have polluted the French race and poisoned French society. Disturbingly, these pamphlets contain the same highly inventive language of his widely admired novels but put their linguistic ingenuity in service of an extreme, even psycho-pathic, form of Jew hatred. An eager collaborator with the Nazis who fled France following World War II, Céline would be sentenced to death *in absentia* after the war. His continues to occupy an ambiguous place within the French literary canon as both an acknowledged liter-ary master and one of the most diabolically hateful writers France has ever produced.

No discussion of representations of antisemitism in 1930s France would be complete without mention of one of the greatest works of the period, the film *The Grand Illusion* (1937), directed by Jean Renoir. Set in a German prisoner-of-war camp during World War I, the film follows a group of French officers, each representing a distinct social type, as they plot a series of escapes. One of these officers is a Jew named Rosenthal (played by Marcel Dalio). Although the character is shown to embody various antisemitic stereotypes – he is from an ostenta-tiously rich banking family, of foreign parentage, slightly effeminate, and uncomfortable in his own body – he is nevertheless embraced by the other prisoners, especially Maréchal (played by Jean Gabin), the embodi-ment of the typical working-class French man, who overcomes his prejudice against Jews during their final, daring escape. Renoir's willing-ness to confront antisemitic prejudice head-on, and to offer a model for its transcendence, sent a powerful message in the late 1930s, when

France was being governed by its first Jewish prime minister – Léon Blum – and Hitler had begun antisemitic persecutions in Germany.

After World War II, the French sought to purge the country of traces of the Nazis and their ideology. One of the leading antisemites of the Occupation – the author and journalist Robert Brasillach – was executed for collaboration in 1945, a sign that literary antisemitism would no longer be tolerated in France. And, indeed, overt expressions of Jew-hatred, which had been commonplace in France in the interwar period, virtually disappeared from French literature after the war. This period also saw the publication of forcefully *anti*-antisemitic texts, such as Jean-Paul Sartre's *Anti-Semite and Jew* (1945–1946), a blistering attack on antisemitism as a form of philosophical "bad faith" and intellectual cowardice. Although Sartre was later criticized for declaring that the Jew exists only because the antisemite defines him as such, in what seemed like a negation of the positive aspects of Jewish identity, the fact that one of the era's leading thinkers and writers spoke up in defense of the Jews was seen by many – including by many Jews – as a sign that France had definitively rejected its legacy of antisemitism.

This does not mean that the French were eager to confront the specificity of Jewish suffering in the aftermath of World War II, at least at first. One of the few French works from the postwar period to discuss the Nazi death camps, Alain Resnais's film *Night and Fog* (1955), did not explicitly mention antisemitism. This reluctance would begin to disappear after the 1972 release of Marcel Ophüls' documentary *The Sorrow and the Pity*, about Vichy France's collaboration with the Nazis. The following decades saw a virtual obsession with the Nazi Occupation period and with the theme of antisemitism in French literature and film – an obsession that has yet to run its course. Every year brings the release of dozens of movies and films about antisemitic persecution during World War II. Some of these works, such as Claude Lanzmann's ten-hour documentary *Shoah* (1985), have been heralded as masterpieces. These works about antisemitism have provided a forum for debates about the nature of French identity and the degree to which Frenchness is open to all who claim it, including Jews and other minorities.

One of the contemporary writers most interested in probing the issue of antisemitism is Patrick Modiano, winner of the Nobel Prize for Literature in 2014. The son of a Jewish father who survived the war living clandestinely in Paris, Modiano cowrote the screenplay for the film *Lacombe Lucien* (1973), directed by Louis Malle, about a young Nazi collaborator. Nearly all of Modiano's subsequent works have been set during the period of Nazi occupation. However, it is his first novel, *La place de l'étoile* ("The Square of the Star," 1968), that offers the most direct confrontation with the issue of antisemitism in his corpus – perhaps in the entire corpus of modern literature. The Jewish hero of this comic novel, named Raphaël Schlemilovitch, takes on a variety of antisemitic stereotypes perpetuated by the French literary tradition. He becomes, in turn, a cosmopolitan, a traitor, a pompous intellectual, and a pimp before winding up on the couch of Sigmund Freud, who tries to cure him of his psychosis by telling him that according to Sartre, the Jew is only a figment of the antisemite's imagination. Confronted with this denial of his very being, Schlemilovitch declares himself nostalgic for the antisemitism of Céline, who at least allowed Jews to exist. Modiano's delirious parody stands as a fittingly absurd end point to France's long and ambivalent literary obsession with its Jewish minority.

Further Reading

Avni, O., "Patrick Modiano: A French Jew?," *Yale French Studies* 85 (1994), 227–247. This short article treats the subject of Jewishness in Modiano's *La place de l'étoile*.

Birnbaum, P., *The Anti-Semitic Moment: A Tour of France in 1898* (Chicago, IL, 1998). This book provides a historical overview of French antisemitism at the time of the Dreyfus Affair and devotes attention to writers, including Drumont.

Carroll, D., *French Literary Fascism: Nationalism, Anti-Semitism, and the Ideology of Culture* (Princeton, NJ, 1995). An analysis of the link between fascism and aesthetics, with analysis of French antisemitic writers from the late 19th century through World War II, including Drumont and Céline.

Freedman, J., "Coming Out of the Jewish Closet with Marcel Proust," in *Queer Theory and the Jewish Question*, ed. Daniel Boyarin, Daniel Itzkovitz, and Ann Pellegrini (New York, 2003), 334–364. This essay interrogates the complexity of Jewish identity in the work of Marcel Proust.

Hertzberg, A., *The French Enlightenment and the Jews* (New York, 1968). A classic exploration of the place of antisemitism in the work of Enlightment philosophers such as Voltaire.

Judaken, J., *John-Paul Sartre and the Jewish Question: Anti-Antisemitism and the Politics of the French Intellectual* (Lincoln, NE, 2009). A thorough study of Sartre's approach to Jews and Jewishness, including his controversial *Antisemite and Jew*.

Kaplan, A., *Reproductions of Banality: Fascism, Literature, and French Intellectual Life* (Minneapolis, MN, 1986). One of the first works to explore how fascist ideology was manifested in mid-20th-century French culture.

Rousso, H., *The Vichy Syndrome: History and Memory in France since 1944* (Cambridge, MA, 1994). This book investigates the postwar French obsession with the period of the Nazi Occupation and the attempt to come to terms with the legacy of French complicity in the deportation of the Jews by writers and filmmakers.

Samuels, M., "Metaphors of Modernity: Prostitutes, Bankers, and Other Jews in Balzac's *Splendeurs et misères des courtisanes,*" *Romanic Review* 97.2 (March 2006), 169–184. An analysis of Balzac's ambivalent treatment of Jews as an expression of his ambivalence toward the culture of capitalism more generally.

The Right to Difference: French Universalism and the Jews (Chicago, IL, 2016). A study of the way that French writers from the Revolution to the present have used the Jews to explore the question of universalism, with sections on Zola, Renoir, Sartre, and Modiano.

Suleiman, S. R., "The Jew in Jean-Paul Sartre's *Réflexions sur la question juive*: An Exercise in Historical Reading," in *The Jew in the Text: Modernity and the Construction of Identity,* ed. Linda Nochlin and Tamar Garb (New York, 1995), 201–218. This essay was one of the first to point to the troubling antisemitic residue in Sartre's supposedly anti-antisemitic defense of Jews after World War II.

The Némirovsky Question: The Life, Death, and Legacy of a Jewish Writer in 20th-Century France (New Haven, CT, 2016). A judicious treatment of Némirovsky's complex relation to her Jewish identity.

20B Antisemitism in Modern Literature and Theater: German Literature, 18th–21st Century*

MICHAEL MACK

This essay analyzes how antisemitic literature in the German-speaking world from the 18th to the 21st century formulated conspiracy theories that dehumanized the Jews, casting them as both foreign and demonic. Reactionary writers (such as H. O. F. Goedsche in his novel *Biarritz*) as well as socialist writers (such as Richard Wagner in his *Ring of the Nibelungs*) fabricated claims that blamed the Jews for having demonically thwarted various promises made by modern, secular versions of redemption. In these fictitious stories, Jews were held responsible for the shortcomings of all forms of modern society. They could thus be demonized as representatives either of capitalism (as in Wagner) or of socialism (as in Goedsche). The term "redemption" highlights the pseudo-theological component incorporated within post-Enlightenment modern German antisemitism in a society that came late to industrialization and nationhood.

A theological-political thematic is particularly striking in the depiction of Jews in 18th-century German literature. The most renowned proponent of Enlightenment thought and practice in the fragmentary German-speaking world was the Lutheran playwright and drama critic Gotthold Ephraim Lessing (1729–1781), whose 1779 drama *Nathan the Wise* was a seminal text of the Enlightenment because of its emphasis on religious tolerance. In it, Saladin, a Muslim ruler, asks the Jew, Nathan, which of the three monotheistic religions is the right one. Nathan answers Saladin's question with a story that is known as the Ring Parable, a tale that Paul Mendes-Flohr and Jehuda Reinharz have called "A Parable of Toleration."[1] A dying father gives each of his three

* I thank the Leverhulme Trust, whose award of a 2019–2020 Leverhulme Research Fellowship made possible the writing of this essay.
[1] Paul Mendes-Flohr and Jehuda Reinharz, *The Jew in the Modern World: A Documentary History*, 2nd ed. (Oxford, 1995), 64.

sons an identical ring, telling each it is the magical original with special powers. Only one ring is original, the other two are copies, but no one can tell the rings apart. The moral is that we should each behave as though our religion is the true one and do our best to follow its teachings. The fact that one of the rings (religions) may be the original (but the other two mere simulacra) should stop bigotry, intolerance and persecution, while reinforcing in its Christian (read: Protestant) readers and audience the assumption that they and they alone have the true ring. While advocating for the diversity and equality of all religions against claims of bigotry and racism, the play simultaneously postulates the existence of a "true" religion.

Moses Mendelssohn (1729–1786), Lessing's contemporary and friend, was the most renowned German Jewish philosopher of the Enlightenment, respected among the intellectual elite as "the German Socrates." He served as Lessing's model for the plea made by his main protagonist (i.e., Nathan the Wise) for understanding amongst different cultures and religions. Privately, Mendelssohn himself was not so sure about the idea that all the Abrahamic religions were equal in their divine mission, maintaining his own sense that Judaism was clearly the point of origin of the others – indeed, was the original "ring." On the other side, there were those who opposed Lessing's view, most especially Friedrich Heinrich Jacobi (1743–1819), an influential German philosopher who, in a "little book" entitled *On the Doctrine of Spinoza*, published in 1785, insinuated that on his deathbed Lessing was not a real Christian and had confessed to being a follower of Spinoza's pantheist philosophy. If true, this would have been scandalous in a German and European 18th-century context, undermining Lessing's influence as advocating for the parallel if not the equivalence of the three "Abrahamic" religions.

Why should following Spinoza (1632–1677), a Dutch Jewish philosopher and one of the foremost exponents of rationalism, be a problem? Even before Jacobi's polemic, Pierre Bayle (1647–1706), a French philosopher and author, had turned Spinoza into the antisemitic representation of "the Jew" because of his atheism and secularism (anything worldly or mundane). Bayle equated Judaism and Jews with what he derogatorily identified as the atheistic and the oriental (i.e., strange and foreign). Bayle's depiction of Spinoza in highly negative terms reinforced the "outsider" image of the Jews throughout Europe. "It is striking to the compulsive need to further Orientalize Spinoza, a figure whose very Jewishness rendered him already 'Oriental' in the eyes of many

Europeans."² Following Bayle, Jacobi further cast Spinoza into a larger-than-life figure representing the additional threats of atheism and fatalism, that is, powerlessness.

The huge controversy sparked by Jacobi's "little book" provoked a comprehensive interest in the work of Spinoza, not only in Germany but throughout Europe – as witnessed by the English writer George Eliot's translation of Spinoza's *Ethics* and her depiction of Spinozist, proto-Zionist thought in her novel *Daniel Deronda* (1876).³ However, Spinoza's legacy became highly ambiguous, not only in Jacobi's depiction of Spinozism as posing the rationalist (i.e., atheistic) threat of modernity but also in the reception of literary representations of modern Jews. For future literary depictions of Jews, the image of Spinoza as the first modern Jew proved to be foundational.⁴

Even though Lessing's *Nathan the Wise* does not overtly question the validity of religion – he is certainly not an atheist – his ring parable blurs the distinctive boundaries separating different religions from one another. From Nathan's peace-loving, quasi-Spinozist, rationalist perspective, it is not the alternative dogmas and doctrine that matter but their interconnected love of one monotheist divinity that unites Judaism, Christianity and Islam, despite their competing claims. Similar to Spinoza in his *Theological-Political Treatise*, Lessing's Nathan argues that any claim to a superior form of revelation where one culture or community triumphs over another is nothing more than an anthropomorphic construction. Just as the ring – the metaphor for the claims of true religion – is the product of human fabrication, so are fractious claims to superiority of one religious community over another. Over against this conception of competition between religions, Nathan's wisdom manifests itself in his love of peace. Ultimately, he convinces the Sultan of the irrationality of religious claims to superiority by individual religions, encouraging instead consideration for the values of individual equality and cultural diversity. To restate this in late 19th-century terms, sectarian theology is abandoned to preserve true religion.

² Jason Josephson-Storm, *The Myth of Disenchantment: Magic, Modernity, and the Birth of the Human Sciences* (Chicago, IL, 2017), 70.
³ For a discussion of this topic, see Michael Mack, *Spinoza and the Specters of Modernity: The Hidden Enlightenment of Diversity from Spinoza to Freud* (New York, 2010), 168–187.
⁴ See Daniel B. Schwartz, *The First Modern Jew: Spinoza and the History of an Image*, (Princeton, NJ, 2012).

The promise of an Enlightened modernity that would realize the right of every individual to flourish in a diverse modern state, premised on the foundation of equality, was an appealing one, especially for those such as the marginalized Jewish philosopher Salomon Maimon (1753–1800), who attempted to pursue a rational life free from what he perceived to be the backwardness of superstition and feudalism in his native Poland by fleeing into Kantian rationalism, only to find himself snubbed by Immanuel Kant himself.

The publication of Maimon's autobiography (*Lebensbeschreibung*) in 1793 functioned for many as an ethnography of the Jews living in 18th-century Germany, as its editor – the writer Karl Philipp Moritz – made clear in his preface: "At a time like now, when the cultural education and enlightenment of the Jewish people has become a special topic of reflection, it [Maimon's *Autobiography*] is a work of close attention."[5] Significantly, Maimon, in the course of his reflections, countered anti-Jewish writings such as Johann A. Eisenmenger's influential *Entdecktes Judentum* (1711) and Immanuel Kant's charge against Judaism as a "religion without religion" (in his *Religion within the Boundaries of Pure Reason*, 1793). By this, Kant meant that Judaism lacked any intellectual or theological elements and was therefore exclusively driven by external values and oriented towards the "goods of this world."[6] Alternatively, Maimon depicts Jews as contemplative people: "the *theoretical*, theological part of Judaism managed to remain pure."[7] Yet, despite Lessing's, Maimon's and Mendelssohn's depiction of Judaism as a contemplative religion, particularly suitable for those who would participate in a modern state premised on equality and diversity, German anti-Semites during the 18th, 19th and 20th centuries increasingly represented Jews and Judaism as irrational, conspiratorial and tribal. They are imaged as a worldly, essentially non-ethical community, which was quasi-demonically rational and aimed to undermine Christianity and its traditions.

Liliane Weissberg has argued that Maimon's literary work perversely served as proof of the antisemitic stereotype of the secular, "worldly" Jew who, in almost diabolical fashion, sets out to conquer the world through his intelligence:

[5] K. P. von Moritz, "Editor's Preface," in S. Maimon, *The Autobiography of Salomon Maimon: Complete Translation*, ed. Yitzhak Y. Melamed and Abraham P. Socher, trans. Paul Reitter, with an afterword by Gideon Freudenthal (Princeton, NJ, 2019).

[6] See Michael Mack, *German Idealism and the Jew: The Inner Anti-Semitism of Philosophy and German Jewish Responses* (Chicago, IL, 2003), 23–42.

[7] Maimon, *The Autobiography*, 70.

A few years after his [Maimon's] death, Wilhelm Friedrich Grattenauer referred to Maimon in his pamphlet *Wider die Juden: Ein Wort der Warnung* (1803) and described him as a man "of sharp intelligence" ("mit grossen Scharfsinn"), who lacked practical wisdom as well as taste.... Grattenauer did not define poverty as a characteristic of the Jew, but a *Verstand* (reason, intelligence) that could be translated into wealth; his Verstand as *Scharfsinn* could turn, however, into the Jew's final downfall, as the term itself assumed the derogatory properties of an anti-Semitic slur.[8]

Importantly, later in the 19th century, Richard Wagner prominently incorporated the antisemitic conception of the worldly, smart, destructive, exploitative Jew in his opera *Ring of the Nibelungs*. Wagner indeed equated "the tragic ring of the Nibelungs" with the "stock-market portfolio that brings to completion the horrid picture of world domination."[9]

The topic of world domination would play a strikingly pernicious role in H. O. F. Goedsche's novel *Biarritz* (1868) and directly influence the legitimization of the infamous Czarist forgery, *The Protocols of the Elders of Zion* (1903). Goedsche, under cover of being a postal employee, worked for the Prussian secret service and published *Biarritz* under the pseudonym of Sir John Retcliffe.[10] Fiction here shapes historical reality posing as factual evidence. The movement from Goedsche's novel to the fabrication of *The Protocols of the Elders of Zion*, and then to the antisemitic propaganda role played by both texts within Nazi Germany, reveals the influential, deleterious effects that the antisemitism evident in German literature exerted on modern European history.

Likewise, Wagner's theme of Jewish world domination, which drives the action of his *Ring of the Nibelungs*, became a substantial and consequential theme in the demonization of the Jews in the 19th and 20th centuries.[11] Wagner used the symbol of the ring to paint the antisemitic image of "the Jew with the prosy stock-market bell" (*der Jude mit der papiernen Börseglocke*).[12] Whereas Goedsche was clearly

---

[8] Liliane Weissberg, "1792–93 Salomon Maimon Writes His *Lebensgeschichte* (Autobiography), a Reflection on His Life in the (Polish) East and the (German) West," in *Yale Companion to Jewish Writing and Thought in German Culture 1096–1996*, ed. Sander L. Gilman and Jack Zipes (New Haven, CT, 1997), 108–115.

[9] Richard Wagner, *Gesammelte Schriften*. vol. 14, ed. Julius Kapp (Leipzig, 1920), 186.

[10] *Biarritz: Historisch-Politischer Roman aus der Gegenwart* (Berlin, 1875).

[11] See David Levin, *Richard Wagner, Fritz Lang and the Nibelungen: The Dramaturgy of Disavowal.* (Princeton, NJ, 1998), and Mack, *German Idealism and the Jew*, 63–76.

[12] Wagner, *Gesammelte Schriften*, vol. 14, 189.

a reactionary, Wagner had been a socialist and therefore identified his fantasy of Jewish world domination with the stock market and capitalism. His antisemitic representation centered round contrasting Europe's purported rulers and those whom they are supposed to dominate, the latter being identified with the native peoples. Thus, in Wagner's literary fabrication, antisemitic representations are employed in order to dehumanize the Jews and depict them as both foreign and nefarious.

Wagner worked on the *Ring* cycle for nearly three decades, between 1848 and 1874, and its significance is widely evident in the representations of the late 19th century. Jews are described as satanic and engaged in a conspiracy for world domination. The pseudo-theological as well as pseudo-scientific preconditions for such highly harmful representations of a conspiracy – in which the Jews were depicted as being engaged – were set in motion through the late 18th century by attempts to characterize the Jews as a people of mundane, worldly and, in Kantian parlance, "heteronomous" (i.e., non-ethical) inclinations. As such, they were contrasted with the asserted Christian characteristics of a meaningful, otherworldly indifference to, and independence from, materialist interests and orientations.[13]

Other novels also contributed to this negative portrayal of Jews and Judaism. Wilhelm Hauff's (1802–1827) historical novel *Jud Süss* (*The Jew Seuss*) depicts in regional terms what would later in the 19th century, and then in the genocidal antisemitism of the Nazis, turn into the fiction of a global Jewish conspiracy for world domination. The work is based on the 18th-century German Jewish banker and financial advisor Joseph Seuss-Oppenheimer. Hauff's novel opens with an edict by the Duke of Württemberg that inexplicably absolves Jud Süss, "cabinet minister and director of finance" (*Kabinettsminister und Finanzdirektor*), "eternally from all responsibility of the past and the future."[14] Because we are not informed of any achievements that would explain the reasons for such an arbitrary act, Hauff represents Jud Süss as irrationally powerful and ill-willed. Indeed, Hauff's 1827 novel established the paradigm of how antisemitic representations in German literature contributed to the historical-political fantasy of a Jewish conspiracy to dominate and change nativist Christian societies.

---

[13] For detailed discussion of this point, see Mack, *German Idealism and the Jew*, 8, 17, 23–41, 76–80, 109–169.
[14] Hauff, *Sämtliche Werke*, vol. 2: *Novellen, Prosastücke, Briefe*, ed. Hermann Engelhard (Essen, 1981), 156.

In Hauff's story, such scheming for power remains local, confined to the land of Württemberg. However, once the Duke has granted special powers to Jud Süss the character of the whole region changes. Hauff has one of his Württemberg nativists complain about the uncanny, almost supernatural power that Jews represent: "since the Jews have become masters of the country, I soon want to become completely Jewish myself." To this exclamation another Württemberg native revealingly responds: "Wait for a few weeks, Hans, then you can become a good Catholic."[15] That is to say, Hauff's novel depicts such change of religion as the prime symptom of Jud Süss's conspiracy. The whole country suffers and as one Württemberg native complains, even the physical shape of its landscape has been distorted: "how this beautiful country is corrupted deep down to its inner heart."[16] The change of state religion from Protestantism to Catholicism represents the corruption that flows from a Jewish conspiracy for power. Sectarian theology overcomes true religion.

The edict that absolves Jud Süss from any responsibility grants him the authority to impose a change of belief or confession that confounds the region's (i.e., Württemberg's) native Protestantism by substituting Catholicism in its place: "they want to make Catholics out of us." In effect, this religious upheaval emerges as the symptom of the corruption of nativist customs and laws.[17] The "they" makes clear that the narrative does not blame Jud Süss alone for this degeneration. The Duke of Württemberg and all those who with him rule the regional country are also responsible for what was occurring.

Hauff's novel ends with the execution of Jud Süss. This ending may shed a different perspective on the opening of the novel in that it depicts Jud Süss as a scapegoat for the general corruption of those in power. Hauff does not simplify the problems that he touches upon, and at the close of his novel Jud Süss emerges as a victim who pays with his life for the corrupt government that controls Württemberg. Hauff represents the Jew as both perpetrator and victim. However, anticipating Wagner's antisemitic representations of the Jew as perpetrator, Hauff's Jud Süss is presented as possessing demonic, almost supernatural, features. Ruth Klüger has convincingly argued that Hauff's romantic depiction of Jud Süss is more balanced than the depiction of Jews in later 19th-century authors like Gustav Freytag (1816–1895), Theodor Fontane (1819–1898),

[15] Ibid., 165.
[16] Ibid., 186.
[17] Ibid., 191.

and Gustave Raabe (1866–1966), who represent Jews as agents of, but not as scapegoats for, the changes brought about by modernity.[18] Nevertheless, Hauff's story stands as the beginning of a distorted tradition that only gets worse as the 19th century unfolds.

However, not all portrayals of Jews were dark and presented in stereotypical images as dishonorable and destructive. For example, Adalbert Stifter's (1805–1868) novel *Abdias* (1841–1847) offers an instructive contrast to the antisemitic representation of Jews as demonized figures. As Mathias Mayer has shown, *Abdias* is Stifter's most modernist work because the narrative of the novel is discontinuous, highlighting contingency and the absence of order in terms of a disconnection between causes and effects.[19] What has so far been ignored in critical discussions of this novel is that its humanizing rather than dehumanizing representation of the African Jew Abdias goes hand in hand with perhaps the first German-language novelistic depiction of the benefits of immigration. Due to the hardship Abdias has to endure in his birthplace, he suddenly (without prior explanation for this move) emigrates from Africa to Europe.

Stifter's novel employs the notion of the "uncanny" or "monstrous" (*das Ungeheure*)[20] in ways that transcend the negative connotations of this and similar terms that are frequently employed to depict Jews as the epitome of what is alien or foreign. Stifter here turns representation against itself, showing in his narration that what we may have taken to be "uncanny" or threatening can actually be beneficial, and what appears to be disappointing may turn out to be promising.[21] Presenting Abdias in positive personal terms, possessing significant virtues, the novel closes with the benefits that Abdias's tough life has brought to the European region to which he emigrated: "The barren valley has from this time onwards [i.e., from when Abdias cultivated it] been fruitful."[22] So not all things Jewish are seen to be negative and despoiling, though the novel is still centrally concerned with the issue of the "Judaization" of Austrian society and culture.

---

[18] Ruth Klüger, *Katastrophen: Über deutsche Literatur* (Göttingen, 1994), 86–93.

[19] Mayer, *Adalbert Stifter: Erzählen als Erkennen* (Stuttgart, 2001).

[20] A. Stifter, *Gesammelte Werke: Novellen*, vol. 1, ed. Dietmar Grieser (Munich, 1982), 362.

[21] For a detailed discussion of literature's capacity to make us question and see anew what we thought to be representative, see Michael Mack, *How Literature Changes the Way We Think* (New York, 2011), 48–90.

[22] Stifter, *Gesammelte Werke: Novellen*, vol. 1, 459.

The literary representation of Jews as alien or foreign has deeply disturbing connotations, as J. P. Stern has shown to be the case in Stefan George's (1868–1933) poetry of the late Weimar Republic, in which he contrasts Jews and Germans:

> The contrasts of "blond and black issuing from one womb," of storm-swept northern cliff and burning desert from which, this pattern of racial antagonism is wrought, strikes us as sensational and crude.... But history is on George's side, for once he really is prophetic. Less than two decades after these poems [i.e., the poems contrasting Jews and Germans in the poetry collection *Der Stern des Bundes*] were written, the lurid contrast ceased to be poetic invention.[23]

Unfortunately, since the Shoah, as Ruth Klüger has argued, the literary representation of Jews has continued to be shaped by what she calls the Shylock paradigm and which she distinguishes from that of Lessing's *Nathan the Wise*.[24] In a most disturbing way, post–World War II German writers, from Günther Grass to Rainer Fassbinder and Martin Walser, have represented Jews along the lines of Shakespeare's Shylock as both victims and perpetrators. This ambiguous representation comes clearly to the fore in, for example, Walser's 2002 novel *Der Tod eines Kritikers (Death of a Critic)*. Walser's work ambiguously describes the fictional murder of a German Jewish literary critic, André Ehrl-König (a satire on the celebrity Jewish critic Marcel Reich-Ranicki), that involves arson and is clearly depicted as a hate crime, pointing to the fact that Germany is not a proper home for the Jews in the eyes of the non-Jewish population.[25] In contemporary antisemitic representations – and there is intense debate regarding whether Walser, who readily uses familiar anti-Jewish stereotypes and characterizations, is an anti-Semite – Jews are yet again portrayed as both alien and demonic. Reich-Ranicki denounced the novel as such, and the question of Walser's resurrection of antisemitic images even after the fall of the Berlin wall (1989), stereotypes still embedded in readers' memories from the Third Reich, condemned him as outside the bounds of acceptable behavior.

[23] Stern, *The Dear Purchase: A Theme in German Modernism* (Cambridge, 1995), 226.
[24] Klüger, *Katastrophen*, 8–29.
[25] Seligman, "Walser der Brandstifter," *Rheinische Post*, May 30, 2002, 12.

Further Reading

Eco, U., *The Prague Cemetery*, trans. Richard Dixon (London, 2010). Historical thriller about how the chapter entitled "The Prague Cemetery" in Goedsche's novel *Biarritz* became the basis for the conspiracy theories propounded in *The Protocols of the Elders of Zion*.

Gilman, S. L., *The Jew's Body* (London, 1999). Detailed analysis of how antisemitic fictions have informed pseudo-scientific medical and popular culture in the German speaking sphere from 1800 to 1945.

Gilman, S. L., and J. Zipes, eds., *Yale Companion to Jewish Writing and Thought in German Culture, 1096–1996* (New Haven, CT, 1997). Contains a variety of highly readable short essays on key issues and events related to antisemitic stereotyping from the 18th century to the end of the 20th century.

Kafka, F., *The Castle*, trans. J. A. Underwood, with an introduction by I. Parry (London, 1997). In quasi-allegorical form, Kafka's 1926 novel depicts the ways in which the antisemitic stereotyping of Jews as strangers determines the protagonist Joseph K.'s experience of being vilified, demonized and excluded by society.

Lessing, G. E., *Nathan the Wise*, trans. E. Kemp (New York, 2004). Spinoza-inspired drama depicting, via Nathan's famous ring parable, the equality of different religions and cultures.

Mack, M., *German Idealism and the Jew: The Inner Anti-Semitism of Philosophy and German Jewish Responses* (Chicago, IL, 2003). Analyzes the pseudo-theological foundations of pseudo-scientific antisemitism in German literature with a focus on Wagner's idealist and socialist antisemitism.

Mendes-Flohr, P., and J. Reinharz, eds., *The Jew in the Modern World: A Documentary History* (Oxford, 1995). Provides an English translation of key documents of German antisemitic literature (such as Wagner's essay "Judaism in Music"). It also contains illuminating introductions and helpful commentary to the translated texts.

20C Antisemitism in Modern Literature and Theater: English Literature

BRYAN CHEYETTE

It was not until 1656 that Jews were officially re-admitted back into Britain under Cromwell's protectorate after being expelled in 1290. During this long absence Geoffrey Chaucer, Christopher Marlowe and William Shakespeare all made Jewish devil-figures part of their literary corpus. These canonical villains have had an enormous influence on how we think of antisemitism in English literature. After all, Chaucer's *Prioress's Tale* (1392) reinforced the medieval blood libel by evoking the "yonge Hugh of Lyncoln" ritual murder story – supposedly "slayn" by "cursed Jewes" – which was popular 150 years before Chaucer's tale was written. Shakespeare, in *The Merchant of Venice* (1600), introduced the world to Shylock and his vengeful desire for a "pound of flesh" from the Christian Antonio. This was to be removed with "extreme cruelty" according to the earliest title page. Marlowe, in a reprise of the medieval morality play tradition, has Barabas in *The Jew of Malta* (1590) replicate every devilish feature of heinous Jews with his red hair, red beard and artificial nose. Friar Jacomo in Act III asks casually of Barabas's whereabouts, "What, has he crucified a child?" But the melodramatic Barabas had already listed a range of his depraved activities in Act II:

> As for myself I walk abroad o'nights
> And kill sick people groaning under walls:
> Sometimes I go about and poison wells;
> And now and then, to cherish Christian thieves,
> I am content to lose some of my crowns,
> That I may, walking in my gallery,
> See 'em go pinion'd along my door.

His "usury" is said to "fill the gaols with bankrupts in a year" but such monstrous boasts and self-conscious villainy are nothing more than an exercise in sensational rhetoric and formulaic horror. Such anti-Jewish fantasies would have been familiar to Elizabethan audiences. The sermons of the poet John Donne, a near contemporary of these audiences, argued that Jews "always keep in readiness the blood of some Christian." As James Shapiro has shown, issues of religious dissimulation – where some forms of Protestantism were deemed to be indistinguishable from an abject Judaism – were a rhetorical feature of the Reformation throughout the 16th century.[1]

But it would be a mistake to assume that Chaucer, Marlowe and Shakespeare originated a single-minded tradition of literary Jew-hatred. Medieval English culture included a wide variety of Jewish images which ranged from venerated Hebrews to reviled child-killers. Such varied images are understandable when we note that Christianity, from its origins, both desired the conversion of "the Jews" to redeem humankind and, equally, gained authority by transcending the supposedly debased Jew. The *Prioress's Tale*, for instance, includes the "new Rachel," the mother of the miraculous "boy singer," who reveals his whereabouts after he is murdered by bursting into pious hymn-singing. In one short tale we have Jewish child-slayers and Rachel, a "beautiful Jewess" (who was said to have anticipated Christ), who is as much a part of medieval morality plays as her villainous counterparts. Shylock's daughter Jessica reaffirms this salvific tradition as does Barabas's daughter Abigail, who is "matchless beautiful." But this divide was not just along the lines of youth and gender. Shylock's famous speech in Act III – "Hath not a Jew eyes? Hath not a Jew hands, organs, dimensions, senses, affections, passions?" – undoubtedly humanized the devil-figure. The many dimensions of Shylock, in stark contrast to the one-dimensional cartoonish Barabas, were reinforced in the hundreds of stage versions of *The Merchant of Venice* from the 18th century onwards.

Most literary historians agree that *The Merchant of Venice*, which remains one of Shakespeare's most popular plays on stage, occupies a "critical position" when it comes to portraying Jews in English literature. Writers who referred to the play over more than a century, when thinking about Jews, included Sir Walter Scott, Maria Edgeworth, Charles Dickens, George Eliot, James Joyce and T. S. Eliot.[2] The influence and authority of Shylock is extraordinary given that he appears in only five scenes of a romantic comedy. But his ambiguity – Is his conversion forced? Are the Christians irredeemably superficial? Is he

---

[1] James Shapiro, *Shakespeare and the Jews* (New York, 1995), 2 and chap. 1.
[2] Michael Ragussis, *Figures of Conversion: "The Jewish Question" and English National Identity* (Durham, NC, 1995), 58 and chap. 2.

on the side of justice or vengeance? Is he, in Portia's words, "the merchant" or "the Jew"? – meant that he could be portrayed in myriad ways. Many great actors gained fame and fortune for their singular interpretation of Shylock, such as Charles Macklin's malignant rendering in the mid- to late 18th century, Edmund Kean's romantic version (seen by Samuel Taylor Coleridge, Lord George Byron, Percy Bysshe Shelley and John Keats) in the early 19th century, or Henry Irving's mid- to late 19th-century depiction of Shylock as a sympathetic victim. By the 18th century, the character of Shylock transcended the play and became a free-floating symbol of what it was to be "exotic," "Hebraic," "oriental" and, above all, a "Jew."[3]

As Shakespeare epitomizes, the founding fathers of English literature bequeathed not a series of unchanging Jewish hate figures but a range of possible attitudes to Jews and Judaism. By the time of the "Jewish Naturalization Act" (or "Jew Bill") of 1753 the rhetoric of Jews as abject others – alien, "black," parasitical – was the stuff of party politics. This ensured that a range of negative images and representations of Jews and Judaism (the malevolent Shylock) were carried over into the 19th century. But, at the same time, a counter-narrative was popularized in the form of the legend of the Wandering Jew. This was taken up by English romantic poets and novelists and offered an alternative version of Jewish difference. The Wandering Jew, known as Ahasuerus, began in the medieval period as a figure cursed with immortality. One version of the legend has Ahasuerus the shoe-maker refusing Jesus a place to rest on his march to Calvary while carrying the cross. As a result Ahasuerus is sentenced by God for eternity to roam over the face of the earth.[4]

This legend was well known during the early modern period, and the cult of Ahasuerus, at its height, was conspicuous by the turn of the 19th century. Romantic poets in Britain and Germany especially thought of the Wandering Jew (akin to the exiled Shylock) as a counterpart for their own sense of timeless alienation from authority. In Britain, most prominently, M. G. Lewis's *The Monk* (1795); Shelley's *Queen Mab* (1813), *The Wandering Jew's Soliloquy* (n.d.) and *Hellas* (1822); Byron's *Cain* (1821); and William Wordsworth's *Song of the*

---

[3] John Gross, *Shylock: Four Hundred Years in the Life of a Legend* (London, 1994), chaps. 8–10. See also Linda Rozmovits, *Shakespeare and the Politics of Culture in Late Victorian England* (Baltimore, MD, 1998).

[4] Galit Hasan-Rokem and Alan Dundes, eds., *The Wandering Jew: Essays in the Interpretation of a Christian Legend* (Bloomington, IN, 1986).

Wandering Jew (1800) all utilized this legend.[5] In *Hellas*, Ahasuerus reveals immutable truths in an age of revolutionary change:

> What has thought
> To do with time, or place, or circumstance,
> Wouldst thou behold the future? Ask and have!
> Knock and it shall be opened – look, and lo!
> The coming age is shadowed on the past
> As on a glass.

The Wandering Jew, in this rendering, is a figure of enduring wisdom. Such tragic nobility was possible only by humanizing Ahasuerus and detaching him from his Christian roots. Ahasuerus – sorrowful, suffering and a victim of divine punishment – was a romantic self-image. Byron's *Cain* and *The Hebrew Melodies* (1815/1824) revived biblical Hebraism for a contemporary audience. The best-known account of the congruence between Englishness, Hebraism and romanticism is Lionel Trilling's "Wordsworth and the Rabbis" (1950). Here Trilling compares Wordsworth's attitude to nature and the rabbinic attitude to the Hebrew Bible, which is characterized equally as "the passionate contemplation and experience of the great object which is proximate to Deity."[6] For Trilling, at least, the alignment between English literature and Hebraism was complete.

But such alignments tell only part of the story. There were also popular images of Jews and Judaism which were utterly opposed to such timeless wisdom. Such doubleness was captured by Coleridge in 1833:

> The two images furthest removed from each other which I can comprehend under one term are Isaiah – "Hear, O heavens, and give ear, O earth!" – and Levi of Holywell Street – "Old Clothes!" – both of them Jews, you'll observe.[7]

It was the ambivalent figure of "the Jew" – messianic and abject, biblical and quotidian – that influenced much 19th-century literature. By

---

[5] Michael Scrivener, *Jewish Representations in British Literature, 1780–1840: After Shylock* (New York, 2011); and Sheila A. Spector, ed., *British Romanticism and the Jews* (New York, 2002).

[6] Lionel Trilling, *The Opposing Self: Nine Essays in Criticism* (New York, 1955), 128. See also Judith W. Page, *Imperfect Sympathies: Jews and Judaism in British Romantic Literature and Culture* (New York, 2004).

[7] "Quakers, Philanthropists, Jews, Epistle to the Romans: August 14, 1833," in *The Table Talk and Omniana of Samuel Taylor Coleridge*, ed. T. Ashe (London, 1888), 244.

1830 there were no more than 25,000 Jews in Britain (out of a population of around 14 million). While a visible number of Jews were itinerant peddlers ("old clothes men"), most were acculturated. Coleridge's Jews, as he shows, were as much a product of textual genealogy as of real-life experience.

Maria Edgeworth's *Harrington* (1819) is a prime example of a novel which engages with the difference between real and imaginary Jews. *Harrington* is written to "atone" after Rachel Mordecai wrote to Edgeworth about the antisemitism in her earlier work for children (Mordecai could also have included three of Edgeworth's previous novels).[8]

The eponymous hero of the novel becomes aware of his own parental-inspired prejudices when he falls in love with Berenice Montenero, whom he assumes to be of a Sephardic (or Spanish) Jewish background following her father's origins. Edgeworth introduces *The Merchant of Venice* into the novel to demonstrate the way in which antisemitism has been transmitted across the generations: "Wherever the Jews are introduced, I find that they are invariably represented as beings of a mean, avaricious, unprincipled, treacherous character."[9] Harrington both falls in love with Montenero and sees how upset she is by Shakespeare's play. Nonetheless, he does not transcend his blinkered assumptions about Jews. He imagines that Montenero, following Jessica, is in need of conversion. But it turns out that she was raised as an Anglican by her Jewish father after the death of her Christian mother.

At the end of the novel, the prejudices of Harrington's parents are reinforced. After hearing of Montenero's upbringing they reaffirm that they always thought that the Jewish woman "looked like a Christian" (as if anyone can "look" like a Christian). They also argue that only a "good Christian" could forgive their enemies in the way that Montenero's father forgives those who falsely accused him of murder. But Montenero's final retort, "and why not a good Jew?" echoes back through the pages of the novel.[10] *Harrington* is set between the anti-Jewish bigotry of the "Jew Bill" (1753) and the anti-Catholic bigotry of the Gordon Riots (1780) which, as Susan Manly argues, associates the recent history of England with "illiberality, xenophobia and deliberate

---

[8] Maria Edgeworth, *Moral Tales for Young People* (1801). See also *Castle Rackrent* (1800), *Belinda* (1801) and *The Absentee* (1812).

[9] Edgeworth, *Harrington* [1817], ed. Susan Manly (London, 2004), 83.

[10] *Harrington*, 291 and 295.

acts of injustice."[11] Being a "good Christian" in these circumstances is denuded of meaning. No longer is a "good Jew" merely a Christian convert.

As Michael Ragussis has argued, many Victorian novels found alternatives to the "ideology of conversion" and, instead, allowed Jewish characters a sense of autonomy outside Christian orthodoxy.[12] Sir Walter Scott's best-selling novel *Ivanhoe* (1819) was the foremost example of this trend. The moneylender Isaac of York and his noble and beautiful daughter Rebecca (following Shylock and Jessica in *The Merchant of Venice*) are openly critical of a "barbarous" England: "The Jews can cure wounds, though we deal not in inflicting them." According to Rebecca, the English were such a "fierce race" that it was not possible for her or her father to remain.[13] Instead, they move to Spain, which is depicted as a more suitable location for such exotic characters. Scott's new English nation, based on the founding myth of reconciling ruling Normans and oppressed Saxons, supposedly transcends a corrupt aristocratic culture that fueled both domestic racial conflict and bloodthirsty crusades. But the embodiment of such liberal tolerance, and also its prophet, turns out to be the eroticized Rebecca, whose refusal (with her father) to convert and stay in England influenced literary texts throughout the century.[14]

The tension between tolerance and exclusion anticipates the two sides of the Jewish emancipation debate (whether Jews should be excluded or not from the nation) which took place between the 1830s and 1850s. The essayist William Hazlitt made the liberal case for the "emancipation of the Jews" by arguing that Jewish emancipation was "but a natural step in the progress of civilization" which would oppose the "prejudice" and "intolerance" of an illiberal England rooted in the past.[15] Charles Dickens, paradoxically, agreed with these arguments but published *The Adventures of Oliver Twist* (1837–39), his second novel, which reinforced the case for Jewish exclusion more than any other

---

[11] *Harrington,* "Introduction," 46.

[12] Ragussis, *Figures of Conversion,* 3.

[13] Sir Walter Scott, *Ivanhoe: A Romance* [1819] (Harmondsworth: Penguin, 1982), 301 and 516.

[14] Nadia Valman, *The Jewess in Nineteenth-Century British Literary Culture* (Cambridge, 2007), chap. 1. See also Cynthia Scheinberg, *Women's Poetry and Religion in Victorian England: Jewish Identity and Christian Culture* (Cambridge, 2002).

[15] William Hazlitt, "The Emancipation of the Jews," *The Tatler,* March 28, 1831, 461–65.

single work of fiction. The figure of Fagin, in particular, reprised the medieval Jew-devil figure (following Barabas and more contemporary stage melodramas) with his "matted red hair," "grizzled red beard" and "perfectly demoniacal" visage.[16] At times Fagin or "the Jew" (as he is known throughout until the 1867 revisions to the novel) is less a person than a "hideous phantom" whose descent into bestiality epitomizes retrogression and degeneracy:

> As he glided stealthily along, creeping beneath the shelter of the walls and doorways, the hideous old man seemed like some loathsome reptile, engendered in the slime and darkness through which he moved: crawling forth, by night, in search of some rich offal for a meal.[17]

When Oliver Twist is first left alone with Fagin, "the Jew" indicates that he might cut the throat of his new occupant with a bread knife. As Frank Felsenstein has noted, "the innuendo of the blood libel is unmistakable."[18] Fagin, in both appearance and behavior, is a medieval bogeyman who abducts Christian children, violates their innocence and even threatens to ritually murder them.

Fagin intends to "blacken" and "change the hue" of Oliver's soul "forever," and the novel is never quite sure whether the forces of individual and national advancement will be enough to save Oliver.[19] The novel is a typically Dickensian *Bildungsroman* with the young orphan finding his way through darkest London (especially the East End) to eventual safety and growth in the English suburbs. And yet, even when he finds relative comfort, there are times when the traumatic memories of Fagin undermine his upward mobility: "Suddenly the scene changed; the air became closed and confined; and [Oliver] thought, with a glow of terror, that he was in the Jew's house again."[20] Like Shylock, Fagin is an isolated figure who is associated mainly with "confined" spaces, not least the prison cell ("No Escape") before his

---

[16] Charles Dickens, *The Adventures of Oliver Twist* [1837–39], ed. Kathleen Tillotson (Oxford, 1966), 50.

[17] Dickens, *The Adventures of Oliver Twist*, 120–21.

[18] Frank Felsenstein, *Anti-Semitic Stereotypes: A Paradigm of Otherness in English Popular Culture, 1660–1830* (Baltimore, MD, 1995), 243. See also Heidi Kaufman, *English Origins, Jewish Discourse and the Nineteenth-Century British Novel* (University Park, PA, 2009), 100–104.

[19] Dickens, *The Adventures of Oliver Twist*, 147.

[20] Ibid., 272.

hanging. His final refusal to accept Christian or Jewish charity separates him from the rest of society and those who once knew him.

By the end of the novel, Oliver, schooled by his new bourgeois family, calls Fagin "the Jew" repeatedly to indicate the distance between them. The fossilized Fagin is no longer an impediment to growth and modernity. His benign equivalent, as Nadia Valman argues, is Rebecca in *Ivanhoe*, whose "mystical assertions of religious loyalty" stand in "opposition to the principles of conciliation and historical progress."[21]

Not unlike Edgeworth's philosemitic revisionism in *Harrington*, Dickens, after complaints from Eliza Davis, eventually made amends for the figure of Fagin. The saintly Mr. Riah in *Our Mutual Friend* (1864–65) was a "venerable man" "long of skirt, and wide of pocket" and also the antidote to Fagin.[22] Davis had accused Dickens of encouraging a "vile prejudice against the despised Hebrew" as Fagin "admits only one interpretation."[23] But, ironically, the insulated Riah admits only a single interpretation as a figure of unmitigated virtue. By playing the role of the Shylockian usurer, for the villainous Fascinating Fledgeby, Riah rightly notes that: "If doing what I was content to do here ... I had been a Christian, I could have done it, compromising no one but my individual self. But doing it as a Jew, I could not choose but compromise the Jews of all conditions and all countries."[24] Riah is both as solitary and as representative as Fagin.

Most Jewish characters in 19th-century fiction veered between these two types, malign or benign, masculine or feminine ("long of skirt"), medieval or modern. William Makepeace Thackeray has a large cast of Jewish characters in his fiction and travel books, but they all tend to be marginal figures having little effect on society as a whole.[25] Anthony Trollope, in contrast, places Jews at the heart of many of his later novels largely because of his hatred of Benjamin Disraeli (a Jewish convert to Anglicanism at the age of twelve), who held political office, including Prime Minister, from the 1860s to the 1880s. But Trollope's

---

[21] Valman, *The Jewess in Nineteenth-Century British Literary Culture*, 30.

[22] Charles Dickens, *Our Mutual Friend* [1864], ed. Stephen Gill (Harmondsworth, 1973), 328.

[23] Cited in Murray Baumgarten, "Seeing Double: Jews in the Fiction of F. Scott Fitzgerald, Charles Dickens, Anthony Trollope and George Eliot," in *Between "Race" and Culture: Representations of "the Jew" in English and American Literature*, ed. Bryan Cheyette (Stanford, CA, 1996), 51 and 44–54.

[24] Dickens, *Our Mutual Friend*, 795–96.

[25] S. S. Prawer, *Israel at Vanity Fair: Jews and Judaism in the Writings of W. M. Thackeray* (Leiden, 1992).

fiction included as many benign Jewesses – such as the eponymous Nina Balatka or Madame Max Goesler in the Palliser series – as powerful Jewish financiers or politicians. By the 1870s, he could rely on his reader's prejudices to identify the "Jewish" characteristics of Augustus Melmotte, the non-Jewish corrupter-in-chief in *The Way We Live Now* (1875).[26]

George Eliot's *Daniel Deronda* (1876) encapsulates just how ambivalent Jewish figures were in the literature of the 19th century. The novel looks back to *Ivanhoe* and prefigures the modernism of James Joyce's *Ulysses* (1922). Eliot's novel is structured around two competing Jewish narratives, one on the side of "race" and nation, the other on the side of art and culture. In this she followed Matthew Arnold's juxtaposing the cultural categories of Hebraism and Hellenism with the racial categories of Semite and Aryan in his *Culture and Anarchy: An Essay in Political and Social Criticism* (1869). That is why *Daniel Deronda* moves from denationalized Leubronn – a fictional city with "Jew dealers" which opens the novel – to the final racially determined vision of a future "Jewish" nation in Palestine. Mordecai and Mirah look to a singular Jewish nationalism, whereas the pianist Klesmer and the opera singer Halm-Eberstein (Deronda's estranged mother) are "wandering" artists.[27] Deronda and Gwendolen move from living as aimless cosmopolitans to a sense of redemptive nationalism in Palestine, for Deronda, and in England, for Gwendolen. By the end of the novel, however, their stories have hardly begun.

Daniel Deronda, following *Ivanhoe*, is full of contradictions. Its plot, in short, is that Jews have to leave England in order to demonstrate the importance of a curative nationalism (or revamped Hebraism) which their British birthplace needs to emulate. What is more, Eliot is assiduous in representing a spectrum of Jews from the mystical Mordecai and the angelic Mirah to those in favor of national equality such as Pash (a "small, dark, vivacious, triple-baked Jew") and the "mongrel" looking pawn-broker, Ezra Cohen, with his "oily cheerfulness."[28] What form national redemption takes is not resolved in the novel. Is it the romantic singularity of Mordecai and Mirah or the civic pluralism of Klesmer and Halm-Eberstein? The one thing that the novel is sure of is that an excess

---

[26] Jonathan Freedman, *The Temple of Culture: Assimilation and Anti-Semitism in Literary Anglo-America* (New York, 2000), chap. 2.

[27] George Eliot, *Daniel Deronda* [1876], ed. Barbara Hardy (Harmondsworth, 1986), 48 and 284.

[28] Eliot, *Daniel Deronda*, 562 and 581.

of rationalism and spirit-less materialism (Pash's call for universalism or Cohen's empty money-making) are precisely what needs redeeming. When the liberal Pash expresses a belief in equal citizenship, or "Jewish emancipation," Mordecai responds with the following:

> What is the citizenship of him who walks among a people he has no hearty kindred and fellowship with, and has lost the sense of brotherhood with his own race?... He is an alien in spirit, whatever he may be in form; he sucks the blood of mankind, he is not a man.[29]

From a nationalist perspective, reinforced by the growth of racial antisemitism from the 1870s onwards, Jews were increasingly castigated as alien blood-suckers who were less than human and no longer deemed worthy of citizenship. With a loss of faith in "Jewish emancipation" as a solution to the "Jewish Question," as *Daniel Deronda* illustrates, Jews were left vulnerable as citizens. No longer are the values of modernity or liberal progress enough. The figure of Deronda shows the limitations of the realist novel and the *Bildungsroman*, as his story remains incomplete with his character left rather formless, not unlike the redemptive nationalism which shapes his future.

Other cruder novelists, such as George du Maurier, chose gothic melodrama rather than realism as a way of grasping Jewish indeterminacy. The figure of Svengali in *Trilby* (1894) is both a dazzling musical genius and a sexually rapacious, racial interloper. But, unlike Fagin, whom Svengali resembles greatly, there is no longer an alternative set of modernizing values in the novel to challenge him. Du Maurier's vulnerable heroine Trilby is utterly determined by Svengali's voraciousness and artistic virtuosity as if society could not progress beyond these unleashed desires.[30]

By the 20th century, the Jew had bifurcated to such an extent that a range of alternative perspectives to mainstream liberalism incorporated figurative Jews. To name just a few of the ambivalent oppositions in English literature up until the 1940s: Jews are represented imaginatively as *both* a bastion of empire *and* one of the main threats to empire; as prefiguring a socialist world state *and* as a key force preventing its development; as the ideal economic man *and* the degenerate plutocrat; as the modern alienated artist *and* the incarnation of a

---

[29] Eliot, *Daniel Deronda*, 587.
[30] Freedman, *The Temple of Culture*, chap. 3; and Daniel Pick, *Svengali's Web: The Alien Enchanter in Modern Culture* (London, 2000).

corrupt worldliness. Writers who exemplified these contradictions include Rudyard Kipling, John Buchan and Rider Haggard in their novels and stories of Empire; George Bernard Shaw and H. G. Wells in their dramas, histories and fictions which imagine a socialist future; and G. K. Chesterton and Hilaire Belloc in their fiction and histories which associated conspiratorial Jewish financiers with the decay of European civilization.[31]

But the group of writers who engaged with the figurative Jew most creatively were the modernists of the first half of the 20th century. These included T. S. Eliot, Wyndham Lewis and Ezra Pound, who veered toward fascism, and Djuna Barnes, James Joyce, Dorothy Richardson and Virginia Woolf, who opposed authoritarianism. The political differences, not least their relationship to antisemitism, was clear to each modernist writer. An authoritarian modernist such as Eliot viewed "the Jew" as a figure of confusion defying all categories, such as the lower-case "jew" who "squats on the window-sill, the owner" in the 1920 poem "Gerontion." Eliot's "jew," in condensed form, is a creature who "squats" as well as who "owns" society, and both versions of "the jew" can only look into the house of Christendom as an outsider from the "window-sill." It was "free-thinking," boundary-crossing Jews that Eliot castigated as they diluted the "European mind" and confused the vital affiliation between "tradition and the individual talent":

> The population should be homogenous; where two or more cultures exist in the same place they are likely either to be fiercely self-conscious or both to become adulterate. What is still more important is unity of religious backgrounds; and reasons of race and religion combine to make any large number of free-thinking Jews undesirable. There must be a proper balance between urban and rural, industrial and agricultural development. And a spirit of excessive tolerance is to be deprecated.[32]

Here we have the fundamental opposition in Eliot's political thought between heretical "free-thinking Jews" and a "homogenous" Christian "unity." What is crucial to Eliot's political aesthetic is the all-important connection between his ideal of using "the right word in the right place" and his political quest to encourage "the great majority of human beings

---

[31] Bryan Cheyette, *Constructions of "the Jew" in English Literature and Society: Racial Representations, 1875–1945* (Cambridge, 1995), chaps. 3–5.

[32] David E. Chinitz, ed., *The Blackwell Companion to T. S. Eliot* (Oxford, 2009), 335–50; and T. S. Eliot, *After Strange Gods: A Primer of Modern Heresy* (1934), 20.

[to] go on living in the place in which they were born."[33] The search for clarity and order on the level of both language and society was crucial for Eliot, and, in these terms, the figure of "the Jew" embodies boundary-crossing disorder and uncertainty.

Unlike Eliot, Joyce embraced the transgressive confusion of the "greekjewish" Leopold Bloom at the heart of *Ulysses*. Bloom was Joyce's equivalent to the militaristic Ulysses but could not have been more different from his mythic counterpart. *Ulysses* was written during the First World War (1914–18), and the Irish war for independence (1919–21), with a sense of heightened nationalism in both Europe and Ireland. Joyce was to subvert such nationalism by locating at the heart of his European mock-epic a "new womanly man," a pacifist and a non-Jewish "Jew" who challenged national and religious certainties. He was well aware of the difference between his politics and those of more authoritarian modernists: "The more I hear of the political, philosophical, ethical zeal and labors of the brilliant members of Pound's big brass band, the more I wonder why I was ever let into it 'with my magic flute.'"[34]

There were modernists, such as Eliot, D. H. Lawrence, Lewis, and Pound, who wished to impose distinct boundaries between Hebrew and Hellene, Aryan and Semite, male and female. This was mainly a masculine tradition ("the men of 1914"), whereas feminist modernists ("the women of 1928"), such as Barnes, Mina Loy, Richardson, and Woolf, embraced the fluidity and transgressive assumptions associated with the figurative Jew.[35] More often than not the images of Jews used in all of these modernist works conformed to conventional discourses of Jewish difference. But authoritarian modernists *reinforced* a sense of difference, whereas transgressive modernists *undermined* such differences.

As George Orwell recognized in his essay on "Antisemitism in Britain" (1945), "there has been a perceptible antisemitic strain in English literature from Chaucer onwards." Orwell included his contemporary Aldous Huxley in his list of "antisemitic" writers, but he could also have included his own fiction.[36] A few other writers were astute

[33] Cited in Maud Ellmann, "The Imaginary Jew: T. S. Eliot and Ezra Pound," in Cheyette, ed., *Between "Race" and Culture*, 90 and 84–101.

[34] Letter to Harriet Shaw Weaver, 2 December 1928, in *The Letters of James Joyce*, vol. 1, ed. Richard Ellmann (London, 1966), 277.

[35] Maren Tova Linett, *Modernism, Feminism, and Jewishness* (Cambridge, 2007).

[36] George Orwell, "Antisemitism in Britain" (1945), in *The Collected Essays, Journalism and Letters of George Orwell: 1943–1945*, 3 vols., ed. Sonia Orwell and Ian Angus (London, 1970), vol. 3, 385. See also Lyndsey Stonebridge, *Placeless People: Writing, Rights and Refugees* (Oxford, 2018), chap. 3.

enough to recognize their own antisemitism after the Second World
War. Graham Greene, for instance, followed Edgeworth and Dickens,
by editing out phrases such as "the Jew" or "the Semite" from his
fiction.[37] But antisemitic images are so ingrained in English culture that
it has been passed down through the generations, as the case of Kingsley
and Martin Amis illustrates. Martin Amis distinguished, in an interview, between his own pronounced philosemitism and his father's literary antisemitism. Both father and son, he tells us, considered Jews to be
"exotic and different." As a result, Martin Amis ended up liking Jews,
whereas Kingsley Amis disliked them.[38] As both father and son are two
of the most characteristic English writers of their generation, one
should not underestimate this statement.

What has been called "civil" antisemitism continues to exist in
contemporary culture, but, as Kingsley and Martin Amis show, it does
not take the form of a monolithic or unchanging hatred.[39] Margaret
Drabble's novel *The Witch of Exmoor* (1996), for instance, characterizes
Nathan Herz, a middle-aged advertising executive, as both "attractive"
and "gross" but, above all, irrevocably different:

> At weekends he overflows into a kind of uncontrolled, deliberate
> grossness. He is crudely and aggressively Jewish: his large fleshy
> nose and his broad fingers, his large dark eyes speak of a rich and
> oriental world he has never visited, a world a thousand miles from
> East Finchley. Hairs sprout, at the weekends, unrestrained from his
> chest. They sprout all year round, day and night, from his ears and
> nostrils and the backs of his hands. Women long to stroke his chest,
> though as far as he knows they do not long to tweak at his nostrils.
> He is an attractive man and he knows it.[40]

Although women find him attractive, Herz is the first to think of
money when his mother-in-law (or the "Witch of Exmoor") is about
to die. He is also involved in "the selling and packaging of England"
and has "the trading instincts of his ancestors." All of these

---

[37] Andrea Freud Loewenstein, *Loathsome Jews and Engulfing Women: Metaphors of
Projection in the Works of Wyndham Lewis, Charles Williams, and Graham Greene*
(New York, 1993), chap. 6.

[38] Martin Amis, "An Arrow Fired backwards Can Still Hit the Target," *Jewish
Chronicle*, 4 October 1991, 19; and Kingsley Amis, *Stanley and the Women*
(London, 1984).

[39] Lara Trubowitz, *Civil Antisemitism, Modernism and British Culture, 1902–1939*
(New York, 2012).

[40] Margaret Drabble, *The Witch of Exmoor* (New York, 1996), 17.

statements – not to mention his overly hirsute body, "large fleshy nose," "dark eyes" and the "oriental world" from whence his ancestors came – could have been part of any English novel with Jewish characters published since the 18th century.

Such exotic and different figures need not be objects of hatred but do leave open the possibilities of exclusion, as Didi Herman has shown in her study of post–Second World War English case law and racialized discourses about Jews in the 20th and 21st centuries.[41] More recently, the "antisemitism" of the Labour Party has shown how constructing Jews as desirable or undesirable, depending on their perceived goodness or badness, is a convention that continues to the present day.[42] Such bifurcations were once used in 19th-century debates concerning Jewish emancipation, then about the mass migration into Britain from Eastern Europe between 1880 and 1920, and finally about excluding Jews from government and national institutions in the interwar period. Only "good," desirable Jews would be welcomed by the state, and many thousands, not fitting this criterion, were repatriated. Modern English literature, with very few exceptions, has reinforced such binary thinking.

Further Reading

Cheyette, B., *Constructions of "the Jew" in English Literature and Society: Racial Representations, 1875–1945* (Cambridge, 1993). A still influential analysis of antisemitism in liberal culture with reference to a wide range of English literature from the late 19th century to the 1940s.

Felsenstein, F., *Anti-Semitic Stereotypes: A Paradigm of Otherness in English Popular Culture, 1660–1830* (Baltimore, MD, 1995). This heavily researched book provides a contextual overview of English Jew-hatred from the restoration to the romantic period.

Freedman, J., *The Temple of Culture: Assimilation and Anti-Semitism in Literary Anglo-America* (New York, 2000). An original and creative account of transatlantic literary antisemitism in the long 20th century.

Kaufman, H., *English Origins, Jewish Discourse and the Nineteenth-Century British Novel* (University Park, PA, 2009). This study explores the conflict between religious and racial definitions of "the Jew" in relation to 19th-century English literature.

Linett, M. T., *Modernism, Feminism, and Jewishness* (Cambridge, 2007). The first book-length study to bring together modernism and feminism in relation to British literary antisemitism.

---

[41] Didi Herman, *An Unfortunate Coincidence: Jews, Jewishness and English Law* (Oxford, 2011).

[42] Cheyette, "Twenty-Five Years After," www.cambridgeblog.org/2020/04/twenty-five-years-after/, accessed 10 July 2020.

Page, J. W., *Imperfect Sympathies: Jews and Judaism in British Romantic Literature and Culture* (New York, 2004). This is the standard work on British romanticism and antisemitism.

Ragussis, M., *Figures of Conversion: "The Jewish Question" and English National Identity* (Durham, NC, 1995). This book investigates the way in which conversionist antisemitism was resisted in 19th-century English literature.

Reizbaum, M., *James Joyce's Judaic Other* (Stanford, CA, 1999). A thorough study of how Joyce used Jews and Judaism to create *Ulysses* which is the most sophisticated account of the subject.

Scrivener, M., *Jewish Representations in British Literature, 1780–1840: After Shylock* (New York, 2011). A wide-ranging and thoroughly researched account of Jews and Judaism in British culture in the long 18th century.

Shapiro, J., *Shakespeare and the Jews* (New York, 1996). The standard work on the perception of Jews and Judaism in the early modern period which extends to the mid-18th century.

Trubowitz, L., *Civil Antisemitism, Modernism and British Culture, 1902–1939* (New York, 2012). A thoughtful study of how antisemitism functions in civil society with reference to anti-immigration legislation, conspiracy theories and a wide range of modern fiction.

Valman, N., *The Jewess in Nineteenth-Century British Literary Culture* (Cambridge, 2007). The first and only book to locate "the Jewess" at the heart of perceptions of Jews and Judaism in the long 19th century.

21 Antisemitism in America, 1654–2020

JONATHAN D. SARNA

Antisemitism, an essay by Jonathan Judaken argues, "requires rethink-ing."[1] The term's manifest lack of clarity, its uncertain periodization, and its complex relationship to other forms of oppression all help to explain why. Antisemitism in the United States, one might argue, likewise requires rethinking. For years, a code of silence enveloped the subject. The Jewish lay leader and scholar Cyrus Adler, longtime presi-dent of the American Jewish Historical Society, insisted in 1898 that he did "not believe it exists," and had "entire confidence in the impossi-bility of its ever existing on the soil of the United States."[2] The word "antisemitism" (with or without a hyphen) did not appear even once in Henrietta Szold and Elfrida Cowen's index to the American Jewish Historical Society's first twenty volumes of publications. Following World War II, historians focused more on anti-Jewish hatred, but tangled over whether it constituted the exception or the rule in America. How, they wondered, did it compare with other hatreds, such as anti-Black racism, anti-Catholicism, and anti-Mormonism? Should antisemitism be understood as grimly eternal, dependably cyclical, or just as an occasional and episodic factor in American history? And how best to interpret it: as a "cultural code," revealing less about Jews than about the culture that stigmatizes them, or with a focus on Jews as historical actors, responsible in many ways for their own melancholy fate?[3] Finally, is antisemitism different in the United States than in other diaspora lands where Jews have lived, or are claims of "American exceptionalism" with respect to antisemitism just a patriotic illusion?

---

[1] Jonathan Judaken, "Rethinking Anti-Semitism: Introduction," *American Historical Review* 123 (October 2018), 1122.
[2] *Reform Advocate* 15 (February 19, 1898), 7.
[3] Shulamit Volkov "Anti-Semitism as a Cultural Code: Reflections on the History and Historiography of Anti-Semitism in Imperial German," *Yearbook of the Leo Baeck Institute* 23 (1978), 23–46; Albert S. Lindemann, *Esau's Tears: Modern Anti-Semitism and the Rise of the Jews* (New York, 1997).

In rethinking American antisemitism, this essay addresses these questions and likewise offers a brief history and periodization. Following Shulamit Volkov's insistence that the historian's role is "to explain how and why a certain form of antisemitism characterizes certain societies at certain times," the focus here is necessarily delimited.[4] The generalizations, nevertheless, carry implications for the study of antisemitism across space and time.

* * *

In a pathbreaking 1957 essay that serves as a starting point for serious scholarship on American antisemitism, historian John Higham argued that antisemitism played a discontinuous rather than a constant role in American history. He showed that it waxed and waned over time, the peaks and valleys closely linked to social and economic crises. He went on to underscore the theme of *ambivalence* that helped to explain antisemitism's cyclical character. "Diverse and conflicting attitudes" toward Jews coexisted in the minds of Americans, he concluded; "many were pro and anti-Jewish at the same time." He also related antisemitism to social problems, such as mass migration, economic dislocation, and the displacement of elites. Through antisemitism, he argued, society "gave a general problem an ethnic focus." Deprivation best explained the three core antisemitic groups of the late 19th century, he believed. Agrarian rebels caught up in the Populist movement, patrician intellectuals in the East, and the urban poor of bustling cities all felt victimized by rapid industrialization. Manifest differences distinguished Kansas farmers, Cambridge intellectuals, and Manhattan day laborers, he knew, but the three groups (like so many other antisemites through the years) shared one great fantasy in common: they believed that Jews lay at the root of their problems.[5] Decades earlier, conspiracy-minded Americans tended to blame similar problems on Catholics, Masons, and Mormons.[6]

Higham's central themes – discontinuity, cultural ambivalence, the link between antisemitism and larger social ills, and conspiratorial

[4] Volkov, "Readjusting Cultural Codes: Reflections on Anti-Semitism and Anti-Zionism," *The Journal of Israeli History* 25 (March 2006), 58.

[5] John Higham, "Anti-Semitism in the Gilded Age: A Reinterpretation," *The Mississippi Valley Historical Review* 43 (March 1957), 559–578.

[6] David B. Davis, "Some Themes of Counter-Subversion: An Analysis of Anti-Masonic, Anti-Catholic, and Anti-Mormon Literature," *Mississippi Valley Historical Review* 47 (September 1960), 205–224.

fantasies – dominate the study of American antisemitism to this day. While Higham's essay focused on the late 19th century, when the word "anti-Semitism" entered the American lexicon, overt forms of anti-Jewish discrimination became commonplace, and immigration spiked, historians soon demonstrated that these same themes applied to earlier and later periods in American history as well.

Antagonism toward Jews, they showed, began with Jewish communal settlement in New Amsterdam (today's New York) back in 1654. The Dutch governor of that colony, Peter Stuyvesant, who considered all forms of religious nonconformity a threat to public order, singled out Jews as "deceitful," "very repugnant," and "hateful enemies and blasphemers of the name of Christ." He sought to expel the bedraggled Jewish refugees who arrived on his doorstep. "Giving them liberty, we cannot refuse the Lutherans and the Papists!" he exclaimed to the Dutch West India Company back in Amsterdam.[7] Those words serve as a reminder that, in America, the fate of Jews and the fate of other persecuted minority groups were, from the very beginning, entwined.

The Dutch West India Company required Stuyvesant to admit the Jewish refugees. Their economic benefit, in a mercantilist economy, trumped religious prejudice. Still, Jews continued to face episodes of rejection, prejudice, and even occasional violence in the colonial era, while anti-Jewish literary stereotypes abounded. "Jew was still a dirty word," the great historian of colonial Jewry, Jacob Rader Marcus, reminded his readers, and he showed that "it was hardly rare to see the Jews denigrated as such in the press."[8] At the same time, he also showed, recalling the theme of ambivalence, that Jews prospered in colonial America and maintained close, sometimes even intimate ties with their non-Jewish neighbors.

The American Revolution effected changes in law and in the relationship of religion to the state that widened the parameters of religious liberty in the new nation. New York, with its long tradition of de facto religious pluralism, became in 1777 the first state to extend the boundaries of "free exercise and enjoyment of religious profession and worship" to "all mankind," whether Christian or not. The Northwest Ordinance, adopted by the Continental Congress in 1787, extended guarantees of freedom of worship and belief into the territories north of the Ohio River. Finally, the Federal Constitution (1787) and the Bill of Rights (1791) outlawed religious tests "as a qualification to any office or

---

[7] Jonathan D. Sarna, *American Judaism* (New Haven, CT, 2004), 2.
[8] Jacob R. Marcus, *The Colonial American Jew* (Detroit, MI, 1970), III, 1335.

public trust under the United States," and forbade Congress from making any law "respecting an establishment of religion, or prohibiting the free exercise thereof."[9]

Significantly, none of these major American documents bearing on religious liberty mentions Jews by name. Jews gained their religious rights as individuals along with everybody else – not, as so often the case in Europe and the Caribbean, through a special privilege or "Jew Bill" that set them apart as a group. It did require a hard-fought bill to win Jews the right to hold public office in Maryland in 1826, and it took another fifty-one years before Jews achieved full legal equality in New Hampshire. Issues like Sunday laws, school prayer, and religious cele-brations in the public square reminded Jews of their minority status long after that. Nevertheless, on the national level and in most of the American communities where Jews actually lived, they achieved legal equality by the end of the 18th century.

Legal equality, of course, did not automatically translate into social equality, nor did it put an end to antisemitic stereotyping. Whenever tensions rose, such as during the closely fought 1800 elec-tion pitting Thomas Jefferson against John Adams, the baiting of Jews formed part of the arsenal of political mud-slingers, even when – as in the case of John Israel of Pittsburgh in 1800 – the candidate in question was not Jewish at all. The range of other antisemitic incidents in the early decades of the young republic spanned the spectrum from literary and cultural stereotyping, social and economic discrimination, attacks on Jewish property, all the way to blood-libel allegations in the *New York Herald* and lurid descriptions of purported anti-Christian senti-ments in classical Jewish texts like the Talmud. In 1820, a newspaper in New York reported to German citizens that the city's Jews were "not generally regarded with a favorable eye; and Jew is an epithet which is frequently uttered in a tone bordering on contempt." It concluded that for all of America's vaunted toleration, "prejudices against the Jews exist here and subject them to inconveniences from which other citizens of the United States are exempt."[10]

In the popular fiction of the antebellum period one likewise discerns a great many antisemitic motifs. For example, a best-selling popular

[9] Jonathan Sarna and David G. Dalin, *Religion and State in the American Jewish Experience* (Notre Dame, IN, 1997), 61–80.

[10] *The German Correspondent* 1 (1820), 6; William Pencak, "Jews and Anti-Semitism in Early Pennsylvania," *The Pennsylvania Magazine of History and Biography* 126 (July 2002), 365–408.

novel by George Lippard entitled *Quaker City, or The Monks of Monk Hall* (1844) portrayed a hump-backed Jewish forger, Gabriel Van Gelt, who swindles, blackmails, and commits murder for the sake of money. Joseph Holt Ingraham's tales, best sellers too, offered a whole cast of dark-eyed Shylocks, beautiful Jewish daughters, and revolting Jewish criminals. But, significantly, Jews rarely appeared as lone villains in these novels. Not only did they have Gentile accomplices, but also in many cases the novels gave expression to more sympathetic understandings of Jewish–Gentile relations. They noted how often Christians oppressed Jews, and observed, perceptively, that people fawned over Jews when they sought to borrow money from them, but cursed those very same Jews if they could not pay that money back.[11]

Ambivalence, so central to Higham's analysis of the late 19th century, turns out to be the key word in understanding how earlier Americans responded to Jews as well. Conflicting emotions, changing experiences, and divergent influences pulled people now one way, now another. At times, the lure of the exotic opened doors to Jews. Rural Americans, for example, sometimes traveled miles just to catch a glimpse of one of God's chosen people. As would also be seen in the case of Asians, however, the lure of the exotic quickly gave way to fear of the unknown. Outsiders came to view Jews as an alien force, a people apart. As patronizing curiosity yielded to xenophobic delusion, doors slammed shut and Jews found themselves excluded.

A second, even more powerful source of ambivalence, beginning before the Civil War, was a pervasive tension between *received* wisdom about Jews and *perceived* wisdom – between, in other words, the "mythical Jew," that cursed figure of Christian tradition deeply embedded in Western culture, and the "Jew next door" who seemingly gave the lie to every element of that demonic stereotype. Usually it was the mythical Jew – the unscrupulous moneylender, the eternal wanderer, the satanic Christ-killer – who was flayed by antisemites. If they sometimes realized that Jews of their personal acquaintance did not fit the mold, that pattern was too deeply ingrained to change; it was easier to live with the contradiction. "Them Jews – I don't mean you" was a phrase that an Upstate New Yorker recalled hearing from her neighbors. Thomas Jefferson, in spite of the liberal sentiments he expressed in correspondence with individual Jews, continued to maintain in other letters that

---

[11] Louis Harap, *The Image of the Jew in American Literature: From Early Republic to Mass Immigration* (Philadelphia, 1975); Louise A. Mayo, *The Ambivalent Image: Nineteenth-Century America's Perception of the Jew* (Cranbury, NJ, 1988).

Jews as a people were morally depraved. Simultaneously, then, individual Jews thrived in the 19th century, often rising to positions of wealth and power. Intermarriage rates, a reliable if sometimes unwelcome sign of religious harmony, likewise spiked to high levels. Yet popular prejudice based on received wisdom continued, nonetheless. When social tensions arose, any purported manifestation of a so-called typical Jewish trait brought all of the old stereotypes back to the fore.[12]

Of course, African Americans, Catholics, and Mormons experienced the brunt of American religious violence during the nation's first century. Nothing in American Jewish history from that time parallels such infamous incidents as the burning by angry white men of the famed Emanuel African Methodist Episcopal Church in Charleston in 1822; the violent anti-Catholic riots that burned and destroyed the Ursuline Convent in Charlestown (today Somerville), Massachusetts, in 1834; or the so-called extermination order issued by the Governor of Missouri in 1838 that declared "the Mormons must be treated as enemies, and must be exterminated or driven from the State." Never were Jews the nation's only out-group, nor was Judaism ever the nation's least favored religion. Whatever prejudice Jews experienced, others suffered far worse.

Still, the Civil War era – a period of heightened racial and religious tension throughout the United States – resulted in an unprecedented surge in antisemitism, "far greater in articulation, repetition, frequency, and in action too," according to historian Bertram W. Korn, "than had ever before been directed against Jews in America."[13] The prominence of several Jews in the ranks of the Confederacy, notably President Jefferson Davis's right-hand man and cabinet secretary, Judah P. Benjamin (dubbed "an Israelite with Egyptian principles," by Senator Benjamin Wade of Ohio), heightened prejudice. Generalizing from the few to the many, one newspaper denounced the entire "stiff-necked generation" of the "Children of Israel" as Confederate supporters, although the majority of the nation's 150,000 or so Jews actually supported the Union. Some likewise blamed Jews for many of the other evils associated with war – smuggling, speculating, price gouging, swindling, and producing "shoddy" merchandise for the military. Indeed, "Jews" came to personify the foulest of wartime capitalism's ills. This helps to explain why General Ulysses S. Grant, on December

[12] Jonathan Sarna, "The 'Mythical Jew' and the 'Jew Next Door' in Nineteenth Century America," in *Anti-Semitism in American History*, ed. David Gerber (Champaign, IL, 1986), 57–78.
[13] Bertram W. Korn, *American Jewry and the Civil War* (New York, 1970), xx.

17, 1862, issued General Orders No. 11, "the most sweeping anti-Jewish regulation in all American history." It expelled "Jews, as a class," from his war zone – an area stretching from northern Mississippi to Cairo, Illinois, and from the Mississippi River to the Tennessee River – for violating "every regulation of trade."

The proximity of Grant's order to the issuing of the Emancipation Proclamation sparked fears in Jewish circles that, with the end of slavery, the status of Blacks would rise and the status of Jews correspondingly fall – a reminder of how much anti-Black racism, before and after the Civil War, shaped the impact of antisemitism in the American setting. Those fears proved groundless, however, for President Abraham Lincoln reversed Grant's order of expulsion as soon as he heard of it, and proclaimed that he did "not like to hear a class or nationality condemned on account of a few sinners." Nevertheless, many Civil War–era Americans (including some in the military) continued to perceive *all* traders, smugglers, sutlers, and wartime profiteers to be "sharp-nosed" Jews, whether they were actually Jewish or not. The implication, echoing a perennial antisemitic canard, was that Jews preferred to benefit from war rather than fight in it. In reality, some 10,000 Jews *did* fight in the Civil War, and some rose to become high-ranking officers. Jews likewise prospered with the rapid growth of the clothing trade during the war. In the Civil War, as earlier, Jews "as a class" suffered because of what the word "Jew" symbolized, while individual Jews won the respect of their fellow citizens and emerged from the fratricidal struggle more self-assured than they had been before.[14]

By all accounts, antisemitism crested in the United States between 1877 and World War II, an era of massive social, industrial, economic, urban, and demographic change that dislocated millions of people, threatened traditional patterns of life, and transformed the whole ethnic and religious character of the United States. Outsiders and newcomers, notably Blacks, Jews, and Catholic immigrants, bore the brunt of the social tensions stirred by these cataclysmic changes. In response, "Jim Crow" legislation enshrined segregation between Blacks and whites; Social Darwinist and racialist ideas spread across the country; nativism and isolationism captured hearts and minds; and as America's Jewish population surged from less than 250,000 to well over 4 million, some persuaded themselves that behind all the changes roiling American life lay a clandestine Jewish conspiracy.

[14] Jonathan Sarna, *When General Grant Expelled the Jews* (New York, 2012).

The term "antisemitism," born in Germany, entered American parlance early in this period. Where Jews had previously been reviled on account of their religion, which some thought conversion could fix, now, like Blacks, they suffered on account of their race; their blood deemed forever inferior to that of the lofty Anglos, Saxons, and Teutons. The late 1870s, consequently, witnessed new forms of discrimination against Jews – similar in kind, if not in degree, to the civil rights violations that characterized the early Jim Crow laws. In 1877, the famed Grand Union hotel in Saratoga, New York, excluded banker Joseph Seligman, friend of President Ulysses S. Grant and one of the country's most respected Jewish figures. "No Israelites shall be permitted in future to stop at this hotel," Judge Henry Hilton, the Grand Union's new owner, announced. Within a few years, "Jews as a class" – the same phrase General Grant had used back in 1862 – were declared unwelcome even at New York's Coney Island, and social discrimination against Jews became commonplace across the country. "The provident hotel-keeper avoids the contact of the Hebrew purse," an 1881 article entitled "Jewish Ostracism in America" reported. "The little child in school finds no room for the Jew in the game at recess.... In social and professional clubs, the 'Jew' is blackballed."[15] A short-lived American Society for the Suppression of the Jews, established in 1879, pledged its members, among other things, not to elect Jews to public office, not to attend theaters where Jewish composers wrote the music or Jewish actors performed, not to buy or read books by Jewish authors, not to ride on Jewish-owned railroads, and not to do business with Jewish-owned insurance companies. "The highest social element," Coney Island developer Austin Corbin explained, "won't associate with Jews, and that's all there is about it."[16]

Antisemitism escalated further in the 20th century. Especially in the years following World War I, Jews faced physical attacks, many forms of discrimination, as well as intense vilification in print, on the airwaves, in movies, and on stage. Immigration restrictions, without explicitly saying so, looked to limit the number of Jews entering the country. Educational quotas, restrictive covenants, occupational discrimination, and physical attacks against Jews limited the civil rights of those who had settled there already. A particularly infamous incident took place in Atlanta where, in 1913, a twenty-nine-year-old Jewish

---

[15] Nina Morais, "Jewish Ostracism in America," *North American Review* 133.298 (September 1881), 265–275.

[16] Sarna, *When General Grant Expelled the Jews*, 126–127.

factory superintendent and local B'nai B'rith leader named Leo Frank was convicted of molesting and murdering one of his employees, thirteen-year-old Mary Phagan, and dumping her body in the basement of the pencil factory where they both worked. The case attracted a frenzy of publicity, and much attention centered on Frank's religion – the mark of his being an outsider to the South, a symbol of otherness and change. Crowds around the courthouse chanted, "Hang the Jew!" When Georgia governor John Slaton, unpersuaded that Frank was the murderer, commuted his sentence in 1915 from death to life in prison, a mob that included many leading local citizens broke into the jail, kidnapped Frank, and lynched him: the first known lynching of a Jew in American history. Years later an eyewitness confirmed what Frank's defenders had long believed: that Mary Phagan was murdered by the janitor of the pencil factory, the "star witness" against Frank. Frank himself was innocent.[17]

Jews' status as founders sometimes determined the extent of antisemitism in a particular place. Comparative studies reveal that "the degree to which Jews were involved in the early growth of a city and had achieved a notable and respected place in public and private life before the era of mass immigration directly influenced how later generations of Jews were received."[18] Jews in Charleston, Cincinnati, and San Francisco, for example, enjoyed "founder" status. While no prophylactic, this significantly helped to mitigate local antisemitism. Jews in Boston, Minneapolis, and San Diego, by contrast, enjoyed no similar advantage. They arrived in numbers long after the founding of their communities, and as perceived "interlopers" the antisemitism they faced was far worse.[19]

Following World War I, as Americans grew "disillusioned with internationalism, fearful of Bolshevik subversion, and frightened that foreigners would corrupt the nation's values and traditions," manifestations of antisemitism rose further. Immigration restrictions, culminating in the National Origins Immigration (Johnson–Reed) Act of 1924, aimed directly at limiting the number of Jews entering the country. Congressman Albert Johnson, an author of that legislation, argued based

[17] Leonard Dinnerstein, *The Leo Frank Case* (New York, 1968); S. Oney, *And the Dead Shall Rise: The Murder of Mary Phagan and the Lynching of Leo Frank* (New York, 2004).
[18] Judith Endelman, *The Jewish Community of Indianapolis* (Bloomington, IN, 1984), 3.
[19] Higham, *Send These to Me: Immigrants in Urban America* (Baltimore, MD, 1984), 141–147.

on a report from the director of the Consular Service that America was in danger of being swamped by "abnormally twisted" and "unassimilable" Jews, "filthy, unAmerican, and often dangerous in their habits."[20] Resulting legislation did not explicitly mention Jews, and other groups faced restrictions as well, but the law's impact on persecuted Jews proved particularly severe. Between 1925 and 1934, an average of only 8,270 Jews were annually admitted into the country, less than 7 percent of those welcomed when Jewish immigration stood at its peak.

More explicitly, the president of the Central Conference of American Rabbis gravely reported that "within three years following the close of the war, there was perhaps more antisemitic literature published and distributed in the United States than in any previous period of its history." What made this literature particularly insidious and incendiary was that so much of it bore the imprimatur of a national hero, automaker Henry Ford. For ninety-one straight issues beginning on May 22, 1920, Ford's weekly newspaper, the *Dearborn Independent*, purported to describe an international Jewish conspiracy based on the notorious antisemitic forgery known as *The Protocols of the Elders of Zion*, first published in Russia in 1905. Four volumes entitled *The International Jew*, drawn from the series, reprinted these scurrilous charges and disseminated them in hundreds of thousands of copies – including such fantastic claims as "Rule of the Jewish Kehillah Grips New York" or "Jewish Jazz Becomes Our National Music." The claims reveal more about Ford and his disdain for changes in American society than they do about Jews. Only in 1927, under intense economic and legal pressure, did Ford publicly apologize "for resurrecting exploded fictions, for giving currency to ... gross forgeries, and for contending that the Jews have been engaged in a conspiracy." But by then the damage had been done.[21]

While Ford attacked Jews in public, numerous American universities and colleges, including Harvard, Yale, and Princeton, privately worked to limit the number of Jewish students they admitted, as did a plethora of private academies and preparatory schools. The extent of the restrictive quotas and the means used to achieve them differed from place to place, but what really mattered for Jews was that they were excluded not on the

---

[20] Roger Daniels, *Guarding the Golden Door: American Immigration Policy and Immigrants since 1882* (New York, 2004), 47–48.

[21] Jonathan Sarna, *American Judaism: A History*, 2nd ed. (New Haven, CT, 2019), 217–218; Leo P. Ribuffo, "Henry Ford and the International Jew," *American Jewish History* 69 (June 1980), 437–477; Neil Baldwin, *Henry Ford and the Jews: The Mass Production of Hate* (New York, 2001).

basis of merit but simply on account of their ancestry and faith. Even harsher restrictions faced Jews in fraternities, clubs, hotels, resorts, and elite neighborhoods – there, in many cases, they were shut out completely. Clubs in fifteen different cities large and small are known to have barred Jews, while discrimination at luxury resorts was "near universal." In addition, bigoted practices and "restrictive covenants" excluded Jews from some of the most desirable neighborhoods in major cities and newly emerging suburbs. Some inviting apartments on Coney Island, for example, shamelessly advertised themselves as being "sensibly priced, sensibly built, [and] sensibly restricted."[22]

Physical violence against Jews likewise became common during this period. In the 1920s, the revived Ku Klux Klan badly frightened Jews, though it directed most of its animus against Blacks and Catholics. Attacks increased in the 1930s, particularly in cities where German Americans sympathetic to Adolf Hitler took to the streets, and where Catholic supporters of the increasingly pro-Nazi radio priest Father Charles Coughlin beat Jews mercilessly. Coughlin, with his reputed audience of 30 million, whipped listeners into a frenzy with his depictions of alleged Jewish misdeeds around the world. He explained Nazi attacks against German Jews on *Kristallnacht* (November 9–10, 1938) as a "defense mechanism" against Communism, for which he held Jews totally responsible. A largely Irish quasi-military organization called the Christian Front (1938–1940), inspired by Coughlin, went on to denounce President "Rosenfelt" for what it called the "Jew Deal," conducted Nazi propaganda meetings, and physically attacked Jews in New York, Boston, and Philadelphia. Meanwhile, the German-American Bund, established in 1936 and secretly funded by the Nazis, distributed anti-Jewish propaganda (including blood libels), organized youth camps on the model of the Hitler Youth in Germany, and conducted mass demonstrations, including one that filled Madison Square Garden on February 20, 1939. By then, more than four in ten Americans told pollsters that Jews had "too much power in the United States." Some, as an antidote, proposed that Jews be driven from the country.[23]

---

[22] Jerome Karabel, *The Chosen: The Hidden History of Admission and Exclusion at Harvard, Yale and Princeton* (Boston, 2005); Dinnerstein, *Antisemitism in America* (New York, 1994), 92–93; Deborah D. Moore, *At Home in America: Second Generation New York Jews* (New York, 1981), 38.

[23] Donald J. Warren, *Radio Priest: Charles Coughlin, the Father of Hate Radio* (New York, 1996); Sander A. Diamond, *The Nazi Movement in the United States: 1924–1941* (Ithaca, NY, 1974); Charles H. Stember, *Jews in the Mind of America* (New York, 1966), 121–123.

Yet for all that it had become widespread, antisemitism never went unopposed. Liberal newspapers and organizations like the Anti-Defamation League of B'nai B'rith openly fought it; a growing interfaith movement headed by liberal-minded clergy worked to counter it; and Jews themselves often found ways to circumvent it, sometimes by patronizing en masse those institutions that accepted them and by creating parallel institutions (Jewish country clubs, Jewish fraternities, etc.) to the ones that excluded them. In comparison to their counterparts in most of Europe, where Jews increasingly feared for their lives, American Jews considered themselves fortunate.

Following World War II, especially as consciousness of the destruction of European Jewry rose and Americans sought to distinguish themselves, ideologically, from the Nazis whom they had defeated, organized antisemitism in America declined dramatically. Between 1946 and 1950, the percentage of Americans who claimed to have heard "any criticism or talk against the Jews in the last six months" dropped from 64 percent to 24 percent. Thanks to federal and state legislation, pressure from returning veterans, government and media exposure (including films like *Gentleman's Agreement*), and the stigma of being compared to the Nazis, discrimination against Jews in employment, housing, and daily life also markedly declined. By the early 1960s, almost all resorts and housing developments had dropped their restrictive clauses; antisemitic college quotas had mostly ended; and professional fields like law, medicine, and banking proved more receptive to Jews than at any previous time in the 20th century. The former director of the Anti-Defamation League, Benjamin R. Epstein, who devoted his career to fighting antisemitism, described the twenty years following World War II as a "golden age" for American Jews, one in which they "achieved a greater degree of economic and political security, and a broader social acceptance, than had ever been known by any Jewish community since the [ancient] Dispersion."[24]

The South served as the major exception to this perceived "golden age." This was surprising since public philosemitism had long characterized the region. North Carolina's late 19th-century governor, Zebulon B. Vance, credited Jews with "all that is excellent on earth or in heaven," and even historians have insisted that the region "exhibited less antisemitism and even nativism than certainly the East and Midwest." A more recent study, however, perceptively argues that southern philo-Semitism

[24] Sarna, *American Judaism*, 276–277.

"was foremost a 'courting' of a somewhat white minority in the struggle for southern white self-determination." It portrays the region's Jews as "integrated outsiders": suspected because they were Jews, accepted because they were manifestly not Black.[25] Jewish support for the civil rights movement threatened this knotty relationship. Fear of Communism (a movement which won support from a noisy Jewish minority, but for which the entire Jewish community was often implicated) and the extraordinary social changes that the South experienced resulted, during the 1950s, in a spate of "bombing outrages" directed against Black and Jewish institutions alike. In just one twelve-month period (1957–1958), "eleven sticks of dynamite were found at a temple in Charlotte; a synagogue in Miami and the Nashville Jewish Center were bombed on the same day; undetonated dynamite was found at a temple in Gastonia, North Carolina; a Jacksonville, Florida synagogue was dynamited; and dynamite with a burnt-out fuse was found at Temple Beth-El in Birmingham, Alabama." Then, in the early morning hours of October 12, 1958, a nitroglycerine bomb equal to fifty sticks of dynamite tore apart The Temple, the oldest and most distinguished Reform congregation in Atlanta. All in all, some 10 percent of the bombs planted by extremists between 1954 and 1959 targeted Jewish institutions – synagogues, rabbis' homes, and community centers. Most of the other 90 percent targeted African American institutions.[26] Attacks on synagogues continued in the 1960s. A widely distributed paperback with the explosive title *165 Temples Desecrated*, published in 1971, chronicled those that took place just between 1965 and 1970. The best-known and most notorious occurred in Jackson, Mississippi, in 1967, where white supremacists bombed Temple Beth Israel's newly dedicated house of worship and then, two months later, returned to bomb the home of the temple's rabbi, Perry Nussbaum.

Even as anti-Semites in the South targeted Jews for supporting civil rights, some African Americans in the North turned on Jews for not supporting civil rights enough. For decades, Blacks and Jews in the North had enjoyed something of a special relationship both as victims of prejudice and as allies in the battle to oppose it, but in the 1960s, the interests, visions, and priorities of the two communities began to diverge. Merit-based educational programs aided Jews far more than

---

[25] Howard N. Rabinowitz, "Nativism, Bigotry and Anti-Semitism in the South," *American Jewish History* 77 (March 1988), 437–451; Anton Hieke, *Jewish Identity in the Reconstruction South: Ambivalence and Adaptation* (Berlin, 2013), 127–133.

[26] Melissa F. Greene, *The Temple Bombing* (Reading, MA, 1996), 6.

they did Blacks, antisemitism declined faster than racism, and Jews moved out to sparkling suburbs while Blacks languished in dangerous inner cities. Subsequently, young radical advocates of "Black Power," in conscious rebellion against their elders, came to view Jews more as obstacles than as allies. Some of them spread the hateful canard that Jews bore central responsibility for slavery; others embraced the Palestinian cause and railed against the State of Israel. A series of well-publicized clashes over public school governance, small business ownership, neighborhood rule, and related grievances culminated, in 1991, in an ugly riot – local Jews dubbed it a pogrom – in the Crown Heights section of Brooklyn. Jews blamed "radical extremists" within the Black community for fanning the flames of hatred, and braced themselves for worse to come.[27]

Contrary to expectations, though, tensions between Blacks and Jews thereafter abated, in part because Blacks and Jews, in most of America, no longer abutted one another, and partly because responsible leaders in both communities labored to tamp down tensions. When Leonard Dinnerstein published the first and only scholarly history of American antisemitism, in 1994, his book ended on a hopeful note. "Greater tolerance and acceptance of diversity in the United States," he concluded, showed that antisemitism "has declined in potency and will continue to do so for the foreseeable future."[28] Members of the millennial generation, born at that time, soon concluded that Jews had finally become "white folks" in America and were past persecution. Only "people of color," now faced hatred, they thought. Academic books supported this thesis; one bore the arresting title *The Death of American Antisemitism* (2000). Journalist Jonathan Weisman reports hearing the popular version of this same thesis from the daughter of a girlfriend. "Anti-Semitism," she told him, "basically doesn't exist."[29]

At the margins of society, antisemitism nevertheless endured. On the extreme political right, Holocaust deniers, conspiracy theorists who maintain that Jews or Zionists control western governments (they label them "Zionist Occupied Governments" [ZOG]), neo-Nazis, and

---

[27] Cheryl L. Greenberg, *Troubling the Waters: Black-Jewish Relations in the American Century* (Princeton, NJ, 2006); Edward S. Shapiro, *Crown Heights: Blacks, Jews and the 1991 Brooklyn Riot* (Waltham, MA, 2006).

[28] Dinnerstein, *Antisemitism in America*, 250.

[29] Karen Brodkin, *How Jews Became White Folks and What That Says about Race in America* (New Brunswick, NJ, 1998); E. Goldstein, *The Price of Whiteness: Jews, Race, and American Identity* (Princeton, NJ, 2007); Jonathan Weisman, *(((Semitism))): Being Jewish in America in the Age of Trump* (New York, 2018).

white supremacists continued to spout hatred against Jews. On the extreme political left, Black nationalists; those who delegitimize, demonize, and apply double-standards to the State of Israel; neo-Communists who blame Jews for capitalism and globalization; as well as advocates for the third world who view America and Jews as inter-linked colonialist oppressors spouted anti-Jewish hatred too. Islamist elements within American Islam, influenced by their Arab counter-parts in the Middle East, joined in these antisemitic attacks, eliding American Jews with Palestinians' longtime enemies, the Israelis. These three groups, much like the antisemitic agrarian rebels, patri-cian intellectuals, and urban poor of the late 19th century, actually had different complaints, different agendas, and little outwardly in common. What they did share, however, was the one great fantasy that so often characterizes anti-Semites: they believed that Jews lay at the root of their problems.

From these margins, antisemitism roared back into the mainstream during the 21st century. The so-called alternative ("alt") right, defined as "a set of far-right ideologies, groups and individuals whose core belief is that 'white identity' is under attack by multicultural forces using 'polit-ical correctness' and 'social justice' to undermine white people and 'their' civilization," developed and gained strength during these years, fueled by social media outlets and online message boards.[30] A particularly popular website, launched in 2013, called itself the *Daily Stormer*, in conscious imitation of the Nazi newspaper *Der Stürmer*.

Due in no small part to the alt-right, the 2016 election was riddled with antisemitic memes and messages. A horrified *Washington Post* correspondent concluded that "Anti-Semitism is no longer an under-tone of Trump's campaign. It's the melody."[31] A "Unite the Right" rally in Charlottesville, Virginia, just one year later, witnessed chants of "the Jews will not replace us." A year after that, on October 27, 2018, a mass shooting at Pittsburgh's Tree of Life synagogue, allegedly perpetrated by a white nationalist who railed on social networks against immigrants and the Hebrew Immigrant Aid Society, left eleven people dead and seven wounded, the deadliest attack ever on a US Jewish community. Another attack six months later on the Chabad of

---

[30] "Alt-Right," SPLC, Southern Poverty Law Center, www.splcenter.org/fighting-hate/ extremist-files/ideology/alt-right.

[31] Laura E. Adkins, "Anti-Semitism in the U.S. Isn't Usually Violent. What If That's Changing?," *Washington Post*, December 19, 2019, www.washingtonpost.com/ outlook/2019/12/19/anti-semitism-us-isnt-usually-violent-why-is-that-starting-change/.

Poway Synagogue, charged to a gunman who accused Jews of planning "genocide of the European race," reinforced fears that alt-right extremists had Jews in their sights.

The alt-right, however, is not alone in fomenting contemporary antisemitism. An attack in 2019 that killed five people at a kosher market in Jersey City and another that same year on the Hanukah party of a Hasidic rabbi in Monsey that killed one and wounded five demonstrated that militant African Americans on the extreme left have likewise committed antisemitic violence. More commonly, left-wing antisemitism has been concealed under the guise of "anti-Zionism." It demonizes those who support Israel and insists, as Columbia University Professor Joseph Massad put it, that "The Jews are not a nation"' and that "The Jewish State is a racist state that does not have a right to exist." Nearly three quarters of all Jewish students surveyed in one 2015 study reported being victimized by antisemitic canards, mostly from left-wing faculty and students, "including the claims that Jews have too much power and that Israelis behave 'like Nazis' toward the Palestinians."[32]

Radical Islamists in the United States have been particularly prone to extend their hatred of Israel to all Jews. One Muslim, in 2006, shot up the Jewish Federation of Greater Seattle. Another, in 2018, aimed his car at Jews exiting a Los Angeles synagogue. A Muslim congresswoman from Minnesota, Ilhan Omar, while denying that she is an Islamist, charged that American politicians get paid to support Israel. "It's all about the Benjamins," she explained.

Fully 88 percent of American Jews described antisemitism as a "very serious problem" or "somewhat of a problem" in a 2019 Anti-Defamation League poll. Almost a third admitted that they avoided "publicly wearing, carrying, or displaying things" that might identify them as Jews. These statistics reflected a record number of antisemitic incidents in 2019, with more reports of assault, vandalism, and harassment than in any year since the Anti-Defamation League began tracking such incidents forty years earlier. Although one study found that "the perpetrators of anti-Jewish hate crimes seem to have nothing clearly uniting them – race, age, political affiliation – except their anti-Semitic intent," and although many linked antisemitism to an overall

[32] Massad quoted in Bari Weiss, *How to Fight Anti-Semitism* (New York, 2019), 95; Leonard Saxe et al., *Antisemitism and the College Campus: Perceptions and Realities* (Waltham, MA, 2015).

climate of hatred and divisiveness in the United States, the existence
of antisemitism within American society could no longer seriously
be questioned.

* * *

Antisemitism's return raised anew the question of American exceptionalism. Is America really different from other countries with respect to
antisemitism? Might extremists – from the right or from the left –
someday turn on Jews? Could something parallel to the Nazi
Holocaust ever happen in the United States? In looking to history to
help answer these questions, five key factors that have long lent a
special color to American antisemitism, differentiating it from the
history of antisemitism elsewhere, must be taken into account.

**In America, Jews have always been able to fight back against anti-
semitism freely**. Never having received their emancipation as an
"award" (which was the case in Europe), Jews have had no fears of losing
it. Instead, from the beginning, they made full use of their freedom,
especially freedom of speech. As early as 1784, a "Jew Broker," probably
the famed Revolutionary-era Jewish bond dealer Haym Salomon,
responded publicly and forcefully to the antisemitic charges of a prominent Quaker lawyer, not hesitating to remind him that his "own religious sectary" could also form "very proper subjects of criticism and
animadversion."[33] A few years later, Christian missionaries and their
supporters faced Jewish responses no less strident in tone. Where
European Jews often prided themselves on their "forbearance" in the
face of attack, Rabbi Isaac Mayer Wise, the great Reform Jewish leader,
once boasted that he was a "malicious, biting, pugnacious, challenging,
and mocking monster of the pen."[34] In more recent times, Jewish
defense organizations have taken on anyone who maligned Jews, including national heroes like General George S. Patton, and even multiple
Presidents of the United States.

**American antisemitism has always had to compete with other
forms of animus**. Racism, nativism, anti-Quakerism, Anglophobia,
Islamophobia, anti-Catholicism, anti-Masonry, anti-Mormonism, anti-
Orientalism, anti-Teutonism – these and other waves of hatred have

---

[33] Jacob R. Marcus, *American Jewry Documents: Eighteenth Century* (Cincinnati, OH, 1959), 41–46.
[34] Isaac M. Wise, *Reminiscences* (New York, 1945), 273.

periodically swept over the American landscape, scarring and battering citizens. Americans have long been extraordinarily pluralistic in their hatreds. Precisely because the objects of hatred have been so varied, hatred has generally been diffused. No one outgroup experiences the full brunt of national odium. Mosques and Black churches today are as much at risk as synagogues. Furthermore, most Americans retain bitter memories of days past when they or their ancestors were *themselves* the targets of malevolence. The American strain of antisemitism is thus less potent than its European counterpart, and it faces a larger number of natural competitors. To reach epidemic proportions, it must first crowd out a vast number of contending hatreds.

Antisemitism is more foreign to American ideals than to European ones. The central documents of the Republic assure Jews of liberty; its first president, in his famous letter to the Jews of Newport, conferred upon them his blessing. The fact that antisemitism can properly be branded "un-American," although no protection in the formal sense – the nation has betrayed its ideals innumerable times including in our own day – still grants Jews a measure of protection. Elsewhere antisemites could always claim legitimacy stemming from times past when the *Volk* ruled, and Jews knew their place. Americans could point to nothing even remotely similar to that in their own past.

America's religious tradition – what has been called "the great tradition of the American churches" – is inhospitable to antisemitism. Religious freedom and diversity, church–state separation, denominationalism, and voluntarism, the key components of this tradition, militate against the kinds of us/them dichotomies ("Germans and Jews," "Poles and Jews", etc.) so common in Europe. In America, where religious pluralism rules supreme, there has never been a single national church from which Jews stand apart. People speak instead of American Protestants, American Catholics, American Jews, American Muslims, and American Buddhists – implying, at least as an ideal, that all faiths stand equal in the eyes of the law.

American politics resists antisemitism. In a two-party system where close elections are the rule, neither party can long afford to alienate any major bloc of voters. State-sponsored antisemitism, so common in Europe, has never factored in American politics. For the most part, the politics of hatred have been meted out against nonvoters like African Americans (until they won the vote), or nonvoting immigrants, or confined to noisy third parties like the anti-Catholic Know Nothings in the 19th century, or to single-issue fringe groups. America's most successful politicians, now and in the past, have more commonly sought support from respectable elements across the political spectrum. For the most part, appeals to unity have won more elections than appeals to narrow provincialism or to bigotry.

These five factors, historically *distinguishing* the American strain of antisemitism from other varieties, are as vital to recall as those *common* factors that are familiar to students of antisemitism everywhere in the world. As a "cultural code," antisemitism reveals as much (or more) about America as about Jews. Historically, as John Higham observed back in 1957, the study of American antisemitism has risen and fallen along with antisemitism itself. Calls to "rethink" American antisemitism are thus, among many other things, a sign of trouble.

Further Reading

Baldwin, N., *Henry Ford and the Jews: The Mass Production of Hate* (New York, 2001). The best-researched study, which also sheds light on the factors that shaped Henry Ford's antisemitism.

Diamond, S., *The Nazi Movement in the United States: 1924–1941* (Ithaca, NY, 1974). A pathbreaking study of the "Nazi Movement," particularly in the 1930s when support for Nazism in America peaked.

Dinnerstein, L., *Antisemitism in America* (New York, 1994). The only scholarly history of American antisemitism from colonial America through the 1990s.

Gerber, D., ed., *Anti-Semitism in American History* (Urbana, IL, 1986). An invaluable collection of fresh, thoughtful, and well-researched articles covering diverse and sometimes surprising aspects of American antisemitism.

Goldstein, E., *The Price of Whiteness: Jews, Race, and American Identity* (Princeton, NJ, 2007). An award-winning, deeply researched study of the shifting place of Jews in America's racial hierarchy.

Greene, M. F., *The Temple Bombing* (Reading, MA, 1996). A well-researched study of the bombing of Atlanta's Hebrew Benevolent Congregation ("The Temple") on October 12, 1958, contextualized within the civil rights movement and the white southerners who violently opposed Black equality.

Higham, J., "Anti-Semitism in the Gilded Age: A Reinterpretation," *The Mississippi Valley Historical Review* 43 (March 1957), 559–578. This pathbreaking article began the serious study of American antisemitism and articulated concepts that remain fundamental to its comprehension and study.

Karabel, J., *The Chosen: The Hidden History of Admission and Exclusion at Harvard, Yale and Princeton* (New York, 2005). Karabel tells the story of college "quotas" that limited Jewish admissions, focusing on the three premier Ivy League universities. An exhaustive, well-researched study.

Oney, S., *And the Dead Shall Rise: The Murder of Mary Phagan and the Lynching of Leo Frank* (New York, 2003). The definitive study of the Leo Frank case which rocked Georgia and much of the American Jewish community from 1913 to 1915 and resulted in a torrent of antisemitism. Leo Frank was kidnapped from jail and lynched on the night of August 16, 1915.

Sarna, J. D., *When General Grant Expelled the Jews* (New York, 2012). The only full-scale study of Ulysses S. Grant's General Orders No. 11 expelling Jews from his war zone in December 1862, amid the Civil War. Abraham Lincoln overturned the order and Grant subsequently atoned for it.

22 Antisemitism in the Weimar Republic and the Third Reich

STEVEN T. KATZ

THE SITUATION AFTER WORLD WAR I

Jews and Judaism survived into the modern age despite two millennia of intense prejudice and hatred. Here again, despite the liberal programs and philosophies of the Enlightenment and post-Enlightenment period, they were still confronted by both old and new forms of anti-Jewish myths and arguments. The new canards covered accusations that Jews were disloyal anti-nationalists and therefore should not be granted citizenship in the states in which they lived; that they were economic exploiters; that they acted together in a conspiratorial plan to dominate the world; that Jews were uncreative and parasitic. Then, in the second half of the 19th century, the powerful idea of racial antisemitism emerged, that Jews *by nature* were inferior and parasitic beings.

These modern lies increasingly influenced the public perception of Jews, but, even as they spread, it appeared to many intellectuals and ordinary people alike that anti-Jewish prejudice was declining in the 19th century and would continue to decline under the economic, social, and political forces of modernity and liberal politics. The failure of specifically antisemitic political parties in Europe in the two to three decades before World War I supplied what appeared to be decisive evidence of this positive improvement. But World War I and the defeat of Germany undid the then widely held belief in "progress" and put a halt to the gradual improvement in the "Jewish Condition" that was taking place across Western Europe.

The crisis that arose in Germany as a result of its military defeat in 1918, and the subsequent imposition by the winners (France, England, and America) of the crushing conditions of the Versailles Peace Treaty (1919), plus the creation of the Weimar Republic to replace the Kaiser Reich, unintentionally undid the possibility of continued political liberalization in the new Germany.

The Weimar Republic was detested by sizable segments of the German population on both the left and the right. Political life grew increasingly unstable through the 1920s and led to a circumstance in which political radicalization became the norm. This tendency to the extreme was driven by the hyperinflation that destroyed the national economy, and then by the devastating impact of the Great Depression in 1929. The eight general elections held in the Weimar Republic between June 6, 1920, and March 5, 1933, are the clearest evidence of the political and economic weakness and vulnerability that overtook German society.

There are four issues of particular importance that were exploited by antisemites in the Weimar Republic: (1) the defeat of 1918 and the charge of Jewish treason in World War 1, (2) the unfavorable Versailles Treaty and conditions of peace that were attributed to Jewish influence, (3) the stereotype of the Jew as a revolutionary, and (4) the caricature of the Jew as a supranational capitalist and economic exploiter. In the context of the German defeat of 1918, these issues were now given an especially radical, racial interpretation by right-wing political parties and in particular by Hitler for whom they would remain central to his political *Weltanschauung* until his death.

Unpacking these four themes through the lens of racial antisemitism, Hitler argued that it was not German military weakness that had caused Germany to lose World War I but, rather, the betrayal of the country by Jews. They had, in what became his most famous accusation, "stabbed Germany in the back," the *Dolchstoss*.

Though the German Jewish community of 500,000 had supplied 80,000 soldiers for the German army, 12,000 of whom died in the fighting, and Jews like Walter Rathenau and Fritz Haber had played major roles in the organization of the war economy, Hitler ignored all these facts and made the defeat a "Jewish issue" involving Jewish betrayal of the Fatherland. "Not the defeats have overthrown us, but we were overthrown by that power [the Jews] which prepared these defeats by robbing our people systematically, for many decades, of its political and moral instincts and forces which alone enable and entitle peoples to exist in this world."[1] That is, defeat was completely the result of "moral contamination by the Jews." Therefore, "solving the Jewish problem" became "the core problem" for National Socialists regarding all the central issues facing German society.

[1] *Mein Kampf* (German edition, Munich, 1941), 388 and 452–53. The English edition, trans. R. Manheim (Boston, 1943).

The Versailles Treaty at the close of World War I ended the Kaiser Reich and created the Weimar Republic, at the same time imposing draconian reparations. Looking for an explanation as to how the new government could have accepted such a punitive and one-sided treaty, veterans' organizations and antidemocratic politicians who opposed the new republic and could not face the truth of their own military weakness had a ready answer: the Jews. In 1923 Hitler wrote: "The Versailles dictate is the death sentence for Germany as an independent state and as a *Volk*." That is, the Treaty was seen by Hitler and his allies not as a political contract between nations but rather as a declaration of racial war by Jews against Aryans. Therefore, what was needed was not a political revolution but rather a racial revolution that would occur in a Social Darwinian–like struggle. In this conflict the world's different "races" would vie for living space (*Lebensraum*) and control against world Jewry. "Race" in this view is not just biology, it is metaphysics; it not only determines what an individual or a group looks like – for example, brown hair, blue eyes, tall or short – but also decides – causes – the rise and fall of nations and the ultimate fate of civilizations.

The explanation given for why Jews worked against Germany rested on the idea that Jews were, by virtue of their nature, revolutionaries, Marxists, and Communists. Their aim was to undermine the established order and replace it with a "Jewish" form of leftist government that would transfer the world's main economic and political power centers to Jewish control. To the antisemites, including Hitler, the revolutionary events in Bavaria in November 1918, led by the Jewish socialist activist Kurt Eisner; the growing strength of the left wing and Communist parties in Germany; and the Soviet Revolution in Russia were clear proofs of this present danger. These events appeared to prove the truth of *The Protocols of the Elders of Zion*, revealing the existence of a worldwide Jewish conspiracy to dominate the world in their own interest. Hitler even claimed that it was a Jew, Paul, who "virtually invented Christianity to undermine the Roman Empire." Thus the necessary aim of National Socialism became: "Annihilation and extermination of the Marxist [i.e., Jewish] worldview."[2]

This analysis was linked to the view that Jews were not, and could not be, loyal citizens integrated into any state. Jews worked only for their own advancement, prosperity, and power, and therefore "the Jew" did not deserve the usual rights and protections that modern states

---

[2] Ibid., 465.

guaranteed to their citizens. Already in the 1920s Hitler insisted that "A rational antisemitism must lead to the systematic legal fight against and the elimination of the prerogatives of the Jew.... Its ultimate goal, however, must unalterably be the elimination of the Jews."[3] This principle would lead to the reversal of Jewish emancipation in Germany once Hitler gained power in 1933, negating all the progress that had been made since the Enlightenment.

The thesis of the Jew as an eternal outsider also manifested itself in the powerful assertion that the Jew stood against German culture and always represented degenerate aesthetic values and parasitic dependence on non-Jews in art and literature. As for the radical creativity in the arts, theater, literature, and painting that marked the Weimar Republic and involved many Jewish artists and performers, Hitler and the Nazi party viewed it all as "Un-German" and decadent. Alfred Rosenberg, one of the chief ideologues of the NSDAP, labeled it "mongrel art."[4] Hitler said of Weimar that its "cultural activity consists in bowdlerizing art, literature, and the theatre ... The Jew makes night into day, he stages the notorious night life, and knows quite well that it will slowly but surely destroy [German culture]."[5]

The economic chaos of the 1920s in the Weimar Republic also gave great weight to the charge that the Jews manipulated national and international financial markets for their own profits. This claim, already popular in leftish political circles in the 19th century, now gained particular resonance in inflation-ridden, and then depression-reduced Germany. That this was false is best shown by the fact that these factors also seriously impacted the local Jewish community. For example, according to the tax register, the number of upper-middle-class Jews dropped nearly 50 percent during the 1920s, while the Berlin Jewish community alone was forced to open nineteen soup kitchens and seven shelters for the homeless.[6]

But economic troubles proved an enormously effective tool for antisemitic propagandists. This showed itself in the election results of the 1920s. When the economy worsened, especially in the depression-affected September 1930 election, Hitler won 18.3 percent of the

---

[3] Hitler's memo of September 16, 1919, in *Hitler: Eine Politische Biographie*, ed. Ernst Deuerlein (Munich, 1969), n. 88.

[4] Alfred Rosenberg, *Mythus*, cited in *Race and Race History and Other Essays*, ed. Robert Pois (New York, 1970), 149.

[5] *Mein Kampf*, 273–74.

[6] Cited from Donald Niewyk, *Jews in Weimar Germany* (Baton Rouge, LA, 1980), 18.

national vote. In the November 1932 election, when the economy had improved slightly, the NSDAP lost 2 million votes.[7]

All the antisemitic arguments, repeated daily throughout the 1920s and early 1930s, successfully undermined the accepted assumption of Jewish emancipation and Jewry's legitimate collective participation in a modern pluralistic Europe. It set the stage for what would happen after Hitler assumed power in Germany.

HITLER AND THE BEGINNING OF ANTI-JEWISH LAWS

When Hitler became Chancellor of Germany on January 30, 1933, all of his hateful views of Jews, repeatedly expressed during the Weimar years, and most fully and explicitly set out in *Mein Kampf*, came into office with him. During his twelve-year reign, an unwavering commitment to the uprooting and eventually genocidal elimination of the Jewish People – the "Final Solution to the Jewish Question" – became the core program of the Third Reich. From the start of Hitler's rule, antisemitism as state policy grew increasingly radical, reaching its exterminationist form after the beginning of the war with Russia in June 1941.

Surprisingly, Hitler's antisemitic program was underdeveloped vis-à-vis its practical implementation when he took control of Germany. Beyond the idea of denying Jews citizenship, the repatriation of Jewish immigrants to their home countries, and talk about instituting laws against *Rassenschande* – race-mixing – there was no fully developed anti-Jewish program. In fact, what practical steps the Reich began to implement were drawn mainly from earlier anti-Jewish Church legislation that had been formulated over the centuries. As a result, between 1933 and 1935, there was a proliferation of anti-Jewish propaganda, sporadic anti-Jewish violence, and the boycotting of Jewish shops, but no national program for eliminating Jews and Jewish influence from German life.

This changed radically with the passage of the Nuremberg (racial) Laws in 1935. This legislation defined who was a Jew according to racial criteria and gave the Hitler state a clear idea of who exactly the Jewish enemies in their midst were. Essentially, the key principle endorsed by this legislation was that one's blood made one a Jew. Despite complexities that we need not enter into, the basic rule was that someone with two Jewish parents was a Jew, and for those with one Jewish parent,

[7] See Gordon Craig, *Germany 1866–1945* (Oxford, 1980), 562–63.

their present religious practice would be utilized to decide whether or not they were Jews. On the basis of this new legal-racial understanding, Jews lost their German citizenship and were excluded from all normal social, economic, and political life. As a result, all of the natural relationships that existed between Jews and their non-Jewish neighbors were dissolved. Once applied, this criterion for belonging to the *Volk* came to exclude Jews from all civil service jobs, all teaching and university positions, and Jewish students from primary and secondary schools, while Jewish doctors and lawyers could have only Jewish patients and clients. By the end of 1937 and early 1938, Jews had been denied all ordinary civil rights in Germany, and the program of the Aryanization of Jewish property, that is, the forced sale of Jewish stores and other assets at low prices to non-Jews, completely marginalized the Jews and pauperized the Jewish community.

Then came the major blow of Kristallnacht, the burning of synagogues and Jewish businesses on the night of November 9, 1938. This was provoked by the killing in Paris of a minor German official named Von Rath, by a Jewish Polish teenager named Herschel Greenspan. During this one evening, the SS and Brown Shirts[8] killed thirty-six Jews, seriously wounded another 300, and burned 131 synagogues to the ground.

Compounding the effects of this violence, Reich Minister Hermann Goering ordered the Jewish community to pay an "atonement" penalty of one billion marks for "causing" the event. This sum represented 15–20 percent of the total assets still held by the Jewish community.

However, though Jews had been murdered and injured, and Jewish property stolen or destroyed, Hitler and the Reich leadership were not altogether happy with what had occurred. They understood that this was not the way a civilized, 20th-century, Western European country carried out its policies. Thus, now began a new, intensive, discussion of how to solve the "Jewish problem."

It needs to be recognized that even at this relatively late date of November 1938 the main solution envisioned by the Third Reich for ridding itself of Jews was their emigration – if they could find somewhere to go. And between 1933 and 1938 German Jews did find such places. Consequently, of the 500,000 Jews in Germany in 1933, 304,000 Jews had emigrated by 1938, many to Palestine, which was then governed as a

---

[8] The black-shirted SS and the Brown Shirts were two semi-military forces created by Hitler; the Brown Shirts was the older of the two organizations, having their origins in the 1920s.

British mandate. This option, however, became less available as the British, in order to placate the Arabs, issued a White Paper in 1936 that curtailed the number of Jews permitted to enter Palestine. Nevertheless, emigration would still be the Nazis' preferred solution, and they applied it also after the Anschluss, the military takeover of Austria on March 13, 1938. Adolph Eichmann, who was sent by Himmler to oversee Jewish policy in Austria, allowed Austrian Jews to leave the country if they were willing to forfeit their wealth and possessions.

The crisis of Jewish migration, that is, of finding safe places for Jews to migrate to, also precipitated an intense conversation around the world that forced the League of Nations to call an international conference on refugees, that came to be held in Evian, France, in July 1938. But the meeting was largely a public relations exercise; few countries agreed to open their doors to Jews. Hitler even offered the organizers of the conference a deal: they could buy the freedom of individual Jews for $250, and a family for $1,000. But there were few takers. For example, despite unclaimed visa slots, the United States admitted only 27,000 Jews between 1933 and 1938.

START OF WORLD WAR II AND THE GHETTOS

On September 1, 1939, the Wehrmacht (German army) invaded Poland and World War II began. With it came a dramatic change in Nazi policy toward the Jews. Once the fighting in Poland was over – it lasted only three weeks – two new, crucial circumstances arose: (1) the Germans found themselves masters of 3,300,000 Polish Jews, and (2) emigration in the new wartime context had become impossible. Moreover, under the cover of war, new possibilities for solving the Jewish problem began to be examined by the Nazi leadership, with the lead in Jewish affairs being assumed by Heinrich Himmler and his SS lieutenants, Reinhard Heydrich and Adolf Eichmann.

In Poland, the Nazis, under the direction of Heydrich, continued the policy they had started in Germany; that is, they began to separate the Jews from the general population, demanded that they wear a yellow star on their outer clothing identifying them as Jews, and began to confiscate Jewish property and assets. By the spring of 1940, this grew into the policy of ghettoization that would apply wherever German forces gained control in Eastern Europe and, later, would complement the mass murders carried out by the Einsatzgruppen (killing squads) in the conquered Baltic states, the western half of the Soviet Union, and the Ukraine. Ultimately, there would be between

1,100 and 1,200 ghettos housing millions of Jews, their existence and survival ranging from a few weeks to many years.

As the name indicates, ghettos, unlike the death camps, were not meant to be killing centers. However, the Nazi view of the Jews as "subhuman," especially those from Poland and Eastern Europe, allowed them to create hellish conditions in which nearly 500,000 Jews would die during the course of the war. The main reasons for this outcome were lack of food, absence of medical care, and the poor conditions under which Jewish ghetto labor was utilized.

Lack of Food. Initially, the rules under which the ghettos were established prescribed that Jews should receive the same number of calories per day as prisoners in German jails. However, corruption meant food supplies intended for the ghettos were often stolen, and then, after the middle of 1941 and the agreement on pursuing the "Final Solution," the official decision was made not to feed Jews at anywhere near survival rates because they were all destined to be exterminated. It is estimated that by 1941 Jews in the Warsaw Ghetto were receiving only 184 calories per day, dooming everyone to starvation and death. Only the smuggling of food into the ghetto, mainly by children, slowed this process. In February 1941, 1,000 people in the ghetto died from malnutrition; by May the monthly total was 3,800. Food policy and extermination policy had now been successfully linked. Likewise, in Łódź, the official quota in 1941 called for 330 grams of food per day, causing rising mortality rates every month. Then, in August 1941, Reichsmarschall Goering announced that of the 1.3 million Jews in the Polish ghettos, only the 300,000 Jews working for the Nazi economy would be fed. The other Jews were defined as "useless eaters" and would not be given a food allowance.

Medical Care. In the ghettos, the combination of extreme food shortages, breakdown of sanitation, overcrowded housing conditions, lack of clean water, and the overworking of ghetto residents proved lethal. By 1942, all toilet facilities and water pipes had broken and no longer functioned. Furthermore, consistent with the Nazi policy of annihilation, the Nazis ruled that no medicine or medical supplies were to be sent into the ghettos. Emmanuel Ringelblum wrote in his diary on August 17, 1941, that the hospitals in the Warsaw ghetto had "lost their therapeutic character. They have become 'places of execution.'" Typhus and tuberculosis in particular became very common. Nazi medical officers and physicians in charge of ghetto medical policy consciously disregarded the need for medical intervention, with predictable results.

Two additional factors need also to be remembered. The Germans demanded that all Jewish women abort their pregnancies – no Jewish children were to be born. Second, the notorious experiments, associated most commonly with Dr. Mengele at Auschwitz, were begun in the ghettos.

Use of Jewish Labor. Ultimately, millions of Jews were incarcerated in ghettos. Due to severe shortages of manpower the Nazi leadership decided to employ a very small percentage of these individuals as slave labor. However, of the 400,000 Jews in Warsaw in 1940, by October 1942, 305,000 had been murdered or died from hunger and disease, rather than be fed enough to be useful workers. In late 1942, Himmler ordered a further reduction of 40 percent in the number of Jews allowed to remain alive as laborers for by now he was obsessed with completing the "Final Solution" without regard to its economic consequences.

Violence and Mocking Religious Practice. There were two further dehumanizing conditions that prevailed throughout all the ghettos and the concentration camps: gratuitous violence and mocking Jewish religious practice. Violence of all kinds against ghetto residents was primarily ideological. It was not aimed to increase production or put down resistance. Instead, it represented *state-approved* beatings, whippings, and then later gassing and shootings, to demonstrate that Jews were lesser beings and therefore outside the circle of moral obligation. Second, because of the unbreakable association of Jews with the practice of Judaism, it is important to recognize that for National Socialism not only Jews but also Judaism was the eternal enemy. To the Nazis, Judaism represented Jewish corruption and the embodiment of Jewish diseased subhumanity. Accordingly, Jews were forbidden to practice Judaism, for example, by keeping kosher, keeping the Sabbath, or celebrating Jewish holidays.

EINSATZGRUPPEN

On June 22–23, 1941, Hitler invaded Russia, home to 3 million Jews. Hitler saw the invasion not only as a war of conquest fought against a territorial and military enemy but also as a massive race war to destroy "Judeo-Bolshevism." That is, this was an ideological war based on the assumption that racially degenerate Jews controlled the Soviet Union and, consistent with *The Protocols of the Elders of Zion*, planned to dominate the world. To fight this unique sort of war the Third Reich created special killing squads known as Einsatzgruppen whose task it was not only to subjugate Russia but also to kill the political and racial enemies – that is, Bolshevik officials and Jews – of the Hitler state. In total, 3,000 men, divided into four units and led by reliable senior SS men, were formed. They were instructed to follow close behind the invading Wehrmacht troops, find Communist officials and important Jews, and kill them on the spot.

As the German troops moved into the Soviet Union, the Einsatzgruppen began their killing operations. Einsatzgruppe A began in the Baltic region; Einsatzgruppe B entered Belorussia; Einsatzgruppe C was responsible for operations in the North and Central Ukraine; and Einsatzgruppe D, led by Professor Otto Ohlendorf, the best known of the commanders of these units, initiated mass murder in the southern Ukraine and the Crimea. Making swift progress into Soviet territory as the Soviet army collapsed, large numbers of Jews – mostly men – were rounded up, shot, and buried in mass graves, or were set on fire in buildings and murdered in other grotesque rituals of murder. In carrying out this slaughter, the Einsatzgruppen were assisted by Order Police battalions comprised of 12,000 men and, in many locations, local anti-Jewish militias. In addition, the army was told, in an order given on May 19, to take "ruthless action" against the representatives of Judeo Bolshevism.[9]

The killing went on daily for over two years as the murderers made their way through the main cities in the western portion of the Soviet Union where almost 90 percent of Russian Jews lived. By the end of 1941, 600,000 Jews in the areas overrun by the four Einsatzgruppen had been savagely slaughtered, and by the end of 1943, over 1,400,000 Jews had been murdered. In addition, on July 17, 1941, Reinhard Heydrich, the chief of Reich Security and second in authority only to Himmler and Hitler as the main architect of the Nazi plan to murder the Jews of Europe, ordered the killing of all Russian Jewish prisoners of war.

The most common method of mass killing was described by a German soldier who participated in the killing of 33,772 Jews at Babi Yar on September 29–30, 1941. The Jews – men, women, and children – were made to march to the ravine at Babi Yar, five and a half miles outside Kiev (in the Ukraine). There they were made to undress. As the German soldier described the scene:

> The Jews had to lie face down on the earth by the ravine walls. There were three groups of marksmen down at the bottom of the ravine, each made up of about twelve men. Groups of Jews were

[9] Saul Friedlander, *Nazi Germany and the Jews* (New York, 2008), 134.

sent down to each of these execution squads simultaneously. Each successive group of Jews had to lie down on top of the bodies of those that had already been shot. The marksmen stood behind the Jews and killed them with a shot in the neck.... I had to spend the whole morning down in the ravine. For some of the time I had to shoot continuously.[10]

Though the squads had initially been ordered to kill only a certain class of Jew, by early August (2 or 3) Himmler ordered the commander of an SS unit near Pinsk to also begin killing Jewish women and children. He told a select group of SS and Wehrmacht officers that: "As a principle, I gave the order to kill women and children ... [because] we must constantly recognize what kind of primitive, primordial mutual race struggle [*Rassenkampf*] we are involved in."[11]

THE WANNSEE CONFERENCE

The early success of the Einsatzgruppen campaign, and the remarkable initial German military victory that occurred in the first three months of the war in the Soviet Union, gave Hitler and Himmler an overwhelming sense of their absolute military superiority. In this state of near euphoria they began to consider the possibility of killing all the Jews in Europe. In the fall of 1941, Hitler and Himmler appear to have reached an agreement to undertake this task immediately.[12] Himmler ordered Rudolph Höss to begin the establishment of Auschwitz, and Reichsmarschall Göring ordered Reinhard Heydrich to call together a high-level conference to announce the decision to exterminate all the Jews of Europe to the senior officials of the Third Reich. Fourteen officials were invited, plus Heydrich and his assistant, Adolf Eichmann. Initially scheduled to be held on December 7, 1941, the Japanese attack on Pearl Harbor on that date caused the meeting – known as the Wannsee Conference after the Berlin suburb where it was held – to be delayed until January 20, 1942.

Heydrich began the conference by explaining to the assembled audience that Göring had given him responsibility to organize a discussion regarding "the preparation of the Final Solution to the Jewish

---

[10] Cited from Richard Evans, *The Third Reich at War* (New York, 2009), 227.

[11] See the discussion in Peter Longerich, *Heinrich Himmler* (Oxford, 2012), 539.

[12] There is debate over this. Some scholars put the date of agreement between Hitler and Himmler on the "Final Solution" in September–October 1941; other scholars date this agreement somewhat later in the fall of 1941.

Question in Europe." He reviewed the anti-Jewish measures that had been taken to date and then concentrated on what was to be done to the Jews in the conquered areas of Eastern Europe and the Soviet Union. He described the policy to be adopted – Jews were to be put to work in Eastern Europe at heavy labor that would eventually cause their deaths, and for "the strongest element of the [Jewish] race and the nucleus of its revival" they would be "treated accordingly," which was a euphemism meaning extermination. Moreover, and crucially, the plan was not limited to the conquered Eastern areas but was to be actively applied in all the occupied states in Europe that were to be "combed from West to East." Indeed, the map used at the conference to indicate the extent of this all-encompassing assault, involving 11 million Jews, included substantial areas not yet under German control, such as Great Britain, Switzerland, Sweden, and Spain.

Heydrich, employing another euphemism, "transport to the east," described the program to annihilate Europe's Jews and the plans that had already begun to be made in this direction. The carrying-out of this gigantic undertaking would be under SS control "without regard to geographic boundaries."

The minutes of the meeting – which lasted an hour and a half – were kept by Adolph Eichmann. There were no objections from any of the bureaucrats or state secretaries present to the idea of murdering all the Jews of Europe; the only point that generated some discussion was the fate of the *Mischlinge* (individuals of mixed Jewish and non-Jewish race). The suggestion was made that they should be sterilized rather than deported, after which the participants went to lunch.

KILLING CENTERS

The task outlined at Wannsee was enormous. To carry it out, the Hitler state needed to expand its killing apparatus. Therefore, six killing centers – to be distinguished from concentration camps – were created, all located in Poland: Chełmno, Auschwitz, Majdanek, Sobibór, Bełżec, and Treblinka. These six sites all had gassing operations and crematoria and three also had establishments that were created to exploit Jewish labor, where workers were utilized under the principle of "annihilation through work," and when exhausted were sent to be gassed. All of this activity was, in theory, to be kept secret from the German people and from everyone else, though in reality secrecy was impossible given the number of individuals needed to carry out this plan, especially civilians working for the German

railways that carried Jews to the killing centers, and the many German
soldiers active in killing Jews who were writing letters home.

In connection with the death camps, experiments were conducted
to choose the most efficient method of killing and after a number of
trials it was agreed that the most efficient way was the use of Zyklon
B gas, unloosed into specially created chambers. This became the main
method of extermination, though it was complemented by other cruel
and sadistic methods in all the camps. The personnel chosen to operate
the six camps were SS men and reliable party members. The total
number of Jews killed at the six sites (according to German documents)
were as follows: at Auschwitz, 1,000,000; Treblinka, 800,000; Bełżec,
434,500; Sobibór, over 150,000; Chełmno, over 150,000; and Majdanek,
over 50,000. This came to a total of 2,585,000.

Jews were shipped to the camps from all over Europe. Nazi documents record the following: 300,000 from Poland, 69,000 from France,
60,000 from Holland, 55,000 from Greece, 46,000 from Czechoslovakia
(and the Protectorate of Bohemia and Moravia), 27,000 from Slovakia,
25,000 from Belgium, 23,000 from Germany, 10,000 from Croatia, 6,000
from Italy, 1,600 from Austria, 10,000 from Belarus, 700 from Norway,
and 394,000 Jews from Hungary.[13] Of these men, women, and children,
at least 90 percent were killed immediately on arrival at the Camps, or
very soon thereafter.

The first stage in the movement of Jews "to the east" involved
approximately 2,000 train journeys between 1941 and 1944. These
journeys brought 800,000 Jews to central Poland where the death
camps were located. Organizing the trains involved thousands of bureaucrats, technocrats, police officers, and German railway officials.
Jews were shipped in trains meant for cattle, each person being charged
a third-class group fare by the railroads, except for children under four,
who traveled free. To economize, the trains were lengthened, and each
car was packed very tightly as Jews were considered "freight," not
human beings. They were given no food or water and the cars were
unheated. One bucket for waste was supplied for up to ninety or 100
people. (In many cases Jews were also forced to fill out "change of
address" forms to be used to deceive others about their sudden
disappearances.)

On arrival at the camps, the train doors were opened, camp guards
with dogs screamed *"Raus! Raus!"* (Out! Out!), and thus began the

---

[13] Evans, *The Third Reich at War*, 304.

quick procedure that led most of those arriving to the gas chambers. The victims were told to undress for a shower; women had their hair cut; and the men, women, and children were violently herded into the gas chambers. The gas was introduced and in 15–20 minutes everyone was dead.

Though the victims had no value when alive, once dead they had value. The cut hair was sold and made into felt, gold teeth were extracted, and unusual body features or tattoos were made into lampshades and other souvenirs. After the bodies were cremated the ashes were spread around the watery parts of the camp to make the ground firmer.

The few Jews who were not immediately killed but who were selected for slave labor were housed in overcrowded huts and suffered inhumane treatment. One central truth must be understood: all the violence, sadism, sexual exploitation, and dehumanization that occurred at the death camps was intentional in order to confirm Hitler's belief that Jews were, by nature, a public health menace that needed to be destroyed. As such, they were *Untermenschen*, outside moral obligation. They were subjected to beatings and separation of families, were given rough, dirty clothing stained with human waste and wooden clogs that regularly created blisters, and were given numbers for identification as nonhumans don't have names. There was no privacy, with three people assigned to one bunk. They were given starvation rations and inadequate drinking water. They were physically punished for any infraction, real or imagined, and *"sportmachen,"* that is, tormenting the Jews to relieve the boredom of the camp guards, was allowed. There was sadism of all sorts, in both the men's and women's camps, rape and sexual exploitation of both men and women, and the shaming of Jews through what has been called "the excremental assault," that is, systematically subjecting Jews to filth and seeing them as waste. So one finds sadistic practices such as the following:

> ... latrines consisted of open pits ... and "one of the favorite games of the SS" ... was to catch men in the act of relieving themselves and throw them into the pit ... These same pits, which were always overflowing, were emptied at night by prisoners working with nothing but small pails.... The location was slippery and unlighted. Of the thirty men on this assignment, an average of ten fell into the pit in the course of each night's work. The others were not allowed to pull the victims out.

When work was done and the pit empty, then and then only were they permitted to remove the corpses.[14]

In sum, every sign of dignity and humanity was intentionally denied to those Jews kept alive for a short period while they were being worked to death.

MEDICAL EXPERIMENTS AND JEWISH CHILDREN

Perhaps the most ghoulish behavior of the Third Reich was its encouragement of medical experiments on Jewish men, women, and children. This began in the late 1930s and continued throughout the war, with sterilization experiments on Jewish women (and men) carried out by Dr. Carl Clauberg (and others), primarily at Auschwitz, beginning in July 1942. The initial medical intervention carried out on the Jewish women, who came primarily from Holland and Greece, consisted of three separate injections into their uteruses, spread over several weeks. The injections contained lipiodol, iodiprin, and F12a that had been diluted by Novocain. After receiving the injections, the women experienced peritonitis, inflammation of the ovaries, and a high fever. The ovaries were then surgically removed, usually in two separate operations, and then dispatched to Berlin for further study. If the women survived, they were, as a rule, sent to be gassed.

The most infamous experiments at Auschwitz were conducted by Dr. Josef Mengele, who especially enjoyed linking the suffering of Jewish mothers and infants. Feiga Lea Horowitz, a Jewish prisoner at Auschwitz, attested at the Nuremberg War Crimes Trials held after the war that "She had seen him [Mengele] order pregnant women to lie down on their backs so he could kick them in their stomachs to force induced labor."[15] Other witnesses gave evidence that he infected mothers-to-be with typhus to see what effect this might have on their infants. On other occasions he ordered the breasts of new mothers encased in plaster so they would be unable to nurse their children and he could see how long newborns could live without feeding.[16]

---

[14] Terence des Pres, *Survivor: An Anatomy of Life in the Death Camps* (New York, 1976), 64–65.

[15] Lucette Matalon Lagnado and Sheila Cohn Dekel, *Children of the Flames: Dr. Josef Mengele and the Untold Story of the Twins of Auschwitz* (New York, 1992), 80–81.

[16] A report about this practice is referenced in Nechama Tec's *Resilience and Courage: Women, Men, and the Holocaust* (New Haven, CT, 2003), 163.

Jewish children were also experimented on. The most extensive trials were again directed by Dr. Mengele in collaboration with the Kaiser Wilhelm Institute for Anthropology, Genetics and Eugenics in Berlin. His research on children focused on twins and, separately, the pathology and physiology of dwarfism. He would separate sets of twins arriving at Auschwitz and send them to his laboratory connected to Crematorium II. The children were of both sexes and ranged in age from two to sixteen. Many of these youngsters went blind from chemicals put in their eyes, and some of the very youngest died soon after the first medical examinations. Moshe Offer, a survivor of Mengele's twin experiments, remembers: "One day my twin brother, Tibi, was taken away.... Mengele made several operations on Tibi. One surgery on his spine left my brother paralyzed.... Then they took out his sexual organs. After the fourth operation, I did not see Tibi anymore."[17]

Finally, particular mention must be made of the absolutely singular Nazi assault on Jewish children from all over occupied Europe who were sent to death camps to be annihilated. According to German documents, 216,300 Jewish children and adolescents were sent to Auschwitz. Of these, over 215,850 were murdered. When the Russians arrived and liberated the Camp, only 212 adolescents and 239 children were still alive, one-fifth of 1 percent. At Treblinka, Sobibór, and Bełżec the percentage of child survivors was even lower: not one child survived in these camps. Often the children, rather than being asphyxiated in the gas chambers, were simply thrown alive into open fiery pits. Annani Silovich Pet'ko, a Russian survivor, attested after the war that she was present when a group of Jewish children were thrown into an open fire. The youngsters were, she remembered, "all under five years old. I heard that they had brought either an entire kindergarten or an orphanage from Dnepropetrovsk." Severina Shmaglevskaya, a Polish prisoner at Auschwitz, testified: "At that time when the greatest number of Jews were exterminated in the gas chambers, an order was issued that the children were to be thrown into the ovens.... The children were thrown in alive. Their cries could be heard all over the camp. It is hard to say how many there were."[18]

---

[17] Lagnado and Dekel, *Children of the Flames*, 71.
[18] The Nuremberg testimony is taken from *Trials of the Major War Criminals before the International Military Tribunal* (New York, 1971), vol. 8, 319–20.

FINAL COMMENTS

It was Hitler's racial metaphysics that justified this intentional, total extermination of the Jewish people, and the "Final Solution" was meant to actualize his plan to make the world *Judenrein* ("free of Jews"). This ambition represented Hitler's deepest beliefs and thus became a central operational aspect of the workings of the Third Reich. Had the war continued, the killing of Jews, seen as a crucial "public health" measure, would also have continued. No compromise with this goal was permissible.

One needs to recognize, however, that National Socialism's anti-Jewish policy from 1933 to 1945 did not evolve linearly. To understand its progress one must continually triangulate what was happening regarding the "Jewish Question" with what else was taking place in the Third Reich and within war-torn Europe more generally. Despite this, the extermination of the Jews was pursued throughout the war in an ever-more radical direction. In the end, the pursuit of the "Final Solution" transcended in importance all other issues on Hitler's agenda.

On April 29, the day before his death by suicide, Hitler left the world his final ideological testament. In it he repeated his never-ending fantasy about Jewish power. "It is untrue," he wrote, "that I or anyone else in Germany wanted the war in 1939. It was desired and instigated exclusively by those international statesmen who were either of Jewish descent or who worked for Jewish interests." He then encouraged the German/Aryan people to continue his anti-Jewish campaign. "Above all I pledge the leadership of the nation and its followers to the scrupulous observation of the racial laws and to an implacable opposition against the universal poisoner of all peoples, international Jewry."[19]

In closing this analysis of Nazi racial antisemitism there is one methodological issue that readers need to be aware of, namely, the "intentionalist" versus "functionalist" debate. These terms indicate two different ways of interpreting the Holocaust. Intentionalists believe that the murder of European Jewry was essentially determined by the acting-out of Nazi ideology and was authorized from the center in Berlin. Functionalists attribute more influence to nonideological and serendipitous factors. However, the reality is that the main events of the Holocaust – the creation of ghettos, Einsatzgruppen, and the

---

[19] Hitler, *Reden und Proklamationen, 1932–1945*, ed. Max Domarus, 4 vols. (Leonberg, 1987–88), vol. 4, 2226.

death camps – occurred only because of the annihilationist doctrine endorsed by Hitler and his chief lieutenant, Heinrich Himmler.

Further Reading

Cesarani, D., *Final Solution: The Fate of the Jews 1933–1949* (New York, 2016). The most recent, complete study of the Holocaust using newly available documentation.

Des Pres, T., *The Survivor: An Anatomy of Life in the Death Camps* (New York, 1976). A powerful depiction of life in the death camps and the origin of the notion of "excremental assault."

Friedlander, S., *Nazi Germany and the Jews*, 2 vols. (New York, 2008). A highly influential history of the Holocaust noted for its heavy use of Jewish sources.

Hilberg, R., *The Destruction of the European Jews* (New York, 1985), student one-volume edition. The most influential of all histories of the Holocaust. Draws mainly on German documents and answers the question, How did it happen?

Katz, S. T., *The Holocaust and New World Slavery*, 2 vols. (Cambridge, 2019). Volume 2 has detailed discussions of the Nazi treatment of Jewish women and children including their abuse in the ghettos and death camps.

Kershaw, I., *Hitler: A Biography*, 2 vols. (New York, 2000). The most thorough and well-constructed biography of Hitler in English.

Lagnado, L. M., and S. C. Dekel, *Children of the Flames: Dr. Josef Mengele and the Untold Story of the Twins of Auschwitz* (New York, 1991). Mengele's special interest in experimenting on twins is explained and documented in this study.

Longerich, P., *Heinrich Himmler* (Oxford, 2012). The main study of the man who directed the day-to-day murder of European Jewry. Thoroughly researched.

Niewyk, D. L., *The Jews in Weimar Germany*, 2nd ed. (New Brunswick, NJ, 2001). The standard study of antisemitism in the Weimar Republic.

Posner, G. L., and J. Ware, *Mengele: The Complete Story* (New York, 1986). Tells the entire story of this arch criminal in a readable and reliable way.

Schleunes, K. A., *The Twisted Road to Auschwitz: Nazi Policy toward German Jews, 1933–1939*, 2nd ed. (Champagne, IL, 1990). A classic discussion of the turns and twists that Nazi antisemitism took from 1933 to the carrying out of the Final Solution.

Weindling, P., *Health, Race and German Politics between Unification and Nazism, 1870–1945* (New York, 1989). A reliable history of the criminal character of Nazi medical experiments.

23 New Islamic Antisemitism, Mid-19th to the 21st Century

ESTHER WEBMAN

INTRODUCTION

The coronavirus pandemic which gripped the world in early 2020 unleashed a wave of antisemitic manifestations worldwide. In various combinations of the blood libel and *The Protocols of the Elders of Zion*, Jews were accused of spreading the virus either as a means to advance their plans to control the world or as a tool to make huge profits from inventing vaccines for it. The reactions to the virus in the Arab and Muslim worlds were no different, although it seems that the antisemitic manifestations were not as numerous as in past crises, probably due to the limited number of deaths because of the virus and the political rapprochement between Israel and certain Arab states. Nevertheless, the same amalgam of the blood libel and conspiracy theories could be found in newspaper commentaries and social media posts. The virus, explained a Jordanian writer, was the result of "the secret Jewish hatred towards the entire world." When the Jews caused the First World War, he went on to say, they were granted the Balfour Declaration; after they caused the Second World War they managed to establish their "settlement" in Palestine; and now they are instigating a third world war in order to announce their "great kingdom of Israel."[1] Iran, which was badly hit by the virus and perceives Israel and the United States as its bitter enemies, considered the virus as specifically targeting the Iranian genome, and Palestinians equated Israel to the coronavirus and suspected that it would exploit the global crisis in order to apply the annexation of the Palestinian territories.

This essay contends that antisemitism in the Arab and Muslim worlds is a religious, cultural, social and political construction of the contemporary era. This antisemitism comprises religious anti-Judaic and Judeophobic themes as well as imported Christian European

[1] As'ad al-'Azuni, "Corona or/and the Third World War," *Duniya al-Watan*, March 16, 2020, https://pulpit.alwatanvoice.com/articles/2020/03/16/516151.html.

antisemitic themes, and is part of a broader anti-Zionist and anti-Israel discourse, which developed as part and parcel of the Arab–Israeli conflict.

The first antisemitic manifestations appeared already in the 19th century, before the emergence of Zionism. Historians of Islam and the Arab world, such as Bernard Lewis, Norman Stillman and Mark Cohen, consider antisemitism in its present form in Arab and Muslim countries as a modern European import that is related to three major factors: (1) colonialism and the penetration of European ideologies and concepts, among them antisemitism; (2) the emergence of nationalism and the collapse of traditional political systems which undermined some of the pluralism that had existed until then, giving way to nationalist government structures less tolerant in their treatment of religious, ethnic and ideological minorities; and (3) the evolution of the conflict over domination of Palestine, beginning with the Jewish settlements in the late 19th century, followed by the establishment of the State of Israel and the ensuing Arab–Israeli conflict.

Traditional enmity toward the Jews under Islam was "unquestionably historically less malicious than traditional Christian anti-Judaism, in which Jews are represented as the murderers of God and the spawn of devil."[2] Yet there are textual roots to contemporary Islamist Judeophobia in the Islamic scriptures – the Qur'an and the Oral Tradition (*hadith*). Recognized as the People of the Book (*ahl al-kitab*), believers in monotheism, the Islamic attitude toward the Jews and Christians derived mainly from their status as religious communities that were protected by the Islamic state under Islamic law (*ahl al-dhimma*). They were allowed to exercise their religions and their communal life, but had to abide by the rules and duties dictated by a social framework of discriminations that emphasized the superiority of Muslims. It should be noted, however, that until the modern era, Jews lacked demonic qualities and Jew-hatred was on the whole "local and sporadic, rather than general and endemic."[3]

FROM THE MID-19TH TO THE MID-20TH CENTURY

The intensified European political and cultural penetration into a weakened Muslim world in the 19th century created a sense of deep

---

[2] Jonathan Judaken, "So What's New? Rethinking the 'New Antisemitism' in a Global Age," *Patterns of Prejudice* 42.4–5 (2008), 541.

[3] S. D. Goitein, *A Mediterranean Society*, vol. 2 (Berkeley, CA, 1971), 283, as quoted in Norman A. Stillman, "Anti-Judaism and Antisemitism in the Arab and Islamic World Prior to 1948," in *Antisemitism: A History*, ed. Albert S. Lindemann and Richard S. Levy (Oxford, 2010), 215.

crisis among Muslims, causing a worsening in their attitude toward non-Muslim minorities, mainly Christians and Jews, who were identified as the beneficiaries of the growing western influence and of various reform efforts carried out by local rulers. In his book *The Jews of Islam*, Bernard Lewis brings an early illustration of the shift in the balance of power between the western Christian world and the eastern Muslim world. He quotes a British document from November 1806, according to which James Green, His Majesty's consul general "in all the dominions of the Emperor of Morocco," appealed to the Moroccan Sultan on behalf of the Jews of Gibraltar, asking him to annul an order "prohibiting all persons professing the Hebrew religion in general from appearing in any of his dominions wearing the European dress."[4] The case is particularly significant as it symbolizes the beginning of a new tripartite relationship of the West, Islam and the Jews. The Jews sought the protection and intervention of the rising Christian power with the Muslim ruler, while still being under Muslim rule. Opting for the patronage of western Christian colonial powers and increasing identification with western culture caused suspicion to grow over the years suspicion and drove a wedge between Jews and Muslims.

With the colonial penetration came the missionaries, together with Christian Arab graduates of European schools, who started to disseminate anti-Jewish ideas and antisemitic themes. The first and most blatant manifestation of this development was the 1840 Damascus blood libel. This affair was touched off by the mysterious disappearance of an Italian Capuchin monk and his native Muslim servant in Damascus. The monks of the Capuchin order, supported by the French Consul Ratti-Menton, accused the Jews of the murder of the two men in order to use their blood for the approaching Passover holiday. A Jewish barber was arrested, and he confessed in his interrogation under torture, implicating seven more members of the Jewish community in the crime. Two of them died under the interrogation and the others were released through the intercession of two prominent Jews – Moshe Montefiore from England and Adolphe Crémieux of France – who interceded with the Ottoman Sultan, Abd al-Majid I, and the ruler of Egypt, Muhammad Ali. This affair not only marked the introduction of the blood libel to Arab and Muslim societies but reflected the growing interference of Great Britain and France in the affairs of the region, the growing reliance of the Jews on their mediation, and the growing involvement of European Jews

---

[4] Bernard Lewis, *The Jews of Islam* (Princeton, NJ, 1984), 154.

in the affairs of the local Jews. The blood libel in all kinds of derivatives became very popular in the Arab antisemitic discourse, especially in times of crisis.

The rise of antisemitism is also related to the rise of political Zionism at the end of the 19th century, when Jewish nationalism began to clash with nascent nationalism in the Middle East after the increase in Jewish immigration to Palestine. The newly established political and geographical order in this region in the wake of the First World War, the Balfour Declaration in November 1917 and the imposition of the British Mandate over Palestine in July 1922 all contributed to the exacerbation of tensions between Muslim and Jews. However, the initial Arab objections to Jewish settlement in Palestine were grounded not in anti-Jewish or antisemitic feelings but in "rational objections from an historical or empirical assessment of the situation."[5] There was an attempt to differentiate between Zionism and Judaism and between Zionists and Jews – a differentiation which has gradually been blurred since the end of the second decade of the 20th century.

Parallel to the emergence of nationalism, the last quarter of the 19th century also witnessed the rise of pan-Islamism, aiming at uniting all Muslims, fighting colonialism and restoring Muslim superiority by returning to the true Islamic values which has guided the early Muslim believers to their successes and victories. The Islamic scholars who advocated this view were not preoccupied with Jews, but they could not ignore them in their attempts to define the place of non-Muslims in their Islamo-national vision, and especially in view of the emerging conflict between the Arabs and the Jewish-Zionist settlers in Mandatory Palestine. At the beginning of the 20th century, for example, Rashid Rida, a leading Islamic thinker, denounced antisemitism in France during the Alfred Dreyfus trial and praised Jewish virtues, such as solidarity and preservation of their language and religion, but by 1934 he had developed a strong antipathy toward Zionism, adopting the belief in a global Jewish power and Jewish subversiveness, as reflected in *The Protocols of the Elders of Zion*.[6] The Muslim Brotherhood

---

[5] Yehoshua Porath, "Anti-Zionist and Anti-Jewish Ideology in the Arab Nationalist Movement," in *Antisemitism through the Ages*, ed. Shmuel Almog (Oxford, 1989), 219.

[6] Sylvia G. Haim, "Arabic Antisemitic Literature. Some Preliminary Notes," *Jewish Social Studies* 17.4 (October 1995), 309–10; Sylvia G. Haim, "The Palestine Problem in al-Manar," in *Egypt and Palestine: A Millennium of Association (868–1948)*, ed. A. Cohen and G. Baer (Jerusalem, 1984), 300–305.

movement, which was founded in 1928 by Hasan al-Banna in Egypt, already placed Palestine at the core of its Islamist ideology.[7]

Antisemitism began to make a significant headway in Muslim circles when nationalists adopted it in the 1920s and 1930s as a polemical weapon against Zionism and against the conspicuous overachievement of the Jews under colonialism. The Mufti of Jerusalem, Hajj Amin Al-Husayni, who was the leader of the Palestinian national movement under the British Mandate, consistently used anti-Jewish themes in his efforts to mobilize Arab and Muslim support in the struggle against Zionism. He warned of the Jews' ambitions to occupy Palestine and Jerusalem and to destroy the al-Aqsa Mosque in order to build the Third Temple. The Wailing Wall riots of 1929 were the first most important case of the use of Islam by the Palestinian leadership at the time. The Wailing Wall is the most sacred site in Judaism but is also the western boundary of the Muslim sacred precinct, which includes the al-Aqsa Mosque and the Dome of the Rock (*Haram al-Sharif*).

The incidents started on a religious day, the Day of Atonement, September 24, 1928, when Jewish worshippers at the Wall set up screens to partition men from women. The screens were considered an aberration of the status quo by the Arabs, and following their complaints to the British authorities, the screens were removed. But this did not calm the atmosphere. The riots spread to other locations, including Hebron and Jaffa, and reached their peak in the summer of 1929. The events of 1929 had a strong pan-Islamic impact, and Husayni exploited them to raise international Muslim interest in Palestine. He was the first prominent Arab leader and cleric who based his anti-Jewish incitement on the early Islamic texts, but he also combined the *Protocols* in his speeches with other political and religious arguments. Already in 1937 he was behind the dissemination of an antisemitic tract, *Islam and Jewry*, which combined anti-Jewish texts from Islamic religious scriptures and classical western antisemitic motifs, presenting the Jews as microbes, exploiters and conspiratorial.

Husayni interpreted Zionism as only the most recent manifestation of the supposed age-old Jewish hostility toward Islam, Muslims and Arabs. His anti-Zionism and opposition to the British drove him to pin his political hopes for independence on Nazi Germany as early as 1933. In November 1941, he escaped to Nazi Germany where he broadcast anti-Jewish propaganda, helped recruit Muslim volunteers to the Waffen

---

[7] On the Muslim Brotherhood, see Abd al-F. M. El-Awaisi, *The Muslim Brothers and the Palestine Question, 1928–1947* (London, 1998).

SS and actively tried to prevent any attempts to rescue Jews from Nazi-occupied lands. Although it is difficult to assess the impact of Husayni's virulent propaganda against Zionism and the Jews on the emerging Islamic new antisemitism, it is evident that over the years the Nazi antisemitic vocabulary became part and parcel of Arab and Muslim discourse on the Jews. The notion of an impending Jewish takeover of the world resonated with *The Protocols of the Elders of Zion*. Perceived as a historical fact and as an integral part of Jewish heritage, the *Protocols* were translated into Arabic in the mid-1920s by an Arab Christian in Palestine and, as in other countries, continually assumed new life, meaning and relevance.

During the period between the two world wars, the Arab press was extensively preoccupied with the issue of the Jews, especially in view of the rising antisemitism in Europe and the immigration to Palestine. However, it exhibited a wide and diversified range of attitudes, and was not obsessively engaged in portraying the Jews as inherently corrupt and evil.

FROM THE ESTABLISHMENT OF THE STATE OF ISRAEL TO THE SIX-DAY WAR

An abrupt change in attitude occurred in the immediate post–World War II era due to the intensifying Arab-Jewish struggle over Palestine with the establishment of the state of Israel in 1948. The conflict elicited a fierce public debate on Zionism, its nature, ideology, history and political aspirations, which still continues. Tackling Zionism was perceived as an existential national challenge, part of the anticolonialist struggle for national independence. This led to increasing preoccupation with the Jews and exposed a wide range of negative images and stereotypes of Jews, leading to a more monolithic discourse, which strives to deny Jewish nationhood and historical roots in Palestine.

In contrast to the general recoil from antisemitism in the West after the Holocaust, the Arab world underwent a change in the opposite direction, allowing antisemitism to flourish openly. The quantity and virulence of antisemitic literature published in the Middle East increased, and during the 1950s and 1960s it was printed partially under governmental auspices, and thus was not confined to the margins of society.

The birth of Israel and the Arabs' defeat in the war they launched against it were perceived by many Muslims as contradicting the right course of history and divine order since God had destined the Jews to be inferior and subordinated to Muslims. Moreover, Zionism's success became the most glaring symbol and proof of the deeper crisis of the Muslim world in the modern age. As the conflict deepened, antisemitism underwent a process of Islamization, using the Qur'an and Islamic traditions to rationalize the negation of Zionism, Israel and the Jews. Both nationalist and Islamist discourses on the Jews drew anti-Jewish themes from Islamic sources to prove the Jews' dubious character and to lend the animosity historic depth and continuity.

Pan-Arabism, the notion that all Arabs form one nation and should be politically united in one Arab entity, which was during the 1950s and 1960s the dominant political and ideological movement, became the primary carrier of antisemitism. Its champions, the populist-military regimes in Egypt and Syria, promoted it as a state policy from above. The pan-Arab worldview perceived Israel as an obstacle to Arab unity, its removal a precondition for Arab revival and self-fulfillment. Consequently, it portrayed the conflict as an existential one, and exacerbated the demonization of the Jews. The rising hostility toward Jews was a major reason for the mass Jewish exodus of 850,000 Jews from Arab countries after 1948.

During this period the myth of the *Protocols* appeared to be gaining ground in the intensified psychological warfare against the Jewish state. They were retranslated and republished in full or in part in various books and serialized in periodicals and dailies. Egyptian thinker and staunch critic of Nazism Abbas Mahmud al-Aqqad introduced the *Protocols* in his early articles in 1948 while covering the war in Palestine, and his book *International Zionism (al-sahyuniyya al-' ala-miyya)* was published in 1956 in the governmental indoctrination series *We Chose for You (Ikhtarna Laka)*, in order to prove the power of Zionism and to point to the ideological similarities between Nazism and Zionism. In 1951 a complete annotated version of the *Protocols* appeared in Egypt, for the first time translated by a Muslim academic, Muhammad Khalifa al-Tunisi. In his introduction, Tunisi described the Jews' fundamentally evil traits, explaining the importance of the *Protocols* for understanding Jewish conduct and events in the Middle East.[8] The same reasoning guided later translators and publishers, who continued to believe that the *Protocols* were the most important book ever to have been published in the world.

---

[8] Muhammad Khalifa al-Tunisi, *The Jewish Peril: The Protocols of the Elders of Zion* (Cairo, 1951, 1976) (in Arabic).

Another set of themes which started to develop as part of the Arab and Muslim antisemitic discourse since the end of World War II was related to the Holocaust. The diversified attitudes toward the suffering of the Jews exhibited during the 1930s and during the war, which also manifested an empathic and humanitarian approach, were replaced by a more homogenous approach deriving from political considerations. The Holocaust was perceived by Arab politicians, intellectuals, scholars and journalists as the major source of international legitimacy and support for Israel, and thus they developed a dual approach toward it: dissociation and intensive preoccupation. On the one hand, they claimed that the Arabs have nothing to do with it, but on the other hand, they could not ignore it. They felt the need to challenge what they considered as the "Zionist narrative" on the Holocaust, as well as its universal status, by employing a wide variety of themes and arguments, ranging from acknowledgment to denial. These include justification of the Holocaust; accusing Zionism of instrumentalizing the Holocaust and creating a "Holocaust industry"; accusing Zionism of collaboration with the Nazis in the extermination of European Jewry; equating Zionism with Nazism, and the reversal of the role of the Jews from victims to persecutors; comparing the Holocaust to the Palestinian tragedy (*nakba*); minimizing and relativizing of the Holocaust; and outright denial.

All those themes were already raised immediately after the war and were aimed primarily at demolishing the moral-historical basis of Zionism and the state of Israel.

FROM THE SIX-DAY WAR TO THE END OF THE 20TH CENTURY

The swift Israeli victory over the Arab armies in June 1967 dealt an additional blow to Arab self-esteem and generated sociopolitical unrest that continued to be channeled against Israel, Zionism and the Jews. The dominant pan-Arab political and ideological order was challenged by Islamist movements. Israel's image turned overnight from a weak country on the verge of collapsing economically and socially and being thrown into the Mediterranean sea before the war into "an all-powerful state." This shift required a satisfactory explanation, leading to the further entrenchment of conspiracy theories and demonization of Zionism and the Jews. The Israeli came to be demonized as a cruel and aggressive Nazi soldier, as an ugly hairy, hook-nosed and long-bearded Jew, or as a beast in a human body, reminiscent of the *Der*

Stürmer imagery.[9] The change also enabled a fundamentalist Islamism to flourish, which encouraged attempts to view the conflict and anti-semitism as being based in Islamic religious sources.

Jews came to personify the most reviled beings in Arab societies and were constructed to serve as an explanatory master key for all disasters, reinforcing the belief in the hidden hand or the hidden power of world Jewry – a force which if the world cannot confront, the weak Arab world obviously cannot. State-sponsored antisemitism has declined somewhat since the 1970s as Arab states began to change their policy toward Israel. Still, all Arab governments tolerated manifestations of antisemit-ism, which served as a safety valve, shifting the blame from the socio-economic failures of the regimes to an external enemy.

The peace treaty between Egypt and Israel, signed in 1979, did not bring about a significant change in Egyptian–Israeli relations nor a decrease of antisemitic manifestations. On the contrary, debates over the nature of these relations intensified, especially after the collapse of the Soviet Union in 1989, and with the expansion of globalization and the peace process which started with the convening of the Madrid peace conference in October 1991. Two distinct camps emerged on the issue of normalization of relations with Israel among Arab intel-lectuals: an anti-normalization camp and a peace camp. Far from being equal in size and influence, the dominant anti-normalization discourse was loaded with antisemitic overtones, combining conspir-acy theories with Islamist motifs. It continued to perceive the Arab–Israeli conflict as an existential rather than a territorial conflict and drew legitimization from religious figures such as the former Egyptian Grand Mufti, Nasr Farid Basil, Shaykh Yusuf al-Qaradawi, the con-temporary spiritual leader of the Muslim Brotherhood, and the defunct al-Azhar Front, which ruled that any kind of relations with Israel – trade, economic, cultural or social – is canonically forbidden. The anti-normalization discourse exposed a real or imagined fear of Israeli penetration in all walks of Egyptian or Arab life and loss of national and cultural identity.

Nevertheless, the collapse of the Soviet bloc and its impact on world affairs, including the Middle East; the emergence of the notion of a new world order; the 1993 signing of the Israeli-Palestinian accords; and the 1994 Israeli-Jordanian peace agreement provided

---

[9] *Der Sturmer* was a weekly German newspaper edited by Julius Streicher that was published from 1923 to 1945. It was virulently antisemitic and its articles and cartoons were a significant part of Nazi propaganda.

grounds for a revision of the Arab traditional approach toward the Jewish Holocaust among liberal Arab intellectuals. Criticizing the prevalent Arab perceptions of the Holocaust, they called for the unequivocal recognition of the suffering of the Jewish people, which they thought would lead eventually to the recognition of the Palestinian tragedy by the Israelis and facilitate reconciliation and coexistence between the two peoples. This new discourse marked a significant turning point in the Arab discussion of the Holocaust, expanded its dimensions and legitimized diverse views. Despite its relative limited number of propagators, this approach brought about a change in the representation of the Holocaust even among its opponents. It diversified the mainstream discourse, while increasingly confining denial to Islamists, who adamantly continued to oppose any kind of reconciliation with the Jewish state.

But the most conspicuous development after the Six-Day War was the rise of Islamist movements as the major sociopolitical player in several Arab countries. Islamist movements became the main carriers of antisemitism. The 1979 Iranian Revolution gave a further boost to the Islamists' strength, highlighting antisemitism as a basic tenet of the Islamist worldview. Unlike mainstream nationalists and leftists, Islamist movements perceived the Arab–Israeli conflict as an essentially religious conflict between Muslims and Jews and between Islam and Judaism, going as far as advocating genocide against the Jews. The resentment toward the Jews of the early Islamic period was translated into an Islamic, emotional and intellectual Judeophobia in Islamist writing and exegesis. Medieval polemics against the Jews, emphasizing the sins and evil they had committed against Muslims since the early days of Islam, particularly their fight and treachery against the Prophet Muhammad, were revived, as well as the old image of Judaism as a harsh and excessively restrictive religion compared with the more tolerant and humane Islam.

Consequently, Islamists view the Middle East conflict as the culmination of over a thousand-year historical, religious, cultural and existential conflict between Islam and Judaism and between Islam and western civilization, between divine law and man-made laws, between good and evil. Jews are depicted as traitors, warmongers, violators of agreements, Prophet killers, bloodsuckers, "brothers of apes and pigs" (based on a number of Qur'anic verses which state that some Jews were turned into apes and pigs by God, as a punishment for violating the Sabbath), disseminators of corruption on earth and enemies of God and humanity. The Islamists reject any distinction between Judaism and

Zionism, asserting that Zionism is simply a racist movement responsible for translating the aggressive Jewish idea into a belligerent reality. According to this interpretation, the clash is irreconcilable, and the destruction of Israel not only is predetermined but is also imperative in order to save humanity and civilization.

The Jews have become, as in European antisemitic thinking, a symbol of the modern world. Israel is completely identified with the West and considered its arm in the region for assuring its continued control, but at the same time also as manipulating the West against Islam. The Muslim Brotherhood, Muslim scholars and Hamas and similar Islamist movements accuse the Jews of spreading atheism, instigating revolutions and inventing corrupted ideologies. However, Islamists, who consider western cultural influence as anathema to authentic Islamic culture, do not hesitate to borrow anti-Zionist and anti-Jewish themes from the West in the service of their cause. The Hamas charter adopted in 1988, for instance, provides a picture of the Jews and Judaism, which is based on, if not directly taken from, *The Protocols of the Elders of Zion*. Similarly, Shaykh al-Azhar Muhammad Sayyid al-Tantawi, the most senior figure in Egypt's religious establishment, in his book *The Children of Israel in the Qur'an and the Sunna* (1997), described extensively the Jews' atrocious acts against the prophet Muhammad and also surveyed their history in Europe, with extensive quotations from *The Protocols of the Elders of Zion* as a major historical source. In addition to initiating the two world wars of the twentieth century for profiteering, Tantawi accused the Jews of conducting "treacherous acts" against Germany during World War I, which led to its defeat. They were rewarded for their treachery with the 1917 Balfour Declaration, which recognized Zionism's claims to Palestine. The Jews, he argued, had exploited the German people ever since the 8th century, and therefore it was no wonder that they rose up against them on a number of occasions, using all possible means of killing, expulsion and robbery. The Holocaust was but the last phase in this chain of confrontations between Germans and Jews, understandable and justifiable, since Hitler, according to Tantawi, was one of those "who put together all of the treacherous deeds" and took action against them to defend himself and "God's creation."[10]

---

[10] Muhammad Sayyid al-Tantawi, *The Children of Israel in the Quran and the Sunna* (Cairo, 1986–87) (in Arabic), 623, 647–48, 651.

THE SECOND INTIFADA AND 9/11: A SINISTER START FOR THE 21ST CENTURY

Two major events occurred at the turn of the 21st century, which had a lasting impact on antisemitism worldwide: the outbreak of violence in the West Bank in September 2000 in response to the failure of peace negotiations in July and in reaction to the visit of the then prime minister Ariel Sharon to the Temple Mount, and the September 11, 2001, attacks on the World Trade Center in New York and the Pentagon in Washington by the global jihadist movement al-Qaʿida (the Base), led by Usama bin Ladin. The chain of events that started on the West Bank lasted for almost five years and came to be known as the Second Intifada,[11] or Al-Aqsa Intifada; it brought in its wake an upsurge of antisemitic manifestations and incitement in Arab and Muslim countries. Mass demonstrations were held in major Arab and Muslim cities, terrorist attacks were carried out against Israeli targets, and several acts of vandalism were perpetrated against Jewish holy sites in the West Bank. It spilled into the cyber media, as a means to win over world public opinion and mobilize Arab and Muslim masses. The Second Intifada highlighted the religious dimension of the Arab–Israeli conflict and blurred the lines between the national and Islamist discourses. This led to the radicalization of the discourse against Israel, Zionists and Jews, as well as against the United States, and provided a happy hour for the antinormalization movement, which fervently fought the peace process and managed to suppress most of its opponents. This radicalization was manifested in the popularization of antisemitic motifs, such as the blood libel and *The Protocols of the Elders of Zion* in TV programs and drama series, the utilization of the equation of Zionism to racism and Nazism in the struggle against Israel in international forums, the promotion of Holocaust denial and the sanctioning of suicide attacks against Israeli civilian targets and Jewish targets worldwide. Muslims were called on to kill Jews worldwide, since holy war (*jihad*) was seen as a duty incumbent on the entire Muslim *umma* (community) until Palestine and the al-Aqsa mosque are liberated and Jews are pushed either into their graves or back where they came from.

---

[11] Instigated by the rise of Hamas and the Islamic Jihad, the first Intifada erupted in the Gaza Strip at the end of 1987 and lasted for almost four years, eventually leading to peace talks and the Oslo Agreement between the Palestinian Liberation Organization (PLO), led by Yasser Arafat, and the Israelis. See Shaul Mishal and Reuven Aharoni, *Stones Aren't Everything – The Intifada and the Leaflet Weapon* (Tel Aviv, 1989) (in Hebrew).

The sanctioning of suicide attacks and the equation of Zionism and racism were aimed at delegitimizing the occupation of the West Bank by Israel as well as Israel's right to exist, while the resort to the ancient motifs of the blood libel and the *Protocols* sought to delegitimize the Jewish people as a whole. The media became a powerful tool in shaping the collective consciousness, and exacerbated the conflict through the projection of Palestinian victimization, false statements, the justification of violent actions and demonization of Israel and the Jews.

The Second Intifada also brought an upsurge in the antisemitic discourse and incidents in Europe, especially among Muslim immigrant communities. Muslim youths were behind most of the violent incidents. Radical Islamist incitement emanating from Arab countries by satellite TV, audiocassettes, CDs and the internet, in addition to European-based radical preachers calling for violence against the Jews, inflamed anger over the Middle Eastern situation among Muslims. Frustration over their lack of integration in European societies and envy at the more successful Jews probably added to their animosity. Such feelings received additional legitimacy from the growing anti-Israeli discourse, particularly among the left, which increasingly challenged Israel's legitimacy to exist as a state of the Jewish people.

The 9/11 attacks caught the Arab and Muslim worlds, as everybody else, by surprise. But unlike the unequivocal worldwide reaction of horror and denunciation, the reactions in the Arab and Muslim worlds were confused and hesitant, ranging from half-hearted condemnation to sheer jubilation, evincing a deep-seated enmity toward the West. This enmity, exacerbated by a continued feeling of humiliation by the world of Islam and cherished by Bin Laden's Islamist worldview, was the driving force behind the attacks. The struggle, or *jihad*, against "the Jews and the Crusaders" (Christians) is a major theme in the ideology of al-Qa'ida and its offspring ISIS (Islamic State of Iraq and Syria) and constitutes the first stage in a long campaign for the restoration of the Muslim caliphate and the establishment of an Islamic world order. According to this view, the Jews not only are the occupiers of Muslim lands in Palestine but are part of the western Judeo-Christian civilization, perceived as a threat to Islamic civilization and Islamic revival. Hence, the reactions to the attacks were basically composed of two interrelated tiers: anti-Americanism and antisemitism.

Looking for competent perpetrators and conspirators "naturally" led to the Jewish connection and gave rise to a host of arguments linking Jews, Zionism and the Israeli Mossad to the attacks. They were presented as "the act of the great Jewish Zionist mastermind that controls the world's economy, media, and politics." The goal of the operations was to coerce the United States and NATO "to submit even more to the Jewish Zionist ideology" by cultivating fears of "Islamic terrorism" and instigating a war against Islam. Posing the question behind most conspiracy theories, that is, who would benefit most from the attacks, it was argued that Israel stood to benefit most from the bloody operation by accusing Arabs and Muslims of perpetrating it. Moreover, only a highly efficient intelligence agency, with access to facilities and information inside the American system, such as the Mossad, could be behind the events. Five Israeli youth put in custody for photographing the scene of the crumbling buildings provided another proof of Israeli involvement and were said to be Mossad agents. But the most popular claim, allegedly proving the Jews' prior knowledge of the planned attacks, was the claim that 4,000 Jews did not report to work at the World Trade Center on the day of the attack.

The September 11 events unveiled the imminent threat against Jews worldwide as part of the Islamists' war against the West and particularly the United States and led to the further entrenchment of conspiracy theories and antisemitism. The subsequent war on terrorism, the war in Iraq in 2003, the Second Lebanon War in July–August 2006 and the Israeli-Palestinian confrontations in Gaza in December 2008–January 2009, November 2012 and July–August 2014 further exacerbated in the Muslim mind the demonic traits of the Jews. The blood libel, conspiracy theories, and the equation of Zionism with Nazism continue to be used by the media – newspaper articles, cartoons, TV series, films and social media – to popularize the image of the Jew as bloodthirsty and a conspirator striving to control the world.

In 2011, a decade after the Second Intifada and 9/11, a wave of upheavals swept the Arab Middle East. Known as the "Arab Spring," they led to the collapse of the existing regimes in Tunisia, Egypt, Libya and Yemen and to the eruption of long bloody internal wars in Libya, Yemen and Syria. At their outset there were a few rays of hope that the obsessive preoccupation with Israel and the Arab–Israeli conflict would diminish, but soon it was realized that they did not mark any significant change in antisemitic perceptions. Although the volume of antisemitic articles in the Arab press diminished somewhat, and the unrelenting struggle between the nationalist and the Islamist forces diverted attention from the Palestinian issue, the Zionist, the Jew and the Holocaust seem to be so entrenched in Arab public discourse that they continue to be repeatedly invoked.

The most notable new phenomenon in the antisemitic discourse since the outburst of the "Arab Spring" is the widespread usage of the term "Jew" as a derogatory term to bash the adversary Other. Each camp, whether the revolutionaries or the old regimes, not only accuse each other of cooperating or conspiring with Zionism and the Jews but actually expose them as "being Jewish." The "Jew" is thus constructed as a functional metaphor, an all-purpose villain, to explain the changing circumstances and catastrophes that befall Arab societies, particularly in the wake of the Arab Spring. The metaphor "Jew" has become a "cultural code" – "a sign of cultural identity, of one's belonging to a specific cultural camp" and "a short-hand label of an entire set of ideas and attitudes."[12]

CONCLUSION

The antisemitic wave, which has swept much of the world since the eruption of the Second Intifada and the events of September 11, gave rise to a new term: "new antisemitism." The term was needed to clear the theoretical and conceptual confusion between old antisemitism and anti-Zionism and anti-Israel positions. The three terms became insufficient for defining the new global phenomenon of criticizing Israeli policies and Zionism by increasingly intertwining antisemitic motifs. The new term denotes the following: attributing Israel's misdeeds to innate Jewish racial characteristics, deploying antisemitic language and imagery, comparing Israelis and Jews to Nazis, questioning the right of Israel to exist and the definition of the Jews as a nation, and denying the Holocaust. These traits typify Arab antisemitism since the early stages of its development, and they provide the justification for Israel's obliteration.

The proliferation of antisemitic manifestations also triggered a debate over the roots of antisemitism in Arab and Muslim societies, and over the significance of virulent Arab utterances against Israel and the Jews, offering opposite interpretations. The common stance among scholars of Arab antisemitism is that it is a new phenomenon, which developed out of the changing circumstances in the Middle East in the 19th century and particularly in the wake of the Arab–Israeli conflict. Arab antisemitism, according to Yehoshafat Harkabi, was "not a cause of the conflict but a product of it. The Arabs did not oppose Jewish

---

[12] Shulamit Volkov, "Antisemitism as a Cultural Code: Reflections on the History and Historiography of Antisemitism in Imperial Germany," *Yearbook of the Leo Baeck Institute* 23 (1978), 35.

settlement for antisemitic motives; their opposition aroused antisemitic emotions among them." However, once the conflict existed and antisemitism created, it became one of the factors that gave the conflict its character, contended Harkabi.[13] Antisemitism developed as a theme of an ethos of conflict, constructed to support its continuation with language, stereotypes, images, myths and collective memory. With their inculcation, anti-Jewish beliefs became an organic part of Arab/Muslim worldviews.

The opposing school of thought claims that Arab antisemitism stems from a long religious and cultural tradition and that Muslim Jew-hatred dates back to the origins of Islam and is embedded in Islamic doctrines and history. Moreover, it also contends that Arab nationalism and Islamic fundamentalism bear inherent fascist traits.[14] Some scholars also attach to Nazism a significant role in the emergence of antisemitism in the Middle East since the 1930s.[15]

There is no definite conclusion to this controversy. But it seems that scholars of Islam and the Middle East agree that "Islamic culture includes natural antipathy directed against Jews ... that arose from the phenomena associated with the emergence of new religions ... [and] that antipathy is embedded in the Qur'an, the Hadith, and most forms of traditional literature."[16] However, this antipathy was not frequently translated into operational action against the Jews under Muslim rule until the modern era. The latent antisemitism becomes activated when life becomes difficult and people's hopes and dreams are frustrated, when there is a need to blow off steam or find scapegoats for serious disappointment and aggravation. Then, "ancient slanders are re-discovered, old writings and complaints are renewed and stereotypes images revived. The result is the restoration of an old prejudice in new clothes."[17]

The chain of events in the Arab world since 2011, and up to the writing of this essay, does not promise a real change in the perception of Israel, Zionism and the Jews. Israel and the conflict are not the focus of the Arab revolutions, but they still dominate the political discourse as part and parcel of the ideological divisions and the public debate which

---

[13] Yehoshafat Harkabi, *Arab Attitudes towards Israel* (Jerusalem, 1974), 225–26.
[14] Robert S. Wistrich, *The Myth of Zionist Racism* (London, 1976), 9.
[15] Matthias Küntzel, *Jihad and Jew-Hatred: Islamism, Nazism and the Roots of 9/11* (New York, 2007).
[16] Reuven Firestone, "Islamophobia and Anti-Semitism: History and Possibility," *Arches Quarterly* 4.7 (winter 2010), 49.
[17] Ibid., 45.

has been going on in Arab societies for more than 200 years over the nature of Islam–state relations, the interaction with other cultures, and the course of change, liberalization and democratization.

Although Islamists continue to envision a world without Jews, and despite widespread antipathy toward the Jews and the continued rejection of Zionism and Israel in Arab and Muslim societies, there are increasing Arab and Muslim voices that criticize antisemitism and even look at the Jews and Israel as a model worthy of appreciation and emulation. Criticism of antisemitism is part of a self-critical literature, which bemoans the inability of Arab and Muslim societies to overcome their differences and solve their acute predicaments. It increased in the mid-1990s when it seemed that globalization and normalization of relations with Israel would usher a new era of democratization and liberalization; in response to the rise of global Jihadist movements at the turn of the 21st century; and in the wake of the "Arab Spring" in 2011. The new nexus between Islamism and terrorism, embodied in ISIS, increased self-criticism in Arab and Muslim societies, which incorporates criticism of the belief in conspiracy theories and of the antisemitic discourse associated with it.

Further Reading

Bostom, A. G., *The Legacy of Islamic Antisemitism* (Amherst, NY, 2008). A compilation of primary and secondary sources of and on Islamic antisemitism. This book includes a long introduction contending that Islamic antisemitism has a long-established history embedded in the religion and culture of Islam.

Cohen, M. R., "Modern Myths of Muslim Anti-Semitism," in *Muslim Attitudes to Jews and Israel: The Ambivalences of Rejection, Antagonism, Tolerance and Cooperation*, ed. Moshe Maoz (Brighton, 2010), 31–47. Based on his comparative study of Muslim and Christian attitudes toward the Jews in the medieval era, this essay challenges the view that antisemitism is an old phenomenon, rooted in Islamic tradition.

Frankel, J., *The Damascus Affair: "Ritual Murder," Politics, and the Jews in 1840* (Cambridge, 1997). A comprehensive account of the Damascus blood libel from 1840, including an analysis of behind-the-scenes struggles between the big powers.

Herf, J., *Nazi Propaganda for the Arab World* (New Haven, CT, 2009). A study of Arabic broadcasting to the Arab and Muslim worlds from Nazi Germany during World War II, with an emphasis on the anti-Jewish and antisemitic propaganda.

Lewis, B., *Semites and Anti-Semites* (London, 1997). The first and so far the only study fully dedicated to antisemitism in the Middle East from the end of the 19th century to the 1990s.

Litvak, M., and E. Webman, *From Empathy to Denial: Arab Responses to the Holocaust* (London, 2009). This study is a comprehensive account of Arab attitudes toward the Holocaust from the end of World War II to the first decade of the 21st century.

Nettler, R. L., *Past Trials and Present Tribulations: A Muslim Fundamentalist's View of the Jews* (Jerusalem, 1987). This book provides a thorough analysis and translation of the tract "Our Struggle with the Jews" by Sayyid Qutb, which clearly exposes the Islamist perceptions of the Jews.

Sivan, E., "Islamic Fundamentalism, Antisemitism and Anti-Zionism," in *Anti-Zionism and Antisemitism in the Contemporary World*, ed., Robert Wistrich (London, 1990), 74–84. This essay discusses the role of antisemitism and anti-Zionism in the ideology of Islamist movements since the late 1960s.

Webman, E., "Al-Aqsa Intifada and 11 September: Fertile Ground for Arab Antisemitism," in *Antisemitism Worldwide 2001/2*, ed. Dina Porat and Roni Stauber (Tel Aviv, 2003), 37–59. This chapter is a survey of the antisemitic manifestations in the Arab media in the wake of the intifada and the 9/11 attacks.

"The 'Jew' as a Metaphor for Evil in Arab Public Discourse," *The Journal of the Middle East and Africa* 6.3–4 (2015), 275–92. This article traces the historical roots of the use of the term "Jew" as a negative noun. This tendency intensified in the antisemitic discourse in the wake of the "Arab Spring."

Wistrich, R., *Muslim Anti-Semitism: A Clear and Present Danger* (New York, 2002). This booklet, published in the middle of the Second Intifada, discusses antisemitism in Arab and Muslim societies, stressing its Islamic roots and genocidal intent.

Yadlin, R., *An Arrogant Oppressive Spirit: Anti-Zionism as Anti-Judaism in Egypt* (Oxford, 1989). This study presents the negative attitudes toward Zionism, Israel and the Jews in Egypt ten years after the signing of the peace agreement between Israel and Egypt in 1979.

24 Anti-Zionism as Antisemitism

DINA PORAT

Webster's Third New International Dictionary of the English Language defined antisemitism in its 1966 edition as follows: "(1) hostility toward Jews as a religious or racial minority group often accompanied by social, economic and political discrimination; (2) opposition to Zionism: sympathy with opponents of the state of Israel."[1]

Martin Luther King Jr. put it even more clearly, in a letter attributed to him a year later, "Letter to an Anti-Zionist Friend": "You declare my friend, that you do not hate Jews, you are merely 'anti-Zionist.' And I say ...: When people criticize Zionism, they mean Jews – this is God's own truth.... so Know this: anti-Zionism is inherently antisemitic, and ever will be so."[2]

The authoritative dictionary had later other definitions,[3] and research proved that King did not send such a letter – the alleged wording is based on his answer given to a Harvard student. Nevertheless, both were repeatedly quoted by Jewish supporters of Zionism and by Israeli personalities as sympathetic: both the dictionary definition and the answer are perceived to be based on the notion of discrimination – if every nation is entitled to a state, then opposing a national movement struggling for the rights of a nation to reach one is discrimination, which, in this case, originates in antisemitism.

* * *

Anti-Zionism means, semantically speaking, being against Zionism, which is a term signifying the connection between the Jewish people

---

[1] *Webster's Third New International Dictionary of the English Language*, vol. 1 (Springfield, MA, 1966), 96.

[2] Eric J. Sundquist, *Strangers in the Land: Blacks, Jews, Post-Holocaust America* (Cambridge, MA, 2005), 110.

[3] Such as the *Merriam-Webster Dictionary*: "Hostility toward or Discrimination against Jews as a Religious or Racial Group" (New York, 1974), 51.

and their land, Zion, and the longing of Jews to return to it, during the almost 2,000 years of their exile. Zion is the biblical name of the country, as well as the name of Jerusalem and the Kingdom of Judea established by King David. From the end of the 19th century Zionism became the term used for the modern national movement of the Jewish people, which defined national political goals as fulfilling the former longings and connection by returning physically to Zion and reestablishing there a Jewish political entity. Therefore, anti-Zionism means objection to and rejection of the goals of the Zionist movement since its inception and of the state it created, per se or as a Jewish state. It is a well-known term often used in today's political and social discourse – especially in the Western world, as well as in the internal Israeli and Jewish discourse – to define a wide variety of persons, organizations, intellectual and academic tendencies and even a few states as anti-Zionists, opposing the Zionist perception that nourishes a Jewish national perception and/or the existence of the state of Israel.

The Zionist political movement was founded in the 1880s, parallel to the consolidation of a new phase in the long history of Jew-hatred. The political modern antisemitic movement consisted of political parties each active in its local arena and together across Europe, and a host of thinkers, authors and activists, producing a multitude of books, pamphlets, journals, stickers, agendas and platforms, and proposals for parliaments. All these had in common the desire to limit, if not to completely abolish, the civil rights Jews had managed to procure in the previous decades, by pinpointing the Jews as a physically ugly and morally dangerous and cunning entity, wishing from its very inception to dominate the world, unfit to be equal citizens, "a Jewish problem."

While the two movements, the Zionist and the antisemitic, developed side by side, the antisemitic one was not necessarily anti-Zionist. On the contrary: a known slogan at the time urged Jews to "go back to Palestine!" But this was just one idea in a long line of suggestions to get rid of Jewish presence. Still, the meeting point between the two was not late to come, and it occurred in the last years of the century, when – again in parallel – *The Protocols of the Elders of Zion* was being forged; the gathering of the first Zionist congress in Basel, Switzerland, was planned and convened; and the Dreyfus affair started in France.

The *Protocols*, a libel against the Jewish people, known, widely translated and distributed worldwide since the first years of the 20th century, claims that the twelve tribes of Israel, led by their elders, convene every hundred years to advance their plot to dominate the world. The usually small booklet that presents this libel as if there were indeed protocols written by the Elders in their tribal meetings has a host of variations, because it is an imaginary invention and forgery that does not rely on any solid source. Yet it became a crucial text, because it embodies the anxiety that spread over Europe in the second half of the 19th century: Jews would use the emancipation they just got as a tool to dominate the world from Zion, to which they will return to rebuild the Kingdom of David. No wonder, then, that the first edition of the *Protocols*, published in Tsarist Russia a few months after Theodor Herzl, the visionary of the Zionist political movement, passed away in 1904, was later translated into English with an introduction that referred to Herzl and to the Zionist movement: "There is a well-established assumption, that the *Protocols* were written or re-written, in the first Zionist congress that took place in Basel in 1897 under the presidency of the father of modern Zionism, Theodor Herzl, who is not alive anymore."[4]

Here is the first link between antisemitism and anti-Zionism: the antisemitic text par excellence, when translated for worldwide distribution, depicts the Zionist modern movement in its very first steps as "a new variation of the eternal Jewish conspiracy against the non-Jewish world."[5]

Opposition was not late to come from within: the Zionist movement was vehemently opposed by most other intellectual, social and political movements within the Jewish people. On the eve of World War II registered members of the Zionist movement amounted to no more than 10 percent of the world's Jewish population, though a much larger periphery was sympathetic to its ideas. The main movements and parties that rejected Zionism as the wrong way to go, a blasphemy even, while advocating their own solutions to "the Jewish problem," were the following:[6]

- The Bund (union), a Jewish Socialist Yiddishist (Yiddish, the Jewish East European language) party, represented the majority of Jewish workers in Eastern Europe, advocated cultural autonomy for Jews in their respective countries and fostered secular Jewish identity and equal social rights to all;
- Most of the very varied groups within Orthodox Jewry opposed, and still oppose, Zionism, no less vehemently than the Bund. They abhor Zionism as a secular way of life, a movement that did not

---

[4] *Protocols of the Meetings of the Learned Elders of Zion*, trans. from Russian by Victor E. Marsden (London, 1936), 6. The author of the introduction is unknown.
[5] Jacob Katz, "Zionism vs. Anti-Semitism," *Kivunim* 2 (February 1979), 56 (Hebrew).
[6] Haim Avni and Gideon Shimoni, eds., *Zionism and Its Jewish Opponents* (Jerusalem, 1990 [Hebrew]).

wait for the Messiah to come to rescue his people under God's instructions, but rather acted against His will. Orthodox groups living in Israel, in Jerusalem mainly, still do not recognize the authority of the state;[7]

- Jewish Communists, anarchists and ultra-leftists bitterly fought Zionism, being a national movement, believing that communism would bring equality among nations and within each nation, thereby solving the "Jewish problem";
- The Autonomists (a position advanced by the Russian historian Shimon Dubnov) wished for cultural autonomy for Jews wherever they lived.
- The Territorialists dreamt of a territory or, if possible, territories, outside the Land of Israel;
- The Assimilationists rejected the idea of Jewish nationalism and wished to be integrated into the non-Jewish societies, especially those in the liberal West.

All these movements went bankrupt during and following World War II and the Holocaust, proving to be an illusion. The Orthodox, too, killed en masse by the Germans, were at their lowest point in the wake of the war. Zionism suddenly remained the only feasible option, and most of the bitter arguments it had raised subsided once two-thirds of the surviving remnant that left Europe reached the shores of the Land of Israel, and the state was established in 1948. All these movements were staunchly anti-Zionist, yet it was an internal Jewish debate, having no bearing on antisemitism. Moreover, the fathers and visionaries of the Zionist movement held a fundamental belief that a Jewish entity in Zion would change the image of Jews and the relations between them and the non-Jewish world. Jews would leave Europe and other regions of the world and come home; the new Jew would be similar to non-Jews, not to the exilic Jew, and thus the causes for antisemitism would lose their grip, and it would gradually diminish.

The immediate outcome of these aspirations was that antisemitism was not an issue in Israel in its first decades – it belonged to a former, different world, based on centuries-old prejudices and hatred. Anti-Zionism coming from the local Arabs, even when expressed in violence, was considered a legitimate, though unfortunate,

---

[7] Benjamin Brown, *The Haredim: A Guide to their Beliefs and Sectors* (Tel Aviv, 2017 [Hebrew]); Dina Porat, "'Amalek's Accomplices': Blaming Zionism for the Holocaust: Anti-Zionist Ultra-Orthodoxy in Israel during the 1980's," *Journal of Contemporary History* 27.4 (October 1992), 695–729.

misunderstanding of Zionist good intentions to develop the country for the benefit of all its inhabitants, and not an outcome of antisemitism. Arabs are Semites, and cannot, a priori, be antisemites.[8] Antisemitism was considered a product of the far right, fascism and other reactionary ideologies, which were denounced in the wake of World War II. The left, intellectually and politically, supported Israel and the Jewish people. The Soviet Union, the bastion of the left, voted in the UN 1947 resolution in favor of establishing a Jewish state, planning to replace Britain in the Middle East. It sent vital military aid to Israel, via Czechoslovakia, at a crucial point during the 1948 war of independence, and was deeply admired by the Israeli left, then at the center of the political map, for withholding against Nazi Germany during the war. Its attitude to its Jewish citizens, which remained hostile, was still considered a different, though painful issue.[9]

These assumptions, and the political reality they were based on, were overturned in the early 1960s by the Adolf Eichmann trial in Jerusalem when the complete story of the Holocaust unfolded on a global scale. It was during the trial that the extent of the Nazi antisemitism and Jew-hatred, with its horrendous results, manifested itself, and the scornful attitude widely present at that time among high German echelons toward a possible Jewish state – they envisioned a Jewish state as a Vatican, a refuge for criminals, and stronghold from which to attack Germany – was exposed. All this now became known to the younger generation in Israel, that same new generation that was not aware of antisemitism. The possibility of connections between antisemitism and anti-Zionism also surfaced at this juncture, strengthened by the most egregious example that came up during the trial: the Grand Mufti of Jerusalem, Hajj Amin al-Hussayni, was both a fervent anti-Zionist and, at the same time, attempted to encourage Hitler and Eichmann to implement the "Final Solution" in general and in the Land of Israel in particular.[10]

In the Six-Day War, Israel rescued itself from annihilation, defeated the armies of the Arab states who were well equipped with Soviet armaments, and tripled its territory. This victory led to a fundamental change in the position of the Soviet Union, which altered its political

---

[8] Anita Shapira, *Land and Power: The Zionist Resort to Force, 1881–1948* (Stanford, CA, 1999), chap. 4.

[9] Alexey Vasiliev, *Russia's Middle East Policy, from Lenin to Putin* (New York, 2018), chap. 9.

[10] Dan Michman, "Adolf Hitler: The Decision-Making Process Leading to the 'Final Solution of the Jewish Question,' and the Grand Mufti of Jerusalem Hajj Amin al-Hussayni," *The Current State of Research: Lectures and Papers* 28 (Jerusalem, 2017).

alliance toward relations with the Arab countries. After 1967, the Jewish state was not depicted anymore as a small, endangered entity of good-will – the left's apple of the eye; instead, it was now considered a brutal occupying force, denying Palestinians their rights and lands. It was no longer perceived as a country established by victims of the Nazis. Rather, it was now presented as a country that used Nazi methods. The new rapprochement between the Soviet Union and the Arab world, which had formerly adhered to fascist and Nazi ideologies, now turned Asian and African countries against the colonial West, and against Israel as its ally. Nevertheless, Israel's self-perception in the late 1960s and the beginning of the 1970s was still the former one, of a peace-seeking, well-meaning country, and, therefore, it was late in recognizing the new global forces at work and their repercussions on antisemitism and anti-Zionism. The Vietnam War and the 1968 students' uprising brought about a new left, especially among western universities and media, which became hostile to Israel. Facing accusations coming from the left, of which Israel considered itself a part, was far more difficult than facing the rising antisemitism in East European countries and the increasingly blatant Arab anti-Israeli expressions, both orchestrated by the Soviet Union. The New Left and its young followers, fostering remorse and guilt feelings on account of the West's history of imperialism and colonialism, identified Israel with these historical wrongs and with outdated nationalistic tendencies, and saw it automatically as a negative international actor and the Palestinians as righteous, mostly without fully understanding the reality they were responding to.[11]

Not to be forgotten is the fact that following the Six-Day War, the holy Christian and Muslim sites in Jerusalem and Bethlehem were for the first time in history in the hands of a Jewish authority – a blow that scarred the self-image of non-Jewish believers until today, and deeply unsettled religious convictions. When Herzl pleaded with Pope Pius X in 1904 to support Zionist aspirations to help the destitute East European Jews find a haven, the Pope was deeply troubled by the possibility of Jews taking care of Christian holy sites – he considered such a possibility far worse than Muslims taking care of them – and he refused Herzl's request for support in the strongest of terms, disregarding the human plight of the persecuted Jews.[12]

---

[11] Robert S. Wistrich, *A Lethal Obsession: Antisemitism from Antiquity to the Global Jihad* (New York, 2010), chap. 14: "The Anti-Zionist Masquerade."

[12] *The Complete Diaries of Theodor Herzl*, vol. 5, ed. Raphael Patai, trans. Harry Zohn (New Yok, 1960), entries from January 23–25, 1904.

A crucial question to be addressed is why the mighty Soviet Union turned with such force against tiny Israel and why it invested such efforts in depicting it as negatively as possible. The eminent Yad Vashem scholar Israel Gutman offered this explanation: following World War II, antisemitism was considered the main underlying cause of the Holocaust, but the post-Holocaust international community could not internalize the implications of a crime of such colossal scale, and even the very mention of antisemitism was evaded in postwar international declarations and other major texts. Not referring to, or calling attention to, the term made it possible to ignore it as a cause of the Holocaust and to blame others for it, first and foremost the Jews themselves, especially the Zionists. The crucial step in conceiving this issue was to equate the Zionists with the Nazis and to try to do away with the heavy cloud of guilt that hovered over Europe since 1945, the year the war ended. The left, in particular, has needed and continues to need this construal in order to maintain its own sense of self-righteousness.

It is not surprising, then, that the Soviet Union was the first to come up with this equation after a few years of supporting Israel when the memory and history of the Nazi period started making its way to center stage: the left in pre-Nazi Germany, led by the Communist Party, did not have the stamina and unity to stop the Nazis from reaching power in 1933, and thus did not help prevent the Holocaust. Moreover, it was the Soviet Union that signed the notorious August 1939 Molotov–Ribbentrop Pact, which paved the way for the bloody war during which it became possible to carry out large-scale murder, not only of Jews. Close to 20 million Soviet citizens and soldiers perished, and the post-war Soviet leaders, reluctant to shoulder the heavy responsibility for the Pact and for ignoring the signs of an impending German invasion in June 1941, needed an immediate culprit. Therefore, using as always the old tactic of inversion, the Soviet Union, joined first by extreme leftists and later by radical Muslims, first accused the Zionist movement of collaborating with the Nazis.[13]

By equating Israelis and Jews with the Nazis – the most extreme of rightist movements, the ultimate evil – the left establishes itself at the opposite pole: its followers are able to see themselves as righteous and virtuous, an image the left cannot do without. Thus, fascism, colonialism, capitalism and racism are allegedly the true essence of the Zionists, who could have, accompanied by their fellow Jews, cooperated with the

---

[13] Israel Gutman, *Denying the Holocaust: Study Circle on World Jewry in the Home of the President of Israel* (Jerusalem, 1985 [Hebrew]), 12 and 16.

Nazis, their ideological twins. Therefore, it is from the left side of the political map, not only from the Arab-Muslim world, that the call for the abolition of the state of Israel is heard. And since the abolishment of a state, moreover, an equal member in the UN, is, in itself, a colossal crime, justifying this unprecedented objective requires an accusation of an equally colossal crime in order to justify it.[14]

Indeed, Soviet efforts continued, pushed forward by additional interests. On November 10, 1975, the UN General Assembly adopted a resolution, according to which "Zionism is a form of Racism and racial discrimination."[15] Racism, it should be recalled, was the fundamental tenet of the Nazi ideology. The vote, orchestrated by the Soviet Union, which enlisted Communist, Arab and third world countries, resulted in 72 countries voting in favor of the resolution; 35 were against, and 32 abstained. It was clear, given the debate surrounding the vote, that the UN agenda was manipulated by like-minded Eastern-bloc states, drawn together as a result of the Cold War which polarized the world into East and West, to destroy the State of Israel on the grounds that it was an imperialist, colonialist outpost of the West in the Middle East. This resolution ignored the previous Resolution 181 of the UN General Assembly passed on November 29, 1947, which called for the creation of a Jewish state, and the May 11, 1949, one, admitting Israel as a full-fledged member of the international community of nations. The Israeli ambassador, Haim Herzog (later Israel's sixth president), delivered a forceful speech criticizing the new resolution in the strongest possible terms, and at the conclusion of his speech tore the resolution draft in half. Israel and its supporters among the world's Jewish communities considered the UN resolution a slap in the face, especially considering the date it was announced – November 10, the date of Kristallnacht – the night of November 9–10, 1938, when a massive, coordinated assault on the Jews in Nazi Germany took place. As it were, both dates, in 1938 and 1975, proved to be turning points in Jewish and Israeli history. Democratic countries, major liberal opinion-makers and leading newspapers strongly denounced the resolution as unworthy and even shameful, the capitulation of an internationally respected body to spreading hate. The Resolution was revoked and annulled in 1991, following the demise of the Soviet Union and the Eastern bloc, but the UN had already, in general, turned into an anti-Israeli organization.

[14] Ibid.
[15] Resolution no. A/res/3379 (xxx) adopted by the General Assembly on the report of the Third Committee (A/10320).

Revoking the resolution was, however, not enough, for the damage
had already been done. Leftist movements, which started evolving a few
years before the resolution, grew stronger. At the same time, more calls
came from within left-leaning western academia to ban Israeli academ-
ics and universities from international programs and cooperation, and
strongly worded anti-Israeli and anti-Zionist manifestations originating
again in leftist circles were the spearhead for continued anti-Zionist
rhetoric and attacks.

Facing these developments, Jean Amery, the Austrian-born Holocaust
survivor and author, published a series of poignant analyses of the new
form of "antisemitism, that presents itself as anti-Zionism," which
originated, much to his chagrin, in the left, of which he considered
himself a part. "The anti-Semite-in-the-closet-anti-Zionist-in-public
that we are facing," he wrote in 1976, "presents himself as an anti-
Zionist, an idealist, fighting for enlightenment and liberalism, against
the dark brutal powers Israel allegedly belongs to. But anti-Zionism is
simply the actualization of the old, known, irrational Jew-hatred," he
argues, "that has infiltrated the political discourse in a scandalous
manner" (perhaps referring to the 1975 UN resolution). He, therefore,
urges the young Socialists, the followers of Communism, the Maoists,
Trotskyists and other radical groups to first explore what Israel is
really about – and he was quite a sharp critic of Israel himself – and
then to understand that there is no way to disconnect antisemitism
from anti-Zionism, because there is "an existential connection
between every Jew and a sovereign state of Israel ... whether or not
every Jew supports Zionism or rejects it." For Jews, Israel is their tiny,
ancient homeland, offering them a roof over their heads, for the first
time, instead of the dark clouds they lived under for over 2,000 years.
Why, Amery wondered, can't young well-educated, politically minded
thinkers understand this feeling of Jews, and realize that if the Jewish
state, surrounded by burning hatred, falls, it has nothing to offer to its
citizens against the slaughter that awaits them? This new, respected
antisemitism, accompanied by historical-moral pathos, he concluded,
is more dangerous than the classic one.[16]

There were additional developments in the 1970s. Following the
Yom Kippur War, which caught Israel by surprise in October 1973, the

---

[16] Jean Améry, *Jenseits von Schuld und Suehne, Bewaeltigungsversuche eines
Überwältigten* (*Beyond Guilt and Atonement*) (Munich, 1966 [German]); "Anti-
Zionism contains antisemitism like a cloud contains a storm," he wrote in 1969 in
the German newspaper *Die Zeit* (*Der ehrbare Antisemitismus* [Stuttgart, 2005], 133).

state authorities, as well as Zionism as a concept, were subjected to harsh criticism and rethinking within Israel. One of the results of this general soul-searching was the birth of a new, small, yet vociferous, phenomenon of post-Zionism. As usual, there were a few agendas presented to the public at the same time. A major one claimed that the Zionist movement was once the order of the day, but it became non-relevant once its goals were achieved. Therefore, a new goal should replace the former one: to enlist all efforts toward the establishment of a civil Israeli society based on equality, justice and the pursuit of peace for all citizens, first and foremost the non-Jews living in it. Another line was advocated by still more extreme Israeli critics of Zionism, who claimed that it is a colonial western movement which wronged both Palestinians and Jews coming from Muslim countries – "Eastern Jews." It should expiate for this sin by turning Israel into "a state of all its citizens," a binational state for the two people, or at least by adopting the two-state solution. This form of post-Zionism came from the left side of the Israeli political map, and reflected a growing division in Israel between left and right regarding their attitudes toward antisemitism and anti-Zionism. Alternatively, the pro-Zionist right, facing Soviet-Arab anti-Israeli coalitions, on the one hand, and the hostility of the intellectual left, on the other, was convinced that "the whole world is against us," "us" meaning the Jewish people and its state. The left pinpointed Israeli presence in the territories occupied in 1967 as the main source of trouble and argued that Israel can blame no one but itself for the rise of anti-Zionism and antisemitism. The post-Zionist solutions, especially the one advocating a "one-state solution," were all perceived by the right, and actually by the majority of the population, as anti-Zionist – even if the post-Zionists objected to being identified in this way – because they actually meant the demise of a Jewish state.[17] The high point of post-Zionism, which contributed to an intensive and comprehensive debate about modern Jewish and Israeli history's future goals and ethics, took place from the mid-1980s to the mid-1990s.[18]

Following the first Intifada, which started in late 1987, one more inversion took place. In addition to turning Israelis and their Jewish

[17] Eliezer Schweid, "Between Post-Zionism and Anti-Zionism," *Kivunim Hadashim* (*New Directions*) 23 (December 2010 [Hebrew]); Elhanan Yakira and Michael Swirsky, *Post-Zionism, Post-Holocaust: Three Essays on Denial, Forgetting, and the Delegitimation of Israel* (Cambridge, 2010).

[18] Dan Michman, ed., *Post-Zionism and the Holocaust: A Reader* (Jerusalem, 1997 [Hebrew]).

supporters into Nazis, the anti-Israel intellectual community turned them into the anti-Christ, thereby intensifying the connection between classical antisemitism and anti-Zionism. Basic Christian ideas regarding suffering and salvation are still deeply embedded in the culture and art of the western world, even if church teachings have lost much of their former influence. According to these tenets, he who suffers brings salvation, and the duty of Christians is to identify with the supreme sufferer, Jesus Christ. Martyrdom, on this reading, can certainly not be attributed to the Jews, not even after the Holocaust, for they rejected the salvation offered by Jesus. Therefore, from a theological point of view, some other group must embody the role of the martyr. Once this group has been politically designated, the theological and the political aspects of martyrdom merge together. In recent decades, caricatures and other illustrations representing Palestinian suffering featured children nailed to crosses and dripping blood to signify a modern crucifixion version. Such depictions draw on the medieval blood libel and update its message in order to show Israelis as menacing orthodox Jews, as portrayed in *Der Stürmer* or in Mel Gibson's *The Passion of the Christ*.[19]

Within this scheme, he who inflicts suffering must become an anti-Christ, equated, most prominently, in the modern world with the Nazis, the ultimate symbol of modern evil. The Jews were killed in the Holocaust by Christians, but Christians cannot, a priori, be the anti-Christ, so it is up to the Jews to go on fulfilling their medieval role. As the French scholar Shmuel Trigano has observed: "If the European memory of the Holocaust recognizes the Jews only as victims, then the moment they cease being victims [as is the case since the establishment of the state of Israel—D.P.], they become the guilty party and their status is inevitably identified with that of the Third Reich."[20]

The Durban UN world conference, which took place in South Africa in August–September 2001, had been planned as an international effort against racism, hence the choice of the location. Yet, after just a few days of deliberations, the conference turned to become an anti-Jewish and anti-Israel tirade. From demonstrations to proposals to change the agenda, every means of expression was used, from racism in general to

[19] D. Porat, "Holocaust Denial and the Image of the Jew, or: 'They Boycott Auschwitz as an Israeli Product,'" in *Resurgent Antisemitism: Global Perspectives*, ed. Alvin H. Rosenfeld (Bloomington, IN, 2013), 467–481.

[20] Shmuel Trigano, "The Political Theology of the Memory: Europe Is Morally Ready for a Second Holocaust," *Kivunim Hadashim* 17 (January 2008 [Hebrew]), 87.

anti-Zionism, here seen in its most paradigmatic contemporary manifestation. The conference became one more turning point, opening a new phase in the long history of antisemitism and in the new history of anti-Zionism, a phase that was branded shortly after the conference ended as "New Antisemitism." The "New Antisemitism" did not generate a new image of the Jew, but the older image was depicted, denounced and attacked with more intensity and hostility, and the number of violent antisemitic cases increased in the following years. Its political use also changed, since the main arena of antisemitic activity moved from the Christian to the Muslim world, which reinforced its use as a political weapon. The Boycott, Divestment, and Sanctions (BDS) movement took its first steps after this conference, which was heavily funded by Muammar Gaddafi, then ruler of Libya. Muslim radical propaganda deliberately blurred the distinction between the state of Israel and the Jewish communities worldwide. This distinction, made during the first decades after establishing the state in 1948, gradually lost its hold and gave way to a perception of the state and the Jewish communities as one entity, a tendency that reached its peak in the Durban Conference. As a result, the distinction between antisemitism and anti-Zionism, and between the attitudes to the Jewish people and its state, was blurred as well. Once Israel was perceived as a Jewish state, the long alleged, highly negative character traits and image of "Jews" were attributed to it, along with a deep demonizing hatred of Jews.[21] Thus antisemitism and anti-Zionism became the two faces of the same coin, "New Antisemitism."

The very notion of Israel and the Jewish communities being one entity, one nation, was not rejected by Israel: a parallel decades long process moved Israeli self-perception from being Israelis only, "new Jews," different from the weak exilic Jews of the past, to the recognition of themselves as Jews sharing the same fate and heritage as any Jew.

Attributing the term "apartheid" to Israel, as was done in the Durban deliberations, was revoked in the Durban III conference in 2011, but again, the damage had already been done.

Facing the Durban results, accompanied by the Second Intifada in 2000, the link between extreme anti-Israel rhetoric and violent deeds

---

[21] Porat, "Blurring the Distinction between Antisemitism and Anti-Zionism," in *Europe-Israel: A Troubled Relationship – Is There a New Anti-Semitism?*, TAU Conference, November 24–25, 2002, 121–125; D. Porat, "Durban: A Different Attack on Israel and the Jewish People," *Kivunim Hadashim* 7 (September 2002), 51–60. I was a member of the Israeli foreign ministry delegation to Durban.

directed against Jewish individuals and communities has become a discernable global trend, manifested in two ways: blaming Jews for Israel's actions – since Jews and Israel were already perceived as a single evil entity, so that any Jew, even the most anti-Zionist, became a potential target; and the integration of more traditional antisemitic stereotypes into the anti-Israel campaign, with expressions such as "a world power," "an international lobby," manipulating global political and military events behind the scenes – bringing the notions of *The Protocols of the Elders of Zion* back to center stage. There is no better illustration of that development than the conspiracy theory, one of many which mushroomed since 2000, according to which the Mossad was behind the attack on the Twin Towers and the Pentagon, and warned American Jews who worked there about the attack. This happened barely two days after the Durban conference was dissolved, a striking example of how Jews and Israel became one entity in the antisemitic/anti-Israeli mind, working together to achieve their common destructive goals.[22]

Thus, it became quite clear that most surveys and deliberations pointed at the need to define when anti-Zionism and anti-Israelism are imbued with antisemitic motives. In answer to this need, a Tel Aviv–based first definition was published in 2003:

- When the language, images and character traits attributed to Israel are imbued with known antisemitic stereotypes.
- When Israelis and Jews are depicted as a cosmic evil, are blamed for world-wide disasters, and compared to the Nazis, the ultimate evil.
- When Israelis and Jews supporting the state of Israel are singled out and attacked and are treated in a disproportionate manner in relationship to the issue at hand and in comparison, to the actions of other nations.
- When the very right of Israel to exist as a Jewish state is delegitimized.
- When the Holocaust is distorted and made a political weapon. When claiming it is misused by the Jews to extort financial support and to make political gains.[23]

But this definition did not change the realities on the ground.

---

[22] Porat in *Antisemitism Worldwide*, Annual Report, 2003/4, the Stephen Roth Institute for the Study of Contemporary Antisemitism and Racism at Tel Aviv University, 5.

[23] Ibid., quoted by Alex Grobman in www.infoisrael.net, November 23, 2006. On my role as the initiator of the first definition, acknowledged by Kenneth Stern (though I was part of the joint effort), see https://electronicintifada.net, a Palestinian blog.

The Durban impact continued and the year 2004 was one of the worst in the decade. Violence doubled in comparison to the previous year, and other expressions of antisemitism increased as well. The German government convened a major conference in Berlin, which resulted in a unanimous decision: it was crucial to craft a definition of antisemitism in order to fight efficiently against this malign ideology. Hence, the European Union Monitoring Center (EUMC) came up with a one-page-long "Working Definition of Antisemitism" (WDA), written as a joint effort of a large number of scholars and organizations, and this was adopted in 2005 at an international Organization for Security and Cooperation in Europe (OSCE) conference in Spain.[24] This WDA, with a few cosmetic changes that had no bearing on its contents, was adopted unanimously in May 2016 by the International Holocaust Remembrance Alliance (IHRA), which then had thirty-one member states. Since then the WDA has been adopted by ten more countries and by hundreds of organizations, churches, municipalities, football teams and universities,[25] and the process of adoption continues. It serves as a tool that helps identify antisemitic cases, collect data and improve monitoring, and it is introduced into court proceedings to provide evidence. Its importance was recently recognized when public and legal pressure was applied to the international social media servers to identify multitudes of antisemitic messages posted on their sites and delete them immediately.[26] It has become a sort of a yardstick, a declaration of values, that is part of a larger struggle, not just against antisemitism but against all forms of discrimination. The "Working Definition of Anti-Gypsyism/Anti-Roma Discrimination" adopted by the IHRA grew out of the momentum generated by the WDA definitions.[27]

Not surprisingly, since the IHRA adopted the WDA, it has become the subject of a fierce international debate over defining when anti-Zionism is antisemitism.[28] The WDA and anti-IHRA opponents, coming mainly from leftist and academic circles, claim it stifles freedom of speech and muzzles criticism of Israel by labeling it as antisemitic. But over and against these objections, it needs to be understood

---

[24] The American Jewish Committee gathered comments from scholars and organizations and elaborated on the final wording.

[25] Cambridge University adopted the WDA in November 2020.

[26] See letters and press releases sent to Facebook by 145 organizations in September 2020, urging it to adopt the WDA. As of August 2020, FB announced that it has updated its policies to better combat antisemitic speech.

[27] On October 8, 2020, after a few years of deliberations.

[28] See Appendix 1. These points were formulated based on TAU 2003/4 points, see n. 22.

that the WDA is a non-legally binding document, adopted as a recom-
mendation, and has no enforcement power. Moreover, the WDA was
adopted by the IHRA international membership even though some of its
members are sharp critics of Israel. The WDA explicitly states that
"criticism of Israel similar to that leveled against any other country
cannot be regarded as antisemitic." It can be regarded as such only when
it relates to one of the four points in the WDA that define it.

Can one say that anti-Zionism is antisemitic in principle, in its very
basic tenets, outside the debate around the four points? Yes, says Robert
Wistrich, one of the top researchers of antisemitism and anti-Zionism:
it is antisemitic in its very nature because it is based on the same
mental and ideological structures that underlie antisemitism, and
anti-Zionism reflects former antisemitic convictions:

1. Israelis are mainly Jews, and Jews constitute a danger, a threat to
   humanity. They are, according to the government of Iran, the "little
   Satan," supported by the US, which is the "Grand Satan." As such,
   they are the opposite of the human and the Godly;
2. Jews have always been strangers, no matter how hard they tried to
   integrate, and the Jewish state is a stranger in the area – Muslim
   critics of Israel call its Jewish inhabitants Crusaders, in order to
   emphasize the notion of "foreigners" for Christian ears;
3. Antisemitism and anti-Zionism share the same Manichaean character. That is, they divide humanity categorically, using the language of classical Manicheanism, into "the children of light," and
   the "children of darkness," with Jews preeminent among the latter;
4. Jews, by nature, are criminals. This claim is central to both classical
   and modern antisemitism and now to anti-Zionism;
5. Antisemitism has always been potentially genocidal, and now, the
   equation of Israelis to Nazis manifests this same potential.
   Accordingly, the State of Israel has no right to exist.

Wistrich concluded his lecture with the following estimation: "The
Christian and Muslim world have not yet fully accepted the fact that
the Jews have returned to their homeland and built themselves a state –
they were not supposed to; this was not included in the unwritten
agreement between them and the rest of the world, which allocated
them a particular, different place."[29]

* * *

[29] Robert Wistrich remarks during a panel discussion with Alan Dershowitz on
   "Antisemitism and anti-Zionism," Tel Aviv, 24 April 2009.

On October 22, 2020, a memorandum of agreement was signed in Washington between the State Department special envoy to monitor and combat antisemitism and the King Hamad Global Centre for Peaceful Coexistence of Bahrain, according to which Bahrain accepts that anti-Zionism is a form of antisemitism, that the IHRA Working Definition of Antisemitism includes examples to that effect, that Jews are a people (and not only a religion), that both nations are Semites, and Israel is the nation-state of the Jewish people.[30]

Further Reading

Ben-Itto, H., *The Lie That Wouldn't Die, The Protocols of the Elders of Zion* (London, 2005). Judge Ben-Itto analyzes the sources of the *Protocols*, the formation of their first text, their dissemination worldwide and the trials in which the libel was exposed and refuted.

The Elder of Zion blog.

The Electronic Intifada blog.

Fine, R., and S. Philip, *Antisemitism and the Left: On the Return of the Jewish Question* (Manchester, 2017). The authors juxtapose two results of universalism, one that offered a progressive way to emancipate Jews and one of suppressing Jewish particularity, while relying on the works of Karl Marx, Hannah Arendt and Juergen Habermas.

Harrison, B., *Blaming the Jews: Politics and Delusion* (Bloomington, IN, 2020). Analyzes the persistent antisemitic belief held by groups at both ends of the political spectrum that Jews dominate world affairs and are the root of all the world's evils.

Herf, J., ed., *Convergence and Divergence: Anti- Semitism and Anti-Zionism in Historical Perspective*, a special issue of the *Journal of Israel History* 25.1 (March 2006). This special issue includes thirteen essays, all dealing with antisemitism and anti-Zionism from a variety of angles, places and movements.

Lewis, B., *Semites and Anti-Semites; An Inquiry into Conflict and Prejudice* (London, 1987). This analysis of the terms "Semites" and "Jews," the wars against Zionism and against the Jews, and even New Antisemitism (termed as early as the 1980s) has become a classic in the field.

Litvak, M., and E. Webman, *From Empathy to Denial: Arab Responses to the Holocaust* (London, 2009). This Washington Institute winner examines attitudes crystallized in the Arab and Moslem world toward the Israeli-Arab conflict in the wake of the Holocaust, from 1945 to 2000.

Marcus, L. K., *The Definition of Anti-Semitism* (Oxford, 2015). This book deals with the Working Definition of Antisemitism, adopted by the International Holocaust Remembrance Alliance in May 2016, which has since stirred an intensive cross-national debate, regarding freedom of speech versus freedom of incitement, and regarding anti-Zionism as antisemitism.

---

[30] Elder of Ziyon blog, http://elderofziyon.blogspot.com, October 26, 2020.

Nelson, C., *Israel Denial: Anti-Zionism, Antisemitism and the Faculty Campaign against the Jewish State* (Bloomington, IN, 2019). Nelson's study addresses the phenomenon of anti-Zionism and antisemitism in North American colleges and universities, where parts of the faculty, as well as students, launch an attack on Israel that allegedly contradicts values they believe in.

Rosenfeld, A. H., ed., *Anti-Zionism and Antisemitism, the Dynamics of Delegitimization* (Bloomington, IN, 2019). This volume features seventeen essays, collected following an April 2016 Indiana University conference, under the same title, in which seventy scholars from sixteen countries participated.

The Stephen Roth and the Kantor Center Annual Reports on Antisemitism Worldwide, 1994–2019, Tel Aviv University, www.Kantorcentertau

Wistrich, R., *Anti-Zionism and Antisemitism in the Contemporary World* (New York, 1990). In both this book and the one listed below, Wistrich explores how the left has come to betray both the Jews and Israel: Jews whose political, traditional home was the leftist parties and Israel, which began as a socialist country, were gradually depicted by the political left as symbolizing the opposite values.

From Ambivalence to Betrayal: The Left, the Jews and Israel (Lincoln, NE, 2012).

25 New Issues

DEBORAH E. LIPSTADT

This essay begins with a definition of antisemitism. It then moves to structural analysis of Jew-hatred as a prejudice and from there to an analysis of the unique elements of this hatred, elements that differentiate it from other forms of prejudice. The final section examines how the age-old antisemitic charges have morphed into a contemporary and relatively new form of antisemitism. It makes the argument that, though the form in which antisemitism presents may be new, in its essence, this hatred has remained the same.

DEFINING ANTISEMITISM

There are many variations on the definition of antisemitism. Since 2010, the United States State Department together with many other nations have adopted the following working definition of antisemitism:[1]

> Anti-Semitism is a certain perception of Jews, which may be expressed as hatred toward Jews. Rhetorical and physical manifestations of anti-Semitism are directed toward Jewish or non-Jewish individuals and/or their property, toward Jewish community institutions and religious facilities.[2]

Under the rubric of this formulation, the following are considered to constitute contemporary examples of antisemitism:[3]

---

[1] Working Definition of Anti-Semitism by the European Monitoring Center on Racism and Xenophobia, as cited by United States Department of State, "Defining Antisemitism." https://2009-2017.state.gov/j/drl/rls/fs/2010/122352.htm.

[2] This definition has been adopted or endorsed by a significant number of other countries, including Germany, France, Israel, Cyprus, Bulgaria, and an array of other European nations. www.jewishvirtuallibrary.org/international-holocaust-remembrance-alliance-definition-of-anti-semitism.

[3] The State Department's formulation of antisemitism, as well as these examples, were adopted from the International Holocaust Remembrance Alliance (IHRA), an

- Calling for, aiding, or justifying the killing or harming of Jews (often in the name of a radical ideology or an extremist view of religion).
- Making mendacious, dehumanizing, demonizing, or stereotypical allegations about Jews as such or the power of Jews as a collective – especially, but not exclusively, the myth about a world Jewish conspiracy or of Jews controlling the media, economy, government, or other societal institutions.
- Accusing Jews as a people of being responsible for real or imagined wrongdoing committed by a single Jewish person or group, the state of Israel, or even for acts committed by non-Jews.
- Accusing the Jews as a people, or Israel as a state, of inventing or exaggerating the Holocaust.
- Accusing Jewish citizens of being more loyal to Israel, or to the alleged priorities of Jews worldwide, than to the interest of their own nations.
- Using the symbols and images associated with classic antisemitism to characterize Israel or Israelis.
- Drawing comparisons of contemporary Israeli policy to that of the Nazis.
- Blaming Israel for *all* interreligious or political tensions.

Although this essay does not address the specific issue of when hostility toward Israel crosses over into antisemitism, it must be noted that criticism of Israeli policies per se cannot and should not automatically be categorized as antisemitism. Many Israelis are, themselves, critical of aspects of their country's policies. Similarly, one can be critical of America or any other country's policies without being against that particular country. Much depends on the shape, specific content and context of those critiques.

There are, of course, other definitions. Helen Fein, a historical sociologist, offers a definition with some added additional elements:

> A persisting latent structure of hostile beliefs towards *Jews as a collectivity* manifested in *individuals* as attitudes, and in *culture* as myth, ideology, folklore, and imagery, and in *actions* – social or legal discrimination, political mobilization against Jews, and

intergovernmental organization that is mandated to focus on Holocaust-related issues, including antisemitism and Holocaust denial. The United States is a member of IHRA: https://www.holocaustremembrance.com/working-definition-antisemitism.

collective or state violence – which results in and/or is designed to distance, displace, or destroy *Jews as Jews*.[4]

There are a number of important concepts embedded in this definition that help us better understand antisemitism, both as a prejudice, in and of itself, and as a sentiment that is rightfully called the longest or oldest hatred.[5] Fein defines it as a *persisting*. This is one of the striking aspects of antisemitism. It doesn't go away; it's not a one-time event. That is true of most prejudices. But the age-old nature of this hatred and its ability to morph into different forms over millennia is notable. As shall be examined in this essay, its essential elements remain constant even as its outer form evolves.

Fein, however, describes it not just as persisting but as *latent*. Something that is latent always had the ability to become blatant. One might compare it to a herpes infection. In certain forms of this ailment, medication may cure the symptoms. However, the infection persists, albeit in a dormant fashion. But when the circumstances change and the moment is opportune, it can reemerge in a different incarnation: the outer trappings look different, but the essence is the same. Alleviate the symptoms, but the infection itself lies dormant and may reemerge at an opportune moment in a new incarnation, a different "outer shell."

Fein also notes that it can be directed at a Jew individually or as Jews collectively. In this sense, it is not dissimilar from other prejudices. The individual person can be subjected to a prejudicial hatred, not for what they are or what they have done, but simply because of who they *are*. Finally, Fein's final italicized phrase, *Jews as Jews*, reminds us of an important point about antisemitism and, by extension, prejudice in general. Antisemitism is not caused by what a Jew *does*. There are Jews, just as there are people who are objects of other prejudices, who are deserving of contempt. Antisemitism is hating someone *as* a Jew or because they *are* a Jew, not because of what they have done. Alternatively, it is attributing their wrongdoings to the fact that they *are* a Jew, for example, saying, "Jews are like that."

---

[4] Helen Fein, "Dimensions of Antisemitism: Attitudes, Collective Accusations, and Actions," in *The Persisting: Sociological Perspectives and Social Contexts of Modern Antisemitism*, ed. Helen Fein (Berlin, 1987), 67. Emphasis in the original.

[5] Robert S. Wistrich, *Antisemitism: The Longest Hatred* (London, 1991).

THE PREJUDICE OF ANTISEMITISM:
A STRUCTURAL ANALYSIS

Antisemitism is a form of prejudice. As such it shares many character-istics associated with other forms of prejudice.

First of all, it is irrational, as are all prejudices. Consider its etymol-ogy: to pre-judge. A prejudiced person determines the nature of another person's character, intellectual abilities, financial acumen, or political leanings not on the basis of the individual's actions or behavior but on the basis of the negative stereotypes associated with the group to which the person "belongs." (Sometimes the animus is directed at people whom the haters perceive to be part of the group in question, when, in fact, they are not. Prejudicial remarks or actions directed at someone who is not part of the group in question, e.g., someone the prejudiced person thinks is Jewish when in fact the person is not Jewish, are expressions of prejudice.) Without even laying eyes on the person in question, preju-diced people assume they know what this person will be like because of the particular group with which the person is identified. This is, of course, an illogical way of judging someone. But for the damage it has too often done, it could be dismissed as simply ludicrous, if not just silly.

Second, prejudices, including Jew-hatred, are not premised on dis-liking a person for a specific behavior or action. As we noted above regarding antisemitism, prejudice is about disliking other people *because* they are members of a particular group. Often, when a Jew or a member of another oft-reviled group does something despicable, a prejudiced person will point to that action as proof that the entire group should be reviled. Yet if a Caucasian or left-handed person were to do something equally despicable, the prejudiced person would be unlikely to proclaim: "That's how white/left-handed people behave and that's why I don't like them."

Third, the prejudicial person attributes the actions of the member of the minority group to the fact that that these were the actions of, for example, a Jew/Black/Latinx person, saying, "Well, Jews/Blacks/Latinx are like that." This can also work in the reverse; for example, when the member of the minority group does something that the prejudicial people approve of, they might say, "Well he's not like the rest of *them*."[6]

Fourth, Jew-hatred, like other prejudices, relies on stereotypes. Irrespective of the hatred in question, prejudicial stereotypes always

---

[6] Charles Y. Glock and Rodney Stark, *Christian Belief and Anti-Semitism* (New York, 1966), 102.

share certain characteristics: (1) They are based on a person's affiliation with a particular group. (2) Stereotypes assume that all members of the group in question share precisely the same characteristics and act in the same fashion. (3) Stereotypes assume there can be no variations within the group. (4) Even when a prejudicial stereotype is used in an affirmative fashion, it is rooted in a negative idea. "He's Black *but* he's a hard worker." "He's a Jew *but* he's very honest when it comes to money." Implied in that "but" but left unspoken in this backhanded compliment are the words "though" and "nonetheless." "*Though* he is Black, he's *nonetheless* a hard worker." "*Though* he is a Jew, he's *nonetheless* honest about money."[7] (5) Stereotypes gain traction by frequent repetition. Repeated often enough, the stereotype moves from a disparaging comment to an accurate-sounding assessment. When someone uses the stereotype of "the rich Jew" they are not reflecting a social reality. If they referred to "the rich Christian," "the rich Muslim," or the "rich atheist," it would not have the same impact because those other descriptions do not "evoke any mythic or archetypal associations." In "western Christian culture ... the Shylock myth has tremendous resonance."[8]

Every set of prejudicial stereotypes relies on group-specific charges. Charges associated with one set of prejudicial stereotypes are *not* interchangeable with another. The stereotypes used by the racist against Blacks or the homophobe against gays are quite different from those used by the antisemite against Jews. For example, the racist stereotypes and code words associated with Blacks often include, but are certainly not limited to, thuggish, inarticulate, lazy, and dumb. The Black person is portrayed by the racist as someone who is not as smart, accomplished, or possessed of the positive attributes as a white person.

In contrast, antisemitic stereotypes are quite different from most other stereotypes, particularly those that are racist in nature. In fact, they depict the Jew as smarter and more accomplished – but in an evil or nefarious way – than the non-Jew. Antisemitic stereotypes are rooted in four different elements or characteristics: (1) An association with

---

[7] Yaacov Schul and Henri Zukier, "Why Do Stereotypes Stick?," in *Demonizing the Other: Antisemitism, Racism and Xenophobia*, ed. Robert Wistrich (Amsterdam, 1999), 31–34. In a recent legal decision in the United Kingdom, a judge ruled against a person who was dismissed from his job for saying, "Jews are the cleverest people" and are "good at physics" because such a remark was "potentially offensive" and could be considered to "demean their personal intellectual ability/hard work." www .thejc.com/news/uk/lecturer-who-called-jews-cleverest-people-in-the-world-loses-unfair-dismissal-claim-1.501785

[8] Wistrich, ed., *Demonizing the Other*, 123.

money or financial power; for example, all Jews are rich or obsessed with money. (2) The notion that Jews are smart, but they use their intellect for malicious purposes. (3) The accusation that the Jews are possessed of a disproportionate degree of control or power over the levers of society. (4) The claim that Jews use that power to advance their own interests at the specific expense of the non-Jew.[9] According to the antisemite, because Jews have these attributes – money, intellect, and power – they are not only to be *loathed* but to be *feared* because of the existential danger they pose to the non-Jew.

ANTISEMITISM'S DISTINCTIVE ELEMENTS: A CONSPIRACY THEORY

While antisemitism shares these characteristics with other prejudices, it has certain unique elements, two in particular, that differentiate it from most other prejudices. Most prejudices tend to "punch down," while antisemites generally perceive themselves to be "punching up." For example, racists look upon the person of color as "lesser than" the white person. Racists contemptuously perceive of people of color as not as industrious, smart, talented, nonviolent, clean-cut, or ambitious as the white person. A typical racist trope might be: "If *they* move into *our* neighborhood, it will ruin the neighborhood." "If *their* kids go to *our* kids' schools, it will ruin the school." And, most contemptuous of all, "If *they* marry *our* kids, it will destroy the purity and standards of our gene pool." In short, they will bring us down. This "looking down upon" applies to other prejudices as well.

In contrast, antisemites "punch up." The antisemite, relying on the aforementioned stereotypical elements associated with Jew-hatred, contends that the Jew is "richer" "more powerful," "cleverer," and "more influential" than the non-Jew. Not only are they all these things, but, the antisemite contends, they use these attributes to harm non-Jews. It is this punching up that makes it difficult for some people to grasp two things. First, they think of prejudice as directed in the main against people who seem vulnerable and powerless. Second, Jews do not "present" as the prototypical victims of prejudice. They appear to be comfortably financially situated, well-educated, and solidly middle-class. And, above all, they seem to have the choice to "pass" as whites. In short, they "appear" to be quite different from traditional victims of prejudice.

---

[9] Deborah Lipstadt, *Antisemitism Here and Now* (New York, 2019), 11–22.

The second unique element of antisemitism and one that flows from this "punching up/punching down" construct is the conviction that Jews are engaged in a conspiracy to existentially damage white society. Acting as those engaged in a conspiracy generally do, they make their plans secretly and surreptitiously, out of view of the non-Jew. The non-Jew is generally unaware of these evil endeavors until it is too late to act against them. Adolf Hitler, in his *Mein Kampf*, numerous speeches, and myriad public and private comments, depicted German Jews as collectively conspiring to harm and dominate the so-called Aryan population. In fact, according to the Nazi theory of the "back stab," Jews had already done so by ensuring that Germany lost World War I.

But this notion of a Jewish conspiracy that was promulgated by Germany's Third Reich was not something new. It had long roots dating back to the Middle Ages (10th–16th centuries). It was these age-old roots that facilitated its ability to gain traction among 20th-century Germans. They were familiar with this depiction of the Jew as a threat to their well-being. Consequently, when the Nazis began to spout these ideas, non-Jews were inclined to believe them to be accurate. (Had the Germans accused the bicycle-riders of conspiring against Germany, people would have dismissed that as ludicrous. Yet there was as much evidence for a conspiracy of bicycle-riders as there was of Jews.)

Long before the Holocaust, the notion of a conspiracy of Jews against non-Jews existed. In the Middle Ages, as Christian leaders increasingly depicted Jew as adherents to a degenerate faith, as opposed to just a different faith, they bolstered their accusations with horrific and completely fanciful claims. Jews were accused of engaging in "blood libel," kidnapping and murdering young Christian children in order to drain their blood. They would then, the antisemites claimed, use that blood to prepare matzah, the unleavened bread used at Passover.[10] It was irrelevant to the accusers that Jewish kashrut practices (the dietary laws) strictly eschew the use of any blood. According to these practices, it is necessary to drain the blood from an animal that is about to be consumed. The accusations were so far-fetched that even some popes condemned these claims as "false" and "fantastic" (as in fantasy).[11]

[10] Matt Goldish, *Jewish Questions: Response on Sephardic Life in the Early Modern Period* (Princeton, NJ, 2008), 8. "In the period from the twelfth to the twentieth centuries, Jews were regularly charged with blood libel or ritual murder – that Jews kidnapped and murdered non-Jews as part of a Jewish religious ritual."
[11] Massimo Introvigne, "The Catholic Church and the Blood Libel Myth: A Complicated Story," *Covenant* 1.2 (April 2007).

A similar illogical conspiratorial accusation, but one with horrific consequences, was made during the "Black Plague." Despite the fact that Jews were also struck by the plague, church and secular leaders accused Jews of having poisoned the wells of Europe as a means of spreading this disease in order to wipe out Christian society.[12] Yet another oft-repeated accusation was that Jews would sneak into churches with a knife or some other implement and stab the wafer used in Mass. During that religious ceremony, the wafer becomes, according to Catholic theology, the body of Christ the wafer, and when stabbed, the accusers claimed, spouted blood.

Underpinning these accusations, particularly the blood libel and desecration of the Host, was the notion that Jews were conspiring to reenact the murder of Jesus.[13] That these accusations were not just illogical but without any basis in fact was irrelevant to much of the European Christian public at large. Many among them accepted them as valid.[14] Generally, these accusations served a political purpose. The Jew became a convenient scapegoat. If something went wrong in the society – the crops failed, the plague spread, a child went missing, or there was a drought – leaders found the Jew to be an easy target to blame. The population, having been repeatedly told that the Jews were guilty of doing terrible things, was prone to believe the charges were legitimate. As a result, thanks in great measure to these far-fetched claims, Jews increasingly became objects not just of loathing but of fear.[15]

A modern expression of this conspiracy is contained in *The Protocols of the Elders of Zion*. At the beginning of the 20th century, Russian czarist secret police took a 19th-century French novel about a

[12] Tzafrir Barzilay, "Well Poisoning Accusations in Medieval Europe: 1250–1500," *Columbia University Academic Commons*, 2016, https://academiccommons.columbia.edu/doi/10.7916/D8VH5P6T.

[13] Miri Rubin, "Desecration of the Host: The Birth of an Accusation," *Studies in Church History*, vol. 29: *Christianity and Judaism* (1992), 169–85, https://doi.org/10.1017/S0424208400011281.

[14] Consider, for example, the preachings of St. Agobard (779–840), Bishop of Lyons, who, fearful that some Christians might be attracted to Judaism, advocated strict legal separations between Christians and Jews. He described Jews as *"filii diaboli"* ("children of the devil"). Arguing that the secular leaders should not allow Christians to mix with Jews, he preached "that the Church of Christ, who should be considered immaculate and unblemished to her heavenly bridegroom, [not] be defiled by contact with the unclean, senile, and corrupt synagogue." Jeremy Cohen, *Living Letter of the Law: Ideas of the Jew in Medieval Christianity* (Berkeley, CA, 1999).

[15] On the split between Christianity and Judaism, see the analysis by the Christian theologian James Parkes, *The Conflict between Church and Synagogue* (New York, 1961).

supposed Napoleonic plot to gain control over the world and turned it into what has become one of the most enduring pieces of evidence for a Jewish conspiracy to control the world. Although the original work, which the czarist police plagiarized, had no connection to Jews, the Russians turned it into a Jewish story. In its revised form, Jews were now the main characters. The fraudulent work was supposedly the records – the protocols – of meetings of a group of Jewish elders who were conspiring how to best exert their power. Despite the fact that it was plagiarized, the book, now known as *The Protocols of the Elders of Zion*, claimed to "prove" that Jews were engaged in a vast conspiratorial plot to destroy Christian culture. It was brought to the United States and widely popularized by Henry Ford.

In 1921, the *London Times* declared the *Protocols* to be "clumsy plagiarism." In 1935, a Swiss court fined two Nazi leaders for circulating a German-language edition of the *Protocols*. The judges in the trial declared the *Protocols* "libelous," "obvious forgeries," and "ridiculous nonsense." The assistant director of the US Central Intelligence Agency, Richard Helms, testified in 1961: "The Russians have a long tradition in the art of forgery. More than 60 years ago the Czarist intelligence service concocted and peddled a confection called The Protocols of the Elders of Zion." In 1965, the United States Senate declared the *Protocols* to be "fabricated" and their contents "gibberish."[16] The Senate based its conclusion on a report issued the previous year by the Senate Judiciary Committee which repudiated the *Protocols*.[17] Despite all these critiques and exposés of the *Protocols*, it continues to this day to be republished and "updated" in many forms.[18]

One of more recent manifestations of antisemitic conspiracy theories is Holocaust denial. Denial of the Holocaust is completely illogical. While there are numerous documents and other forms of evidence attesting to the Holocaust, one need not be familiar with the history to recognize the ludicrous nature of deniers' arguments. If the deniers

---

[16] *The Protocols of the Elders of Zion*, in *Holocaust Encyclopedia*, United States Holocaust Memorial Museum, https://encyclopedia.ushmm.org/content/en/article/protocols-of-the-elders-of-zion.

[17] The political scientist Stephen Bronner has described the *Protocols* as "probably the most influential work of antisemitism ever written... what the *Communist Manifesto* is for Marxism, the fictitious *Protocols* is for antisemitism." Stephen Bronner, *A Rumor about the Jews: Reflections on Antisemitism and the Protocols of the Learned Elders of Zion* (New York, 2003), 1.

[18] For examples of contemporary iterations of the *Protocols*, see Dina Port, "The Protocols of the Elders of Zion: New Uses of an Old Myth," in Wistrich, ed., *Demonizing the Other*, 323ff.

were to be correct, their claims would fly in the face of evidence from an array of sources: survivors, bystanders, and, above all, perpetrators.[19] The admission by Germany, as well as its myriad allies, that the Holocaust is an established historical fact is particularly significant. They would have the most to gain from demonstrating that this did not happen. It is important to note that in not one war crimes trial after the war did a perpetrator say it did not happen. They may have claimed – and many did – that they had no choice but to follow orders, but they did not claim that it did not happen.[20] Yet another group that would have to have been "in on" the hoax or have been duped are the thousands of historians who conducted research on myriad aspects of the Holocaust. They would have had to either be tricked or be essential parts of this conspiracy.

Logic also upends one of their most oft-heard claims. Deniers demand that they be shown the document signed by Hitler ordering the Holocaust. This, they continually claim, would allay all their doubts. At the same time that they make this demand, deniers dismiss any document that demonstrates there was a Holocaust – and there are a myriad of them – as a forgery. Logic compels one to ask: If, as the deniers contend, the Jews were so adept at forging documents, why did they not forge this one document?

---

[19] For survivor testimonies, see Yale University Library, Fortunoff Video Archive for Holocaust Testimonies, http://web.library.yale.edu/testimonies; University of Southern California, SHOAH Foundation, https://sfi.usc.edu/full-length-testimonies; United States Holocaust Memorial Museum, www.ushmm.org/remember/the-holocaust-survivors-and-victims-resource-center/survivors-and-victims/survivor-testimonies. Many of the witnesses from the areas in which these murders occurred have spoken of what they saw. See, for example, Patrick Desbois, *The Holocaust by Bullets: A Priest's Journey to Uncover the Truth behind the Murder of 1.5 Million Jews* (New York, 2009). See also the interviews conducted by Claude Lanzmann for his documentary *Shoah*, www.ushmm.org/online/film/docs/shoahstatus.pdf.

[20] Many perpetrators who were tried for war crimes after World War II argued that they had no option but to follow orders and kill the victims; otherwise, they would have been killed. However, this does not seem to have been the case. As David Kitterman concludes after an investigation of over 100 cases of Germans who refused to execute civilians, "the most remarkable conclusion about this investigation is the failure to find even one conclusively documented instance of a life-threatening situation (shot, physically harmed, or sent to a concentration camp) occurring to those who refused to carry out orders to murder civilians or Russian war prisoners. In spite of general assumptions to the contrary, the majority of such cases resulted in no serious consequences whatever." David Kitterman, "Those Who Said 'No!': Germans Who Refused to Execute Civilians during World War II," *German Studies Review* 11.2 (1988), 241–54.

There are many other illogical arguments on which deniers make their case. They posit that, given that the Germans were so efficient and powerful, they never would have allowed any witnesses to remain alive at the end of the war and thus able to testify to the existence of a murder program. This contention by deniers is premised on their ability to achieve any goal they set out for themselves. The absurdity of this argument is evident in its premise. If the Germans were able to fulfill all their goals, how is they did not win the war, which was, of course, their primary goal?

Holocaust denial is, quite plainly, a form of antisemitism. It is not about history. It is about attacking, discrediting, and demonizing Jews. The claims of the deniers – that the Jews planted evidence, got German prisoners of war to admit to crimes they did not commit, and forced Germany to shoulder a tremendous financial and moral burden when the war ended – are predicated on the notion of the mythical power of the Jews, which, they firmly believe, was extensive enough to realize this vast conspiracy. Unconcerned about how their actions would affect millions of people and with only their own political and financial benefit in mind, the Jews created the myth of the Holocaust in order to obtain a state of their own and extract vast amounts of money from Germany. Then, according to this theory, they proceeded to displace another people from their land in order to gain sovereignty for themselves. These assertions rely on classic antisemitic tropes, the same ones found throughout 2,000 years of antisemitic accusations. Just as the Jews persuaded the Roman Empire and then the rulers of Palestine to do their bidding and crucify Jesus, so, too, they persuaded the Allies to create evidence of a genocide for their own financial and political gain.

THE PSEUDO-SCIENCE OF RACIAL ANTISEMITISM: CONTEMPORARY MANIFESTATIONS

Holocaust denial forms a pivotal role in one of the more contemporary versions of the antisemitic conspiracy theory, namely, that the contemporary equivalents of the *Protocols'* so-called Jewish Elders are engaged in a racialist conspiracy with the aim of perpetrating a "white Genocide."[21] This genocide, its adherents contend, will eliminate white people and replace them and their culture with black and brown people,

---

[21] Julie Nathan, "As the Pittsburgh Synagogue Massacre Shows, Fears of 'White Genocide' Are Incitement to Murder," *ABC Religion and Ethics*, October 29, 2018, www.abc.net.au/religion/white-genocide-is-incitement-to-murder/10442966.

among them Muslims. This racialist fantasy theory posits that Jews are the driving force behind this white genocide.[22]

The roots of the strain of antisemitism on which this accusation is built began to emerge in the 19th century.[23] It was embedded within a pseudo-scientific racial "theory." Its proponents contended that the world was composed of different racial groups. According to these racial theorists, known as eugenicists, there was a "science" of race. The eugenicists argued that people have genetic characteristics which impact not only their height, weight, health, and appearance, but their loyalty, bravery, honesty, wisdom, and uprightness.[24] Race was the determining factor in which civilizations succeeded and which failed. The races were, eugenicists contended, of "unequal" value. According to this theory of eugenics, white societies would always dominate "yellow" or "black" societies.[25] According to eugenicists, Jews were not just biologically and racially inferior, but their racial qualities made them evil, corrupt, and a threat to "white races." Though the charges against them had been made previously by church leaders, according to this racial theory their nefarious qualities were not a result of their religious or political beliefs. Their evilness was rooted in their "blood."[26] This pseudo-scientific theory asserted that, though Jews might look white, they were not. They had distinctly Jewish "blood." Consequently, even if a Jew had no connection with other Jews or chose to convert, their "essence" was still Jewish. If they had only one parent who was a Jew, they were still essentially Jewish. This became an operative aspect of the persecution of the Jews in Nazi Germany. If even one of a person's four grandparents was a Jew, that person was considered to be of mixed heritage and, for purposes of racial classification, a Jew.

Over the course of the 20th century, this concept of "race" melded with deep-seated "nationalism." This science of race had a strong presence in America and was the basis of discrimination in the late 19th and

[22] Andrew Wilson, "#whitegenocide, the Alt-Right and Conspiracy Theory: How Secrecy and Suspicion Contributed to the Mainstreaming of Hate," *Secrecy and Society* 1.2 (2018).

[23] For background on the emergence of racial antisemitism, see Poliakov, *The History of Anti-Semitism* (Philadelphia, 2003), vol. 3, pt. 3.

[24] George Fredrickson, *Racism: A Short History* (Princeton, NJ, 2015).

[25] Michael Burleigh and Wolfgang Kiperman, "Racism," in *How Was It Possible? A Holocaust Reader*, ed. Peter Hayes (Lincoln, NE, 2015), 21.

[26] For a discussion of how this concept of race was medicalized and used to justify the Third Reich's programs for sterilization of the so-called disabled, medical experiments and ultimately genocide, see the iconic work by Robert J. Lifton, *The Nazi Doctors: Medical Killing and the Psychology of Genocide* (New York, 1980).

early 20th century against those who were considered not to be white Anglo-Saxon Protestants (WASPs).[27]

One might assume that, in the wake of the Holocaust, this theory would have been relegated to the ash heap of history and the realm of pseudo-science, worthy only to be disregarded or recognized as ludicrous. Sadly, that is not the case. Today, these conspiratorial and racist notions about Jews have been melded together to create something known as "white replacement/genocide" theory. Rooted in the conspiratorial anti-semitic themes discussed above, this theory contends that Jews are intent on wreaking havoc on "white Christian" civilization, with an ultimate goal to destroy it. In the 1990s, this theory gained traction in the United States among those who were part of the white power or white suprema-cist movement. David Lane, a committed white supremacist, authored a tract entitled "The White Genocide Manifesto." He contended that there was a "Zionist conspiracy to ... exterminate the white race." He created a pledge, which white supremacists call the "Fourteen Words," which is often recited at their gatherings – it was frequently heard at the Charlottesville "Unite the Right" rally in August 2017 – and on their social media platforms: "We must secure the existence of our people and a future for white children."[28]

According to adherents of this theory, the Jews' accomplices or lackeys in this effort are an array of people of color, among them Muslims and African Americans. In order to avoid this catastrophic takeover, whites must band together, arm themselves, and go on the offensive.[29] When these racialists speak of creating a white ethno-state for European whites, they are specifically excluding Jews. The Christian Identity movement, a religious expression of white supremacy, argued that whites were the lost tribes of Israel and that Jews, together with people of color, are the descendants of Satan and animals.[30]

---

[27] Steven Farber, "U.S. Scientists' Role in the Eugenics Movement (1907–1939): A Contemporary Biologist's Perspective," *Zebrafish.* 5.4 (2008), 243–45. doi:10.1089/zeb.2008.0576.

[28] Kevan A. Feshami, "Fear of White Genocide: Tracing the History of a Myth from Germany to Charlottesville," *Lapham's Quarterly* (September 6, 2017), www .laphamsquarterly.org/roundtable/fear-white-genocide.

[29] Sara Diamond, *Roads to Dominion: Right-Wing Movements and Political Power in the United States* (New York, 1995); Leonard Zeskind, *Blood and Politics: The History of the White Nationalist Movement from the Margins to the Mainstream* (New York, 2009).

[30] Michael Barkun, *Religion and the Racist Right: The Origins of the Christian Identity Movement* (Chapel Hill, NC, 1996). The Christian Identity movement proclaims the following: "We believe that there are literal children of Satan in this

This fear of active replacement by the Jew, derived directly from the historical underpinnings of antisemitism, is a central feature of contemporary antisemitism and is an oft-heard theme on white supremacist social media sites. The Traditionalist Worker Party, one of the groups that organized the "Unite the Right" Charlottesville rally, produced an official propaganda video instructing their members to attend the rally. It began with the following statement: "Genocide doesn't always happen with guns and bombs, the European people are facing genocide ... the international Jewish system, the capitalist system, and the forces of globalism want to destroy our people, they are doing this through mass immigration," and encourages members to attend the rally in order to say "we will not be replaced."[31] Those adhering to this ideology argue that Jews pose a specific danger because, while they are not white, they can "pass" as white.[32]

This view of the Jew is also deeply embedded in the Christian Identity Movement, where Jews are depicted as the arch enemy because of their intention to vanquish Aryans by relying on "economic enslavement, colored immigration and race mixing."[33] The *Daily Stormer*, a publication that advocates for white supremacy, described the effort to convert the masses into a "pro-white, antisemitic ideology."[34] Another member of the *Daily Stormer* editorial board complained that "our country is being usurped by a foreign tribe, called the Jews."[35] Another prominent white supremacist has written that "the Jew is the enemy of the human race. He has been for as long as we've got written language to record it."[36]

world today.... We believe that the Canaanite Jew is the natural enemy of our Aryan (White) Race. The Jew is like a destroying virus that attacks our racial body to destroy our Aryan culture and the purity of our race." Barbara Perry, *In the Name of Hate* (London, 2001), 144.

[31] Matthew Heimbach, Unite the Right! August 12 – Charlottesville, VA at Lee Park, Traditionalist Worker Party (July 8, 2017), https://web.archive.org/web/20190330210127/https:/notimeforsilence.wordpress.com/charlottesville/, at 0:00–0:22 and 4:24–4:40.

[32] "Betty A. Dobratz and Stephanie L. Shanks-Meile, *The White Separatist Movement in the United States: "White Power, White Pride!"* (New York, 1997).

[33] Nicholas Goodrick-Clarke, *Black Sun: Aryan Cults, Esoteric Nazism, and the Politics of Identity* (New York, 2001), 234.

[34] Andrew Anglin, "Alternative Right's Colin Liddell Attacks Andrew Anglin for Defending Robert Ransdell against RamZPaul," *Daily Stormer* (September 28, 2014). https://dailystormer.su/alternative-rights-colin-liddell-attacks-andrew-anglin-for-defending-robert-ransdell-against-ramzpaul/.

[35] Hawes Spencer, interview with Robert "Azzmador" Ray, the Hook (August 11, 2017) https://twitter.com/Suarez_CM/status/896196179456917504.

[36] Christopher Cantwell, "Taxing Truth," chriscantwell.com (August 20, 2018), NOCUSTODIAN00001842. https://christophercantwell.com/2018/08/20/radical-agenda-s04e010-taxing-truth/.

Those adhering to this form of antisemitic ideology view the Jew as the "Puppeteer" behind white replacement. According to the antisemite, people of color are not adept enough to engineer such a massive takeover of white Christian society on their own. There must be someone manipulating them. And that someone is the Jew. For white supremacists, Jews are a prime source of evil. The racist ideology associated with white supremacist organizations is inexorably linked to its Jew-hatred. For adherents to this ideology, the Jew is as "nonwhite" as a black person and, therefore, poses an existential threat to the white person.[37]

These newly emerging forms of antisemitism have age-old roots. The vessel in which the hatred is contained may change. The shape it may assume can be different, yet at its heart both its essence and its potentially lethal nature remain the same.

Further Reading

Almog, Shmuel, ed., *Antisemitism through the Ages* (Oxford, 1988). A series of essays tracing the history of antisemitism, based on the lectures and symposia held in Jerusalem by the Zalman Shazar Center for Jewish History.

Ben-Itto, Hadassa, *The Lie That Wouldn't Die: The Protocols of the Elders of Zion* (London, 2005). An accessible presentation of the history of one of the most influential antisemitic forgeries by a judge involved in investigating and litigating cases concerning the *Protocols*.

Berger, David, ed., *History and Hate: The Dimensions of Anti-Semitism* (Philadelphia, 1997). A series of essays by leading Jewish historians on antisemitism from antiquity to the modern era.

Brustein, William I., *Roots of Hate: Anti-Semitism in Europe before the Holocaust* (Cambridge, 2003). A systematic and comparative study of antisemitism prior to the Holocaust and its religious, racial, economic, and political roots.

Chanes, Jerome A., *Antisemitism: A Reference Handbook* (Santa Barbara, CA, 2004). A global survey of antisemitism covering many countries and biographical sketches of influential figures in the history of antisemitism including Father Charles Coughlin, John Chrysostom, and David Duke.

Herf, Jeffrey, ed., *Anti-Semitism and Anti-Zionism in Historical Perspective: Convergence and Divergence* (London, 2007). Reflections from Israeli, European, Canadian, and American historians comparing and contrasting the similarities and differences between anti-Zionism and antisemitism and the manner in which it has spread to different regions of the world.

Kertzer, David I., Arthur Morey, et al. *The Popes Against the Jews: The Vatican's Role in the Rise of Anti-Semitism* (New York, 2001). Arguing that the Roman Catholic Church played a major role in the development of

[37] Kathleen Belew, *Bring the War Home: The White Power Movement and Paramilitary America* (Cambridge, MA, 2018), see introduction, n. 24.

European antisemitism, the book contends that, although the Vatican did not approve of the genocide of the Jews, its teachings and policies helped make it possible.

Levy, Richard S., *Antisemitism: A Historical Encyclopedia of Prejudice and Persecution* (Santa Barbara, CA, 2005). An important resource containing 612 articles by over 200 scholars from many different countries, this historical encyclopedia provides a broad range of information, history, and analysis of antisemitism.

Michael, Robert, ed., *Dictionary of Antisemitism from the Earliest Times to the Present* (Lanham, MD, 2007). A very useful reference resource on the history of antisemitism.

Nirenberg, D., *Anti-Judaism: The Western Tradition* (New York, 2013). An intellectually powerful examination of the way Jew-hatred is foundational to the history of Western civilization. Examines how different societies and countries rendered Judaism as the internal enemy, something to be feared, fought, and destroyed.

Parkes, James W., *Antisemitism* (London, 1963). A classic work by a man who was a scholar and an Anglican clergyman. This book helped propel Christian theologians and clerics to reevaluate Christianity's role in the development, spread, and inculcation of antisemitism.

Poliakov, Leon, *The History of Anti-Semitism*, 4 vols. (Philadelphia, 2003). A comprehensive, multivolume history of antisemitism that surveys the history of this hatred from ancient to modern time. Among other things, it demonstrates that Jews did not even have to be present in a society for antisemitism to thrive.

Wistrich, Robert S., *A Lethal Obsession: Anti-Semitism from Antiquity to the Global Jihad* (New York, 2010). A compelling and comprehensive examination of the both known and often ignored roots of Jew-hatred through the ages.

26 Antisemitism in Social Media and on the Web

MARK WEITZMAN

Scholars have increasingly recognized that the impact of antisemitism is linked to the means of its transmission.[1] Reporting on a recent study, Monika Schwarz-Friesel wrote, "The spreading of antisemitic texts and pictures on all accessible as well as seemingly non-radical platforms, their multiple distribution on the World Wide Web, a discourse domain less controlled than other media, is by now a common phenomenon within the space of public online communication."[2]

In her acclaimed study of the blood-libel myth, the historian Magda Teter reminded us that antisemitism, which the scholar Robert Wistrich notably describes as the "Longest Hatred,"[3] requires a channel of communication in order to spread its message. Teter's study linked the evolution and persistence of this staple of antisemitism to the printed word, emphasizing that "it turned out it mattered what people read ... It was the printed books, not personal contacts that became accepted knowledge."[4] And, she continued, "Rumors and lore became 'facts' once they entered reputable printed books."

Teter notes the "disheartening fact that the long early modern paper trail continues to be relevant in the modern era ... This is also why

I want to acknowledge my thanks and appreciation to my colleagues, Rick Eaton and Emily Thompson, for their comments on an earlier draft of this chapter. I have consistently drawn on their deep knowledge of this topic and I am deeply grateful for their cheerful willingness to always be of assistance.

[1] For the purposes of this discussion I define antisemitism and Holocaust denial in accordance with the IHRA Working Definition of Antisemitism and the IHRA Working Definition of Holocaust Denial and Distortion (both at holocaustremembrance.com).

[2] Monika Schwarz-Friesel, "'Antisemitism 2.0': The Spreading of Jew-hatred on the World Wide Web." Available at www.researchgate.net/publication/337034786_Antisemitism_20-The_Spreading_of_Jew-hatred_on_the_World_Wide_Web, accessed November 21, 2020.

[3] Robert Wistrich, *Antisemitism, the Longest Hatred* (New York, 1992).

[4] Magda Teter, *Blood Libel* (Cambridge, 2020), 9.

antisemitic websites and chat groups are filled to the brim with
articles ... that are, as one white supremacist online user announced,
'backed up by records going back many centuries.'"[5]

The use of the Internet, representing the latest technological innovation to espouse bigotry, radicalization, and even to assist terrorism has
its precedents. Joseph Goebbels, the Nazi propaganda chief, was quick
to credit the power of radio and film, saying of radio that "the German
revolution, at least in the form it took, would have been impossible
without ... the radio" and that film was "one of the most modern and
scientific means of influencing the masses."[6]

Following Goebbels's example, modern antisemites were quick to
also recognize the potential of the new technology. George Dietz, a
West Virginia neo-Nazi, was perhaps the first, using the old Bulletin
Board System (BBS) in 1983. In Dietz's postings, which served as a model
for later websites, he used his own articles, as well as a collection of
writings by other antisemites and racists, to create a rich library that
included both new and old sources. These gave his site an impression of
both numbers and historical credibility.[7]

Dietz was followed in 1984 by Louis Beam, who was responsible for
getting the Aryan Nations Liberty Net (based on the Aryan Nations
ideology) online. A key figure of the racist movement during that period,
Beam emerged from the Texas Ku Klux Klan (KKK) to serve as an
"Ambassador at Large" for the Aryan Nations and was also one of the
founders of the Militia movement, which flourished in the United
States in the 1990s. By the spring of 1984 Beam was circulating a
manifesto titled "Computers and the American Patriot" that introduced
the Aryan Nation Liberty Net, allowing "any patriot in the country ...
to tap into this computer at will in order to reap the benefit of all
accumulative knowledge and wisdom of the leaders."[8] Beam was
shortly followed by Tom Metzger, a veteran Californian anti-immigrant
neo-Nazi activist, and others, who understood quite early in the digital

[5] Ibid., 383.
[6] Joseph Goebbels, *The Radio as the Eight Great Power*, www.calvin.edu/academic/cas/gpa/goeb56.htm, accessed November 21, 2020.
[7] Mark Weitzman, Testimony US House of Representatives Committee on Homeland Security, "Using the Web as a Weapon: The Internet as a Tool for Violent Radicalization and Homegrown Terrorism," November 6, 2007; Chip Berlet, "When Hate Went Online," CiteSeerX – When Hate Went Online (psu.edu), (adapted from a paper presented at the Northeast Sociological Association, Spring Conference, Sacred Heart University, Fairfield, CT, April 28, 2001), accessed December 1, 2020.
[8] Louis Beam, "Inter-Klan Newsletter, 1984" (undated), 1984.inter-klan_newsletter.pdf (simson.net), accessed December 1, 2020.

revolution that the Internet not only could facilitate communications and marketing, but might also serve to link and empower members and sympathizers of the movement.⁹ By 1985 the *New York Times* was reporting on this new phenomenon, describing how "An Idaho- based neo-Nazi organization has established a computer-based network to link rightist groups and to disseminate a list of those who it says 'have betrayed their race.'"¹⁰

The growing sophistication and radicalization of the extremists also began to manifest in the technological domain. From the mid-1980s crude versions of Nazi computer games began appearing. These games, with titles like *Aryan Test, Clean Germany, Anti-Turk Test,* and *KZ* [German for Concentration Camp] *Manager* appeared in both US and European websites. Designed to mock victims of genocide and racism and clearly aimed at younger users, hate games serve the triple purposes of dehumanizing the enemy, while entertaining and recruiting youngsters. An Internet culture was emerging that normalized violence, advanced it as a form of problem-solving, and mocked victims, who were invariably members of minorities. Today these games continue to proliferate online, with even the older games continuing to attract visitors. For example, a more advanced version of *KZ Manager* can be found online today. This game uses allusions to the Nazi gassing of Jews and applies that to a contemporary minority target in Germany: the Turkish minority. The deploying of such games enormously expanded the potential reach of bigots on both sides of the Atlantic.

The Oklahoma City bombing marked a new phase in the extremist's war against the US government. It also marked the start of the digital age of extremism, with Don Black's Stormfront website generally considered as the first extremist site online. A veteran of the KKK, where he was a colleague of David Duke, Black served three years in federal prison for being part of an armed attempt to take over the island of Dominica. Black used his time in jail to hone computer skills and began Stormfront in 1995. The site quickly became the most important and largest white nationalist site online. Using the Celtic cross as its

⁹ For Metzger, see his November 22, 2020, obituary in the *New York Times,* "Tom Metzger, Notorious White Supremacist, Dies at 82." For an early analysis of extremism online, see Mark Weitzman, "'The Internet Is Our Sword': Aspects of Online Antisemitism," in *Remembering for the Future: The Holocaust in an Age of Genocide,* ed. John K. Roth, Elisabeth Maxwell, Margot Levy, and Wendy Whitworth (London, 2001), 911–925.
¹⁰ Wayne King, "Computer Network Links Rightist Groups and Offers 'Enemy List,'" *New York Times,* February 15, 1985.

logo, Stormfront.org had a large library, an active forum, and an Internet
radio program and was available in up to ten languages.[11]

A young racist, Alex Curtis, used his website to distribute an article
calling for a "Lone Wolf" strategy, which asserted that "true believers"
could best achieve their goals by staying under the radar screen, invisible to the authorities and researchers. The most notorious example of a
"lone wolf" was Timothy McVeigh, who was unknown until his arrest
after the Oklahoma City bombing. Curtis also posted a "point system,"
targeting judges, civil rights leaders, and others. Curtis was convicted of
hate crimes charges in 2000.[12]

For the veteran American antisemite and neo-Nazi David Duke the
Internet is a godsend, as can be seen in the advice he gave to his followers
to "Develop computer and other technical skills. The computer and
Internet revolution give us untold possibilities to awaken our people all
over the world and to build our Movement."[13] In July 2020, after years of
activity online, Twitter "permanently suspended" Duke's account.[14]

And, of course, no mention of the Jewish conspiracy to control the
world would be complete without a reference to the classic text of
antisemitic propaganda, *The Protocols of the Elders of Zion*, which
remains a staple of antisemitic conspiracy theorists. The *Protocols*,
which appeared over 100 years ago, embodies the theme of the alleged
Jewish conspiracy aimed at dominating the world, which is still pervasive, often signified today through thinly veiled antisemitic attacks on
liberal Jewish financier George Soros.[15] Today, it is accessed online by
extremists and antisemites, ranging from neo-Nazis to Islamic extremists to conspiracy theorists, via scores of websites and languages.[16]

[11] For a profile of Black, see the Southern Poverty Law Center (splcenter.org), while
Stormfront is profiled at Southern Poverty Law Center (splcenter.org), both undated,
accessed December 8, 2020.
[12] See the FBI Report on Operation Lone Wolf, "FBI Operation Lone Wolf," 2000,
accessed December 8, 2020.
[13] Mark Weitzman, "Transmigration of Antisemitism: Old Myths; New Realities," in
Not Your Father's Antisemitism, ed. Michael Berenbaum (St. Paul, MN, 2008).
[14] "Twitter Bans White Supremacist David Duke after 11 years," *The Guardian*, July
31, 2020.
[15] "Demonization of Soros Recalls Old Anti-Semitic Conspiracies," Voice of America,
English, May 15, 2007 (voanews.com).
[16] The classic text about the *Protocols* is Norman Cohn's *A Warrant for Genocide*
(London, 1967). *Dismantling the Big Lie: The Protocols of the Elders of Zion* by
Steven L. Jacobs and Mark Weitzman (Los Angeles, CA, 2003) is a detailed refutation
of the text. See also Juliane Wetzel, "The Protocols of the Elders of Zion on the
Internet: How Radical Political Groups Are Networked via Conspiracy Theories," in
The Global Impact of the Protocols of the Elders of Zion: A Century Old Myth, ed.

The 9/11 attacks on the United States signified a new stage in
Internet extremism, with Islamist extremism rapidly exploding
online. (I use the term "Islamist" to signify the radical jihadist and
extremist ideology, distinct from the religion itself.) As could be
expected, antisemitism in its various manifestations has been a staple
of this radical discourse. Israel is excoriated as a cancer or a colonial
enterprise without legitimacy and one that engages in Nazi-like
behavior. Jews are regularly described as enemies of Mohammad and
Islam, and even as enemies of humanity. They are accused of engaging
in all sorts of terrible behavior, with blood libels updated to the
present. According to an analysis of ISIS's online English-language
magazine in the years 2014–2016, Jews are even conspiring with the
Shia Muslims to destroy Islam; thus, eliminating Jews becomes a
major religious obligation.[17]

It can easily be seen from the above that there is certainly a
commonality of antisemitic tropes that are shared by both extreme
right-wing and Islamist digital discourse. This pattern reflects the
historical migration of many antisemitic tropes from Europe to the
Middle East, from Christianity to Islam. For example, the historian
Jonathan Frankel has noted that the Christian communities "were the
source from which the accusations of ritual murder had emanated" in
Damascus in 1840.[18]

It is clear that for both radical Islam and radical antisemitism,
"Antisemitic beliefs often serve as a key entry point for individuals to
radicalize, join extremist groups, and progress into violent mobilization."[19] For example, according to some scholars, a fundamental narrative in radical Islam concerns the theme of betrayal. In this narrative,

Esther Webman (London, 2011), and Richard Landes and Steven T. Katz, *The
Paranoid Apocalypse: A Hundred Year Retrospective on the Protocols of the
Elders of Zion* (New York, 2012).

[17] Daniel Rickenbacher, "The Centrality of Anti-Semitism in the Islamic State's
Ideology and Its Connection to Anti-Shiism," *Religions* 10.8 (2019), 483; https://doi
.org/10.3390/rel10080483, accessed December 8, 2020.

[18] Jonathan Frankel, *The Damascus Affair: Ritual Murder, Politics and the Jews in
1840* (Cambridge, 1997), 54. Frankel drew on earlier work by the Israeli scholars
Jacob Landau and Moshe Ma'oz in making this point.

[19] Alexander Meleagrou-Hitchens, Bennett Clifford, and Lorenzo Vidino,
"Antisemitism as an Underlying Precursor to Violent Extremism in American
Far-Right and Islamist Contexts," 3, https://extremism.gwu.edu/sites/g/files/
zaxdzs2191/f/Antisemitism%20as%20an%20Underlying%20Precursor%20to%
20Violent%20Extremism%20in%20American%20Far-Right%20and%20Islamist
%20Contexts%20Pdf.pdf, accessed December 8, 2020.

"the Battle of Khaybar (629 CE) is a tale of treachery and the dire consequences of plotting against Allah and His Prophet. However ... the role of the traitor is assumed by an entire group, rather than a single individual, and that group (tribe) was Jewish, not Muslim."[20] This narrative can then be viewed as the Islamist version of the traditional Christian charge of deicide, and both of these highly charged accusations lead to antisemitic discourses that become fundamental elements of belief.[21] These narratives often have "persuasive power" that can fuel radicalization.[22]

And there is no question that jihadist radicalization has often been traced to online activity. In order to test that thesis, the RAND Corporation engaged in a study of fifteen test cases in the United Kingdom which "confirmed that the internet played a role in the radicalisation process of the violent extremists and terrorists whose cases we studied."[23] It is also clear that the "Internet is used to target young people. Terrorist organizations use cartoons, popular music videos and computer games to get their attention."[24]

These efforts are very sophisticated. For example, ISIS released a forty-four-minute-long video on the battle for Mosul (2016–2017) that is aimed at creating a counternarrative to the Netflix version of the battle. Not only does their video use the Netflix logo, which might fool viewers into believing they are watching the original film, but by positioning the Netflix logo over the ISIS flag they cover up the ISIS symbol, which might be recognized and then banned by social media platforms on the lookout for terrorist symbols.[25]

Holocaust denial is a recurring theme as well. Iran, the only country where Holocaust denial is a matter of official state policy, maintains a vigorous social media presence where even the highest leaders of the

[20] Jeffry R. Halverson, H. L. Goodall Jr., Steven R. Corman, "The Battle of Khaybar," in Jeffry R. Halverson, H. L. Goodall Jr., and Steven R. Corman, *Master Narratives of Islamist Extremism* (New York, 2011), p. 67.

[21] Ibid.

[22] Ibid., 80.

[23] Ines Von Behr, Anaïs Reding, Charlie Edwards, and Luke Gribbon, "Radicalisation in the Digital Era: The Use of the Internet in 15 Cases of Terrorism and Extremism," 2013 (rand.org), accessed December 7, 2020.

[24] Raphael Cohen-Almagor, "Jihad Online: How Do Terrorists Use the Internet?," in *Media and Metamedia Management*, ed. Freire F. Rúas Araújo X. and Martínez Fernández V. García X (Switzerland, 2017).

[25] "ISIS Responds to Netflix Film about Mosul," Middle Eastern Media Research Institute (MEMRI), accessed December 8, 2020.

country engage in supporting denial.[26] Denial is a pervasive theme, as it is believed that negating the Holocaust undercuts and destroys Israel's legitimacy, as the state of Israel exists only to assuage Europe and the West's guilt over the Holocaust.[27]

Conspiracy theories are also prevalent. From 9/11 to the coronavirus pandemic, Jews are blamed for every disaster and accused of fomenting or manipulating the event for their own nefarious purposes.[28] They are accused of undermining morals ("spreading homosexuality")[29] and, in terms chillingly reminiscent of Nazi propaganda, ultimately of being "'a cancer to society.'"[30]

Although the origins of social media can be found already in the 1990s, the concept of social media did not begin to find widespread use until the mid-2000s. Based on user-generated content, social media in all its manifestations broke down editorial boundaries and controls and opened up the internet to a new era of uncontrolled material. It rapidly has become the most important means of communication in today's world, with an estimated 4.33 billion users worldwide.[31] The dominant platforms such as Facebook and YouTube, along with others such as TikTok, WeChat, Instagram, Twitter, Tumblr, LinkedIn, Telegram, WhatsApp, Snapchat, Viber, Pinterest, Reddit, and more have become the primary means of obtaining and sharing information, marketing, facilitation of social networks, and influencing public opinion.[32]

---

[26] Tweet by Ayatollah Ali Khamenei, "Why Is It a Crime to Raise Doubts about the Holocaust?," October 28, 2020, quoted in Golnaz Esfandiari, "Iran's Supreme Leader Criticized for Equating Cartoons of Prophet Muhammad with Holocaust Denial" (rferl.org). The best full treatment of Holocaust denial in the Arab world remains Esther Webman and Meir Litvak, *From Empathy to Denial: Arab Responses to the Holocaust* (New York, 2009).

[27] See for example Osama Al-Alfi, "The Truth about the Holocaust," Al-Ahram, February 1, 2019; translated and excerpted in "Columnist for Egyptian Government Daily Denies Holocaust," MEMRI. This example was taken from the Tom Lantos Archive maintained by MEMRI, which is an invaluable archive of relevant material, accessed December 9, 2020.

[28] 2020 MEMRI TV clips and reports from the MEMRI 9/11 Archives Project, MEMRI; "Pakistani Taliban: Coronavirus Was 'Hidden like an Atom Bomb,'" MEMRI; "Iraqi TV: COVID Vaccine Will Control People via Satellite," MEMRI, December 10, 2020.

[29] MEMRI Weekly, November 21–December 4, 2020: MEMRI, "Fmr Hamas Official: Jews Spread Homosexuality," MEMRI, December 3, 2020.

[30] Kafa Al-Zou'bi, "Jordanian Writer: Cancer of Judaism Harms Humanity," Al-Awal News, April 9, 2020, MEMRI.

[31] DataReportal, "Digital around the World," April 2021, Global Digital Insights.

[32] For example, according to the Pew Research Center, "More than half of U.S. adults get news from social media" and "Facebook is the dominant social media news source." Elisa Shearer and Elizabeth Grieco, "Americans Are Wary of the Role

This meant that antisemitism, Holocaust denial, and conspiracy theories quickly migrated to these platforms and proliferated there. One report by a Jewish advocacy group found over 382,000 antisemitic postings on social media in 2016.[33] Two years later another report found over 4 million antisemitic tweets, and by 2020 a US government official was estimating that in the first eight months of 2020 there were 1.7 million antisemitic posts just on Facebook and Twitter.[34]

This rise of digital antisemitism has been accompanied by an increase in antisemitic hate crimes and acts in Europe and the United States. A 2018 survey by the human rights arm of the European Union found that in the eleven countries with the largest Jewish populations in Europe, 89 percent of the Jews who responded felt that antisemitism had risen over the past decade.[35] At the same time, FBI hate crime statistics showed that in 2019 Jews were the victims of over 60 percent of religiously motivated hate crimes, more than four times greater than any other group.[36]

The proliferation of antisemitic material did not go unnoticed. By 2017 antisemitic memes, such as Pepe the Frog, were swirling around the internet and became a part of the discourse in the US presidential campaign. As antisemitism grabbed headlines, both civil society advocacy groups and political leaders began advocating for changes to the rules that appeared to protect blatant hate speech. Under pressure, Facebook and then others began to address the issue by announcing policy changes. For example, in August 2020 an NGO in the United Kingdom released a report which demonstrated that Facebook's own algorithms "actively promote" Holocaust denial by recommending links to other Holocaust denial material.[37] While Facebook had long claimed to act against hate speech, and had indeed had previously banned some antisemitic stereotypes, it still maintained that freedom

Social Media Sites Play in Delivering the News," Pew Research Center (journalism. org), October 2, 2019, accessed December 1, 2020.

[33] See the World Jewish Congress' 2016 report, "The Rise of Antisemitism on Social Media," antisemitismreport.pdf (crif.org), accessed December 1, 2020.

[34] Elan S. Carr, "Taking Aim at Online Anti-Semitism," The Hill, October 20, 2020, accessed December 1, 2020.

[35] "Experiences and Perceptions of Antisemitism – Second Survey on Discrimination and Hate Crime against Jews in the EU," European Union Agency for Fundamental Rights, December 10, 2018 (europa.eu), accessed November 21, 2020.

[36] "Muslims, at 13.3 percent, were the next highest number of victims." FBI Uniform Crime Report Hate Crime Statistics, 2019, p. 3, incidents-and-offenses.pdf (fbi.gov), accessed December 8, 2020.

[37] Jakob Guhl and Jacob Davey, "Hosting the Holohoax: A Snapshot Denial across Social Media," Hosting-the-Holohoax.pdf, August 10, 2020 (isdglobal.org), accessed December 1, 2020.

of speech was the overriding principle that obliged it to allow some hard-core antisemitism and other forms of hate speech to be posted.

Indeed, in August 2018 Facebook founder Mark Zuckerberg had controversially stated that "I'm Jewish, and there's a set of people who deny that the Holocaust happened. I find that deeply offensive. But at the end of the day, I don't believe that our platform should take that down because I think there are things that different people get wrong."[38] However, in the face of the ensuing critical reaction Facebook eventually reversed course. In a post on his blog (October 2020) Zuckerberg announced a new policy, writing, "But with rising anti-Semitism, we're expanding our policy to prohibit any content that denies or distorts the Holocaust as well."[39] This policy change was amplified in a letter by Monika Bickert, Facebook's VP of Content Policy, in which she put the move into the context of both their banning of hate speech ("We took down 22.5 million pieces of hate speech from our platform in the second quarter of this year"), hate groups ("We have banned more than 250 white supremacist organizations"), and the "well-documented rise in anti-Semitism globally and the alarming level of ignorance about the Holocaust, especially among young people."[40]

Google has had its own issues with antisemitism. In 2004 a campaign ("Google bombing") led to an antisemitic site (Jew Watch) run by a neo-Nazi to appear first in response to Google searches for the word "Jew." This site was still appearing on the first page of Google searches for "Jew" in 2013.[41] In 2014 the alt right pushed the use of triple parenthesis ((( ))) as brackets to identify Jews online, and in 2016 Google removed an extension of its Chrome browser that automatically assigned the brackets to Jewish names.[42] In the United Kingdom alone a recent study found that over 170,000 antisemitic searches were made on Google last year, and 10 percent of those could be classified as "searches [that] involve violent language or intentions."[43]

---

[38] Kara Swisher, "Zuckerberg: The Recode interview," Mark Zuckerberg: The Recode interview, Vox, October 8, 2018, accessed November 30, 2020.

[39] Mark Zuckerberg, "Today we're updating our hate speech," Facebook, October 12, 2020, accessed Dec 1. 2020.

[40] Monika Bickert, "Removing Holocaust Denial Content," Removing Holocaust Denial Content, About Facebook (fb.com), October 12, 2020, accessed December 1, 2020.

[41] Tal Frost, "Anti-Semitism in Information Era" (ynetnews.com), August 4, 2013, accessed December 8, 2020.

[42] "Google Bans Plug-In That Picks Out Jews," BBC News, June 6, 2016, accessed December 8, 2020.

[43] "Hidden Hate: What Google Searches Tell Us about Antisemitism Today," Blog, CST – Protecting Our Jewish Community, January 11, 2019, accessed December 8, 2020.

Twitter has also been a major source of antisemitism online, with issues including politicians and celebrities who either post or retweet antisemitic content.[44] In 2017–2018 researchers found 4.2 million antisemitic tweets (and 3 million antisemitic handles).[45] Its recent policies regarding Holocaust denial have been somewhat confusing. Holocaust denial, appearing with handles like #holohoax, have proliferated on Twitter. Following Facebook's lead, Twitter announced that it would also remove Holocaust denial posts.[46] Two weeks later, in a hearing in the US Senate, Twitter CEO Jack Dorsey said, "We don't have a policy against that type of misleading information."[47] However, Dorsey's statement was walked back by a company spokesman, who reiterated that "our glorification of violence policy prohibit [sic] glorification of genocide including the Holocaust."[48]

Other mainstream platforms were not exempt from antisemitism either. Reports of harassment of Jewish TikTok creators have surfaced[49] along with many instances on Instagram.[50] And after having been a prime source of Holocaust denial videos, YouTube banned Holocaust denial videos in 2019, calling such conspiracies "hateful."[51]

But while the mainstream companies were finally taking action against antisemitism, the reality was that some of the most extreme and virulent expressions of hate were originating and circulating on lesser-known platforms. One of these was VK, or VKontakte (InContact), a Russian-based social media and networking service that is one of the most popular in the world. VK has served as a communications bridge between US and Eastern European antisemites and

[44] See, for example, Kareem Abdul-Jabbar, "Where Is the Outrage over Anti-Semitism in Sports and Hollywood?," Hollywood Reporter, July 14, 2020, accessed December 9, 2020.
[45] "Quantifying Hate: A Year of Anti-Semitism on Twitter" (adl.org), May 7, 2018, accessed December 8, 2020.
[46] "Twitter, like Facebook, to Remove Posts Denying the Holocaust," Bloomberg, October 14, 2020, accessed December 8, 2020.
[47] Ben Sales, "Two Weeks after Twitter Bans Holocaust Denial, CEO Jack Dorsey Says It's Still Allowed," Jewish Telegraphic Agency (jta.org), October 28, 2020, accessed December 9, 2020.
[48] Ibid.
[49] Kalhan Rosenblatt, "Jewish Teens Say Life on TikTok Comes with Anti-Semitism," (nbcnews.com), September 25, 2020, accessed December 9, 2020.
[50] See, for example, Gordon Rayner, "Twitter and Instagram Must Explain Why Rapper's 'Abhorrent' Anti-Semitic Posts Were Left Up for so Long, Says Priti Patel," July 26, 2020 (telegraph.co.uk), accessed December 9, 2020.
[51] "YouTube Bans Holocaust Denial Videos in Policy Reversal," Voice of America – English (voanews.com), June 7, 2019, accessed November 30, 2020.

extremists.[52] In the United States a great deal of alt-right and other forms of radical antisemitism was linked to networks like Discord, Reddit, 4chan, 8chan (now 8kun), and Gab. These sites often had rooms devoted to specific themes or topics, and some served as incubators of extremism.[53] Abetted by sympathetic moderators who did not attempt to control the discourse, antisemitism and other forms of hate speech created a toxic atmosphere. In one notorious case in the months leading up to the infamous violent 2017 "Unite the Right" rally in Charlottesville, Virginia, "the far-right movement used the online chat room Discord to encourage like-minded users to protest" in Charlottesville.[54] Reddit has been described as "worse than Stormfront" and was also one of the ten most popular sites in the United States.[55] Robert Bowers, the murderer of eleven Jews in the Tree of Life synagogue in Pittsburgh, the worst case of antisemitic violence in American history, posted his infamous last message on Gab right before he entered the synagogue and started shooting.[56] Currently, Telegram, which originated in Russia where it was started by one of the founders of VK and is now based in Dubai, has seen a significant surge in antisemitic and extremist use. Telegram was originally popularized by Islamist terrorists because it promises greater security and almost total freedom of speech (it now claims that it will act only against "terrorist" material, which has diminished its popularity in those circles).[57] Gab also became attractive to antisemites and other extremists because of its refusal to moderate and apply any

---

[52] By one measure VK is the fourteenth most popular network in the world, and second in Russia. Vk.com, "Analytics – Market Share Data & Ranking," SimilarWebVK. com, January 2020 overview. On VK's links to the United States, see Anti-Defamation League, "Linking American White Supremacists to International Counterparts" (adl.org), July 2, 2019, accessed December 1, 2020.

[53] See, for example, Anonymous, "At Age 13, I Joined the Alt-Right, Aided by Reddit and Google" (fastcompany.com), December 5, 2019, and James Damore, "Google, and the YouTube Radicalization of Angry White Men," *The Guardian*, August 13, 2017, accessed December 1, 2020

[54] Kianna Gardner, "Social Media: Where Voices of Hate Find a Place to Preach," Center for Public Integrity, August 30, 2018, accessed November 30, 2020.

[55] Keegan Hankes, "How Reddit Became a Worse Black Hole of Violent Racism than Stormfront" (gawker.com), March 10, 2015, accessed December 9, 2020.

[56] Abby Ohlheiser and Ian Shapira, "Robert Bowers Gab Account: How Gab Became a White Supremacist Haven," *Washington Post*, October 29, 2018, accessed November 30, 2020. See also Alex Amend, "On Gab, Domestic Terrorist Robert Bowers Engaged with Several Influential Alt-Right Figures," Southern Poverty Law Center (splcenter. org), November 1, 2018, accessed December 9, 2020.

[57] swc-telegram-briefing-july.pdf (wiesenthal.com), July, 7, 2020, accessed December 8, 2020.

standards to posts by its users, which contrasted with the restrictive steps being taken by the larger, more mainstream companies.

But perhaps the most significant event to change the social media landscape is currently unfolding. It is clear that the insurrection in the Capitol in Washington on January 6, 2021, was incited by the combustible combination of President Trump's urging his followers to come to Washington in an attempt to intimidate congressional certification of the vote and the receptiveness of the extreme right wing to read those messages as confirmation of the violent conspiracy theories that had been circulating online for the past few years.[58] Even before the riot, at least one FBI report warned of online threats, reporting about a thread that incited followers to "Be ready to fight. Congress needs to hear glass breaking, doors being kicked in, and blood from their BLM and Antifa slave soldiers being spilled. Get violent. Stop calling this a march, or rally, or a protest. Go there ready for war."[59]

The rioters comprised a mélange of extremist groups as well as individuals with no specific connection to organized extremism. Groups such as the Proud Boys were prominent in the lead-up and in the riot itself. Although the Proud Boys proclaimed that they are not racist or antisemitic and point to the Latino background of the group's leader as evidence, their members have a detailed history of antisemitic statements and memberships in hard-core antisemitic and neo-Nazi groups.[60] During the presidential campaign they received a quasi-endorsement from then President Trump, who during a campaign debate in September said, "Proud Boys stand back and stand by." While Trump's statement might have been ambiguous, the extremist right took it as an endorsement of the Proud Boys and their beliefs and as a signal that violence would be a legitimate reaction if the election results were not as they desired. As the neo-Nazi Andrew Anglin wrote, "He is telling the people to stand by. As in: get ready for war."[61]

<hr/>

[58] See, among many, Craig Timbrell and Drew Harwood, "Pro-Trump Forums Erupt with Violent Threats ahead of Wednesday's Rally against the 2020 Election," *Washington Post*, January 5, 2021, accessed January 6, 2021.

[59] Devlin Barrett and Matt Zapotosky, "FBI Report Warned of 'War' at Capitol, Contradicting Claims There Was No Indication of Looming Violence," *Washington Post*, January 12, 2021. BLM refers to Black Lives Matter, while "Pantifa" is a term used by the far right to denigrate the Antifa movement.

[60] "Proud Boys' Bigotry is on Full Display," Anti-Defamation League (adl.org). December 24, 2020.

[61] Amy Gardner, Joshua Partlow, Isaac Stanley-Becker, and Josh Dawsey, "Trump's Call for Poll-Watching Volunteers Sparks Fear of Chaos and Violence on Election Day," *Washington Post*, September 30, 2020; and Neil MacFarquhar, Alan Feuer,

The Proud Boys were not the only antisemitic extremists identified at the riot; others included Nick Fuentes of the Groyper Army, who posted a video on a livestreaming service (DLive) prior to the riot stating, "What can you and I do to a state legislator – besides kill him?", and the antisemitic conspiracy theorist Joseph "Tim" Gionet, known as "Baked Alaska."[62] Antisemitic images were highly visible at the riot, including denial of the Holocaust.[63] One widely circulated photo featured a rioter rampaging through the Capitol wearing a "Camp Auschwitz" sweatshirt that was sold online, along with other items, by a New York company.[64] That image outraged House Speaker Nancy Pelosi, who cited it as one of the spurs for her establishment of a commission to investigate the riot.[65]

One of the most prominent influencers in the loose coalition of informal groups (which included some Christian conservatives and far right-wing extremists) that incited the insurrection was the shadowy conspiracy theory known as QAnon, which exists primarily online.[66] Originating on 4chan and then migrating to 8chan (now 8kun), QAnon essentially claims that a secret satanic cabal of Democratic pedophiliacs that include prominent figures ranging from Hillary Clinton to Pope Francis controls the "deep state," and former President Trump was viewed as their hero and savior. Antisemitism features as an essential

Mike Baker, and Sheera Frenkel, "Far-Right Group That Trades in Political Violence Gets a Boost," *New York Times*, September 30, 2020.

[62] A. C. Thompson and Ford Fischer, "Members of Several Well-Known Hate Groups Identified at Capitol Riot," Frontline, January 9, 2021, www.pbs.org/wgbh/frontline/article/several-well-known-hate-groups-identified-at-capitol-riot/, accessed January 9, 2021. For the Groyper Army and antisemitism, see Ron Kampeas, "In the US, the 'groyper army' seeks to make anti-Semitism mainstream," *Times of Israel*, December 9, 2019, www.timesofisrael.com/in-the-us-the-groyper-army-seeks-to-make-anti-semitism-mainstream/, Dec. 9, 2019, accessed January 18, 2021. For an incisive look at Gionet's journey by a former colleague, see Ben Smith, "We Worked Together on the Internet. Last Week, He Stormed the Capitol," *New York Times*, January 10, 2021 (updated January 21, 2021).

[63] Elana Schorr, "Anti-Semitism Seen in Capitol Insurrection Raises Alarms," *Associated Press*, www.usnews.com/news/politics/articles/2021-01-13/anti-semitism-seen-in-capitol-insurre, January 13, 2021, accessed January 13, 2021.

[64] Lisa Rozner, "Capitol Chaos: Anti-Semitic Apparel Worn during Riot Traced to Website Based in New York City," CBS New York (cbslocal.com), January 11, 2021, accessed January 11, 2021. The rioter was later identified and arrested.

[65] Nathan Baca, "House Appoints Retired Lieutenant General to Lead Capitol Riot Investigation," Congressional investigation into Capitol riots, Nancy Pelosi, wusa9.com, January 15, 2021, accessed January 15, 2021.

[66] David D. Kirkpatrick, Mike McIntire, and Christiaan Triebert, "Before the Capitol Riot, Calls for Cash and Talk of Revolution," *New York Times*, January 16, 2021.

component of QAnon, with Q adherents posting antisemitic images and
targeting prominent Jewish figures.[67] QAnon's impact would even be
felt in Congress, as the November elections saw at least two known
supporters of the movement (Reps. Marjorie Taylor Greene, a
Republican from Georgia, and Lauren Boebert, a Republican from
Colorado) winning seats. Greene shared an antisemitic video online in
2018 and Boebert has been accused of using antisemitic language.[68]

The shock wave caused by the insurrection reverberated throughout
every level of American society. While the political structure of the
United States was most visibly threatened, the responsibility of the tech
industry as the incubator of the conspiracy theories and violent fantasies that flamed up in Washington also came under intense scrutiny,
even from industry leaders and employees themselves. As a result,
several major companies took significant steps to rein in or even ban
hate speech, misinformation, and conspiracy mongering, with antisemitic postings being included. For example, Twitter decided to "permanently suspend accounts that are solely dedicated to sharing QAnon
content," while Google, Apple, and Amazon all took steps against
Parler. Google suspended Parler from distribution on its Play Store,
while Apple removed Parler from their App Store and Amazon dropped
them from their server.[69] Amazon stated that its action was the result of
Parler continuing to host threads that included "calls to hang public
officials, kill Black and Jewish people, and shoot police officers in the
head."[70] As a result Parler was briefly offline before being able to find a
new host in Russia and resuming limited services.[71]

Big Tech engendered a counterreaction that united some free
speech advocates with extremists and antisemites in protesting the

[67] On QAnon in general, see the report by the Simon Wiesenthal Center, "QAnon –
From Fringe to Conspiracy," qanon-from-fringe-conspiracy.pdf (wiesenthal.com). For
QAnon and other antisemitic symbols at the riot, see Jonathan Sarna, "The Symbols
of Antisemitism in the Capitol Riot," Brandeis NOW, accessed January 12, 2021.
[68] For Greene, see Ben Sales, "Marjorie Taylor Greene Shared Antisemitic and
Islamophobic Video," Jerusalem Post (jpost.com), August 27, 2020, accessed
January 19, 2021. Boebert, who has expressed strong support for Israel, was accused
of using Nazi terminology to describe Colorado's Jewish governor's efforts to combat
the COVID-19 pandemic. See, for example, Malka Benoni, "Letters to the Editor,"
Pueblo Chieftain, January 17, 2021, accessed January 29, 2021.
[69] Richard Nieva, "How Silicon Valley Has Responded to the Deadly Pro-Trump Riot at
the Capitol," CNET, January 13, 2021.
[70] Russell Brandom, "These Are the Violent Threats That Made Amazon Drop Parler,"
The Verge, January 15, 2021.
[71] Jason Murdock, "Parler Hopes for U.S. Host as Russian Firm Provides Temporary
Website," msn.com, January 20, 2021.

"censorship" being imposed by the companies.[72] Others migrated from the mainstream social media into TikTok or the fringe platforms like Gab and Telegram.[73] While this migration removed some mainstream access and might have lessened the large-scale impact of hate and conspiracy theories, by pushing users into private groups and encryption it also had the unintended consequence of making it more difficult to track extremism online. Another unanticipated effect was the use of photos, screenshots, and online video by both law enforcement and private citizens, including family members disgusted by the events, to identify and then arrest participants suspected of committing crimes during the insurrection.[74] While the ultimate impact of the violent insurrection is still unclear, the participants' agenda of "Overthrowing the government. Igniting a second Civil War. Banishing racial minorities, immigrants and Jews" continues to fester online and fuel recruitment and more potential violence in the near future.[75]

The reality is that antisemitism (and other forms of extremism) has permeated the internet and the genie cannot be put back in the bottle. The efforts of mainstream tech companies like Facebook or Google can have an impact, but they cannot resolve the situation. As it stands now there is simply too much hate speech online for even the most ambitious effort to control. And of course the situation is even more acute on those platforms that offer a less controlled environment. The eminent British historian Sir Richard Evans recently wrote that "the gatekeepers of opinion formation have been bypassed through the Internet and anyone can put out their views into the public sphere, no matter how bizarre they might be."[76] Hate speech and conspiracy theories "are powered by the rise of the Internet and social media";[77] they weaken truth and undermine civil society. Antisemitism, in the words of Ahmed Shaheed, the United Nations' Special Rapporteur on Freedom

[72] Jessica Guynn, "'They Want to Take Your Speech Away,' Censorship Cry Unites Trump Supporters and Extremists after Capitol Attack," *USA Today,*, January 15, 2021.

[73] Tina Nguyen and Mark Scott, "Right-Wing Extremist Chatter Spreads on New Platforms as Threat of Political Violence Ramps Up," *Politico*, January 12, 2021.

[74] Hannah Knowles and Pauline Villegas, "Pushed to the Edge by the Capitol Riot, People Are Reporting Their Family and Friends to the FBI," *Washington Post*, January 16, 2021.

[75] Neil MacFarquhar, Jack Healy, Mike Baker, and Serge F. Kovaleski, "Capitol Attack Could Fuel Extremist Recruitment for Years, Experts Warn," *New York Times*, January 16, 2021.

[76] Richard J. Evans, *The Hitler Conspiracies* (New York, 2020), 216.

[77] Ibid., 1.

of Religion and Belief, is "toxic to democracy ... and threatens all societies in which it goes unchallenged."[78] Today, as recent events have emphasized, the internet is the arena in which that challenge must be met if antisemitism is to be marginalized and rendered powerless to cause further harm.

Further Reading

Daniels, Jessie, *Cyber Racism: White Supremacy Online and the New Attack on Civil Rights* (Lanham, MD, 2009).

Davey, Jacob, "Hosting the 'Holohoax': A Snapshot of Holocaust Denial across Social Media," Institute for Strategic Dialogue (London, 2020).

Oboler, Andre, "Online Antisemitism 2.0. 'Social Antisemitism' on the 'Social Web,'" Jerusalem Center for Public Affairs, *No. 67*, April 1, 2008, https://jcpa.org/article/online-antisemitism-2-0-social-antisemitism-on-the-social-web/.

Schwarz-Freisel, Monika, "Antisemitism 2.0 and the Cyberculture of Hate: Opening Pandora 's Box," in *The Routledge History of Antisemitism*, ed. M. Weitzman, J. Wald, and R. Williams (London, forthcoming).

"'Antisemitism 2.0' – The Spreading of Jew-Hatred on the World Wide Web," www.degruyter.com/document/doi/10.1515/9783110618594-026/html.

Simon Wiesenthal Center Report, "New SWC Report: QAnon: From Freinge Conspiracy to Mainstream Politics," September 2020, www.wiesenthal.com/about/news/new-swc-report.html.

"Parler: An Unbiased Social Platform?," November 2020, www.wiesenthal.com/assets/pdf/parler_report_final-2020.pdf.

"Telegram: A Briefing," July 2020, www.wiesenthal.com/assets/pdf/swc-telegram-briefing-july.pdf.

Weimann, Gabriel, and Natalie Masri, "Research Note: Spreading Hate on TikTok," *Studies in Conflict & Terrorism* (2020), 1–14.

Weitzman, Mark, "Antisemitism and Terrorism on the Electronic Highway," in *Terrorism and the Internet*, ed. Hans-Liudger Dienel, Yair Sharan, Christian Rapp, and Niv Ahituv (Amsterdam, 2010), pp. 7–26.

"The Internet Is Our Sword: Aspects of Online Antisemitism," in *Remembering for the Future: The Holocaust in an Age of Genocide*, ed. John K. Roth, Elisabeth Maxwell, Margot Levy and Wendy Whitworth (London, 2001), pp. 911–925.

Wetzel, Juliane, "The Protocols of the Elders of Zion on the Internet: How Radical Political Groups Are Networked via Conspiracy Theories," in *The Global Impact of the Protocols of the Elders of Zion: A Century Old Myth*, ed. Esther Webman (London, 2011), pp. 147–160.

---

[78] Ahmed Shaheed, A/74/358 - E - A/74/358 -Desktop (undocs.org), accessed November 30, 2020.

27 Theories on the Causes of Antisemitism

BRUNO CHAOUAT

PROLOGUE

Understanding antisemitism is a daunting task. The plethora of explanations bears witness to the complexity and the lability of what scholars have called "the longest hatred" or a "lethal obsession."[1] Antisemitism is not monolithic. Its expressions have varied considerably throughout history and continue to morph in unpredictable ways. One of the most recent studies regarding those variations is David Nirenberg's book *Anti-Judaism: The Western Tradition*.[2] After surveying a broad corpus of documents and philosophies hostile to Judaism, Nirenberg suggested that the Western civilization since antiquity needs to define a negative "other" so as to establish its own identity and continuity. This other has been Judaism.

In several compelling theories, Judaism is construed as the West's *internal outside*. By that phrase, I mean that Jews stand at the origin of the West, but the West also perceived the Jews as alien, as though the very origin were somehow beside or outside itself. As a result, it makes the West always different from itself and triggers an anxiety with respect to identity.

Presently, there are fierce debates regarding what qualifies as antisemitism, how to define it semantically and legally. Those semantic and legal debates determine state policies. In some countries, indeed, hate speech and incitement are punishable by law, and in order to identify whether we are dealing with hate speech we must clearly define antisemitism. Are anti-Zionism, "Israel bashing," or the Boycott, Divestment and Sanctions (BDS) movement antisemitic? Does antisemitism necessarily originate from traditional Christian or post-Christian

---

[1] Robert Wistrich, *Antisemitism: The Longest Hatred* (New York, 1991); Robert Wistrich, *A Lethal Obsession: Antisemitism from Antiquity to the Global Jihad* (New York, 2010).

[2] David Nirenberg, *Anti-Judaism: The Western Tradition* (New York, 2013).

quarters (far right or revolutionary left), or can it also come from the
former colonized who are themselves the target of prejudice – Muslims
from the Maghreb, the Middle East, or Africa? If the answer is yes, are we
dealing with the same phenomenon? Should the critique of the Jewish
religion, tradition, or legal doctrine be considered antisemitic, or is it the
object of legitimate intellectual debate? Do Philip Roth's fictional character Alexander Portnoy's rants against the Jewish law and its sexual
repression qualify as "auto-antisemitism," "Jewish self-loathing," or are
they part of an individual's normal rebelliousness against external limitations?[3] Those questions are fraught with misunderstandings and I will
hardly be able to formulate all the answers in this chapter.

Antisemitism's tendency to morph does not mean that there is no
invariable accounting for the extraordinary persistence of the phenomenon over time – a persistence mirrored by the unusual resilience of the
Jewish people throughout history.[4] Jewish sites (such as cemeteries) in
Western democracies continue to be desecrated, and Jews are assaulted
and murdered decades after the Shoah. Sadly, antisemitism coexists
with old and new forms of prejudice. And even more sadly, at times
anti-Jewish hatred arises among ethnic, racial, and religious minorities,
fueled by a rhetoric uncannily reminiscent of centuries-old antisemitism. Even though there is in Islamic tradition some potential for justifying rivalry with the Jews (after all, Islam, like Christianity, is a
younger sister to Judaism among the Abrahamic faiths, and there is
sibling rivalry), Islamic antisemitism has been strongly influenced by
its European, Christian, or secular counterpart – especially throughout
the last century. As we have seen since the Pittsburgh synagogue mass
shooting, xenophobic and racist antisemitism has resurfaced at least in
the United States. But we are also witnessing, in the United States, Jews
persecuted by oppressed minorities that reclaim the status of ... *real*
Jews. I am thinking of attacks on orthodox Jews by so-called Black
Hebrew Israelites[5] (more on antisemitism based on a claim to be the
"real" Jews later).

In the following I will focus on old and new theoretical trends that
I find particularly helpful in identifying some invariables of antisemitic

---

[3] Philip Roth, *Portnoy's Complaint* (New York, 1969).

[4] On Jewish historic resilience, see Danny Trom, *Persévérance du fait juif – Une
théorie politique de la survie* [*Persistence of the Jews: A Political Theory of
Survival*] (Paris, 2018).

[5] See Sarah Maslin Nir, "Black Hebrew Israelites: What We Know about the Fringe
Group," *New York Times*, December 11, 2019, www.nytimes.com/2019/12/11/
nyregion/black-hebrew-israelites-jersey-city-suspects.html.

bigotry. Insofar as antisemitism, perhaps more than any other form of prejudice, is multifaceted, we need to consider multiple theories. Readers should not be discouraged by the diversity of theories and hypotheses. This very diversity enriches our understanding of the antisemitic obsession.

I do not aim at exhaustiveness and I will engage only with theories that are rooted in psychoanalytic, philosophical, and religious hypotheses. My goal is merely to trigger curiosity and entice the reader to think and read further. Unfortunately, the work of some of the theorists with whom I engage has yet to be translated into English. As a literary and humanities scholar I will leave it to social scientists, more familiar with materialist, economic, and social thought, to propose further explanatory grids. I am not generally satisfied with sociological explanations despite some brilliant insights because they tend to limit antisemitism to socioeconomic contexts. However, those contexts are by definition always changing, whereas antisemitism persists. In 1992 Werner Bergmann published a cogent survey of social and psychological theories of antisemitism.[6] He broke them down into psychological theories of personality, deprivation theories, theories of social perception, group psychology, and theories of crisis.

More recently, Sander Gilman and James Thomas have explored postwar psychopathological theories of racism and antisemitism.[7] The most salient examples of those theories are two: the narcissistic identification with the leader adapted from late 19th-century Gustave Le Bon's *Psychologie des foules* revisited by Freud's 1921 *Group Psychology and the Analysis of the Ego*, and the Frankfurt School's psychosociological portrait of the "authoritarian personality." Those theories have deessentialized our understanding of antisemitism – for instance, they constitute a rebuttal of the theories of the singularity and even uniqueness of German Jew-hatred – and have anchored antisemitism in psychosocial, empirical circumstances.

Theories are useful, albeit by nature limited. One limitation of social and psychological theories is their tendency to underestimate the specificity of antisemitism and to conceive of racism and antisemitism in the same terms. If the overlap between the two phenomena is obvious, by equating the two bigotries one runs the risk of missing their

[6] Werner Bergmann, "Psychological and Sociological Theories of Antisemitism," *Patterns of Prejudice* 26.1–2 (1992).
[7] Sander L. Gilman and James Thomas, *Are Racists Crazy? How Prejudice, Racism, and Antisemitism Became Markers of Insanity* (New York, 2016).

distinctive features.[8] I will thus not revisit psychosocial theories in the following remarks but will try to complement them with philosophical and religious explanations. Those explanations will not be less limited, obviously, but it is my hope that they will provide new intellectual means toward understanding antisemitism.

SARTRE

In the last years of the Second World War Jean-Paul Sartre used his existential analytic method to understand antisemitism.[9] He partly succeeded and partly failed. Those who contend that he failed argue that he was not able to understand the Jew qua Jew. The Jew, for Sartre, was a product of the antisemite's fantasy, of his gaze. It is the gaze of the antisemite that creates the Jew. The objection to Sartre's approach is legitimate. But it does not take away that *Anti-Semite and Jew* remains until today a virtuoso portrait of the antisemite of French stock, of the then recent collaborator with the Nazi regime and Vichy's "national revolution."

Wherein consists this portrait? For Sartre the antisemite is a text-book case of the man of bad faith. The latter is the man who lives in accordance with the belief that human beings have a predetermined essence and who does not realize that the essence of man is to have no essence at all, to exist before being anything in particular, before any determination. Sartre famously summed it up in the proposition, "existence precedes essence" – his axiom of freedom. In other words, the man of bad faith – in this case the antisemite – is not free. He submits himself to beliefs in natural and cultural determinations, blood and soil, social classes, race or religion, and so on. For him, man is a tree, rooted in a landscape, be it social or natural, and the Jew is precisely the one who does not belong to that landscape. Reactionary thought fails to embrace the core principles of existential-ist humanism. Existentialist humanism can be understood as a form of universalism that makes every human being equal before existence and death and therefore every human being not only free to choose his own fate but also forced to choose it – sentenced, as it were, to freedom. To wit, Sartre's antisemite is an alienated consciousness. He wallows in the primitive world of the "in-itself," of beings and

---

[8] See Karin Stögner, "Intersectionality and Antisemitism: A New Approach," *Fathom*, May 2020, https://fathomjournal.org/intersectionality-and-antisemitism-a-new-approach/.

[9] Jean-Paul Sartre, *Anti-Semite and Jew* (New York, 1948).

things that are glued or riveted to their essence rather than capable of transcending it. He is an inauthentic being.

This diagnosis was remarkable, to be sure, yet it may have missed the point, that is, that the Jew is neither a free "for-itself" (a consciousness freed from its supposed essence) nor an "in-itself" riveted to his essence. Jewish being (what I call Jewish factualness) has determinations that indeed precede existence. The marking of the law in the flesh (circumcision), the inscription within a filiation and within a chain of generations – such things allude to the fact that the Jew is not just a *free-floating for-itself*, a definition that applies better to Sartre's intellectual than to the Jew. The Jew is indebted. Being Jewish entails obligation to a past. As a result the Jew is far from emancipated from the past. He is not a pure project. This is what Sartre was reproached with at the time of the publication of his book and until today – his ignorance of Jewish factualness, of the fact that there are actual Jews who exceed or rather precede construction by the gaze of the antisemite. Jewish existence, in contrast to Sartre's "human reality," does not amount to indeterminate existence and self-projection into the future. And so if Sartre was able to grasp something important about the psychology of French antisemitism, he fell short of understanding the specificity of antisemitism insofar as he did not engage with Jewish factualness, with the concreteness of Jewish existence and even with this troubling fact that the "authentic" Jew does not entirely choose his fate. What Sartre finally helped us understand was more the essence of xenophobia, racism, and French bigotry than the enigma of antisemitism.

REPLACEMENT

One particular trait of Jewish existence is particularism. Even though Sartre was sensitive to existence "in situation," that is, concrete conditions of experience, and suspicious of abstract universalism, he did not dwell on the subject of Jewish "particularism" – a stumbling block throughout the history of anti-Judaism and antisemitism. In a few pages I cannot retrace that history. I will limit myself to some thinkers who have recently engaged either favorably or critically with the doctrine of Paul of Tarsus, arguably the first "intellectual" of Christianity. It is well known that the apostle brought to the Western world the idea that to be a true Jew, a "fulfilled" Jew, one had to renounce particularism. Paradoxically enough, to be a real Jew one had to cease being a Jew. Or, at least, one had to overcome a limited loyalty to the particular and a "narrow" understanding of Jewish existence. One had to open one's mind to the message of Jesus and accept him as the Messiah.

In the 1st century CE Paul's doctrine as laid out in his epistles to the Gentiles promoted the replacement of the letter with the spirit, the law with faith, and the circumcision of the flesh with that of the heart. Arguably, Paul's constituted the first narrative of emancipation – emancipation from an identity rooted in the flesh, in filiation and genealogy. Paul wished to replace embodied filiation (vertical) with symbolic brotherhood (horizontal) – Christians were to be brothers in Christ. This opened up the possibility of broadening the community – a community of love (*agape*) rather than a community rooted in law and embodied filiation. Paul's community could potentially embrace and include all the nations (Gentiles, or *goyim*) and turn particular Judaism into a universal creed. This was the meaning of Catholicism: the universal, apostolic Church.

In the 1980s French philosopher Jean-François Lyotard, mainly known for an intriguing book on the postmodern condition,[10] wrote very critically of the attempt by Paul and by Christianity in general to overcome Jewish particularism.[11] For Lyotard, indeed, Paul provided the first theory of emancipation; he was the first "modern." For Lyotard, "modern" designates a belief in the possibility of total emancipation. As such, Christianity constituted the first grand narrative of modernity. Faith in Christ was supposed to free the Jews from their enslavement to the Law, and the sacrifice of Jesus on the Cross was meant to have freed all humankind once and for all. Then Lyotard considered the Enlightenment, Marxism, modern science, all narratives that promised the emancipation of humankind from the shackles of heteronomy (the transcendent Law) and childhood. Recall Kant's definition of Enlightenment as "man's emergence from his self-incurred immaturity."[12] Modern, for Lyotard, is any narrative that claims to free humankind from all forms of subjugation, inequality, and injustice. To be sure, this was a very idiosyncratic understanding of the concept of modernity, but perhaps a useful one when it comes to grasping Paul's formidable intellectual and political *coup de force*.

[10] Jean-François Lyotard, *The Postmodern Condition* (Cambridge, MA, 1987).
[11] Jean-François Lyotard, *The Hyphen: Between Judaism and Christianity* (Atlantic Highlands, NJ, 1998).
[12] Immanuel Kant and H. B. Nisbet, *An Answer to the Question, "What Is Enlightenment?"* (London, 2013).

THEORIES ON THE CAUSES OF ANTISEMITISM   503

For Paul, the Law and the letter condemned the Jews to a form of enslavement and even symbolic death. "The letter kills," Paul famously declared. Under the Law one cannot be alive – the Jew must therefore free himself from the letter and liberate the spirit. Universalism, the "catholic," arises from that liberation; the life of the spirit arises from the overcoming of the fossilized letter. The Gentiles are invited to join the Church and to become *verus Israel* – the true Israel. In other words, the Jews, once converted, will become accomplished Jews, real Jews. Under the Law, they will always remain incomplete, archaic, anachronistic – an unfinished work. The Jews had a great intuition – monotheism and the rejection of idolatry – but Paul's epistles suggest that they failed to turn that intuition into a universal creed.

Lyotard intimated that the Pauline narrative effected a symbolic violence that opened up the history of Christian antisemitism. He called this violence that of the "hyphen" (the *trait d'union* between Jew and Christian). For Lyotard, this hyphen, rather than uniting or bridging (*unir*) Jew with Christian, meant instead the erasure of the Jew – *falsus Israel* – and its replacement with the Christian – *verus Israel*. Lyotard rooted his philosophy in the idea that total emancipation is, strictly speaking, not possible. The Jews, for Lyotard, bear witness to this structural impossibility of overcoming an original "grip" – heteronomy, which means, literally, the law of the Other. To be sure, this grip or stranglehold (*mainmise* in French) was, for Lyotard, neither the Law delivered to Moses on Mount Sinai nor God's demand that Abraham sacrifice Isaac. Incidentally, Lyotard was an agnostic thinker. For him human beings are unable to overcome entirely the state of childhood and to achieve total autonomy, to overcome completely the handicap of having been an infant (*infans* meaning the one who does not speak). Lyotard took seriously the notion that humans are always born too soon, and that prematurity is indeed an important feature of the human condition. He always considered that this condition of prematurity is impossible to overcome entirely. Infancy, dependence, and vulnerability, for Lyotard, transcends biological age and remains with us in adulthood. Hence Lyotard's critique of all narratives of emancipation, starting with the Pauline one.

Against Lyotard's critique of the hyphen between Jew and Christian, French communist philosopher Alain Badiou in the 1990s reclaimed the legacy of Pauline universalism.[13] For Badiou, Paul had

---

[13] Alain Badiou, *Saint Paul: The Foundation of Universalism* (Stanford, CA, 2003).

coined the very first universalism – the one that would open up all
ensuing narratives of emancipation, especially the Marxist-communist
one. Drawing on Paul's overcoming of differences ("there is neither Jew
nor Greek," etc.), Badiou claims that Christian universalism indicates
the promise of genuine equality. Such a conception of universalism
reproduces the Pauline *coup de force* denounced by Lyotard – and turns
the Jew in the flesh again into some obstacle to the promise of equality.
Hence a certain embarrassment for the neo-Pauline philosophy (in that
case the Marxist revolutionary one) to acknowledge the national form of
Judaism – namely, the State of Israel. Contemporary anti-Zionism is
often formulated in the name of a universalist and internationalist
conception of humankind that precludes particular political and
national expressions. To be sure, one can also argue that the State of
Israel represents an attempt at total emancipation through national
sovereignty (a collective adulthood), and as such it is not surprising that
Lyotard avoided engaging with Zionism in his consideration of Jewish
experience. If Lyotard took seriously the carnal dimension of transmission (the Jew-in-the-flesh), "Jews" as he called them, with scare quotes,
were nonetheless somewhat metaphorical. As I will further suggest,
they were a metonymy of heteronomy, a representative of the law that
comes from the Other – a heteronomy that is inscribed in the flesh and
transcends the difference between Jews and Gentiles.

More recently, the problem of universalism and replacement has
taken a new turn. Historian Enzo Traverso, for instance, argued that
antisemitism itself, since the creation of the State of Israel, has been
replaced with other forms of bigotry, more specifically with
Islamophobia.[14] For Traverso the Jews are no longer the targets of the
anti-Jewish West. They are instead part of the dominant group (white,
colonial, or neocolonial European) that discriminates against European
Muslims. Interestingly, Traverso's narrative mimics the grammar of
replacement theology and Christian universalism. In the case of
Traverso, the Jews, indeed, are authentically Jewish insofar as they are
revolutionaries struggling against oppression, insofar as they fight for
the universal liberation of humankind. Strangely enough, for Traverso,
those authentic Jews are pre-Shoah and pre–Jewish State Jews. In this
perspective, as soon as they acquired a sovereign state, in the aftermath
of the Holocaust, the Jews were on the side of the oppressor and of
political conservatism. Jews in this narrative are construed as

[14] Enzo Traverso, *The End of Jewish Modernity* (London, 2016).

anachronistic and as an obstacle to the movement of history – a movement toward progress, emancipation, and equality. If they were truly
modern, Jews in the West would continue to be revolutionaries and
forces of progress and they would oppose national sovereignty at the
expense of an oppressed minority (the Palestinians).

Today's Jews in Traverso's narrative have thus not been able to
measure up to the universal message of original Judaism – the message
of the Prophets, the message of dissidence and revolution. The Jews whom
he alleges remained faithful to that message were the diaspora Jews. Once
Jewish national sovereignty was restored, Jews became the agents of
conservatism, inequality, and capitalism. Those who will take over the
message of universality are the new oppressed (the new Jews, perhaps a
new avatar of the *verus Israel*?) – namely, the Muslims in Europe.

If Traverso never reclaims the legacy of Paul or of Christianity, the
grammar of replacement seems to be strikingly recycled through the idea
that Jews are not what they should be and therefore find themselves on
the wrong side of history understood as an ineluctable movement toward
progress. We are dealing here not with antisemitism proper but with a
dubious understanding of the Jews as a "prismatic category," to use
sociologist Zygmunt Bauman's phrase.[15] While the conservative prism
sees Jews as dangerous revolutionaries, from the revolutionary perspective Jews are conservative and capitalists. This prismatic perception has
nurtured anti-Judaism and antisemitism in modernity.

In 2003 linguist Jean-Claude Milner proposed one more critique of
European universalism.[16] It was in the aftermath of September 11, 2001,
the Second Intifada and the War in Iraq, when a new wave of violent
antisemitism broke out in France and Europe. Milner diagnosed that
postwar democratic Europe and its project of indefinite geopolitical
expansion and perpetual peace (*Pax Europea*), far from having overcome
the plague of antisemitism, prospered on the very erasure of the Jews. The
New Europe, for Milner, was virtually criminal with regard to the Jews.
The striving for universal peace, the post-Shoah "Never again" motto,
was a way of promoting what Milner called an "easy universalism"
rooted in the empty expansion of human rights. That easy universalism
he opposed to a "demanding universalism" exemplified by Jewish difference and to a principle of limitation (the nation-state, for instance) rather
than indefinite expansion. Not unlike Lyotard, Milner saw modern

---

[15] Zygmunt Bauman, *Modernity and the Holocaust* (Ithaca, NY, 1989).
[16] Jean-Claude Milner, *Les Penchants criminels de l'Europe démocratique* [*The
Criminal Leanings of Democratic Europe*] (Paris, 2003).

democracy as a project that sees the Jews as an obstacle to indefinite progress and emancipation. Finally, Jews, according to Milner, are the embodiment of an irreducible difference that Enlightenment and modernity have attempted to suppress. Since the emancipation in the 18th and 19th centuries, the Jews have always been construed as a problem in need of a solution. Based on two cornerstone differences – generational (children/parents) and sexual (male/female) – Judaism resists being resolved or liquidated in a democratic modernity that tends to level down all differences.

I leave it to the reader to appreciate the limits and even the risks of Milner's theory, the least of which being that Jews somehow do not belong to European Enlightenment, that the rise of early 21st-century antisemitism is structurally linked to the European Union, and that the latter is a disguised rehash of Nazi imperialism.

ID

I will now turn to the psychoanalytic explanation for antisemitism. American scholars are notoriously no longer well disposed toward psychoanalysis. Even the disciplines of psychology and psychiatry have rejected Freud's legacy as some sort of relic of the prescientific method. And yet there is something quite intriguing in an analysis of antisemitism based on an exploration of the Western id. Freud, persecuted by the Nazis in Vienna and in exile in London, published his *Moses and Monotheism* in 1939.[17] That book, a testament of sorts, was not meant to be scientific, but quasi-literary. In fact, Freud presented it as a "historical novel." He was in search of what he called the "historical truth" – not so much the factual truth but the unconscious one. Therefore, the reader could not expect sound factual, empirical evidence. In his theoretical fiction, Freud argued that Moses was not a Jew but an Egyptian, that the monotheism he imposed on the Hebrew slaves whom he liberated and then led to the Promised land came from previous Egyptian avatars of monotheism, and that the Hebrews, who resented the imposition of such a constraining and repressive legislation, murdered or at the very least attempted to murder Moses, a father figure. That murder, actual or attempted, was then forgotten (repressed, in Freudian parlance) and returned in the form of guilt. Jews would be bound by that guilt based on the return of the forgotten attempted

---

[17] Sigmund Freud, *Moses and Monotheism* (New York, 1939).

murder of their symbolic "father," Moses. Granted, such speculation is far-fetched. And yet, even though the account is purely speculative and factually fragile, it offers an inspiring theory, what we could call a theoretical fiction. Again, Freud, in that book, was not aiming at scientific truth. His was an attempt at laying out a very personal speculation about the archaic origins of antisemitism, based in part on the psychoanalytic method. But what does that theoretical fiction, if I may use that paradoxical phrase, have to do with antisemitism? What does it accomplish for our understanding of antisemitism?

Recall that Freud was writing his book in the midst of antisemitic persecutions. One of his purposes was to understand the irrational violence unleashed upon European Jews. The Jews, in Freud's Oedipal scenario, are the people who refused to acknowledge the murder of (or the wish to murder) the father. The Christians, by contrast, acknowledged it and in the Christian narrative, the Son is put to death in order to cleanse the sins of humankind. But what is interesting is that Jewish refusal to admit the murder (or the attempted murder, for that matter, since for the unconscious a death wish also triggers guilt) became a curse for the Jews throughout the history of Christian Europe, as if the Jews were the incarnation of a lingering, interminable guilt that could not be cleansed because it is repressed, deeply buried in the unconscious. The Jews, as it were, stand as the living witnesses to a suppressed, traumatic memory.

Lyotard, whom we have already encountered, took up where Freud left off. In a book dedicated to the Nazi philosopher Martin Heidegger and his at best contemptuous relation to Judaism, Lyotard took Freud's historical novel seriously.[18] For him, "the jews" (in this sense written without a capital) designate an original, unconscious affect, that Lyotard characterized as the "memory of the forgotten." They designate a disturbance within the West and Europe. This unconscious affect would haunt the West and the West will never cease trying to get rid of that haunting disturbance. Lyotard was reproached for using scare quotes to mention "the jews," thus suggesting that he was not talking of real, historical Jews and that he was turning them into a mere metaphor. It may be true, but at the same time, antisemites do not consider the real Jews either in their hatred (it is well known that antisemitism can bloom even in the absence of Jews). Instead, the antisemite reacts to a psychic representation of the Jews. To be sure, that psychic, repulsive

---

[18] Jean-François Lyotard, *Heidegger and "the Jews"* (Minneapolis, MN, 1990).

representation has effects in the real world and on real Jews, from forced conversion, ghettoization, and pogroms, up to genocide.

In a 2018 book French philosopher Jean-Luc Nancy, a disciple of Jacques Derrida, argues that the Jews constitute an "internal outside," or an external inside, of Europe.[19] In the European unconscious, provided that such a thing exists, Jews are a destabilizing principle. Nancy's speculation is very close to Lyotard's. The European psyche, he claims, is split between a striving for autonomy (to wit, modernity) and the remainder of heteronomy – to wit, an archaic attachment to the call from God. Nancy further suggests a psycho-anthropological theory of sibling rivalry. Built on Judaism, Christianity is yearning for a self-foundation. It strives to be its own origin. The younger does not forgive the elder. In the most compelling part of his argument, Nancy identifies antisemitism as a case of European self-loathing, a phenomenon that is inscribed in the genetic code of European civilization. Nancy argues that European civilization is split between, on the one hand, a striving for autonomy and rationality and, on the other hand, a longing for an ideal and spiritual accomplishment – the sacrifice of power, materiality, and wealth to something higher. Nancy sees this split at work in the history of the Christian Church (the Catholic Church has built its worldly empire by preaching its rejection of mundane affairs and worldly considerations). As a result, European antisemitism appears as a case of psychological projection. *The Jew comes to embody everything that modern Europe hates about itself –* money, power, democracy, and technique. Nancy concludes his argument with the metaphor of paranoia, a paranoia at the level of a whole civilization: a threat that originates in oneself is turned into a threat that originates from the other. Nancy's analysis both in terms of sibling rivalry and in terms of a projection onto the Jews of an anxiety about oneself would apply very well to Islamic antisemitism. His analysis of European antisemitism should be extended to the paranoid structure of extra-European antisemitism. Indeed, as Avishai Margalit and Ian Buruma have shown, Islamist hatred of the West recycles European self-hatred and the projection of its own anxiety vis-à-vis modernity onto an enemy (the Jew, America).[20]

---

[19] Jean-Luc Nancy, *Exclu le juif en nous* [*Excluded the Jew within Ourselves*] (Paris, 2018).

[20] Avishai Margalit and Ian Buruma, *Occidentalism: The West in the Eyes of Its Enemies* (New York, 2004).

MYTH

By the end of the war, the same year that Sartre was writing *Anti-Semite and Jew* and one year before his death (1944), philosopher Ernst Cassirer published a *pièce de circonstance* that purported to understand the Nazi campaign that led to the final solution.[21] Cassirer's hypothesis rests on a distinction between Judaism, especially prophetic, and "political religion," especially Nazism. Where prophetic Judaism disrupted myth and replaced it with ethics, Cassirer claims, Nazism marked an interruption of ethics and a return to myth. To be sure, such return was not a return to the original experience of myth in ancient Greece, but to what we may call a *myth of myth*, an artificial, manufactured production of myth for industrial times and modern man. This myth was laid out in Alfred Rosenberg's notorious *Myth of the Twentieth Century* (1930), a major inspiration of Nazi ideology and an influence on the remythification of politics by the Third Reich. Prophetic Judaism, according to Cassirer, had defined a religious ethics that does away with images as conveyors of myth. No myth can exist without images, Cassirer tells us, and thus Nazi politics had to return images to the front stage. To understand Cassirer more concretely, one should think of the cinema of Hitler's official filmmaker Leni Riefenstahl, and the collective narcissism that her movies nurtured. At the movie house ordinary Germans would be invited to recognize an imaginary, ideal version of themselves as though in a mirror. The so-called Aryan race was meant to be a race of gods, and Josef Goebbels, in his interwar novel *Michael*, declared that politics was "the plastic art of the state."[22] The "aestheticization of politics" was Walter Benjamin's thought-provoking definition of fascism in the 1930s.[23] A *Volk* had to be shaped from an amorphous mass. Indeed, in some images of Nazi propaganda the Führer appeared as a sculptor who molds the ideal *Volk*. The "plastic art of the state," politics, must extract forms and images out of the formless. To produce those forms and images, one had to invent a formless, abject other and eliminate it in the same way as a sculptor shapes his material by removing matter.[24] This formless other will be the "anti-mythic" people – the

[21] Ernst Cassirer, "Judaism and the Modern Political Myths," *Contemporary Jewish Record* 7.2 (1944).

[22] Joseph Goebbels, *Michael: A Novel* (New York, 1987).

[23] Walter Benjamin, "The Work of Art in the Age of Mechanical Reproduction," www.marxists.org/reference/subject/philosophy/works/ge/benjamin.htm.

[24] See Eric Michaud, *The Cult of Art in Nazi Germany* (Stanford, CA, 2004).

Jews, whose collective and individual body makes neither image nor race – a counterimage and a *Gegenrasse* (anti-race).

Cassirer further argues that by condemning idolatry Judaism had renounced anthropomorphism, the very idea that the gods are human and the converse proposition that humans (Aryans) are like gods. By contrast, the likeness to God in Judaism is not anthropomorphic. It is a likeness without likeness, as it were, a similitude without simile.

But Judaism brought about yet another disruption, Cassirer intimates, that is, the interruption of human sacrifice – an interruption willed by God Himself when He stays Abraham's offering of Isaac. This would radically transform the relation of man to God. With the interruption of sacrifice arises a conception of individual responsibility – the emergence of conscience. By contrast, Nazism, through its claim to returning to primitive religion, abolished individual responsibility and replaced it with collective guilt and punishment. Furthermore, Nazism unleashed the instincts allegedly repressed by monotheism. Literary critic George Steiner went as far as to suggest that Nazism was a natural reaction to the stifling of the soul brought about by the Jewish repression of the animist and pagan tendencies.[25] The Jews were slaughtered in the Holocaust not so much for having killed God, Steiner argues, but for having invented Him and thereby stifling human aggressive tendencies. Via such intellectual construction, Steiner illustrates the risks inherent in theorizing antisemitism. His extreme rationalization suggests that explaining antisemitism can amount to justifying it.

To go back to Cassirer, his musings have value only if one agrees to limit Judaism to prophetic Judaism – a Judaism that strives for universalism, the overcoming of nationalism, and peace among nations. It is nonetheless an intriguing theory, especially if one sees prophetic Judaism as a herald of Christian universalism and even of Marxist revolution and if one admits that Nazi antisemitism was also a delayed rebellion against the Christianization of pagan Europe and an attempt at recovering a Nordic, pre-Christian past.

Historians have noted a return to myth in the early 20th century – thus before Nazism and Alfred Rosenberg[26] – in the resurgence of the occult tradition.[27] An experience of fragmentation in the multinational

---

[25] George Steiner, *In Bluebeard's Castle: Some Notes towards the Redefinition of Culture* (New Haven, CT, 1971).

[26] Alfred Rosenberg, *The Myth of the Twentieth Century* (Torrance, CA, 1982).

[27] Nicholas Goodrick-Clarke, *The Occult Roots of Nazism: Secret Aryan Cults and Their Influence on Nazi Ideology* (New York, 1992).

Austrian state and a more general disenchantment in the modern world led some German intellectuals to harness the occult tradition to their conservative revolution. Occultist politics, the cult of an elite made up of initiated bearers of a secret legacy, set in motion a dynamic whereby the revolution of the future was meant to be a return to a mythological past (or Golden Age). The politics of the occult was Manichean through and through, positing a struggle between the forces of evil (financial institutions, parliamentarianism) and the forces of the good (the old Aryan-Germanic hierarchy).

One often thinks of Nazi antisemitism as based on modern scientific or pseudo-scientific developments such as eugenics and hygienics. But this concentration on pseudo-science, this idea that Nazism is a modern phenomenon, underestimates the role of mythic imagination in the elaboration of the mystique of the superior race. Indeed, occultism was used to elaborate a racial mystique. An esoteric exegesis of the Bible mixed with pseudo-science, for instance, led Jörg Lanz von Libenfels to fantasize that the source of all evil in the world comes from the racial compromising of the Aryans through wicked interbreeding with lower animal species. That pseudo-science was known as "theozoology."[28]

One name never fails to pop up in any genealogy of the modern revival of the occult in relation to racial mystique – that of the mysterious Madame Blavatsky, née Hahn, Russian emigrée and self-proclaimed medium and magician who published in the late 19th century *The Secret Doctrine*. Her race theory rests on the myth of the lost city of Atlantis. Instead of locating Atlantis between Europe and the Americas, Blavatsky's Atlantis is situated in the far North, near the pole.[29] From Atlantis descended the root-race of the Aryans. Blavatsky distinguishes between Aryans and Semites, with the latter taking up the negative characteristics of the Jew according to the antisemite – concealment, malice, materialism, and so on: "with *The Secret Doctrine*, antisemitism now acquired cosmological importance. The Jews suddenly stood in the way of the great preordained progress of the races."[30] (More shortly on this return of a Manichean and millenarian worldview in the context of conspiratorial thinking.)

In the wake of Madame Blavatsky's revival of the myth of the Atlantis, Nazi ideologues would later locate the birthplace of the Aryans

[28] Ibid., 94.
[29] Dan Edelstein, "Hyperborean Atlantis: Jean-Sylvain Bailly, Madame Blavatsky, and the Nazi Myth," *Studies in Eighteenth-Century Culture* 35 (2006), 267–291.
[30] Ibid., 275.

in some imaginary North Hyperborea or Arktogäa. What we observe at the turn of the 20th century is a racist and geomythical imagination in which pseudo-science, myth, and the occult collude.

CONSPIRACY

At this juncture I propose to reflect on the new challenges posed by a siege-like mentality in the age of post-truth, social media, and fake news, and its correlation with antisemitism. Such thinking involves the fear of being under siege from an imaginary enemy; it is a form of collective paranoia that nurtures a conspiratorial mindset. In the last century, totalitarian regimes have exploited the manufactured feeling of besiegement by a vaguely defined enemy via state propaganda. In the cyber era, conspiratorial thinking travels at the speed of light, and anyone with access to social media can spread fake news. If propaganda is still the monopoly of the state in totalitarian or autocratic regimes, in Western democracies it has become privatized and tailored to the expectations of specific communities and specific collective or even individual prejudices.

The conspiracy theory that has had an ongoing impact on European and, later, on world Jewry is the one expounded in the notorious *Protocols of the Elders of Zion*, at the turn of the 20th century.[31] One can even say that the *Protocols* constitutes the matrix of modern conspiracy theories. Centuries after the age-old blood libel, centuries after Christian accusations of Jews' poisoning wells, the *Protocols* spread rapidly in space and time and heralded the age of transnational anti-semitic propaganda. We find it in print and online today in the Middle East, South America, and even Japan. The 1987 Covenant of the Palestinian militant organization Hamas mentions the *Protocols* in a positive light.[32] At the core of this Franco-Russian forgery rests the belief in the malevolent power of the Jews with hidden hands – a construct that will spawn a vast number of conspiracy theories. One of the main conspiratorial fabrications and assaults on truth in the postwar era concerns the perversion of Holocaust memory. Holocaust denial erases facts and blames the Jews for having forged the story of their own extermination in order to draw financial and political benefits

---

[31] See Richard Landes and Steven T. Katz, eds., *The Paranoid Apocalypse: A Hundred-Year Retrospective on The Protocols of the Elders of Zion* (New York, 2011).

[32] Hamas Charter, Article 32, the Avalon Project, https://avalon.law.yale.edu/20th_century/hamas.asp.

from victim status. Holocaust denial is not limited to the West and has spread in the Arab and Muslim world.[33]

The theme of a conspiracy to enslave the Gentiles to Jewish masters has recently been recycled via the myth of the Jews as initiators and main beneficiaries of slave trade. But it was already one of the themes of racist antisemitism in the 1930s and '40s – an antisemitism built on the belief in the Jewish plan to weaken and subjugate the so-called Aryans.

To conclude, I shall submit a hypothesis on the relation between conspiratorial thinking and antisemitism, and suggest that conspiracy theory may have some ancient, archaic, and mythic roots. Scholars of mysticism Gershom Scholem and Hans Jonas have argued that the gnostic worldview has long overlapped with anti-Judaism.[34] Historians of religions identify as Gnosticism the heterogeneous collection of writings that form the corpus of heterodox gospels deemed heretical by the Church. In the 2nd century of our era, Marcion of Sinope uncoupled the Gospel from the Hebrew Scripture. For Marcion the God of the Hebrew Scripture was evil, while the God of the Gospel was good and loving. Jesus could not be Jewish because he was the embodiment of love. It is not by chance that Nazi theologians turned to Marcion to de-Judaize Jesus. The gnostics believed that the world was created by an evil, inferior demiurge, none other than the God of the Hebrew Scripture, and that the true God was alien to this world. I would suggest that the evil power attributed to the Jews builds on such ancient beliefs, which were later on secularized in racial pseudo-science. The conspiratorial worldview, likewise, rests on a Manichean and apocalyptic struggle between those who are endowed with a special knowledge (the gnostics) and the agents of evil.

Furthermore, it is possible to understand conspiratorial thinking as an inversion of the all-powerful hand of God and of theodicy (divine justice). For the believer in conspiracy theories, a hidden hand is the *prima causa* of all the negativity in the world, of all the machinations that contribute to the ills of the age. We are witnessing today a resurgence of conspiratorial thinking, amplified by the exponential growth of new technologies. I would argue that conspiracy theory is a form of Manichean gnosis (gnosis = knowledge) that allows a group of self-proclaimed initiates (the gnostic

[33] Meir Litvak and Esther Webman, *From Empathy to Denial: Arab Responses to the Holocaust* (Oxford, 2011).

[34] Hans Jonas, *The Gnostic Religion* (Boston, 2001). On Scholem, see John G. Gager, *The Origins of Anti-Semitism: Attitudes toward Judaism in Pagan and Christian Antiquity* (Oxford, 1985), 168.

is the one who is endowed with a secret knowledge) to point to an enemy and divide the world into light and darkness. Such thinking transcends the political opposition between left and right. Esoteric, hermetic ways of interpreting the world and society can be found among new populists on the far right and the far left. In the wake of the death of God and the disruption of the belief in divine justice, at a time of great disorientation in a globalized world, we are witnessing the emergence of new forms of religious thinking and the return of so-called stigmatized, repressed, or marginalized knowledge. The manufacture of conspiracies is the vehicle of this new religious thinking. What we call fake news and post-truth testifies to a new collective magical thinking – that there is a demonic cause to the disorientation and alienation of man in the new global disorder. That demonic cause will rarely fail to be the Jews.

Further Reading

Cassirer, E., "Judaism and the Modern Political Myths," *Contemporary Jewish Record* 8.2 (April 1944), 115–126. An essay that underscores the Nazi revival of paganism and myth and rejects Judaism and the Jews as bearers of an abstract ethics.

Consonni, M., and W. Liska, eds., *Sartre, Jews, and the Other: Rethinking Antisemitism, Race, and Gender* (Munich, 2020). An edited volume on the relevance of Sartre for understanding not only antisemitism but also other forms of prejudice such as sexism and racism.

Freud, S., *Moses and Monotheism* (New York, 1967). Freud's last book, written while in exile in London. A testimony to his ambivalence toward Judaism, a work of free-wheeling speculation, and an analysis of collective trauma and repression.

Goodrick-Clarke, N., *The Occult Roots of Nazism: Secret Aryan Cults and Their Influence on Nazi Ideology* (London, 1992). A major contribution to the study of some irrational, religious roots of Nazi ideology.

Landes, R., and S. T. Katz, eds., *The Paranoid Apocalypse: A Hundred-Year Retrospective on The Protocols of the Elders of Zion* (New York, 2011). An edited volume that surveys the history of the Franco-Russian forgery and a reflection on the social and intellectual mechanisms of conspiracy theories.

Lyotard, J.-F., *The Hyphen: Between Judaism and Christianity* (Atlantic Highlands, NJ, 1999). A close reading of Paul of Tarsus that suggests that anti-Judaism is rooted at the core of the Christian tradition.

Nancy, J.-L., and P. Lacoue-Labarthe, "The Nazi Myth," *Critical Inquiry* 16.2 (Winter 1990), 291–312. An original revisiting of Cassirer's analysis of Nazism in terms of myth, with a psychoanalytic twist based on the theory of narcissism.

Nirenberg, D., *Anti-Judaism: The Western Tradition* (New York, 2013). A major contribution to the understanding of Western civilization from antiquity to modernity based on the West's vexed relation to Judaism.

Sartre, J.-P., *Anti-Semite and Jew* (New York, 1948). The first postwar philosophical attempt at grasping the logic of antisemitism and establishing the
portrait of the antisemite.

Taguieff, P.-A., *Rising from the Muck: The New Antisemitism in Europe*
(Chicago, IL, 2004). The first major contribution to the understanding of
the return to an older paradigm; the core hypothesis of the book is that from
the beginning of the third millennium we have seen the rise of an antisemitism in the name of antiracism and antinationalism.

Appendix The International Holocaust Remembrance Alliance: Working Definition of Antisemitism

In the spirit of the Stockholm Declaration that states: "With humanity still scarred by ... antisemitism and xenophobia the international community shares a solemn responsibility to fight those evils" the committee on Antisemitism and Holocaust Denial called the IHRA Plenary in Budapest 2015 to adopt the following working definition of antisemitism.

On 26 May 2016, the Plenary in Bucharest decided to adopt the following non-legally binding working definition of antisemitism:

> Antisemitism is a certain perception of Jews, which may be expressed as hatred toward Jews. Rhetorical and physical manifestations of antisemitism are directed toward Jewish or non-Jewish individuals and/or their property, toward Jewish community institutions and religious facilities.

To guide IHRA in its work, the following examples may serve as illustrations.

Manifestations might include the targeting of the state of Israel, conceived as a Jewish collectivity. However, criticism of Israel similar to that leveled against any other country cannot be regarded as antisemitic. Antisemitism frequently charges Jews with conspiring to harm humanity, and it is often used to blame Jews for "why things go wrong." It is expressed in speech, writing, visual forms and action, and employs sinister stereotypes and negative character traits.

Contemporary examples of antisemitism in public life, the media, schools, the workplace, and in the religious sphere could, taking into account the overall context, include, but are not limited to:

- Calling for, aiding, or justifying the killing or harming of Jews in the name of a radical ideology or an extremist view of religion.
- Making mendacious, dehumanizing, demonizing, or stereotypical allegations about Jews as such or the power of Jews as collective – such as, especially but not exclusively, the myth about a world

Jewish conspiracy or of Jews controlling the media, economy, government or other societal institutions.
- Accusing Jews as a people of being responsible for real or imagined wrongdoing committed by a single Jewish person or group, or even for acts committed by non-Jews.
- Denying the fact, scope, mechanisms (e.g. gas chambers) or intentionality of the genocide of the Jewish people at the hands of National Socialist Germany and its supporters and accomplices during World War II (the Holocaust).
- Accusing the Jews as a people, or Israel as a state, of inventing or exaggerating the Holocaust.
- Accusing Jewish citizens of being more loyal to Israel, or to the alleged priorities of Jews worldwide, than to the interests of their own nations.
- Denying the Jewish people their right to self-determination, e.g., by claiming that the existence of a State of Israel is a racist endeavor.
- Applying double standards by requiring of it a behavior not expected or demanded of any other democratic nation.
- Using the symbols and images associated with classic antisemitism (e.g., claims of Jews killing Jesus or blood libel) to characterize Israel or Israelis.
- Holding Jews collectively responsible for actions of the state of Israel.

Antisemitic acts are criminal when they are so defined by law (for example, denial of the Holocaust or distribution of antisemitic materials in some countries).

Criminal acts are antisemitic when the targets of attacks, whether they are people or property – such as buildings, schools, places of worship and cemeteries – are selected because they are, or are perceived to be, Jewish or linked to Jews.

Antisemitic discrimination is the denial to Jews of opportunities or services available to others and is illegal in many countries.

Index

Printed in the USA
CPSIA information can be obtained
at www.ICGtesting.com
CBHW072218190924
14704CB00011B/448

9 781108 714525